What's New in
Virtual Reality Madness 1996

- The Buyer's Guides have been greatly expanded to include three times as much information and are now included on the accompanying CD-ROMs.

- VR is exploding all over the Internet, and we've got it covered for you. Learn about VRML—the emerging standard for VR worlds on the web.

- Expanded coverage of new games and other fun products, including Descent; Magic Carpet; Under a Killing Moon; Gadget; *Star Trek, The Next Generation* Technical Manual; Myst; DOOM II and DOOM add-ons; and many more.

- Three CD-ROMs, including many new products: Superscape Visualizer, Virtus VR Stereo, Virtek 3-D Ware Personal Edition, The Journeyman Project Turbo (complete game), PhotoMorph 2.0, Vistapro 1.0, The Netscape Navigator, and many more.

- Coverage on updated virtual reality software. Learn about Vistapro 4, VREAM, Superscape, Distant Suns, Virtus WalkThrough Pro, and Virtus VR.

- Expanded tutorials for 3D Studio, Virtus WalkThrough Pro, VREAM, and many other programs to show you how to access key features step by step.

- In addition, the book is packed with new images, a completely new color section, and more!

VIRTUAL REALITY MADNESS 1996

Ron Wodaski

PUBLISHING

201 West 103rd Street
Indianapolis, IN 46290

This book is dedicated to my kids: Chanel, Chris, and Justen; and to my wife, Donna

Copyright © 1995 by Sams Publishing

THIRD EDITION

International Standard Book Number: 0-672-30865-7

Library of Congress Catalog Card Number: 95-74704

98 97 96 95   4 3 2 1

Interpretation of the printing code: the rightmost double-digit number is the year of the book's printing; the rightmost single-digit, the number of the book's printing. For example, a printing code of 95-1 shows that the first printing of the book occurred in 1995.

Trademarks

Composed in 1 Stone Serif and MCPdigital by Macmillan Computer Publishing

Printed in the United States of America

Publisher and President	Richard K. Swadley
Acquisitions Manager	Greg Wiegand
Development Manager	Dean M. Miller
Managing Editor	Cindy Morrow
Marketing Manager	Gregg Bushyeager

Acquisitions Editor
Christopher Denny

Development Editor
Kelly Murdock

Software Development Specialist
Wayne Blankenbeckler

Production Editor
Fran Blauw

Technical Reviewer
Alfonso Hermida

Editorial Coordinator
Bill Whitmer

Technical Edit Coordinator
Lynette Quinn

Formatter
Frank Sinclair

Editorial Assistant
Sharon Cox

Cover Designer
Tim Amrhein

Book Designer
Alyssa Yesh

Production Team Supervisor
Brad Chinn

Production
Mary Ann Abramson
Angela D. Bannan
Carol Bowers
Mona Brown
Charlotte Clapp
Jeanne Clark
Terri Deemer
Cheryl Dietsch
Mike Henry
Louisa Klucznik
Kevin Laseau
Paula Lowell
Steph Mineart
Casey Price
Bobbi Satterfield
Tina Trettin
Mark Walchle
Angelina Ward

Overview

Contents

PART II   Virtual Fantasies

Acknowledgments

I have received an amazing level of cooperation from the hundreds of companies whose software and hardware are described, reviewed, and illustrated in this book. It takes a lot of effort to ship dozens and dozens of products in both directions, and I'd like to take this opportunity to publicly thank everyone who helped out in this regard.

A big thank you goes to my three kids—Justen, Chris, and Chanel—who had to wait sometimes while Daddy finished his chapters.

Two people assisted in the preparation of this edition of the book, and deserve special mention. Robin Conforto spent hours and hours and hours on the phone contacting the companies listed in the Hardware and Software Buyer's Guides. Thanks to Robin's efforts, the guides have expanded enormously in coverage, and are now included on the CD-ROMs that come with this book. You'll now be able to find many more references to products in every category. Tim McNitt developed the detailed tutorials for trueSpace and WorldsChat, and was instrumental in developing many of the Internet and virtual reality materials you'll find on the CDs, in the book, and on our home page at **http://www.mcp.com/sams/vrmadness**.

I also want to tip my hat to all the folks in the various multimedia- and virtual-reality-related forums on CompuServe. If you aren't already a member of CompuServe, you're missing out on one of the world's best idea exchanges. We visit the various forums every day, both to answer questions and to learn. Multimedia in general and virtual reality in particular are fast-evolving fields. Electronic communication is the most effective way to keep up to date.

About the Author

Ron Wodaski resides on the shores of Puget Sound in Washington, where he uses the back roads to the information highway to keep up with the latest advances in multimedia and virtual reality.

Ron started out as a journalist, but caught the computer bug when he bought one of the original Osborne computers as a word processor.

He designed and wrote custom software using BASIC and dBASE II for several years, eventually joining the dBASE team at Ashton-Tate until it was merged with Borland. Somewhere along the line, he graduated to C and then retired to Visual Basic and Toolbook. He has worn a number of different hats in the computer industry, including programming, test management, project management, and product design.

He currently writes books on a variety of computer subjects. He also writes science fiction stories, with an emphasis on virtual reality. When no one is looking, he avoids computers entirely while kayaking or sailing the waters of Puget Sound.

Introduction

Virtual Reality

Wow. What a year it has been for virtual reality. This edition of my book contains a wealth of new information. There's so much that's new that it's hard to summarize it for you.

The biggest news is almost certainly the arrival of low-cost headsets for games. They come with all the goodies you could want: clear images, head tracking, and support for all the best games. This is an area that is going to get better and better as time goes on. The future has arrived! See Chapter 7 for my personal reviews of the units I tested. The Buyers Guides on the CD-ROMs contain detailed product information.

The number of companies involved in virtual reality has grown enormously since I wrote the last edition of the book. Check out the VR Hardware and Software Buyer's Guides, which are now located on the CDs included with this book. They are crammed with hundreds of products. Many are new, and many are available at drastically lower prices.

The advances in software are nearly as dramatic as those in hardware. A number of companies have delivered new versions of their software. VREAM has evolved into VRCreator. Superscape is moving into the mainstream. Virtus has shipped a Pro version of WalkThrough for Windows. trueSpace, formerly only a 3D product, is expanding to cover many areas in VR.

The arrival of VR on the Internet is another revolution in the making. VRML is the hot topic—it's a language for describing a virtual universe over the web. Several VRML tools are included on the CD-ROMs with this book. We also have a home page you can visit. Its a starting point for a complete exploration of everything VR on the Internet. Join us at **http://www.mcp.com/sams/vrmadness**.

The bottom line is very simple: VR has arrived. The cool tools that we have been waiting for are waiting to be used. Join me as we explore every nook and cranny of the virtual universe!

What's New in *Virtual Reality Madness 1996*

This edition of *Virtual Reality Madness* represents a major update and revision of the material. Consumer-level VR has changed for 1996, and we've managed to collect the best of the new products for you under one virtual roof. Heres a partial list of what's new and hot in this edition:

- The Buyer's Guides have been greatly expanded—we have included three times as much information in this edition. You'll be able to find up-to-date information about everything virtual—gloves, headsets, world creation, programming, garage VR, etc. These Guides are now located on the CDs with this book.

- VR is exploding all over the Internet, and we've got it covered for you. You'll find shareware you can use to browse VR sites on the net, tips on creating VR for the net, and gateways to dozens of key VR treasures on the net. You'll also learn about VRML—the emerging standard for VR worlds on the web.

- We received many more hardware items for testing, and Chapter 7 is now stuffed with detailed, personal reviews of the key VR products. You'll learn what's hot, and what isn't. See how the i-glasses!, CyberMaxx, VFX1, CyberEye, and other headsets measure up against each other.

- Coverage has been expanded in all chapters. Chapter 4, "Virtual Fun," covers a bunch of new games and other fun products, including Descent; Magic Carpet; Under a Killing Moon; Gadget; *Star Trek, The Next Generation* Technical Manual; Myst; DOOM II and DOOM add-ons; and many more. Every chapter has coverage of new products.

- New products are included on the CD-ROMs that accompany this book. You get a valuable assortment of VR software, including complete, fully functional versions of Superscape Visualizer, Virtus WalkThrough Stereo, Virtek 3-D Ware Personal Edition, The Journeyman Project Turbo, PhotoMorph 2.0, and Vistapro 1.0. There are also new demos of virtual reality products and games, video clips of cutting edge VR, and much more.

- Coverage on updated virtual reality software is included. Learn about Vistapro 4, VREAM, Superscape, Distant Suns, Virtus WalkThrough Pro, and Virtus VR. In addition, you'll find dozens of new software entries in the VR Software Buyer's Guide on the CD-ROMs.

- Many software products now offer advanced features. I have expanded the tutorials for 3D Studio, Virtus WalkThrough Pro, VREAM, and many other programs to show you how to access key features step by step.

■ In addition, the book is packed with new images, a completely new color section, and more!

As I write this, the image that comes to mind is of the three witches in *Macbeth*. "Bubble, bubble, toil and trouble..." That's the recipe for virtual reality. Mix and match reality and imagination in the strongest concentrations you can stand and see what comes out—goblins and ghosts, major distortions of space-time, or a fly-through of your new kitchen. The only limit to what you can do with virtual reality is right between your ears. Hold on tight, get ready for adventure: it's time for the amazing, 16.7-million color journey into the computer/mind spaces of *Virtual Reality Madness 1996*!

Ron Wodaski
August 1995

I

VIRTUAL REALITY IS HERE

1

VIRTUAL REALITY HAS ARRIVED

The first edition of this book began with a simple assertion:

Virtual Reality has arrived.[1]

What was true two years ago is even more true today. In fact, virtual reality has more than arrived: It's moving in and settling down. Consider the evidence:

■ Head-mounted devices[2] have come down from around $6,000 to the $500 to 1,000 range.[3]

■ More and more games are using either a full 3D or a virtual reality design.

■ Even Nintendo has announced a VR product: Virtual Boy.

■ Several competing software products now are available for creating your very own virtual universes. Several even work in Windows, formerly the wasteland of virtual reality. Many of them are available for just a few hundred dollars. Several of them are free, included with this book!

■ Fancy VR trackballs and six-degrees-of-freedom[4] gizmos are now in the price range of mere mortals (translation: less than $200, down from $1,000 or more).

■ One powerful (Caligari's trueSpace) and several economy, easy-to-use 3D-modeling packages for Windows now are available.

For decades, virtual reality has been nothing more than speculation and promises. Today, you can buy virtual reality hardware and software right in your favorite computer store. Science fiction buffs have been waiting with barely suppressed glee for just this moment. Now that is has arrived, the big question is, "What can I do with VR?" This book holds the answers.

But even with these rapid-fire advances in affordable VR technology, we are only at the beginning. We haven't arrived at the culmination of virtual reality; this is the moment of its birth. There is plenty of room to grow. You still can't get taste from your computer; nor can you surround yourself with the smell of the ocean shore in

---

[1] I have chosen to make liberal use of footnotes throughout the text—sometimes for fun, and sometimes to expand a thought or follow a useful tangent. You have been warned!

[2] In the movies, when you see folks with half or more of their heads covered in a spacey-looking helmet, that's an HMD. *Lawnmower Man* was a good example.

[3] Although you still can spend $6,000 and more if you really feel that you have to.

[4] The *six degrees of freedom* (don't you just love that phrase out of context?) are up/down, left/right, forward/backward, pitch, roll, and yaw. Still confused? There is more on this kind of stuff later. Stay tuned.

the morning. Headsets are still bulky. The action is still all about sight and sound, with just a touch of tactile sensation thrown in for a tease.[5]

I have to confess that it is enormous fun to write about virtual reality. *VR*, as it often is called, is by far the coolest thing to happen on computers since electrons first danced to the whims of programmers. In the first edition, I wrote: "I can't tell you how many times I went storming through the house to find my wife or one of the kids to show them some stunning apparition on my computer screen." This edition marks my third time around the VR merry-go-round, and I found just as many reasons to run screaming around the house as I have in the past. Low-cost helmets, great new game controllers, lower software prices, and much faster screen graphics are just a few of the things that got me excited, and I can only hope you'll have as much pleasure discovering the possibilities of VR as I did.

This book is arranged like a cookbook. You'll find cool recipes that you can mix up in your own home. We have tried to stick mostly with software and hardware that anyone can afford, but sometimes we found stuff so utterly cool and amazing that we included it even if it was expensive. Examples include such software as 3D Studio[6] and SuperScape, and such hardware as head-mounted devices and fancy VR input devices like the Spaceball.

In this chapter, you start with a form of VR that is easy to visualize and work with: 3D world design using Vistapro. As you move through the book, you learn more and more about the concepts and techniques of virtual reality. Along the way, I've tried my best to include lots of fun stuff.[7]

Beginning at the Beginning

Virtual reality is an extremely broad term. It has come to refer to almost anything that has anything at all to do with three dimensions on computers. The original use of

---

[5]Example: data gloves. Still in the development stage, these devices enable you to use your hands as an input device without benefit (or encumbrance) of a mouse or keyboard. Much like a padded glove, these babies still sport wires all over the place and outrageous price tags. With any luck, by the time we're ready to write the next edition of the book, real data gloves will be available. For now, there's not much beyond the Mattel Power Glove.

[6]Release 4 of 3D Studio is a good example of an entirely new class of products. Formerly, you needed a super computer to do animations as powerful as what you see on TV or in the movies. This latest release of 3D Studio, while not exactly cheap, cuts the cost of wild 3D animation by a factor of 10 or more.

[7]This reflects my theory of learning: We learn better and faster when we are having fun. Remember advanced math and how boring it was? What if you had been using what you were learning to build a remote-controlled airplane, or to design a more efficient racing-boat hull? It seems so obvious, you gotta wonder sometimes about the educational system.

the word, back when VR was all in the imagination, referred mostly to complete immersion systems. This meant complex headsets to project a 3D visual space, and a bodysuit full of electronics to send and receive signals about your own body position. Using such a system, you would feel just like you were in a virtual world. More important, you could interact with that imaginary universe.

Such hardware is, in fact, available today. It requires a lot of supporting hardware, however, and represents the farthest edge of VR—in terms of cost and capability. It is not necessary, though, to start with such complex hardware and software at all. To my way of thinking, virtual reality starts in the imagination. Mankind was born with the ability to visualize in three dimensions—that's where VR begins. The computer can only build on or enhance our own built-in VR abilities. For our purposes, virtual reality will encompass the full range of 3D and virtual software and hardware.[8] Some of it will be interactive, and some will be static. But everything will meet the critical requirement for inclusion in this book: It has to be fun.

One of the most fascinating aspects of virtual reality is the creation of virtual landscapes. In this chapter, you learn how to build natural and fantastic landscapes using a product called Vistapro. Vistapro is a wonderful program that I enjoyed a great deal. It isn't often that I find a program that is this enjoyable and fun to use. I have included an earlier version of Vistapro for DOS on the CD-ROMs. It does not have all the features described in this chapter; you need to upgrade to the latest version to enjoy all the features. It is a complete version, however, and you can save the files and images that you create with it to your hard disk. It's not just a demo: It really works.

---

[8]The purists will be on my case for this, but let's face it: VR has many faces. The best current VR technology has its start in 3D—when we get more computing power, we can move from 3D to virtual. I prefer to see the technology as a continuum.

Planets 'R' Us Vistapro 3.0

RECIPE

1 Copy program
2M or more available extended (XMS)[9] memory
1M hard disk space
1t patience

Instructions: Load the landscape of your choice and arrange ingredients in a pleasing setting. Render slowly on a fast machine until done. Serve with animation or morphing, or season with 3D Studio or VREAM for exciting variations. Good rendering is like homemade bread: It has to sit a while before it's ready. Don't be in a hurry.

Vistapro now ships on a CD-ROM, and most of the stuff that was optional last year now is included. The Vistapro CD-ROM edition includes the following goodies, most of which are covered in this chapter:

- Vistapro itself
- MakePath Flight Director for animation
- Vistamorph for landscape special effects
- Landscapes, including Ayers Rock, Mars,[10] and National Parks—a total of more than 3,000 landscapes for your rendering pleasure
- Image and animation samples
- MIDI and audio-music tracks
- A 3D bungee-jump animation

---

[9]It's easy to get confused between EMS and XMS memory. *XMS*, or *extended memory*, is faster because your computer can work with bigger chunks of it. *EMS*, or *expanded memory*, is slower because it requires a lot of juggling of memory space. If the software gives you a choice, choose XMS.

[10]More than 200M of Mars data is included.

Figure 1.1 shows a typical landscape created with Vistapro.[11] It is based on a natural landscape in southwestern Oregon: Crater Lake. The vertical scale has been enhanced to emphasize details; and the sky, lighting, and angle of view were chosen to reflect the purpose for the image: a desktop for Windows. There's lots of clear space in the sky for icons.

Figure 1.1
A landscape created
with Vistapro 3.0.

This image appears exactly as it was created in Vistapro. As you learn how to work with Vistapro, you can control precisely how the image appears: realistic or dreamy, sharply defined or obscured by fog. And after creating a landscape, you can enhance realism further by altering the image using paint programs, such as Photoshop from Adobe. Figure 1.2 shows a fanciful Mars landscape at local dawn, including an artificial lens flare for a nice touch of ultra-realism.

It's easy to create a landscape in Vistapro. The program includes mapping data for a number of real locations, from Big Sur in California to the Alps in Europe. You also can create *fractal landscapes*—scenes based on the science of fractal[12] imagery. To create

---

[11]The CD-ROM includes numerous generated landscapes as well. These landscapes come in all sizes, so you can have fun no matter what computer you have. Images range from basic 8-bit images to 1024×768, 24-bit, photo-realistic images. There are even some 3D images for use with red/blue 3D glasses.

[12]*Fractal* comes from the word *fraction*. It refers to the use of fractional dimensions to create interesting, lifelike images. You draw on paper in two dimensions, and experience life in three dimensions, for example. A fractal image might have a dimension of 2.65, instead of a simple, straightforward 2 or 3.

a landscape, you just set a number of parameters and click the Render button (see Fig. 1.3 to view a rendering in progress). To make life even easier, Vistapro comes with presets you can use to quickly set up for rendering.

Figure 1.2
A Vistapro image enhanced in Adobe Photoshop for Windows.

Figure 1.3
A Vistapro land-scape partially generated.

I have included demo versions of Vistapro 3.0 for DOS and Windows on the CD-ROMs that accompany this book. You can use the demo versions to explore the capabilities of the program. Unlike most demo programs, it is full-featured; you can even save your work to disk. You also can get Vistapro add-on products that enable you to create morphs[13] and animations. With these add-ons, you can create landscapes that grow and change before your eyes, or you can animate a fly-through of a landscape.

The opening screen of Vistapro is shown in Figure 1.4.[14] The landscape is on the left, and various controls are on the right. In this section, we look at how you can use the controls to create fractal landscapes, to modify existing landscapes, and to render landscapes in a variety of interesting ways.

Perhaps the nicest thing about Vistapro is that you can use it to do wonderful things without having to worry a whole lot about the complexities of 3D. Drawing software is awkward to use in 3D, because it requires you to think in three dimensions. With Vistapro, you can rely on basic map-reading skills.

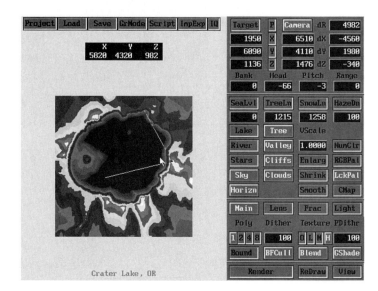

Figure 1.4
The Vistapro screen.

---

[13]The term *morph* is a shortened version of the word *metamorphosis*. A morph involves a visual transformation of one image into another. The movie *Terminator 2* used numerous morphs of a police officer turning into the liquid-metal terminator. Many commercials also feature morphs these days, such as a car morphing into a tiger.

[14]Vistapro originally was written for the Amiga, so the interface isn't PC standard. However, Vistapro is easy to use and shouldn't present any usage problems once you learn a few quirks. Quick tip: A gadget is really a text box (Windows style), and you have to press Enter to complete your entry.

Setting Up for Rendering

Vistapro normally involves three steps. You can spend more or less time at each step to perfect your landscape:

- Create or select a map
- Set scene parameters
- Render

You can create a map in various ways, and you always can load one of the many maps supplied with the program. Vistapro uses Digital Elevation Modeling (DEM) to describe the 3D coordinates of a landscape. The sample files included with the program rely on USGS[15] mapping data and are extremely accurate.

Instant Virtual Reality

In the following sections, you learn how to fine-tune the various settings available in Vistapro to produce exactly the kind of landscape you want. You don't have to twiddle the dials, however, to get results. To follow along with this example, you can use the demo version supplied on disc or the regular version of Vistapro 3.0. To begin, load one of the supplied DEM files by clicking the Load menu and dragging to the Load DEM option. (Refer to Fig. 1.4 to locate the menu bar at the top left of the Vistapro screen.) Pick any file on the list, such as CRATERLA.DEM, and click it. Click the Load button at the upper left to load the file.

There's a tiny little button at the right of the menu, labeled IQ. Click this button to display a list of predefined settings:

Low—This setting renders very quickly, but the results are crude. Low is useful when you want to check the general appearance of the landscape quickly.

Medium—This setting is useful for slower computers or to get a (relatively) quick look at your landscape.

High—This setting yields useful results—images that look realistic and can be used in desktop publishing or other situations that require detailed images.

Ultra—This sets Vistapro for extremely high-quality rendering. It takes longer to render images, but the results often are stunning.

User—You also can define your own settings.

---

[15]That's the United States Geologic Survey.

The button you pick depends on what you would like to see, and also on the speed of your computer.[16] If you are using a 386/25 or slower machine, I recommend the Medium setting for your first rendering. For faster computers, High or even Ultra is fine.

Clicking one of the IQ buttons sets numerous parameters; you might notice some of the settings on the right side of the screen changing. Don't worry about those settings yet. The only button you are interested in is at the bottom left of the controls: Render. Click it, and watch as the landscape is created bit by bit on-screen. The speed of rendering varies dramatically with the speed of your computer and with the level of quality you set. Rendering can take from a few seconds to a minute.

The border of the screen flashes when the rendering is complete. To save the rendering, press Esc, and then click the Save menu. Select the image type you want to save. For this exercise, I suggest using Save PCX. This option saves your landscape rendering as an 8-bit PCX image.

Basic Settings

One setting makes a dramatic difference in the appearance of your rendered images: the screen resolution. By default, Vistapro assumes that you have the most basic VGA display hardware installed.[17] If you have a Super VGA card, however, don't despair: If it includes support for VESA,[18] you can use Super VGA resolutions for rendering.

Display cards support the VESA standard in two ways:

■ Right in the hardware
■ Using a TSR[19] program

---

[16]Rendering is a CPU-intensive activity. Until recently, personal computers were simply too slow to be used for rendering. If you feel badly about the time it takes to render, consider this: Until the 486 CPU came along, most rendering was done on supercomputers like the Cray.

[17]The default resolution is 320×200 and 256 colors (sometimes called MCGA). This is a standard VGA resolution.

[18]There is a long story behind VESA. Every display adapter has its own way of doing Super VGA; for a long time, there was no standard way of implementing Super VGA. This was a big problem for software companies, who had to write different software for each Super VGA display card or pass up support for Super VGA. VESA changed that by creating a standard interface for Super VGA resolutions (800×600, 1024×768, and so on).

[19]*Terminate and Stay Resident.* These are programs that load into memory when your computer starts, and stay there all the time you use it. They are typically found in your CONFIG.SYS and AUTOEXEC.BAT files.

If your card supports VESA in the hardware, you don't need to do anything to use Vistapro at Super VGA resolutions.[20] Vistapro checks your video card to see whether it supports VESA automatically.

If your card uses a TSR to support VESA, you need to load that program before you run Vistapro to get Super VGA support. Consult the documentation that came with your video card for information.

If you have VESA support (and most recent video display cards do support VESA), you gain access to the Super VGA resolutions. Vistapro supports a number of Super VGA resolutions, ranging from 640×400 to 1,280×1,024. Most video cards that support 1,280×1,024, however, don't support it under VESA, so the highest resolution you are likely to be able to use is 1,024×768. This is more than adequate for most needs. To set the resolution, use the GrMode menu button. This menu also enables you to turn on support for 24-bit color. If you choose to use 24-bit color, keep in mind that the file sizes for high-resolution images can get very large—1,024×768×24 bits is 2,359,296 bytes (2,304K).

Not all video-card drivers support VESA as well as they should. If you encounter problems—such as a black or gray screen, vertical bars, or scrambled images—you should contact the video-card manufacturer for an updated VESA driver.

If you are working with the demo version of Vistapro 3.0 from the CD-ROMs, disk file size doesn't matter—you can't save to disk anyway. However, if you only have the minimum amount of memory required by Vistapro installed (2M), you might be limited to the lower screen resolutions.

Camera and Target

In the "Instant Virtual Reality" section earlier in this chapter, the view you saw used the default camera and target locations. In this section, you learn how to set up your own camera and target positions.

Figure 1.5 shows the controls for camera and target. Notice the three columns at the top, and the row of settings at the bottom. The first column, at the left, defines the target location in 3D coordinates. The middle column defines the camera location,

---

[20]The demo version of Vistapro supplied on the CDs might not support some or all of your computer's Super VGA resolutions.

and the far right column shows the delta[21] between the Target and Camera coordinates. You can use the small buttons between the Target and Camera settings to lock one or more of the settings. You use the bottom row of settings to change the orientation (heading) of the camera. All distances are measured in meters, and all headings are measured in degrees.

Figure 1.5
Camera and target controls.

When you work in two dimensions, only two coordinates are needed to specify a location: height and width. Working in three dimensions requires three coordinates to specify a location: height, width, and depth. The first two dimensions, height and width, are referred to using the letters **X** and **Y**.[22] The third dimension, depth, uses the letter **Z**. These letters are a standard shorthand way of referring to the three dimensions; you'll see these letters over and over in this book and elsewhere.

You can see the letters X, Y, and Z in the columns under the Camera and Target controls. Notice the column of buttons between the Camera and Target columns; you use these buttons to lock the current position of the camera and target along any one dimension. If you want to prevent any changes to height, for example, simply click the Z button before moving the camera or target.

Moving the camera or target is very easy. Click the appropriate button at the top of the column—either Camera or Target. Then click anywhere on the map; the camera or target then moves to the new location. Both are marked by a tiny square, and the camera angle is displayed by two lines radiating from the camera. Objects within the angle are included in the rendering.[23]

The third column shows the delta, or difference, between the target and the camera. The top number, dR, is the actual range distance (a straight line, in meters) from the camera to the target. The three figures below dR—dX, dY, and dZ—represent the distance in the X, Y, and Z directions. For example, if the camera is at 1,000 meters and the target is at 500 meters, then dZ is equal to –500 meters.

---

[21]*Delta* is a Greek letter used by scientists and mathematicians to indicate change or difference.

[22]These are called *Cartesian coordinates*, as you may have learned in high school algebra or math class.

[23]Because the Camera view is 3D and the Map view is 2D, you will find that objects outside the angle might show up in the rendered landscape. If you set the camera overlooking the valley, for example, objects in the valley show up for some distance outside the indicated angle.

Four settings are located at the bottom of the camera/target area. These settings control the orientation of the camera, including such things as tilt and rotation. Vistapro uses the technical terms[24] for each kind of orientation. To understand the terms, imagine that you are five years old again and playing airplane with your friends. Your arms are out to the side and serve as your wings. Most of these measurements describe a rotation of one kind or another, so most measurements are expressed as degrees:[25]

> **Bank**—If you lower your left wing (arm),[26] that is a bank to the left (counterclockwise), and it is expressed as a negative number. If you lower your right wing, that is a bank to the right and is expressed as a positive number. A bank of –10 means that the left wing is lowered 10 degrees.
>
> **Head**—Heading describes the direction you are facing. North is 0; south is 180 degrees. Rotation to the right (clockwise) is a positive number; rotation to the left is a negative number. If you refer back to Figure 1.4, where the heading is –66, you see that this means the camera is facing roughly west northwest.
>
> **Pitch**—If you lean forward or backward, you can change your pitch. If you pitch forward (nose down), that's a negative number. If you pitch backward (nose up), that's a positive number. A positive pitch of 90 degrees puts your nose right on the ceiling.
>
> **Range**—This is not a measurement in degrees; it uses meters. It is a setting you can use to eliminate portions of the view from the rendering. If you enter 1,000 meters, for example, objects more than 1,000 meters away are not rendered. Similarly, if you enter –500, objects closer than 500 meters are not rendered.

By default, the camera is placed 30 meters above the height of the landscape at the location you choose. This placement prevents nearby objects from obscuring the view. You can change the camera height by entering a new number in the Camera Z control.[27] You don't need to make any changes to Bank, Head, Pitch, or Range to get useful renderings. Vistapro sets these when you locate the target or camera.

---

[24]These terms are taken from aviation and often are used to describe the movements of an aircraft.

[25]There are 360 degrees in a complete circle. Thus, a quarter rotation is 90 degrees, and a half rotation is 180 degrees.

[26]Of course, the right wing (arm) goes up at the same time.

[27]You can change the settings in any of the controls manually at any time before rendering.

For a dramatic point of view, change the camera height to 500 or 1,000 meters above the height of the map location.

Trees and Clouds, Lakes, and Rivers

The middle portion of the control panel contains a number of parameters that have a major impact on the appearance of your rendered landscape (see Fig. 1.6). You can add a number of natural features, including such things as lakes and rivers, clouds, stars, cliffs, and so on.

Figure 1.6
The Vistapro middle control panel.

The middle control panel also includes settings for various boundaries, such as the distance at which haze becomes apparent and the tree line. Using these settings, you can create a very natural-looking landscape.

Four kinds of settings are located on the middle control panel:

■ Boundaries

■ Natural features

■ Scale and textures

■ Colors

You learn about each of these settings in the following subsections.

Boundaries

The Boundaries settings enable you to establish the location of basic natural boundaries in the landscape. You can use these settings to make subtle adjustments to the landscape. You can add haze to increase the sense of distance in the landscape, for example.

There are four Boundaries settings you can control:

> **SeaLvl**—Use this setting to change sea level. If you enter 500, for example, all portions of the landscape at or below 500 meters are changed to 0 meters.

All portions of the landscape above 500 meters are lowered by 500 meters. The result is that everything at or below sea level is flattened. To set sea level based on the map, click the SeaLvl button and then click the map to indicate an elevation.

TreeLn—Vistapro can render trees in the landscape. This number defines the height in meters above which trees will not grow. This reflects the way trees actually grow in natural settings. As with many of its features, Vistapro uses artificial intelligence to decide where, exactly, to put trees. Steep slopes have a lower treeline and flat surfaces have a higher tree line. Again, this reflects the way trees behave in nature. To set a tree level based on the map, click the TreeLn button, and then click the map to indicate an elevation.

SnowLn—This is the lowest level at which Vistapro draws snow on the landscape. As with the tree line, Vistapro bends the rules to generate a realistic-looking snow line. To set a snow level based on the map, click the SnowLn button, and then click the map to indicate an elevation.

HazeDn—This is the haze distance; a value of 0 eliminates haze, values up to about 1,000 give progressively more haze, and values over 1,000 generate a thick fog.[28] To have Vistapro calculate a typical haze value, click the HazeDn button.

Natural Features

Version 3.0 of Vistapro gives you control over a number of natural features of the landscape. Such features can make a dramatic difference in the appearance of the rendered image. Table 1.1 lists the various settings you can control.

Table 1.1. Natural Features in Vistapro 3.0.

Feature	Description
Lake	Click this button, and then click a point on the map. All points at that elevation then define a continuous shoreline surrounding a lake. Be careful with this setting; if there is a break in the proposed shoreline, the lake might spill over into places you didn't intend.

continues

---

[28]In most cases, such foggy scenes aren't very useful—almost all of the detail from the landscape is lost. One type of landscape that sometimes benefits from severe haze is a seacoast, where some fog can look terrific.

Table 1.1. continued

Feature	Description
River	Click this button, and then click a point on the map. Vistapro then calculates a river course for you. If the river isn't wide enough for your needs, click an adjoining point to widen the river.
Stars	Use this option in place of Sky for a nighttime effect. You can choose large or small stars. Unless you intend to output to videotape, small stars are your best bet. **Important:** If you don't change the landscape colors, they still render in daytime colors!
Sky	Causes Vistapro to render a sky. If you have a bitmap you want to use as a sky, turn off Sky and use the Load/Background menu selection to load your bitmap.
Horizon	Causes Vistapro to render a horizon line. If you don't want a distant horizon, or if you have your own background, click to turn off this setting. In most cases, you will want Horizon on.[29]
Tree	Causes Vistapro to add trees to the landscape. You don't see the trees until you render. The dialog box that you use to define the type and density of trees is described later in this section.
Valley	Determines the extent to which a valley changes the tree line or snow line. Clicking this setting opens a dialog box with two values. **Valley Width** determines how much valley effect is used. The default value is 100. **Valley Scale** determines the extent of valley effect at each valley point. Larger numbers expand the range of the valley effect, and smaller numbers restrict the range. The default is 8.
Cliffs	Defines which portions of the landscape are steep enough to be considered cliffs. Special colors are used to render cliffs. In some cases, a more natural look results if Cliffs is turned off. You need to experiment to see the effect on a given landscape.

---

[29]If you set a very high camera elevation, having Horizon on usually improves the appearance of the image. A high camera elevation might show the edges of the map, and a carefully chosen horizon color can make this less noticeable.

Feature	Description
Clouds	Causes Vistapro to add clouds to the sky. You don't see the clouds until you render. The dialog box that you use to define the type and density of clouds is described later in this section.

All these controls have noticeable effects on the rendered image, but several have a big impact on the final rendered image. We'll look at those controls in detail now.

Lake

The Lake setting is powerful and dangerous, but it can add a touch of realism to a scene. You can change the colors for water to create different moods.[30] The most important thing to learn is the relationship between the point you click and the shape of the lake. Fortunately, Vistapro enables you to preview the appearance of the lake before you finalize it.[31]

River

It takes a little experimentation to develop a knack for getting rivers to look right. A single click to create a river is seldom enough to get a useful river effect; it's more like a creek effect. To create natural-looking rivers, look for the characteristic land forms on the map. Figure 1.7 shows a close-up of a portion of a map, and the best areas for starting a river are marked. Figure 1.8 shows the results of a single click to create a river; Figure 1.10 shows a river created from multiple clicks. Note that there are several tributaries to the river, and that the river is wider.

Figure 1.9 shows the results of rendering the river in Figure 1.8. Note that the river is almost invisible. Figure 1.11 shows a rendering of the river in Figure 1.10. In this case, the river fits the scale of the landscape much better.

---

[30]See the "Colors" section, later in the chapter.

[31]Unfortunately, the dialog box that asks you `Accept Lake?` often covers the preview area. You need a quick eye to determine whether the lake will work for you, because you might see only the preview for a fraction of a second. If in doubt, I highly recommend saving your work before creating a lake!

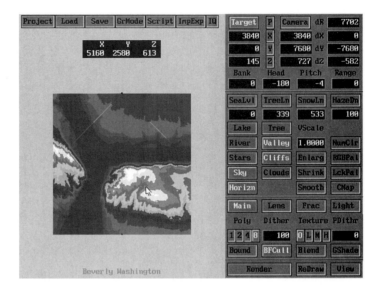

Figure 1.7
A detail of a map, showing good locations for originating a river.

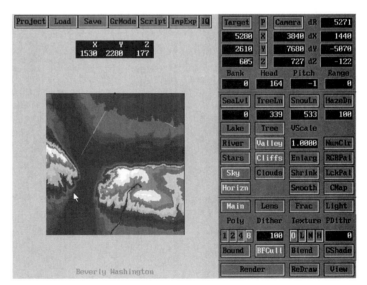

Figure 1.8
A river created with a single click of the mouse.

Figure 1.9
A rendering of the river created in Figure 1.8.

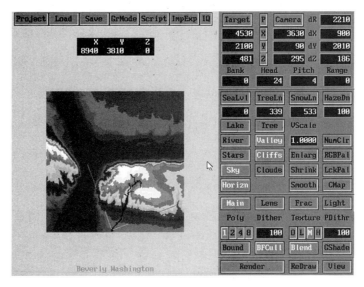

Figure 1.10
A river created with multiple mouse clicks.

Figure 1.11
A rendering of the
river created in
Figure 1.10.

Stars

It's easy to add stars to your images: Just click the Stars button to enable that feature. This action only changes the appearance of the sky, however, which now includes a dark background and lots of stars. The landscape colors don't change. The resulting image won't look bad, but if you want a realistic nighttime scene, you need to edit the landscape colors. Refer to the "Colors" section later in this chapter for more information.

Like other additions to the landscape, such as trees and clouds, the starry sky renders consistently. If you create an animation, you can count on the stars behaving like real stars. That is, they appear to move as the animation's point of view changes.

Trees

The newest version of Vistapro, version 3.0, improves greatly on the original version in this area. Vistapro 3.0 is capable of rendering realistic-looking trees. You pay a price for such realism, however: Rendering time increases dramatically if you set the quality of tree images very high. Unless you are rendering a final image, you probably want to render trees at modest settings.

Clicking the Trees button when it is off displays the Tree Control Panel shown in Figure 1.12.

The first thing to notice is that there are four kinds of trees: Pine, Oak, Cactus, and Palm (see Fig. 1.13 for an example of pine trees). Most types of terrain in Vistapro are similar to this figure. Each terrain type has a range of colors used to render the terrain. The default colors for trees are four shades of green, naturally. Because Vistapro offers several colors, you can generate more varied and interesting textures for the many kinds of terrain.

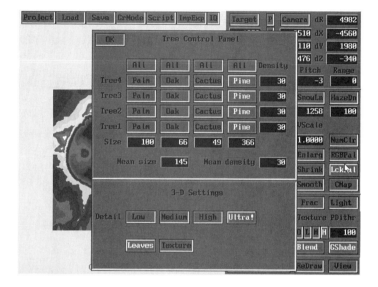

Figure 1.12
The Tree Control Panel for defining the characteristics of trees.

Figure 1.13
Vistapro pine trees.

The Tree Control Panel is a lot like a program within a program. It controls the rendering of trees, which are complete, discrete, fractal objects. The top half of the Control Panel enables you to define the types of trees that appear at specific elevations, as well as the size and density of trees at each elevation.

If you want to have more pine trees at high elevations and more oak trees at low elevations, for example, you can set Tree4 as Pine, Tree3 as both Pine and Oak, Tree2 as Pine and Oak, and Tree1 as Oak.

The density of trees you use varies with the landscape. If you want a sparse look, try settings of 10 to 30. If you want a loose forest, try a setting of 50. Higher settings give you a full forest, and you cannot see individual trees. Size also varies, depending on the landscape. You might need to experiment with different sizes until you get the look you want. A flat landscape probably looks best with smaller trees, and a deep valley with steep cliffs might look better with taller trees. When in doubt, simply accept the default settings.

You can control the overall size and density of all tree types by using the Mean Size and Mean Density settings.

The Tree Control Panel also contains settings for 3D rendering of trees. You can choose different levels of detail: Low, Medium, High, and Ultra. As a general rule, match the tree detail to the image size. If you are rendering at 320×200, Low detail is fine. Any additional detail simply gets lost. Even at 1,024×768, only trees closest to the camera benefit from the extra detail.

The two buttons at the bottom of the Tree Control Panel, Leaves and Texture, further refine the appearance of trees. The Leaves button does just what you would expect: It adds leaves to the trees. The Texture button adds fractal textures to leaves and branches of trees. If you don't use 3D settings for trees, they are created as stick figures, as shown in Figure 1.14. Figure 1.15 shows a rendered image with leaves, and Figure 1.16 shows image 1.15b with texture instead of leaves. All these images were rendered at 1,024×768 with an IQ setting of Ultra.

a

Figure 1.14
Two-dimensional trees: oak (a) and palm (b).

b

Figure 1.15
Oak (a) and palm
(b) trees with leaves.

Figure 1.16
Palm trees with texture. Note that these are not substantially different from trees without texture at this resolution (640×480).

Clouds

Your landscape needs a good set of natural-looking clouds to be complete. It just wouldn't do to have a gorgeous, natural landscape sitting under a completely artificial sky, now would it? A click of the Clouds button displays the Cloud Control Panel shown in Figure 1.17. This box contains just a few buttons and controls, but it doesn't take much to create a pleasing sky.

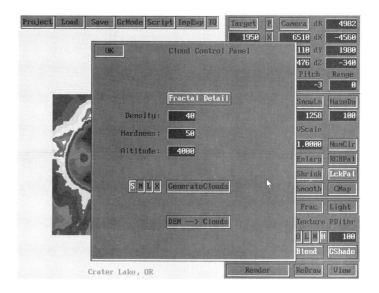

Figure 1.17
The Cloud Control Panel.

Table 1.2 lists the various cloud controls.

Table 1.2. Vistapro Cloud Controls.

Control	Description
Fractal Detail	Adds fractal details to clouds for a more realistic effect.
Density	Determines the total cloud coverage. Higher numbers result in more clouds.
Hardness	Sets fluffiness. Lower settings result in fluffy, fleecy clouds.
Altitude	Determines the height of clouds. Clouds always are created higher than the camera's height.
S/M/L/X	Click one of these buttons to determine the size of the clouds, ranging from small to extra large.
GenerateClouds	After you have the settings the way you want them, click this button to generate the clouds.
DEM —> Clouds	Creates clouds based on the DEM data of the current landscape. You can use this setting to create clouds and then save them with the Save/Clouds menu item.

You can use the DEM —> Clouds button for a very interesting effect: skywriting. Create a PCX file in your favorite Image Editor that contains text, and then load it into Vistapro using the PCX —> DEM selection on the ImpExp[32] menu. Then use the DEM —> Clouds button to create clouds shaped like the text.

Figure 1.18 shows simple, medium clouds without any fractal detail, and Figure 1.19 shows clouds with fractal detail added. The differences are subtle, but then so are clouds.

---

[32]Import/Export

Figure 1.18
Clouds without fractal detail.

Figure 1.19
Clouds with fractal detail (most noticeable just to the right of the top center).

Scale and Textures

Just to the right of the controls for natural features is the third column of buttons in the middle control panel: scale and texture settings (refer to Fig. 1.10). The three scale settings and one texture setting are shown in Table 1.3.

Table 1.3. Vistapro Scale and Texture Settings.

Control	Type	Description
VScale	Scale	Determines the vertical scale factor.
Enlarg	Scale	Enlarges a portion of the map to full map size.
Shrink	Scale	Shrinks multi-part maps to the next smaller size.
Smooth	Texture	Smoothes rough edges in the map.

Vertical Scale

Every point on the map is multiplied by the number you enter into the VScale box. This number increases or decreases the height of all points on the map. If you enter a value of 2.0000, for example, every point becomes twice as high. If you enter a value of 0.5000, every point is half as high. Because the lowest level on the map is always 0, numbers greater than 1 have the effect of increasing the vertical relief of the map.[33] Numbers between 0 and 1 reduce vertical relief.

You also can enter negative numbers. These numbers turn the map "inside out." That is, mountains become valleys and valleys become mountains. This can produce some very interesting effects.

Enlarge

This control enables you to enlarge a portion of a map to full map size. This setting can be useful when you generate a map using fractals[34]—if you see an interesting portion of the map, you can enlarge it and work with just that portion of the map.

After enlargement, the map is smoother than it was because the partial map does not have the same level of detail as the full map. You can use the Fractalize button in the lower control panel to artificially add realistic detail.

Shrink

Shrink is not the exact opposite of Enlarge. A little background is necessary. Vistapro can work with several sizes of maps. The smallest size, 258×258 data points, is appropriately called Small. The standard-size map is called Large, and it is 514×514 data points. You can load one standard Vistapro DEM file or up to four small DEM files. The largest size, Huge, is 1,026×1,026 data points. This can contain up to 16 small files, four standard files, or one giant, extra-big, huge file.

---

[33]This is a fancy way of saying that the mountains get higher in relation to the valleys.
[34]See the "Fractal Magic" section.

The Shrink command shrinks the current map by one step in this hierarchy. Thus, a huge file shrinks to large, and a large shrinks to a small. You cannot shrink a small file any farther.

This business of combining DEM files to view larger areas is new in version 3.0 of Vistapro. Vistapro loads all files in a larger view if you set the image size to Automatic.[35]

Smooth

You seldom need to use smoothing with a DEM file that represents real data, but smoothing can be very useful when you are creating maps by other means. Smoothing removes the "rough spots" in the data. Look at Figure 1.20, for example, which shows a map generated using fractals. The texture is extremely rough. Now look at Figure 1.21 after smoothing has been applied; the texture is noticeably smoother.[36]

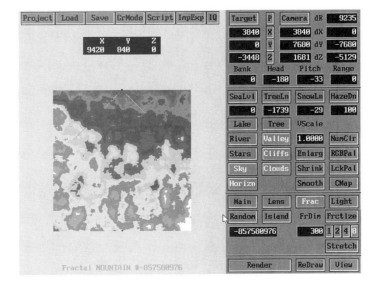

Figure 1.20
A map with very rough texture.

---

[35]This is set on the Project menu: Set DEM Size.

[36]You can use smoothing several times to tame a particularly rough landscape. Smoothing tends to affect high points more than low points, however, so overuse can reduce the overall height of the terrain. You might need to apply a larger vertical scale after repeated smoothing.

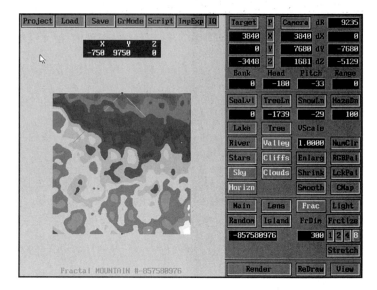

Figure 1.21
*The same map after
smoothing has been
applied.*

Use smoothing when the map details are too complex to make out clearly.

Colors

This brings us to the last column of controls in the middle control panel (refer to Fig. 1.21). There are four buttons, as explained in Table 1.4.

Table 1.4. Vistapro Color Controls.

Control	Description
NumClr	Rendering normally uses all 256 colors in the 8-bit palette. If you plan to edit the image in a paint program, this setting enables you to use fewer colors for a rendering. You then can use the remaining palette slots for additional colors in a paint program. If your paint program supports 24-bit color, this setting is not necessary.
RGBPal	Normally, Vistapro selects the colors for a palette prior to rendering the image. This button enables you to force Vistapro to select a palette based on colors that actually appear in the rendered image. You must enable 24-bit support on the GrMode menu first, however.

Control	Description
LckPal	This setting locks the color palette. Normally, Vistapro calculates a separate palette for each image. This button forces Vistapro to use the current palette for rendering.
CMap	Clicking this button activates the ColorMap Control Panel, which is described in this section.

Under most conditions, you don't need to do anything at all with this group of buttons. You can blissfully go on generating image after image without ever visiting this section of the screen. However, for special purposes, these are handy settings to have around.

After you have played around with Vistapro for a while, it can be fun to play around with the colors in a scene. You might want to render a nighttime scene, for example, or perhaps a Mars landscape appeals to you. The CMap button gives you the power to completely control the colors used by the system to render images. You can even save color settings to disk for later use. Figure 1.22 shows the ColorMap Control Panel.

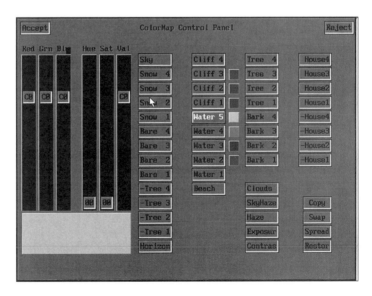

Figure 1.22
*The ColorMap
Control Panel.*

The ColorMap Control Panel has a zillion buttons, and it's both easy and complex to use. The easy part is setting individual colors. To set a color, click the button (such as Sky) and then adjust the Red/Green/Blue or the Hue/Saturation/Value sliders until you have the color you want. The hard part is creating a set of colors that gives you scenes that look the way you want them to look.

I've tried many techniques for developing a coherent set of colors, and only one method works consistently well: working within groups of colors, and then with groups of colors. Generally, I make one pass through all the color buttons, starting with Sky and working through the buttons, one color at a time. When I get to the first color in a group, I spend some time creating a color that is just right. The higher numbered colors, such as Snow4, are located at higher elevations and are usually the brighter colors.[37] If I set a bright color in the 4 position, I then can set the exact same color in the 3 position, and then use the Value slider to darken it a little. This method enables me to maintain tight control over color values inside a group. If you want to vary hue or saturation instead of value, of course, you simply can change that slider instead.

Using this technique, you wind up with four colors that change predictably. The color might not be exactly what you want, or it might not work well with other color groups, but you now have a controlled situation that makes it easier to edit the entire color group, if that is necessary.

After I set up all the colors in all the color groups, I render a sample image to see the effect of the colors. If it is not the effect I want, I go back to the ColorMap Control Panel and adjust the colors in whichever groups are causing a problem. If the snow is too dark, for example, I lighten each of the colors in the Snow group by the same amount.

This process requires a light touch and some patience, but you can create some amazing-looking scenes if you are willing to take the trouble to create your own color map.

Bottom Control Panels

The bottom control panel can take on four different appearances, depending on which of the four buttons at the top of the panel you click (refer to Fig. 1.21). These panel variations are listed in Table 1.5, and are described in detail in this section.

Table 1.5. The Vistapro Bottom Control Panel.

Variation	Description
Main	Enables you to set rendering parameters and to establish basic geometry for rendering. You also need to have this panel active to start rendering.

---

[37]If you have some special color scheme in mind, of course, you might want the reverse.

Variation	Description
Lens	Enables you to adjust the angle of view for the camera and to create red/blue 3D images.[38]
Frac	Gives you access to fractal features, which include such goodies as adding fractal detail to a map or creating a complete fractal landscape.
Light	Enables you to adjust lighting angle and to set shadow style.

The controls in the bottom control panel are settings that you use frequently. The most important panel to understand is the Main Control Panel, because its controls have a major impact on the appearance of your rendered image.

Main

Getting the right settings on the Main Control Panel can make or break your rendering (see Fig. 1.23). Knowing what to expect for various settings is the key to both natural and fantasy landscapes. You learn about the Main Control Panel button by button in this section.

Figure 1.23
The main version of the bottom control panel.

Poly

A properly rendered landscape doesn't show it, but it is made up of perfectly ordinary polygons.[39] These four minibuttons determine the size of the polygons used for rendering. Smaller polygons lead to more detailed renderings. Thus, a setting of 1 uses the smallest polygons and a setting of 8 uses the largest polygons. Figure 1.24 shows a landscape rendered with a Polygon setting of 8, and Figure 1.25 shows the same landscape rendered with a setting of 1. For these examples, to emphasize the effect of changing the Polygon setting, no special smoothing or texturing capabilities were used.

---

[38]You need red/blue 3D glasses to get the stereo effect.

[39]If you didn't learn about polygons in geometry class, read on. A *polygon* is a flat shape bounded by three or more lines that meet at vertices (a *vertex* is a fancy name for a corner). The simplest polygon is a triangle, and most 3D programs build more complex objects out of triangular polygons. A rectangle or an octagon is also an example of a polygon. Polygons with sides of equal length are called *regular polygons*.

Figure 1.24
*A landscape
rendered with a
polygon setting of 8.*

Figure 1.25
*A landscape
rendered with a
polygon setting of 1.*

Large polygons are useful in the early stages of designing a landscape. You can check lighting angles, for example, without taking a lot of time for a detailed rendering. If all you want to know is whether a given cliff face is in light or shadow, a quick rendering is all you need.

After you have the gross features of the landscape worked out, however, you need to use progressively smaller polygon settings to see what your landscape looks like.

Dither

Vistapro determines what color to use for a given polygon based on its altitude.[40] By itself, this creates a banding effect that doesn't look natural. You can use this setting to determine the amount of dithering between adjacent bands of color.[41]

A value of 100 provides a modest amount of dithering—just enough to blend adjoining areas slightly. Higher values smooth the transitions more; values of more than 1,000 make it impossible to distinguish one area from another. A value of 0 turns off dithering completely.

Texture

Texture is a very powerful feature that has a lot to do with how natural your landscapes look. Without texture, color alone is used to suggest landscape features. Unless you want an unnatural look to your landscape, texture is a good idea. However, texture adds quite a bit of time to the rendering process.

Vistapro offers four minibuttons for setting texture levels. O stands for Off, and the remaining buttons set texture levels of Low, Medium, and High. When you set the texture level to Low or more, you are asked to choose between Shading and Altitude texturing.

Shading texture is less CPU-intensive than altitude texture. If you click Shading, Vistapro breaks each polygon into smaller polygons and uses a slightly different color for each polygon.[42] Altitude shading uses fractal technology to break the larger polygons into smaller polygons, each of which is shaded and colored individually. This shading creates extremely realistic features. If realism is your goal, make sure that you set Altitude shading to On.

---

[40]Strictly speaking, this is not true. Vistapro considers other things besides altitude when deciding what color to use. A polygon on the side of a mountain might be below the snow line, for example, but Vistapro might decide to render it as snow or as a cliff instead of basing the color on height. Vistapro takes a large number of values into consideration during rendering. Many of these values are intended to create the most natural-looking landscapes.

[41]*Dithering* is a simple mixing of pixels from one area with the pixels in an adjoining area.

[42]If you choose to use shading texture, try clicking the GShade button as well. This turns on *Gouraud shading*, a technique that is very effective for fantasy-style landscapes. It normally is not useful to use Gouraud shading with altitude, because Gouraud obliterates the details generated by altitude shading.

PDithr

PDithr stands for *pixel dithering*. Pixel dithering is different from regular dithering. Regular dithering affects the boundaries between landscape colors. *Pixel dithering* applies to every pixel in the image. Generally, a little pixel dithering—100 to 250 units—is a good thing. This is particularly useful in the sky. Vistapro uses only a few colors for the sky, and pixel dithering improves the situation.

Bound

Clicking this button enables you to *mark* (set a boundary for) an area. During rendering, only the portion of the map within the boundary area is rendered.

BFCull

BFCull stands for *back-face culling*. When this button is enabled, polygons facing away from the point of view are not calculated. It's hard to think of a situation in which you wouldn't keep this feature turned on. The only example that comes to mind involves putting the camera inside a mountain, where you would want to see the complete underside of the mountain.

Blend

Blend is yet another control that is easy to confuse with dithering. If the Blend button is enabled, Vistapro averages the colors of a polygon with those of the polygons surrounding it. This action improves the appearance of distant portions of the rendering, and you have to decide for yourself whether the reduced intensity of color in the foreground is worth the result.

GShade

The GShade button controls Gouraud shading. This form of shading is used by a variety of 3D software products, including 3D Studio. GShade is very effective at eliminating boundaries between polygons. However, this setting also has a tendency to make the landscape look less realistic because it decreases the apparent level of detail in the image. GShade is very useful for creating fantasy landscapes with a romantic feel to them. Figure 1.26, for example, shows a landscape generated with a realistic effect, and Figure 1.27 shows the same landscape using Gouraud shading.

Figure 1.26
*A landscape
rendered without
Gouraud shading.*

Figure 1.27
*A landscape
rendered with
Gouraud shading*

Lens

Vistapro uses the image of a camera to describe the point of view used for the rendering. The analogy isn't carried very far,[43] but it is useful and it does make it easier to get a feel for what the rendering looks like. After all, who hasn't had at least some experience with a camera these days?

---

[43]For example, 3D Studio uses extensive camera terminology and techniques. You can *roll* or *dolly* the camera, and you can set a very wide range of lens characteristics.

Figure 1.28 shows the appearance of the bottom control panel when the Lens button is enabled. Many buttons are located on this panel, but most of them are for special purposes. In fact, for most uses, you don't need to mess with the Lens settings at all.

Figure 1.28
*The Lens version of
the bottom control
panel.*

The primary control you have over the lens is *focal length*. In nontechnical terms, your choices range from wide angle to telephoto. However, the numbers don't correspond to the focal length values for the most common lens in use today for 35-mm cameras. Lower numbers represent wider fields of view, and higher numbers represent narrower fields of view. If you click the Wide button, you get a 90-degree field of view. This view is useful for most situations. In real life, a wide-angle lens is the lens of choice for landscape photography, and that's generally true for Vistapro as well.

The manual for Vistapro points out that you can set very, very high values for the focal length, but you need to move the camera very far away from the scene. You can enter a value of 30,000, for example, but the camera must be 1 million meters away from the scene to get any kind of useful image. (That's because the field of view is so narrow that you must "step" *way* back to see anything useful.)

The remaining controls enable you to create 3D images using red/blue images (you need red/blue glasses to view the images) and panoramic images. The procedure for creating red/blue 3D images is straightforward and is explained well in the Vistapro manual. However, even though the actual procedure is simple, it takes some intense experimentation to determine the correct values for effective 3D images. Expect to spend some time getting the hang of it. The key variables are *camera separation* and *image separation*. To get started, follow the manual's instructions exactly, and then vary the settings for your own viewing requirements.

TIP

If you do render 3D images, avoid large foreground objects when you are getting started. Large objects can make it difficult to get a good 3D effect. I also suggest making sure that there is no glare on the screen; bright reflections will almost certainly spoil the 3D effect.

Figure 1.29 shows what a red/blue 3D image looks like. This image is in black and white, but there are a number of images on the CD-ROMs that you can view with special glasses.

Figure 1.29
A red/blue 3D image (see text for explanation of double image).

To create a panoramic series of images, you need to render three times: once in the usual way, once with the Port[44] button enabled, and once with the StrBrd (Starboard) button enabled. To make sure that the images meet properly at the edges, use a setting of 16 for the focal length (just click the Wide button). Figure 1.30 shows a single image created from three views (Port, Normal, and Starboard).

Figure 1.30
A panoramic image created from three separate renderings.

---

[44]Do you, like most of us, get confused when it comes to *port* and *starboard*? As a public service, I am offering some assistance in getting these two terms into your brain. Ignoring the fact that *left* and *right* would be just as easy to put on the buttons in Vistapro, there are some easy mnemonic devices you can use to tell your port from your starboard. Device 1: The word *left* has four letters, and so does *port*. Ergo: *port* is *left*. Device 2: *Left* comes before *right* in the dictionary, and *port* comes before *starboard*, so *port* is *left* and *starboard* is *right*. Device 3: As Phil, my development editor noted, "the ship left port" is also a convenient way to remember that *port* is *left*. The interesting thing about both of these words is that they are based on words that describe both sides of a ship. *Port* comes from the word *porthole*, meaning a small circular hole in the side of a ship; portholes can be on any side of a ship. *Starboard* comes from *steer bord*. A *bord* is the side of a ship (any side), and steering is just what you think it is. How these came to refer to specific directions is anyone's guess; the terms have been in use in English for more than 400 years! I guess it's too late to make a change.

Fractal Magic

The Fractal bottom control panel enables you to modify an existing landscape with fractal details or to generate random landscapes. Figure 1.31 shows the controls available in this control panel.

Figure 1.31
The Fractal version of the bottom control panel.

The Random button enables you to generate random fractal landscapes. Below the Random button is a text window where a random number appears if you click the Random button.[45] Vistapro generates the fractal landscape as a new map. The other controls in the Fractal Control Panel affect the nature of the new landscape.

A number such as 1,232,832 generates a completely different landscape than its opposite, –1,232,832. You also can enter numbers directly into the text window and press Enter to generate a landscape.

The Island button generates the landscape as an island; that is, the edge of the map is at 0 elevation. As with all landscapes, you have to fill the sea with water yourself; use the SeaLvl button or the Lake button—either will work well.

The FrDim setting controls the height and roughness of the generated terrain. The default value is 100. Higher values result in higher, rougher landscapes; lower values result in smoother, lower terrain.

The Frctlze button adds fractal detail to existing landscapes. It uses the setting of FrDim to determine what to do. High values of FrDim result in a roughening of the landscape, and low values smooth out the landscape. This button also relies on the setting of the Fractal Divisor buttons immediately below it. The Fractal Divisor buttons determine the scale of the fractalization. A setting of 1 adds fractal noise in very tiny changes, whereas a setting of 8 probably changes the overall look of the landscape. These buttons work exactly in reverse when you generate a landscape; a small fractal divisor generates large landscape features and a high setting results in many small mountains.

The Stretch button changes a landscape by stretching it vertically. Peaks get higher, and valleys get deeper. If you set a low value in the Fractal Divisor buttons, only small

---

[45]You can enter your own number here as well. In fact, if you find a random landscape that you like, you can note the number and re-create it anytime you want.

features get stretched—a good effect for nightmare landscapes. At high values of the Fractal Divisor, only larger features are stretched. You can stretch repeatedly with different Fractal Divisor settings to get different effects. Figure 1.32 shows a landscape before stretching, and Figure 1.33 shows the same landscape after stretching. Yes, that's Mount St. Helens in both figures.

Figure 1.32
A landscape before stretching.

Figure 1.33
A landscape after stretching with a fractal divisor of 4 (twice) and with a fractal divisor of 1 (once).

Lighting

The Lighting Control Panel also affects the appearance of the landscape map. A set of concentric circles is overlaid on the map, as shown in Figure 1.34. Each circle represents a different lighting angle. At the 0 circle, the light is right on the horizon. At the circle marked 45, the light is exactly halfway between zenith[46] and the horizon. The number represents the number of degrees the light is above the horizon; zenith is 90 degrees. To set the light location,[47] click the Custom button on the Light Control Panel, and then move the mouse around on the map until the light is coming from the direction you want, at the angle you want.

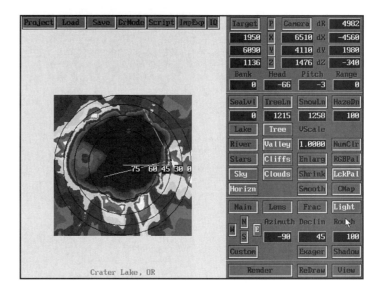

Figure 1.34
*The Lighting version
of the bottom
control panel.*

The angle of lighting and the direction in relation to the camera can make a huge difference to the appearance of the landscape. Generally, you want to light from the side at intermediate angles. A bad lighting location can ruin your rendering, however, while a creative lighting angle can create a mood or effect that enhances the appearance of the rendering. For examples of the effects of different lighting setups, see Figures 1.35 through 1.40. All figures show the same landscape, with shadows turned on and exaggeration turned off. Roughness is set to 100 in all figures.

---

[46]YATT: Yet Another Technical Term. *Zenith* is the point in the sky directly overhead.

[47]It might help to think of the light as the sun in a cloudless day, because that's the effect you get from setting the lighting angle and position.

Figure 1.35
A landscape with the light right behind the camera; note how flat-looking the scene is.

Figure 1.36
The same landscape as Figure 1.35, but lit from the right side at a 45-degree angle.

Figure 1.37
The same landscape
as Figure 1.35, but
lit from the left side
at a 45-degree angle.

Figure 1.38
The same landscape
as Figure 1.35, but
lit from overhead
(high noon).

Figure 1.39
The same landscape as Figure 1.35, lit from behind and slightly to one side.

Figure 1.40
The same landscape as Figure 1.35, lit from a low angle to simulate sunrise.

You can set basic lighting positions using controls in the Lighting Control Panel (refer to Fig. 1.34). The N/S/E/W buttons put the light at North, South, East, or West. The Declination is the lighting angle, expressed as degrees away from the horizon (which is 0). The Azimuth control refers to the rotational angle of the light, with South being 0 and North 180 degrees. The Rough setting controls the apparent roughness of the landscape, and is used with shading texture.[48] Useful values range from 0 to 300; higher values should be used only when you need an unnatural look. Figures 1.41 and 1.42 illustrate the effect of different roughness settings.

Figure 1.41
A landscape rendered with shadows on and a roughness setting of 0.

The Exager button exaggerates the effects of lighting. Instead of a gradual transition from light to shadow, the transition is more abrupt. This effect enhances the apparent detail in the image, but you should experiment with each landscape to see whether it works. In particular, using exaggeration with low lighting angles can put large, flat areas into near-total darkness.

The Shadow button does just what you would expect: It adds shadows to the landscape. This is a must for natural-looking landscapes. Only terrain casts shadows; trees and clouds do not. Rendering takes longer with shadows on.

---

[48]In case you forgot, you set shading texture in the Main Control Panel when you select the amount of texture to apply—the O/L/M/H buttons control texture, with O being Off (no texture), and the other buttons setting Low, Medium, and High texture values. After you click L, M, or H, you are asked to set the altitude or shading texture.

Figure 1.42
A landscape rendered with shadows on and a roughness setting of 300.

Figure 1.43 shows a landscape rendered with shadows off, and Figure 1.44 shows a landscape rendered with shadows on.

Figure 1.43
A landscape rendered without shadows.

Figure 1.44
A landscape rendered with shadowing turned on.

Using PCX Files as Maps

This is one of the coolest features of Vistapro. You can import PCX files for a variety of applications and in a variety of ways. You can import a PCX graphic that has nothing at all to do with a landscape, for example, such as the face in Figure 1.45.

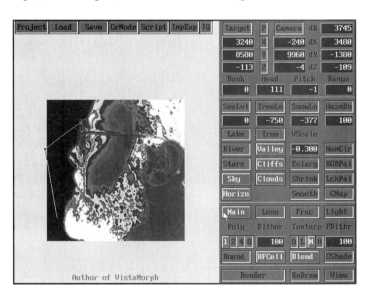

Figure 1.45
The face of the programmer of Vistapro imported as a landscape.

Although the map looks like a face, the rendered landscape doesn't resemble a face at all; Figure 1.46 shows a cliff corresponding to the nose in the map. Before rendering the image, I created a sea in front of the nose and added fog to obscure the medium and distant portions of the landscape. Note that the VScale setting in Figure 1.45 is set to –0.300. As a result, the original peaks were turned into valleys, and the original valleys were turned into mountains.[49] Figure 1.47 shows how the landscape looks with a VScale setting of +03.000; it is a photo negative of Figure 1.45.

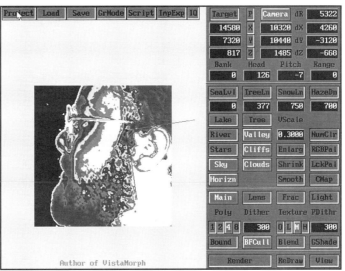

Figure 1.46
A rendered land-scape from the PCX file imported in Figure 1.45.

Figure 1.47
A reversed scale setting for the map in Figure 1.45.

---

[49]Which hints at a more general consideration: Just importing a PCX file is seldom all you have to do to get a good landscape. You might have to make major adjustments in order to get good results. Be prepared to play and massage until you have something workable. Instant art this is not!

As a matter of fact, I preferred working with this version of the file. Figure 1.48 shows why. I call it *The Valley of the Ear in Morning Light.* As you can see if you look at the original on the CD-ROMs,[50] this image is lit by a low light angle. I also massaged this image slightly in Adobe Photoshop for Windows. I selected just the portions of the "snow" that are facing the sun, and tinted them ever-so-slightly pink to make it look more like an authentic sunrise. Vistapro does not support such detailing, but it's not hard at all to add such effects in a photo-realistic paint program; all you need is a "magic wand" tool that selects areas of similar color.

Figure 1.48
The Valley of the Ear in Morning Light.

TIP

Make sure that the PCX file is large enough to fill the map area (which is usually 514×514). If the file is smaller, you might get skewing or other undesired distortion.

It's not as easy as it might look to get a map that looks like the PCX file you import, however. I took a frame from a video I prepared for a different book I wrote (see Fig. 1.49), converted it to a PCX file, and imported it. The resulting map (shown in Fig. 1.50 from a very high camera angle) bore only the slightest resemblance to the image, but as you can see in Figure 1.51, it nonetheless provided some interesting renderings. Figures 1.52 and 1.53 show details from a landscape generated from a slightly different version of the same image. Before converting the image from a BMP to a

---

[50]To find images on the CD-ROMs, look for them by the figure number in the index.

PCX file, I loaded it into BitEdit[51] and reordered the palette according to brightness. Vistapro maps the incoming image according to the order in which colors exist in the palette. If the colors are in random order, you see a random result, as shown in Figure 1.50. If you order the palette entries in some way, you get more consistent results.

> If you don't think you have an interesting landscape for rendering, try different camera angles and target locations. Almost every landscape has features in it somewhere that give you a pleasing rendering.

TIP

Figure 1.49
An image of the author for importing into Vistapro.

---

[51]This is a bitmap editor that comes with the Video for Windows retail package.

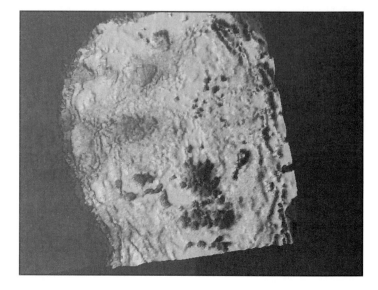

Figure 1.50
A rendering of the image from Figure 1.49; note that it bears little relation to the original image.

Figure 1.51
A rendering at a low camera angle at a point just below the "nose."

Figure 1.52
*A rendering of a
broad valley from a
different PCX image
of the author.*

Figure 1.53
*The same valley as
in Figure 1.52, but
from a much lower
camera angle.*

Figures 1.52 and 1.53 illustrate how important it is to experiment with different camera angles and targets. The mood of your image can vary dramatically with different placements.

Animation

Vistapro does a great job rendering single images, but the program really comes into its own when you generate a series of images and combine them into an animation. You could do this manually, of course, by adjusting the camera angle to a slightly different position for each image. However, you would need at least 15 frames for each second of animation.

If you use fewer than 15 frames per second, the image flickers too obviously. Even more frames per second would be better (cartoons and movies use 24, and video uses 30), but many computers don't support such high frame rates—see my book, *PC Video Madness*, for a complete discourse on this subject—and that can get mighty tedious to do manually. The answer is a Vistapro add-on program called Flight Director. Flight Director, also available from Virtual Reality Laboratories, uses Vistapro's script capabilities to generate a series of images that correspond to a flight path through a landscape.

Figure 1.54 shows a Flight Director screen. It looks something like the Vistapro screen. The concept behind Flight Director is simple. You click a series of points on the landscape map, and this becomes a flight path that a Vistapro camera follows. You can see the flight path superimposed on the map in the left half of the screen in Figure 1.54.

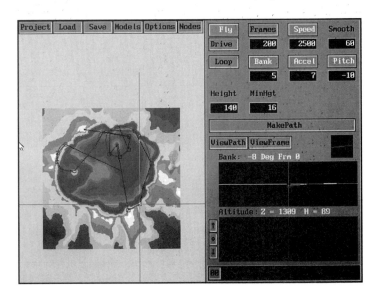

Figure 1.54
The Flight Director screen.

The cross hairs over the map mark the current cursor position. Each of the small squares along the flight path is called a *node*, and each node can have its own target. Flight Director interpolates camera and target positions between nodes, creating a smooth flight path. After you place all the nodes and add any targets,[52] click the MakePath button to generate a path. To see the result in Wireframe[53] mode, click the ViewPath button, which flies you through the animation in the space normally occupied by the map (see Fig. 1.55).

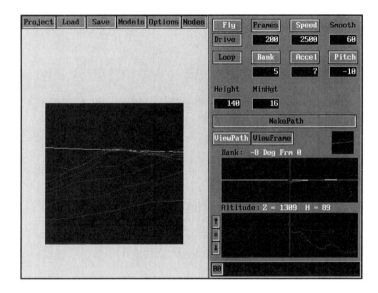

Figure 1.55
Wireframe anima-
tion of the flight
path.

Flight Director enables you to choose the type of imaginary vehicle making the journey from the Models menu (see Fig. 1.56). Not all the vehicles fly; in addition to a glider, jet, cruise missile, and helicopter, you will find a dune buggy and a motorcycle.[54]

---

[52]If you don't add any targets, Flight Director assumes that you simply want the camera to point forward.

[53]*Wireframe* refers to the act of rendering 3D objects using outlines instead of solid shapes. It's a lot easier and faster to render wireframes than solids.

[54]Use caution when working with the land-based vehicles; the path is close to the ground, and actually may go underground if the landscape is very rough. This does not look very good, so watch out for it in the wireframe preview. You can tell you're underground if the landscape is suddenly overhead instead of below.

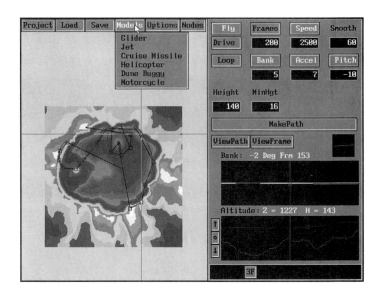

Figure 1.56
Choosing the kind of vehicle.

Let's take a moment to look at the controls in Flight Director. You might never use them; when you pick a vehicle, Flight Director sets default parameters that match the vehicle's characteristics. You might want to fine-tune those characteristics, however, or you might want to try something completely different.

Refer to Figure 1.56, where you can see a number of buttons and text windows at the top right of the screen. You can choose to set Fly or Drive buttons, which correspond to the two types of vehicles on the Models menu. You also can determine whether the pace of the fly-through[55] is adjusted for the number of frames, or whether it proceeds at a constant speed and generates as many frames as are needed. If you want the number of frames to control the animation, click the Frames button and enter the number of frames. If you want speed to be the deciding factor, click the Speed button and enter an appropriate speed. I find that 2,500 is a good starting point for speed, but you can change that number for different effects.

You also can set numeric values for Bank, Accel, and Pitch, which control the limits of these activities for the vehicle. *Banking* refers to action in turns. Aircraft bank one way, while land-based vehicles bank in the opposite sense. A motorcycle, for example, banks into a turn, while a glider banks the opposite way. *Acceleration* controls the degree to which a vehicle changes speed as it rises and falls. A high Accel value means that the vehicle changes speed more dramatically.

You also can control Pitch changes. Higher values enable the vehicle to pitch forward or backward to a greater degree as it ascends or descends.

---

[55]Granted, you can fly or drive, but for simplicity's sake, I'll use the term *fly-through* in this section to refer to both.

The Height text window tells Flight Director how high above the ground elevation to place nodes. For flying vehicles, a good range is from 100 to 200 meters. For ground vehicles, set a low value like 15 to 30 meters. Keep in mind that these numbers are for nodes only. Flight Director makes an effort to ensure that the path doesn't go through the ground, but this is not a guarantee. Raise these numbers for rough terrain to avoid running into the ground. The MinHgt text window tells Flight Director the minimum height above ground to maintain; this is also an effective way to keep from running into the ground. Settings of 5 to 15 meters (15 to 45 feet) will work, but use higher numbers for rough terrain.

The Smooth button also affects the relationship between the vehicle and the ground. High values of smoothing round off the rough edges of the path, but in rough terrain this can run you into the ground. If in doubt, check the path in Preview mode (click the ViewPath button).

The Loop button causes the last node to loop back to the first node, creating an animation that can be looped.

If you don't want to purchase Flight Director, but still would like to create animations, see "Scripting in Vistapro," later in this chapter, for some ideas to help you create simple animations.[56]

The procedure for creating a flight path is simple:

- Click to place nodes indicating the path you want to follow.
- Select a model or set the various control settings manually.
- Click the MakePath button to create the path.
- Check the path with the ViewPath button.

If you find that you want to change a node, you can delete it and add a new one using the Node menu, or you can use the Bank and Altitude windows to move the node with the mouse (refer to Fig. 1.56). After moving a node, you must use the MakePath button again to re-create the path. Use the Save menu to generate a script that you can load into Vistapro.[57]

---

[56]Scripting won't be useful in the demo version of Vistapro that is on the CD-ROMs, because you need to save animation frames to the disk before you can link them to an animation. You need the full working version of Vistapro to create animation with Flight Director or scripts.

[57]To load the script, just use the Script menu in Vistapro. Select one of the Run items (which one you use depends on the kind of file you want to generate: Targa, BMP, or PCX), and then click the name of the Script file you created in Flight Director. You need to supply a base name, such as PIC, to which Vistapro appends numbers for each file—PIC00001.PCX, PIC00002.PCX, and so on. Vistapro now happily creates all the images necessary for the animation. You can load the resulting files into a program such as Animator Pro or VidEdit to create a FLI, FLC, or AVI file. Before you start, make sure that the image size and all settings are correct. The most common mistake with a script is to have the wrong landscape loaded!

Figure 1.57 shows four frames from an animation from one of the files on the CDs. If you look closely, you'll see that each frame is slightly different. The sequence is taken from one of the Crater Lake fly-throughs.

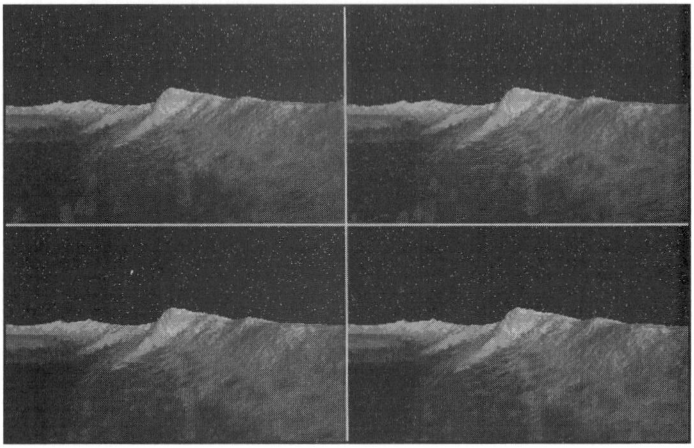

Figure 1.57
Four frames from an animation (a fly-through over Crater Lake, OR).

TIP

Lock the palette before creating animations.[58] This action ensures that a single palette is used for all the files. Locking the palette is necessary for using the animation player that comes with Vistapro, and makes life easier with most other programs. You might get better results, however, with some programs that can create a single palette from multiple palettes. Examples include Animator Pro and good old VidEdit.

To see an example of an exciting landscape animation in 3D Studio, see Chapter 6, "I Can Fly!"

Morphing

Now you'll learn something that literally will make the earth move: how to morph landscapes. It won't exactly happen under your feet, but you can create animations of a wide variety of landscape changes. In this section, you learn how to create an animation that grows a rugged, mountainous landscape out of flat terrain using Vmorph, another add-on program for Vistapro.

---

[58] Use the LckPal button in Vistapro to lock the palette. If you are using Vmorph (see the next section) to create the animation, set Lock Palette on the Setup menu.

Figure 1.58 shows the starting landscape. However, this is not the place to get started; you start with the last frame, for reasons that will be clear shortly. Figure 1.59 shows the last frame.

Figure 1.58
The starting landscape for a morph.

Figure 1.59
The ending landscape for a morph.

I created this landscape using the Fractal Control Panel; I simply clicked the Random button and took what showed up. Because the morph is intended to show a landscape rising up, the key is to use the vertical-scaling capabilities. It's very simple: For the ending image, I used a vertical scale of 2.0 and saved the file as END.DEM. For the starting image, I used a vertical scale of 0.2 and saved it as START.DEM.

> Don't save the file as an extended DEM file. Vmorph can't handle the extended file format.[59] If you want to include such things as clouds in the morph, you need to use scripts. See "Scripting in Vistapro," later in this chapter, for an example.

Figure 1.60 shows the opening screen of Vmorph. Vista Morph is not included on the CD-ROMs included with this book. It is an add-on program that you can purchase from Virtual Reality Laboratories, the folks who sell Vistapro. It's much easier to work with than it looks. There's a menu at the top, frame numbers from left to right,[60] and buttons with actions you can take on the left. You only need to use one of the buttons to create a morph: LOADDEM. You load START.DEM to start the morph and END.DEM to complete it.

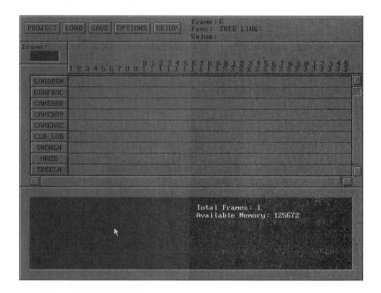

Figure 1.60
The opening screen of Vmorph.

Step 1: Click on the line marked LOADDEM in the space for frame 1 (see Fig. 1.61). A dialog box appears. Enter the name of the file to load (START.DEM) and click OK.

Step 2: Click again on the line marked LOADDEM, but this time in the space for frame 60 (see Fig. 1.62).[61] A dialog box opens. Enter the name of the file to load (END.DEM) and click OK.

---

[59]Extended DEM files contain information beyond simple landscape data cloud settings, tree settings, and so on.

[60]The frame numbers are confusing; they read from left to right and bottom to top. That is, the number 10 shows up with 0 on the top and 1 on the bottom.

[61]Use the slider button at the bottom right to move to frame 60.

Step 3: Click the right mouse button to toggle the menu, and then click the Morph button. The dialog box shown in Figure 1.63 appears. Don't enter text into the text windows directly. Click on the LOADDEM line in frame 1, and then in frame 60. The values are entered into the Morph dialog box automatically. You need to change only one value: Set a value of .75 for Ease.[62]

Step 4: Set global values for the morph on the Setup menu: Lock Palette On and Graphics Mode 320×200. Set the palette to frame 1.

Step 5: Time to generate the script. Click the Save menu and enter a name for the script file in the text window (see Fig. 1.64). After the script is saved, exit Vmorph.

Step 6: Load Vistapro. Click the script menu selection Run PCX, which displays the dialog box shown in Figure 1.65. Click the file name of the script file you created in step 5.

Step 7: After the script loads, you see a dialog box asking for the base picture name. This is a three-character prefix that is used for each of the image files generated. The first file name in the example would be PIC00000.PCX, the next file name would be PIC00001.PCX, and so on. After you click OK, the script runs. The script repeatedly uses Vistapro to create frames; the process can take a long time. I once created a very long fly-through of the Big Sur area. It had more than 1,600 frames and took two and a half days to generate. This isn't as bad as it seems; I added trees, which can triple the rendering time.

Step 8: Enjoy! You can use the PCX2FLC utility to create an animation, or you can load the bitmaps into VidEdit (Video for Windows) as a DIB sequence[63] and add sound appropriate to such earth-shattering goings on. The PCX2FLC utility is easy to use—it has a command-line interface. To create an animation, use the command line

```
pcx2flc pic -b -s
```

where `pic` is the base picture file name, `-b` tells the program to use compression to reduce file size, and `-s` tells the program to optimize for playback speed. These settings ensure playback on the widest variety of hardware. The output file in this example would have the file name PIC.FLC.

See "Scripting in Vistapro" for an example of a script created by Vmorph.

---

[62]*Ease* controls the pace of the morph. If the Ease value is less than 1, the morph starts fast and then slows down. If the Ease value is greater than 1, the morph starts slow and then speeds up.

[63]You can use a utility like Image Pals in Windows to convert all the files in one shot, or you can use the Run BMP24 menu choice instead of Run PCX to generate bitmap files directly. However, 24-bit files are much larger, so you need much more disk space—192,000 bytes per frame, to be exact, for a 320×200 animation.

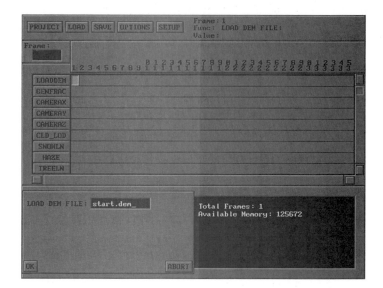

Figure 1.61
Loading a DEM file
in frame 1.

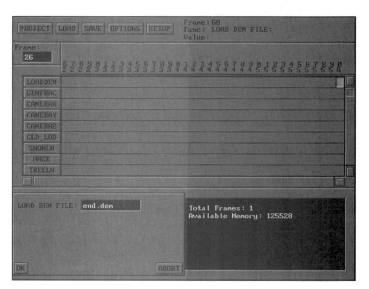

Figure 1.62
Loading a DEM file
in frame 26.

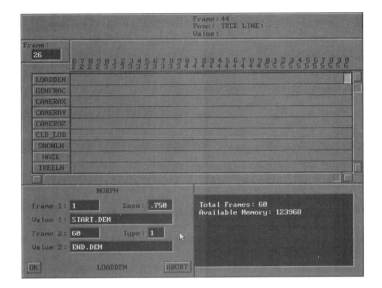

Figure 1.63
*Setting the morph
values.*

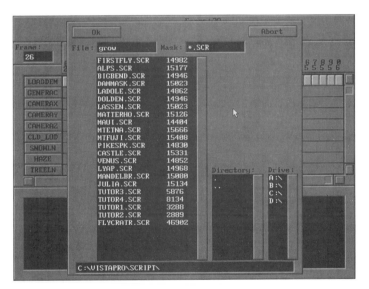

Figure 1.64
*Generating the script
file.*

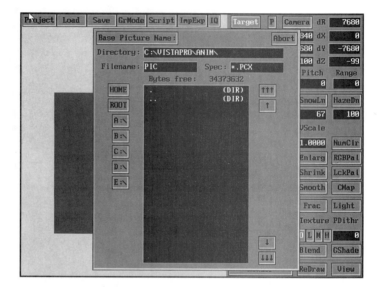

Figure 1.65
Selecting a script.

Figure 1.66
Four sample frames from a morph animation (frames 1, 20, 40, and 60).

Vistapro Gallery

All the images in this section were created with Vistapro. Some of the images were further modified in a paint program. Typical reasons for using a paint program include adding a sun, adding special effects such as a lens flare, adding objects or people to the landscape, and using the landscape as a background.

Figure 1.67
A view of El Capitan, a famous rock-climbing destination.

Figure 1.68
The same view as in Figure 1.67, but using Gouraud shading. Note how this softer shading gives the image a very different feel.

Figure 1.69
A fractally generated landscape in late afternoon light.

Figure 1.70
This landscape is similar to that in Figure 1.69, but no cliffs and a body of water give it a much more serene look. Note that there is no sky haze, giving the landscape a hyper-real look.

Figure 1.71
Even the simplest landscape looks good in a Vistapro rendering.

Figure 1.72
A slightly fractalized version of the Mandelbrot set.[64] A Mandelbrot DEM file is one of the sample files that comes with Vistapro. As supplied, the landscape has sheer cliffs and isn't too exciting. I applied smoothing and a little fractal texture to create a more realistic appearance.

---

[64]The *Mandelbrot set* is a famous set of points in fractal history. See Chapter 7, "Hardware for Virtual Worlds," for information about fractals.

Figure 1.73
Two renderings of a valley using the same data. The rendering on the left was done using normal height, and the rendering on the right used a height setting of 2.000.

Figure 1.74
A fanciful landscape created from one of the DEM files supplied with Vistapro 3.0.

Scripting in Vistapro

One of the most powerful aspects of Vistapro is its support for scripting. Just about every feature of Vistapro can be controlled in a script. The easiest way to create a script is to use Vmorph to generate a script. If necessary, you can edit the generated script in a text editor to make final changes. You usually can accomplish everything you need to right in Vmorph, however.

Figure 1.75
This landscape was created from a PCX image that was imported with the PCX —> DEM menu selection. The extreme vertical drop is typical of an abrupt change in the PCX from a light shade to a dark shade.

Figure 1.76
This landscape also is based on an imported PCX that was converted to a DEM file. The image has a haunting quality that I really like; it's one of my favorite Vistapro landscapes.

In the "Morphing" section earlier in this chapter, I outlined an eight-step procedure for creating a morph in Vmorph. In this section, you learn how to tweak the script to produce the most realistic-looking animations.

Remember that column of buttons at the left of the Vmorph screen? Refer back to Figure 1.61 (and remember to scroll to get to a button you don't see in front of you).

To set up the necessary parameters, all you need to do is click in frame 1 in the rows corresponding to several important buttons. The most important settings are shown in Table 1.6.

Table 1.6. Morph Settings.

Setting	Description
Altitude Texture	One of the most important settings for photo-realism is altitude texture. We are rendering at 320×200, so there's no need for ultimate quality. I used a setting of **ALTITUDETEXTUREMEDIUM**.
Blending	Blending is most effective on distant portions of the landscape. With a setting of **BLENDON**, distant objects are not too sharply defined.
Dithering	With only 256 colors in a palette, dithering is critical for realism. This is one of two dither settings, and it controls dithering between color bands. I used the same value that Vistapro uses as a default: **DITHER 100.00**.
Shadows	Just for fun, I used Vmorph to create a varying sun angle during the animation. Setting **SHADOWSON** emphasizes the movement of the sun.
Lighting Angle (Azimuth)	Moving the sun during the animation gives the impression of time-lapse photography. A setting of **SUNAZIMUTH 90.00** starts the sun in the east. It moves approximately 3 degrees (1/60¥180) in each frame. The exact change from frame to frame is affected by the Ease setting of .75.
Pixel Dither	This is one of two dither settings. This setting controls the amount of dithering in all pixels, whereas the Dither setting refers only to the color bands. I used a setting of **PIXELDITHERRANDOM 100.00**. This provides a modest amount of dithering; too much dithering ruins the realistic effect.
Polygon Size	All the settings listed here are important, but none is more important than Polygon Size. For realism, always use a setting of **POLYGONSIZE1** when rendering. This creates the smallest possible polygons.

Setting	Description
Backface Culling	Rendering speed increases if you set **BACKFACECULLINGON**. This means that unseen portions of the landscape are not rendered.
Palette Locking	Setting **LOCKPALETTE** ensures that all frames use the same palette as frame 1. This is necessary if you are using PCX3FLC to create the animation.

You can set each of these values by clicking in frame 1 in the corresponding row in Vmorph. An appropriate dialog box appears, enabling you to enter or click on the required value or setting. The only exception to this is the lighting angle. This works just like the morphing you did on the LOADDEM line. Click frame 1 in the row marked SunAzimuth and enter a value of 90 (that's East). In the same row, click frame 60 and enter a value of –90 (West). Then click the Morph menu button at the top of the screen to display the Morph dialog box. Click frame 1, then frame 60, and then click OK in the dialog box to create the intermediate settings in frames 2 through 59.[65]

If you set these values correctly, you see the following script lines for frame 1, following the default settings:

```
ALTITUDETEXTUREMEDIUM
BLENDON
DITHER 100.00
SHADOWSON
SUNAZIMUTH 90.00
PIXELDITHERRANDOM 100.00
POLYGONSIZE1
BACKFACECULLINGON
RENDER
LOCKPALETTE
; Frame: 1 END
```

The wide variety of available commands gives you a high degree of control over scripting. With a little effort, you can create some amazing animation. You also can use Vmorph to add such things as cloud-map loading for each frame to increase realism. To load a cloud map, all you need is a command like this for each frame:

```
CLOUDLOAD CLOUD\MORPH1
```

The file name is MORPH1. You do not need to specify the CLD extension.

---

[65]You can use this technique to morph any numeric values in a script, between any two frames.

Listing 1.1 shows an example of a more complete Vistapro script generated by Vmorph. This is an example of a script that creates an animation of a trip through a landscape, including changes in such things as sun angle to make it more realistic.

Creating animations is fun, but it's also fun just to play them. I have included many animations created with Vmorph (as well as an animation player) on the CD-ROMs for your enjoyment.

Listing 1.1. Example of a Typical Vistapro Script (Generated by Vmorph).

```
Vista Script File
CamX, CamY, CamZ, Bank, Hdng, Ptch,
; Frame: 1 BEGIN
DEFAULTDIRDEM DEM\
DEFAULTDIRCMAP CMAP\
DEFAULTDIRCLOUD CLOUD\
DEFAULTDIRSCRIPT SCRIPT\
DEFAULTDIRFOREGROUND TGA24\
DEFAULTDIRBACKGROUND TGA24\
DEFAULTDIRIQ IQ\
LANDSCAPESIZEAUTO
GRMODEVGA320×200
GRMODEVESA640×480
LOADDEM DEM\START.DEM
ALTITUDETEXTUREMEDIUM
BLENDON
DITHER 100.00
SHADOWSON
SUNAZIMUTH 90.00
PIXELDITHERRANDOM 100.00
POLYGONSIZE1
BACKFACECULLINGON
RENDER
LockPalette
; Frame: 1 END
; Frame: 2 BEGIN
SPAWN META DEM\START.DEM DEM\END.DEM DEM\METALTMP.DEM 1 59 1 0.75 1
LOADDEM DEM\METALTMP.DEM
SUNAZIMUTH 83.90
LOCKPALETTE
RENDER
; Frame: 2 END
; Frame: 3 BEGIN
SPAWN META DEM\START.DEM DEM\END.DEM DEM\METALTMP.DEM 2 59 1 0.75 1
LOADDEM DEM\METALTMP.DEM
SUNAZIMUTH 80.85
RENDER
; Frame: 3 END
;
; Frames 4 through 57 are pretty much the same. For each
; frame, the parameters for the SPAWN command are
; incremented, and the sun azimuth angle is changed to give
; the impression that the sun is moving across the sky
 ;during the morph.
```

```
;
; Frame: 58 BEGIN
SPAWN META DEM\START.DEM DEM\END.DEM DEM\METALTMP.DEM 57 59 1 0.75 1
LOADDEM DEM\METALTMP.DEM
SUNAZIMUTH -86.95
RENDER
; Frame: 58 END
; Frame: 59 BEGIN
SPAWN META DEM\START.DEM DEM\END.DEM DEM\METALTMP.DEM 58 59 1 0.75 1
LOADDEM DEM\METALTMP.DEM
SUNAZIMUTH -90.00
RENDER
; Frame: 59 END
; Frame: 60 BEGIN
LOADDEM DEM\END.DEM
SUNAZIMUTH -90.00
RENDER
; Frame: 60 END
```

Vistapro for Windows

I found Vistapro completely addictive—it was just about impossible to stop playing with it. I suppose that it makes one feel like a kind of superman, able to forge complete landscapes out of mere electrons. There was only one thing stopping me from becoming a complete addict: Vistapro ran under DOS, and I spend most of my time in Windows.

I am no longer safe. Virtual Reality Laboratories sent me the Windows version of Vistapro. Now I have this program at my fingertips and I don't know how I'm going to get my work done.

The Windows interface is almost exactly like the DOS interface, as you can see in Figure 1.77. A few of the buttons have moved to new homes, but by and large, people familiar with the DOS version can find their way around in the Windows version. The biggest advantage of the Windows version is simplified support for high-resolution video modes, such as 1,024×768 and 24-bit color. If your video driver supports a mode, then Vistapro does, too.

Figure 1.78 shows an aerial shot of Maui that I created with the Windows version of Vistapro.

As you can see, all the detailed features of the DOS version are available in Windows. The trees are nicely detailed, shadowing is very effective, and the water even has waves. I was extremely pleased with performance on my 486/66. In general, I prefer the

Windows version over the DOS version. Perhaps this is just because of my preference for working in Windows, but the capability to render in the background is an especially useful feature that the DOS version does not offer.[66]

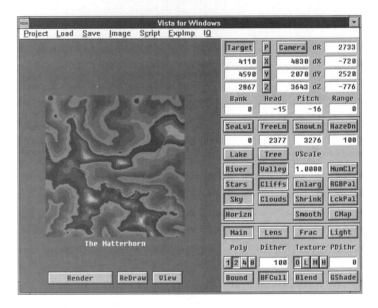

Figure 1.77
The Windows
interface of
Vistapro.

Figure 1.78
An aerial view of
Maui created with
the Windows
version of Vistapro.

---

[66]Watch out, however—rendering uses up a lot of your computer power, and some tasks aren't much fun while rendering is going on. Solitaire is fine; word processing might get tedious.

Figure 1.79 shows another image that I generated with the Windows version. This is a random fractal landscape with a lake of black lava. It is an almost hyper-real landscape—very rich in detail and extremely effective at fooling the eye.

Figure 1.80 shows another side of the capabilities of Vistapro for Windows. This is a nighttime, moonlit landscape from the vantage point of a valley near the Matterhorn. It has an eerie, almost supernatural, quality. It would make a great movie set!

Figure 1.79
An imaginary landscape that looks almost photographic.

Figure 1.80
The Matterhorn and vicinity, rendered in Vistapro with a nighttime sky.

Speaking of the Matterhorn, I learned a little tip that I'd like to pass on to you. In general, when I render, I use the highest possible quality settings. Compare Figure 1.80 to 1.81, however. Note that Figure 1.80 is much more realistic than Figure 1.81. The primary difference between these two figures is the polygon setting. Figure 1.80 uses a very high (and therefore coarse and, one would assume, less realistic) setting of 8. However, when coupled with altitude shading, this gives the rock face of the mountain an extremely realistic look. There is one flaw—that nearly straight line at the base of the Matterhorn, at the boundary of the mountain's base and the snow—but this seems a small price for a touch of reality. (Compare to Fig. 1.81, where the line is still present, but much less obvious.)

Figure 1.81, on the other hand, shows more detail, but the rock face is much less realistic. The small polygon size—a setting of 1 was used—results in a kind of pebbly surface, quite unlike the actual surface of your average mountain.

Overall, I can't overstate how pleased I was with the Windows version of Vistapro. I do try to restrain myself when recommending software, but Vistapro has to be an exception. It has been wonderful fun to play with. The Windows version just makes it that much more tempting.

Figure 1.81
A more realistic view of the Matterhorn, rendered in Vistapro. See text for details and compare to Figure 1.82.

Figure 1.82
A less realistic view of the Matterhorn, rendered in Vistapro. See text for details and compare to Figure 1.81.

Related Products

Several related products are available from Virtual Reality Laboratories that are worth mentioning here. These products use some of the same techniques used in Vistapro, but address different issues and tasks. Three of the more interesting are Mars Explorer, Venus Explorer, and Distant Suns. In addition, I spoke with the chief programmer for Vistapro, John Hinkley, and I have some important information about a new version of Vistapro (version 4) that should be out and available by the time you read this.

Mars Explorer

I recently read a pair of science fiction novels set on the planet Mars. They are *Red Mars* and *Green Mars,* by Kim Stanley Robinson. Both novels include settings at various places on Mars, and use the scientific names for these places: Olympus Mons, for example. As I read along, I got more and more confused. I kept thinking that I would enjoy this so much more if I had a handy reference to the surface features of Mars.

Mars Explorer to the rescue! This program enables you to explore a large portion of our planetary neighbor in detail. The program is supplied on CD-ROM, and has a simple and very handy interface (see Fig. 1.83).

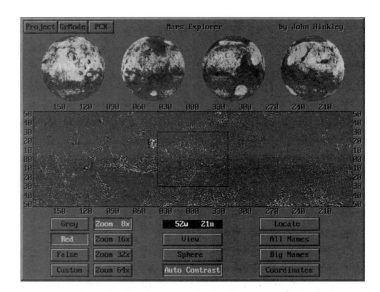

Figure 1.83
The Mars Explorer
user interface.

The four global views of Mars at the top are purely ornamental; the meat and potatoes of this program is the map at the center of the screen. The black box encloses an area of Mars that you can view in greater detail. The exact nature of those details is determined by the buttons at the bottom of the screen. See Table 1.7 for a description of what each button does.

Table 1.7. Mars Explorer Buttons.

Button	Function
Grey	Displays the Mars map in grey.[67] Useful if you are using a monochrome monitor on your portable computer during a Mars landing.
Red	Mars' nickname, the Red Planet, is based on its natural color. Red displays Mars as it was meant to be seen.
False	You also can view Mars in false colors, but I couldn't find a good reason to use this selection for visual use. However, false colors can be used to define regions of constant height, which creates a contour map effect.

---

[67]*Grey* or *gray*? The spelling *grey* is your clue that this program was developed originally in Great Britain, where they have *grey* skies. I live near Seattle, where we have *gray* skies.

Button	Function
Custom	If you care to take the time, you can define your own 256, false-color scheme for viewing Mars.
Zoom buttons	Enable you to see various levels of detail. See Figures 1.84 through 1.86 for examples of zoom capabilities. At larger zoom factors, the little black box gets smaller, because you are viewing a smaller area of the planet.
View	Views the area within the little black box.
Sphere	Displays a revolving sphere animation of Mars. Awesome, but once you've seen it... Figure 1.87 shows a single frame from the animation.
Auto Contrast	These images were collected by a spacecraft orbiting high above the Martian surface, and image contrast is quite poor. The software attempts to correct for this problem if this button is clicked. You also can make manual adjustments to suit your own tastes.
Locate	Displays a list of Martian features to view.
All Names	Shows all names in the Martian place-name database when you view an image of the surface. See Figure 1.88 for an example.
Big Names	Shows just the really important place names when you view an image.
Coordinates	Searches using Martian surface coordinates.

A gallery of Mars Explorer features follows.

Figure 1.84
A view of the area around Olympus Mons at a view factor of 8x. At this setting, you can make out only the major features of the planet. It's hard to get a sense of scale, but Olympus Mons is 600 kilometers across and 25 kilometers high! For comparison, the original Mt. Olympus is a little less than 10,000 feet high.

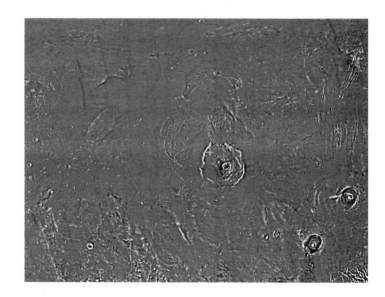

Figure 1.85
A view of the area around Olympus Mons at a view factor of 32x. The mountain now fills more than half the height of the image, and many more details are visible.

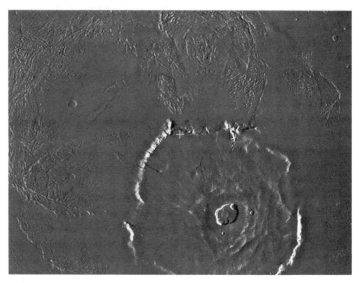

Figure 1.86
A view of the area around Olympus Mons at a view factor of 64x. The mountain now is bigger than can be shown, and the finer details of its surface are clearly visible.

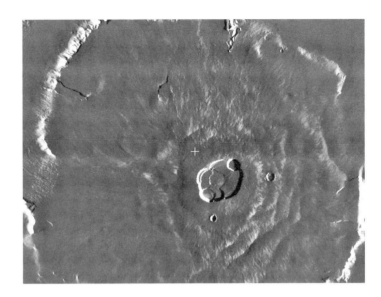

Figure 1.87
A single frame from the animation of a revolving Mars.

Figure 1.88
A view of the Tithonium Chasma showing place names; Perrotin crater is selected at the middle right. Note that the latitude and longitude of the crater are displayed at the bottom of the screen. This example includes only the major place names. With all place names set, dozens of names would be shown.

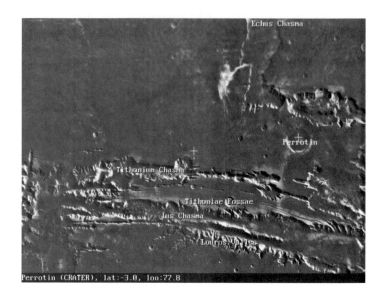

Just for fun, I loaded several of the Mars DEM files that come on the Vistapro CD-ROM into Vistapro for Windows (see Fig. 1.89). I used a total of 12 files, creating a region 4 wide by 3 high in order to encompass all of Olympus Mons.[68]

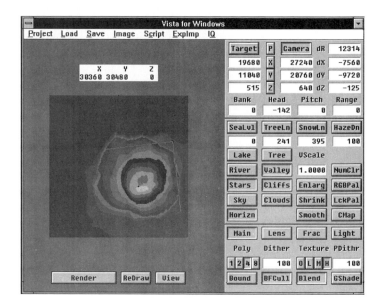

Figure 1.89
Vistapro for Windows with the DEM files for the Olympus Mons region loaded.

---

[68]The files are arranged by latitude and longitude, so they were easy to find using the opening screen of Mars Explorer as a guide.

I rendered the scene with the vertical scale exaggerated by a factor of 7—Olympus Mons is so large that it looks almost flat from any normal vantage point. Figure 1.90 shows the resulting rendering.

The Vistapro CD-ROM comes with a very large number of Mars DEM files, covering a large portion of the planet. You easily can render any scene you want by loading the appropriate region's DEM files.[69]

Figure 1.90
A rendering of the landscape around the Olympus Mons on Mars, courtesy of Vistapro for Windows.

Venus Explorer

Virtual Reality Laboratories' Venus Explorer uses the same interface as Mars Explorer, so it's very easy to move from one product to the other. The Venus images are based on radar data from the Magellan spacecraft. This means that the views of Venus aren't based on visual colors, but on the radar reflectivity of the Venusian surface. You won't see the colors you would see (if you would see much in the soupy atmosphere of Venus!) if you actually set foot on the surface, but you will see the correct topographic information.

Figure 1.91 shows the interface for Venus Explorer. As promised, it is virtually identical to that for Mars Explorer. You have all the same options.

---

[69] As if Vistapro weren't already addictive enough, now I've got another planet to fool around with! No wonder I never seem to get to Comdex.

In addition, you can view the images of the Venusian surface in great detail if you have a video card that supports the higher VESA resolutions, such as 800×600 and 1,024×768 (see Fig. 1.92).

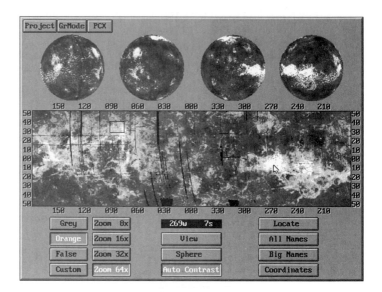

Figure 1.91
The interface for
Venus Explorer.

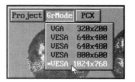

Figure 1.92
Viewing at higher
resolutions.

I had no trouble at all using Venus Explorer. The only down side is that, because it uses the same interface as Mars Explorer, it does not include data for views of the north and south polar regions. Figure 1.93 shows a typical surface image, and Figure 1.94 shows an image with feature names turned on.

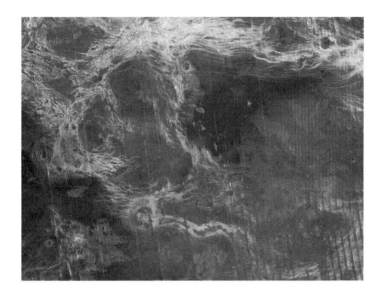

Figure 1.93
A typical view of the surface.

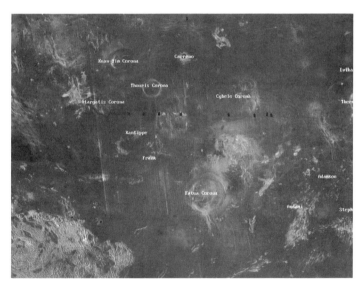

Figure 1.94
A surface view with names superimposed.

You might have noticed in Figure 1.91 that there are some black streaks on the surface map. These are not some strange surface features on Venus; they are gaps in the Magellan data. Figure 1.95 shows an area that has such missing data.

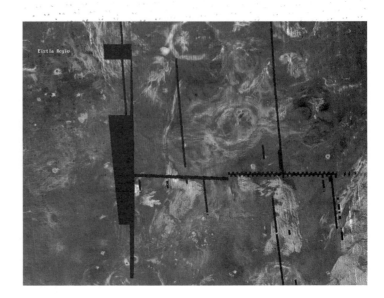

Figure 1.95
Areas of missing data.

Overall, Venus Explorer is just as enjoyable as Mars Explorer. It's a great learning tool if you are interested in planetary science.

Distant Suns

While Vistapro and Mars Explorer use much of the same technology, Distant Suns (also from Virtual Reality Laboratories) is a completely different kind of program. Distant Suns enables you to tour the universe, but the emphasis is on accurate facts, not realism. I have been an astronomy buff since I was knee high to a 14-inch monitor, so I couldn't resist the temptation.[70]

I may be stretching the term *virtual reality* to make it cover Distant Suns, but it's well worth the stretch. Figure 1.96 shows one of the many views of the universe that Distant Suns offers. In Figure 1.96, you are somewhere out in the solar system,[71] watching Halley's comet make its orbit around the sun. The comet is located just above the word Mercury. If you look closely, you even can make out the tail. The toolbar under the Distant Suns menu is set to animate Halley's orbit at the rate of two days per frame, which is just right to give it a nice, graceful transition near the sun.

---

[70]Given my confession of addiction to Vistapro and this reference to temptation, you might be getting the idea that my interests in computers are out of control. You are correct.

[71]From the looks of things, it appears that your viewing position is somewhere beyond Mars and within the orbit of Jupiter.

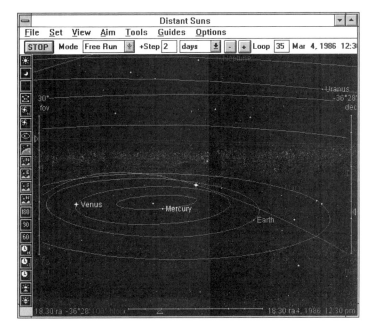

Figure 1.96
Animating the orbit of Halley's comet as of March 4, 1986.

You also can use Distant Suns to view the universe in more traditional, technical, astronomical terms, as shown in Figure 1.97. You can easily center the view on an astronomical object of interest, using the Search & Aim dialog box shown in Figure 1.98. The view is centered on the now famous star Betelgeuse.[72]

Distant Suns is full of neat features. There is a detailed lunar map, for example, as shown in Figure 1.99. Another clever aid to celestial navigation is shown in Figure 1.100—the Rise/Set guide. This guide adjusts to the date you select, and shows graphically the rising and setting times of the principal heavenly bodies.

---

[72]Famous of course, because of the movie starring Michael Keaton some years ago. Fame has its price, of course; how many of us can spell the name correctly?

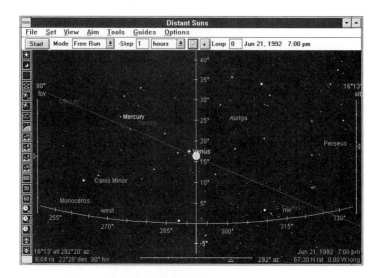

Figure 1.97
A view of the starry skies centered on the sun.

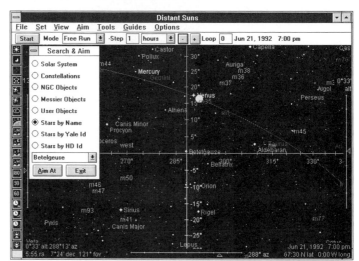

Figure 1.98
The Search & Aim dialog box lets you center the view on just about any heavenly object.

Figure 1.99
*Distant Suns
includes a
lunar map.*

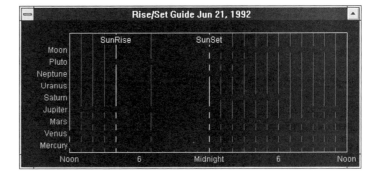

Figure 1.100
*The Rise/Set guide
enables you to see
which heavenly
bodies are available
for viewing in the
night sky.*

It was a lot of fun to work with Distant Suns. The capability to create animation of sky movements was especially interesting, and the detailed and comprehensive nature of the information will amuse and inform anyone with an interest in astronomy. The documentation is straightforward and very useful, and it contains a wide variety of useful facts. You can even learn how to select an appropriate telescope if you tire of virtual skies and want to spend some time gazing at the real thing.

Also included is a huge library of astronomical images. There is a large library of images from the lunar orbiter fly-bys, as well as a number of images from planetary exploration. Figure 1.101 shows just one of the hundreds of images from the CD—a close view of the asteroid Gaspra.

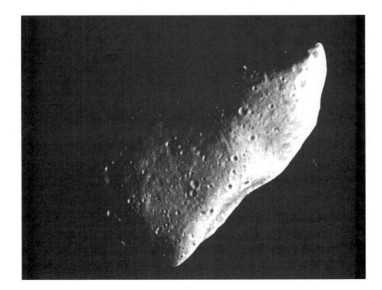

Figure 1.101
*A photograph of the
asteroid Gaspra
from the collection
of images on the
Distant Suns' CD.*

I have hardly covered even the high points of Distant Suns. The program's capabilities go on and on. It was clearly a labor of love by its creator, which makes it doubly enjoyable for the user. At press time, I learned that a new product, called First Light, will be out in 1995 from Virtual Reality Laboratories. It includes a number of new features, all oriented at putting you, the user, into space. You can visit the planets and see their details in 24-bit color. You can create animations. You can tour the planets. A demo that shows you the features of this new program can be found on the CD-ROMs included with this book. It is only a mere slide show, but it will give you a good idea of the features of the program—think of it as Distant Suns on steroids. Figures 1.102, 1.103, 1.104, and 1.105 show scenes from the new product.

Figure 1.102
Jupiter and its
principal moons.

Figure 1.103
Saturn viewed in
First Light.

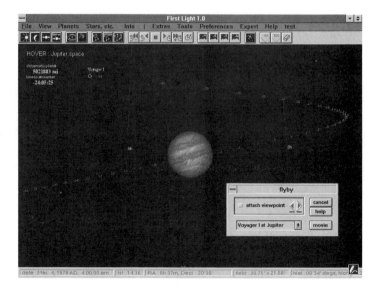

Figure 1.104
Checking out the path of a Voyager fly-by.

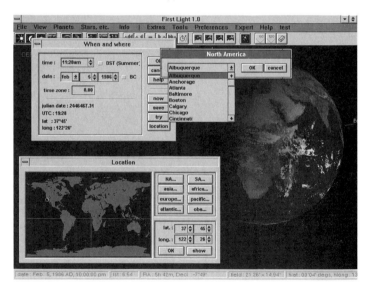

Figure 1.105
Setting up your own position on your home planet.

Vistapro Version 4

I got some exciting news just as I was finishing this chapter: A new version of Vistapro will be out soon—and it may already be on store shelves by the time you read this. The user interface for the new version was not done yet as I was writing, but Virtual Reality Laboratories sent me some images that show the capabilities of the new version. These images speak for themselves, and they say one thing: Version 4 will add some amazing capabilities.

Consider Figure 1.106, which shows an amazingly realistic view of a river. Figure 1.107 shows a sunset. Note how realistic the sun itself is, as well as the subtle reflection of waning sunlight on the landscape.

Figure 1.106
A realistic view of a river created in an early version of Vistapro 4.

Figure 1.107
A sunset view created in an early version of Vistapro 4.

Several other images created in version 4 are included in the color section of this book, and a fantastically detailed video clip (RIVR_RUN.AVI) that shows a long, detailed fly-through of a desert mountain landscape (see Fig. 1.108 for a sample image from the video clip).

Figure 1.108
A realistic view of a desert landscape from a video created in an early version of Vistapro 4.

The evidence from these pictures is, to me, overwhelming: Vistapro 4 will be an improvement on what I had regarded as perfection. Here's a list of the new features to look forward to in version 4:

Texture mapping—Applies texture maps to terrain, buildings, or even waves.

Phong shading—Supports better images and specular reflections such as shimmering leaves, glittering streams, and so on.

Transparent clouds—Enables you to peek through the clouds to the landscape below, or to let the stars shine through.

Stratified cliffs—Provides much more realistic rendering of exposed rock surfaces.

Lens flare—Creates a much more realistic look to any image with bright light sources (sun, lava flows, and so on).

Waves—Enables you to define the wavelength, amplitude, speed, and source of waves—even to animate them.

Walk-about Camera mode—Enables you to move the camera using the mouse and to preview the view from any location.

Sun, moon, planets—Adds these celestial bodies to your sky.

Sun color/ambient light—Gives you complete control over lighting.

Gray-scale import/export—Used for importing and exporting landscape data.

Altitude texturing—Offers greater control in version 4.

Trees—Offers more detail and realism in version 4.

Anti-aliasing—Provides smoother, more realistic boundaries.

Hitch Your Wagon to a Star

I hope that I have been able to convey the excitement and pleasure I experienced using Vistapro. Software comes and goes, but there are certain packages that offer more than usual, and I certainly put Vistapro and Distant Suns into that category. There's something about creating photo-realistic renderings that I find exciting, and Vistapro is easy to use and powerful. Distant Suns has enough meat to satisfy the hungriest astronomical purist. These programs don't offer every single feature you might want, but then again, neither of them costs a fortune, either. Vistapro, in particular, is one program no virtual-reality enthusiast should be without.

There is a demo version of Vistapro 3.0 for Windows and DOS on the CD-ROMs; give it a whirl and see if you don't agree.[73]

---

[73]You might think I get a commission, I'm selling this program so hard. Unfortunately, I don't get a penny.

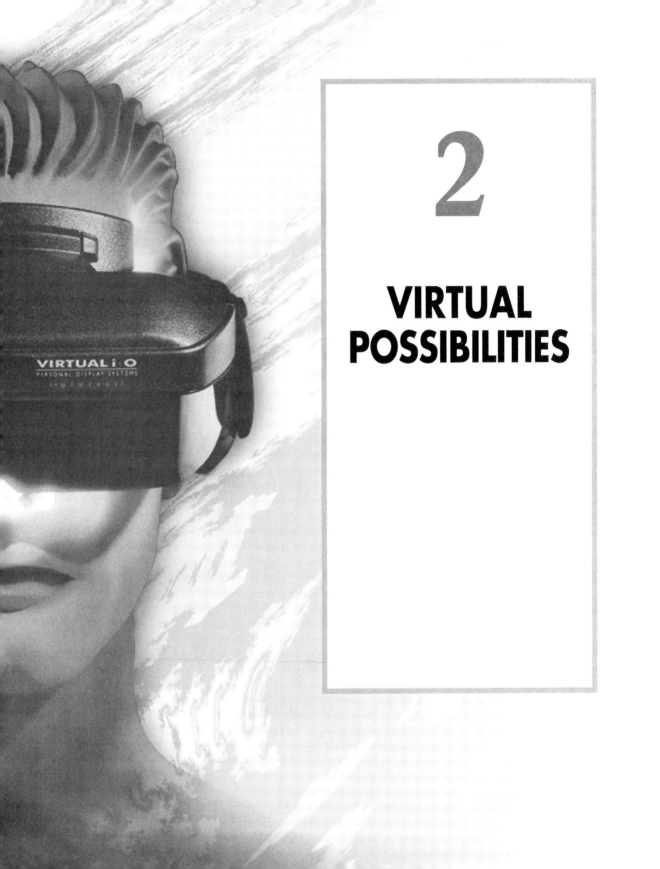

2

VIRTUAL
POSSIBILITIES

In Chapter 1, "Virtual Reality Has Arrived," you learned how to get a running start in virtual reality using Vistapro. In this chapter, virtual reality moves indoors with three (count 'em) affordable and powerful products: Virtus VR, Virtus WalkThrough Pro, and VREAM. Like Vistapro, these programs offer inexpensive ways to explore virtual spaces.[1]

The Virtus programs don't offer all the fancy control and details of the high-end packages, such as Superscape,[2] but they are a blast to use, as you'll see in this chapter. VREAM, on the other hand, offers a great deal of power and depth at a very affordable price.

Before the blast, however, a little background on VR. There's a lot of discussion about just what, exactly, qualifies as VR. Prepare yourself for a radical definition of the concept.

Virtual versus Artificial Reality

Virtual reality are buzzwords these days, and hot ones at that. Virtual reality is so hot, in fact, that the meaning changes almost daily as companies try to associate their products with the words. I'd like to step back from the craziness and intensity of buzzwords and talk in a more generic sense about the underlying concepts of virtual reality.

To begin, let's start with a generic term: *artificial reality*. Not only does using this term avoid the confusion surrounding virtual reality but, in many ways, artificial reality is more accurate. I don't expect everyone to suddenly switch to using new terminology,[3] but it might take some of the heat, confusion, and too-high expectations out of the air. To that end, a definition of the term *artificial reality* is necessary.[4]

---

[1]Virtus WalkThrough is particularly appealing—you already own it. A special version that includes stereo support is included on one of the CD-ROM discs that come with this book. This is a real deal—the genuine article, and already paid for. What's the catch? A simple one—you can have a lot of fun with Virtus WalkThrough, but you also can upgrade to the Professional version. See the back of the book for details.

[2]For information on Superscape, see Chapter 5, "Creating Your Own Reality."

[3]Terminology often takes funny twists and turns. In the late '80s, *cyberspace* often was used to mean the same thing as *virtual reality*. Today, *cyberspace* refers to things like the Internet, which has almost nothing to do with VR. Go figure.

[4]Truth be told, I hate definitions, because as soon as you create one, someone comes along and points out the deficiency of the definition. Defining terms such as *artificial reality* is doubly dangerous because the terms are so vague.

artificial reality—n.; anything at all that stimulates the mind or senses to create a simulacrum of reality in the imagination.

I have deliberately created a definition that stresses results, not the technique used to achieve those results. The emphasized phrase—*in the imagination*—stresses the kind of results that matter. A more narrow definition would define virtual reality in terms of stimulating the senses, but the imagination is far more powerful, and it is capable of filling in the gaps created by technical limitations. Virtual reality need not be virtually real to be interesting, useful, or fun.[5]

For some time, virtual reality had a very definite meaning: full bodysuits, helmets, and other paraphernalia associated with full-body total immersion into an electronic reality.[6] Pieces of that total picture have begun to arrive, and the term *virtual reality* has shifted to describe those first arrivals. The term then has been stretched further to mean just about anything three dimensional. This is an extremely broad range of meaning, and it is useful to break artificial realities into categories. The following sections cover these categories, beginning with the most modest forms of artificial reality and ending with the ultimate forms of virtual reality. The range reflects the current state of the art and projections of what might be possible in the future.

Text

Text might strike you as an unusual form of artificial reality, but it is useful to look at how text serves in that role. For centuries, books have been the cutting edge of artificial reality. Think about it: you read words on a page, and your mind fills in the pictures and emotions—even physical reactions can result. Text is important because all our expectations[7] are based on what we've experienced with books.[8]

Text forms a baseline on which we can measure the success of various kinds of artificial reality. Although there are many ways that images, sounds, and other sensory communication can expand the capabilities of text, there are qualities of the reading

---

[5]The day when virtual reality becomes virtually indistinguishable from reality is a long way down the pike. We can't let that little fact spoil the party!

[6]In some ways, I like that term—*electronic reality*—best of all. But buzzwords have never thrived on accuracy, have they?

[7]Except those based on television.

[8]Kids, of course, who are growing up today don't necessarily base their expectations on books. Many do, however—my son Justen loves books, but he's also a nut about his Sega and Nintendo systems, as well as PC games like Descent. Books provide a depth of stimulation that most games and PC programs can't match. The nonvisual, low-tech nature of text actually gives it an advantage over all other forms of artificial reality. It's a lot easier to simulate, and stimulate, if the technical overhead is reduced. This seems obvious, but it's a critical obstacle that must be overcome in the development of virtual reality.

experience that will be challenging to reproduce. If you are not convinced, think about books that have been converted to movies. Most of the time, even if the movie is regarded as being as good as the book was, the movie has to leave out a lot of the story—the overhead of telling a story in pictures is a lot higher than for text.

2D Still Images

Photographs have been with us for a little more than a century, and their capabilities are described in the phrase "a picture is worth a thousand words." This is true in two senses: a picture—specifically, a photograph—is both accurate and detailed. Nonetheless, comparing pictures and words is, to drag in another old bromide, like comparing apples to oranges. Text is good at certain things, and pictures are good at others. You can't, for example, look behind what is in a two-dimensional picture, nor can you take pictures of many things—the state of a man's mind or a molecule.

Most of the time, pictures and text are used together. This reflects their complementary aspects. Each is good at different things, and best when used together. Neither one is truly superior to the other. The concept of complements is a good one to keep in mind when working with virtual reality. Just because you can make something virtual doesn't mean that virtuality is the best way to convey the information.

3D Still Images

This is a technology that is both common and in its infancy. Primitive 3D still images have been with us for decades, but it has been holograms that have made quality 3D images possible. However, from a commercial standpoint, holography is mostly a failure—there are no widespread commercial uses of holograms as images. Holograms are used for such things as credit cards and packaging precisely because they are complicated to reproduce.[9]

Technically speaking, however, 3D images represent an interesting twist in the move toward more sophisticated artificial reality. The simulacrum of the third dimension is vivid, even if the image quality is often second rate or worse.

---

[9]Not to mention the fact that reproduction of color is a real challenge—we consumers vote with our wallets (or our credit cards) and a largely green hologram of the planet Mars, for example, doesn't necessarily convey useful or interesting information.

Animation

Neither 2D nor 3D images have a quality that reality thrives on: movement. Animation—the trick of using flickering images to fool the eye—adds the dimension of time to artificial reality in ways that still images never can. A series of still images on a page, for example, or even a series of slides, provides only an intellectual sense of movement and change. Animation, even when very abstractly done, conveys a sense of immediacy that is very powerful.

Video

I was tempted to include video with the discussion of animation, but the two technologies are different enough to merit separate consideration. Video, after all, captures an image of reality and preserves it, and that is an entirely different kind of artificial reality than animation. Animation is truly and totally artificial—most of the time.[10]

Converting video to animation starts with a standard video of some real action—a fish swimming or a couple dancing, for example. An artist then uses this as an underlay for an animation, substituting a series of drawings for the video frames. The effect looks like a virtuoso animation, when in reality, it is simply a series of tracings.

But video also can be used to create magic realities. You easily can superimpose a video image either on another video image, or on an animation (2D or 3D). The effect ranges from the mundane (a weatherman in front of his map) to the magical (you as the goalie in a hockey simulation).

Sound

Multimedia computers, upgrade kits, and sound cards are in the process of revolutionizing how we think of computers. The capability to listen to sounds appropriate to a context can make the computer interaction much more pleasant, and often more interesting, effective, and informative. You can use sound for everything from using a cat's meow instead of a beep for errors, to controlling your computer with voice commands.

Unfortunately, the majority of the sound cards installed on computers today aren't of very high quality, and most uses of sound do not use high-fidelity recording techniques. High-quality stereo sound is as important in computer use as it is in a home stereo system. Until there is general use of noise-free, accurate sound equipment on computers, we'll be missing something. In terms of numbers, we must move from

---

[10]Some of the most fascinating animation sequences actually are based on video.

the 8-bit, mono, 22-kHz sounds of today to true CD-quality sound (16-bit stereo with 44-kHz sampling and low noise).

3D Motion

We are just beginning to witness serious efforts to portray the third dimension in ordinary media. Films such as *Jaws III* featured 3D for viewers using special glasses, but the investment in equipment to create such films made them unusual.[11] Technology has just begun to swing to the point where you can create 3D motion pictures on your own.

In most cases, glasses of some kind are required to decode the 3D information in each image of an animation or video sequence. Unlike conventional 3D glasses, video 3D glasses are high tech. They use shutters that direct subsequent frames of the video to each eye in turn. Chapter 12, "The Virtual Future," covers this kind of technology in greater detail.

This kind of technology is right at the edge of what is available to the average computer enthusiast today. Developments in this area will make up the bulk of serious progress in virtual and artificial reality over the next several years.

3D Input Devices

One of the most frustrating aspects of current 3D technology is the lack of a convenient way to manipulate 3D objects. Whether you are using a simple 2D video monitor or sophisticated, 3D, head-mounted displays; if you do not have the capability to manipulate objects with a 3D input device,[12] the possibilities are limited.

As you will see repeatedly in the examples in this book, programmers and game designers have developed many clever techniques for manipulating 3D objects using 3D tools. Almost without exception, this is a tedious, frustrating, and inexact way to work. Current experiments with head-mounted tracking devices, 3D mice, and interactive gloves have not yet resulted in a low-cost, easy-to-use solution to the problem. However, that doesn't stop manufacturers from trying over and over to create the perfect 3D input device. We may yet get an intuitive, cheap, and reliable way of working in 3D!

---

[11]It's also true that, for the most part, there haven't been any artistically satisfying 3D films, either. *Jaws III* was, by far, the worst of the Jaws movies. Maybe the larger cameras used for 3D scare the actors.

[12]The world is waiting for a 3D manipulation device that will make 3D interaction as easy as 2D mouse-based or pen-based interaction.

Head-Mounted Displays

Often called *headsets* or *HMDs*, these range from goggles to full-sized, head-encircling units. You can buy a first-class, head-mounted display today for less than $10,000, but most of the software that uses such expensive hardware is highly specialized. You can find software that enables you to visualize complex organic molecules in 3D, for example, but there is nothing available yet that addresses more pedestrian activities. The high cost of HMDs is the current root of that problem.

Inexpensive head-mounted displays exist, but they tend to make serious compromises. Human vision is marvelously wide-angle, for example. Creating a screen that is small and light enough to be placed in front of your eyes, and still curved enough and wide enough to give you a natural field of vision is beyond the range of affordable technology. Some simple units are available in the $500 to $1,000 price range, but they can't compete with the more costly units. The less than $1,000 headsets tend to be made specifically for game play, because they don't provide a rich enough display environment for serious VR. To get a useful HMD, you need to spend about $2,000.[13]

Another serious problem involves data rates. Filling larger displays with data and keeping track of where your head is pointing takes serious computing power—more than is available on a typical 486, although a fast Pentium probably will do the job.

Wide-Angle Displays

Thus, the next step after HMDs is HMDs with a field of vision approximately the same as we humans take for granted. Personally, I would expect this to be a major step, and one that has the potential to revolutionize artificial reality. Until the field of vision is wide enough to engage the two kinds of vision we possess,[14] the experience will be marred by whatever shows up in our peripheral vision—whether it be simply blackness or "real reality."

Display technology also must advance to a point where the large numbers of pixels needed for true wide-angle displays can be displayed cheaply and, just as important, instantly.[15]

---

[13]I'm referring here to the CyberEye headset from General Reality. It's a cut above the game-oriented headsets but is actually as good as many units that cost two or three times as much money.

[14]That is, central focus and peripheral.

[15]The very nature of digital imaging is both a blessing and a curse. The blessing comes in the form of very exact image representation. The curse takes the form of high data rates to reproduce precise colors and large, complex—and therefore interesting—images.

Tactile Feedback

What would life be like if your mouse went bump when you reached the edge of the computer screen? That's tactile feedback—a physical sensation coming back from the computer to tell you what's going on. Vibrating mice are with us today, but there is a real lack of software that supports such technology.[16]

A mouse represents just the barest beginnings of tactile-feedback technology. Gloves that give you a sensation of picking up objects are a much more advanced form of tactile feedback. Overall, however, it seems likely that tactile feedback will not be a form of virtual reality that finds its way into common use quickly. It's a great challenge to engineer the feel of a fur coat into a glove, for example!

Head and Body Tracking

If only the computer could, like a friend in a conversation, keep track of our head or body position, we could communicate so much more easily with the computer. Voice recognition is nice, but what if you could signal the equivalent of an OK button by just nodding your head? Pointing with a finger is one of the most natural gestures, but it is completely mysterious to a computer.[17]

Current ideas about how to implement tracking are somewhat intrusive. Video games, for example, are making use of large (3 to 4 feet in diameter) circular sensors placed on the floor. Experimental head-tracking devices often require you to wear something on your head, although there are experiments with video cameras built into monitors.[18] The computer analyzes the video image to try to determine where your head is facing. Current systems that use this technology are very expensive, ranging from $10,000 to $120,000 for systems that sense your facial expressions.[19]

Nonvisual Sensory Output

Now we are moving into the realm of future possibilities. Senses such as smell and touch are a lot harder to integrate into a computer connection. The sense of smell, for example, is extremely complex—and very personal. One person's great smell is another person's stink.

---

[16]What we really need is a mouse that will resist movement if we try to do something inappropriate. Wouldn't it be great if the mouse offered resistance when you tried to move the mouse cursor out of a modal dialog box, for example? (A *modal dialog box* is an item that you must deal with before you return to the program that generated it.)

[17]Unless you own a Glidepoint mouse substitute. This is a pad that you touch with your finger to move the mouse cursor. Not exactly VR, mind you, but an interesting product.

[18]How would you feel if the computer were constantly watching you with a video camera?

[19]Most such systems require you to stick white dots on your face. Not ideal for an office environment!

Given that we are only just beginning to be able to reproduce a limited number of scents chemically, and that the most desirable scents are tremendously subtle and natural, the sense of smell might not be computerized for quite some time. Touch is equally complex. Touch receptors are located all over the body, with different kinds of receptors in different areas. It seems highly likely that initial attempts to integrate touch will focus on areas of the body with large numbers of touch receptors, such as the hands.

Extrasensory Input and Output

The possibility of involving nonsensory data in the loop also exists. This can be done as a simulation or by mapping—for example, converting infrared data into sounds (mapping bright objects in the infrared to high pitches, and dim objects to low pitches), or mapping data to the visible spectrum (bright as blue, dim as red, for example). Ultimately, this possibly could be done more directly by mapping sensor data right into the brain.[20]

Total Immersion

The ultimate goal of artificial reality would be to create an experience that would be indistinguishable from the real McCoy. This seems like total hype at this stage of the game, and the proper forum for such ideas may well have to remain on the Holodeck of the Starship Enterprise for the time being.

Artificial Is a Matter of Degree

If there is anything to be learned from my attempt at classifying the forms that virtual reality might take, it is that there are many degrees of artificial. Some degrees are more realistic than others, and some do a better job of creating the experience of reality than others. The "reality" is that there are multiple dimensions involved, and there is no single line from the simple to the complex. Artificial reality is made up of a large number of intersecting needs and technologies, and all of it is bounded by what we actually can afford to do, as individuals and as a society.

Creating Virtual Spaces with Virtus

One big difference between the first edition of this book and the present edition is the power of the available VR software. However, there is a second difference that's

---

[20]This is far out, highly speculative stuff. It is, however, interesting to think about the possibility of extending human senses via computers.

just as important: the software is getting easier to use. Two products from Virtus exemplify the best of both worlds: Virtus VR and WalkThrough Pro. Both products take full advantage of the Windows interface, and that makes them easy to use. Both products also offer significant power for creating virtual worlds.

Virtus WalkThrough Pro offers more pure power, while Virtus VR is designed more for the beginner.

Virtus VR

The universe of virtual reality offers an infinite number of possibilities in every direction. However, there is one thing that virtual reality has in common with everyday reality: to get anything done, you have to know how to do it. Contrary to the expectations created by movies and books, a virtual world is something you have to put together piece by piece. You can't just wave your magic wand and have a completely customized virtual world at your disposal.

As with any software, there are different degrees of power and ease of use available to you. On the one hand, you can go for all the power you can afford—but you better prepare yourself for the time and money it will take to master that power. Superscape is an excellent example of VR power.

On the other hand, you can choose software that is as inviting and easy to use as possible—you can get started with VR instantly. Install the software, and then just pop together a nice, simple virtual world right from the start. Virtus VR, one of the software products included on the CD-ROMs with this book, is a perfect example of that kind of software.

In this section, you learn how to create a simple world in Virtus VR.

Hands On: A Virtual Training Center

There are two ways to learn about VR: in theory and with practice. Theory is useful, of course, but practice is a lot more fun. Let's get right down to business, and see how one goes about creating a virtual world. I'll pop in some theory here and there, in case you need some justification for the fun.

If you haven't already installed the demo version of Virtus VR that comes on the CD-ROMs with this book, now is the time to do it. To get the most out of this chapter, you'll want to follow along on your own computer.

Virtus VR is a Windows program, and this makes it exceptionally easy to learn and to use. Figure 2.1 shows what you see after you double-click the Virtus VR icon to run the program.

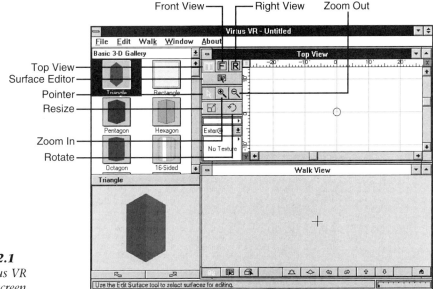

Figure 2.1
The Virtus VR starting screen.

The window is divided into three parts. I know—it does look like four parts, but bear with me here. One of the three parts is further subdivided into two parts (the Gallery). The three parts are

> **Left side**—Gallery
>
> **Upper right**—Design window
>
> **Lower right**—Walk window

Let's take a look at each of these parts in turn. We'll look at how they are used, and you'll learn about the tools and buttons used in each part.

The Gallery

The Gallery contains the objects that you can place into your Virtus VR virtual world. These objects range from simple geometric shapes—cubes, cones, spheres, and other forms that you might remember from solid geometry classes back in high school or college—to realistic objects like chairs, couches, lamps, and doors.

The lower portion of the Gallery window displays a 3D image of the object. You can turn the object to look at it by clicking the arrows at the bottom of the Gallery window. The left arrow rotates the object to the left, and the right arrow rotates it to the right. Figure 2.2 shows a cube that has been rotated.

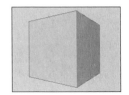

Figure 2.2
A rotated cube.

Design Window

If you have ever seen the plans for a house, you have some idea of how the Design window works. The Design window shows a 2D view of your world—from the Top, Front, or Right view. For house plans, the Top view often is called the Plan view, and the Front and Right views are called elevations. This is a convenient way to work—after all, your monitor is only 2D. You get finer control over your work by operating mostly with the 2D views while you create. You then can move around in the world in 3D using the Walk window.

To add a new object to the Design window, drag it over from the Gallery. You can reposition and resize the object after you place it. You can only view your world from the top, front, and right side in the Design window. This means that you can only see your objects in Plan form—a 2D representation using outlines (also called wireframe). The three top buttons on the toolbar (refer to Fig. 2.1) control the view (T, F, and R correspond to the Top, Front, and Right views).

The button below these is the Surface Editor button; it enables you to change the characteristics of individual surfaces. The five remaining buttons, from left to right and top to bottom are

> **Pointer**—Selects objects and surfaces
>
> **Zoom In**—Magnifies the view in the Design window
>
> **Zoom Out**—Reduces the view in the Design window
>
> **Resize**—Changes the size of an object
>
> **Rotate**—Changes the orientation of an object

Walk Window

The Walk window is where you explore your virtual world. If you have a fast computer, you can view objects in 3D, including shading. You can easily use your mouse to move around in the Walk window. Note the row of buttons at the bottom of the Walk window (see Fig. 2.3). You can use them for various purposes.

Figure 2.3
*The Walk window
buttons.*

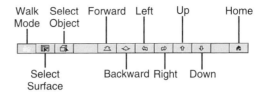

From left to right, these buttons are

> **Walk Mode**—Enables you to move around in the Walk window using your
> mouse. Click left of the central cross hairs to turn left, and click right of them
> to turn right. Click above the cross hairs to move forward, and click below to
> move backward. You can modify movement by using the Shift and Control
> keys, as shown in Figure 2.4. If clicking does not cause movement, that
> usually means that you have clicked one of the Select buttons—click the
> Walk Mode button to activate it.

> **Select Surface**—When this button is down, clicking in the Walk window
> selects a surface for editing in the Surface Editor.

> **Select Object**—When this button is down, clicking in the Walk window
> selects an object.

> **Forward**—Moves forward until the mouse button is released.

> **Backward**—Moves backward until the mouse button is released.

> **Left**—Turns left until the mouse button is released.

> **Right**—Turns right until the mouse button is released.

> **Up**—Moves up until the mouse button is released.

> **Down**—Moves down until the mouse button is released.

> **Home**—Returns the point of view and view direction to the home position.
> This is handy if you get "lost" and can't see anything in the Walk window.

You might want to practice moving around in the Walk window using both the mouse
clicks of Walk mode, and the buttons at the bottom of the Walk window. Open any
of the sample files provided on the CD-ROMs by choosing Open from the File menu.
Some simple sample files also can be found on your hard disk after you install Virtus
VR in the directory *<drive>*:\VIRTUSVR\MODELS, where *<drive>* refers to the letter
of the drive on which you installed Virtus VR. If you want to play around with something more complex, look at the sample files in the *<drive>*:\VIRTUSVR\SCENES directory.

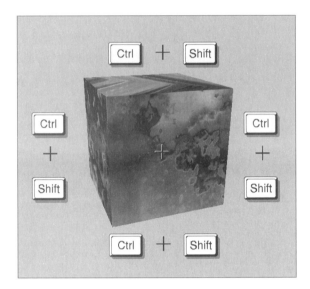

Figure 2.4
*Moving around with
the mouse in the
Walk window.*

Instant VR

Of all the VR software I've tested, Virtus VR is the only product that gives you truly instant virtual reality. While writing this book, I used just about every kind of virtual reality software available. Almost every VR product assumes that you already know something about VR, or that you are willing to spend lots of time learning how to use the software. Virtus VR uses a simple drag-and-drop method of creating VR environments. This makes it the ideal software for an introduction to virtual reality.

Let's take a few minutes to demonstrate just how quickly you can be up and running in Virtus VR. In this section, you'll build a simple one-room house, complete with a door, window, and a painting on the wall. This will be a very simple project, designed to teach you how to get up and running with Virtus VR. For the more adventurous, the next section in this chapter, "Virtuoso Virtus VR," shows how to create much more complex[21] virtual worlds with Virtus VR. If you want to jump right in, feel free to skip ahead.

Begin by clicking the Rectangle icon in the Gallery window. Without releasing the mouse button, drag the cursor into the Design window. Release the mouse button, and the rectangle drops into place in the Design window, as shown in Figure 2.5.

The corners of the rectangle are little black squares. These indicate that the object is selected. Any operations you perform with the menus or the tools are applied only to the currently selected object. You can deselect an object by clicking on the background.

---

[21]And interesting!

Note that there is something else in the Design window along with the rectangle—a small circle. This little circle represents your "eyes"—it controls the direction of your view in the Walk window. (The location of the circle might be different than what you see in Fig. 2.5.)

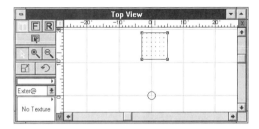

Figure 2.5
Adding a rectangle.

Look again at the Walk window, which should show a 3D view of the newly created rectangle. You'll probably see something similar to Figure 2.6. It isn't very clear, is it? You need to "step back" to see what you have created; the point of view is too close to the rectangle to see what it is. It looks like nothing more than a white patch in a window—not like a rectangle.

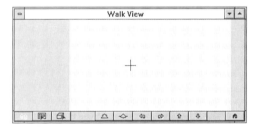

Figure 2.6
*A 3D view in the
Walk window.*

There are two ways to change your point of view. You can use the little circle in the Design window to change the view angle, or you can use the mouse to move around in the Walk window. It takes a little practice to get used to moving around with the mouse, so we'll take the easy way out here, and use the circle in the Design window.

To move the point-of-view circle, click it with the mouse, and then drag it to a new position at the left of the rectangle (see Fig. 2.7). Look at the Walk window—wow! It's blank. Don't worry—this simply means that we aren't looking at anything. When we moved the point of view, we didn't change the direction of view, so we are now looking off into empty space. The little black line at the top of the point-of-view circle tells you the direction of the view. With the line pointing to the top of the Design window (as in Figs. 2.7 and 2.8), the view is straight ahead and the rectangle is off to the right.

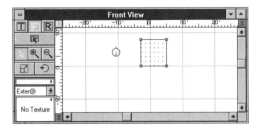

Figure 2.7
Relocating the point-of-view circle.

In order to bring the rectangle into view, we must turn toward the right. Move the cursor to the point-of-view circle (see Fig. 2.8). To change the direction of view, hold down the Control key, click on the circle, and drag toward the right. You will see a dotted line connecting the circle and the mouse pointer, indicating the direction of view (see Fig. 2.9). Hold down the mouse button until you get a direction of view that includes the rectangle.

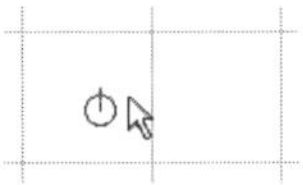

Figure 2.8
Adjusting the point of view: step 1.

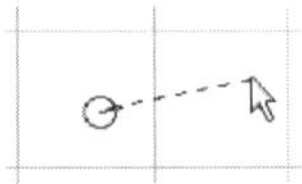

Figure 2.9
Adjusting the point of view: step 2.

When you have set the desired direction, release the mouse. The line extending out of the circle is now pointing in the desired direction (see Fig. 2.10). You might need to try several times to get the exact correct angle for the view; after making a change, look at the Walk window until you see something like Figure 2.11.

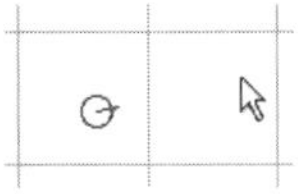

Figure 2.10
Adjusting the point of view: step 3.

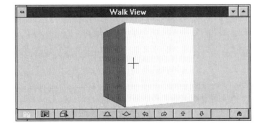

Figure 2.11
The view in the Walk window.

Now that you have "stepped back" from the object, you can see it much more clearly. If you haven't moved back far enough, just drag the little circle around until the view in the Walk window matches the example in Figure 2.11.

So far, all we have is a simple box, with no way to get inside. Our next task is obvious: a door. We'll use the Surface Editor to add the door. Look closely at the toolbar located at the left of the Design window. It has a number of buttons, as shown in Figure 2.12.

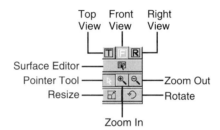

Figure 2.12
The Design window's toolbar.

Take note of the Surface Editor button. It's the deep, dark secret to using Virtus VR to do cool stuff. To use the Surface Editor on a surface, you must first click the Surface Editor button to activate it. Figure 2.12 shows what the Surface Editor button looks like before you click it, and Figure 2.13 shows what the button looks like after it has been clicked (that is, activated). Virtus VR behaves very differently when the Surface Editor is active.

Figure 2.13
When the Surface Editor is active.

After you have activated the Surface Editor icon, you must click on the surface you want to edit. If you are following along with me, your Design window is currently showing the Top view. This means that only the top of the object is visible in the Design window. If you wanted to edit the top surface in the Surface Editor, you could now click on it and—presto—off you go to the Surface Editor.

Often, however, you want to edit something besides the current surface. There are two ways to select a surface to edit:

1. Click in the Design window next to the surface you want to edit. The arrow in Figure 2.14 shows where you would click to edit the left side of the object. Do this now so you'll be ready for the next step in the development of the room.

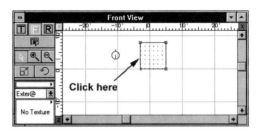

Figure 2.14
Selecting a surface
in the Design
window.

2. Move the point-of-view circle, and adjust the view direction so that the desired surface is visible in the Walk window. Click the Select Surface button (at the bottom of the Walk window; see Fig. 2.15), and then click on the surface in the Walk window to open the Surface Editor. The dot in Figure 2.15 shows where you would click in the Walk window to select the left side of the object.

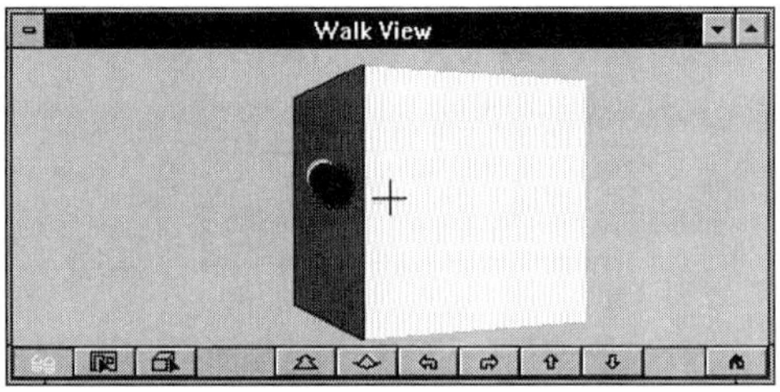

Figure 2.15
Selecting a surface
in the Walk
window.

When you enter the Surface Editor, you will see only the selected surface, as shown in Figure 2.16. It looks a lot like the normal situation in Virtus VR, but if you look carefully, you'll see that the top right window is now labeled `Surface:Outside`. The Surface Editor icon is gone from the toolbar (see Fig. 2.17), replaced with a little arrow that means *return to Design window*. In addition, the top three buttons in the Design toolbar have changed to O, I, and B.

O stands for Outside, I stands for Inside, and B stands for Both. These buttons determine how the 2D shapes in the Surface Editor gallery will be applied to the surface you are editing:

Outside—If this button is pressed, shapes you apply to a surface will be visible only on the outside of the surface.

Inside—If this button is pressed, shapes you apply to a surface will be visible only on the inside of the surface.

Both—If this button is pressed, shapes you apply to a surface will be visible on both the inside and outside of the surface. When creating translucent windows or transparent doors, this is the setting to use!

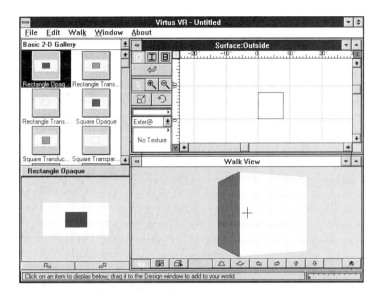

Figure 2.16
*The Surface Editor
in action.*

Figure 2.17
*The toolbar changes
in the Surface
Editor.*

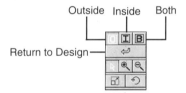

The Resize and Rotate buttons are used in the Surface Editor to change the shapes you apply to a surface.

The Gallery window has also changed. Instead of simple shapes, you now see shapes that can be applied to surfaces. Each shape has three versions:

Opaque—Useful for applying textures to a portion of a surface, or for applying colored shapes to a surface.

Translucent—Useful when you want windows or glass. Enables you to see through the surface, but with a slight reduction in clarity typical of windows.

Transparent—Useful for doors or other openings.

Use Transparent for things like doors, Translucent for windows, and Opaque for things that are "on" a surface.

Let's create a door for our cube, and turn it into a room. We want the door to apply to the inside and the outside portions of the surface, so make sure that the B button is active.

Click Rectangle Transparent in the Gallery window. Figure 2.18 shows the appearance of the transparent rectangle in the bottom portion of the Gallery window, after using the Rotate Right button. The transparent rectangle appears as the hole through the surface of an object. Drag a Rectangle Transparent object to the Surface Editor window.

Figure 2.18
*A transparent shape
in the Gallery
window.*

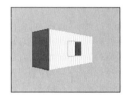

Depending on your screen resolution, you will see the 2D Rectangle Transparent object as a large or small rectangle with an X through it as you drag. Position this X over the surface you are editing, and then release the mouse button. If you do not like where you drop the rectangle, you can click and drag to move it until you have it positioned on the surface as shown in Figure 2.19.

The Surface Editor window should now look approximately like Figure 2.19. The black area is the transparent rectangle. It doesn't look much like a door, but we'll fix that in a moment. The Walk window should look like Figure 2.20. Note that you can see through the surface to the inside of the object.

Figure 2.19
*A door has been
added.*

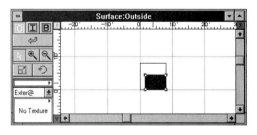

Figure 2.20
*The door appears in
the Walk window.*

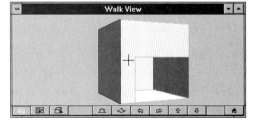

To shape the opening into a doorway, click and drag the corners of the transparent rectangle to the approximate proportions of a doorway. If you want to be exact, you can use the rulers at the top and left to make the doorway exactly three feet wide (that's pretty typical for an exterior door) and about seven feet high (actual door height is usually 6'8"). Figures 2.21 and 2.22 show the result in the Surface Editor and the Walk window.

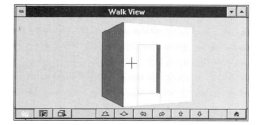

Figure 2.21
A properly propor-
tioned doorway.

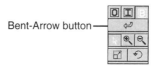

Figure 2.22
The doorway in the
Walk window.

To return to the Design window, click the Bent-Arrow button below the O, I, and B buttons on the toolbar (see Fig. 2.23).

Figure 2.23
The Surface Editor
toolbar.

Bent-Arrow button ——

If the Design window is not already displaying the Front view, click the F button in the toolbar to display the Front view (see Fig. 2.24). The location of the door now is marked by a dashed line.

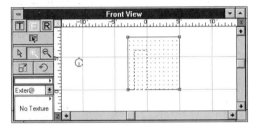

Figure 2.24
The door in front view.

Now let's add a window to the room. Click the R button to change to the Right view. The result is shown in Figure 2.25. The door, now visible in profile, is the thicker black line at the left of the room. The right side of the room is facing you in the Design view. Click the Surface Editor button in the toolbar (see Fig. 2.26), and then click anywhere on the right side to activate the Surface Editor.

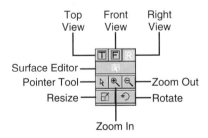

Figure 2.25
The door in right view.

Here's a tip to make it clearer how to use the Surface Editor: First, click the Surface Editor button in the Design window toolbar. The button changes to the appearance shown in Figure 2.26. Now click on the surface you want to edit. Presto—you jump to the Surface Editor.

Figure 2.26
The Surface Editor toolbar

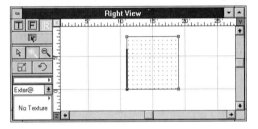

You can use the Zoom buttons to enlarge or reduce the display of the right side in the Surface Editor (see Fig. 2.27, which shows the right side zoomed in a bit).

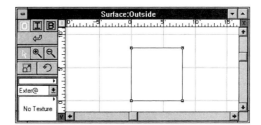

Figure 2.27
*Zoom in the Surface
Editor.*

To create a window in this surface, click on Rectangle Translucent in the Gallery window. If you have a screen resolution of 640×480, you might not be able to see the complete text for each item. The translucent rectangle looks more or less like a window, as you can see in the bottom half of the Gallery window (see Fig. 2.28).

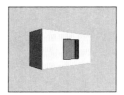

Figure 2.28
*A translucent shape
in the Gallery
Editor.*

Creating a window is just like creating a door. The only difference is that you now are using a translucent shape instead of a transparent one. Click on Rectangle Translucent in the Gallery window, and drag it into the Surface Editor. Position it over the surface, and release the mouse button. Figure 2.29 shows the result.

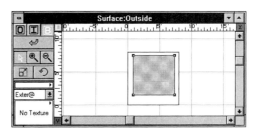

Figure 2.29
A window added.

Use the corner handles to change the shape of the rectangle, or drag the rectangle by clicking and holding the mouse until you have it in a good place for a window. Figure 2.30 shows where I placed my window.

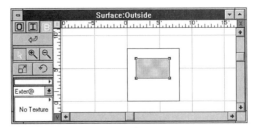

Figure 2.30
A resized window.

Figure 2.31 shows the view of the window and the door in the Walk window (after I moved around using the controls at the bottom of the Walk window, of course!). As I described earlier, you can also use the Design window and the little circle to change your point of view quickly.

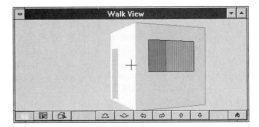

Figure 2.31
*A window and door
in the Walk
window.*

You can easily enter the room by the door, either by using mouse clicks in the Walk window to maneuver around, or by using the buttons at the bottom of the Walk window. Figure 2.32 shows the interior of the room, with the window on the left and the door on the right. Figure 2.33 shows the position of the point-of-view circle in the Top view. It is located just inside the top left corner of the room. As I moved the point of view, I watched carefully in the Walk window to see when I was in the room.

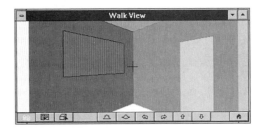

Figure 2.32
*The interior of the
room.*

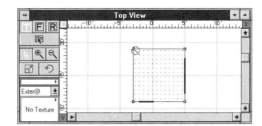

Figure 2.33
*The point of view for
the interior view.*

You can easily add some decoration to the room. For example, click on the pull-down list at the top of the Gallery window to choose a gallery with some interesting objects in it, such as office furniture or household items (or something more bizarre that suits your taste!). Click and drag any object from any gallery to the Design window (Top view works best), and place it anywhere in the room (or outside, if that suits your fancy). You might need to resize the object to fit the size of your room. Click on the object handles (at the corners) and resize as needed by dragging with the mouse. Figure 2.34 shows a cone I placed in the room by dragging it from the Gallery window. When resizing, you might find that the object has floated off the floor (as in this case). Just drag it back down. You might need to switch to a side view first.

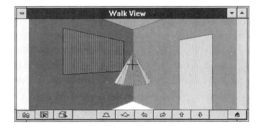

Figure 2.34
*Adding an object to
the room.*

You also can decorate an inside wall using techniques like those we used to create the door and the window. Click on either one of the two blank walls in the Walk window, using the Walk window's Turn Left button to bring one of the walls into view (see Fig. 2.35). Click the Surface Editor button, and then click on the blank wall. This displays the wall in the Surface Editor, as shown in Figure 2.36.

Figure 2.35
*Walk window
controls.*

Surface Editor   Turn Left

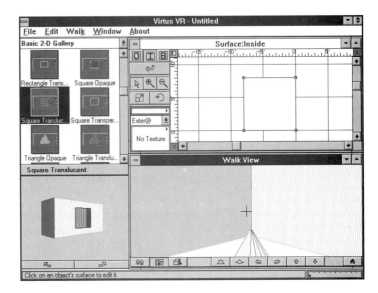

Figure 2.36
The interior wall in the Surface Editor.

In the 2D Gallery, highlight the Rectangle Opaque option (scroll down if it doesn't show in the window) and drag it into the Surface Editor. Place it on the surface, and resize as shown in Figure 2.37. Figure 2.38 shows the result in the Walk window.

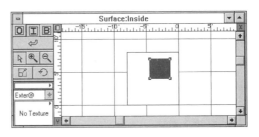

Figure 2.37
An internal wall with an opaque rectangle.

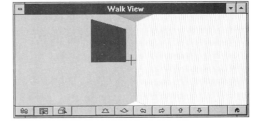

Figure 2.38
An opaque rectangle added to the wall.

As artwork goes, this is very boring—let's use the texture feature of Virtus VR to apply a flower pattern to the rectangle. In the toolbar, note the Texture button (it now says No Texture). Click the pull-down list just above it, and select Exterior Textures. Then click the Texture button to open the Texture list shown in Figure 2.39.

Figure 2.39
The Texture list.

Click Impatiens Shaded, and the rectangle takes on this texture. Figure 2.40 shows the view of the wall in the Surface Editor. Figure 2.41 shows the appearance of the textured rectangle in the Walk window.

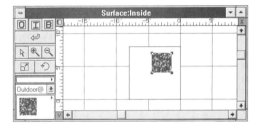

Figure 2.40
A wall in the Surface Editor.

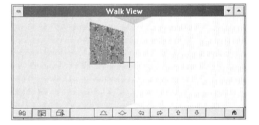

Figure 2.41
A wall in the Walk window.

Just for fun, why don't you take a walk in the little virtual world you have created? You can get started using the Top view to position the point-of-view circle in front of the door, where you can look in at your handiwork (see Fig. 2.42). You then can use the mouse (or the control buttons at the bottom of the Walk window) to explore your world.

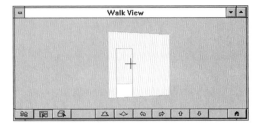

Figure 2.42
Outside the completed room.

If you want to record your movements and replay them later, click the Walk window to activate it and then choose Record from the Walk menu (see Fig. 2.43). All your movements will be recorded. The recording is saved to disk after you choose Save from the File menu to save your work. Only one recording can be saved as a recorded walk sequence, but you can create an animation of any recorded set of movements.

Figure 2.43
Recording a walk.

To save the walk as an animation file on your hard disk, choose Snapshot from the File menu. This displays a small submenu; choose Animator Pro (see Fig. 2.44).

> You also can save a bitmap image of the current contents of the Walk window by clicking the BMP option on the Snapshot submenu.

Animator Pro is an animation program from Autodesk that is used by many professional animators to create 2D animations. The file format for this program has become a standard file format for animations created by other programs as well. Early versions of Virtus VR had a few bugs in their animation files, and some video card drivers also can cause trouble with animation files. If you experience problems playing the animations, contact Virtus for an update, or contact the vendor for your video display card for more recent drivers. It's always a good idea to check for video driver updates every three to six months, in any case.

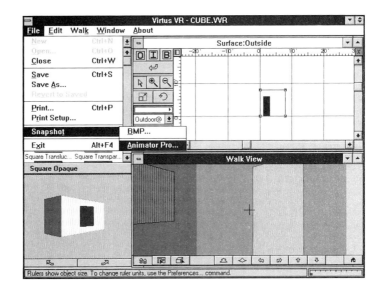

Figure 2.44
Creating an
animation file.

If you choose Animator Pro from the menu shown in Figure 2.44, the dialog box shown in Figure 2.45 appears. It's usually a good idea to click in the Smooth Path check box to place an X in it; this option removes any jerkiness in the animation. Clicking this option causes Virtus VR to add extra frames to make the walk speed constant throughout the animation.

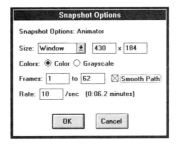

Figure 2.45
The Snapshot
Options dialog box.

You also can change the size of the animation, the rate, and the number of frames. The size of your animation will probably vary from the numbers shown in Figure 2.45, since the animation is based on the actual size of the Walk window.

Until you are more familiar with the effects of these options, I recommend using the default values. When everything is correct (refer to Fig. 2.45 if you accidentally make changes), click the OK button, and supply a file name for the animation in the dialog box that appears. During creation of the animation, you'll see a status bar, as shown in Figure 2.46.

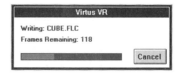

Figure 2.46
*The animation
status indicator.*

You can add additional rooms using the techniques we have explored here, or you can add more items from the various galleries to get the look you want. You also can apply textures to entire walls; explore the textures included on the CD-ROMs. If you want doors between rooms, remember to create two doors: one for each of the adjoining rooms.

Virtuoso Virtus VR

You can create much more than just simple rooms with Virtus VR. In the last section, you learned many of the basic operations needed to work with Virtus VR. In this section, you'll see how a more complex room environment is created. A few of the basics are repeated here, for those who chose to skip the detailed tutorial in the earlier section.

Figure 2.47 shows what Virtus VR looks like when you start it. The left portion of the window, called the Gallery, contains objects you can place into a virtual environment. The Top window is where you do your work of creating and modifying objects and the environment. It's called the Plan view. The bottom window is the Walk window, where you easily can walk through a virtual environment using the mouse.

For beginners, there is a collection of buildings, environments, and objects that enables you to get started right away. In Figure 2.47, the objects were pretty ordinary—cylinders and boxes and other boring (but necessary!) 3D shapes. Virtus VR also comes with some pretty detailed objects for various kinds of environments—the home, kitchens, offices, and even farms. As an example, let's decorate the Oval Office of the White House.[22] Figure 2.48 shows the Plan view of the White House, and Figure 2.49 shows an outside view.

---

[22]You guessed it: The plans for the White House are conveniently included with Virtus VR.

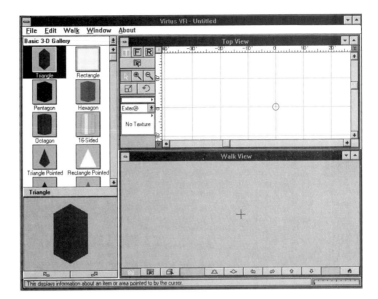

Figure 2.47
Virtus VR looks like this before you start building a world.

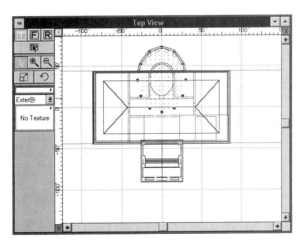

Figure 2.48
A plan of the White House.

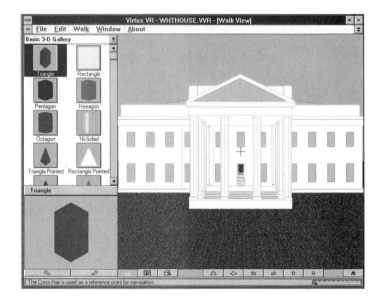

Figure 2.49
An outside view of
the White House.

You can use the Walk window to get to the Oval Office. By clicking above the cross hairs at the center of the window, you can move forward. To move backward, click below the cross hairs. Clicking to the right or left makes a turn. You can combine these moves by clicking on a diagonal.

By combining these moves, you easily can find your way in any virtual world. To move from the view in Figure 2.49 to the inside of the Oval Office, you would move forward and down to enter the front door, and then go straight back to the office. Figure 2.50 shows the unfurnished interior of the Oval Office, as included with Virtus VR.

Notice in Figure 2.50 that I have selected the Office 3D gallery instead of those boring simple shapes. Now you'll find chairs and desks at the left of the Virtus VR window. To place one of these objects in the virtual Oval Office, just click and drag the object into the Plan view, placing it where you want. You can resize the object, move it, rotate it, and change the color or surface texture of the object.

For fun, look at the little window at the bottom of the gallery—you can use the left and right arrows to rotate an object and see it from all sides. Figure 2.51 shows an office chair as it is being rotated.

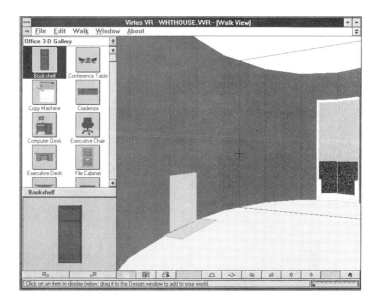

Figure 2.50
Inside the Oval Office.

Figure 2.51
Various views of an office chair.

Figure 2.52 shows the Plan view and the WalkThrough window, with a chair and desk now installed in the Oval Office. Both items can be seen in both windows.

You also can create your own buildings and rooms from scratch, or create an outdoor scene. Figure 2.53 shows a fun living room, with fireplace and furniture, that I created in about 15 minutes with Virtus VR.

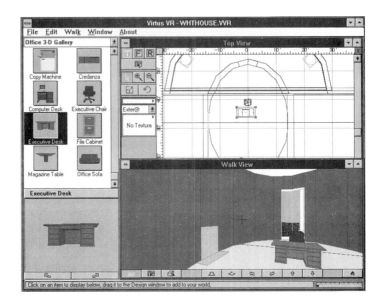

Figure 2.52
A partially furnished oval office.

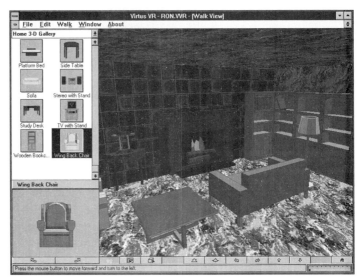

Figure 2.53
A living room created from scratch with Virtus VR.

Let's look at how the living room was created. I began with a simple box, as shown in Figure 2.54.

To do anything interesting with this box, we'll need to use some of the tools in the toolbox. The toolbox is located at the left of the Plan view.

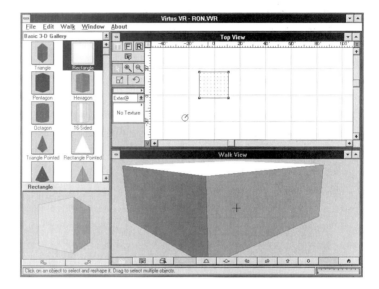

Figure 2.54
Starting a new virtual world with a basic box.

The easiest thing to do is to change the object's color. Click and drag downward on the Color panel to display the Color Selection palette (see Fig. 2.55). The last 30 colors you used are displayed at the top, with a larger number of colors below. If you want to be very precise about the color you use, click on the Little Palette icon, and you get a standard Windows Color Picker dialog box. Figure 2.56 shows the object with color applied.

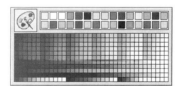

Figure 2.55
Selecting a color for an object.

Colors are nice, but there are more interesting ways to add details to an object in Virtus VR. Click and drag downward on the Texture panel to display a list of available textures you can apply to an object.[23] Figure 2.57 shows a few of the textures supplied with Virtus VR, and Figure 2.58 shows an object that has a texture.

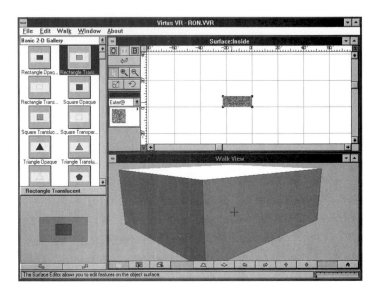

Figure 2.56
Applying a color to the object.

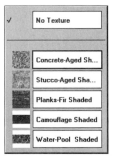

Figure 2.57
Some of the textures supplied with Virtus VR.

Now we have a box with a texture, but that's still hardly an amazing feat. Let's add a window and a door—then we'll have something! To switch to a new gallery, click on the small panel at the top of the Gallery, and select one of the Window galleries. To place a window on what is now becoming a building, simply click and drag the

---

[23]There are several Texture libraries supplied with Virtus VR. The small panel above the Texture panel enables you to select from the available collection of textures.

window of your choice into the Plan view.[24] Figure 2.59 shows a window on the building, and Figure 2.60 shows a door added. I switched to the Door Gallery, of course, before clicking and dragging the door into place.

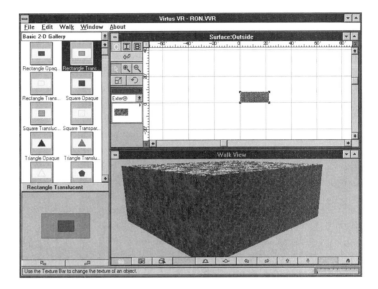

Figure 2.58
An object with a texture applied to it.

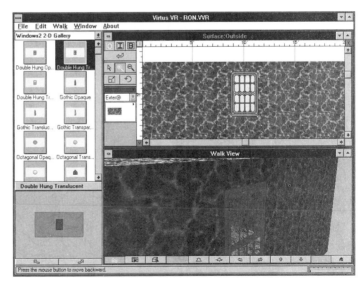

Figure 2.59
A window turns the box into a building.

---

[24]Of course, you should rotate the Plan view to make sure that the surface you are looking at is the one that gets the window!

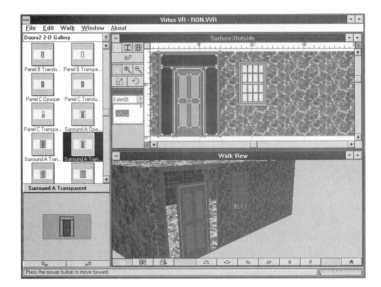

Figure 2.60
Adding a door makes it a bit more real.

You now can use the mouse to move through the door and into the interior of the building. Switching to the Home 3D Gallery gives us some very useful objects to add to our burgeoning virtual world, such as the fireplace shown in Figure 2.61.

Next, I added a couch, a small table, and a lamp. The room looked a little spare, so I dressed it up with a row of bookcases on the right-hand wall (see Fig. 2.62).

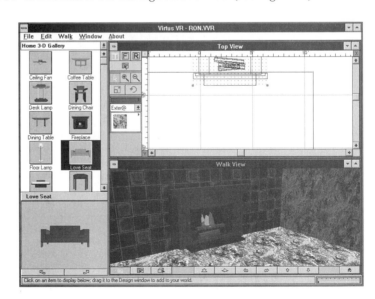

Figure 2.61
Adding a fireplace to the interior.

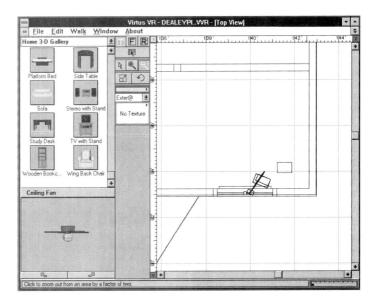

Figure 2.62
Adding more furniture to the room.

I had thought that the bookcases would add a nice realistic touch, but they wound up looking so bare that I just had to make some books to put on the shelves. This was very easy to do—I simply created a box, decreased it to the size of a book, and gave it a brown color (see Fig. 2.63 for the Plan view of the book in the bookcase). One book, of course, makes hardly any difference. I used the Object Duplicate command to create a whole row of books; Figure 2.64 shows the result.

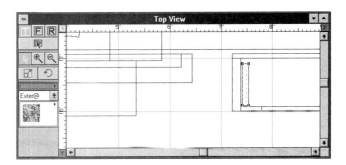

Figure 2.63
One book created in Virtus VR.

To make the scene a bit more realistic, I took a moment to "knock" the books out of their perfect alignment (see Fig. 2.65). I then added one more book in one of the other bookcases, and tilted it to suggest realism (see Fig. 2.66). I could have gone on to add more books, but the scene looks like someone is in the process of moving in, and that was realistic enough for me.

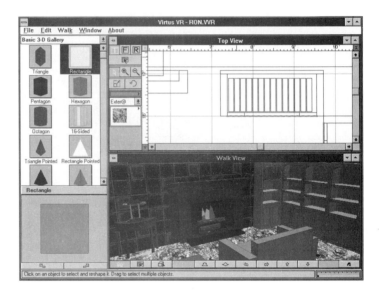

Figure 2.64
*Adding some books
to a bookcase.*

I did add a few more touches, such as a wing chair and a floor lamp, to create the final scene, as shown in Figure 2.67.

Of course, you could take the scene further. You could add one of the characters from the People Gallery to our virtual world. In Figure 2.68, I added a woman seated on the couch, and moved the point of view to a position on the couch looking at her.

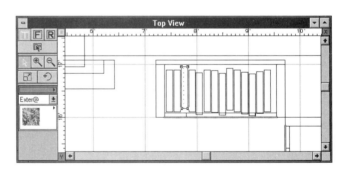

Figure 2.65
*Loosening up the
arrangement of
books.*

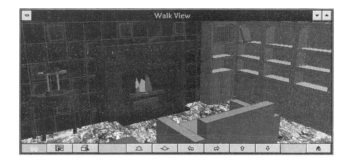

Figure 2.66
The scene with more books in the bookcases.

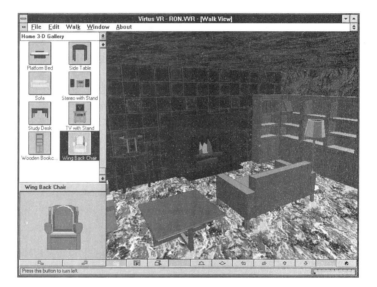

Figure 2.67
The completed virtual world.

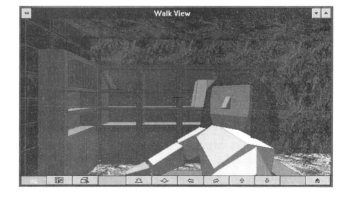

Figure 2.68
People in the virtual world.

If you want, you can record your movements in a virtual world for later playback. You also can export recorded movements to a FLC file. This animation format is supported by many products, such as Autodesk's Animator Pro.

I enjoyed Virtus VR a great deal. It's simple, it's very easy to use, and it provides enough entertainment and flexibility to make it a really good deal. If you have any interest in exploring the possibilities of virtual reality, this is a great place to start.

Virtus WalkThrough Pro

Earlier in this chapter, you learned some of the basic techniques of virtual reality using Virtus VR. Virtus VR has much to recommend it for the beginner, but the very features that make it easy to learn also limit its power. In this section, you'll learn about a related, but more powerful, product called Virtus WalkThrough Pro.

There are many significant differences between Virtus VR and WalkThrough Pro. The key difference has to do with the way that you create virtual objects. In Virtus VR, you simply plop basic shapes into your virtual universe, and then alter them in simple ways, or combine them to make more complex objects. In WalkThrough Pro, you can create objects by drawing them in the 3D space. You also can alter an object's fundamental shape by adding or deleting faces.

This enables you to create more complex and interesting objects for your virtual world. However, you'll find that you must give up some of the drag-and-drop simplicity of Virtus VR to gain this much power. There are also more tools—some of them quite exciting. Using WalkThrough Pro, you'll be able to create more realistic (and more accurate) virtual objects.

This is made possible by a completely different set of tools. In WalkThrough Pro, you retain much more control over objects as you create them. Instead of dragging and dropping objects, you define how large they are and how they are oriented as you create them. This enables you to position objects and size objects immediately. It also offers you great control over the proportions of width, height, and depth.

In this section, our primary focus will be to examine the tools included with WalkThrough Pro. To learn more about creating objects and buildings, see the section "Creating Objects," later in this chapter.

WalkThrough Pro Basics

You've already learned many of the things you need to know about WalkThrough if you read the tutorial for Virtus VR earlier in this chapter. If you haven't, you'll want to review that material, and then follow the new material here. Many of the navigating, moving, rotating, enlarging, and other techniques used in Virtus VR are also used in WalkThrough Pro.

The look and feel of the two programs is also similar, as you can see from the view of WalkThrough Pro in Figure 2.69. There is a floating toolbar to the left of the main window, a Design window, and a Walk window. The toolbar changes as you use different areas of the program, and we'll look at each version as we go along. The Design window is very much like the one found in Virtus VR, although it's more flexible. The Walk window lacks the control buttons found at the bottom of the Virtus VR Walk window.

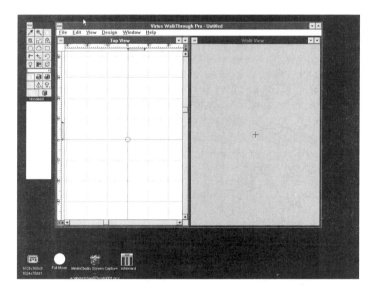

Figure 2.69
Virtus
WalkThrough Pro.

Let's start with the floating toolbar (see Fig. 2.70). When the Design window is active, this is what you will see. If the Walk window is active, the toolbar looks like the version shown in Figure 2.71. I'll show you how to use that version of the toolbar later, when we look at the Walk window. For now, if the Walk version of the toolbar shows up, just click anywhere in the Design window to activate the Design Toolbar.

Figure 2.70
*The Design window
floating toolbar.*

Figure 2.71
*The Walk window
toolbar.*

Some of the tools in the toolbar should be familiar from Virtus VR. Others are new, and add substantial power. One key feature of WalkThrough Pro is that some of the tools are stacked. Stacked tools have a small arrow at the bottom right, indicating that there are more tools than meet the eye.

As shown in Figure 2.70, the tools are arranged in groups, and we'll look at them by the rows in which they appear. There are 15 tools in the top group, followed by the color bar, and then eight more tools. That big area of white space at the bottom is the Layers list. You can put objects in different layers, and each layer can have a name for easy reference. Layers help you keep track of what's what, and what's where. Layers also help you avoid object clutter—too many objects on the screen at one time can be confusing. This is the old 2D screen, 3D world bugaboo: it's hard to visualize three dimensions on a two-dimensional computer monitor.

Let's go over each of the tools, one by one, to see what they can do for you.

Basic Tools

 Color Lifter—"Picks up" a color anywhere on-screen and makes it the current color. All newly created objects will automatically use the color you pick.

 Magnify/Zoom—Zooms in on the current view in the Design window. The view doubles each time you click. To zoom out, hold down the Control key while you click this tool.

 Select Object—Operations are performed only on the currently selected object. To select an object or surface, click this tool, and then click the object you want to select. Hold down the Shift key to select more than one object at a time. Clicking again on an object deselects it.

 Tape Measure—Finds the distance between two points. To measure, click to activate this tool, and then click and drag in the Design window. The distance is shown in a pop-up window.

 Scale Object—Changes the size of objects. Click and drag to change size along any axis, or hold down the Shift key to scale in all axes.

 Skew Object—Deforms an object. Click and drag to lean the object in any direction. If you click a container (such as a room), the objects within it are not skewed.

 Lock Object—Locks objects (Design window) or surfaces (Surface Editor) so that they cannot be edited. To unlock objects, hold down the Control key. To unlock all objects, double-click this tool.

 Hide Object—Hides one or more objects. To hide an object, click on this tool, and then click on the object. To unhide all objects, double-click this tool.

Drawing Tools

 Create 8-Sided—Creates an eight-sided object.

Create 6-Sided—Creates a six-sided object.

Create Square—Creates a four-sided object.

Create Triangular—Creates a three-sided object.

 Create N-Sided—Creates an object with the number of sides that you specify.

 Create Irregular—Creates an object with irregular sides—sides can be of different lengths, and angles between sides may vary.

 Create Rectangular—Creates a rectangular object.

More Basic Tools

Connect Surfaces—Used only when you have two objects that share a common opening. By connecting the adjacent surfaces, you can make sure that the opening passes through both of them.

Add/Remove Handle—Handles define the edges of objects. This tool enables you to change the number of edges. You could add handles to the side of a house to create a bay window, for example. To add a handle, click on the edge of a surface. To remove a handle, click on it.

Rotate Object—Rotates objects about an axis in the Design window. The angle of rotation appears in the Coordinates window, if it is displayed.

The WalkThrough Editors

The bottom three icons in the toolbar are used to open special windows for editing. From left to right, these buttons open the Lighting Editor, the Surface Editor, and the Tumble Editor.

Lighting Editor

The Lighting Editor button enables you to add lighting to your virtual world. Lights are attached to individual objects, so you can set up complex lighting arrangements to suit your needs.

In the example in Figure 2.72, a cube is shown in the Lighting Editor, and one of four lights is selected. The lights are listed in the toolbar, which changes dramatically for the Lighting Editor.

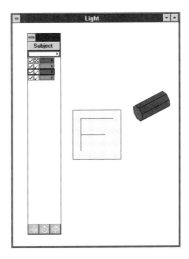

Figure 2.72
A cube in the Lighting Editor.

To select a light, click on the colored bars near the top of the toolbar. In Figure 2.72, the third bar from the top is selected. There are three boxes for each light. From left to right, the boxes are On/Off, Light Type, and Light Color.

You can use the mouse in the Lighting Editor to change the angle and position of each light. In Figure 2.72, the light is placed slightly above and behind the object, and the light color is a medium grayish green.

The three small buttons at the bottom of the toolbar are used to define which axes of rotation are active. As a general rule, it's safest to adjust one axis of rotation at a time. Trying to control several angles of rotation with the mouse is difficult at best.

Surface Editor

The WalkThrough Pro Surface Editor is very much like the one found in Virtus VR. To invoke the Surface Editor, click the Surface Editor button and then click on the surface you want to edit.

A typical Surface Editor session is shown in Figure 2.73. Note that the toolbar changes for each Editor, showing you tools that are appropriate for that Editor.

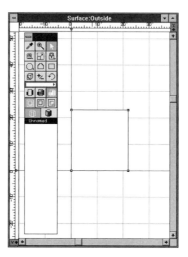

Figure 2.73
The Surface Editor.

The Surface Editor doesn't look like much, but it is a very powerful tool for creating both objects and environments. You can apply surfaces, create openings, or add windows.

There are three additional tools you need to master to use the Surface Editor effectively:

 Place on Front—If this button is pressed, new surfaces are placed on the front of an existing surface.

 Place Through—If this button is pressed, new surfaces are placed on the front and the back of an existing surface. Always use this setting for doors and windows.

 Place on Back—If this button is pressed, new surfaces will be placed on the back (hidden side) of an existing surface. Useful for modifying the interior of a room.

Tumble Editor

The Tumble Editor, like the Lighting Editor, is specific to WalkThrough Pro—you won't find either of these editing tools in Virtus VR. The Tumble Editor is something like a 3D pair of scissors. You can use it to make major modifications to your shapes.

There are two basic steps involved in using the Tumble Editor effectively. The toolbar changes to include a cube at the bottom (see Fig. 2.74). As in the Lighting Editor, there are three buttons that enable you to control axes of rotation. As in the Lighting Editor, I strongly advise trying to rotate along a single axis at a time. You can do some dramatic rotations with two or more axes active, but you can also get completely lost. If you do get lost while rotating, close the Tumble Editor and start over—it's just about impossible to reorient yourself!

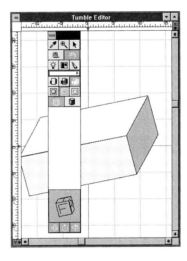

Figure 2.74
The Tumble Editor.

You can use the following tools in the Tumble Editor:

Tumbler—When the hand at the left of the toolbar is clicked, you can rotate the object in whatever axis or axes are active. Tumbling won't change the position of the object in the Design window.

Knife—Activate the knife, and you can draw a line that will cut the object in two. Only one half of the object will remain. Experiment with the knife to learn which side stays and which side disappears. Use Edit/Undo often!

Object Modifiers

You might think we are about to dive into a grammar session, but object modifiers don't have anything to do with adjectives and adverbs. When you are creating objects in the Design window, you can modify the opacity, inflation, and appearance of the object. The Opacity modifiers also apply to surfaces in the Surface Editor. To modify the properties of an object that already exists, select the object and then double-click on the modifier's button in the toolbar.

Opacity Modifiers

 Make Opaque—If this modifier button is pressed, all objects and surfaces you create will be solid—you won't be able to see through them. In most cases, this is the setting to use.

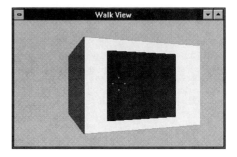

Figure 2.75
An opaque surface object.

 Make Translucent—This is most useful when you need to create a window. You'll be able to see through the opening or object, but you'll still be aware that a surface is present because the objects you see will be slightly dimmed.

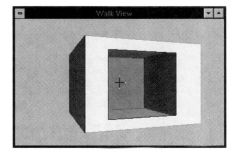

Figure 2.76
A translucent surface object.

 Make Transparent—This can be used for doors, or for altering the apparent shape of an object by creating an opening.

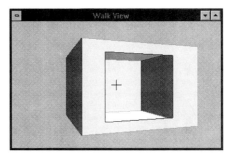

Figure 2.77
A transparent surface object.

Inflation Modifiers

 Inflate Straight—The object is "inflated" into the third dimension with vertical sides. A square, for example, is inflated into a cube when you create it.

 Inflate Double-Point—The object has a point at the top and the bottom. A square can be inflated into an object that looks like a pair of tetrahedrons (see Fig. 2.78).

Figure 2.78
Some Inflate Double-Point objects.

 Inflate Double-Rounded—Similar to Double-Point, but the resulting object has a rounded top and bottom.

 Inflate Pointed—The object has a flat base and extends upward to a point.

 Inflate Rounded—The object has a flat base and extends upward to a rounded top.

 Inflate Pointed Flip—The object is flat on top and extends downward to a point.

 Inflate Rounded Flip—The object is flat on top and extends downward to a rounded bottom.

Figure 2.79
Various types of inflation.

Appearance Modifiers

 Flat Shading—By default, all your 3D models use flat surfaces to represent curves. This is the fastest way to render curves. However, it doesn't look as realistic as curves would. If you have a very fast machine, experiment with Smooth Shading. If the screen updates too slowly, switch back to Flat Shading.

 Smooth Shading—Use this setting to create more natural-looking curves on your models and objects. However, curves take longer to render. If the screen updates too slowly, switch to Flat Shading.

Layer List

As you add objects to your virtual world, you can get confused about what line represents what edge of what object. By placing objects in layers, you can control what you see and what you work on.

The Layer list appears at the bottom of the Design window toolbar (see Fig. 2.80). When you start a project, there is just one layer, with the clever name of "unnamed." If you have objects that overlap, you will find that using layers makes your work much simpler.

To create a new layer, choose New Layer from the Design menu and enter the name of the new layer. The new name will be highlighted in the Layer list—it is now the current layer; new objects are placed in the current layer. You can hide individual layers, color all objects in a layer, or lock a layer.

Figure 2.80
The Layer list, at the bottom of the toolbar.

To remove a layer, choose Delete Layer from the Design menu. To move an object to a different layer, select the object and double-click the name of the layer you want to move it to. To perform operations on a layer, click on the layer name and hold the mouse button until the Layer menu appears.

Creating Objects

That's a lot of tools. It's easy to get the impression that WalkThrough Pro is so complicated you'll never get the hang of it. Nothing could be further from the truth. Using just a few of these tools, you can create many different kinds of objects for your virtual world. Don't try to learn everything at once. Fundamentally, WalkThrough Pro is easy to use. But it does have a lot of depth, and it will take time to learn everything there is to learn.

Let's begin by building a simple table using WalkThrough Pro. When you start the program, you'll see the two windows: Design and Walk (see Fig. 2.81). You'll also see the toolbar to the left of the Design window. I've shown it here inside the Design window for convenience. This is your blank slate—your *tabula rasa* with which you can create the virtual world of your dreams.

Let's define some specifications (specs, for short) for the table: 6 feet long, 4 feet wide, and 3 feet high. To begin, click the Create Rectangle tool (shown pressed in Fig. 2.82). Then click and drag in the Design window, using the rulers at the top and left to make sure that the table has the correct dimensions. This is quite a small object in the Design window, as shown in Figure 2.83.

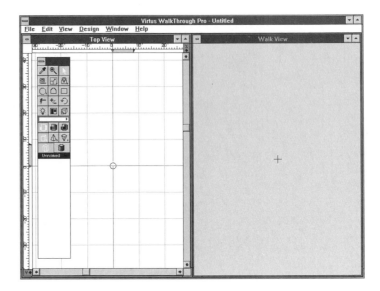

Figure 2.81
*Design and Walk
windows.*

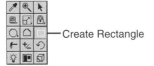

Create Rectangle

Figure 2.82
Creating a rectangle.

Figure 2.83
*By default, Snap to
Grid is always on.
However, the grid
size changes as you
zoom in and out. At
the default zoom
level (shown at the
left), there is a grid
point every 6 inches.
This means that you
can't create an
object smaller than
6 inches. To create
smaller objects,
zoom in.*

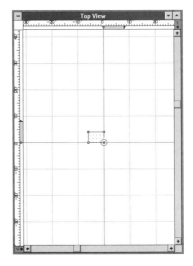

Many 3D and VR tools allow you to snap to a grid. *Snap* simply means that, no matter where you click, the result will occur at a point on the grid. For example, if you set up a grid that has points every foot, you could create rectangles that are exactly so many feet on a side—2×3, 4×8, etc. This is especially useful when you want objects to meet each other exactly. In fact, in most cases, you'll want to work with the grid on. How you turn the grid on will vary from product to product.

Click the Magnify tool (shown pressed in Fig. 2.84), and click several times in the Design window to zoom in. The result should look like Figure 2.85. Verify the size of your table by checking the rulers at the top and the left of the Design window. It should be 6 feet long and 4 feet wide.

Magnify

Figure 2.84
The Magnify tool.

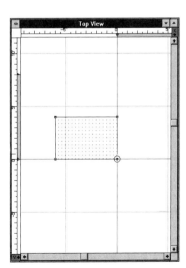

Figure 2.85
A magnified view.

Now let's switch to the Front view to check our work. From the View menu, choose Change View, and then choose Front (see Fig. 2.86).

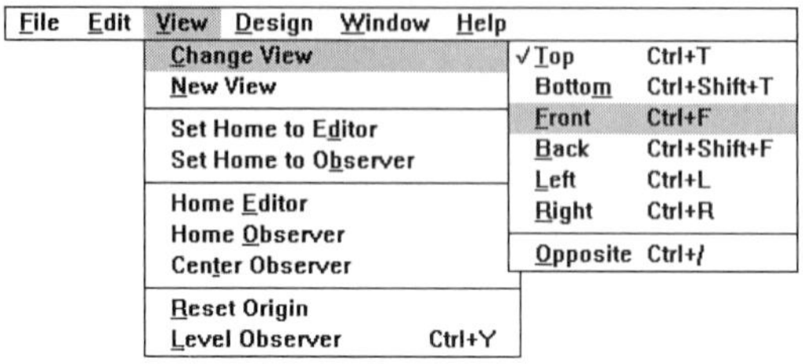

File	Edit	View	Design	Window	Help		√Top	Ctrl+T

Change View √Top Ctrl+T
New View Bottom Ctrl+Shift+T
Front Ctrl+F
Set Home to Editor Back Ctrl+Shift+F
Set Home to Observer Left Ctrl+L
Right Ctrl+R
Home Editor
Home Observer Opposite Ctrl+/
Center Observer

Reset Origin
Level Observer Ctrl+Y

Figure 2.86
Selecting the Front view.

This displays the Front view, as shown in Figure 2.87. Oops! What we have is a box 8 feet high! That's not a very good table.

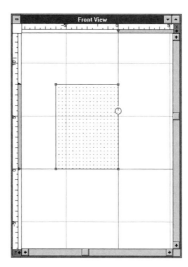

Figure 2.87
The Front view.

Why is the table 8 feet high? The height of new objects created in the Top view is controlled by the ruler marks in the Front and Side views. You'll learn how to set up the ruler marks shortly.

You can adjust the height of the table by clicking the midpoint of the top line, and then dragging it down to the 3-foot mark (refer to the ruler at the left of the Design window). The result should look like Figure 2.88.

Now we have a 3-foot-high table, but it's still just a box sitting on the ground. This is supposed to be the table top! Click the midpoint of the bottom line, and drag it up so that the table is 6 inches thick, as shown in Figure 2.89.

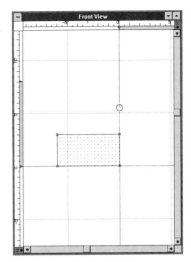

Figure 2.88
Adjusting table height.

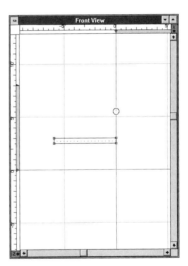

Figure 2.89
Adjusting the thickness of the table.

As you may recall from our discussion of Virtus VR, the dark areas next to the ruler determine how a new object will be inflated. *Inflation* simply refers to what happens when an object is changed from the 2D representation you draw in a view to a 3D object. In the case of the table top, think of it as a rectangular balloon.

Note that, by default, the height of new objects is 8 feet—from 0 to 8 on the ruler at the left. Our next job is to create legs for the table. By changing the top point of that dark area, we can make sure that the legs will be inflated from floor level (the line at 0 on the ruler) to the underside of the table top. Click and drag the black mark at the top of the dark area until it is 2'6" high (see the area inside the circle in Fig. 2.90).

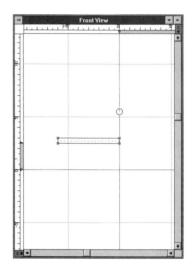

Figure 2.90
*Adjusting the
inflation level.*

Now switch back to the Top view by choosing Change View from the View menu and then choosing Top. Click the Create Rectangle tool (see Fig. 2.91), and click and drag a small object at the upper left of the table top (see Fig. 2.92).

Figure 2.91
Creating a rectangle.

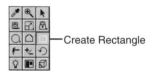

—Create Rectangle

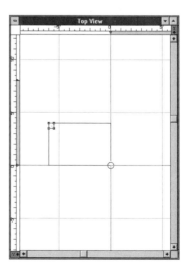

Figure 2.92
Adding a leg.

Now add the other three legs, as shown in Figure 2.93. You should have no difficulty getting all the legs the same size because, unless you turn it off, Snap to Grid is already on. Make each of the legs 6 inches square.

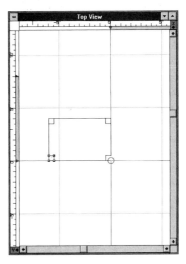

Figure 2.93
Adding the remaining legs.

Before moving on, make sure that each leg is exactly in the corner of the table top. If not, click the Selection tool, and then click and drag the leg into position.

Switch to the Front view to check your work. The results should look like Figure 2.94. If the legs do not exactly touch the floor and the table top, you can delete them, reset the marks at the top and bottom of the dark area, and try again.

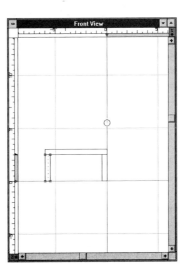

Figure 2.94
The table in Front view.

At this point, you can't really see the table in the Walk window (see Fig. 2.95). If you already are familiar with moving around in the Walk window, this is a good time to explore all sides of the table. If you are not, move away from it by clicking a bit below the cross hairs in the center of the Walk window. The result should look like Figure 2.96.

Figure 2.95
The table doesn't show up in the Walk window.

Figure 2.96
Moving back from the table.

To apply color to the table, choose Select All from the Edit menu, and then click and hold the mouse on the Color bar in the toolbar. Click an any appropriate color.

At this point, you can combine the five objects into a single object. This is handy when you want to move the table, for example. This is called *grouping*, and it's easy to do. Select all objects that make up the table (four legs, one top), and then press Ctrl+G. You also can choose Group from the Design menu to accomplish the same task.

Let's add a vase to the top of the table. First, change the way that new objects are inflated (unless, of course, you'd like to create a rectangular vase). Click and hold on the Inflate Flip button on the toolbar until the choice for this button "flies out" to the side, as shown in Figure 2.97. Click the Flip Rounded button.

Figure 2.97
A fly-out tool selection.

Now go to the Design window, and adjust the inflation markers at the top and bottom of the dark area to the appropriate positions for a vase, as shown in Figure 2.98. If you have trouble moving the bottom marker, drag the floor marker downward, move the lower marker up, and then replace the floor marker at 0.

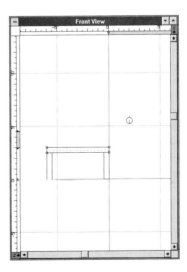

Figure 2.98
Adjusting inflation.

Click the Create 8-Sided object to activate it (see Fig. 2.99), and then click and drag out a vase on the table (it's that small circular object on the table at the left in Fig. 2.100).

Figure 2.99
Creating an eight-sided object.

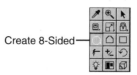

Create 8-Sided

Figure 2.100
A proto-vase on the table.

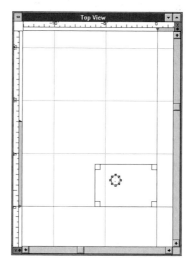

The view in the Walk window should look like Figure 2.101. While the vase is still highlighted in the Design window, double-click the Smooth Shading button on the toolbar (see Fig. 2.102). Now the vase appears more like a round vase (see Fig. 2.103).

NOTE

> If you experience problems with WalkThrough Pro, the cause might be your video card drivers. WalkThrough Pro pushes the video system very hard, and if you haven't recently upgraded your card's drivers, you can wind up with unpleasant crashes. Contact the manufacturer of your video card for information about obtaining updated drivers.

Unfortunately, no one would expect a sharp-pointed vase to stand on a table. The vase needs a flat bottom.

Figure 2.101
The view in the
Walk window.

Figure 2.102
Smooth shading
added.

Figure 2.103
The vase appears
rounded.

You can flatten the vase in a few quick steps. Click the Tumble Editor button (the lower right button in Fig. 2.104) to activate the Tumble Editor. When you first open the Tumble Editor, the vase is too small to work with. Click the Magnify tool (see Fig. 2.105) to activate it, and then click in the Design window until the vase is large enough to work with (see Fig. 2.106).

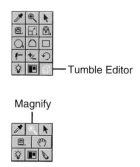

Figure 2.104
Using the Tumble Editor.

Tumble Editor

Figure 2.105
Using the Magnify tool.

Magnify

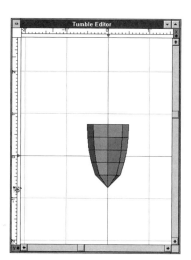

Figure 2.106
Zooming in on the vase.

Now click the Knife tool (see Fig. 2.107). Draw a line from the right to the left near the bottom of the vase.

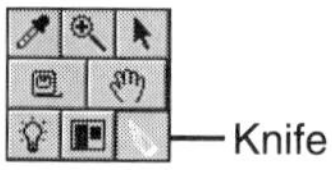

Figure 2.107
Using the Knife tool.

Knife

Make sure that you draw from right to left! It's easy to make a mistake, so now is a good time to tell you that the Edit menu has an Undo command.

NOTE

When you release the mouse button, the bottom portion of the vase disappears, as shown in Figure 2.108.

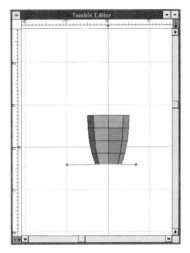

Figure 2.108
The bottom of the vase is gone.

The Walk view of the vase should look like Figure 2.109, and the Front view should look like Figure 2.110.

Figure 2.109
A Walk view of the vase.

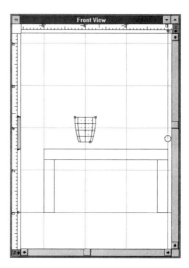

Figure 2.110
A Front view of the
vase.

The vase is the correct shape, but it is floating in the air.

To lower the vase to the table top, click the Selection tool (see Fig. 2.111), click on the vase to highlight it if it is not already selected, and then drag it downward. Be careful not to click on an edge, or you might change the shape of the vase. Stop when the vase touches the table (see Fig. 2.112). Figure 2.113 shows the Walk window view of the vase.

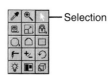

Figure 2.111
Using the Selection
tool.

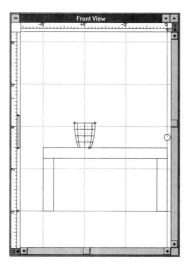

Figure 2.112
The vase at the table
top level.

Figure 2.113
A Walk window view of the completed vase.

This is just one example of a table; there are many different designs that you could create with WalkThrough Pro—rounded legs, for example, would be an easy change.

However, there are limits to the kinds of objects you can create with WalkThrough Pro. A bowling ball, for example, would be impossible—WalkThrough Pro only allows positive curvature; you couldn't do the finger holes.

Nevertheless, you can do a lot with WalkThrough Pro. For example, you could quickly embellish the simple table and vase by adding some fruit to the arrangement. Use the settings shown in Figure 2.114: Opaque, Inflate Double-Rounded, and Smooth Shading. Create several rounded shapes, and color them appropriately as shown in Figure 2.115. You can add touches to make them look more like fruit. The lemon, for example, is yellow and slightly elongated to look more natural. I have added a tiny cylinder to the red apple to act as a stem. I started with a fairly large cylinder, and then shrank it dramatically and rotated it away from vertical to make it look more natural.

Figure 2.114
Settings for adding fruit to the table top.

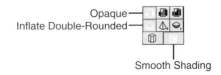

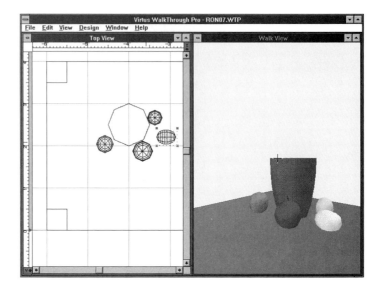

Figure 2.115
The colors are changed to make the objects look more like fruit.

WalkThrough Libraries

Virtus WalkThrough offers a lot of power for creating objects, but you don't have to create everything from scratch. Several libraries of objects can save you a lot of time and trouble. Even more important, as your skill with WalkThrough grows, you can create your own objects and store them in your own libraries. This is an extremely powerful technique for building more and more sophisticated virtual worlds.

When you install Virtus WalkThrough, you also install a number of useful libraries. You can order many different add-on libraries from Virtus—see the tear-out card at the end of the book. Libraries give you enormous power, because whatever you can create, you can store in a library.

Figure 2.116 shows a typical Library view. The list of library contents appears on the left, and a standard WalkThrough window appears on the right. You can view the object from any angle and switch easily from one object to another.

Adding a library object to a virtual world is simple: copy it to the Clipboard, and then paste it into your world. That's all there is to it.

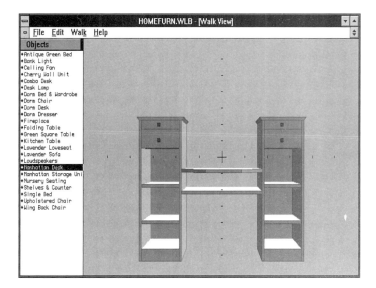

Figure 2.116
*A typical
WalkThrough
library object.*

There are a large number of preferences for maneuvering through a library; the navigation preferences are shown in Figure 2.117.[25] You can choose a wide-angle or telephoto lens, or even change the type of lens to match the view.

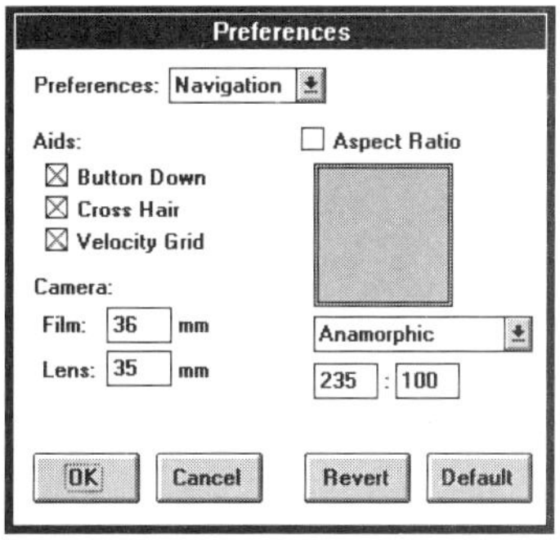

Figure 2.117
*Setting
WalkThrough
preferences.*

One of the more fascinating libraries contains human figures—every one of which is named Brutus. Some of the figures are very amusing; four are shown in Figure 2.118.

---

[25]You also can use these same preferences in WalkThrough itself.

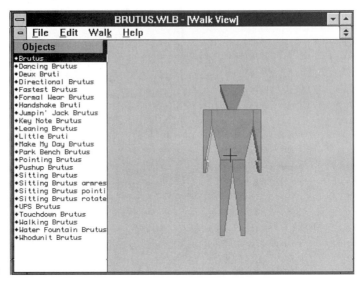

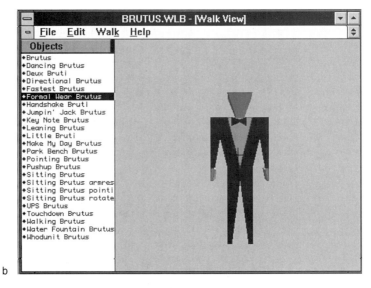

Figure 2.118
Brutus, hero of the Virtus libraries, in four different incarnations.

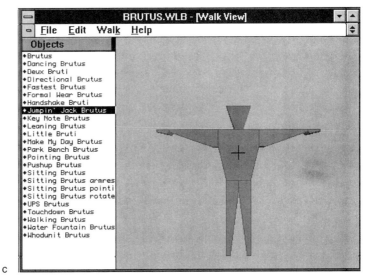

c

d

Building a WalkThrough House

Let's take everything you've learned about Virtus WalkThrough and apply it to a virtual world. I always seem to gravitate to building virtual houses—let's try a house with a bow window. The window will demonstrate the finer points of creating details in Virtus WalkThrough.

We'll start with some of the techniques you learned earlier. Start with a rectangle, just like the one we created earlier. This will be the basic shape of our house. Now create a smaller rectangle at the "front" of the house, using the Rectangle tool in the Plan view.

If you did not already create the second rectangle touching the house, drag the window so that it lines up with the front edge of the house now.

This smaller rectangle will become the bow window. The first step toward that goal is to add two new handles to the front of the window by using the Add/Remove Handles tool.

The window needs more curvature, so, one at a time, move the front corners back. Simply click on a handle and drag it to move it.

We're getting close—just one more thing to do. Make sure that the Plan view is the active window, and then press Ctrl+F to switch to the Front view. Click on the window you are building to select it, and then click on the top edge and move it down a small amount (see Fig. 2.120 for guidance). Then do the same with the lower edge. The result should look like Figure 2.119.

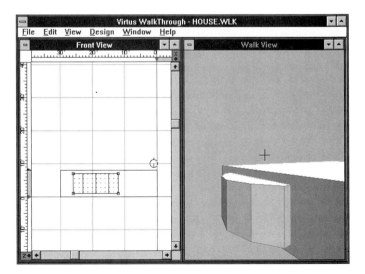

Figure 2.119
The basic shape of the bow window is completed.

We now have the shape of a bow window, but it's not transparent. We'll need to add some window panes. This part can get a little tricky, so pay close attention. We are going to select each panel of the bow window, and operate on it in the Surface Editor. Selecting the panel you want might require some experimentation, because it's not always obvious which line to click on to select a panel.[26]

To start, click to select the window, and then click the Surface Editor icon. Now click on any of the vertical lines that border the panels; this opens the Surface Editor with a single panel, ready for editing.[27] Click the Rectangle tool and draw a window pane, as shown inside the panel (see Fig. 2.120). Click the Transparent tool, and that should make the window look like glass.

Repeat these steps for each of the panels. Experiment with using different vertical and horizontal lines to activate the Surface Editor—it's not always obvious which line to click to select a panel. You'll wind up with four panes in four panels, as shown in Figure 2.121. You'll also want to make the back of the window transparent; simply select that surface, click the Surface Editor icon to activate the Surface Editor, and then activate the Transparent icon.[28]

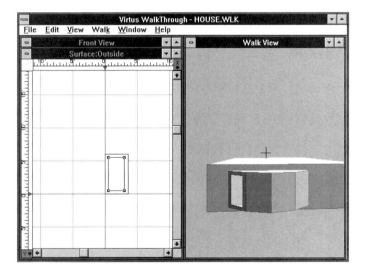

Figure 2.120
*Adding a pane to
one of the panels.*

---

[26]This is mostly annoying, rather than a big bother. If you select the wrong panel, you know it immediately in the Surface Editor. Just close the Surface Editor and try a different line. If clicking on the two vertical sides of a panel doesn't do the trick, for example, try clicking on the top or bottom line of the panel. Eventually, you'll get the surface you need.

[27]Make sure that the Place Through icon is active; otherwise, the objects you are creating will be above or below the surface, instead of on it.

[28]Otherwise, the back of the window object will prevent you from seeing into the house.

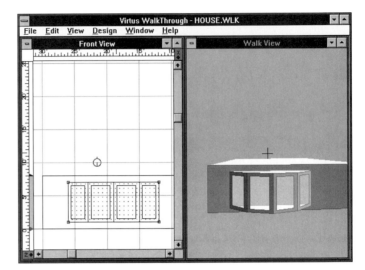

Figure 2.121
The completed bow window.

A window is nice, but a door to get into the house would be even nicer. We'll use the Surface Editor again, but this time, select the front of the house after you activate the Surface Editor icon. Align the Plan view so that you can see and work on the right side of the front surface. Again using the Rectangle tool, drag out a rectangle for a large entryway (see Fig. 2.122).

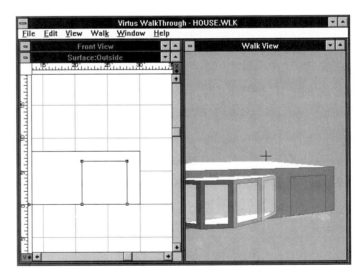

Figure 2.122
Adding a rectangle for a large entryway.

While you have the front wall selected, you'll need to make an opening in it for the window—otherwise, you'll look through the window box and see just the front wall of the house! Simply drag out a rectangle the same size as the bow window, using the rulers to guide placement.[29]

Let's add some additional detail for the entryway. You'll be adding four elements, in the following order (peek ahead to Fig. 2.123 to see where the objects go):

1. Add a side light to the entryway, and make it translucent.

2. Add the door.

3. & 4. Add two windows to the door, and make them translucent.

You can select each of these objects in turn and give them a color. I chose dark brown for the entryway frame, a lighter brown for the door, and a slight blue tint for the glass. You can give the front of the house a color, but I wanted my house all one color, so I didn't add any color until after I closed the Surface Editor.

Figure 2.124 shows the results of adding the additional detail (including adding color). It's now very clear what the overall object is—the window and door are detailed sufficiently to read clearly.[30] What we need now, of course, is a roof.

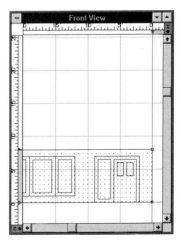

Figure 2.123
Adding details to the entryway.

---

[29]**Hint:** Look at the house in the Plan view from the front, and note the exact boundaries of the window object.

[30]If you are feeling ambitious, try creating a little doorknob for the door. **Hint:** Create a box, and then modify the inflation to rounded on both ends.

When you are building a complex model, the new WalkThrough Pro version enables you to create separate layers for each group of objects. The New Layer menu option in WalkThrough Pro opens the dialog box shown in Figure 2.125; all you have to do is name the layer. Layers make it easier to manage a large environment with lots and lots of objects.

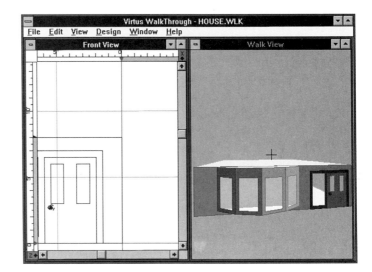

Figure 2.124
A view of the front of the house.

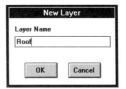

Figure 2.125
Adding a new layer in WalkThrough Pro.

When creating the roof, it's important that we locate it above the house. Look at Figure 2.126, which shows the roof already added, from a Front view. See that little gray bar along the left-hand ruler? That bar has small black handles that you can use to define the inflation height of new objects. Before creating the roof, I simply set that bar to 8 feet. To create the roof, switch to Top view and drag out a rectangle, being sure to slightly overlap the house—that's what a roof does in real life.

The roof is just a blocky box so far, however, as you can determine by moving around in the WalkThrough window. Let's use the Slice tool to lop off pieces of that box, leaving a nice, normal roof. Select the roof, and then select the Tumble Editor icon. This displays the Tumble Editor, and you can change the orientation of the roof object by dragging the mouse over the little cube in the toolbar. Arrange the roof object so that you are viewing it from the front; you can double-click on a face of the roof to level it in the Tumble Editor. The result of your effort should look like Figure 2.127.

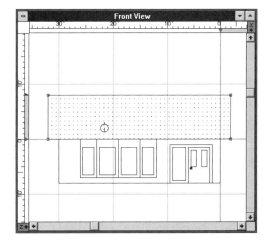

Figure 2.126
Adding a roof of the correct height.

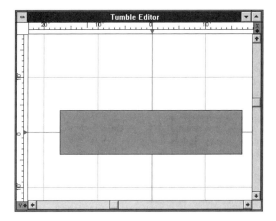

Figure 2.127
Using the Tumble Editor.

Now select the Slice tool, and position the cross hairs at the midpoint of the top of the roof. Click and drag to the lower right-hand corner of the roof and release the mouse button. The result should be a removal of a section of the roof, as shown in Figure 2.128.

To create a matching slope on the other side of the roof, place the cross hairs at the lower left corner. Then click and drag to the top center and release the mouse button. This removes a corresponding section of the roof object, leaving a much more normal-looking roof profile (see Fig. 2.129).[31]

---

[31]If, instead, you click and drag from the top center to the lower left, you'll remove the roof, and leave the part that was supposed to be removed. If you make this mistake (or any others!), press Ctrl+Z to undo the error.

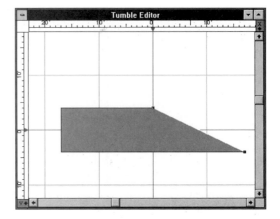

Figure 2.128
*Removing a portion
of an object with the
Slice tool.*

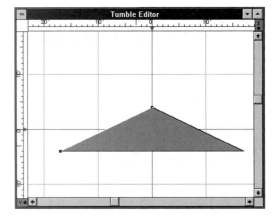

Figure 2.129
*A roof created with
the Slice tool.*

If you would like to create a hip roof, tumble to a side view, double-click on the roof to orient it to face you, and then use the Slice tool to remove additional portions of the roof object (see Fig. 2.130).

Figure 2.131 shows the completed house and roof in the WalkThrough window. Note that you can see through the windows, as though they were glass.

You can add a ground object by dragging out, for example, an eight-sided object with only 1 foot of inflation—use the gray bar at the side of the Plan view to limit the size of the inflation.

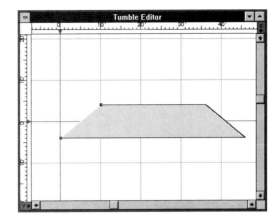

Figure 2.130
The roof modified to the hip roof style.

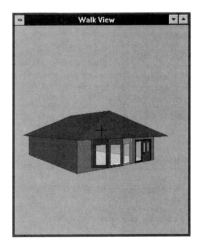

Figure 2.131
The house now has a roof.

Other nice touches include adding furniture using the various libraries. To open a library, choose Library from the File menu and double-click on the LIBRARY subdirectory. When you find an object you want to add to the house, choose Copy from the Edit menu in the Library window, and choose Paste from the Edit menu in the Plan view window.[32]

---

[32]There are a number of interesting models included with the Virtus software when you install it onto your hard disk.

Getting Started with VREAM

Every software package comes with a set of good points and bad points. In most cases, it's easy to tell what's good and what's bad. In other cases, the good stuff is hidden, and it takes time and a clever eye to discover it. VREAM is one of the products with many, many good features that are not obvious at first glance. Let me state the value of VREAM up front: it's the most powerful virtual reality software product for the price. Nothing else puts total VR power on your desk for such a small investment. Yes, you can spend $5,000 or more to get a somewhat more polished interface, but if that number doesn't fit your budget, how about a few hundred dollars for VREAM?

Why am I so excited about VREAM? There is a simple reason: VREAM is very powerful. Powerful software has to make trade-offs. You can't have a zillion tools at your disposal and also have a simple, easy-to-use package. Something has to give. With VREAM, you gain a tremendous number of new tools. VREAM gives you power well beyond products such as Virtus VR and Virtus WalkThrough. The Virtus products focus on providing the tools that are easy to use. VREAM, on the other hand, exists to provide power. It's going to take you some time to learn how to use it, and to understand just what it's capable of. In this chapter, you'll learn about the various tools included in the VREAM development environment. You'll also learn a little bit about how to use some of the most interesting tools. The capability to add VR hardware such as HMDs, data gloves, goggles, motion trackers, and so on is just one of the things that sets VREAM apart from the pack at the affordable end of the VR software universe. These are also the things you'll need to take time to learn about in order to use VREAM effectively.

Figure 2.132
A typical VREAM
runtime screen.

VREAM Basics

VREAM consists of two parts: a Design tool and a Runtime tool. If you start VREAM, the very first thing you see is a screen that enables you to choose which tool you want to work with, as shown in Figure 2.133. The VREAM 3D World Editor is used to create objects and to design your world. The VREAM Runtime System (refer to Fig. 2.132 for a sample view) is used to explore the virtual world.

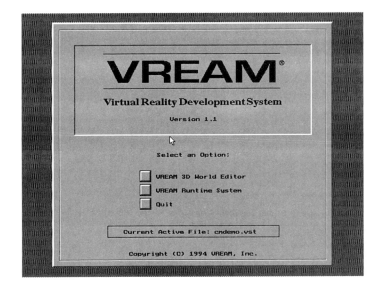

Figure 2.133
The VREAM opening screen.

There is also a third way to work with VREAM, and it is a technique that will be especially attractive to anyone with computer programming experience: direct editing of VREAM files, using VREAM's powerful script language.

If you choose to start with the VREAM 3D World Editor, you'll see a screen similar to the one shown in Figure 2.134.[33] VREAM is not a Windows product, which means that the menu system and program operation aren't as convenient as they would be for a Windows program. On the other hand, this makes it much easier to support fancy 3D hardware (those helmets and glasses and other goodies). Since VREAM does not have to limit itself to standard Windows video capabilities, it can bend and stretch itself to provide all kinds of support for high-end display technologies. Not all of these are expensive, either.

If you choose to start with the runtime system, you'll see a screen display showing a view of a VREAM virtual world. Depending on the speed of your computer and video card, this can range from 320×240 to 640×480, using 256 colors.

The key to using VREAM, however, is the World Editor. In this chapter, you'll learn about each of the icons at the bottom of the VREAM window, and you'll also explore some of the key tools found only on the menus.

---

[33]In Figure 2.134, one of the VREAM demo worlds is shown in the Editor. By starting your own world from scratch, the entire central area would be blank. If you have ever used WordPerfect for DOS, with its blank screen, you have some sense of what it's like to start up a world in VREAM. Fortunately, that toolbar at the bottom is a lot more friendly than WordPerfect.

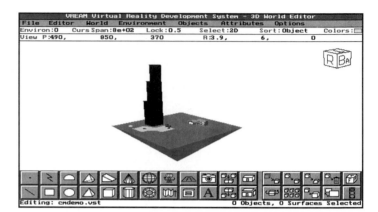

Figure 2.134
The VREAM 3D World Editor.

Using VREAM Tools

There are a total of 34 buttons (tools) at the bottom of the VREAM window. This is a daunting number of tools to learn at one time. However, there are some characteristics that the tools share. Let's take a look at tool behavior, and then we'll look at each of the tools in detail. The tools are divided into two sections, separated by a small gray space. The tools on the left side of the toolbar are for object creation and editing, and are shown in Figure 2.135.

The tools on the right side of the toolbar are for moving, copying, deleting, and otherwise working with objects or the World Editor itself, and are shown in Figure 2.136.

Figure 2.135
Tools for object creation and editing.

Figure 2.136
Tools for working with existing objects.

In many cases, once you start using a tool, VREAM expects you to keep right on using it. If you create an object, VREAM is prepared for you to create another one right away—the tool stays active. When you are done using a tool, click the left and right mouse buttons simultaneously to put it away. You can observe the current status of a tool or action by watching the prompt line at the bottom of the VREAM window—short, cryptic, but vital prompt messages are displayed there. When working with a tool, pay very close attention the prompt line—you often will see messages such as Click L button to continue.[34] In general, if VREAM doesn't seem to be acting right, check the prompt line to see what's up.

There are also two status bars at the top of the window that provide useful information such as present location in the workspace. This is especially useful when working in the third dimension (just how far back from the front of the object am I?).

There are three working modes in VREAM: Viewer Position, Cursor Position, and Point Tracker. Choose Status Bar from the Editor menu, and then choose Status Bar Mode to change modes. When the Viewer Position mode is active, the status bars show the current position and rotation of the viewer's point of view. When the Cursor Position mode is active, the status bars show the current position of the cursor in both viewer-coordinate space (V) and world-coordinate space (W). When the Point Tracker mode is active, you can display the coordinates of any point in the status bars. Just click on a point to get its coordinates. This is valuable when creating, moving, and editing objects—you can use any existing point or points as references.

You can even change modes right in the middle of creating or editing an object by using the F3 key.

The VREAM Toolkit

When you use a tool, the prompt line at the bottom of the screen tells you what actions to take. For example, if you create a cube, you are prompted for various points on the cube, one at a time. This is very different from Virtus VR or Virtus WalkThrough Pro, where you could drag out a cube or rectangle interactively with the mouse.[35]

By default, the mouse moves the cursor in the X/Y plane. This plane extends up and down, left and right. To move the mouse cursor forward or backward (into or out of the 3D work area), hold down the right mouse button while you drag.[36]

---

[34]That L refers, of course, to the left mouse button.

[35]Think of it as the price of power—the folks at VREAM spent more time adding features than they did adding convenience.

[36]This takes some getting used to, and I highly recommend practicing your VREAM mouse technique before you attempt any serious world building.

Let's take a look at each of the tools available in the VREAM World Editor:

 Point—Creates a succession of individual points. Point objects are usually used as reference objects for creating a series of other objects using Point Tracker mode.

 Line—Creates a line by defining the two endpoints of the line. Successive lines are not connected to each other; each line is a separate object.

 Polyline—Creates line objects with complex outlines, consisting of multiple line segments. The endpoint of one line becomes the starting point for the next line. Successive lines are connected and make up one object.

 Surface—Enables you to create three-, four-, and N-sided 2D objects by clicking the points that define the surface. Always define surface points in a counter-clockwise order; this makes the side facing you the front of the object. Do not try to create surfaces with concave edges; group objects as you did in WalkThrough Pro. Surface objects are actually 2D objects in 3D space; always select points in the same plane!

 Arc—Creates a 2D object based on an arc of a circle. The shape is defined by a center point, an arc, start and stop angles, and the number of line segments along the arc. The larger the number of segments, the harder your computer must work to display the image in the runtime system.

 Circle—Creates a circular, 2D object. The shape is defined by the center point, radius, and number of line segments along the circumference. This means that you will get a rounded polygon, not a pure circle. For smooth edges, choose higher numbers of segments.

 Tetrahedron—So far, we've been covering 2D objects; this is the first in a series of 3D objects you can create. You are prompted for the various points on the tetrahedron during creation.

 Pyramid—Creates a pyramid with a four-sided base.

 Wedge—Creates a wedge-shaped object.

 Cube—Creates a cube.

Cone—Creates a cone defined by the radius of the base, height, and number of sides.

 Cylinder—Creates a cylinder defined by the radius, height, and number of sides.

 Sphere—Creates a sphere defined by the radius and the number of longitudinal and latitudinal segments.

 Torus—Create a torus (doughnut-shaped) object defined by the center of the torus, the inner and outer radius, and the number of segments.

 Revolution—Creates a surface-of-revolution object. First, create a polyline object, and then click this tool to rotate the polyline. There is an example of this process later in the chapter.

 Extrusion—Creates a surface-of-extrusion object from a polyline. The polyline is lofted into a third dimension to create the object. See the example later in this chapter.

 Mesh—Creates a surface object with four sides, subdivided into a series of four-sided polygons. In plain English, you can create an object that's something like a window screen, and then manipulate individual points to create complex shapes. As with other complicated tools, look for the example later in this chapter.

 Solid Cut—Cuts holes in existing surface objects.

 Texture—Applies a PCX image to an object.

 Text—Creates text objects. You can specify the characters, position, font style, and font size.

 Group—Creates a group of objects from a series of individual objects. Each object group has a unique name.

 Ungroup—Breaks a group object down into its component objects. Many tools only work on single objects, not groups.

 Room—Creates a room object. Room objects are a special class of objects. You can create a room from 2D surface objects, or from a 3D object primitive (such as a cube). Rooms are discussed in more detail later in this chapter—they are a key VREAM concept.

Unroom—Breaks a room down into its component 2D surface objects. This is useful when you want to perform an operation on only one surface of an existing room.

Move—Moves objects within the World Editor workspace.

Rotate—Rotates objects within the World Editor workspace. Rotation is performed by entering numeric values for yaw, pitch, and roll. To enter values, click in the field with the mouse, and then edit the contents of the field.

Copy—Copies objects within the World Editor workspace.

Array—Creates multiple, evenly spaced copies of an object. You can create rows and columns of a selected object.

Change—Enables you to alter the position of a single point on an object. This is particularly useful when working with Mesh surface objects.

Resize—Resizes the currently selected object(s).

Delete—Deletes the currently selected object(s).

Viewer Distance—Moves the viewer (that's the point of view, the place you are viewing the world from). You specify a distance to move.

Viewer Position—Moves the viewer to a new position and orientation. There are 15 predefined positions, including initial, front, back, left, right, top, bottom, and so on. You can also specify a unique position using X,Y,Z coordinates.

Viewer Walk—Enables you to "walk" through the world you are creating. Normally, you work in Edit mode, and the icon for this tool has a red light. In Walk mode, it turns to a green light. In Walk mode, any input devices defined in the VREAM file are active (such as a Cyberman or mouse). High-resolution screen modes are not active.

VREAM Menus

Exploring the various VREAM menu selections can be either a rewarding or a frustrating experience. If you proceed cautiously and learn how to use the choices one at a time, you'll be rewarded with a growing list of cool tools you can use. If you try to digest all of them at once, you will suffer a serious brain jam. With that little caution in mind, let's attack the VREAM menus one at a time.

Because the VREAM menus are so wide and deep, it's impossible to cover every menu selection. I will point out the most useful and/or interesting options available to you, and provide a general tour of each menu.

Start VREAM at the DOS command line by typing **VREAM** *<filename>*, using the file name of an existing world you want to edit or a new one you want to create. When you start VREAM, you see the Grand and Glorious Opening Screen (GAGOS), shown in Figure 2.137. Yes, my tongue is firmly in cheek; VREAM is a straightforward, no-frills software package, designed to get the job done with a minimum of fuss. VREAM is the Swiss Army Knife of virtual reality software; you get a whole pile of tools you can carry around for a very attractive price.

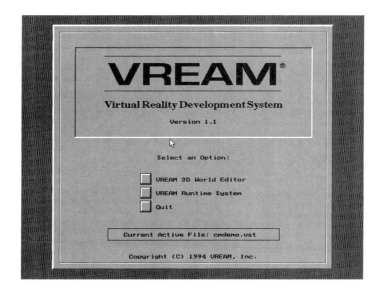

Figure 2.137
The VREAM
GAGOS.

To enter the World Editor, click the VREAM 3D World Editor button in the GAGOS. This transports you to the virtual world whose name you typed on the DOS command line. VREAM is not a Windows product, and menu navigation might feel odd to anyone already familiar with Windows. For example, if you click on a menu selection and change your mind, the entire menu disappears when you click on a different menu item. There are other differences, too, such as a need to press Enter whenever you enter a value in a dialog box. Then you must click the Set button or Cancel button—the Enter key doesn't automatically close the dialog box. These differences are annoying, but they don't seriously detract from the value of the program. They are like the foibles of a good friend.

File Menu

The File menu (shown at the left), like any File menu, is for opening, saving, creating, and other file-related activities. The most important items to note on the File menu are Load DXF and Save DXF. The DXF file format is a 3D file format that many, many 3D and virtual reality software packages can read and write. Ideally, the DXF format enables you to create a 3D object in one package and import it to another.

This is a great idea, but the practical application of the idea leaves something to be desired. I have found that there are wide variations in the successful use of the DXF format. For example, I created a 3D chair in trueSpace (see Chapter 3 for details on working with trueSpace, a wonderful 3D modeling and animation program), and exported it as a DXF file. When I tried to import the DXF file into Virtus WalkThrough Pro, the result was very disappointing—the object didn't import, and sometimes crashed the program.

When I tried importing the very same DXF file into VREAM (see Fig. 2.138), the result was much better (see Fig. 2.139). The import was quick, easy, and painless. Figure 2.140 shows the result in solid modeling format using the VREAM runtime viewer.

Figure 2.138
Importing a DXF
file into VREAM.

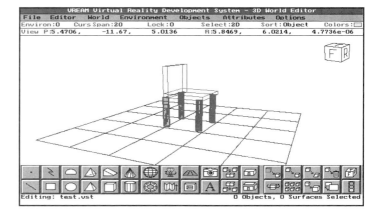

Figure 2.139
A wireframe model of the imported chair.

Figure 2.140
A chair from trueSpace imported into VREAM via DXF format.

There are many variations in the DXF format, and many complex sets of information stored in it. The result: not all software packages support the same DXF features. When you find a combination of software that works well together (one to easily create DXF files, and another to import them for VR work), consider yourself lucky and stick with it!

Editor Menu

The Editor menu (at the left) is used primarily to control the 3D World Editor itself. You can change the way that objects are shown (wireframe or solid, for example), or change settings for the title bar, status bar, cursor, grid, and so on.

Some of the more useful Editor menu selections include

> **Wireframe Color**—All objects drawn in the World Editor use the same color for wireframe. The default color, a medium blue, might not be suitable for best viewing, and you can change to a more comfortable color.

> **Status Bar**—This selection enables you to change the status bar mode (Viewer Position, 3D Cursor Position, or Point Tracker). When creating any complex environment, you will find yourself changing modes frequently.

Object Selection—This selection enables you to choose the appropriate object-selection mode for your work. The Selection Type submenu enables you to pick either 2D or 3D object selection. 2D is easier to use and is best for general work. 3D object selection is handy when the object you want to select is behind another object.

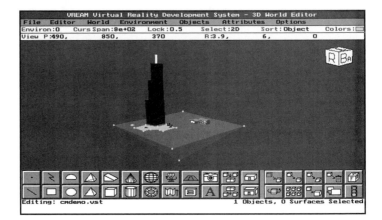

Figure 2.141
A VREAM world at runtime.

World Menu

The World menu contains a very important group of commands that provide key support for some of the exciting VR hardware now available. If you have purchased—or plan to purchase—a headset, 3D video display card, input device, or other cool tool, this is the menu for you!

The key items of interest are

Graphics Display—This is one item that doesn't require fancy hardware. Use this menu selection to determine the screen resolution for your virtual world. You can go with a high-resolution screen at 640×480, or you can speed up display by using a smaller screen size.

Stereoscopic—Here's the key to exciting 3D hardware. If you have CrystalEyes glasses (or a compatible), dual monitors, or a Cyberscope (the economy method—see Figs. 2.142 and 2.143), you can turn on the appropriate display for these devices.

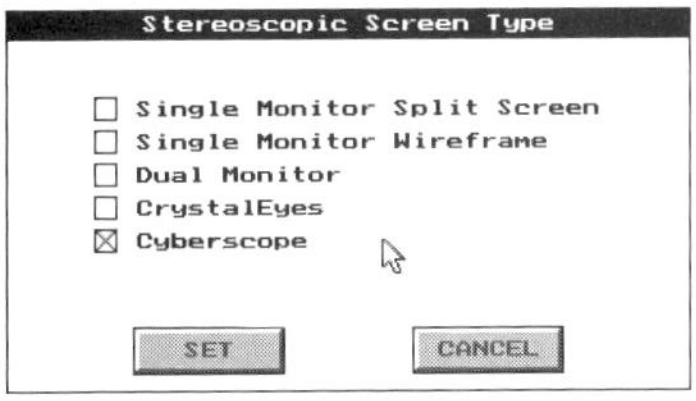

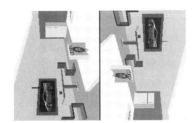

Figure 2.142
Selecting Cyberscope for screen output.

Figure 2.143
Stereo screen output format for the Cyberscope.

Interface Devices—There are a lot of choices in version 1.1 of VREAM for all kinds of input devices (see Fig. 2.144). You can start easy with traditional input devices (keyboard, joystick, or mouse), or add support for a wide variety of devices. For each type of input device, you can turn support for navigation or the grabbing hand on and off (see Fig. 2.145). For example, you can navigate with the keyboard, and use the mouse to grab objects with the hand. (See the next section, "Environment Menu," for details about the hand.) Or you can use the mouse to navigate, and use a Mattel Power Glove for grabbing objects! The Power Glove is no longer manufactured but is available used at great prices ($30 and more, depending on its condition). A Power Glove makes a great low-cost VR toy.

Figure 2.144
Selecting an input device.

Initial Viewer Pos.—Sets the point in space where a user starts from. You can also set jump points—positions in the virtual world that the user can go to instantly.

Figure 2.145
*Changing input
device parameters.*

Environment Menu

The Environment menu enables you to control many different aspects of the virtual world, including lighting effects, the screen size, the grabbing hand, gravity, and so on. You can create more than one environment for a virtual world, using different settings and objects. You can instantly switch from one environment to another at runtime.

The key features of the Environment menu are

Light Source—Enables you to set the exact position of the light source in the world.

Screen Size—Sets the size of the active screen within the virtual world. You set values for the four corners of the screen. A background image can be used to fill the area around the active screen. This option is used to allow a virtual world to work smoothly on less powerful computers, or when a game requires a background image.

Hand—Determines whether the 3D grabbing hand will be displayed at the start of a runtime session. The hand can appear in three predefined shapes: a hand (see Fig. 2.146), a gun, or a wand. You can also set the color of the hand, its size, and the relative starting distance of the hand, as shown in Figure 2.147.

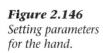

Figure 2.146
*Setting parameters
for the hand.*

Figure 2.147
The VREAM hand
looks like this on
your screen.

Gravity—Gravity is one of the key features found in VREAM. This sets it apart from the many purely visual 3D/VR products on the market. Using gravity, you can add many useful and interesting features to your virtual worlds—objects can be thrown, balls can bounce, and so on. You can set gravity on or off, you can set a value for gravity (higher or lower than Earth Normal), and you can establish ground level for gravity (the level to which objects fall, when they fall).

Viewer Speed—Sets the standard rate of motion of the viewer through the virtual world.

Viewer Limits—Enables you to set the movement and rotation limits for the current environment.

Objects Menu

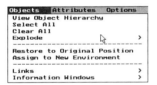

The Objects menu (at the left) gives you the capability to work with objects in ways that go beyond the toolbar at the bottom of the VREAM window. You can select objects, delete them, explode them into their component parts, or move objects from one environment to another.

The key features of the Object menu are

View Object Hierarchy—Enables you to examine the types, number, attributes, and relationships of objects in an environment. You can also use View Object Hierarchy to select one or more objects. This is handy when you have many objects, or when you want to refer to objects by their names.

Restore to Original Position—Restores an object to its original position in the Editor. This is defined as the position of the object when the current world was loaded from the hard disk.

Explode—Enables you to break down an object into the surfaces that make up the object. For example, a cube object would be broken down into six 2D surface objects—four sides, a top, and a bottom. Only object primitives can be exploded. You cannot explode groups—only single objects.

Links—You can link objects using conditions. You can turn links on and off, set conditions, and add links using the Links submenu. For example, you can create a link that will cause an action when the hand grabs an object, or when objects collide. This is a very powerful feature, but it requires some study to use it effectively. VREAM offers many different conditions and responses, giving you a great deal of power for interactive and animated sequences. For example, you can have music play when a viewer enters a room.

Attributes Menu

The Attributes menu (at the left) enables you to change the attributes of objects. There are a huge number of attributes, and it takes some time to learn all the possibilities. Even using just a few attributes, you can add a lot of features to a virtual world.

The key features of the Attributes menu are

General—Enables you to set names for objects.

Display—Turns wireframe on and off, turns solid display on and off, changes the solid color used for an object, and offers many other features related to the visibility of an object. Interestingly, the inside and the outside of an object can be controlled individually, so that an object can be invisible from the outside, but visible once you are inside it. The exterior and interior colors can be different. You can also set a particular color in a texture to be invisible, making that color transparent. This is very useful when you want to create windows.

Physical—This is a very powerful submenu that enables you to control a wide variety of physical attributes of an object. Key selections include

Touchable—Determines whether an object can be manipulated with the grabbing hand.

Moveable—Determines whether an object can be moved.

Rotatable—Determines whether an object can be rotated.

Throwable—Determines whether an object can be thrown with the grabbing hand.

Penetrable—Determines whether the viewer can go inside an object. By default, all objects can be penetrated. If you create a wall, remember to set penetration to Off.

Weight—Determines how far an object can be thrown. The heavier the object, the faster it responds to gravity (that is, the faster it falls).

Elasticity—Determines how an object bounces when dropped onto the gravity base level or a gravity surface. The higher the number, the more the bounce.

Gravity—Determines whether an object responds to the force of gravity.

Gravity Surface—Defines a surface that will stop another object's fall. All gravity surfaces should be flat, horizontal surfaces. To select a surface, first select the object, and then click on the surface while pressing the Alt button.

Motion—Enables you to set automatic rotation for an object, or to translate an object to a predefined location.

Group—Enables you to group objects into larger objects. You can also define the level of grouping, or group objects loosely (to allow access to individual objects within the group after grouping).

Optimization—Contains various settings to improve the performance of your virtual world.

Options Menu

The Options menu (at the left) is a very brief menu, which is used to check the amount of memory available and to redraw the screen. You can use Memory Check to verify that sufficient memory is available for your world, or to verify that the memory used doesn't exceed your requirements. Screen redraw will clean up the display if it becomes "dirty" from partial redraws.

VREAM Power Tools

Several of the tools included in VREAM are very powerful, and they deserve a closer look. These are the Revolution, Extrusion, Mesh, and Room tools. In this section, you'll get a chance to see how these tools work, and how they can be used to create virtual objects. In each case, the process starts with a new, blank virtual world in the VREAM 3D World Editor (shown in Fig. 2.148). Choose New from the File menu to create a new world.

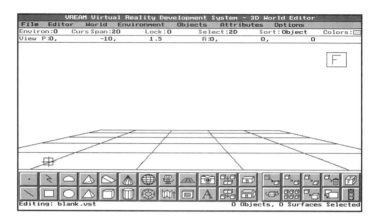

Figure 2.148
Starting with a blank world.

Surface of Revolution

Polyline tool

It's actually very easy to create a surface of revolution. The process starts with a polyline. Next, define a center of rotation. VREAM rotates the polyline in 3D space to create a 3D object. For this example, we'll create a goblet. To begin, click the Polyline tool (click the icon shown in the margin). The prompt line at the bottom of the VREAM window then asks you to enter point #1. You could type the 3D coordinates (X,Y,Z), but that's tedious. Instead, just click in the VREAM window. To create additional points, just keep clicking.

Figure 2.149 shows the first several points of a goblet in the VREAM window. Continue clicking points to outline the goblet. Figure 2.150 shows a completed goblet profile using a total of nine points. You can use any number of points, and feel free to shape the goblet to your taste.[37]

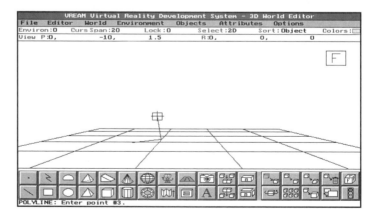

Figure 2.149
Creating a polyline.

---

[37]Too many points, though, will slow down display speed at runtime.

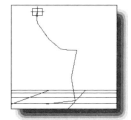

Figure 2.150
A completed polyline.

To complete the process of creating the polyline, click the left and right mouse buttons at the same time. The polyline will show up as a thin blue line. This indicates that the polyline is not selected. You'll need to select it before you use it for a revolution.

To create the surface of revolution, click the Revolution tool (which, oddly enough, just happens to look like a goblet. Clever, eh?). If you forgot to select the polyline, you'll see the error dialog box shown in Figure 2.151. The polyline looks like Figure 2.152 when it is selected and the Revolution tool has been clicked.

Revolution tool

Figure 2.151
The consequences of forgetting to select an object before clicking!

Figure 2.152
A selected polyline displays points as small black squares.

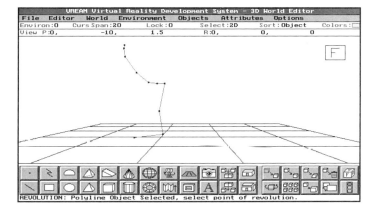

The prompt line (at the bottom of the VREAM window, shown in Fig. 2.152) is asking you to identify the point of revolution. This point defines the center around which the polyline will be revolved. To create a goblet from the polyline, the point of revolution must be close to the stem portion of the polyline—otherwise, the stem will be too fat. Figure 2.153 shows the cursor at a good spot for a point of revolution for the goblet. **Important:** note that the cursor is slightly to the right of the rightmost point on the polyline!

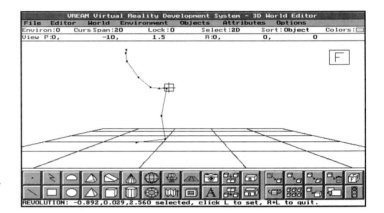

Figure 2.153
Selecting the point of revolution.

The prompt line now asks for a starting angle. If you wanted a partially revolved object, you could enter an appropriate start angle. In our case, we want all 360 degrees, so the start angle is zero. Press Enter, and you are asked for a stop angle; press the Enter key to accept the default of 360.

This completes the process; the result is shown in Figure 2.154. Figure 2.155 shows the goblet at runtime. Notice that you can see the polyline that served as the basis for the goblet. Depending on the exact shape of your goblet and where you put the point of revolution, your result may vary.

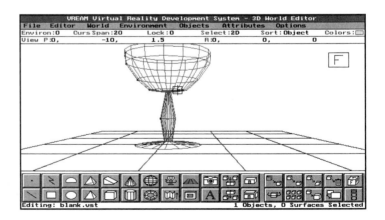

Figure 2.154
The goblet in the 3D World Editor.

Figure 2.155
The goblet at
runtime.

That's all there is to surfaces of revolution. You can easily create all kinds of complex 3D shapes using this technique—anything from bowling pins to table legs, and lots in between.

Surfaces of revolution are excellent tools to use when you want the most realistic world possible. However, it takes time to draw all those surfaces—they can slow down screen display! Use revolved objects sparingly if you need a fast, interactive world.

Extrusion

Extrusion works a lot like revolution: you create a polyline and then extend it into three dimensions. In the case of an extrusion, the process is more like working with a pasta maker. The polyline defines the mold, and then VREAM makes the pasta. As you'll see in the following example, you can get some funny looking pasta with the extrusion tool.

*Polyline
tool*

To begin, click the Polyline tool and click several points to create a new polyline (see Fig. 2.156). You don't need anything fancy; any random line with three or more points will do. Click the polyline to select it, and then click the Extrusion tool (just below the Revolution tool). VREAM will ask you to supply a *base point*—an arbitrary point that serves as the zero point for measuring the length of the extrusion.

*Extrusion
tool*

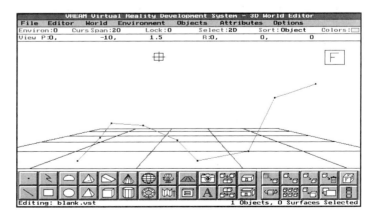

Figure 2.156
Creating a polyline.

Now the prompt line asks you to select an extrusion point. This point defines the length and direction of the extrusion, relative to the base point. (Remember to click and hold the right mouse button to move into and out of the scene if you want the extrusion to occur at an angle). Figure 2.157 shows a line that runs from the base point to the extrusion point.

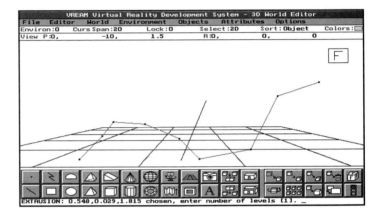

Figure 2.157
Setting the extrusion point.

The prompt line now asks you for the number of extrusion levels. This is the number of intermediate points along the extrusion path. If you will not be editing the extruded object, enter 1 for the number of levels. If you want to make changes later, enter a larger number. We'll use four levels for this example. Press Enter, and then follow the instructions on the prompt line to complete the extrusion. The result should look like Figure 2.158.

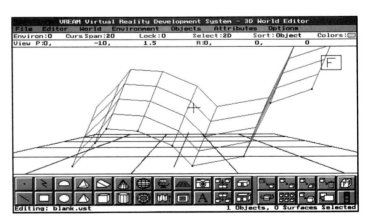

Figure 2.158
An extrusion.

You can choose the Solid On/Off option from the Environment menu to display the extruded object as a 3D object (see Fig. 2.159). You can also click the Walk button (at the lower right of the VREAM window) to move around and see the new object from different perspectives. Figure 2.160 shows the view from the right side.

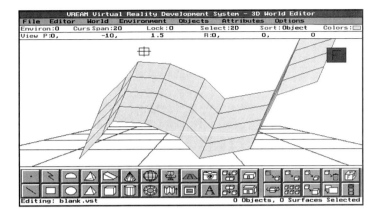

Figure 2.159
Viewing in 3D.

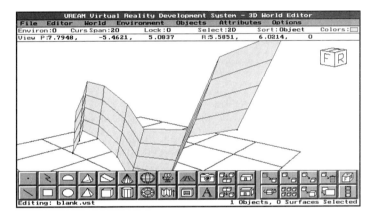

Figure 2.160
*Changing the angle
of view.*

By default, VREAM uses the keyboard for navigation. Here are the keys for moving around:

Q	Move left
W	Move right
E	Yaw left
R	Yaw right
A	Move backward
S	Move forward
D	Pitch down
F	Pitch up
Z	Move down
X	Move up
C	Roll left
V	Roll right

You can also set up VREAM to use the mouse for navigation, but this only operates in the VREAM at runtime, not while walking in the World Editor.

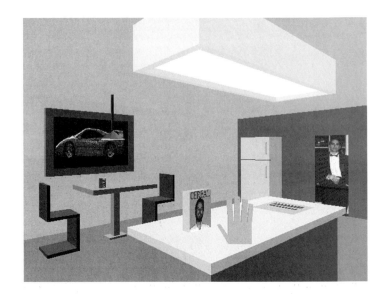

Figure 2.161
A sample VREAM world.

Mesh

With revolutions and extrusions under your belt, you'll find mesh objects very easy to create. A mesh object is a 2D surface object. It's like creating an extrusion using a line with one segment—not a polyline. It's a useful way to create fast walls.

Mesh tool

To begin, click the Mesh tool (just to the right of the Revolution tool). The prompt line will ask you to enter four points. These points define the outline of the mesh (see Fig. 2.162). With the Extrusion tool, you defined the number of levels. With the Mesh tool, you define the number of columns and rows. The final result, using four columns and four rows, is shown in Figure 2.163.

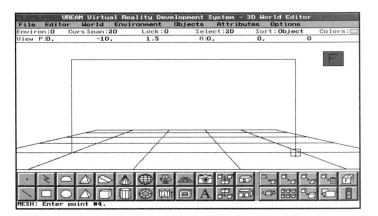

Figure 2.162
The outline for a mesh object.

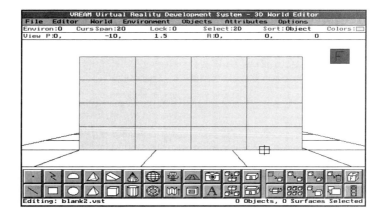

Figure 2.163
A completed mesh object.

You can move individual points in a mesh to create complex shapes, such as faces or bowls. This takes a bit of work to get right—it's always hard to create 3D shapes using a 2D screen. But it's a very powerful tool for the determined and creative VR enthusiast.

You can also move or rotate the mesh as an object. For example, to rotate the mesh, click the Rotate tool (at the upper left in the rightmost group of tools). The dialog box shown in Figure 2.164 enables you to enter rotation values for yaw, pitch, and roll.

Rotate tool

Figure 2.164
Setting yaw, pitch, and roll.

VREAM dialog boxes aren't like Windows dialog boxes—you must click in a field before you can type values, and you must press Enter to conclude the entry. Click the Set button when done.

NOTE

The result of a rotation is shown in Figure 2.165.

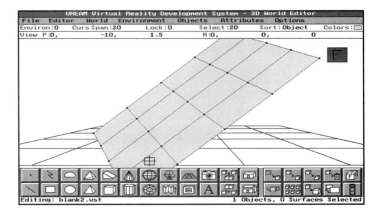

Figure 2.165
A rotation of a mesh object.

Rooms

VREAM uses a fairly complex logic to determine which objects are in front of other objects. What it can't do easily is handle objects that are inside other objects. Virtus WalkThrough has similar problems. However, VREAM has a solution to the problem: rooms. You can quickly create a room from an object primitive (cubes, cylinders, and so on), or you can carefully build a custom room from 2D surface objects.

For this example, we'll create a rectangular 3D object, break it into its component parts, add a door and window, and then assemble the final result into a custom room.

Cube tool

To begin, click the Cube tool. The prompt line asks you to lay out the width of the object. As shown in Figure 2.166, click once at the left of the VREAM window to set the start point, and once at the right of the window to set the width.

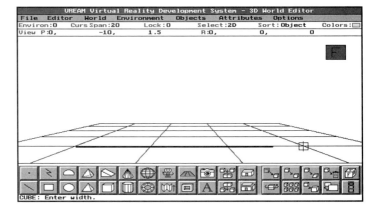

Figure 2.166
Laying out the width.

Next, the prompt will ask for the depth; click and hold the right mouse button to set a point for the depth (see Fig. 2.167).

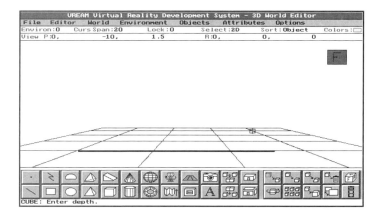

Figure 2.167
Setting the depth.

To set the height, move the mouse upward from the depth point (see Fig. 2.168). When you are done, you will have an object that looks like Figure 2.169.

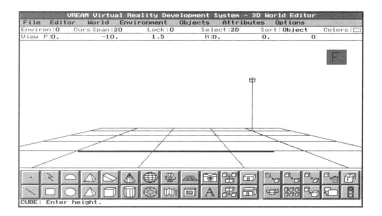

Figure 2.168
Setting the height.

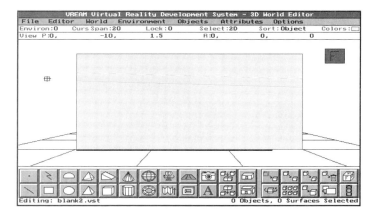

Figure 2.169
The completed object.

> If you don't need any windows or doors, you can quickly turn the object into a room. Select the object and click the Room tool. You'll see the dialog box shown in Figure 2.170. Verify that the Create Room from Primitive option is selected, and click the Set button.

Room tool

Figure 2.170
Selecting a room-creation method.

But don't create that room just yet! Let's have some fun and add a door and a window. Our first task is to explode the object into its component parts. Choose Explode from the Objects menu, and then choose Explode into Component Surfaces (see Fig. 2.171). You won't see any visible change, but there are now six surface objects instead of a single cubic object.

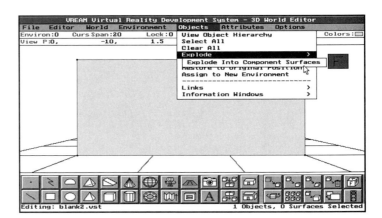

Figure 2.171
Exploding an object into its component parts.

Solid Cut tool

We'll now cut the door and window into the front surface object. First, let's make sure that no other objects are selected. Choose Clear All from the Objects menu to deselect all objects. Then click on the front surface to select it, and only it. Now click the Solid Cut tool (just below the Mesh tool). The prompt line asks you to enter Point #1. See Figure 2.172 for the location of the first point.

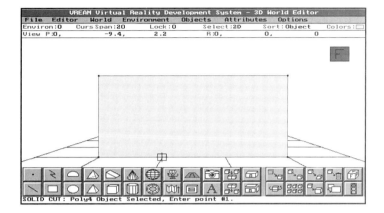

Figure 2.172
*The location of the
first point.*

> Always set the points for a Solid Cut in counter-clockwise order—otherwise, the cut will remove the portion you want to keep!

Figure 2.173 shows the fourth point for the solid cut that will make our door. Follow the instructions on the prompt line to complete the process of creating the door.

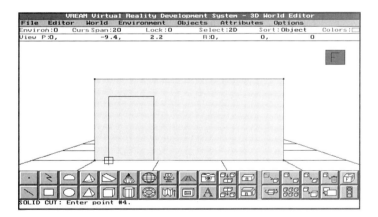

Figure 2.173
*The fourth line in
the solid cut for a
door.*

Figure 2.174 shows the completed result—a nice cut in the front wall. Note that the floor of the room's interior looks odd. If this happens to you, choose Redraw Screen from the Options menu to clean up the mess.

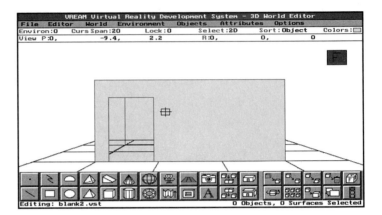

Figure 2.174
The cut in the wall.

Now add a window, following the same sequence of steps. Figure 2.175 shows the result. This is a good example of extreme screen weirdness. During editing, VREAM gets confused about what's in front of what, but redrawing the screen will clean things up. Figure 2.176 shows the result after a screen redraw.

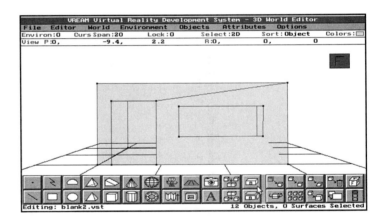

Figure 2.175
Adding a window.

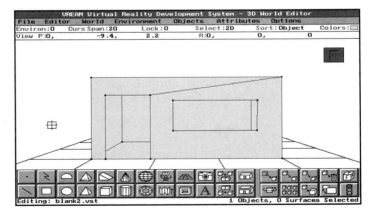

Figure 2.176
The cleaned-up display after redraw.

To turn this collection of 2D surfaces into a room, just click the Room tool. You'll see the dialog box shown in Figure 2.177. It's the same dialog box shown in Figure 2.170 but, this time, make sure that the Create Custom Room option is selected, and click the Set button.

*Room
tool*

Figure 2.177
*The room-creation
method, revisited.*

The display shouldn't change in any way when you create the room; it should still look like Figure 2.176. Creating a room simply tells VREAM how to display the room itself, as well as any objects that are placed inside the room. That's the main reason for rooms in the first place: to distinguish what is inside from what is outside.

To prove that we really have created a room, let's add an object to the interior of the room. Any object primitive will do; I chose a cone (see Fig. 2.178). To make the cone stand out, you can change its color. Choose the Solid Color option from the Attributes menu to display the dialog box shown in Figure 2.179. Pick a color you like, and click the Set button. You can also change the wireframe color by choosing Wireframe Color from the Attributes menu. Figure 2.180 shows the result of changing both the solid color and the wireframe color. You can't see the colors in black and white, but you can see the difference in shades of gray.

Cone tool

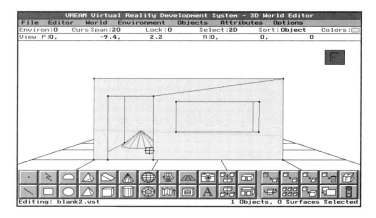

Figure 2.178
*Adding a cone to the
room.*

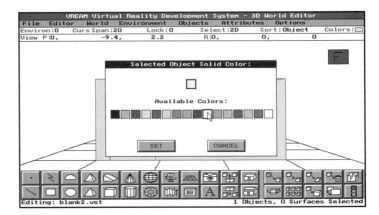

Figure 2.179
Selecting a color.

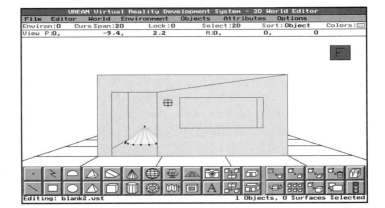

Figure 2.180
Can you tell that the colors have changed from Figure 2.178?

You can also change other attributes of any object in the room. Figure 2.181 shows the physical properties you can change, including such goodies as Throwable and Weight. Choose the Physical option from the Attributes menu, and then choose Throwable to display the dialog box shown in Figure 2.182; click the Throwable selection. To give the object some weight, choose Physical from the Attributes menu and then choose Weight. The prompt line asks for the weight value. To be throwable, an object must weigh less than 100 pounds. The lighter the object, the farther you can throw it.

You can also have fun by making the object respond to gravity. Choose Physical from the Attributes menu, and then choose Responds to Gravity to display the dialog box shown in Figure 2.183. Verify that the Respond to Gravity option is checked, and then click the Set button. You now have an object with some fun physical properties. To explore these properties, you'll need to load the object into the runtime viewer. Save your changes to the hard disk, and then use the File menu to exit. Then click in the GAGOS to start the runtime viewer.

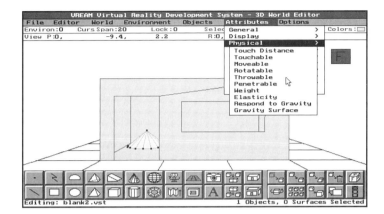

Figure 2.181
Changeable physical properties.

Figure 2.182
Determining whether an object is throwable.

Figure 2.183
Choosing the Respond to Gravity option.

Figure 2.184 shows the starting view at runtime. Note that the hand is active; you can press the F5 key to turn the hand on and off.[38] In this example, you'll be using the mouse to operate the hand, but you can also use alternate input devices such as the Fifth Dimension glove or the Mattel Power Glove to operate the hand. Click and hold the right button to move the hand in and out of the scene. Figure 2.185 shows the hand moved farther into the scene.

---

[38]In other words, if the hand isn't visible, just press the F5 key.

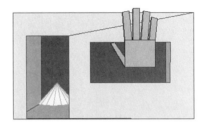

Figure 2.184
The view at runtime.

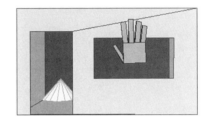

Figure 2.185
*Moving the hand
into the scene.*

Let's have some fun with the object in the room by throwing it around. Begin by using the S key to move forward into the scene until the hand is inside the room (see Fig. 2.186). Move forward just a bit more and then click and hold the left mouse button to close the hand around the conical object (see Fig. 2.187). You'll know whether the hand has closed around the object because the object will move with the hand (see Fig. 2.188).

Figure 2.186
*Moving forward
moves the hand as
well.*

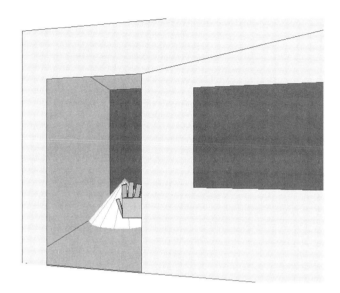

Figure 2.187
Moving the hand to the cone.

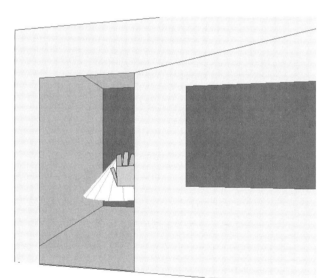

Figure 2.188
(a) Gripping with the hand.

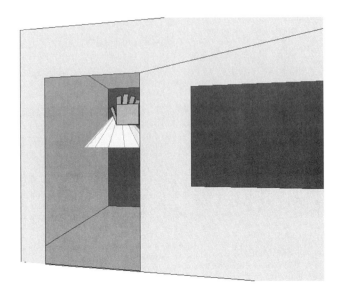

(b) *Moving with the hand while gripping.*

To throw the object, first move it to the right (see Fig. 2.189). Then move the hand to the left and, while the mouse is still moving, release the object. It will drift off to the left at the same velocity the mouse had at the moment you released the button. It's very important to keep the mouse moving while you release the object. If the object does not get "thrown," it's usually because you did not keep the mouse moving.

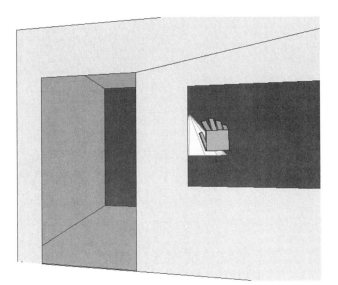

Figure 2.189
Throwing the object.

Figure 2.190 shows the thrown object in flight. Throwing is much simpler in practice than it looks when you are reading about it!

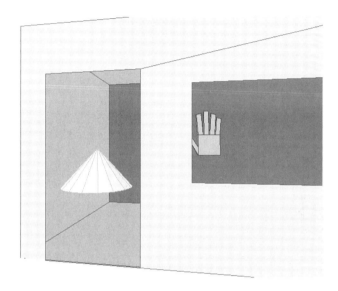

Figure 2.190
The object in flight
after being thrown.

This overview of the tools of VREAM only hints at what the product is capable of. Figure 2.191 shows what you can accomplish when you push VREAM to its limits.

Figure 2.191
A sophisticated
VREAM virtual
world.

3

VIRTUAL
POWER

3D Modeling

Most of the pictorial art throughout history was created without any accurate attention to the third dimension. At best, the third dimension was stretched in virtually[1] unrecognizable ways. There are good reasons for this. The most important reason is simple to state:

> **Drawing in three dimensions is not natural.**

Before you start calling me an idiot for making such an inane pronouncement, think about this for a minute. What is natural about 3D is *viewing* in three dimensions. Living in three dimensions does not automatically qualify anyone for drawing in three dimensions. There is some effort involved. If you don't believe me, pull out pencil and paper and draw a circle. Heck—don't even worry too much about getting the sides perfect; if you were working on a computer, the computer could align things for you.

Done with the circle? Good. Now draw a sphere.

Not as simple, right? Good. Now we're on the same wavelength.

I am making this point as a warning. If you have never drawn in three dimensions with a pencil, don't expect the computer to suddenly make it easy. It's not the mechanics of drawing in 3D that are difficult; it's thinking in 3D that's hard. Once you break through the barrier, however, and start thinking in 3D, it gets easier and easier. If you haven't already had a 3D-drawing "Aha!" experience, you will at some point. It might seem like work until you reach that stage, however. So don't give up if it seems frustrating—you'll miss the best part of 3D if you do. Which leads me to the following statement:

> **With a little effort, you can make drawing in three dimensions a perfectly natural activity.**

In other words,[2] 3D drawing is an acquired taste.

Working in Three Dimensions

There are two ways to work in three dimensions: intuitive and mechanical. The intuitive method is exciting, once you acquire the skills, but good old mechanical drawing has its advantages, too. For starters, it offers a frame of reference that I can describe. It's like the notes in a musical score—it's a way of describing something, but it is not that something. Just as it takes practice to turn notes into music, it takes practice to turn mechanical drafting into interesting virtual spaces.

---

[1] Unintentional play on words, but I'll take credit for it anyway.

[2] And in keeping with the recipe idea, of course.

When working in two dimensions, we traditionally use Cartesian[3] coordinates to define points in the 2D plane. Figure 3.1 shows a typical Cartesian coordinate system. There is a vertical axis, called the Y axis, and a horizontal axis, the X axis. The point where these two axes meet is called the *origin*. The origin is at distance zero on both axes, and we can describe this point as (0,0).

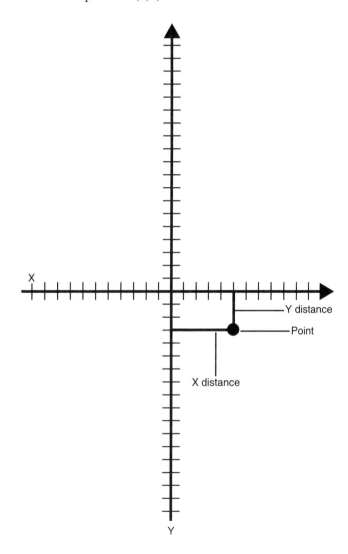

Figure 3.1
The Cartesian (X,Y)
coordinate system.

---

[3]Named after the great mathematician René Descartes, who slept until noon. They never tell us those things about famous people, and we don't find out until it's too late to develop such delicious eccentricities in ourselves.

To define a point, we need merely mention its distance from the origin along both axes. A point 5 units to the right of the origin along the X axis and 3 units below the origin on the Y axis, for example, has the coordinates (5,−3). By convention, the X coordinate is given first. An infinite number of such points exists in the 2D plane.

To describe points in 3D space, we add a third dimension. The third axis is called the Z axis.[4] A three-dimensional coordinate system is shown in Figure 3.2. That figure is a 2D representation of a 3D concept, so it can be hard to read.

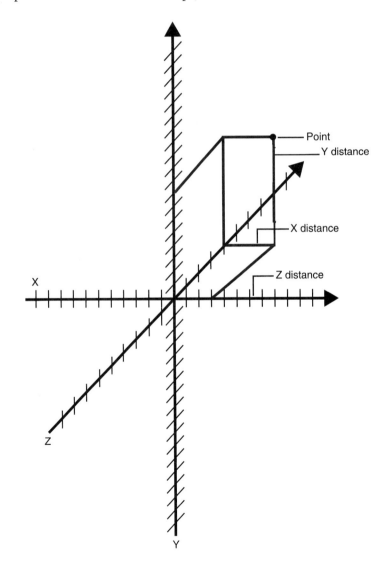

Figure 3.2
A three-dimensional
coordinate system.

---

[4] I'll bet you saw that coming.

Figure 3.3 shows a 3D model of a similar point in space, created in 3D Studio. Notice how much easier it is to visualize a 3D image when there are more visual cues (lighting, different materials, and so on) in the image.

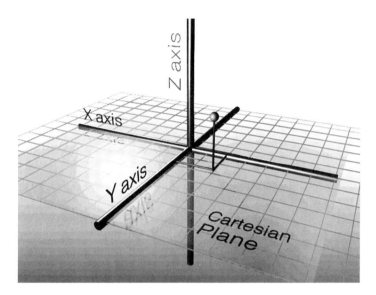

Figure 3.3
A clearer picture of a
3D coordinate system.

To specify a point in a three-dimensional system, we need to supply three numbers. Each number represents the distance from the origin along each respective axis—X, then Y, then Z. If we take the same point as in the preceding example, and lift it 83 units up from the origin, its coordinates are (5, –3, 83).

Now, we have not merely an infinite number of points in a plane, but an infinite number of planes in space—and each plane has an infinite number of points in it. The level of complexity has just gone from infinity to infinity squared.[5]

I suppose all those infinities would be more manageable if we didn't have to find a way to represent them on two-dimensional surfaces. Paper is two-dimensional; the computer screen is two-dimensional. Thus, the allure of fancy, virtual-space-creating goggles: They offer the promise of being able to draw and work in three dimensions using clever tricks to fool the eye (see Chapter 8, "Seeing is Believing").

---

[5]Of course, I'll leave the question of how one squares infinity to the mathematicians.

The problem is, such goggles cost thousands of dollars, have limited capabilities,[6] and the range of software written for them is, well, almost zero.[7] For a while yet, we'll have to make do with representing three dimensions in two dimensions. The rest of this chapter is dedicated to the proposition that as long as we're calling it virtual reality, degrees of virtuality are a reality—for the time being. After all, a perfectly rendered, highly detailed 3D scene on your computer monitor beats the heck out of nothing at all.

trueSpace from Caligari

RECIPE

1 copy trueSpace
1 glance at documentation

Instructions: Make a few basic shapes, and then stretch 'em around a bit so they look like real stuff. Paint liberally, then render. Great for hors d'oeuvres, parties, screen savers, and so on. When done, watch out for animation among the party-goers.

One of the great truisms of working in 3D is that it's horribly difficult to create 3D objects while working with a 2D interface like a computer screen. Elsewhere in this book, we talk about the costs and benefits of various kinds of 3D and six-degrees-of-freedom input devices, as well as about various 3D viewing devices. The primary hazard with anything truly 3D is cost. In addition, you are limited to software that supports the 3D devices of your choosing.

---

[6]Don't move your head too quickly, for example—the computer will choke trying to update the scene to keep up and will shatter any illusion of reality.

[7]Not that there aren't software programs, of course, but so far there aren't any spreadsheets or word processors—that is, the kinds of software you and I use every day. Drawing programs are limited to special-purpose applications, such as rendering the chemical structure of complex molecules.

Until 3D input and output becomes more economical, what we really and truly need is a 3D-modeling environment that works well in a 2D computer world. I'm a big fan of the interface in 3D Studio, but I'm also the first to admit that it takes serious study and practice to use it effectively—and even after a year of close study, you will find that there are things that are just plain hard to do with it. 3D Studio's first requirement is power, and sometimes that requires some sacrifice in the interface. This is fine if you absolutely must have it all, but sometimes it would be nice to just have a comfortable, easy-to-use interface for 3D modeling.

Well, there is one, and it's called *trueSpace*. With most 3D modelers, I find myself going through a frustration phase, where nothing makes any sense, and I keep waiting for everything to click into place.[8] With trueSpace, I was up and modeling in minutes, and I could hardly wait to learn about the next cool feature. I have arranged for a trial version of trueSpace on the CD-ROMs, and I recommend it highly. It's not cheap, but it's not thousands of dollars, either. It's what I would call affordable, and it's plenty good enough for real work, even if 3D Studio still is the professional's choice.

The version of trueSpace shown in detail in this chapter and included on the CD-ROMs is version 2.0. Several important improvements have been introduced in this new version that make it both easier to use for beginners and more powerful for professionals:

- trueSpace 2.0 enables you to see objects as 3D solids while you work. The previous version could render 3D objects as solids, but you could manipulate objects only as wireframe models. Now, you can draw a cube and then shape it, deform it, and move it, and see the results instantly. You can still work with wireframes and, as you will see from the tutorials, it can be very useful to do so.

- The new version offers 3D Boolean operations, simulating the real-world effects of chiseling, drilling holes, and fusing 3D shapes together.

- Accelerated, real-time 3D graphics with video cards such as the Matrox Impression Card are now supported.

- New tools are included to enhance photorealism, including motion blur, which replicates the human perception of an object or scene in motion, as well as procedural textures that change during an animation.

trueSpace Explained

Because I'm really impressed with trueSpace, I'm going to provide an extra-detailed tutorial. Even so, I simply can't go into all the cool and interesting 3D stuff you can do with this product. If you like what you see, start exploring with the trial version on the CDs.

---

[8]Actually, it's usually more like a squishing sound, as my hopes get dashed by reality.

The trueSpace interface, shown in Figure 3.4, might seem overwhelming at first, but it's very well organized and slowly will begin to arrange itself into accessible categories after several hours of use. trueSpace runs in Windows, but the default interface plays around a bit with the realities of life in Windows. I wound up preferring the upside-down interface, although it put me off at first. I found it more natural to have the vast array of toolbars at the bottom of the working window, but if you don't like that arrangement, you can change it with the Preferences settings.

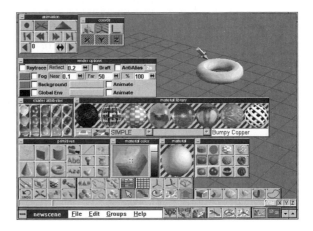

Figure 3.4
A few of the trueSpace tools.

Let's take a detailed look at the interface, because it's at the heart of using trueSpace effectively. The Caption bar, located at the bottom left of the screen, contains some of the usual Windows stuff: the Control menu, the window caption, and a menu (File, Edit, Groups, and Help). To the right of the menu is a row of icons. These icons control the 3D viewpoint in the main window. They don't affect objects—just your view of the objects.

Above the icons, you will find a status bar. Pointing at any icon or tool displays a text message letting you know what that tool does. This makes it easier to learn how to use trueSpace—of all the kinds of software that benefit from a status bar, 3D modeling is at the top of the list.

Above the status bar are two rows of icons/tools. These seem intimidating at first, but you'll find that the tools are arranged logically into groups. It takes a while to get a good feel for which groups contain which tools, but once it falls into place, trueSpace really starts to feel like a 3D-modeling sports car.

When you first start, some of the tools are gray, because they can't be used until you have created an object. If you haven't created an object, you can't exactly rotate one, for example.

Figure 3.5 shows an example of a Control Panel located above the tool groups and to the left. The Control Panel contains several basic geometric shapes[9]—a cube, a sphere, a torus,[10] and others. To create an object, just click on a shape and—presto!—you've got one.[11]

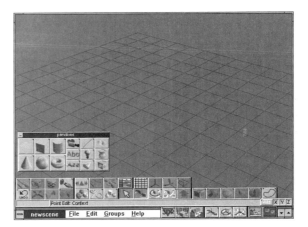

Figure 3.5
The trueSpace opening screen.

The trueSpace Toolbox

Before we try to create any models, let's take a look at the basic complement of trueSpace tools. I hope you are impressed with the number of tools, because I have a nice surprise for you—many of those tools expand into two additional possibilities. By clicking and holding on a tool, you often can display a row of variant tools, from which you can pick one tool to work with. When you click the tool for picking only part of an object, for example, you can choose among picking a vertex, a face, an edge, and so on.

By right-clicking a tool, you often can open a dialog box for establishing settings for the tool. Right-clicking the Rotation tool, for example, enables you to determine which axis you can rotate around (X, Y, and/or Z).[12]

I can't cover all the possibilities here in the book, but you can explore using the trial version on the CDs.

---

[9]Referred to in 3D-speak as *primitives*.

[10]*Torus* is the technical term for a doughnut shape.

[11]One of the things I like about trueSpace is that it doesn't make you think in strict terms. With most 3D modelers, you can't just create a shape—you have to decide how big it should be and where it should be right off the mark. That's nice and scientific, but some of us would rather just get a default shape, and then push and shove it into place and shape afterward.

[12]Each axis can be selected independently, so you can rotate using one, two, or all three axes—yet another example of flexible, high-powered modeling in trueSpace.

What I can do here is to provide a breakdown of the basic tools in the basic tool groups. Let's take a look at the tools available in trueSpace first, and then look at how they are used for modeling, surface mapping, and rendering.[13]

Editing Tools

Figure 3.6
The Editing tool group.

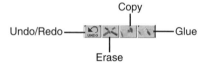

Undo/Redo—Does just what you would expect: undoes your last action or redoes an action that you just undid.

Erase—Deletes the current object.

Copy—Makes a copy of the currently selected object. Note that the copy will initially occupy the same space as the original and must be moved to be seen.

Glue—Enables you to attach objects hierarchically. An object can be a child or a sibling of another object, and you can unglue it if necessary. If you create a torso, for example, an arm normally would be attached as a child object.

Library Tools

Figure 3.7
The Library tool group.

Material Library—Opens the current Material library in a dialog box, enabling you to select a material to apply to an object or a face.

Paths Library—Opens a dialog box with a list of predefined spline paths.

Primitives Panel—Enables you to instantly create simple geometric shapes, such as cubes and spheres. Also contains the tools for creating lights, text, cameras, and deformation objects.

Navigation Tools

Four groups of navigation tools exist: Object, View, Point, and Deform. All these groups make use of the Coordinates Property panel (see Fig. 3.8).

---

[13]Keep in mind that many of these tools have variants. A tool with a little triangle in the upper right corner has variants. A tool with a little triangle in the upper left corner has a Control Panel for settings.

Figure 3.8
*The Coordinates
Property panel.*

This panel enables you to select the active axis or axes for allowable movement. The left mouse button controls movement on the X and/or Y axis, while the right mouse button controls movement on the Z axis.[14] The top row of buttons in the panel is used to constrain motion to three, two, or one plane.

Figure 3.9
*The Object Naviga-
tion tool group.*

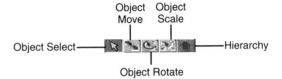

Object Select—Selects an object. When this tool is active, click it.

Object Move—Moves the current object by clicking and dragging.

Object Rotate—Rotates the current object along one or more axes by clicking and dragging.

Object Scale—Increases or decreases the size of the current object by clicking and dragging in one or more dimensions.

Hierarchy—Moves up or down in an object hierarchy.

Figure 3.10
*The View Naviga-
tion tool group.*

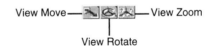

View Move—Moves the viewpoint.

View Rotate—Rotates the view.

View Zoom—Zooms in or out.

Figure 3.11
*The Point Naviga-
tion tool group.*

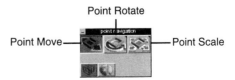

---

[14]In other words, to move on the X axis, deactivate the Y axis in the Coordinates Control panel, and then drag the left mouse button in the view to make the change. To move on both the X and Y axes, activate both axes and then drag with the left mouse button pressed. To move up and down on the Z axis, click with the right button and drag. It sounds complicated, but after you do it a few times, you'll see how easy and convenient it is.

Point Move—Moves the currently selected point(s).[15]

Point Rotate—Rotates the currently selected point(s).

Point Scale—Scales (enlarges or shrinks) the currently selected point(s).

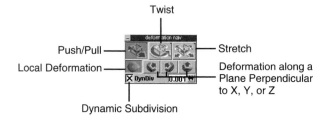

Figure 3.12
The Deform Navigation tool group.

Push/Pull—Deforms object by moving the selected surface.

Twist—Rotates selected part of the object.

Stretch—Scales (enlarges or shrinks) the selected part of the object.

Local Deformation—Sets deformation to occur around a specific point on the object.

Deformation along a Plane Perpendicular to X, Y, or Z Axis—Each restricts deformation to cross sections perpendicular to the chosen axis.

Dynamic Subdivision—Retains the smoothness of an object by subdividing a deformed face into a mesh of many faces. This can be a slow process, requiring your computer to perform a huge number of calculations.

Modeling Tools

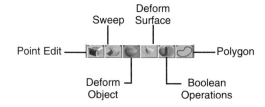

Figure 3.13
The Modeling tool group.

Point Edit—Edits portions of an object. Variants are Edit Points, Edit Edges, Edit Faces, Delete Face, and Edit Context. (Edit Context enables you to edit a combination of points, edges, and/or faces.)

Sweep—Sweeps an object or face through space to create a more complex object. Variants are Sweep, Tip, Lathe, Macro/Sweep, and Bevel.

---

[15]Use the Point Edit tool in the modeling group, of course, for selecting points. You'll see a little P below the arrow cursor when you are in Point mode. Always select an object before you select Point mode—you can select only points on the current object.

Deform Object—A very powerful tool! Enables you to deform objects into complex, free-form shapes. This tool and the next are enough to make trueSpace a first-class 3D modeling product.

Deform Surface—Enables you to just grab any place on the object and pull a shape smoothly out of the surface.

Boolean Operations—Creates new objects from the space defined by the union, intersection, or subtraction of one object and another. (Remember learning about sets in grade school math? Well, here they are again! Fortunately, this time the computer does all the math.) These are more super tools that enable you to build complex shapes quickly and easily. Variants are Object Subtraction, Object Intersection, and Object Union.

Polygon—Creates a polygon in a single plane, and enables Boolean operations on the polygons. Variants are Regular Polygon, Freehand Polygon, and Spline Polygon.

Rendering Tools

Figure 3.14
The Rendering tool group.

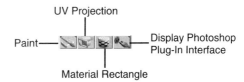

Paint—Creates new materials and applies the materials to objects or portions of objects. Variants are Paint Object, Paint Over Existing Material, Paint Face, Inspect, and Paint Vertices.

UV Projection—Applies textures to objects. There are three methods of mapping textures: Planar, Cylindrical, and Spherical. (*Planar mapping* is flat mapping. *Cylindrical mapping* applies a texture the way a label is applied to a can of refried beans. *Spherical mapping* is like a planet's surface.) The Control Panel clearly displays examples of each method of mapping.

Material Rectangle—Creates material rectangles that can be positioned on an object's surface interactively.

Display Photoshop Plug-In Interface—Enables you to use a number of image-filtering effects from Adobe Photoshop.

Animation Tools

Figure 3.15
The Animation tool group.

Animation Editor—Opens the Animation Control Panel. You can add animation frames, set key frames, and play an animation. See the tutorial that follows for details.

Path—Draws or edits paths for objects that are animated.

Constraints—Forces an object to behave in certain ways. There are two variants: one that forces an object to always face some other object, and one that forces an object to always face in the direction in which it is moving.

Project Editor—A timeline-based window that enables you to adjust the timing and relationships involved in an animation.

Utility Tools

Figure 3.16
The Utility tool group.

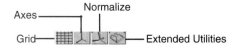

Grid—Turns Snap to Grid on and off.

Axes—Displays and/or modifies the axes for an object.

Normalize—Returns an object to its original state. Variants are Normalize Location, Normalize Rotation, Normalize Scale, and Move Axes to Center of Object.

Extended Utilities—A miscellaneous assortment of useful modeling tools. Includes tools to subdivide, mirror, triangulate, and clean up any bad geometry of objects, and other tools.

Window (View) Tools

Figure 3.17
The Window (View) tool group.

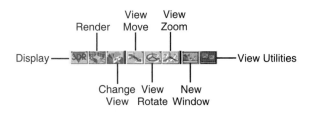

Display—Enables you to choose between Wireframe or Solid Render display. Right-click either icon to open a panel where you can set additional parameters for the display.

Render—Shows you the materials painted on the surfaces of objects. Variants are Render Object, Render Scene, and Render Scene to File. Rendering can be stopped by pressing the Escape key or by double-clicking the right mouse button.

Change View—Changes to a different view, such as Top, Front, Side, or Perspective. Camera view changes the viewpoint to that of any selected object.

View Move—Moves your viewpoint. Use the left mouse button and drag in the workspace to move in the X and Y coordinates; use the right button to move up and down. Click this tool with the right mouse button to open a Control Panel that enables you to constrain movement to just one or two coordinates.

View Rotate—Rotates the view; left and right mouse buttons work as for View Move.

View Zoom—Zooms in or out of the view; mouse buttons work as for View Move.

New Window—Opens a new window with its own View controls.

View Utilities—Variants include Look at Current Object, Reset View, Close All Panels, and Dock All Panels.

The Menu Bar

Figure 3.18
The menu bar.

> File   Edit   Groups   Help

File—Loads or saves objects or entire scenes. Also opens a Preferences panel that enables you to adjust various global settings, including default lighting and scene detail.

Edit—Includes the Undo, Redo, Erase, and Copy options, as well as an Image Utilities panel with several image-conversion functions.

Groups—Specifies which groups of tool icons are displayed.

Help—Includes the About and On-Line Help options, and enables you to toggle display of the context-sensitive Help bar.

Getting Started with trueSpace

Allow me to introduce you to our resident expert on trueSpace, Tim McNitt. Tim is the guest author for this part of the book. He'll take you on a journey into the world of 3D modeling with trueSpace. One of the key uses for trueSpace is to create 3D models that can be imported into virtual worlds, or into VRML worlds for use on the Internet (see Chapter 12 for more about VRML and VR on the Internet).

Because I'm really impressed with trueSpace, I'm going to provide an extra-detailed tutorial. Even so, I simply can't go into all the cool and interesting 3D stuff you can do with this product. If you like what you see, start exploring with the trial version on the CDs.

If the amount of detail in the section "The trueSpace Toolbox" seemed overwhelming, I need to make two things perfectly clear:

■ This is typical of life with 3D software and should not be held against trueSpace.[16]

■ There's a lot more to trueSpace than what you've seen so far.

If this seems to be a bit much, think for a moment about what's going on when you use a product like trueSpace. Not only does the software have to deal with all the variables of point of view and object rotation and all the rest, but it has to provide you with the easiest possible ways to interact with itself. This is a major job, and until recently, it has taken a tremendous amount of computing power and very sophisticated software to get the job done. So don't be daunted; be impressed and hang in there. If there is one product that offers a (relatively!) easy path into 3D modeling, it's trueSpace.

Enough talk; let's create something![17] Open trueSpace. Click and hold on File, then drag your pointer up to Scene, then over to New to clear the workspace. Click the Solid Render Display (3DR)[18] icon in the Window group in the bottom row of the toolbar. If 3DR is not visible, it is in a pop-up menu under Wireframe Display.

Begin the way any universe must begin: with a little light. Click File and then click Preferences. In the Preferences panel that opens, select White Light from the Lights pop-up menu at the lower right corner of the panel (see Fig. 3.19).

---

[16]If you did not already know this, then you probably skipped ahead to this chapter.

[17]The following tutorial is based on the tutorial you'll find in the documentation for trueSpace. I have spiced it up with my own comments and observations, of course.

[18]If you get lost as we discuss the various tools, refer back to the section "The trueSpace Toolbox," which describes the tools. Most of the icons and descriptions of what they do are covered there.

But there is no one to see this light—let's create a camera to record the scene. Click the Primitives icon in the Libraries group, and then click the Camera tool in the Primitives panel. (see Fig. 3.20). It's not an impressive-looking camera, but its only job is to provide a point of view—it won't show up if you render the scene.[19]

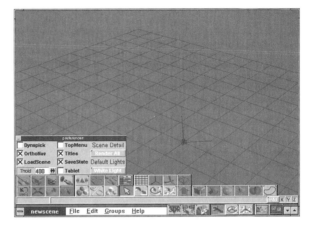

Figure 3.19
A universe with lights in it.

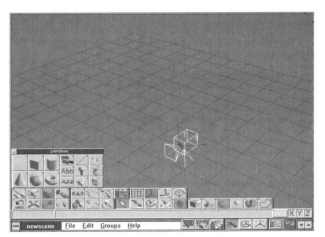

Figure 3.20
A camera in the universe.

A camera[20] can be moved just like any other object. If you look closely at Figure 3.20, you'll note that the camera is just pointing off in any old direction, and we need it to point toward the scene we are about to create. To move the camera, click the Object tool, and then click on the camera. The camera turns white to show that it is selected. To rotate the camera, click the Object Rotate tool, and then drag the mouse to perform the rotation. **Hint:** You usually want to rotate the camera in only one plane at a time, and that's usually the horizontal plane. To do this, you must rotate the

---

[19]Try it if you aren't the trusting kind.
[20]And lights, for that matter.

camera about its vertical axis (the Y axis). To constrain movement to just the Y axis, right-click the Object Rotate tool to open the Coordinates Control Panel (see Fig. 3.21). By default, all three axes are active (X, Y, and Z), so all three buttons are pressed.[21]

To deactivate the X axis, click the X button—it turns lighter (refer to Fig. 3.22). Now, when you click and drag, the object rotates only around the Y axis. You do not need to turn off the Z axis; to rotate about the Z axis, you must click and drag with the right mouse button.

Figure 3.21
The Coordinates Control Panel can be used to constrain rotation about an axis.

Figure 3.22
The Coordinates Control Panel with the X axis deactivated.

Click the Object Rotate tool once more to activate it.[22] Now click and drag anywhere in the scene to rotate the camera. Experiment with dragging left and right, up and down, and observe the effect it has on object rotation. The camera should wind up pointing straight ahead into the scene, as shown in Figure 3.23. Now click the Object Move tool and move the camera a little to the left so that it isn't right on top of the lights.

Figure 3.23
Rotating the camera to face into the scene.

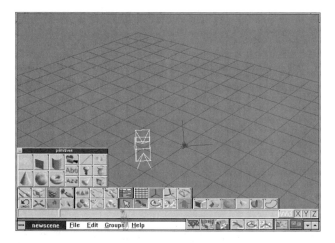

---

[21]A button looks darker when it is pressed. Sort of like people, I guess.
[22]And, at the same time, dismiss the Coordinates Control Panel.

It is often convenient to create a second, smaller window in which to work. Click the New Window tool in the Window group to open a new window. Position the new window in the upper right of the main window, as shown in Figure 3.24.

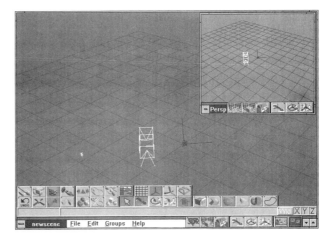

Figure 3.24
Adding a new window.

You can control the point of view in the new window independently of the main window. To make the new window show what the camera sees, click and hold on the new window's Change View tool, and then slide the mouse pointer up to the Camera icon and release.

Now to the meat of this exercise: Let's create something interesting! Click the Vertical Text tool on the Primitives panel, and then click somewhere in front of the camera to place a large cursor in the drawing space. Type a word, such as **Multimedia!** (see Fig. 3.25). If only outlines show up in the workspace where letters should be, click the 3DR icon.

All we've done so far is create a flat bit of text—let's make it 3D. Click the Sweep tool in the Modeling group and drag the mouse to extend the text into the third dimension, as shown in Figure 3.26.[23]

We are going to use the view in the working window at the upper right for rendering this scene later on. Right now, we can't see very much of the text in this window. To move the text, click the Object Move tool and then click and drag the mouse until the text shows clearly in the working window, as shown in Figure 3.27. You might need to click and drag more than once to get the text where it needs to be. If you

*Change
View
pop-up
menu*

---

[23]By doing this, we are using the default settings for a Sweep. Right-click the Sweep tool to change the default settings.

have trouble keeping track of your position, think in terms of moving the text in front of the camera. To move the text up and down, you can use the right mouse button instead of the left.[24]

Figure 3.25
Adding text to the scene.

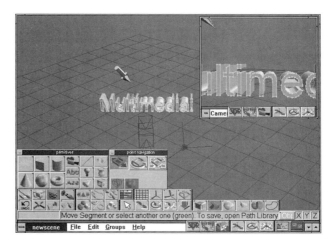

Figure 3.26
Now the text is 3D.

---

[24]If you feel up to it, you can also move the camera around to point at the text, but this is much trickier!

Figure 3.27
Moving the text so
that it appears
centered in the
working window.

At this point, it might be nice to give the text and background a little color. Right-click any tool in the Paint pop-up menu and several panels will open up. Left-click the slider beside the colored hexagon of the Material Color panel and drag it to create whatever color you want (see Fig. 3.28).

Figure 3.28
Changing the
material color.

Paint
pop-up
menu

Select Paint Object from the Paint pop-up menu to apply the color to the text. To change the background color, right-click whichever of the Render icons is visible next to 3DR in the small working window. A Render Options panel opens, as shown in Figure 3.29. Click the button to the left of the word Background, and then experiment with sliding the three bars across the color swatches in the Background Color panel until you produce a color you like (see Fig. 3.30).

Figure 3.29
Selecting the back-
ground from the
Render Options panel.

Figure 3.30
Changing the
background color.

By this time, your workspace is probably getting pretty cluttered with panels, so before proceeding any further, you might want to close them all by selecting the Close All Panels tool from the pop-up menu at the lower right of the toolbar.

Close All
Panels
tool

Creating an Animation

We now have an object, but it's nothing fancy so far. To make it more interesting, let's create an animation using the Animation Editor. It's surprisingly easy to do. Begin by clicking the Object Move tool, and then click and drag the text away from the camera to the far corner of the grid while trying to keep the text centered, as shown in Figure 3.31.

Next, click the Animation tool to bring up the Animation panel (see Fig. 3.32). Change the current frame number to 30 by clicking the double arrow to the right of the number and dragging right or left to increase or decrease the setting. Alternatively, you can double-click the number itself and enter a new value from your keyboard. After you change the number, press Enter, and the cursor will stop blinking.

Using the Object Move tool, drag the text until it fills the frame of the working window from side to side, as shown in Figure 3.33. To record the changes in this frame and make it a key frame, click any tool (such as Object Rotate, because we'll be using it next), and then click the Record button in the Animation panel. This locks the changes to the current frame.

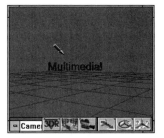

Figure 3.31
Moving the text away from the camera before beginning the animation.

Figure 3.32
The Animation panel.

Figure 3.33
Moving the text to a new position in frame 30.

What's a Key Frame?

When cartoons and animation first were created, the artists had to draw every frame of the animation by hand. Before they did this, however, they would render certain frames in the animation. They might draw every tenth frame, for example, and then fill in the frames between. This is an early example of key frames. It didn't save much time overall, but it did help the animators to get a handle on the huge task before them.

When you are creating an animation on a computer, you have a huge advantage. You can specify just the key frames, and have the computer fill in the other frames for you. A key frame usually marks a point where an object's animation starts or stops, changes direction, or otherwise becomes different. In the tutorial, you created a position for the text object at frame 0 and again at frame 30. The computer calculates all the intervening positions for you.

This makes your job as master animator easy. Think how tedious it would be to have to position the object in every frame—and how much harder still to make it move smoothly!

That's it! You have just created an animation. To view the animation, click somewhere in the small working window to make it the current window, and then click the large Play button at the upper right of the Animation panel.

Not bad, but a little slow and jerky. That's because trueSpace is drawing each frame of the Animation in the small window and the full-size window simultaneously. Due to the huge demands that animations place on memory, the best results generally are produced when animations are run only in small windows. To specify that the animation run only in the small window, right-click the Play button (see Fig. 3.34) and select Scene from the Animation Parameters panel (see Fig. 3.35). Now click somewhere in the small window to be sure it is the current window, and then click Play. Much better!

As amusing as this animation is,[25] we can do better. Go back to frame 0 (just click the Go To Start button in the Animation panel), and then click the Object Rotate tool (rotation about the X axis should still be disabled), as shown in Figure 3.36. Rotate the text so that it faces away from you, giving you a side-on view of the first letter in the word. Now advance to frame 30 (click Play or Advance To End). You might need to rotate the text back so that it faces you and again fills the frame.[26]

---

[25]Yes, my tongue is firmly in my cheek.

[26]If you are having difficulty getting the animation just right, I have included a file on the CD-ROMs with the scene as it should be up to this point. Just load scene TRUSP001.SCN into trueSpace. See the *Guide to the CD-ROM* menu application on Disc One to locate the scene files referenced in this chapter.

GUEST
AUTHOR

Figure 3.34
*Right-click Play to open
the Animation panel.*

Figure 3.35
*Select Scene to play
the animation in the
small window.*

Figure 3.36
*Rotating the text
at frame 0.*

The text object now has two (count 'em!) motions at the same time—it is moving toward the camera, and it is rotating as well. To see the result in action, click the Play button.

But there's more! Begin with the frame counter at frame 30, and then change the number to 75 and press Enter. We'll add two motions: tilt and fly-over. First, tilt the text backward about 45 degrees, as shown in Figure 3.37. **Hint:** Right-click the Object Rotate tool and re-enable rotation about the X axis if you have not already done so; then disable the Y axis.

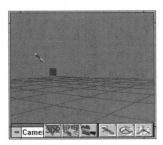

Figure 3.37
*Rotating the text
backward using the
Text Rotate tool.*

Next, click Object Move and drag the text toward the camera until a letter from the center of the word fills the frame (see Fig. 3.38). Finally, drag the text up, out of view, as shown in Figure 3.39.

Figure 3.38
Moving the text to
fill the frame with
a single letter.

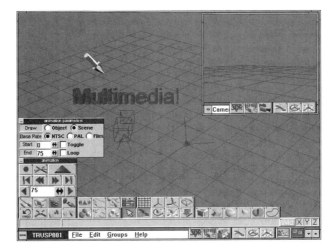

Figure 3.39
Moving the text
until it disappears
from the camera's
view.

The result of these combined movements (which occur between frames 30 and 75) is a rotation and flying out of the scene—a nice dramatic finish to the animation.[27] You can play the animation using the Play button on the Animation panel, but that only displays the animation at whatever speed your computer can draw each frame, and the grid is still visible. To create a fully rendered version, click and hold on the Render button in the small working window and select Render To File.

This opens a dialog box where you can specify the file name and directory for the resulting file, as shown in Figure 3.40.[28]

Render
to File
tool

---

[27]A file (TRUSP002.SCN) with the completed animation scene is on the CD-ROMs.

[28]**Note:** The trial version of trueSpace on the CD-ROMs may not enable you to render to file. If you want to get a look at the completed animation, it is on the CD-ROMs as TRUSP001.AVI. Just for fun, I've included another text AVI file on the CDs: Check out TRUSP002.AVI.

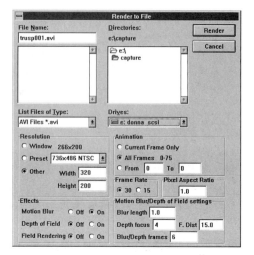

Figure 3.40
This dialog box
enables you to
render your anima-
tion to an AVI file.

To save the animation to an AVI file, make sure that you select AVI Files *.avi in the List Files of Type box. You can set a number of other parameters for the video rendering, but the only critical one to select is Animation of All Frames. Motion Blur is a nice effect that smoothes animation, but it results in very long rendering times (sometimes hours).

After you click the Render button, another dialog box appears where you can specify a video-compression method (see Fig. 3.41). This saves some file space. RLE encoding gives you a relatively clean image, but Cinepak or Indeo usually provides significantly higher compression rates. Once the long process of rendering is over, you can finally view the completed video on whatever video playback software you have (see Fig. 3.42).

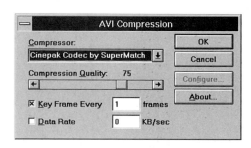

Figure 3.41
Choosing an AVI
compression method.

Figure 3.42
*A rendered scene
from the animation.*

Building a Starship with trueSpace 2.0[29]

Open trueSpace. If trueSpace is already open, click on File, and then drag your pointer up to Scene and over to New to clear the workspace (see Fig. 3.43).

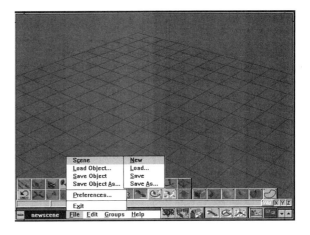

Figure 3.43
*Selecting a new
scene to clear the
workspace.*

You can choose to work in either Wireframe display or Solid Render display (3DR) by clicking the Display Selector button in the Window Group in the bottom row of the toolbar. Or, you can access a pop-up menu by holding down the left mouse button and then dragging the mouse up. This allows you to select one of the display modes. Solid Render display provides the most realistic modeling environment, but Wireframe display is useful when working with the individual edges or vertices of a model. The

*Select a
display
mode*

---

[29]By including a tutorial for creating a starship, I don't want to give the impression that trueSpace is only for outer space stuff. You can just as easily create mundane earthly objects like buildings and furniture. In fact, trueSpace can be a valuable tool for technical illustrations. But let's have some fun!

speed of rendering in Solid Render mode depends on your computer: the faster your video card and CPU, the faster the solid will be rendered.

Start with a Cylinder

Click the Primitives icon in the Libraries group to bring up the Primitives panel.

Right-click the Cylinder icon. This opens a panel where you can specify the parameters of the cylinder you are about to create. Set the parameters by clicking on the double arrow to the right of a number and dragging your mouse right or left to increase or decrease the setting. Alternatively, you can double-click on the number itself and enter a new value from your keyboard.

Set the latitude to 2; this gives the cylinder a top and a bottom, but no additional cross sections. Set the longitude to 24 to give the cylinder enough sides to appear circular. Finally, set the top radius to 1. Now, click the Cylinder icon and a cylinder will be drawn in the workspace (see Fig. 3.44).

*Specifying
cylinder
parameters*

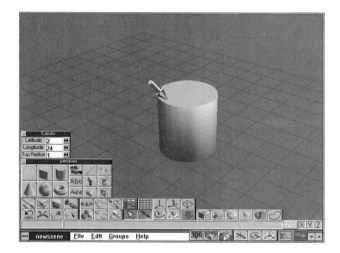

Figure 3.44
*Creating a simple
cylinder.*

Next, you will need to rotate the cylinder 90 degrees, so that it is lying on its side. Do this by first left-clicking, and then right-clicking the Object Rotate icon in the Object Navigation group. Left-clicking selects the tool. Your right-click opens a Coordinates panel. Left-click the X button to temporarily disable rotation about the X axis. Now, to lay the cylinder on its side, all you need to do is click anywhere on the workspace and drag your mouse downward (see Fig. 3.45).

Figure 3.45
*Rotating the cylinder
90 degrees.*

Squash it

Practicality aside, I don't find cylindrical spacecraft to be that interesting, so let's squash the cylinder to give it an oval cross section, as shown in Figure 3.46. Click the Object Scale tool. Then, click anywhere in the workspace and drag your mouse down and to the right. A finished oval about five grid spaces wide and one grid space high is a good, workable size.

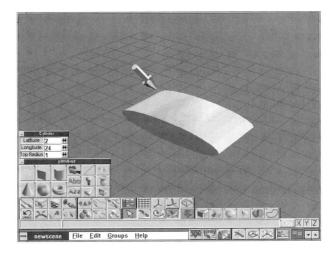

Figure 3.46
*Squashing the
cylinder to create the
basic cross-section of
the starship.*

Stretch it

Next, you will use the Point Edit and Sweep tools to lengthen the squashed cylinder. First, click and hold on the Point Edit tool in the Model group. This opens a pop-up menu with several tool variants. While still holding down the left mouse button, move

Selecting Point Edit Faces

Selecting Sweep

your mouse pointer up until Point Edit Faces is highlighted. When you let go of the mouse button, the highlighted tool is selected.

Notice that your mouse pointer now has a letter P attached to it, to remind you that you are in Point Edit mode.[30] Move the mouse pointer to somewhere in the oval face of the model, and click. This selects the face, as shown by the green outline. Click three times on the Sweep tool in the Model group. If the Sweep icon is not visible, you might need to access it from its pop-up menu.

Each time you click Sweep, a new section is added to the model. Figure 3.47 shows several sections added to the model. Each of these sections will be manipulated separately in later steps.

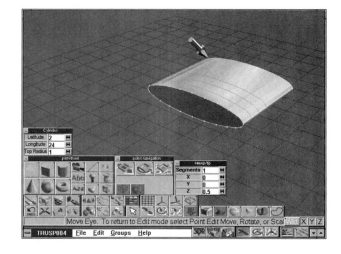

Figure 3.47
Adding new sections to the model with the Sweep tool.

Now go to the Point Navigation panel and click the Point Scale tool (see Fig. 3.48). Then move your mouse pointer to anywhere on the workspace, and then click and drag diagonally down and to the left. This reduces the selected face to a smaller oval (see Fig. 3.49).

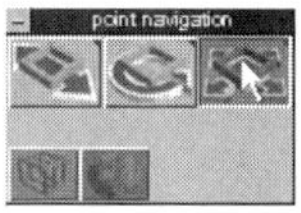

Figure 3.48
Selecting Point Scale from the Point Navigation panel.

---

[30]Also notice that the Point Navigation panel has opened. You can ignore this panel for now, but you will use it after the next couple of steps.

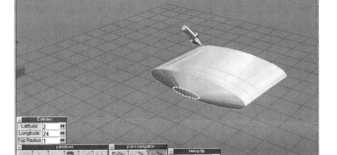

Figure 3.49
Reducing the face of the model to a smaller oval.

Click the Deform Object tool in the Model group. The Deformation Navigation panel appears, as shown in Figure 3.50. Left-click, and then right-click the Push/Pull button in the upper left of this panel. Left-clicking selects the tool. Right-clicking opens a Coordinates panel. Click the Y button to temporarily disable deformation along the Y coordinate.

Click and hold in the center of the small oval face of the model. Still holding the left button, drag the mouse to the left to stretch out the nose of the starship (see Fig. 3.51).

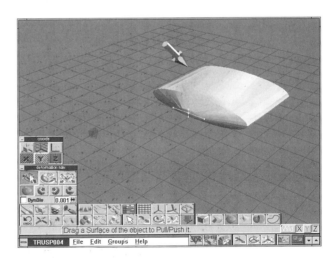

Figure 3.50
Selecting the Push/Pull tool from the Deformation Navigation panel.

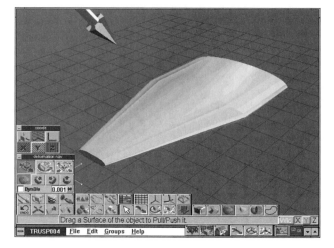

Figure 3.51
*Using Deform Object
to stretch out the
nose of the starship.*

Add a Couple of Engine Mounts

Before you build the engines, you are going to need a place to mount them on the ship (details! details!). Click and hold on the Point Edit icon and slide your mouse up to Point Edit Edges; then release the button to select Edges. An Alert window appears, reminding you that the object has animatable deformation[31] associated with it (see Fig. 3.52). Click Yes to release the deformation connections.

Figure 3.52
*Choose Yes
to release the
animatable
deformations.*

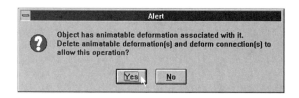

*Changing
to
Wireframe
mode*

To select the precise edges you want, it is helpful to change to Wireframe display if you are not already there. Select Wireframe Display from the pop-up menu under the 3DR icon.

One of the edges you will be selecting is on the opposite side of the model, so you need to change your viewpoint. Click the Eye Rotate icon in the Window Group at the bottom of the toolbar (see Fig. 3.53). Now click and hold anywhere in the workspace and drag your mouse to the left until the ship is pointing at you and down slightly.

---

[31]Now there's an obscure phrase for the record books!

Figure 3.53
The Eye Rotate icon.

Now comes the really tricky part: selecting the right edges to make the engine mounts symmetrical on both sides of the ship. The edges you want are at the back of the ship, along the top, just in from the sides. (Look closely at Figure 3.54 to be sure.) Hold down the Control key and click one of the edges, and then the other. Both edges should be highlighted. If not, click Undo and try again.

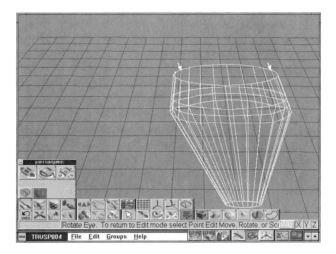

Figure 3.54
Selecting the two edges for the engine mounts.

In the Point Navigation panel, click the Point Move tool (see Fig. 3.55). Then right-click anywhere in the workspace and hold; then drag the mouse up to give the ship a couple of ears, as shown in Figure 3.56.[32]

Figure 3.55
Selecting Point Move from the Point Navigation panel.

---

[32]If you have trouble getting the engine mounts right, a file with the scene up to this point is on one of the CD-ROMs (TRUSP003.SCN).

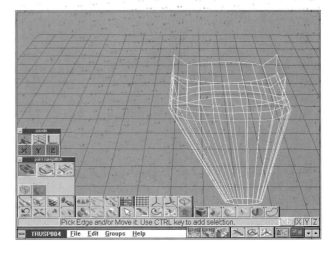

Figure 3.56
*The completed
engine mounts.*

Then Add the Engines

In the Primitives panel, click the Cylinder icon to draw another cylinder. There it is, right in the middle of the ship (see Fig. 3.57)! Don't worry—one of the advantages of working in Wireframe display is that you can manipulate models inside other models.

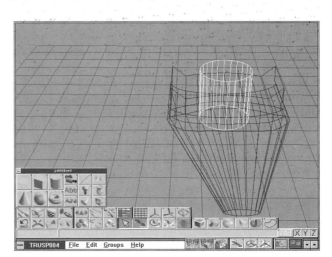

Figure 3.57
*Manipulating one
model inside another
is no problem in
Wireframe mode.*

At this point, it will be easier if you go back to the original viewpoint, so you can see the ship from an angle, rather than straight on. You could click the Eye Rotate button, and then click and drag to the right, but there is an easier way: Click on the

pop-up menu at the bottom of the toolbar on the far right, next to the Minimize arrow. One of the choices in the pop-up menu is Reset View. Select it, and the workspace returns to the original view.

Now rotate the cylinder so that it is lying on its side, just like you did at the beginning of this exercise. Left-click, and then right-click on Object Rotate. Check to be sure that the X coordinate button is still disabled. Then left-click and drag the mouse downward anywhere on the workspace to rotate the cylinder.

To change the size of the cylinder, click the Object Size tool. Then, right-click anywhere in the workspace and drag the mouse to the right to lengthen the cylinder to about five grid spaces (see Fig. 3.58). To make the cylinder narrower, click and drag the mouse diagonally down and to the left. You can leave the engines as cylinders or make them oval by dragging the mouse more left than down.

Selecting Reset View

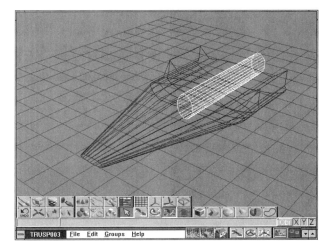

Figure 3.58
Making the engine the right shape and size.

When you are satisfied with the shape and size of the engine, click the Copy tool in the Edit group to make a duplicate of it. After making a copy, both engines will be occupying the same space, so until one is moved, you won't see them both.

Placing the engines evenly on their mounts will be easier if you shift between a couple of *orthogonal* (right angle) views. Start by clicking and holding on the Perspective View icon in the Window group at the bottom of the toolbar. While still holding down the button, slide the pointer up to Top View, and then release.

Copy tool

Selecting
Top View

Click the Object Move tool in the Object Navigation group. Then, click anywhere in the workspace and drag up and to the right to align the engine with its mount. Click on the other engine, and then click again and drag down and to the right to align it (see Fig. 3.59).

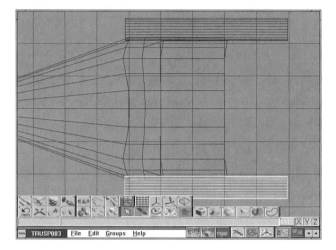

Figure 3.59
The engines aligned
in Top view.

To finish aligning the engines, select the Left view from the same pop-up menu you used to get to Top view earlier. To move the engine, click and drag up to place the engine. Then click on the other engine, and click and drag again to place it (see Fig. 3.60). **Hint:** The final model will look more natural if the engines overlap the vertical surface of the engine mounts.

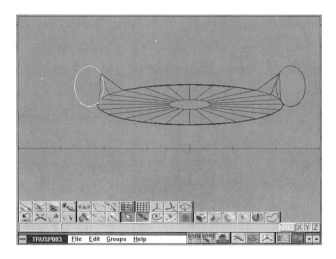

Figure 3.60
The engines
overlapping the
engine mounts, as
seen in Left view.

The engines now should be in place, so it is time to step back and see what your starship looks like so far. Select Perspective view from the same pop-up menu where you found Top view and Left view. At this point, with the engines moved out of the belly of the ship, you can go back to Solid Render display by selecting the 3DR icon from the Display Selection pop-up menu (see Fig. 3.61).

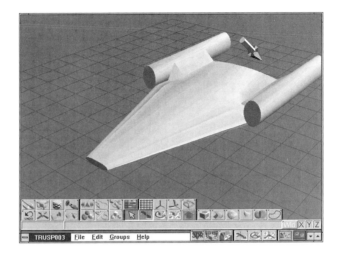

Figure 3.61
The engines placed
on the starship, as
seen in 3D mode.

If you are satisfied with the placement of the engines, it is time to glue them to the main body of the ship. If not, go back to Top view or Left view and move the engines where you want them. To glue the engines, click somewhere on the main body of the ship, and then click on the Glue pop-up menu in the Edit group and select Glue as Child. Your mouse pointer now turns into a glue bottle. Click on one of the engines, and then on the other. Now the ship and its engines can be moved as one.

This final modeling step is optional, but I think it improves the overall look of the ship, so I'm including it. Go back to Wireframe display for a moment. From the Point Edit pop-up menu, select Point Edit Faces. Click on one of the four square faces on the top center of the ship. Hold down the Shift key and click on the other three faces. All four faces now should be selected, as shown in Figure 3.62.

Glue as
Child
icon

Left-click, and then right-click on the Point Move icon in the Point Navigation panel. Click the Y button to disable movement along the Y axis. Click and hold the left mouse button and drag upward a short distance to raise the center section of the ship. When you think it is raised enough, click the Object Tool to exit Point Edit mode. Go back to Solid Render Display (3DR) to see how it looks, as shown in Figure 3.63.[33]

---

[33]Okay, so it doesn't make a huge difference! I think it's an improvement! The difference between a model that looks like a toy and one that gives the illusion of reality is details. Hours or days could be spent adding minute details to your model but, for now, let's turn to giving it some color. By the way, a scene with the completed model is on the CD-ROMs (TRUSP004.SCN).

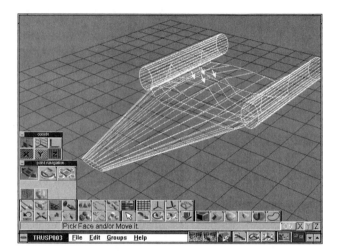

Figure 3.62
Selecting the four square faces on the top center of the ship.

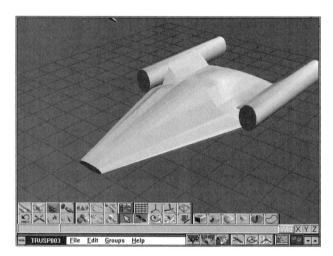

Figure 3.63
The completed starship model.

And Now, for a Little Color

Right-click any tool in the Paint pop-up menu, and several panels open: Material, Material Color, Attributes, and Shader Attributes (see Fig. 3.64). Changing any of the settings in the last three panels changes the character of the sample sphere in the Material panel.

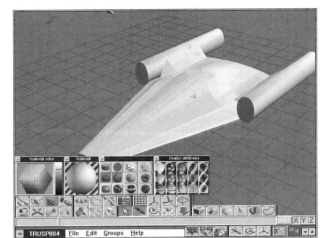

Figure 3.64
The Material Settings panels.

You also can choose one of the materials supplied with trueSpace by clicking the Material Library icon in the Libraries group.

Material Library tool

To select one of the materials, just click on it, and it will appear on the sample material sphere. To bring up one of the other Material libraries, click the button showing the name of the current Material library. Then choose Load, and a standard Windows file requester opens, from which you can choose one of the Material Library files (see Fig. 3.65).

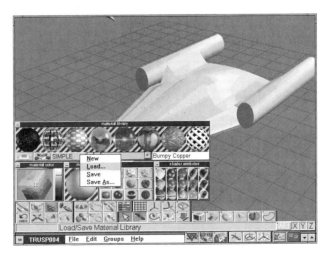

Figure 3.65
A Material library.

*Paint
Object tool*

*Render
Current
Object tool*

*UV
Projection
tool*

To apply the material to your starship, choose the Paint Object tool from the Paint pop-up menu.

To see what your painted starship looks like, select Render Current Object from the Render pop-up menu at the bottom of the toolbar.

You can also have trueSpace show the material painted on the starship in real time as you continue to work on the model. Right-click the Solid Render Display (3DR) icon to open a Render Quality panel (see Fig. 3.66, under the arrow cursor), and then click Toggle Use of Textures in Solid Render.[34]

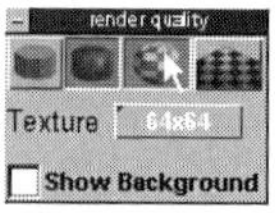

Figure 3.66
*Selecting Toggle Use
of Textures from the
Render Quality panel.*

trueSpace provides three different mapping techniques for applying materials to objects. To change the mapping technique, click the UV Projection icon in the Render group.[35]

A UV Map panel opens, from which you can choose Planar, Cylindrical, or Spherical UV Projection. Click one of the choices, and then click Apply.

Experiment with different materials and UV projections until you find a combination you like. You can also paint individual faces of your starship with different materials by clicking the Paint Faces tool in the Paint pop-up menu. Your mouse pointer now looks like a paintbrush. Click on any face of your model to apply the current material, as shown by the sample sphere in the Material panel, to the selected face. To turn off the Paint Face tool, click the Object tool.[36]

Stars

A starship looks pretty lame rendered against a plain gray background, so let's spice up the scenery a bit. trueSpace can use images of several formats as backgrounds. If you don't already have an image of a starfield on file, here's how you can make one using standard Windows applications. In case you didn't already know it, Windows

---

[34]The cost of seeing objects rendered is slower performance. In a few years, when our personal computers have a gigabyte of RAM, we will be able to manipulate complex scenes of photographically rendered three-dimensional objects.

[35]*UV projection* refers to a mathematical technique for describing the location of a point on an object's surface. It has nothing to do with ultraviolet light.

[36]A scene with the completed and painted starship is on the CD-ROMs (TRUSP005.SCN).

comes with an animated starfield screen saver. We are going to take a screen capture of the starfield, convert it to a bitmap, and import it into trueSpace for a background.[37]

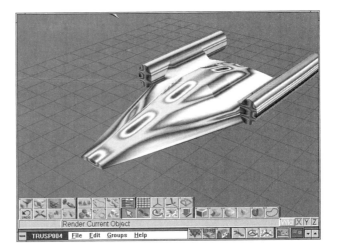

Figure 3.67
The starship with material mapped in planar UV projection.

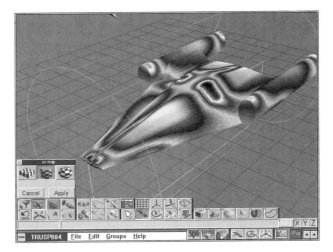

Figure 3.68
The starship with material mapped in cylindrical UV projection.

Leave trueSpace temporarily and open the Control Panel (probably in your Main group if you are using Program Manager). Select Desktop, then click on the down arrow next to the Screen Saver Name window. Select Starfield Simulation. Click Setup, increase

---

[37]The starfield simulator screen saver creates square stars on some computer configurations. If yours is one of these, and you would like a better starfield, I have included a couple on the CD-ROMs (STARS1.BMP and STARS2.BMP).

the number of stars to 200, and then click OK. Now click Test, and the starfield simulation begins. While the starfield is visible, press the Print Screen key on your keyboard. This copies the starfield to your Clipboard. If you move your mouse slightly, the starfield disappears, and you can click Cancel or OK in the Desktop window.

You can use any Image Editor to convert the Clipboard image to a bitmap or other trueSpace-compatible format. I don't generally use Paintbrush, but it comes with Windows, so here goes: Open Paintbrush, and then maximize the window. From the View menu, choose Zoom Out. From the Edit menu, choose Paste, and then choose Paste again.[38] From the View menu, choose Zoom In. Finally, from the File menu, choose Save As, and then save the image as STARS.BMP in your trueSpace directory.

Go back to trueSpace and right-click any one of the Render icons from the Render pop-up menu at the bottom of the toolbar. A Render Options panel opens, as shown in Figure 3.69. Click on the gray bar to the right of Background.

Figure 3.69
Selecting a background from the Render Options panel.

A standard Windows file requester opens, from which you can select your starfield bitmap. When you have selected the file, its name appears in the gray bar to the right of Background in the Render Options panel. To see the results, select Render Scene from the Render pop-up menu at the bottom of the toolbar. You can also have trueSpace show the background in real time as you continue to work.[39] Right-click the Solid Render Display (3DR) icon to open a Render Quality panel, and then click Show Background (see Fig. 3.70). Now click the 3DR icon again, and the background appears behind the grid, as shown in Figure 3.71. Not bad—all you need now is a planet to orbit.

Figure 3.70
Selecting Show Background in the Render Quality panel.

---

[38] I don't know why you need to select Paste twice, but it seems to work.
[39] Again resulting in slower performance.

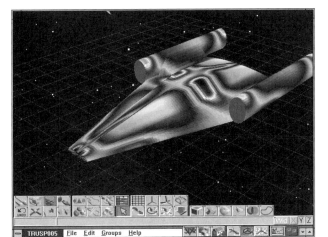

Figure 3.71
The starship with a starfield background.

Planets

Click the Primitives icon, and then right-click on the Sphere to open a panel where you can specify the parameters of the sphere you are about to create (see Fig. 3.72). Give the sphere 16 lines of Latitude and 24 lines of Longitude to create a smooth surface.[40] Now click the Sphere icon in the Primitives panel to draw a sphere.[41]

Figure 3.72
Specifying the parameters of the sphere.

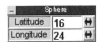

Move the planet over to the side and behind the ship, and make it larger. Click the Object Move icon, and then click anywhere in the workspace and drag the planet to the upper left corner of the screen (see Fig. 3.73). To make the planet larger, click the Object Scale tool, and then hold down both mouse buttons and drag the mouse diagonally up and to the right.

Click the Material Library icon, and then select a material to apply. Select the Paint Object tool from the Paint pop-up menu.

---

[40]The more lines, the smoother the sphere, but it takes more memory to draw it.

[41]Don't worry if your ship temporarily disappears; it will return after you move the planet out of its belly. Remember, we are pushing the capabilities of existing memory.

GUEST
AUTHOR

If you want to make truly realistic planets, you can import images into trueSpace and apply them as textures.[42] Right-click the Use Texture Map tool to open a Texture Map panel, as shown in Figure 3.74. Click the Get Textures button, and a standard Windows file requester opens from which you can select the image file to use as the basis of your new texture (see Fig. 3.75). Now when you select the Paint Object tool, your imported image is mapped onto the planet.

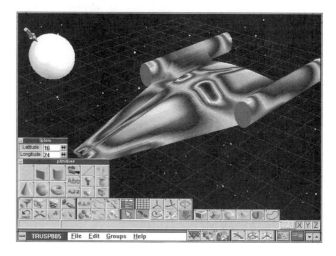

Figure 3.73
*Moving the planet
to the side.*

Figure 3.74
*Right-clicking Use
Texture Map.*

Figure 3.75
*Selecting the Get
Textures icon to
import an image
as a texture.*

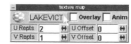

To see the final result of all this work, select Render Scene from the Render pop-up menu at the bottom of the toolbar. Feel free to move the ship and planet around to improve the scene. When you are finished, take a break. You just created a virtual universe, so you deserve a virtual day of rest.[43]

---

[42]Surprise—I've included on the CD-ROMs a couple of bitmaps that make pretty good planet surfaces (PLANET1.BMP and PLANET2.BMP).

[43]This universe is available ready-made as a scene file on the CD-ROMs (TRUSP006.SCN).

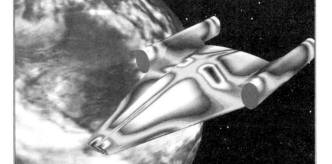

Figure 3.76
A virtual universe
with a starship,
planet, and stars.

Fly Your Starship Through a Gravitational Anomaly

You are going to need a little elbow room on the workspace, so let's shrink the starship and move it out of the way. Click the Object Scale tool, and then hold down both mouse buttons while dragging the mouse down and to the left until the ship is about two grid squares wide. Now click the Object Move tool and then click anywhere in the workspace and drag the ship to the far corner of the grid, as shown in Figure 3.77.

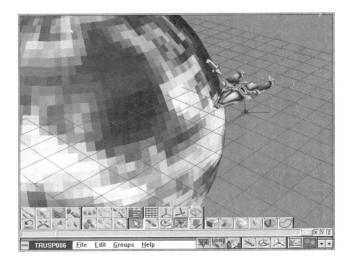

Figure 3.77
Shrinking the
starship and moving
it out of the way.

Build the Deformation

Click the Primitives icon to bring up the Primitives panel. Click the Free Standing Pipe for Deformation icon, as shown in Figure 3.78. A deformation pipe then is drawn in the workspace, as shown in Figure 3.79.

Figure 3.78
*Choosing the Free
Standing Pipe for
Deformation icon.*

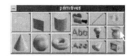

Figure 3.79
*A free-standing pipe
for deformation.*

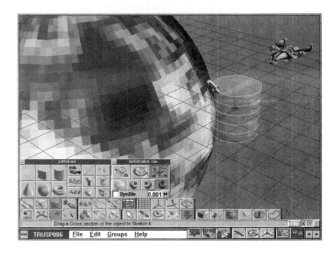

Click the Deformation Along a Plane Perpendicular to Z Axis icon in the Deformation Navigation panel (see Fig. 3.80). The pipe should have a green circle at the top, center, and bottom. Increase the number of rings to six by clicking anywhere in the workspace and dragging the mouse upward.

Figure 3.80
*The Deformation
Navigation panel.*

Now turn the pipe into a two-ended funnel (hourglass shape), as shown in Figure 3.81. Click the Stretch icon in the Deformation Navigation panel. Then click on one of the inner green rings of the pipe. The ring turns white. Hold down both mouse buttons and drag down and to the left to reduce the diameter of the selected ring. Reduce the other inner rings to produce a shape that looks like a two-ended funnel.

Lay the deformation funnel on its side by clicking the Object Rotate icon, and then clicking anywhere in the workspace and dragging diagonally down and to the left.

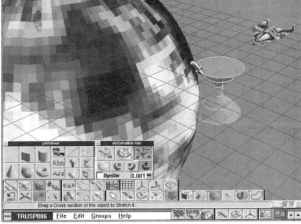

Figure 3.81
Turning the deformation pipe into a two-ended funnel.

Warm Up the Engines

Move the ship so that it is positioned to fly into one end of the funnel, as shown in Figure 3.82. Click the Object tool, then the Object Move icon, and then click on the ship. Now click and drag the ship in front of one end of the funnel. The ship needs to be lined up precisely for the effect to work, so use the Top view and Side view to refine the alignment. When you are satisfied with the alignment, go back to Perspective view.

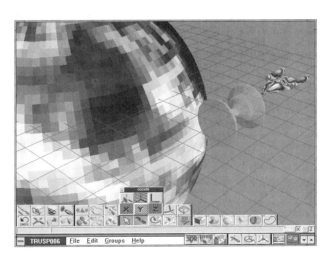

Figure 3.82
Positioning the starship to fly directly through the deformation funnel.

*Start
Deforming
by Stand-
Alone
Deforma-
tion Object
tool*

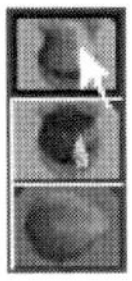

*Animation
tool*

Right-click the Object Move icon to bring up the Coordinates panel. Disable movement along the Y coordinate by clicking the Y button. Select the Start Deforming by Stand-Alone Deformation Object tool from the Deformation pop-up menu. Your mouse pointer now looks like a glue bottle. Click on the deformation funnel to associate it with your starship.

Click the Animation tool to bring up the Animation panel (see Fig. 3.83). Change the current frame number to 30 by clicking on the double arrow to the right of the number and dragging your mouse right or left to increase or decrease the setting. Alternatively, you can double-click on the number itself and enter a new value from your keyboard. After you change the number, press Enter, and the cursor will stop flashing.

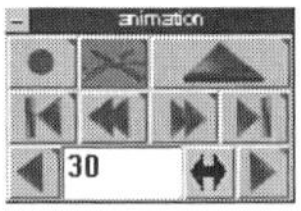

Figure 3.83
*Change the frame
number to 30 in the
Animation panel.*

Now move the starship through the funnel to the other side, as shown in Figure 3.84. You just created an animation. To see the animation, click Play on the Animation panel (see Fig. 3.85). Engage![44]

Figure 3.84
*Moving the starship
to a new position in
frame 30.*

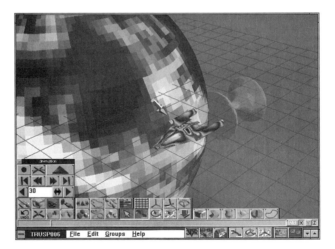

---

[44] A file with the completed animation scene is on the CD-ROMs (TRUSP007.SCN). A couple of AVI files with the starship are also on the CDs (TRUSP003.AVI and TRUSP004.AVI). Enjoy!

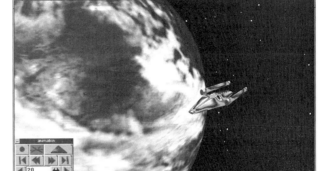

Figure 3.85
*A rendered frame
from the completed
animation.*

Video and 3D Modeling Software

One of the most fascinating ways to work with 3D modeling packages is to add video images. Many 3D packages support some form of animation, and video lets you mix virtual and real in sometimes powerful ways. In this chapter, you explore ways to use 3D modeling to enhance videos. In Chapter 10, "You Are the Star," you learn how to put video images into a virtual space. You can put an image of yourself in a dream reality, or you can put a product video inside a virtual-space presentation for a sales meeting.

Working with video adds a whole new dimension to 3D modeling.[45] And the reverse is true as well: Adding 3D modeling to video creates some visually stunning possibilities. In this section, you learn how to use several 3D modeling packages to create digital special effects for video files.

Issues with Video

Using video is not a trivial step. The results can be stunning, but if you are not already working with video, you might be surprised by the effort and technology required. It's not daunting by any means; with a minimum investment of time and money, you definitely can add videos or use 3D software to enhance your videos. Read through this section carefully to see whether you will be able to assemble the components you need. A minimum setup requires the following:

■ **A video source.** Right now, it's expensive to buy video clips, so you'll probably want a video camera. You can spend anywhere from $400 to $2,000 for a new camera (more if you want professional Windows software). The retail price of

---

[45]Did he really say that? Ouch!

this piece of the puzzle is the least of your worries—street prices are around $100, and it might even wind up as an integral part of Windows.

- **A tripod.** This is a minor item that can make a huge difference in quality. A tripod ensures steady images, which is very important when working with small image sizes. Make sure that you get a true video tripod with a fluid head.[46]

- **A video capture card.** A card that compresses video in real time is ideal; expect to spend around $500 for such a board. The Intel Smart Video Recorder is a good choice, but more boards are coming out all the time.

- **A fast computer.** I recommend at least a 486/66, 500M of hard disk space, fast seek time (12-millisecond average seek or better), and a very, very fast Windows accelerator video display card.

- **Video for Windows software.** The retail price of this piece of the puzzle is the least of your worries—street prices are around $100, and it might even wind up as an integral part of Windows.

- **3D modeling software.** Good choices include the two packages I describe in detail later in this chapter: 3D Studio from Autodesk and Imagine from Impulse. Imagine is much more affordable ($495 retail) than 3D Studio ($2,995).[47]

Some optional goodies make life a little easier:

- A video monitor for displaying the incoming video signal.

- Remote controls for all your equipment so you're not jumping up and down all the time to adjust things.

- A video output card to send animation to videotape.

- A second deck for dubbing and editing video material outside the computer. (If you do this, consider Video Director from Gold Disk; it could make your life substantially easier.)

- A high-end video-capture system. Standard video-capture cards, like the Intel Smart Video Recorder, are limited to image sizes of 320×240 and 15 frames per second (fps). Full-motion, full-frame video is 640×480 and 30 fps. For many applications, the smaller image size is fine—it enables you to display text as well as the video image on your computer screen. If you want to output edited video to tape, however, you'll need high-end equipment. Expect to pay from $5,000 to $50,000 for a full setup.

---

[46]A *fluid head* smoothes out motion when you pan the camera. Don't get a tripod for a still camera; it probably won't have a fluid head.

[47]Don't let the price difference fool you—Imagine is extremely powerful. Autodesk markets 3D Studio to folks who already are using things like AutoCAD, which is a limited market—thus the high price. If all you want to do is work in 3D modeling, then Imagine may be all you need. A warning, however: Imagine is extremely idiosyncratic. If you don't have an artistic orientation, you might find it frustrating. It also is challenging to learn to use well. The bottom line with Imagine is that a minority of folks who use it fall madly in love, while most folks simply never figure it out.

Obtaining Source Material

If you haven't worked with video before, you might be surprised to find out what's involved. It's not as simple as pointing a camera and clicking the Record button. After you get the steps down, however, it's pretty easy to do. There are many nuances to learn, of course, but I've had so much fun integrating video into my applications that it has never been a bother.

Let's assume that you are working with the Intel Smart Video Recorder,[48] and that you have a videotape with a sequence you want to capture. It might be a shot of a new product showing how it is used, or it might be the president of a company making pithy comments during a keynote address at a symposium on flywheel manufacturing. The complete process works like this:

1. Before you do anything else, defragment the hard disk you will use for capture. This is a must! A fragmented disk can seriously cut into your capability to capture video. The time spent hunting for the next available sector results in lost data. After you defragment, run VidCap (the Video for Windows Capture program) and use File/Set Capture File to create a large capture file. Allow from 10M to 25M per minute of video, depending on the card you are using and the image size you plan to capture. Refer to the manual that comes with your capture card for guidance, or experiment.

2. Queue the videotape to a point several seconds before the beginning of the sequence you want to capture. Most decks take a few moments to get started. Don't stop the tape at this point—just pause it. If you stop it, it will take even longer for the tape to get up to speed. Until the tape gets up to speed, there will be no audio.

3. Run the VidCap application that comes with Video for Windows (or any other application that supports video capture, such as Premiere from Adobe). Click the Capture Video icon or choose Capture/Video from the menu.

---

[48]I keep mentioning this card because it is far and away the most convenient to use. Just in case you think I'm biased or that Intel is paying for the endorsement, I'll mention some other cards that also do a good job. The Video Spigot, from Creative Labs, has excellent image quality, and comes with some clever options that give you more choices when it comes to playback. The Pro Movie Spectrum, from Media Vision, also does a good job, but I thought the image quality wasn't quite as good as in the Spigot. If you need overlay, consider the Bravado 16 from Truevision. It comes with an add-on, real-time, compression module; has room for a VGA-to-video daughter card; and has excellent image quality. The only hassle is that it won't enable you to have more than 15M of memory in your system.

4. Set the Capture options you want to use. For general use, I suggest Video Options set to 15 fps, 160×120, and the Indeo Video codec.[49] For audio, start with 8 bits, 22 kHz, and mono. After you get this much working, you can experiment with other settings. Click OK when everything is set the way you want it.

5. Another dialog box appears; clicking OK starts recording. Don't do that yet! Every second of video capture chews up lots of disk space. Start video play-back, and after about a second (or when your deck is up to speed and playing with a clean image), click the OK button to start capture. When you have the entire sequence (plus a little extra, just in case), press Esc on your keyboard and then click the Stop button on the video deck.

6. You now have the video sequence on your hard disk, but you are not done. Run VidEdit (it also comes with Video for Windows), and open the Capture file. Use Video/Compression options to set parameters for the file. If you want the file to be able to play satisfactorily on 386 machines, set the following compression options:

- CD-ROM 150K/second
- No Recompression or No Change, depending on what software you use for this step.
- Key frame set to 1

If you want the best possible image quality because you plan to use the file in a 3D animation, set the following compression options:

- Full Frame
- Data Rate will be gray
- Key Frame will be gray

> An important point to keep in mind: Saving a file without compression takes up an enormous amount of disk space. You can compromise by setting a very high data rate (say 300k/sec or more) and No Recompression. You'll learn more about this in the next section, "Image Quality."

Now use File/Save As to save the file with a new name. You now can use the Capture file to capture another sequence. This technique has the advantage of enabling you to use the same unfragmented Capture file over and over.

---

[49]*Codec* is a made-up word that has two possible origins. Some say it refers to encoding and decoding, and some say it refers to compression and decompression. Either way, it refers to a computer algorithm that handles both capture and playback. Take your pick.

In addition, it gives you the most compact file sizes and data rates for the best play-back on slower machines.

If you want more detailed information about using video, you can find it in my book, *PC Video Madness*, also from Sams Publishing. It contains a wealth of information about working with video on the PC.

Image Quality

Because you will almost certainly be working with video-image sizes in the range of 160×120 to 320×240, you'll need to pay special attention to image quality at several steps in the overall process. When you are shooting video, try to fill the frame with the subject. This makes the subject stand out, even at smaller image sizes. A steady camera is also very important—use a tripod whenever possible. You can find a decent video tripod for as little as $50, and it will be suitable for a typical miniature camcorder. If you own a larger or heavier camcorder, you'll need to spend more—anywhere from about $100 to $300.

During or after capture, when you compress the video[50] you need to make some decisions that maintain image quality. Uncompressed video isn't practical; full-motion, full-frame video occupies 1.5 gigabytes per minute![51] The more you compress, the lower the image quality. You need to find a balance point between quality, image size, frame rate, and the speed of the playback machine.

Life with Palettes

I have a saying regarding video playback: "24 bits or bust." A little history is necessary to explain why this is so.

When Windows was born, only 4 bits of data were available for specifying colors. That yields a grand total of 16 possible colors. You cannot do photographic-quality images with 16 colors. You can fake it using dithering, but the results are not very pleasing.

The next step forward was to 8-bit color; that gives us 256 colors to work with. Actually, it's a little better than that; the design used to implement 256-color support lets you pick which 256 colors you want to use at any one time from a universe of more than 16 million colors. The selection of colors in use at any one time is called a *palette*. If you want to display an image that uses colors different from those in the current palette, you need merely switch to a different palette. Presto! You can display images that use a wide variety of colors.

---

[50]Compression is a complex area. There are no general guidelines for how to compress. Trade-offs are involved. Higher compression results in smaller files and enables you to play back on slower machines. Image quality is reduced, however. You have to experiment to find out what you prefer.

[51]That's why video is supported mostly in small sizes like 160×120 or 240×180.

The reality isn't quite so presto. If you have an image displayed on-screen when you change the palette, the colors in that image get changed—there's only one palette, and if you change it, everything changes. This is the Achilles heel of using palettes. Every time you change the palette, any images already on-screen get their colors scrambled. This can be so severe that you can completely lose any suggestion of what the first image actually showed. Fortunately, when you go back to the original image (give it the focus, in Windows-speak), its palette gets restored, and it looks fine. Any other images in the background, of course, will look odd because *their* palette isn't currently in use.

Thus, my slogan: 24 bits or bust. 24-bit color gives you instant, simultaneous access to all 16+ million colors. And at today's prices—less than $100 for 24-bit video at 640×480—24-bit color is very affordable. Not only that, but 24-bit color looks dramatically better than any palette ever will. If you don't want the overhead of pushing all 24 bits around for every pixel on your screen, 16-bit color does a good job. It avoids the palette problems, provides enough color for general use, and has one-third less calories than true color.

And here's the clincher: The best codecs automatically store video data as 24-bit color. If you don't have 24-bit in your system, it fakes it—it dithers the image to use the current set of 256 colors to display the image. This is OK, but you miss seeing how good the video image really is. If you are going to work with video, use the best possible video display card you can afford. The results are worth it. If you must keep costs down, or if you want to work at high resolutions like 1,024×768 or 1,280×1,024, 16-bit color is also very good and is an excellent compromise.

At the very high end, 32 bits of color data are used. This includes 24-bit color, plus an 8-bit alpha channel. The alpha channel is used to define transparent and translucent areas of the image. Some hardware, such as color scanners, uses 32, 48, or even 64 bits of color information, but these are not often encountered in the everyday computer world. All of this says nothing about display technology; would you believe there is already research being done on using lasers to project images directly onto the retina of your eye? Now there's a technology that has **SAFE** stamped all over it!

3D Studio

Have you ever been in a situation where you knew what you had to do, didn't like doing it, and had to do it anyway? That's the position that I'm in when it comes to writing about 3D Studio from Autodesk. First, the good news: I love what I can do with this program. Next, the bad news: the software costs almost $3,000 and uses a hardware dongle[52] as well. These are major inconveniences in this day and age of

---

[52]The word *dongle* has an interesting origin, or so I've read in the ads from a company that sells them to software vendors. The ad said that the inventor of the little hardware clump (which you attach to your parallel port so the software knows you are the true and legal owner of the software) was named *Don Gull*. I'm just a teensy-weensy bit skeptical on that one.

$99 software. Why, in the very next section, I'll be describing the wonders of a product that retails for one-sixth of that. The question becomes, "Why bother with an expensive product like 3D Studio?"[53]

Because there are times when nothing else will do. As you see in this section, 3D Studio can produce some really fantastic effects.

RECIPE

1 Video for Windows file
1t Premiere 4.0
4 cups 3D Studio
8M to 16M of memory
1 hot CPU

Instructions: Convert the AVI file to a FLC file, and then attach it as a texture map to an object in 3D Studio. Animate the object to create a digital special effect—wipes, explosions, flips, flying videos—you name it. Convert back to AVI and serve.[54] Makes an excellent appetizer in multimedia titles, or serve between courses to clear the palette. Don't forget to reserve audio and put it back into the AVI file when you do the final conversion!

Getting Started

Before you can use a video file in 3D Studio, you need to convert it to a file format that 3D Studio can read: FLC or FLI. These are animation file formats.[55] The conversion process is easy, but you need extra software to pull it off. Almost any video-editing software will do the trick. In this example, I'll show you how to pull it off using Premiere 4.0 from Adobe. Premiere is a very powerful video editor. We won't be exposing any of the power under the hood, but if you are interested in video editing, Premiere is, well, the premiere product in this category.

---

[53]Especially when Autodesk sent it to me at no cost, and I should be grateful and keep my mouth shut.

[54]Actually, this concoction might best be described as a kind of club sandwich: 3D Studio in the middle, Animator Pro on both sides of that, and VidEdit on the outside. A little mayo, and you've got lunch at your desk.

[55]FLI is the original animation file format from Autodesk, and is limited to 320×200 size animations. The FLC format is much more efficient, and also is flexible in image size. Whenever possible, use the FLC format.

Premiere is a complex product, as you can guess from looking at the program in Figure 3.86.

The Premiere interface is very intuitive. To load the AVI file of your choice, simply double-click in the window at the lower left: the Project window. This opens the Import dialog box, shown in Figure 3.87.

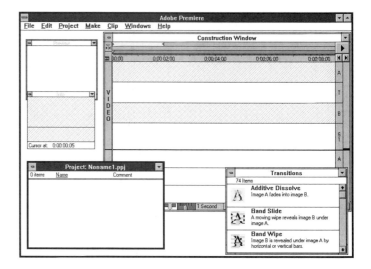

Figure 3.86
The Premiere window, showing the principal program components.

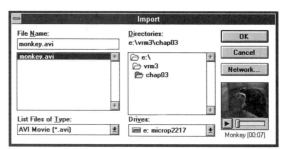

Figure 3.87
Importing a Video for Windows file.

In this example, I'm loading a file called MONKEY.AVI. Note that the first frame of the video clip is previewed at the lower right of the Import dialog box. Figure 3.88 shows the file imported into the Project window.

Before you can do anything with the video clip, you have to add it to the Construction window at the top right. This is easy to do—click and drag the image of the clip from the Project window to the top horizontal band in the Construction window. Figure 3.89 shows the result.

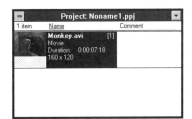

Figure 3.88
A file in the Project window.

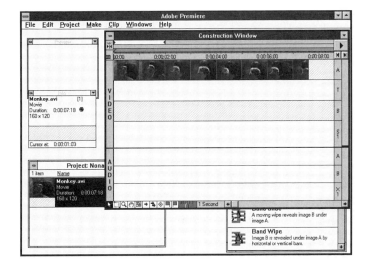

Figure 3.89
Adding the clip to the Construction window.

That's the bulk of the real work. You could, if you wanted, add special effects, combine video clips, or perform other magic on the video using Premiere. But that's a subject for a different book! All that remains is to set the parameters for the output file. Because Premiere is normally used to output AVI files, we need to make a number of changes to set it up to output a FLC file.

Click the Make menu, and then click the Make Movie menu selection. This opens the Make Movie dialog box, shown in Figure 3.90. Look at those two buttons at the bottom of the dialog box: Output Options on the left and Compression on the right. Click the Output Options button to display the dialog box shown in Figure 3.91.

There are three things to pay attention to here. First, make sure that the drop-down box at the upper left shows the Entire Project option. Second, make sure that the size of the output is correct. It should be the same as the input file size. Third, at the upper right, make sure that the drop-down box shows the Autodesk FLC/FLI option. This is the file format 3D Studio will use later. Click OK when the settings are correct.

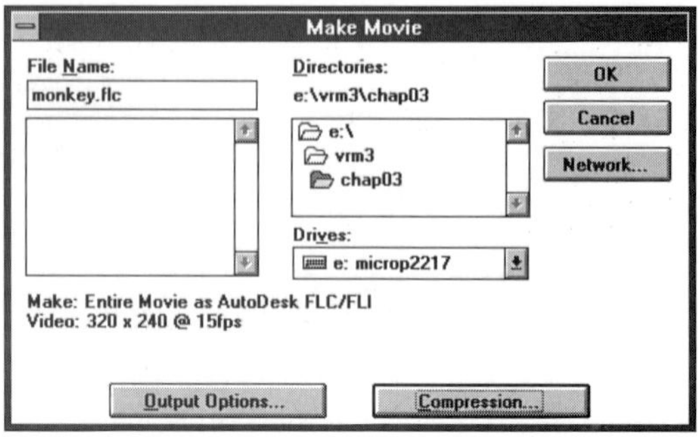

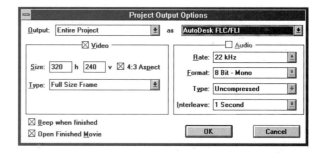

Figure 3.90
Making a Movie.

Figure 3.91
*Setting output
options.*

Because we are not outputting a Video for Windows or QuickTime video clip, the Compression options do not apply, and can be safely ignored. Enter a file name (MONKEY.FLC, in this example) and click the OK button in the Make Movie dialog box. This starts the process of making the movie. There are two steps, both shown graphically by Premiere. First, Premiere creates a palette for the FLC file, showing progress using the graphic shown in Figure 3.92. Premiere then converts the video to an animation, frame by frame, showing progress as it goes (see Fig. 3.93).

When the clip is complete, Premiere displays the animation in a Clip window, as shown in Figure 3.94.

Once you have a FLC file, it's time to run 3D Studio.

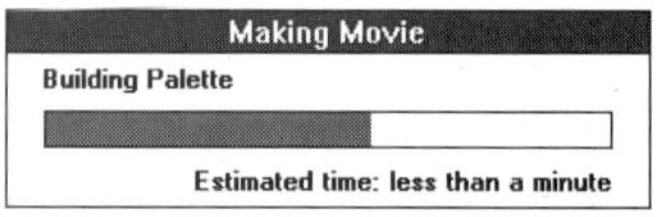

Figure 3.92
*Creating a palette for
the animation file.*

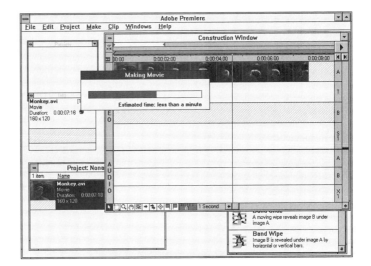

Figure 3.93
*Saving the
animation file.*

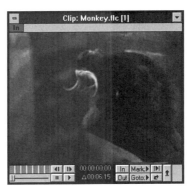

Figure 3.94
*The animation in
a Clip window.*

Creating Objects in 3D Studio

The opening screen of 3D Studio is shown in Figure 3.95. There are four viewports, a menu at the upper right, and several icons at the lower left.

The standard types of viewports follow:

Top—This shows your 3D creation from above.

Front—A front view of the scene.

Left—A view from the left side.

User—A 3D view, sometimes referred to as an *orthographic projection*.

There are additional viewport types available, but you can only display up to four at one time.

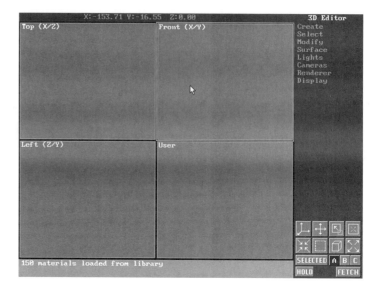

Figure 3.95
*The opening screen
of 3D Studio.*

Unlike the menus you might be familiar with in most graphics programs, 3D Studio's menu is vertical. Clicking a top-level menu item, such as Create, displays the next level of commands (look ahead to Fig. 3.98 to see an example).

The icon group at the lower right of the screen gives you access to a number of common actions (see Fig. 3.96).

In this example, you learn how to use 3D Studio to create one style of video transition. You can apply the same basic techniques to a wide variety of special effects, however. I'll offer some suggestions at the end of this section. In the example, we'll shrink one video to reveal another video behind it.

You need precise sizes for your objects, so turn on Snap using the View menu (see Fig. 3.97). I also turn on Grid Points to show the locations that I'm snapping to. The most common video file size is 160×120 pixels, so we'll create an object with exactly those dimensions. To create an object, choose Create from the menu at the upper right, and then click Box (see Fig. 3.98).

Click anywhere in the upper left of the Front viewport, and drag the mouse until you have a rectangle that is exactly 160 units wide and 120 units high.[56] You can verify the exact size at the top of the screen (see Fig. 3.98). Note that 3D Studio prompts you for the required action at the bottom of the screen in a status bar.

---

[56]3D Studio doesn't use any specific real-world measurement system; a unit can be anything you want it to be—feet, inches, meters, miles, and so on.

After you define the rectangular shape, you are asked to set the depth of the box. Unless you want to attach the video to a box with depth, set the depth to be minimal by clicking twice in the same place—once to anchor the depth setting and once to define its length as zero. The completed, ultra-thin box is shown in Figure 3.99.

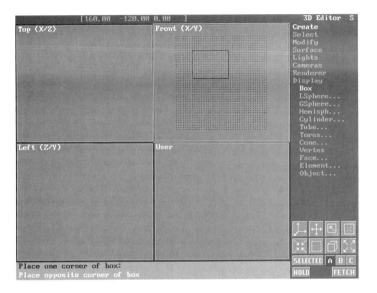

Figure 3.96
*The 3D Studio
icon group.*

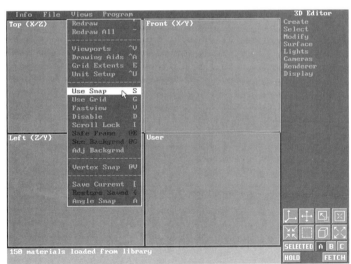

Figure 3.97
*Turning on Snap
in 3D Studio.*

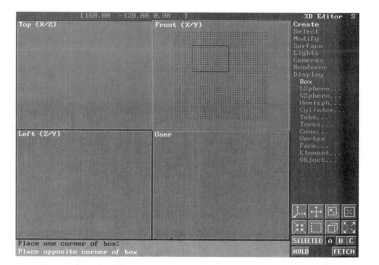

Figure 3.98
Creating a box.

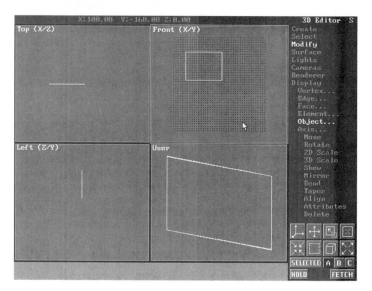

Figure 3.99
A 160×120 box defined in 3D Studio.

Now click on the Modify menu and choose Object/Move. To create the second object,[57] hold down the Shift key when you click on the object we just created. This clones the object, giving us a second ultra-flat box just the right size, as shown in Figure 3.100. After creating the clone using Move, you need to reposition the new object to cover the first object.

---

[57] For the second video sequence, of course.

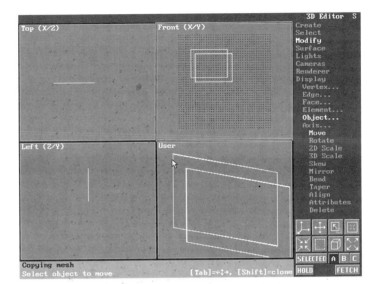

Figure 3.100
A cloned object.

Mapping

You add a video sequence to an object as a texture map. To apply a map, you need to define mapping coordinates so that 3D Studio knows where to position the bitmaps and at what scale. In this case, the object is the same proportion as the video, 160×120, so the easiest way to do this is to fit the map to the object. Use the Surface/Mapping/Aspect/Region Fit[58] menu option to display the mapping coordinates. Figure 3.101 shows (in the upper right viewport) mapping coordinates that are both offset from and larger than the object. The cross hairs are located at the upper left corner of the object to define the upper left extent of the map, and you just need to click and drag to the lower right corner of the object to properly fit the mapping coordinates.[59]

Figure 3.102 shows mapping coordinates properly applied. The image has been zoomed in to show just the object being worked on. Note that there is a small vertical line at the top of the rectangle; this little handle defines "up" for the map. Fortunately, it's already pointing in the right direction. If it weren't, we would use the Surface/Mapping/Adjust/Rotate option to change it.

---

[58]This business of putting slashes between menu commands is the standard way of referring to 3D Studio menu options, and is used throughout this section.

[59]If you try to render an object that has a map but no mapping coordinates, you get an error message. It can't be done!

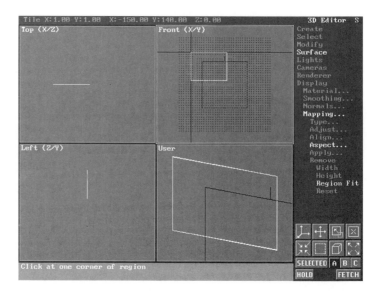

Figure 3.101
*Default mapping
coordinates.*

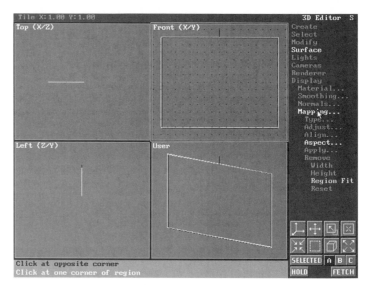

Figure 3.102
*Mapping coordinates
fitted to an object.
Note the handle at
the top, indicating
"up."*

The next step is to apply the coordinates to both objects, using Surface/Mapping/
Apply/Object. In order to apply the mapping coordinates, we need to select an object. With one object on top of the other, as in this case, however, you can't do that
by clicking—the click always selects the object on top. To select an object by name,
simply press the H key instead of clicking. This displays a list of objects from which
to choose (see Fig. 3.103). When you choose the object from the list, the action specified by the current menu option is applied to that object. You can apply the same
mapping coordinates to both objects.

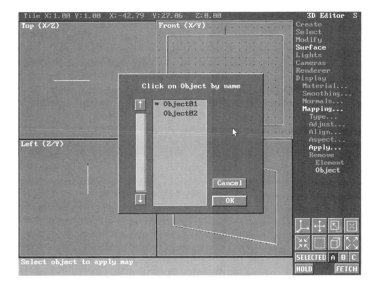

Figure 3.103
*Selecting objects
by name.*

Materials

After you have added mapping coordinates, the next step is to apply a material. This material will, in effect, paste the FLC file's images onto the object. Creating custom materials like this is easy with 3D Studio. You use the Material Editor to create new surface materials. To start the Material Editor, press the F5 key. The Material Editor screen is shown in Figure 3.104.[60] The blank squares at the top of the screen are slots for showing the appearance of new materials. The controls at the middle of the screen are used to set the color and other characteristics of the material. The four groups of buttons at the bottom of the screen are the ones we are interested in—they control mapping. Before we start, however, move the mouse to the top of the screen to activate the menu and click Option/Cube. The default setting renders to a sphere; because you'll be rendering to a flat surface, the cube gives a more representative example.

It's very easy to create a texture map. Click on the Texture 1 file name button (see Fig. 3.105), under the words Map Type. This opens a dialog box that enables you to select the file you want to use. Click the file name (MONKEY.FLC, for this example), and then click OK. The file name is displayed on the Texture Map file name button. To see what the texture map will look like, click the Render Sample button at the bottom right. A small-scale rendering is displayed in the current material slot at the top of the screen.

---

[60]Due to the limitations of the screen-capture software, I had to use a reduced screen resolution to show 256 colors in the Material Editor. The images in this section were taken at 320×240×256 colors; if you have a Super VGA adapter, you almost certainly will want to use 640×480×256 colors.

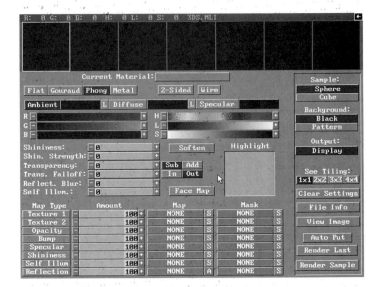

Figure 3.104
The Material Editor screen in 3D Studio.

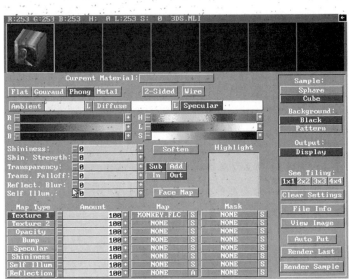

Figure 3.105
An example rendering of a texture map.

That's all there is to it. We won't be using any of the other features in the Material Editor for this example. If we want to, we can set characteristics such as shininess, rendering quality, transparency, and more. We also can create bump maps (to determine surface texture based on an image file) or reflection maps (to determine what will reflect off the surface).

To save the material, press the P key to put the material into the Material library. A dialog box asks you for the material name; enter any name that fits in the space provided. Spaces are OK. Because we have two objects, each with a different AVI file, in this case, you also would create a second material using a second FLC file. After you place both materials into the library, press the F3 key to return to the 3D Editor.

Next, you'll want to apply the new material to the objects. Use the Surface/Material/Choose option to select one of the new materials, as shown in Figure 3.106. In this case, the material is called Monkey Antics. Click OK when you have the right material selected.

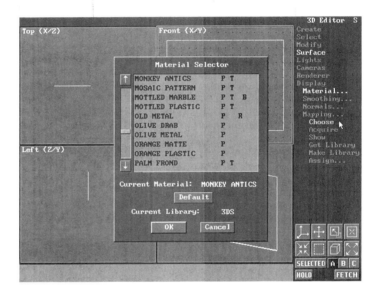

Figure 3.106
Selecting a new material with the Material Selector.

To apply the material to an object, use Surface/Material/Assign/Object. Then choose the second new material and apply it to the other object.

At this point, both rectangles are in the same plane, and you need to move one of them in front of the other. You can use Select/Object/Single to make one of the rectangles the current object, and then move the selected object. Press the H key to open the Click on Object by Name dialog box, and select the object that you want to move to the front; then click OK.

Now use Modify/Object/Move, which changes the cursor to a small box with arrows, as shown in Figure 3.107. Click in the Top viewport to activate it,[61] and then press Tab until the little arrows are pointing up and down. To move the currently selected object, click the Selected button at the bottom right, and then use the mouse to move

---

[61]Only if it is not already activated.

the selected object just ever so slightly downward. Because we are working in the Top viewport, this has the effect of moving the object toward the front. Figure 3.107 shows how little of an offset is necessary.

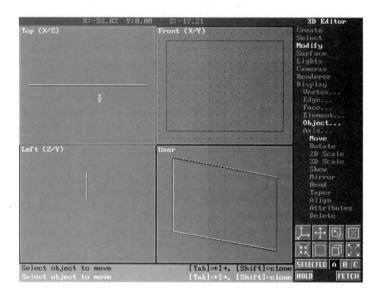

Figure 3.107
Moving an object.

This is a good time to check your work. Use the Renderer/Render menu option, and click in the User viewport to select it as the view to render. You should see the Render Still Image dialog box (see Fig. 3.108); if you don't, click the User viewport a second time.[62] Make sure that the Disk button is not highlighted, and then click the Render button to render to the screen. During rendering, you see a Rendering in Progress dialog box (see Fig. 3.109).

After a few moments, you see a rather dim image, as shown in Figure 3.110. You probably won't be able to recognize the image at all. The reason for this is simple: This is virtual reality—there is almost no light to illuminate the scene unless we add the light.

---

[62]If the User viewport wasn't the active viewport, it won't render on the first click. The first click in a viewport always has the effect of activating it, rather than carrying out a menu action. This is a safety feature; it prevents you from taking actions you don't want to take and enables you to move to a different viewport and continue the current operation there.

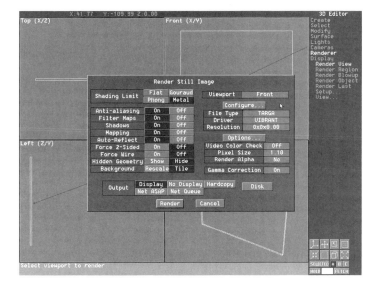

Figure 3.108
Rendering a still image.

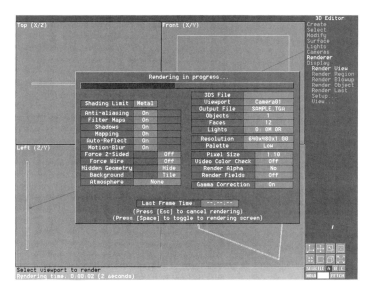

Figure 3.109
The Rendering in Progress message box.

By default, the ambient light in a scene is set to a value of 77. There are 256 possible values, from 0 to 255; a value of 77 represents 77/256 or 30 percent of full lighting—not much at all. The default value is displayed if you choose Lights/Ambient from the menu, as shown in Figure 3.111. I suggest a setting in the range of 200 to 255 for adequate lighting. If you want colored lighting for special effects, use the RGB or HSL settings to create the color you want.

Figure 3.110
*A rendered scene,
but with inadequate
lighting.*

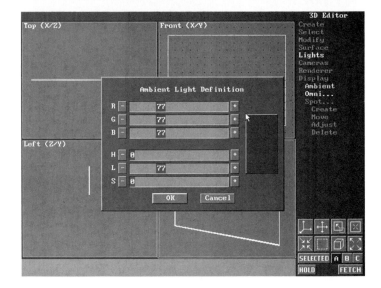

Figure 3.111
*Adjusting ambient
lighting.*

If you choose Renderer/Render again and render the scene to the screen, you see more natural results (see Fig. 3.112).

3D Studio also enables you to create two special types of lights. These are *omni lights*, which are point sources of light; and *spotlights*, which cast shadows and have adjustable light cones. You can create quite intricate lighting arrangements by using several kinds of lights in different positions.

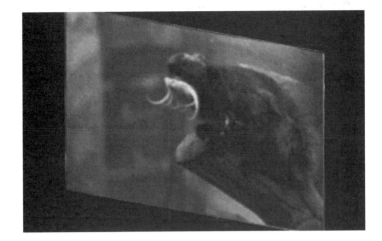

Figure 3.112
A scene rendered with adequate lighting.

Animating

Here's a summary of what we've done so far:

- Converted the AVI file to a FLC file or a series of TGA files
- Created two objects the same size as the video images
- Applied mapping coordinates to the objects
- Created two materials using texture maps—one for each video file
- Assigned the new materials to the objects
- Adjusted lighting values

Everything is now in place; it's time to animate. Animation takes place in the Keyframer, which you can access by pressing the F4 key. The opening screen of the Keyframer is shown in Figure 3.113. It's similar to the 3D Editor screen, but there are some important differences. The four viewports are the same, but the menu is different. There are two new buttons above the icons: Track Info and Key Info. These buttons enable you to modify key points along the animation track to fine-tune the animation or to delete key animation events.

The buttons below the icons are standard VCR-style controls for moving from frame to frame or for playing the animation sequence.

You can view an animation in several ways. You can use a standard viewport, such as Front view, which gives you a Plane view (flat, with no perspective). You also can render from the User viewport, which gives you an orthogonal view (3D, with no perspective). Or, you can create a camera, which gives you full 3D and perspective. For our purposes, the flat, no-perspective view is ideal—there will be no distortion of the rectangle during the special effect. The Front viewport is best, of course, but there is empty space around the objects. We want to fill the frame with the image.

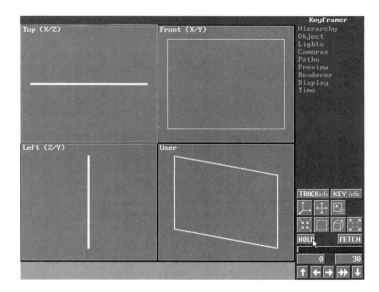

Figure 3.113
The Keyframer
screen.

Figure 3.114 shows the Zoom icon in action. The upper left corner of the object has been clicked, and you then can drag the mouse to mark the lower right boundary of the viewport.

Figure 3.115 shows the result of this zoom. The left and right borders of the object now are coincident with the viewport. Don't worry about the fact that the top and bottom of the object aren't lined up with the viewport. You can set the aspect ratio of the rendering so that only the actual object appears in the scene. Of course, if you wanted black space around the image, you would adjust the zoom factor accordingly.

Using the Keyframer, you do not have to create every frame of the animation. In fact, in this case, we can create a single key frame, and the Keyframer generates all the intervening frames. Use the controls at the bottom right to move to the last frame. By default, the Keyframer creates 30 frames. At 30 frames per second, that's two seconds of video—about right for an effect.

This is a good point to talk about how to select the proper parts of your video sequence for the effect. Let's suppose that you have one video sequence that is 33 seconds, and a second sequence that is 14 seconds. For this example, you would export the last two seconds of the first video, and the first two seconds of the second video. After you complete the generation of the effect, you splice the pieces together like this:

31 sec. of first video + 2-second effect + last 12 sec. of second video

This yields a total of 45 seconds of video. We lost two seconds because two seconds of each video now are playing simultaneously.

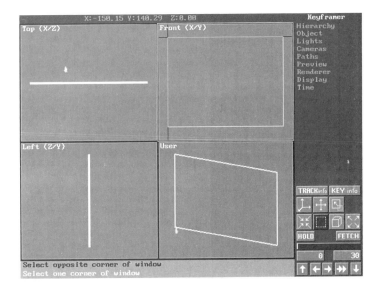

Figure 3.114
Adjusting the zoom factor of a viewport.

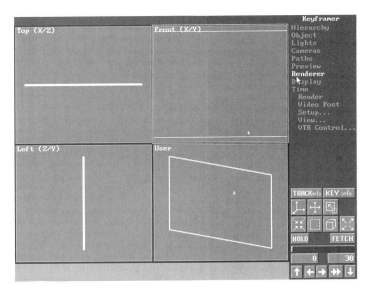

Figure 3.115
The zoom has been adjusted to match the object and the viewport.

Back to the Keyframer: We now are at frame 30, the last frame in the sequence. The desired effect is to have the front video shrink away to nothing at the center of the other frame. Choose Object/Scale, and then click on the front object (use the H as described earlier if you want to select it by name). Drag the mouse sideways to change the scale of the object. Depending on your screen resolution, you might need to zoom in and scale the object a second time to make it small enough to "disappear" during the rendering. Any size below 1 unit will be smaller than a single pixel in the final rendering. Figure 3.116 shows the scaling operation in progress, and Figure 3.117 shows the completed scaling.

To show that the Keyframer really does create all the intervening frames, look at Figure 3.118. It shows frame 15 of the animation—yes, the front object is exactly halfway along in the shrinking process.

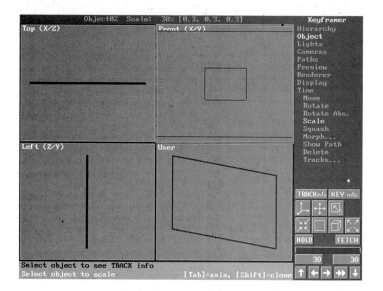

Figure 3.116
The scaling operation in progress.

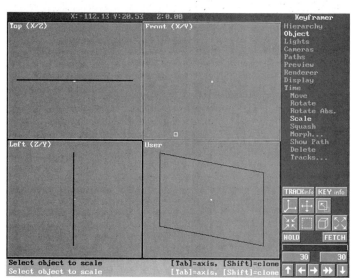

Figure 3.117
The scaling operation completed.

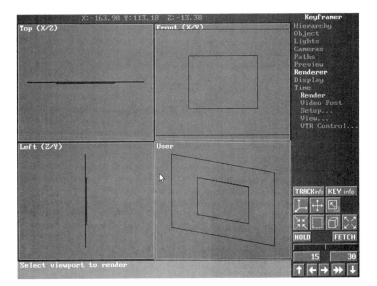

Figure 3.118
Frame 15 of the animation.

Rendering the Animation

After you create the animation sequence as a wireframe model, as outlined earlier, you are ready to render the animation as a FLC file. Before you render, you need to configure the system. Choose Renderer/Setup/Configure, which displays the dialog box shown in Figure 3.119.

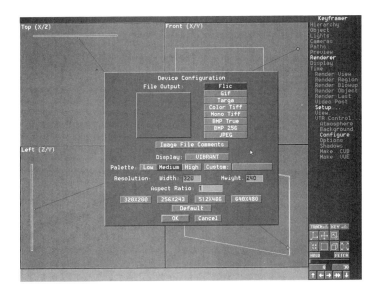

Figure 3.119
Configuring for rendering.

I suggest turning off compressed output—make sure that the Compressed button is not highlighted (this button will be invisible if compression is not available for the chosen file format). This keeps image quality at the highest possible level. You have the option of outputting as a FLC file or a series of images. If you plan to use Animator Pro to output BMP files, go ahead and save your work as a FLC file. If you want to use a utility to convert numbered files to bitmaps, select the file format you want—GIF, TGA, or TIF.

There are three palette choices listed, but only two of them are worth considering: Medium and High. See Table 3.1 for information about the palette choices. For most cases, the Medium setting is fine.

You also need to set an appropriate image size. You can set three parameters: Width, Height, and Aspect Ratio. Width and Height are obvious: Use numbers that are in the same proportion as the objects. In this example, I have used 320×240, exactly twice the size of the originals. The primary consideration when deciding on image size is the machine you plan to use for playback. The smaller the image size, the better it plays on slow machines. Set the aspect ratio to 1. This is the ratio of pixel width and height.

After you have the configuration set, it's time to render. Choose Renderer/Render from the menu, and click in the viewport you want to render (Front). This displays the dialog box shown in Figure 3.120.

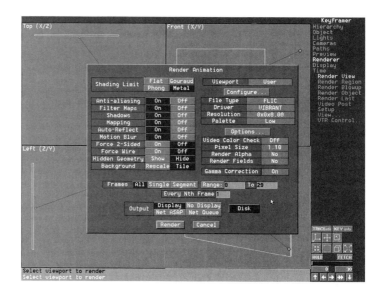

Figure 3.120
Setting up for
rendering.

Table 3.1. Rendering Palette Choices.

Choice	Description
Low	The Renderer creates an optimal 256-color palette for the first frame and then uses that palette for all subsequent frames. Unless the first frame is highly representative of the remaining frames, this is not a good option.
Medium	The Renderer creates an optimal 256-color palette for each frame in the animation and then combines the palettes into one optimal palette.
High	Each frame is rendered with 24-bit color. After rendering is complete, a single, 256-color palette is calculated. This option takes the most time, but gives the best results. It also uses a lot of disk space—72M in the case of a 562-frame animation I created.

For this example, accept the default settings for rendering. You can test the animation by picking a representative frame and rendering a single frame. Click the Single button, make sure the Disk button is not highlighted, and then click the Render button. You are asked whether you want to render to the screen only; click OK. When rendering is complete, you see an image like the one in Figure 3.121. This is frame 15—the front image has shrunk halfway.

If the image meets your approval, it's time to render the complete animation. Choose Renderer/Render to redisplay the Render dialog box. This time, click the Disk button to highlight it and click the All button. After you click the Render button, you are asked to supply a file name. If you chose to render as a series of numbered frames, enter a name like **FILE*.GIF** or **FILE*.TGA**, depending on the file format you want. Otherwise, enter a file name of up to eight characters. Depending on the complexity of the animation, the image size, and the palette setting, the time to render each frame can vary from a few seconds to a few minutes.

If you rendered the animation as a FLC file, there are two ways to import it into VidEdit. You can run a program like Animator Pro or Animator Studio and then save the file as a series of BMP files. You then can load the files as a DIB Sequence in VidEdit using the File/Insert menu option (see Fig. 3.122). Or, you can simply use the File/Open command and load the FLC file into VidEdit. In many cases, using File/Open works just fine. In some cases, you may find that the conversion did not work properly.[63] In such a case, you have to go back and create bitmaps to insert.

---

[63]Symptoms of incorrect importing include bits of prior frames floating around in the current frame, misalignment of images (horizontal or vertical offsets within the image frame), size distortion, and so on.

Figure 3.121
A rendered frame
from the animation.

If you rendered the animation as a series of image files, use a utility like Image Pals or Graphic Workshop to convert the files to DIBs with a BMP extension. You then can use File/Insert to import the images.

Figure 3.123 shows the entire 30-frame animation as a series of bitmaps loaded in the Image Pals utility program. The first frame is at the upper left, and the animation progresses from left to right, and top to bottom.

Figure 3.122
The File/Insert menu
in VidEdit.

Figure 3.123
A 30-frame animation as a series of bitmap images in Image Pals.

Finishing Up with VidEdit

After you have a series of bitmaps, you are ready to finish up the process using VidEdit. Figure 3.122 shows the File/Insert menu option, and Figure 3.124 shows the dialog box that this menu option opens. To load a DIB sequence, first select DIB Sequence in the List Files of Type drop-down list at the bottom left of the dialog box. Note that the default extension is *.DIB. Change it to *.BMP and press Enter. This displays all BMP files in the current directory (left of center in Figure 3.124). Click the first file name in the sequence you want (FADE0001.BMP, in this example) and click the OK button. This displays the dialog box shown in Figure 3.125. Click DIB Sequence in the Select the File Format box, and then click OK.

VidEdit reads in the file. A message box appears, showing the progress of the operation if there is a large number of DIBs to load. Figure 3.126 shows the sequence loaded into VidEdit. After you have the sequence in VidEdit, you can fine-tune frame rate, add audio, and so on—all the things that VidEdit is designed for.

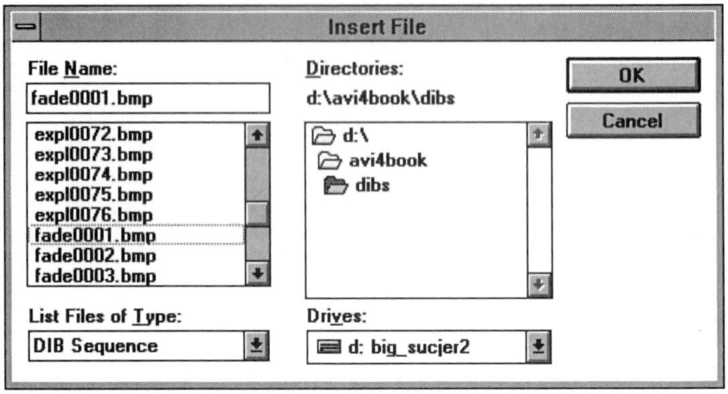

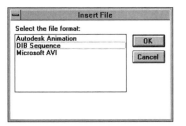

Figure 3.124
Selecting the first file in a DIB sequence.

Figure 3.125
Inserting a DIB sequence.

Figure 3.126
A video special effect loaded into VidEdit.

If we assume that we started with one video sequence of 33 seconds and a second one of 14 seconds, you need to perform the following steps in VidEdit to complete the process:

1. Open another instance of VidEdit and use Edit/Copy to copy the first 31 seconds of the first video to the Clipboard.

2. Go to the original instance of VidEdit, move to the beginning of the special effect, and use Edit/Paste.

3. Go to the second instance of VidEdit and open the second video file. Use Edit/Copy to place the last 12 seconds of the video into the Clipboard.

4. Go to the original instance of VidEdit, move to the end of the file, and use Edit/Paste.

5. If you will be saving the video using a 24-bit codec, skip to the next step. If you will be using an 8-bit codec, choose Video/Create Palette and click the Paste Palette button when it appears. Then save the file as described in the next step.

6. To save the file, use the appropriate settings. If you want to ensure that the video will be viewable on the widest range of computers, use the parameters shown in Figure 3.127. When using Indeo in particular, a key frame setting of 1 ensures that you will avoid any ghosting or weird delta frame[64] effects on slower machines.

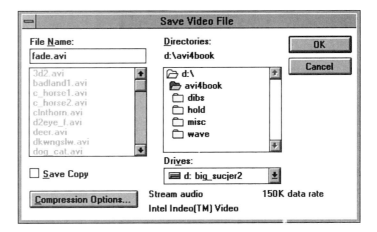

Figure 3.127
Setting Compression options in VidEdit.

Imagine

Imagine is a 3D modeling package that originated on the Amiga. I can sum up Imagine in one sentence: It is a really cool product that can be frustrating to learn how to use. A love/hate relationship is almost inevitable with Imagine. There are times while using the program when I ask myself, "Why am I using this program?" Sooner or later, the answer comes knocking: I'll find a way to create a truly organic object that would be nearly impossible to create using a different program.

But that doesn't quite describe what it's like to get started with Imagine. After all, you can't use a program until you learn *how* to use it! Without qualification, I would say that Imagine was the hardest program to learn that I have encountered. You would think that it would have to be pretty darn useful to still get reviewed in this book,

---

[64]A *delta frame* is a frame between key frames. The Greek letter *delta* has been used for many years by mathematicians and scientists to indicate change; a delta frame only contains information about changes, not an entire frame of data.

and you would be correct. To give you a clear idea of how Imagine works, I will take you through its operations one tiny step at a time. For that reason, this particular section is much more detailed than many other sections.[65]

RECIPE

4 cups Imagine
4M to 8M of memory
1M expanded memory
1 math coprocessor/486 CPU
1 VESA-compatible video display card
1 truckload patience

Instructions: Allow adequate time for preparation; ingredients may not blend properly at first. Using Imagine is a lot like making whipped cream: Stop too soon, and you'll have nothing but the time you spend; get it just right, and you'll have a delight. This is a real chance to let out your inner artiste.

The opening screen of Imagine is appropriately perplexing. It's just a logo, with no menu in evidence (see Fig. 3.128). To access the menu, you need to click at the top of the screen. To get started, click on the Project menu, and then click New.[66] If you never even got to the opening screen, chances are you don't have any expanded memory. It's easy to add. Look at the line for emm386 in your CONFIG.SYS file. If it

---

[65]I almost feel obligated to do this—the manual that comes with Imagine has a long list of faults. #1: The manual was written for the Amiga, where Imagine was born, and there is absolutely no attempt to translate for the PC user. #2: There is no index. #3: (and I'm just getting started) It's nearly impossible to find the information you need in the narrative because it wanders around quite a bit. #4: The manual is written as though the author knows what you want to do and why, and I think that's patronizing and out of place in a good software manual. #5: The entire manual is written as a single tutorial. There's no reference section at all. One good point: The information is all there if you can be patient enough to extract it. Author Phillip Shaddock, a good friend of mine, wrote the manual for version 3.0 of Imagine at the same time that I wrote the second edition of this book. Phil's efforts have dramatically improved the manual for Imagine.

[66]Many menu selections also have corresponding key sequences to activate them. I've never used an Amiga, so I can't judge the portions of the interface that were carried over from the Amiga. However, some of them make no sense at all on the PC. To activate Alt key sequences, for example, you must use the right Alt key. The left Alt key—the one most of us use—won't do it.

says noems, change it to 1024 instead. This gives you 1M of expanded memory. You can allocate more if you have 8M or more of system memory.

After you name the project, you see the screen shown in Figure 3.129. Click the New button to create a rendering subproject, which displays the dialog box shown in Figure 3.130. There are many buttons and text windows, but you only need to understand a few of them to get started. Most important: Rendering Method and Picture Size. Set Scanline for the rendering method; this gives you most of the features you want in solid modeling, but without ray-tracing features.[67] This is good for seeing what your image looks like without spending a lot of time getting there. When you finish the design, you can render with the Trace setting, which gives you full ray-tracing capabilities. Set an image size that meets your needs—320×200 or 640×480 is a good starting place.

Figure 3.128
*The Imagine
opening screen.*

Imagine comes from the Amiga, so the text windows take a little getting used to. You can't just enter text; you must press Enter to "lock in" the text you've entered. If you don't press Enter, the text change does not take place. Exiting an Imagine dialog box is a two-step process: press Enter to exit the text window, and click an OK button to exit the dialog box.

---

[67]*Ray tracing* involves creating an image by tracing the path of light rays in the scene. This is a very exact way of handling complex phenomena like reflections, but it takes longer to render this way.

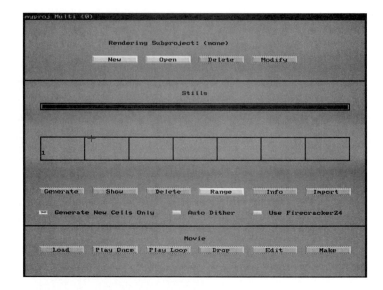

Figure 3.129
*The Project Editor
screen.*

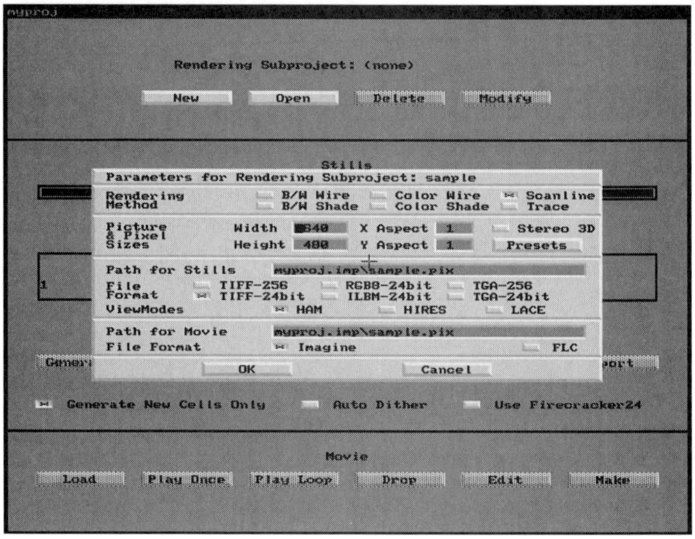

Figure 3.130
*Creating a rendering
subproject.*

Completing this step takes you back to the Project Editor. Click at the top of the screen to activate the Editor menu, shown in Figure 3.131.

Imagine uses a number of what it calls *Editors*. Each Editor is its own distinct program, although some Editors resemble each other. Table 3.2 contains a brief description of each Editor and its capabilities.

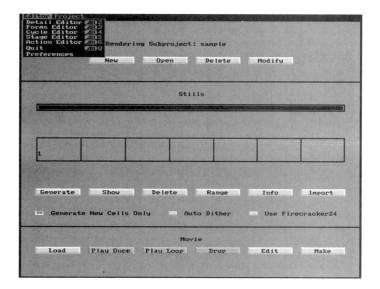

Figure 3.131
The Imagine Editors.

Table 3.2. Imagine Editors.

Editor	Description
Project	Where you manage your entire 3D project.
Detail	Does just what its name implies: Enables you to finish the details on objects that you created elsewhere. You can apply surface textures, for example, to objects you created in the Forms Editor.
Forms	Where you can create forms or objects interactively by moving the points on the surface of the object. You can create amazingly organic objects with this Editor. Typically, you'll create a basic form for an object here and then finish it in the Detail Editor.
Cycle	Enables you to set up repetitive motions for an animation.
Stage	Enables you to load various objects and put them into motion. It uses tweening[68] to create intermediate frames.
Action	You can apply the finishing touches to your animation here, including many special effects like explosions and rotations.

---

[68]*Tweening* is a common concept in animation programs. It's similar to morphing: You create a start position and an end position, and the software creates all the intermediate positions.

For this example, you'll start with the Forms Editor. In many ways, it's one of the most impressive aspects of Imagine. Short of the day when you can have a headset and gloves that enable you to modify a 3D object directly, Imagine gives you some interesting tools to work with in the Forms Editor. That's the good news. The bad news is that it's going to take time and practice, practice, practice to get good at it.

Figure 3.132 shows the opening screen of the Forms Editor.[69] There are four windows on the screen. Clockwise from the upper left, they are

Top—The object viewed from above.

Perspective—An adjustable perspective view of the object.

Right—The object viewed from the right side.

Front—The object viewed from the front.

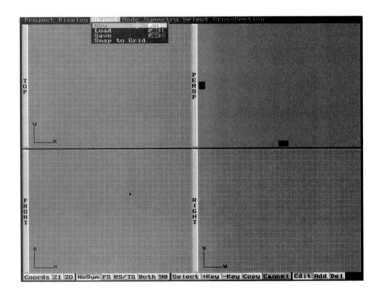

Figure 3.132
The Forms Editor screen.

This is a fairly standard variation on the presentation of 3D objects but, as you see shortly, it's not exactly what it seems to be. To create an object, use the Click menu at the top of the screen and choose Object/New. This displays the dialog box shown in Figure 3.133.

There are a lot of things going on in this dialog box that require an explanation. What are slices? What's a former view?[70] Let's interrupt the tutorial for a bit here to talk about how Imagine creates objects.

---

[69]To get to the Forms Editor from any other Editor, use the Click menu at the top of the screen. It's right there on the Editor menu.

[70]It's not the last view, I'll tell you that much!

An object is made up of points and slices. *Points* are just what you expect—a point is a point is a point.[71] *Slices* also are just what the name implies. They are important because they enable you to establish some degree of control over your 3D objects. Think of a cucumber. It's basically a cylinder with its ends closed over. But it's a rounded shape; where do you put the points? The answer: at the slices. Take that cucumber and slice it up at intervals of, say, one inch. Then put it back together and you've got a typical Forms Editor object.

Keep that image in mind and refer again to Figure 3.133. You are being asked to supply the number of points and the number of slices. If you enter 8 for the number of slices, it's like cutting the cucumber into 8 equally spaced slices. If you enter 16 for the number of points, you get 16 points—on each slice. That's a total of 128 points for the object.

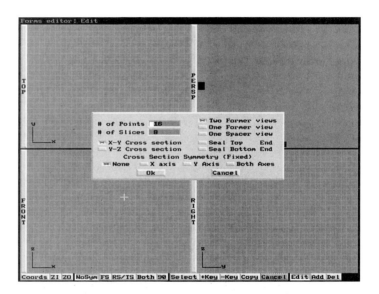

Figure 3.133
Creating a new object in the Forms Editor.

As for the other items in the New Object dialog box, a *former view* is nothing more than a view window in the Forms Editor. For certain kinds of objects, you can work with fewer windows when you need to modify only one or two dimensions of the object. For now, click the One Former View button. X-Y and Y-Z Cross Section refer to the orientation of the object in the Forms Editor view windows; for now, accept the default. The Seal Top End and Seal Bottom End options close off the object instead of making it a hollow tube.

---

[71]With apologies to Gertrude Stein.

The buttons near the bottom of the dialog box regarding symmetry can be safely ignored for now; click None. These buttons enable you to create objects that are symmetrical in one or two directions. Your face is bilaterally symmetrical, for example—there is a single axis down the middle of your face with the same features on either side of that line.

Click OK to close the dialog box, and you see something like Figure 3.134.

It's time for another digression into the ways and means of Imagine. There are some minor points about the display that make a big difference in how you work with Imagine compared to, say, 3D Studio.[72] The first thing to notice, if you can make it out in the figures, is that each of the view windows[73] has a small axis indicator in the lower left corner. There are two axes in each view—one pointing up and one pointing to the right. Each axis is labeled with a letter: X, Y, or Z. It takes a while to get used to thinking in terms of axes, but this might help: The X axis goes from left to right, the Y axis goes from front to back, and the Z axis goes up and down.

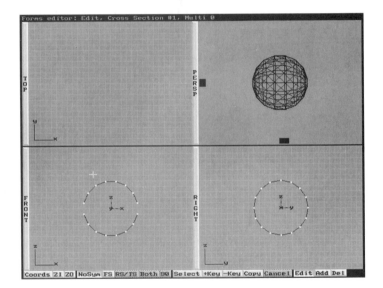

Figure 3.134
A newly created object in the Imagine Forms Editor.

---

[72]Think of it this way: Imagine is a right-brain kind of program. Any sense it makes probably will appeal to the creative side of your brain. 3D Studio is more of a left-brain, intellectual type of program. Here's another way to look at it: Learning to use Imagine is like learning to play a musical instrument. Learning to use 3D Studio is like learning calculus.

[73]Except for the Perspective window, which uses sliders to adjust the point of view.

Look closely at the Front view in Figure 3.134. This is not just an ordinary Front view of the object. Notice that the last two points on the right and left of the circle are not connected like the other points are. Let's go back to that cucumber idea. Think of Figure 3.134 as a Front view of a very, very fat cucumber. Those unconnected points are the two tips of the cucumber, and each pair of points defines a slice of the cucumber. Here's the punch line: If you move one of these points, you aren't really moving a point. You are adjusting a slice. We'll move some points and slices around shortly; for now, let's get back to describing the interface.

The Perspective view in Figure 3.135 uses wireframe modeling. This makes it hard to visualize the object when there are many points and, in 3D modeling, there are almost always too many points. Imagine also lets you display the Perspective view as a solid, or even shaded.[74] Use the Display/Shaded menu option to change the Perspective display (see Fig. 3.136 for the result).

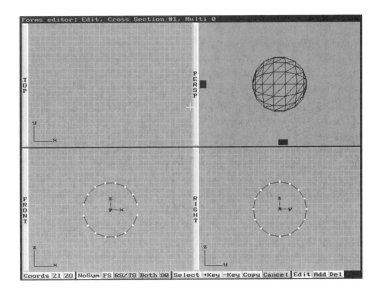

Figure 3.135
Using solid modeling to display the Perspective view.

Clicking on the left margin of any view window enlarges it to full screen, as shown in Figure 3.136. Because we selected shading, a light source has been added to show the object more clearly as a 3D object. You can switch to the other view windows using the buttons at the right of the screen labeled Front, Right, and Top.

---

[74]The shaded view actually only shows up under certain circumstances. You can enlarge any one view window to full screen by clicking on the vertical bar to the left of the view window. In full-screen mode, the Perspective window shows shading. If you must, peek ahead to Figure 3.136.

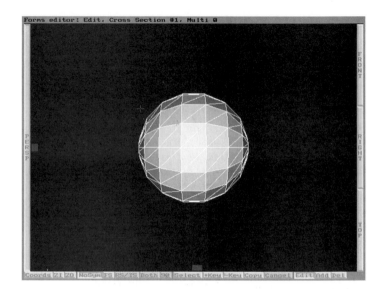

Figure 3.136
A shaded view of the object.

Let's get daring and move a point. Click on a point near the middle top of the Front view and move it close to the center of the object.[75] When you are done moving the point, look at the Perspective view (the upper right of Figure 3.137). Notice that you didn't move just one point; you adjusted an entire slice of the object. Figure 3.138 shows a 3D shaded view of the object.

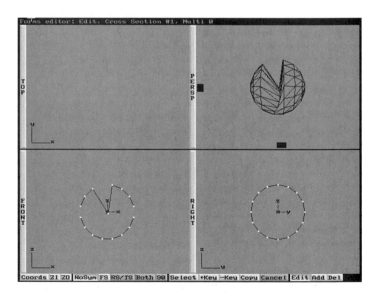

Figure 3.137
Moving a point on a slice in the Front view.

---

[75]While you are moving the object, you'll see a little axis indicator telling you that the Z axis is up and the X axis is to the right. This duplicates what already is being displayed in the lower left of the Front view window, so I don't exactly understand why it happens.

Because we created this object without any symmetry, we are free to move any point on any slice. If we create an object with bilateral symmetry, moving one point on a slice moves the corresponding point on the other side of the slice like a mirror image. Look at Figure 3.139, for example. It shows an object that is bilaterally symmetrical.[76]

Time for another lesson in the ways and means of Imagine. Notice that the Right view window hasn't changed one bit, even though we have made dramatic changes to the shape of the object. Remember that the Front view isn't really a true Front view. The Right view isn't really a true Right view, either. You aren't seeing a Front view of the entire object. You're seeing a Front view of a single slice. Because all the slices are still circular (even if they are different sizes), the Right view is still circular, too. To change the slice that is shown in the Right view, use the Select button at the bottom center of the screen. You can display only key slices in the Right view. To make a slice a key slice, click the +Key button (to the right of the Select button). You can use the -Key button to make a slice a non-key slice again. The idea behind key slices is simple. If a slice is not a key slice, it adapts itself to changes made to key slices. In other words, non-key slices assume positions between key slices.

Figure 3.140 shows a shaded 3D view of the new object.

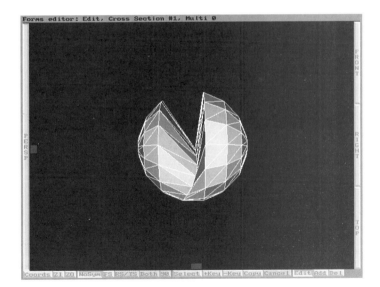

Figure 3.138
The result of moving a point on a slice.

---

[76]Most of the time, when you create a new object, it shows up as a sphere. You then can deform it to whatever shape you want. You can use a type of Snap to Grid feature to easily make perfectly square or rectangular objects.

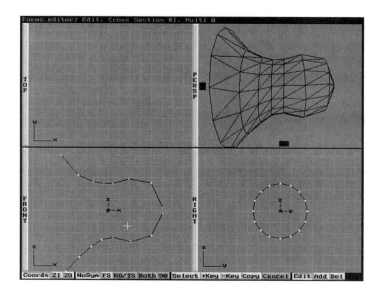

Figure 3.139
An object with two-
fold symmetry.

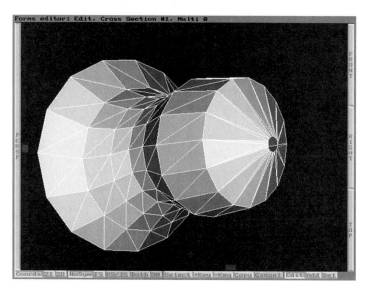

Figure 3.140
A shaded view of the
new object.

You can work with more than one point at a time in Imagine. The Select menu enables you to pick the method you'll use for selecting active points: Click, Drag Box, or Lasso. Click is the method we've used so far; to modify a point, you just click on it. The Drag Box method is familiar to anyone who has used a Windows drawing program (see Fig. 3.141). To drag a box around some points, choose Select/Drag Box from the Click menu at the top of the screen, and then click and drag a box around the points you want to select.

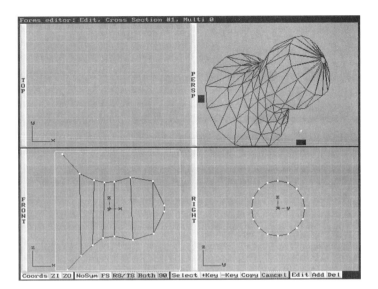

Figure 3.141
*Selecting points
with a drag box.*

The points you selected, and the lines between them, now are highlighted and you can work with just those points. The Object/Snap to Grid menu option, for example, would operate on the selected points, moving them to the nearest grid points.[77]

You can create some pretty fancy shapes with the Forms Editor. Look at Figure 3.142, which shows a car form from the samples that come with Imagine. A shaded view of the form is shown in Figure 3.143. It doesn't look exactly like a car; you can add things like wheel wells and fenders in the Detail Editor.

Fun with the Forms Editor

Let's try a little experiment to see if I can make it clear how an object responds to your manipulations in the Forms Editor. To start, create an object with eight slices and eight points. Before you click OK to create the object, choose One Former View. In the Front view, rearrange the points to make a rough outline of the letter A (see Fig. 3.144).

Make one of the slices near the center of the letter form a key slice, and then use the Select button to select it. This slice is now the one showing in the Right view. Click Select/Lock to turn on Snap to Grid. Now move the points in the Right view to form a square. Look at the Perspective view, and note the contortions the form makes to switch from a circular slice, to a square slice, and then back again.

---

[77]This is dangerous! If more than one point gets moved to the same grid point, you'll have no indication of the situation. This can get very confusing if you are not aware of the possibility.

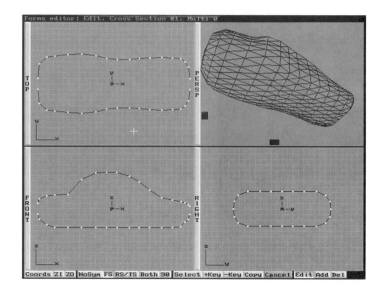

Figure 3.142
A more complex shape created with the Forms Editor.

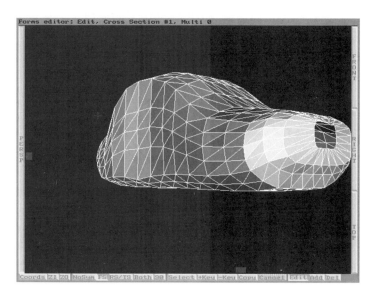

Figure 3.143
A shaded view of the object in Figure 3.142; it's a car! Sort of.

Now rearrange the points in the Right view to form a diamond shape, as shown in Figure 3.145. In addition, change the angle of view in the Perspective view to show the object more clearly. Note that the middle slice does, indeed, now have a diamond shape.[78]

---

[78]With a little more effort, we could have a great robot shape here!

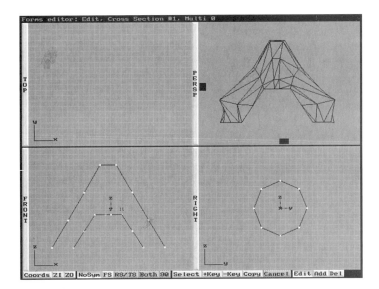

Figure 3.144
Fun with the Forms Editor.

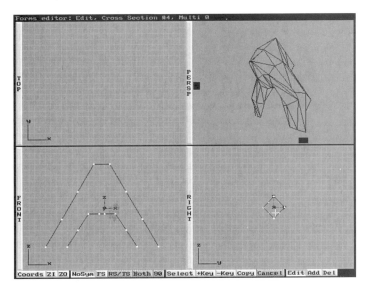

Figure 3.145
*Yet another varia-
tion of the middle
slice.*

Now let's get weird. Move the top point of the diamond in the Right view way to the right, as shown in Figure 3.146. Look at the Perspective view—there is the point way out to the right. Notice how the lines from other slices automatically adjust themselves to create intermediate positions.

Let's try a more useful set of transformations in the Forms Editor. Create a new object, again with eight slices and eight points. Choose No Symmetry and Two Former Views. In the Front view, rearrange points until you have something like what I've done in Figure 3.147. That's right: We're making a fish. Figure 3.148 shows a shaded view of the fish form.

The form is a little fat for an angel fish. In the Top view, move the points to narrow each slice (see Fig. 3.149). Align the points that define the tail until they actually touch each other. Note how this changes the appearance of the slice in the Right view. This is not thin enough, however; you also need to move the points in the Right view to about the same distance apart as you did in the Top view.

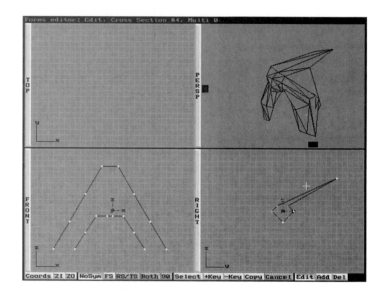

Figure 3.146
Far out to the right in the Forms Editor.

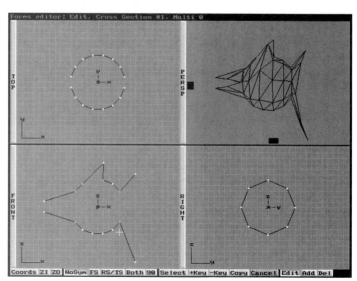

Figure 3.147
Creating a fish in the Forms Editor.

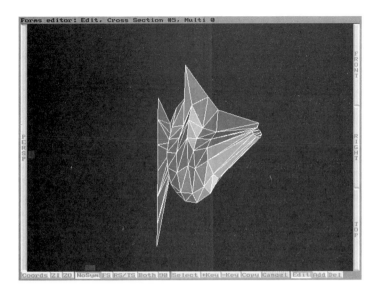

Figure 3.148
A fish form.

So far, we have just a fish floating in space. There is no reference point, but we can create one easily by adding something called a *ground*. The result is shown in Figure 3.150.

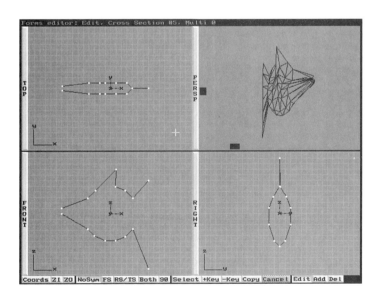

Figure 3.149
Narrowing the fish form for a realistic appearance.

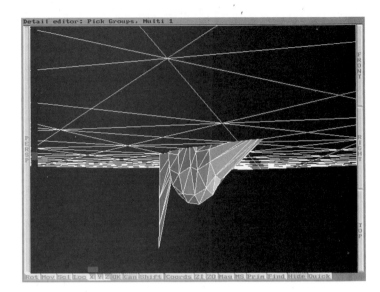

Figure 3.150
*Oops—fish and
ground share a
common center.*

Because objects are all created at the origin of the workspace, the ground cuts the fish
in half. We need to move either the fish or the ground, and it's easy to do. Click the
Move button at the bottom left, and then use the mouse to click and drag the ground
below the fish (see Fig. 3.151). The result of the move is shown in Figure 3.152.

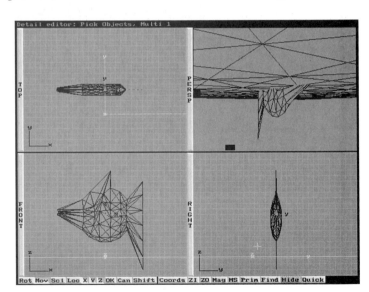

Figure 3.151
*Dragging the ground
to a new position
after clicking the
Move button.*

Now you can do a quick render by clicking the Quick button at the lower right of the screen. The result is shown in Figure 3.153. Hmm... it sort of looks like a fish, but we're definitely not done yet! It's time for the Detail Editor.

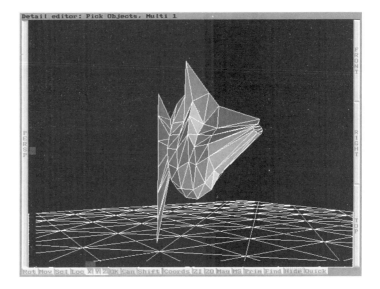

Figure 3.152
The result after moving the ground below the fish.

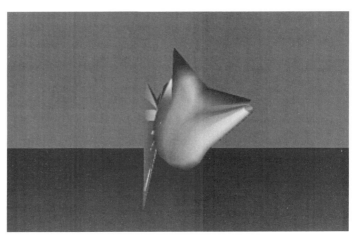

Figure 3.153
A fish rendering.

The Detail Editor looks like the Forms Editor, but the menus are quite different. Once again, there are strange but important new concepts to learn. The most important concepts are Select and Pick. *Selecting* appears to mean nothing more than making an object appear orange, but you can't *Pick* an object unless it's *Selected*. There's a menu option called Pick Selected, and that's what it does.[79] There are also several other methods for picking an object, such as Pick Last. Whatever method you use, Pick the fish. This enables you to access the Object/Attributes menu option, and this is where the fun really starts. This displays the Attributes Requester (Amiga talk for the Attributes dialog box), as shown in Figure 3.154. You can set a large number of attributes—color, reflectivity, hardness, shininess, textures, and more. Providing a complete description of attributes is beyond the scope of this book, however. For this example, I gave the fish a bright blue color and made it mildly reflective and shiny. This gives a quick approximation of the surface attributes of a typical tropical fish.

Even so, there's more to do. At the very least, we should add an eye to our fish. We can create a simple sphere, and then Move it and Scale it so that it looks just right (see Fig. 3.155). I set attributes of color black, shininess 100%, and white spectral reflection for the eye. Again, these are just quick approximations of the natural characteristics of an eye. The result isn't too bad (see Fig. 3.156).

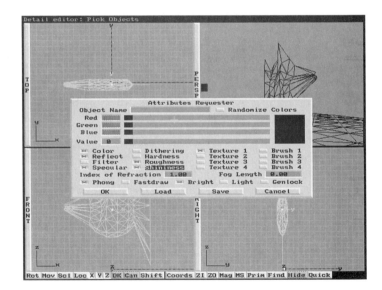

Figure 3.154
The Attributes Requester in the Detail Editor.

---

[79]Editorial comment: This complexity about selecting and picking makes the Detail Editor more painful than it needs to be, but, like the other quirks of Imagine, you get used to it if you stay with it long enough. It adds significant difficulty to the learning process.

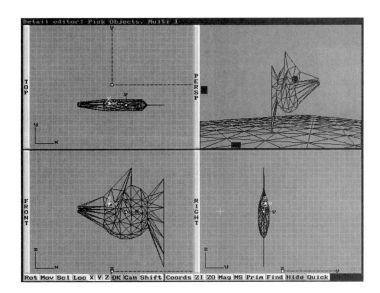

Figure 3.155
*Adding an eye to
the fish object.*

Figure 3.156
*A rendering of
the fish, eye,
and ground.*

Imagine Summary

This section only hints at what you can do with Imagine. Despite its idiosyncratic interface and poor documentation, Imagine has some interesting and powerful capabilities. If you have time and patience, you can do much more than what I've shown here, including sophisticated animation.

Architectural Space

Computers are digital. That means that some things are easier than others. When it comes to virtual reality, straight lines are easier than curves. For that reason, some of the most advanced VR applications involve architecture. Not that buildings don't have curves, but the vast majority of the lines, edges, and faces are straight. This makes for a certain degree of simplicity.

Not so simple is the sheer number of those lines, edges, and faces. In fact, this is a good place to illustrate the volume of data involved in creating a virtual space. Consider the lowly Cape Cod style of home, for example. What would it take to simulate the process of opening the front door, crossing the living room, walking up the stairs, and then examining the details of an upstairs window frame?

Indoors

The answer is, it would take a lot. I want to impress upon you just how much it does take, however, because this is the central issue of virtual reality. Until there are ways of handling the massive amounts of data involved, all the headsets in the world won't help a bit.

Let us go then, you and I, up to that front door. What do we see as we stand before it? There's the door itself, of course. This one is made of wood. "What kind of wood," we must ask. And is the wood painted, stained, oiled, varnished, or covered in some other way? Is there a window in the door? How many panes of glass are in the window? Is the glass simple, clear, flat glass; or is it stained glass; or perhaps cut or etched glass? How fancy is the frame around the window? What about the hardware on the door—brass, pewter, chrome, or something else? Is there weather stripping at the base of the door? What about the threshold at the base of the door frame? And what about the door frame—what kind of wood is used there, and is it a fancy molding with difficult-to-reproduce, complex curves? And then there are the latch and the notch for it in the door frame. And don't forget to consider where the light is coming from. Is it a sunny day? Are there any clouds? Is there a porch light—or, for that matter, a porch? Light surfaces reflect light; what effect does that have on the scene?

Assuming that we've been able to generate an image that can handle all of that, now we have to put it in motion—and that means starting all over again. Even a little motion changes things. As we open the door, the lighting angle changes constantly. But that's just part of the problem. As the door opens, it reveals a bit of the living room inside—with its rugs, walls, paintings, trim, couches, chairs, baseboard, electrical outlets, and more.

Now that I have you convinced of the difficulty of the task, it's time to look at a software package that does (sort of) just the things I've described. If you think this was merely a clever ploy to prevent you from being overly disappointed with the limited capabilities of low-end architectural-rendering software, you're right.[80] In order to render 3D scenes, or to enable you to move through the scenes, low-end software had to make some serious compromises.

Let's look at a software package called 3D Plan from Autodesk. It's a very easy program to use, and it provides some intriguing VR capabilities in an inexpensive package. Figures 3.157 and 3.158 show two views created with 3D Plan. Figure 3.157 shows a view across a backyard pool, and Figure 3.158 shows a view through sliding glass doors into the interior of a cabin.

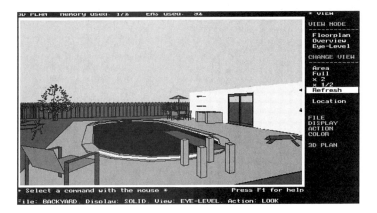

Figure 3.157
A backyard virtual reality.

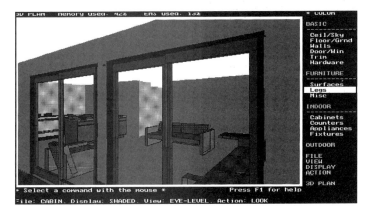

Figure 3.158
A view into the interior of a cabin.

The opening screen of 3D Plan is shown in Figure 3.159. The bulk of the screen is the area where the 3D view will be shown. Information about the current view is displayed at the bottom, and the menu is located at the right of the screen. There are five menu options, and they are listed in Table 3.3.

---

[80] It's easy to expect too much from VR software if you don't consider the true nature of the task at hand.

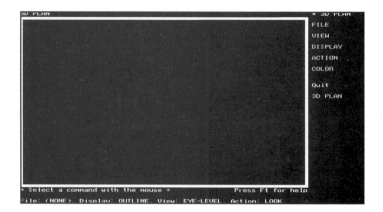

Figure 3.159
The 3D Plan opening screen.

Table 3.3. 3D Plan Menu Options.

Option	Function
File	Loads and saves files.
View	Establishes your point of view and the basic type of rendering.
Display	Contains parameters for fine-tuning the rendering.
Action	Enables you to move your point of view.
Color	Changes the colors of objects in the rendering.

RECIPE

1 DWG file
4 cups 3D Studio
2M of expanded memory
1 EGA or better display card

Instructions: This is an easy-to-prepare, light dessert. Images aren't very detailed—no Super VGA support—but the results are quick. Plan ahead: You can't do anything unless you have prepared some DWG files in advance. Use Generic 3D, AutoCAD, or any of the Home Design modules available from Autodesk.

3D Plan works with any EGA or better color display card, but I highly recommend using a VGA display. 3D Plan does not use any Super VGA capabilities you may have. This is unfortunate, because VGA resolution—and its 16 colors—doesn't provide a very realistic image.

To create a rendering, click the File menu at the upper right of the screen. This displays a menu with several items; click Load 2D. You can load only a 2D drawing that uses the DWG file format. You can use products like Generic CADD (also from Autodesk) to create plan drawings, or you can use the much simpler Home Series of drawing products (yes, also from Autodesk). The Home Series software comes in packages labeled Kitchen, Bathroom, and so on. You can create a plan in one of the Home Series packages and then view it in 3D with 3D Plan.

3D Plan comes with several sample DWG files. Figure 3.160 shows the plan file HOME.DWG during the loading process. 3D plan applies a little artificial intelligence during the loading process. It follows a few simple rules to determine what is, and is not, a wall in the plan drawing. When it has things pretty well figured out, 3D Plan displays only the walls. Most of the walls are in bold, indicating that they are selected. You can click on a wall to deselect it, and it does not appear in the 3D rendering. This can be useful. If you want to look at a kitchen in 3D, for example, it might be easier if you eliminate a wall or two. If you deselect a wall accidentally, just click on it again to reselect it.

Press Enter when you have the walls the way you want them.[81] 3D Plan then completes the loading process. You see the complete Plan view, including any 3D objects that were placed in the view with the drawing program used to create the plan. Figure 3.161, for example, shows a complete Plan view from the HOME.DWG file.[82]

Your next task is to establish your position and point of view. Click anywhere on the Plan view to set your position; cross hairs with one long leg appear (see Fig. 3.162). Slide the mouse back and forth to face the long leg in the direction you want to view. In this example, the viewpoint is just inside the front door in the living room, looking off toward the dining area.

---

[81]If the drawing has no walls—for example, a landscape drawing showing just trees and shrubs—3D Plan does not pause during loading to ask about walls.

[82]This is a good spot to put in a few words about what a Plan view is. If you have ever taken a class in mechanical drafting (I had one in high school), you are familiar with floor plans. That's all a Plan view is—a view from above showing the location of objects in the plan. Objects include walls, furniture, electrical lines, and anything else that might exist in an architectural drawing.

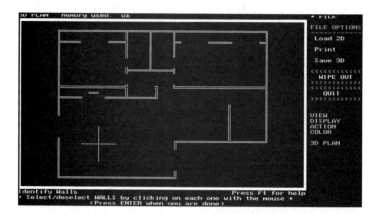

Figure 3.160
Selecting walls
during loading.

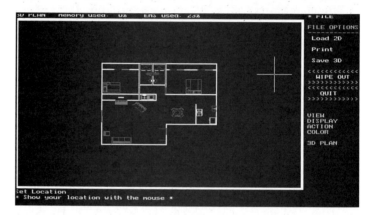

Figure 3.161
A Plan view in
3D Plan.

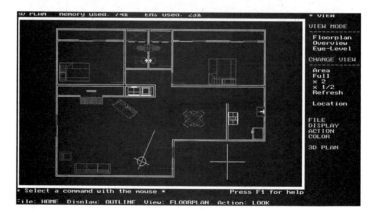

Figure 3.162
Setting the point
of view.

Click View to go to the View menu, where you see three possible View modes:

Floorplan—Shows the Plan view. This is a 2D-viewing mode.

Overview—A 3D view of the entire plan. This view ignores the viewpoint you just set.

Eye-level—A view at eye level from the viewpoint you just set.

You also can use this menu to change views. You can zoom in or out, for example, or use the Area selection to pick a specific area to view. To select an area, just click and drag out a box with the mouse.

Click on Eye Level, and you see something like the view shown in Figure 3.163. The first thing you will no doubt notice is that it is a Wireframe view. If you have even a moderately fast computer, you can switch to a more pleasing rendering mode.

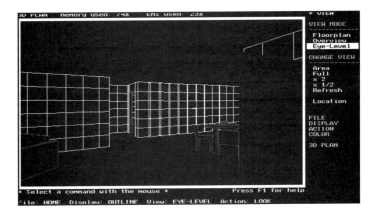

Figure 3.163
An eye-level view in 3D Plan.

Click Display, which switches you to the Display menu. You see three Display modes listed on the menu:

Outline—This is Wireframe mode.

Solid—Colors all objects in the scene using the current color scheme.

Shaded—Shades the solid view using simple rules about lighting. There is also a subchoice: Edge. If Edge is on, you see a black line at the edge of each object.

Figure 3.164 shows a view using the Solid display mode. This is an improvement, but it's hard to tell where one wall ends and the next begins. Let's try Shaded mode (see Fig. 3.165). This is as good as it gets. 3D Plan isn't a photo-realistic rendering program. It does, however, provide an inexpensive way to visualize what a new kitchen layout will look like, or to get an idea of what your new house will feel like. You could even use it to try out a new furniture layout. These are minor but worthy applications for virtual reality.

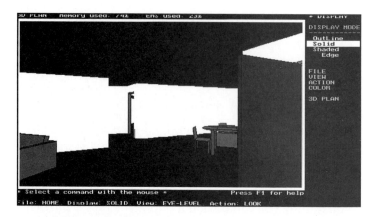

Figure 3.164
The Solid display mode.

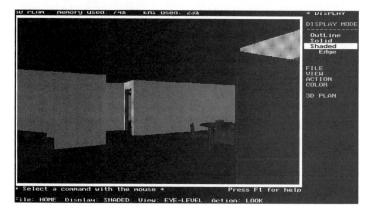

Figure 3.165
The Shaded display mode.

The rendering quality might not be detailed, but 3D Plan does have some additional VR features. You can move through the virtual space using the arrow keys, for example. There is a short delay while the program recalculates the view. The left- and right-arrow keys turn left and right, and the up- and down-arrow keys move the point of view forward and backward. Figure 3.166 shows a view of HOME.DWG from the dining area into the living room, for example. Figure 3.167 shows the view a few steps toward the living room.[83] This is much more intuitive than resetting the viewpoint using those cross hairs. In fact, it is this simple feature of being able to move through the 3D space that makes 3D Plan useful.

---

[83]This movement is precise. Each key press moves you the same number of feet or rotates you the same number of degrees. You can use the Ctrl key to magnify the motion. Pressing the left-arrow key, for example, rotates you one degree to the left, and holding down the Ctrl key and pressing the left-arrow key rotates the view 15 degrees.

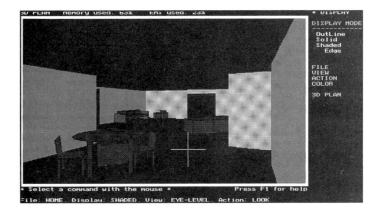

Figure 3.166
*Another view in
3D Plan.*

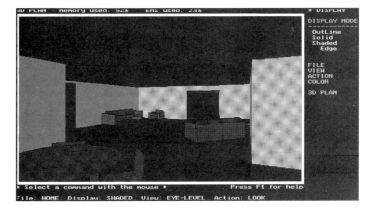

Figure 3.167
*A step forward in
the virtual space.
Compare to Figure
3.166.*

If you aren't happy with the appearance of the image, you have limited control over the colors used. 3D Plan is limited to VGA's 16 colors, and there are more than twice that number of object categories, so colors have to be shared. You can set the color of a variety of object types. You can assign different colors to furniture, carpet, walls, ceiling, doors, door frames, and so on. Figure 3.168 shows the same view as in Figure 3.167, but with different colors.

In addition to the Eye-Level view, you can look at your project using the Overview mode, as shown in Figure 3.169.

3D Plan is one of the plainer programs that makes use of virtual reality, but it does a great job within its limited sphere.

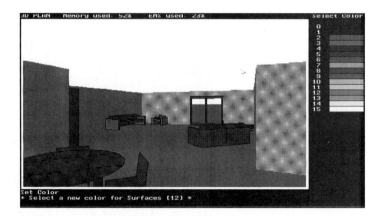

Figure 3.168
Setting different colors in 3D Plan.

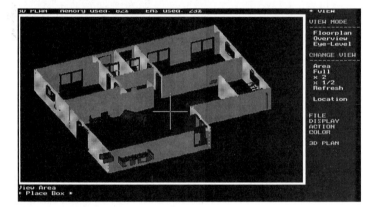

Figure 3.169
Using the Overview mode.

Rendering, Inside and Out

If playing with indoor spaces is challenging, rendering of both indoor and outdoor scenes is even more so. The variables that are so overwhelming when working with floor plans become even more numerous. In addition, when working with outdoor scenes, nature enters the picture—grass, clouds, trees, and other detailed, complex objects.[84] Granted, there are techniques for dealing with such objects, but this greatly increases the load on the computer. One of the best ways to deal with that level of complexity is to use an Image library such as those offered by ImageCels (see the VR Software Buyer's Guide on the CD-ROMs). Still, rendering provides some pretty sweet results, as you can see in Figure 3.170. The model for the scene was developed entirely in 3D Studio.

---

[84]The science of fractals is what enables computers to render such objects in anything even approaching a reasonable amount of time. It would be impossible to render every blade of grass in a lawn or every leaf on a tree.

Figure 3.170
*An office scene
created and rendered
with 3D Studio.*

One way around this is obvious: Don't bother to render all the details. Of course, it helps if you do a great job with what you do render—the missing details are less noticeable. Figure 3.171 shows a rendering of a cathedral created in 3D Studio.[85]

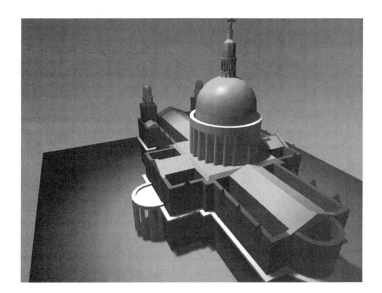

Figure 3.171
*A rendering of a
cathedral in 3D
Studio.*

---

[85]The source file is one of many, many samples provided with 3D Studio. 3D Studio comes with a CD that has hundreds of files of all kinds that you can use to create renderings, or to use within your own renderings.

There's no lawn, no trees, and the windows look glued on, but this rendering is still impressive.[86] If the rendering itself isn't sufficient to impress you, there's a flying animation of a trip around and over the cathedral on the CD-ROMs included with this book.

Sometimes, the problem isn't too many details; sometimes, in order to achieve a realistic rendering, you need to remove details. Objects fade with distance—in the real world, a distant mountain shows almost no details.[87] Fog is similar (see Fig. 3.172).

Figure 3.172
Virtual fog.

Unfortunately, a lack of detail is sometimes simply unavoidable. It takes time to add the little details that add the extra touch of realism, and time isn't always available.[88] Figure 3.173 shows a portion of the same virtual space used for Figure 3.172. This portion of the file doesn't have a lot of detail. That doesn't matter in the view of Figure 3.172, because the street level is so far away and obscured by fog as well. If you look at Figure 3.172 carefully, you'll see that there are several cars down there on the street—just enough to suggest the idea of cars on the street. You don't realize how empty the streets are until you get down there and look.

Speaking of details, I decided to render a view of this cityscape at night, using low light levels. The first rendering looked wrong, and it didn't take long to figure out why: There were no lights at street level. The cars didn't have headlights or taillights.

---

[86] It's even more impressive in color, of course.

[87] You can create a hyper-real landscape by leaving out the haze, of course.

[88] At least right now it takes time. Perhaps someday, after we've all taken the time to create all the wonderful details of everyday life electronically, all we'll have to do is pull virtual stuff out of a virtual library—light bulbs, sidewalks, front doors, pottery, sofas, and ice cream cones.

There were no streetlights. The traffic signals (you can see a few in Fig. 3.173) didn't signal. It would take a lot of effort to add all those lights. To see just how much work it would take, I added headlights to each of the cars.

Figure 3.173
A cityscape without a lot of details.

A lot more work was involved than I expected.[89] I couldn't just go to the Car menu and click Headlights; I had to use what was available to create headlights. I'll describe what it takes to create a single headlight. Step one is to create a light located just above a car's bumper. This involves clicking in one view to place the light, and then clicking a second time to place the light's target.[90] I then had to zoom in and out a bit to make sure that the light was, in fact, next to that car's bumper. "Why," you ask? When working in Front, Top, or Side view, an object might look like it's where it is supposed to be. However, it might actually be a million miles away—there's no way to tell what's going on in the third dimension without switching to another view. This is the bane of existence in the virtual fast lane.

Once the list exists, you must adjust it. A light has a couple of nested cones: the central cone (the *hotspot*), where the light is brightest, and the outside cone, where the light is weaker (called *falloff*). I set the width of the hotspot at 15 degrees, and the falloff at 45 degrees. I then made sure that the light was aimed slightly downward, just like a real headlight. Unfortunately, when I rendered the scene, I couldn't see any evidence whatsoever that I had just spent some time creating headlights. I had to make two changes to make the lights visible.

---

[89]I did this in 3D Studio; I don't know why I expected that it wouldn't take time.
[90]In 3D Studio, lights have targets.

The first problem was with the street. A very dull, black material had been created to simulate the street, and it wasn't reflecting any of the light. A real street, of course, is black, but it reflects some light. I had to go into the Material Editor and muck around with the characteristics of the street. I added a little shininess and modified the way that the material responded to light. I went back and forth a few times until I had it right.

The second problem involved the nature of lights in 3D Studio. You can see the effects of a light, but you won't see the light itself. So I had to add little globes just behind each light and set properties in the Material Editor so that the globes glowed enough to look like headlights.

The result of all this effort is shown in Figure 3.174. It's like one of those Waldo books: Can you find the headlights? After all the work, you can't even see them at this point in the animation (frame 92 of 150). That's more of life in the virtual fast lane.

In the last few frames of the animation, when the point of view is much closer to street level, the headlights are quite noticeable (see Fig. 3.175).

Figure 3.174
The city at night,
courtesy of 3D
Studio.

Of course, while working with the model in Wireframe mode, I had little idea of what the headlights would look like. Figure 3.176 shows a screen from 3D Studio during the creation process. The view at the upper left shows a car from above, with two lights and two targets (the vertical lines connect lights and targets). The view at the bottom left is a close-up from the side of the small spheres that show up as the bright lights in Figure 3.175, and the view at the bottom right shows an overview of a portion of the city with cars in it.

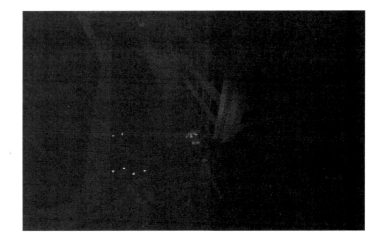

Figure 3.175
Virtual headlights in
frame 143 of 150.

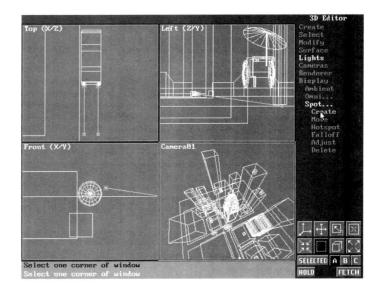

Figure 3.176
Creating headlights
in 3D Studio.

The point of this is that there is an enormous amount of effort and care that goes into a photo-realistic virtual space. It gave me a real appreciation for the details of everyday life. Virtual Rome cannot be built in a day.

4

VIRTUAL
FUN

Even the most hard-core computer user probably wishes computers were more fun. Not that software vendors haven't tried—the next time you visit your local software store, compare the shelf space used for software and for games. In most cases, you'll see at least as much space devoted to games as to business software—sometimes more. The disparity is even more obvious when you limit yourself to multimedia software—the vast majority of titles are games, or close enough to games to be called such.

While you're in the store, ask the manager a simple question: Which games are selling the best? The answer: 3D games sell better than any other category. The same is true of shareware games—titles like DOOM and Heretic are the hottest things going. As a public service,[1] you'll find a number of 3D shareware games and trial versions of commercial games on the CD-ROMs that come with this book. Check the table of contents on the discs for instructions.

3D and the Inner Child

A little kid lurks inside every computer user. That much is clear from the huge number of games on dealer shelves. What is it about 3D games, and even the use of 3D in business software, that makes it so appealing? Was it the new features that made Windows 3.*x* such a smashing success, or was it really those 3D buttons?

Without a moment's hesitation, I'll assert that Windows succeeded because it used 3D in small but important ways. The 3D look gave Windows legitimacy in a way that no other feature could. Think about it: Before the 3D look, Windows was an interesting also-ran, sitting on as many bookshelves as hard disks. Put a little 3D in, and wham!—a revolution occurs.

Microsoft offers a lot of reasons for the success of Windows 3.*x*, such as

■ The huge product roll-out, with live video conferences in cities all over the United States;

■ The all-new GPF to replace the all-too-common UAE;[2] and

■ The addition of sound and other multimedia support

These are not the reasons why Windows became a success. No one who actually buys Windows ever goes to such conferences; they're for guys in suits with big offices. GPF, UAE—gimme a break here; a crash is a crash, even if it only brings down the system

---

[1] As if putting games on the CD is anything but a cold-blooded appeal to the child in every reader. Hi. I'm the author's alter-ego, Clarence. The author has certain obligations to his editor and society, but I don't. I'll be watching over Ron's shoulder throughout this chapter, and you can count on me to give you the real story.

[2] These are, of course, the good-old Windows program crash errors. A UAE was an unexplained application error, and a GPF is a general protection fault.

half as often. As for multimedia, how many computers were already set up for multi-media when Windows was introduced?

I'm exaggerating here, of course,[3] but I'm doing it to make a point. Maybe 3D didn't put Windows on tens of millions of computers overnight, but it makes a Big Difference:[4] Buttons are really buttons now, not just little pictures with lines around them.

More precisely: virtual buttons. Remember those Fisher-Price crib toys that provide a row of buttons? Each button does something cute when the baby pushes it—a cow makes a "moo" sound, a door opens to reveal a picture of a turkey,[5] or a bell rings. That's what a toolbar is: the adult version of that old crib toy.

Many[6] psychologists define play as "anything that provides a large reward for a small effort." Do you see the connection? A simple little click on a toolbar button gives you big dialog boxes. No need to hunt through menus to find the commonly used tools (that's work); just click on a picture (that's play).

What does all this have to do with virtual reality? The answer is coming right up.

Virtual Reality as a Game

When a new computer product enters the market, it tends to sputter and flop around a bit before it becomes well known and successful.[7] During this time, whole legions of news reporters, computer columnists, and magazine editors spend infinite hours of their time theorizing about

- Why the new product came into being;
- Whether it represents an Entire New Category of hardware software;
- Who will use the new product;
- What implications for the industry are inherent in the new product; and
- Whether anyone will actually spend money on it.[8]

---

[3]Like heck! He's silly enough to believe every word of what he's saying.

[4]With apologies to Douglass Adams for stealing the device of capitalizing Big Ideas.

[5]Hey—this is sounding more and more like software as we go along!

[6]Some.

[7]Unfortunately, some flounder, sputter, and do painful things to your computer even after they become successful!

[8]Do you know why we face a glut of monstrously huge software products these days? It's harder to pirate a piece of software that requires 10 pounds of documentation. If you ever spent some time at the photocopier making pirate documentation, those days are now officially over.

If you look through the computer press, you find exactly these kinds of discussions going on about such subjects as the PowerPC, multimedia, and virtual reality. Everyone is acting as though VR is some kind of New Thing. It's not new at all. In fact, at every stage of computing, as soon as the CPU power grows enough to support the next level of VR, it gets added. The most notable additions of VR to the common computing repertoire are listed in Table 4.1.

Table 4.1. Virtual Reality That We Already Use.

Item	VR Justification
The mouse[9]	A device that, although not as sophisticated as a Power Glove, still allows you to move around in a virtual space.
GUI (Graphical User Interface)	Virtual desktop—that's what they called it at first, remember?[10]
3D buttons	Buttons have evolved from a mere box-shaped outline to a complete simulation with an animated click—how virtual does it have to be?
The toolbar[11]	Crib toy for adults
Headsets	Yes, the 3D headset (complete with head tracking) is now officially a consumer device; just ask the folks at Virtual I/O or VictorMaxx.

Soon, we'll have useful speech recognition and other advances, too.

Cool Games

Since shortly after computers first arrived into our lives, one category of software has been driving the development of new technology more than any other: games. It is in games that the latest advances in multimedia and VR show up first. Games are where the risks are taken, the advances made. In my endless search for knowledge and cool stuff to pass on to you, dear reader, I have left no CD unturned in my effort to find the coolest of the cool—the games that make your hair stand on end, that make you dizzy with excitement.

---

[9]Can anyone explain why the price of a mouse varies from $19.95 to more than $100 for exactly the same functionality??? I mean, let's get real here.

[10]And you thought virtual reality was new...

[11]Didn't anybody patent this thing? They're everywhere—even places where they don't work. Somebody could've made a mint on this idea.

I looked at many games, and some were good and some were (horror of horrors!) boring. There are three major categories:

■ Action games like DOOM, Dark Forces, Hell, Blake Stone, Raptor, and Bio Menace. You are involved in a life-or-death struggle with an enemy and must shoot your way out of danger.

■ CD adventure games like Myst, Under a Killing Moon, Bio Force, Iron Helix, Return to Zork, and Stunt Island. These are less adrenaline-raising games that sometimes offer subtle clues to unlocking puzzles.

■ "Educational" games like SimCity 2000. You build, test yourself, answer questions, or otherwise engage your mind in fun and playful ways.

Many games run only in DOS,[12] and they will test your ingenuity before you even play them. The DOS games require a *lot* of memory in order to run. Blake Stone, for example, requires 615,000 bytes of free conventional memory. You shouldn't even think of playing such a game without DOS 6.2. If you haven't already done so, you should set up separate game-only CONFIG.SYS and AUTOEXEC.BAT files that set up your system for absolute minimum memory requirements, or use the multi-configuration menuing options in DOS 6.2*x*. Before playing games, reboot with a configuration that gives you the maximum amount of memory while still loading all your multimedia drivers. If you are unsure about how to set up for lots and lots of memory, I have some good news: Most of the games we reviewed had a Help or README file that gave tips on how to optimize your system memory. MS-DOS 6.*x* manuals can help you out, too.[13] The bottom line is to get everything you don't actually require for multimedia or mouse support out of your configuration.

A few adventure games run under Windows, and many of these, too, have unique system requirements that are listed with the game. When it comes to games, ignore the README files at your peril.

---

[12]Windows adds some overhead that can slow down games. Microsoft has been working on enhancements to Windows that will improve game performance. The first round was called WinG, but it didn't go far enough. Look for game support of Windows to evolve further in future editions of Windows 95.

[13]The MS-DOS 6 manuals have a detailed section in the User's Guide on how to make more memory available. It has step-by-step instructions on how to optimize memory by using MemMaker. MemMaker looks over your existing memory configuration and suggests an optimum memory configuration for your machine. It increases efficiency by moving device drivers and memory-resident programs into available UMBs (upper memory blocks), and fine-tunes memory by changing the order of commands in your startup files. If you don't like the new memory configuration, you can always undo it. Once you find a satisfactory memory configuration, you can set up separate CONFIG.SYS and AUTOEXEC.BAT files for each configuration. See your DOS manual for details. I experimented with MemMaker and came up with a bare-bones configuration that I use for all VR DOS games. A word of warning, however: MemMaker is playing with fire and may occasionally backfire. When this happens, you should have a backup copy of your original configuration files to fall back on.

Windows 95 will create some changes in the game world. Windows 95, for one thing, has much better support for games than Windows 3.*x* did. This means that more games will run under Windows—even if they weren't designed for Windows originally. It also means that memory issues may (finally!) fade into the background and allow us to launch games without crossing our fingers for good luck first.

On the other hand, don't expect Windows 95 to fix everything at one time. The need to be patient when installing a game is likely to be around for some time to come.

Don't assume anything when you start out to play a new game. These puppies are pushing the outer envelope of what can be done on a PC, and each game probably has some special requirements you'll need to know about. Read the README file carefully, and look for items relating to specific hardware or software you use regularly. Many games never run at all on some PCs, and games are the most-often-returned software purchase.

Installation procedures for several of the DOS games will ask you to specify an interrupt (IRQ), I/O, MIDI port address, DMA channel, and so on. If you have not already installed your sound card, keep track of this information as you go. If you installed your sound card some time ago (like I did) and didn't record the settings, run the configuration or setup program, find out what they are, and write them down. One of those yellow stickies on the side of your monitor makes for a convenient way to get at this information.

I have a Sound Blaster sound card, and the configuration program (SBCONFIG.EXE) is located in the SB16 directory. See "Setting Up Your Sound Card," later in this chapter, for information about setting up a Sound Blaster 16; other sound cards will have similar procedures.

Memory management for DOS games is critical. Some third-party memory managers may not work properly with some games. Read the game documentation carefully if you are using a memory manager other than the one that ships with DOS or Windows.

Action Games

When it comes to games, action is the essence—action games far outsell other categories by a wide margin. There are occasional exceptions to this rule (Myst, for example), and not all action games are worth your attention. But it is the *action* that makes best use of the various 3D and VR technologies available. In this section, you'll learn about the games that excite me the most.

Descent

When I wrote the second edition of this book, a brand-new game had just hit the streets and was all the rage. That game was DOOM. At the time, nothing else could touch DOOM in two categories: It was a ton of fun, and it jumped 3D graphics to a whole new level. In fact, DOOM is still a hot game, and has spawned an entire generation of DOOM-alikes, such as Heretic and Rise of the Triad. Unlike many of the 3D games, DOOM holds its own as a game—not just as a 3D game.

However much fun it is to play DOOM, the 3D technology that once took our breath away is now just typical. The primary limitation of the DOOM interface is that you cannot move up and down. Oh, you'll go up and down stairs, but you can't look up—and if you did, there would be nothing to see.

Descent adds that extra dimension. In Descent, you are totally immersed in a 3D world. Instead of exploring a flat level, you are free to truly roam 3D space in every direction. You can fly in every direction, spin, turn, and zoom in and out—full six-degree-of-freedom movement is yours in Descent. Figure 4.1 shows an example of looking up and down.[14] This up/down business isn't a luxury, either! There will be plenty of times when the enemy will attack from above or below, and you had better be prepared to respond.

You see, the enemy has the same freedom of movement that you do. Figure 4.2 shows an enemy attack in progress. You have a number of weapons at your disposal, but some you will have to find by exploring the world of Descent.

One of the goals of your mission is to rescue hostages. They are hidden in various places; Figure 4.3 shows a few happy hostages, glad for their rescue.

---

[14]Of course, you can also move up and down just as easily!

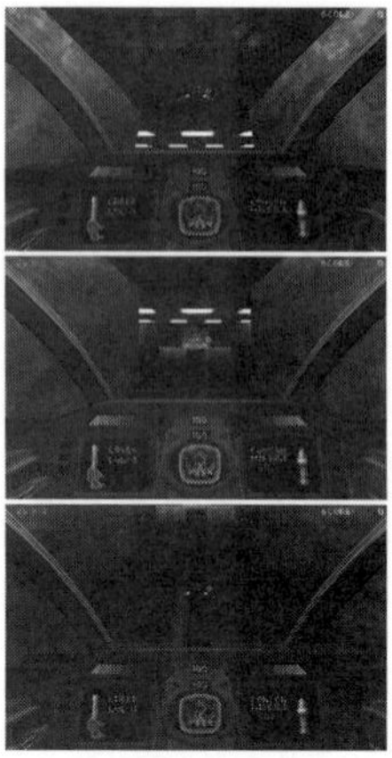

Figure 4.1
*Moving/looking up
and down is easy in
Descent.*

Figure 4.2
An enemy attacks!

Figure 4.3
*Rescuing the
hostages.*

The cockpit interface shown in the previous figures is just one way to interact with Descent. You can also use a smaller information display, as shown in Figure 4.4, or do away with the display and see the full-screen view. Figure 4.5 shows the Options screen. Descent has layers upon layers of options to set, and you can completely customize the way that your joystick or other game device works within Descent. For example, my son Justen likes to be able to move forward without having to use the keyboard, so we set up the joystick support for his Thrustmaster so that the middle button, when moved up, moves him forward. This adaptability is a great feature, and adds to the pleasure of playing Descent.

Figure 4.4
*An alternate
information display.*

Figure 4.5
Setting options.

Unless you are using one of the advanced joysticks, you will almost certainly have to use the keyboard as well as the joystick to access Descent's fast feature list. Figure 4.6 shows the most important keys; note that you can reprogram Descent to use key combinations of your own by using the Configuration setting in the Options menu.

Figure 4.6
*The most common
keystrokes used in
Descent are just a
press of F1 away.*

As much fun as it is to play Descent, you haven't really played it until you've tried either the Spaceball Avenger game controller or a game headset, such as the i-glasses! from Virtual Vision. The Avenger makes movement with six degrees of freedom unbelievably easy,[15] and the i-glasses! will simply blow you away with a game like Descent. Descent supports full stereoscopic 3D images while using game headsets, and the clear, crisp image of the i-glasses! makes it a blast. However, most other headsets will also give you a 3D experience with Descent; it supports all the major players.

Of course, for the ultimate Descent experience, pop on the CyberEye headset, which has even smoother, clearer graphics. Wow! Gaming will never be the same around our house.

---

[15]Although you had best do some practicing to get the hang of it.

DOOM, DOOM II, Heretic

DOOM is a shoot-'em-up action game that really gets the adrenaline going.[16] I (Donna) had never played an action game like DOOM, and none of the video arcade games prepared me for this experience. Probably the closest experience I can think of was sitting in the theater watching the *Terminator* movies. This is what it's like to actually lose yourself in an alternate reality. No helmet, no tactors,[17] not even total immersion, but each time I play the game, I am totally caught up in this nightmare reality.[18]

I experienced an interesting physical reaction after playing some VR games. I am particularly susceptible to motion sickness, which may explain why I was affected and the rest of my family wasn't. After playing Raptor for about an hour, I felt very dizzy. The computer monitor was moving up and down as if I were sitting in a boat that was rocking up and down.

Something similar occurred after I had been playing DOOM for several hours. I had had a particularly busy morning, and decided to take off an afternoon and play DOOM—to really get a feel for the game and see how far I could get. There were no phone calls or interruptions, and I lost track of time. For that period of time, I was a marine fighting for my life.

When I came back to my "normal" reality, I realized I was staring at my computer screen, completely tense. My back was stiff and my palms were sweaty. I got up and walked out to the mailbox to relax. For a brief period of time, I was disoriented. My eyes had trouble adjusting to the sun, and I was slightly dizzy. I had no idea I had been so intensely involved in the game, but I can see how moving from one reality to another can affect you physically. I've read the reported side effects from extended use of HMDs and can see how this is

---

[16]I have always preferred the tamer sort of adventure games, such as Myst or Return to Zork, that challenge a player to find clues and unlock hidden mysteries. But I have to admit, I got a real rush the first time I played DOOM. I could hear beasts growling in the background, and cautiously crept forward, peering around corners. I totally panicked when I saw a monster coming at me, and reacted at a very primal level. I experienced the same emotions I would in any life-threatening situation—and received an adrenaline rush that lasted throughout the game. So this is what all the fuss is about—you get a natural high! And the game is addictive. I watched Ron and my son sit at the computer for several hours trying to shoot their way out of a maze—and die several times before finally succeeding. Playing DOOM is a great way to get out your frustrations after a particularly trying day. "Take that, Sucker!" has a whole new meaning when you're standing with a machine gun in your hands facing a huge monster belching flames and smoke at you!

[17]*Tactors* are devices that provide tactile feedback.

[18]That's why we measure virtual reality success in human terms, not in artificial terms such as interactivity. Like a good book, good VR is involving. If it makes you sweat, it's good VR.

possible. Although the effects quickly passed, I thought I'd pass this along. The moral of the story: Stay cool. Remember! It's just a game. Isn't it?

Setting Up Memory

DOOM uses DOS-protected mode, which means that it takes advantage of extended memory.[19] To configure DOOM for best use of memory, set up a minimum memory configuration and do the following:

■ DOOM requires that you have 4M of RAM installed to run. Also: Make sure you have 3M of *free* RAM available. Disable unnecessary resident programs, such as SmartDrive, on 4M machines.

■ Do not use any memory managers that provide expanded memory, such as EMM386 or QEMM, and so on. If you must use one, use the NOEMS option. Extended memory managers, such as HIMEM.SYS, are not included; you do need those. Yes, this is complicated; welcome to the world of DOS games.

■ Do not use any disk-caching programs like SMARTDRV.

■ Load all the drivers and TSRs high that you can using DEVICEHIGH (CONFIG.SYS) or LOADHIGH (AUTOEXEC.BAT), as appropriate.[20]

■ Use the MEM command with the /c switch to examine the layout of your machine's memory. This tells you how much memory each driver or TSR is using, and the size of contiguous memory blocks available for loading high. For best results, type

```
mem /c ¦ more
```

to avoid information scrolling off the screen.[21] You can also type

```
mem /c>OUT.TXT
```

to save the output to a text file (name: OUT.TXT), which you can read later.

---

[19]Some games use expanded memory; always check their documentation. We (like many folks running Windows) use the NOEMS parameter on EMM386.EXE in our CONFIG.SYS file. That meant changing the CONFIG.SYS file before using some games.

[20]I would strongly recommend not loading DOS games onto DoubleSpace compressed drives. When you use DoubleSpace, you lose about 50K of conventional memory—and that's a big chunk that your games may require. You can free up additional conventional memory by not loading your DoubleSpace driver into memory. If you have a minimum memory configuration in your startup files and have DoubleSpace drives you don't need, reboot your system setup with mini-mum memory configuration. When the message Starting MS-DOS... appears, press Ctrl-F8. This tells DOS not to load the DoubleSpace drives. Press Y to step through the commands in CONFIG.SYS and AUTOEXEC.BAT.

[21]**Suggestion:** Put this line in a batch file so you can run it easily and often.

■ Load your mouse driver, because you'll want the option of using your mouse and keyboard simultaneously with DOOM. You also can use a joystick as an alternative, but the keyboard/mouse combination worked very well for us.

Okay—Let's Play

Before you begin the game, read the README file by typing **readme** in the DOOM directory. It contains the DOOM manual and getting started instructions, provides registration information, and lists brief descriptions of new features in version 1.2 and bugs fixed from version 1.1. The README file also provides background information on the game to give you some perspective on your adventure. It also provides the details of your mission, should you decide to accept it. You'll learn about the weapons provided, armor and health bonuses, and all the other features of the game. The end of the README file contains instructions for multiplayer and network play.[22]

Figures 4.7 and 4.8
Beginning screens for DOOM to select the game and episode.

When you are ready to begin the game, you are presented with a series of menu options. You can select a new game, load or save an existing game, or quit. The Options item lets you exit the game; turn messages (displayed at the top of the screen) on or off; and change the level of graphic detail, screen size, mouse sensitivity, or sound

---

[22]Yes, you can involve your friends in the frenzy of DOOM. You can play by modem or over a network. You can join with your friends to kill the bad guys, or you can try to kill each other. DOOM is very flexible that way. One Sams editor reports that it's fun to play DOOM by modem while using speaker phones for a conference call!

volume. The Read This! item contains an About screen and a brief list of navigation keys. You can access this menu at any time during the game by pressing Esc. I soon developed a habit of saving my game at the beginning of a level. I used the Quicksave feature whenever I completed a sticky task and didn't want to start over again.[23]

If you choose the option for a New Game, you are given an opportunity to choose between three games.[24] Once you choose a game, you must determine your skill level. The highest level (naturally!) is Pray to God.

If you do not select any of the options, the game begins a self-running demo.[25] The demo takes you through a quick tour of the game and is useful for finding secrets, hidden passageways, and other hints and tips. When I get stuck on a level, I go through the demo again and try to pick up some tricks. But there's nothing like the first time you play the game and get to navigate through the corridors and up the stairs by yourself. Turning a corner, not knowing what to expect, is what DOOM is all about.[26]

Figure 4.9
In the lobby with only a pistol for protection.

You begin DOOM in the lobby with a pistol in front of you. The only weapons you have at your disposal at first are a pistol and your fists. The optimum fun for me is using a mouse for navigating and firing your weapon, and the keyboard for switching weapons or pressing the space bar to open doors.

---

[23]And there are plenty of sticky tasks. There are times when you will be overwhelmed by the challenges, and it's nice to have a quick way of returning from the dead to have at it again.

[24]If you are playing the shareware version (that is, you haven't registered), you have only one game to play—the first in the series. To play the other two games, you must register, and they will be sent to you.

[25]You will be amazed the first time you watch the demo—particularly when you find yourself with a chainsaw in your hand. Ugh! My son's reaction? "Oh, wow! Who's the bad guy? Are we the bad guy? Can I play?" **Hint:** You'll see some interesting possibilities during the demo. It moves at a very fast pace, but pay attention—you can get some great ideas for later, when you are playing the game.

[26]I often find myself shouting out things like "Take that!" or "Yikes!" as the game unfolds—DOOM is very involving.

It takes a while to get the hang of navigation. I found myself bumping into walls or falling off stairs, with an echoing grunt from the character I'm playing. Or shooting at every strange sound. In the background are the growls and gun shots from your opponents.[27]

It doesn't take long to learn how to position yourself to go around corners or to climb a stairway. Unlike some VR products (VREAM, for example) you cannot go through objects. They provide resistance. Walls, for example, act just like walls.[28]

One of my first accomplishments was to successfully climb the stairs off the lobby and recover a vest and armor bonus. As you can see, the graphics are realistic but not high resolution. Color is used effectively to help clue you in. The vest is a bright green, while the armor bonus has a dull green fluorescent glow. The object of the game is to gather bonus points, weapons, ammunition, and secrets before moving to the next level. And, of course, to blast your adversaries to smithereens!

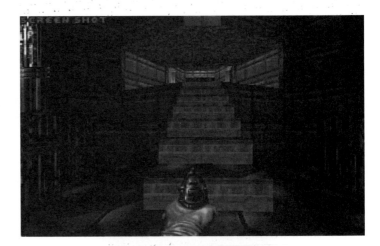

Figures 4.10 through 4.13
Navigating stairs to gather armory points and armor.

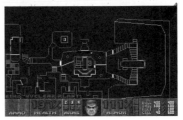

---

[27]You will even hear grunts from the other side of a wall—that's your clue that there's something there. After you've killed all the bad guys, if you still hear growls and grunts, there's more to do. Your job becomes finding the hidden doorway that will lead you to the next battle.

[28]Some walls are actually secret doors, but I won't spoil the fun by revealing too much.

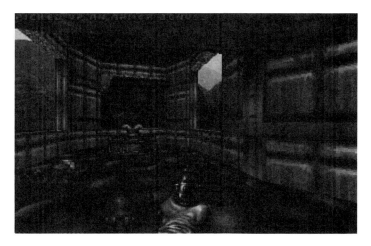

When you kill an enemy, his carcass lies there. Figure 4.12 shows the remains of an enemy on the left side of the screen under the window. Not only must you look at the carnage, but you can pick up his ammunition if you move over his body. Gruesome, huh?

You soon learn how to use your weapons to your greatest advantage. Although the machine gun is extremely effective at picking off a large number of opponents, you quickly run out of ammunition. If you find a backpack, you can carry extra ammo. But the most effective way to fight your enemy is by alternating between a variety of weapons. Skill is important: You can nail even the baddest of bad guys with your shotgun if you fire without missing a beat.

You learn how to advance, retreat, and take cover behind corners or panels. Rather than bumping into walls, you learn how to use them to protect you from oncoming shots and blasts of fire. For some real fun, try charging your enemies and engaging them hand-to-gun.

One of my most important discoveries was learning how to use the mouse to move around and turn.[29] Your movements are bi-directional, and you cannot jump or crouch. But you have the ability to control the speed and direction of your character. In the screen shots shown in Figures 4.14 through 4.23, you get a 360-degree view of the turret. The room looks outside onto some mountains and an outdoor area, and you can see from the screens how realistic the graphics are.

Figures 4.14 through 4.23
A view of 360-degree rotation in the tower.

---

[29]DOOM also supports the Logitech Cyberman, an inexpensive six-degrees-of-freedom input device. The hand controller buzzes and shakes when you are shot.

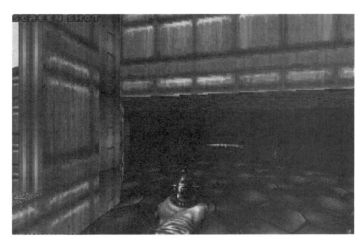

During your travels, you will encounter rooms with a switch on the wall. If you press the space bar (or double-click the mouse button), you activate a switch that will open a door or reveal a hidden passageway. You have to go searching to find the door or passageway, as it isn't always obvious. And some of the hidden accesses have a time limit. If you don't move fast enough, you lose out.

Notice the status bar at the bottom of the screen in Figure 4.24. It provides useful information on the amount of ammunition you have available, the percentage of health left (0% means you die!), the weapons at your disposal, and the percentage of armor you have for protection against oncoming fire. The "mug" in the middle is more than a self-portrait. It alerts you to the direction in which an enemy can be found, and as you lose health, the face shows the effects. There is also a color indicator if you find color-coded keys to high-security areas, and the information on the far right tells you how many bullets you have for each of your weapons.

Figure 4.24
Flip the switch.

Sometimes you have to swim through pools of poison to flip a switch. If you take too long, the poison kills you. If you aren't careful and fall into a deep well of poison, you may not be able to get out.

Figure 4.25
A pool of poison.

Figure 4.26
A suit of armor, ready to be picked up (just walk up to it and it's yours).

Occasionally, you will be lucky enough to find protective gear like these radiation suits. They are only effective for a brief period of time, so you must act fast before the effects wear off. They are good protection if you must swim through poison to reach secret rooms.

In some screens, you can see a medical kit in the far left background. Take note of these, even if your health is good and you aren't in need when you find one. If you have a particularly rugged shoot-out, you may want to backtrack to a secure area and pick up some health bonuses, medikits, and stimpaks. They can mean the difference between life and death.

Figure 4.27
An automap diagram of the nuclear plant.

There are many mazes and corridors you must search through. It's easy to get lost and end up going in circles. The Tab key lets you easily toggle to a map that displays a schematic diagram of the building you are in. You can't see your opponents, but you can find entrances and corridors and get a different perspective on things.

Each level has an Exit door. When you have killed as many opponents as you can find, gathered as many items as you can use or carry, and can't find any more secrets, it is time to exit. If you are not ready to exit, simply go back out the way you came, take note of where the exit was for future reference, and go look around some more.

Figure 4.28
Tally your points at the end of a level.

When you press the lever to exit, you are presented with a screen that tallies up the percentage of kills, items recovered, and secrets found. The goal, naturally, is to have 100 percent before exiting. You carry the items found with you to the next level. So, if you found a shotgun, chain gun, or chainsaw, you have the option of using it in the next level. Otherwise, you must rapidly search out new weaponry.

Figure 4.29
*Your new target is
the nuclear plant.*

When you have completed one level and are ready to move on to the next, you are given a topographical map that shows the next building you must secure. You can press the Tab key to see an automap with a schematic diagram of the building.

Be on your guard when you begin a new level. The beasts get bigger and meaner as the game progresses. Some of them are nearly invisible—just an outline of a figure that comes out of the middle of nowhere.

You can save up to six games and start wherever you left off. The Pause button on your keyboard temporarily pauses the game if you are interrupted.

DOOM is the kind of game that will keep your interest for hours on end. It's a real blast![30]

DOOM II

DOOM II is a lot like DOOM—the same interface, the same cool 3D graphics, the same fluid, demon-smashing motion through a hellish virtual world. However, the more things stay the same, the more different they become, as evidenced by the amusing and dynamic twists of fate evident in the new version. How about point-to-point transporters, new hidden secrets, and a bunch of new levels? DOOM II is also a great treat for anyone who likes to play custom versions of DOOM—try up to 32 levels of alternate DOOMish reality.

The basic look and feel that we all loved, however, is pretty much intact, as you can see in Figure 4.30. What is different is a greater variety of details in the various settings; Figure 4.31 shows a typical example.

The bottom line on DOOM II is that if you liked DOOM, you'll love DOOM II. The interface is familiar enough to be easy to learn, and the challenges and settings are different enough to make DOOM II interesting in its own right.

---

[30]If you will pardon the pun.

Figure 4.30
DOOM II uses the familiar interface of DOOM in new settings.

Figure 4.31
A corridor from DOOM II.

Heretic

Heretic takes the DOOM interface into the world of magic. Like DOOM II, if you loved DOOM, there's a good chance you'll feel the same about Heretic. There are the usual demons (see Figs. 4.32 and 4.33), and the weapons are different (does a crossbow appeal to you?), but it has the good old DOOM feel through and through. There are new features, though, and the farther you go into Heretic, the more you will find. For example, when you kill one of the demons shown in Figure 4.33, you can watch its "soul" rise up and disappear.

Figure 4.32
Heretic features demons like this one.

Figure 4.33
Another Heretic demon.

Also like DOOM, Heretic features a map that you can view by pressing the Tab key. Figure 4.34 shows a typical map scene; note that the edges of the map fade away to nothing—I guess that's to make it more like magic.[31] Figure 4.35 shows another re-worked DOOM trick: a switch.

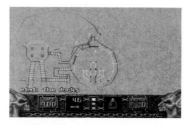

Figure 4.34
A Heretic map.

Figure 4.35
The Heretic version
of a switch.

Heretic is fun, but it does vary from the DOOM standard, focusing on blasts of magic force instead of traditional weapons. It has a less gory feel overall, and that will either appeal to you or make the game less desirable, depending on your tastes.

D!Zone

D!Zone is a DOOM add-on. It works with DOOM and DOOM II. While it is a little piece of heaven for any DOOM addict, it's also a lot of fun for even the casual DOOM player.

I wasn't sure what D!Zone does, and looking at the package you may also wonder the same thing. I'll solve that problem by giving you the tour here. However, you can save yourself some reading: If you have DOOM and like it, you'd be crazy to pass on D!Zone. It's a wonderful addition to your DOOM arsenal.

When you run D!Zone, you'll see what looks like an awful mess (see Fig. 4.36). That mess, however, is a wonderland of DOOM features. D!Zone will run DOOM after you set custom settings for your DOOM (or DOOM II) session. So you can drift through this and two other pages and configure DOOM just the way you want it. D!Zone even

---

[31]Tongue is firmly in cheek.

gives you control over some stuff that DOOM itself does not, such as the ability to visit levels out of order, or to randomize certain settings during play.

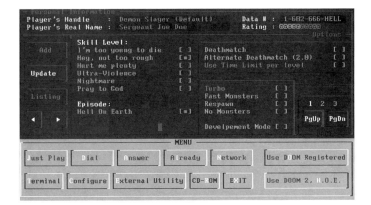

Figure 4.36
The D!Zone opening screen.

But that's just the easy part of what D!Zone offers. Look now at Figure 4.37, which shows the real strength of D!Zone. It comes with hundreds of alternate DOOM games and levels. You can see a number of these already selected for play at the left of the screen. Right-clicking on this area displays the screen shown in Figure 4.38.

Figure 4.37
More custom DOOM settings.

When you first see the screen shown in Figure 4.38, it will tell you that you need to pick a location to view files. If your CD-ROM drive is drive D, this is D:\LEVELS\PWADS. Once you set the location, you'll see all the PWAD files at that location, as shown in Figure 4.38. These are simply the usual cryptic, DOS, eight-character file names, but highlight a file and click the View Desc. File button to see more information.[32]

---

[32]Not all files will have information, however; sometimes you just have to try a file to see what it's about.

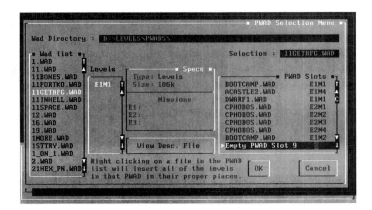

Figure 4.38
Picking from the hundreds of DOOM alternate games and levels.

The vast bulk of the files is actual DOOM levels of more or less complexity. Some have a single level; some have 10 or more levels, and are almost a game of their own. Still other files (in the Specials directory) are simply music and graphics files.

I'll pass on a few hints about using the screen shown in Figure 4.38; it's not at all obvious how to work with it, although the README file that comes with D!Zone is reasonably clear about most things.[33] The procedure is:

1. Click on a file name at the left to highlight it. This displays one or more levels in the box immediately to the right of the file names. Ignore that for now.

2. Click on a PWAD slot at the right of the screen; in Figure 4.38, the bottom slot is highlighted (you can scroll to additional slots—up to 32 with DOOM II).

3. Click on the level in the list of levels that you want to add to that slot. The level's file name appears in the list of PWAD slots at the right of the screen.

This probably sounds much more complicated than it actually is; once you get familiar with the process, adding levels is trivially easy. After you add the levels you want, click the OK button, and then click the Just Play button on the main screen. You'll be asked to select a conversion script; for starters, just choose the default. D!Zone then builds a custom PWAD file (the default name is T.WAD) in your DOOM or DOOM II directory; Figure 4.39 shows what the screen looks like while the PWAD file is being built.

---

[33]And full of funny, even weird, comments; it's worth a read even if you do know how to use the software.

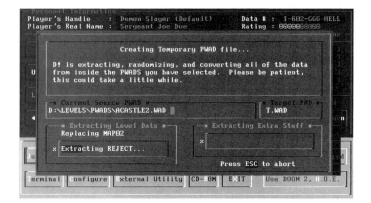

Figure 4.39
*Building the
temporary PWAD
file.*

When the process is over, D!Zone runs DOOM and starts you at the first level you selected. D!Zone even shows you the DOOM command line you can use to run the combination yourself (see Fig. 4.40). Figure 4.41 shows scenes from some of the DOOM levels that are included with D!Zone. The top scene shows just how different some of the levels are from conventional DOOM levels; note particularly the gorgeous sky and the odd-looking trees. Even the walls are unique. The bottom figure shows a river of lava in a somewhat DOOM-like setting. In all levels, the beasties you fight are all the familiar DOOM beasties.

Figure 4.40
*Starting DOOM
with D!Zone.*

Figure 4.41
*Scenes from various
DOOM levels
included with
D!Zone.*

Overall, D!Zone is quirky and amusing, not terribly intuitive, and absolutely essential for anyone who is mad about DOOM.[(34)]

Dark Forces

This is another game built on the legacy of the 3D interface of DOOM. Like DOOM, you move around in 3D using the keyboard, mouse, joystick, or other input device; kill the bad guys; and try to keep yourself alive and well.

There are subtle but very important differences between Dark Forces and the DOOM games, however. The use of sound in Dark Forces is much more effective. Where DOOM and its siblings mostly present you with the grunts, groans, and mumblings of monsters; in Dark Forces, you'll be facing foes who are more or less human, and they talk. Sudden cries of "There he is!" and similar alert cries will get your blood boiling in a hurry. The use of sound in Dark Forces creates a much more immediate sense of immersion in the game, and makes game play significantly more enjoyable.

The game interface is what you would expect, as shown in Figure 4.42. It features familiar figures from the *Star Wars* universe, but it goes well beyond such earlier (and fun) games as Star Wars Rebel Assault and Star Wars X Wing. Game play is very, very smooth in every respect.

Figure 4.42
*Encounter some of
your favorite Star
Wars enemies in
Dark Forces.*

I found the puzzles in Dark Forces to be just a bit harder than those found in DOOM and DOOM II. The implementation of various features is also a cut above, such as the map shown in Figure 4.43. Instead of having to flip to a completely different map view, the map appears superimposed over the game screen—allowing you to refer to the map without becoming vulnerable to attacks by the enemy. I found this map technique extremely useful for certain situations, such as complex mazes.

Overall, the game play of Dark Forces is superb—it's one of the best out there. It doesn't allow the swooping and turning in six degrees of freedom that Descent does, but there are some crouching and jumping capabilities that are lacking in most DOOM-class games. This is a smooth, well-designed game in just about every respect.

---

[34]Enthusiasts might want to take a gander at *Tricks of the DOOM Programming Gurus,* also from Sams Publishing, for down-and-dirty DOOM advice.

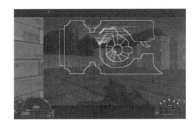

Figure 4.43
*Maps float on the
screen while you
play, if desired.*

Raptor

Raptor is a DOS-based game that puts you in the cockpit of a plane with turbine engines. You earn money on each mission, with which you can purchase additional weapons.[35]

During setup and installation, you select the game control type: mouse, keyboard, or joystick; music card; and sound device. If you have a sound card, the music and sound effects greatly enhance the game. The music in the opening sequence is really deep and full, and creates a feeling of anticipation.

If you select the option for a New Mission from the main menu, you are given the opportunity to select your call sign. You can select your pilot ID picture by clicking on ID with the mouse button. I chose a red-headed female and gave her the call sign *Babe*. Is this fantasy time, or what?

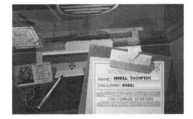

**Figures 4.44
and 4.45**
*Raptor's main menu
and call sign.*

---

[35]Unless, of course, you fail and go down in flames.

Figures 4.46 and 4.47
Choose the level of difficulty and your weapons.

After you select your call sign, you have to select the level of difficulty. Training mode lets you familiarize yourself with the game and its controls, but you can't earn any money. Rookie is the easy level, with Veteran for medium difficulty, and Elite for the brave (or foolhardy).

After you pick the difficulty level, you enter the Hangar, where you have the opportunity to save the game (press F2 inside the Hangar), enter the Supply Room to purchase supplies with money awarded in previous missions, fly a new mission, or leave the Hangar and return to the main menu.

Figure 4.48
The Hangar.

The Supply Room offers an opportunity to select as many weapons as you can afford. I recommend starting out with lots of shields. It took me a while to figure out I had tons of ammo and could shoot it out the entire game. But I took a lot of hits and went down in flames the first couple of times. The plane is maneuverable, and a smart pilot will dodge incoming fire.

Figure 4.49
The Flight Computer for Raptor.

After you select your weapons, you select a mission. The flight computer is displayed on your screen as you approach your destination. Be ready, 'cause you are about to take on several types of aircraft, ending with the mother of all aircraft!

Figures 4.50 and 4.51
Some aircraft give off a golden glow that awards you extra money. And you can increase your weaponry by destroying some land-based operations.

Ever watch the movie *Top Gun*? That's what Raptor reminded me of. On a much smaller scale, of course, but this is the first flight simulator I've used and it was fun to feel like I was flying an aircraft.

Navigation is pretty simple. Moving the mouse sideways causes a lateral move of the plane, and moving forward and backward repositions the plane accordingly.

The graphics may not be at the level of games like Myst or Zork, but they were good enough to make the game really enjoyable. Some of the planes produce a golden glow when destroyed and give you a bonus if you pick them up. Missiles also destroy buildings on the land, and occasionally they can add to your firepower.

***Figures 4.52
and 4.53***
*An enemy plane
going up in flames,
and the mothership.*

The graphics are pretty detailed, and enemy planes go up in flames. And just when you thought you had it made, you hear a deep rumble, see a large shadow coming in your direction, and encounter the mothership.

If you successfully complete your mission, you have money with which to buy additional weapons.

The game has limited navigation; for example, you can't turn your ship around. But you have quite a bit of maneuverability; you can move forward on the screen to take an aggressive posture, or fall back if you run into too many oncoming planes at once.

Raptor requires quick reflexes and an itchy trigger finger. You can outmaneuver the enemy if you play the game a couple of times. But it is a low-stress way to release a little frustration and have some fun. Raptor comes with an 11-page pamphlet but is intuitive enough to play by just sitting down and poking around.

Blake Stone

Blake Stone comes with a colorful manual that includes a comic book. My expectations were high for this game: It is the follow-up to Wolfenstein 3D, a classic of 3D gaming.

The colorful flyer gives the game a PC-13 rating, stating that it is not recommended for younger viewers due to realistic depictions of violence. What a hoot!

I was impressed with the PC-13 screen that displays when you start up Blake Stone but still wasn't sure whether the game's creators were putting me on.

Figure 4.54
The banner displayed when you start up Blake Stone.

Figures 4.55 and 4.56
Startup screens for Blake Stone (choosing a mission and difficulty level).

The next two screens are pretty standard stuff, so that you can choose a mission and difficulty level. Pretty realistic graphics in the difficulty screen.

Figures 4.57 and 4.58
The initial startup screens of Blake Stone.

The opening screen bears a strong resemblance to DOOM, with the hand-held pistol looking down a corridor. And there are strong similarities between the two games, which reflect id Software's influence on the game. But I consider any contributions from DOOM to be on the plus side.

If you successfully defeat your opponent, you can pick up his weapon. However, if you encounter an informant (dressed in a white lab coat), you can query him and get important information. Of course, you take the risk that he has no information to offer and will shoot you.

Blake Stone has 3D-texture mapping in 256 colors and feels like a VR game. You have the ability to maneuver and explore anywhere you have access. Once again, I found myself bumping into walls trying to round corners or go through doorways. But the main difference between Blake Stone and DOOM is that Blake Stone has bright primary colors. This contributed to the feeling that it was just a game, and the lack of realism gives it less of an adrenalizing effect than DOOM.

There were enough similarities that my experience with DOOM made it easier to play Blake Stone without reading the instructions. Eventually, I read the background story so I could learn more about the game's nuances.

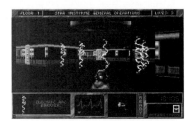

Figures 4.59 through 4.61
Barrier switches, shut-off arcs, and posts.

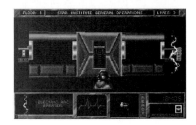

Blake Stone has great graphics, including detailed floors and ceilings. Sometimes, you encounter ugly enemies hidden behind arches and posts. If you find the barrier switch, you can shut them off and gain access.

You can access the automap feature by pressing the Tab key. The automap provides a color-coded map of the current floor. The right side gives you a tally of total points for the game, number of informants alive, and number of enemies destroyed.

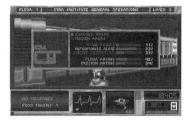

Figure 4.62
*The built-in
automapping feature
from Blake Stone.*

You move from one level to another via the elevator, but it will not operate unless you have the red access card—typical game stuff.

**Figures 4.63
and 4.64**
*Looking at the
eating lounge and
food unit.*

I enjoyed coming upon the eating area. The room is colorful and is complete with tables, chairs, and a food unit. If you have any tokens, you can buy food from the dispenser. This has the additional bonus of increasing your life expectancy.

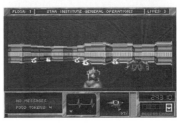

Figures 4.65 and 4.66
If you successfully defeat the big enemies, you may find them guarding treasure.

In Blake Stone, you aren't just fighting for your life or the cause—if you can survive the onslaught of Dr. Goldfire's enemies, you may stumble onto some booty.

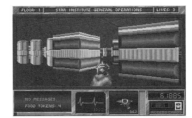

Figure 4.67
Check for hidden passageways.

You can sometimes find hidden passageways if you move along the wall and press the space bar.[36]

Figure 4.68
A blood-spattered maze.

---

[36]Sound familiar? If you've played DOOM, you discovered this trick. However, in DOOM you were alerted to a secret passageway by discoloration of the wall or the sound of a door opening and closing. I had no such clues to this movable wall in Blake Stone.

When I came upon the passageway shown in Figure 4.68, I realized why the game had a PC-13 rating. This room was pretty graphic and realistic, and could easily put you off if you're sensitive to violence.

Figure 4.69
One of the slimy "boss" enemies you encounter in Blake Stone.

I enjoy Blake Stone as much as DOOM, but for different reasons. I like the challenge of exploring each of the levels to see what kinds of surprises I might find. And I love the detailed graphics and bright colors of Blake Stone; DOOM is dark and eerie.

The music and sound effects are fun and add a lot to Blake Stone. I really enjoy the ability to maneuver and explore areas without having to point and click. There's nothing that compares to real-time navigation, and Blake Stone offers detailed graphics with true VR-type navigation.[37]

3D Action Games

The following games were sent to us by Apogee Software when we put out the call for VR games, but they are more 3D than VR. They remind me of computerized versions of Nintendo and Sega games. But they're fun and colorful, so here are some samples.

Duke Nukem II

Duke Nukem II has vivid, parallaxing VGA graphics; music; and digitized sound effects for Sound Blaster or compatible sound cards. It also supports keyboard and joystick modes. The game is designed for all skill levels and has 32 levels in four episodes. It includes a Save and Restore feature that can be accessed from the main menu.

---

[37]I can't help myself; I find myself continually comparing Blake Stone to DOOM. DOOM was the first game I played that offered real-time navigation through corridors, up stairs, and so on. And the menacing sounds and feeling of being hunted—as well as of hunting—in DOOM hit me at a guttural level that Blake Stone never touched. Blake Stone has cartoon-like monsters, so you remember it's a game. DOOM has more menacing-looking opponents, which gives a feeling of realism. I find Blake Stone more benign and more playful. But it would be difficult to choose between the two if I had to pick a favorite. Somehow, I can't see Blake Stone ever becoming the cult favorite that DOOM is.

Figure 4.70
*Duke Nukem is
back!*

**Figures 4.71
and 4.72**
*Duke goes after the
bad guys in a big
way.*

Halloween Harry

The All-American values of sex and violence are alive and well in this game, as can be
seen from the opening screen.

Figure 4.73
*The opening screen
of Halloween Harry.*

**Figures 4.74
through 4.77**
*Earth is under
attack by alien
invaders, and Harry
is the man for the
job.*

The story unfolds with a series of images that set the scene. It's the year A.D. 2030, and New York City is under attack by alien invaders. Halloween Harry is the hero of the hour. Duke Nukem fans should find a lot to like in the Halloween Harry game.

Figure 4.78
Halloween Harry
encounters a
zombie.

Figure 4.78 shows the 256-color scrolling graphics, which are supplemented with sound effects and music. Harry has the ability to fly through levels with his jetpack.

The system requirements for Halloween Harry are a VGA graphics adapter and an 80286 or better IBM-compatible machine. Joystick and Sound Blaster are optional.

Bio Menace

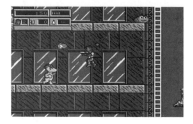

Figures 4.79
and 4.80
Super agent Snake
Logan facing some
of the mutants
created by Dr.
Mangle.

Bio Menace has colorful, smooth-scrolling graphics that are supplemented with AdLib music and sound effects. The system requirements are an EGA graphics adapter or higher, an IBM or compatible 286 processor or higher, and support for an AdLib music card or compatible.

Adventure and Puzzle Games

This class of games offers some excellent opportunities for virtual environments. However, the classic VR trade-offs are evident; you often must choose between fluid movement in the environment and good graphics. You will seldom get both with today's technology.

Myst

Myst is an adventurous mystery game that runs under Windows. The game runs from CD-ROM, which makes it possible to have very detailed graphics. Installation is very simple. To install Myst, you must have Windows running. Then simply choose the Run option from File Manager and type **D:\INSTALL**, where *D*: is your CD-ROM drive letter. Consult the instructions included with the game for step-by-step guidance.

The system requirements for Myst follow:

- IBM/Tandy personal computer or 100 percent compatible
- 386 DX 33 MHz processor or higher (486 recommended)
- 4M RAM
- Windows 3.1; MS/PC-DOS 5.0 or higher
- Super VGA graphics card (640x480, 256 colors)
- MPC-compliant sound card
- Mouse
- Hard disk with 4M of free space
- CD-ROM drive (preferably, double-spin)

Myst requires a 256-color, palletized display driver; you will get better results at smaller screen resolutions. If you normally use 1,024x768 screen resolution or 16- or 24-bit graphics, you will need to change to 640x480, 8-bit mode and restart Windows in order to run the game. The payoffs are high-resolution graphics and video clips that add a lot of pleasure to the game.

I was quite unprepared for the level of detail in Myst's graphics; it sets new standards for what is possible. The game makes excellent use of music to intensify the experience. The sound is so full, and the sound effects are so well orchestrated that I found the music as pleasurable as the graphics. For instance, down by the water you can hear the ocean lapping on the shore. On top of the island, you can still hear the ocean in the background. There are different sounds for each of the areas on the island. The sounds add a great sense of realism. Metal doors clank, wooden doors squeak, but the overall effect is to enhance the sense of being in a different world.

The trade-off—there's always a price—is that although Myst provides beautiful graphics and sound, it offers jumpy, point-and-click navigation. In a game like DOOM, you have an opportunity to navigate around corners, proceed forward or go backward, or make a 360-degree turn by moving the mouse. Myst allows limited navigation by clicking the mouse. You can move forward by clicking the mouse in the center of the screen, or turn to the right or left by clicking on the right or left side of the screen. You are cued by a pointing hand on the left and right edges of the screen. Sometimes you can rotate 90 or 180 degrees by clicking, but some portions of the game restrict the places you can go. There is always a pause before you move, and you don't get any sense of the movement. You are in one place before you click, and then you suddenly arrive in a new place. There are some animations that provide transitions, but realistic movement is not what Myst is about.

After you have visited an area of the island, you can use Zip mode to quickly move between areas. Zip mode is signified by the cursor changing to a lightning bolt. This helps speed up the process of moving, which can be tedious when you want to move quickly between one place and another.

You can save your game and start it up at a later time by accessing a menu at the top of the screen. To show the menu (it's normally hidden), place the cursor at the top of the screen to see the File and Options menus. The File menu lets you begin a new game, restore a previous game, save your existing game, or exit. The Options menu lets you decide whether to use transitions. If transitions are on, Myst uses a dissolve effect whenever you move from one screen to another. You can also turn on Zip Mode. The Options menu also includes information about the game.

I found the level of detail in the graphics very rewarding, and enjoyed spending time and energy trying to solve the puzzle. Myst is most definitely not an action-oriented game. It is thought-provoking and challenging.[38] The object of the game is to explore an island world and to use various clues to solve puzzles that provide access to unexplored areas. The game is steeped in mystery and keeps you coming back for more.

The story unfolds in a most unusual way. Myst is actually a book describing an island world that you get to explore. As you read the book, you realize you are actually there—exploring the island described in the book.

---

[38]For those of you using CompuServe, the Gamers Forum has a lot of hints on how to play Myst.

Figure 4.81
The first page of the book Myst.

The story begins with a page from an open book. If you click on the picture, you are drawn into it and find yourself standing and looking at a mountain with a big gear on top.

Standing on the boardwalk, you can hear the water lapping at the shore. There are several directions you can explore, and it is fun to just choose any direction and begin. I chose not to get a closer look at the gears, but to head up the steps to some buildings.

You must keep a sharp eye out for clues, but this one is pretty obvious, and the first one I happened upon. It is a personal note with a clue. The game provides a nice journal that you can use to keep track of clues. I started out jotting things on yellow Post-Its, but they kept getting lost or covered up. The journal is much better for keeping notes.

Figure 4.82
The pathway and gears have several colors, with high-lights and shade that add to the realism.

Figure 4.83
Notice the shadows
falling across the
steps, and the scrap
of paper on the right
side of the board-
walk.

Figure 4.84
Click on the scrap of
paper, and you can
read it easily. Note
the rich detail in the
texture of the paper.

Figure 4.85
Notice the stone
pillars on this
building and the
level of detail,
including the brass
emblem on the door.

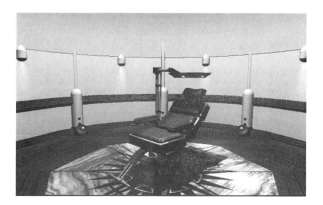

Figure 4.86
*Inside the building is
a time machine.*

To solve the puzzle, it is important to observe every area carefully. Later, you can use clues to unlock mysteries, like how to use this time machine.

**Figures 4.87
through 4.94**

*A 360-degree view of
one of the buildings.
The wood is a rich
mahogany color,
and even the ceiling
is ornamented. The
paintings on the
walls provide
important clues, so
check them out.
Each image in this
sequence is one click
away from the next.*

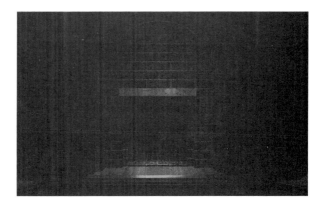

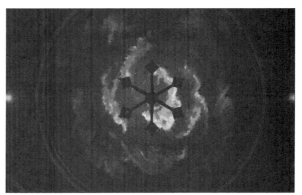

Notice the level of detail inside this building. The wood has a nice texture and reddish color, and the floor has a circular design. Clicking on one of the pictures reveals a hidden staircase.

***Figures 4.95
through 4.98***
*The shadows on the
buildings and on the
path through the
trees add an eerie
feeling and enhance
the sense of realism.
This sequence shows
the screens you
would see along
your way down the
path.*

As you explore the island, you encounter new paths and buildings. And once you have visited an area, you can always use Zip Mode to zip between areas.[39]

Figures 4.99 and 4.100
Solving the puzzle will reveal new areas, or ages, to explore.

---

[39]Zip mode is active when your cursor turns into a lightning bolt. You can choose Zip mode by accessing the menu at the top of the screen.

When you have successfully gathered enough clues to solve portions of the puzzle, you will discover new areas to explore. I had to piece together clues found in four or five locations to discover the building shown in Figure 4.99.[40] And I feel like I've barely scratched the surface of the game's potential.

Magic Carpet

Like Descent, Magic Carpet is a game that supports full six-degrees-of-freedom movement. Your carpet can take you up, down, and around; you can tilt and pitch and roll—it was realistic enough to make me dizzy, and that's saying something. No other game I played was quite as responsive as Magic Carpet. One reason: Magic Carpet is played in an outdoor setting, unlike the caves and caverns of Descent. You can get a lot dizzier a few thousand feet up in the air.

Also like Descent, Magic Carpet has full support for 3D stereo. It will work with red/blue glasses, and it supports a number of the better game headsets, such as the i-glasses! and CyberMaxx. Figure 4.101 shows the configuration page; one of the many combinations for headsets is shown (headset and joystick). This is better than many other games, which require you to use a relatively complex command-line sequence to support a headset. Since many headsets support head tracking, you may wind up not using the joystick for navigation.

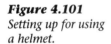

Figure 4.101
*Setting up for using
a helmet.*

Speaking of navigation, Magic Carpet must be very well programmed—navigation is extremely responsive on even a 486 computer. The game starts with what you see in Figure 4.102—perhaps a corner of a personal library in some magic kingdom. The globe takes you to the world of Magic Carpet, while the molecular model is used to start network play. You can save games to and from disk using the books stacked at the right.

---

[40]When I've been working several hours on the book or trying to get software to run, Myst is a nice way to take a break. Sometimes I begin a new game to see if I can find fresh evidence. And sometimes I feel like picking up where I left off to see how much farther I can go. The whole family got involved in comparing notes and sharing clues we found. If you get frustrated, it's fun to compare notes with someone else. Each of you may have pieces of the puzzle that will unlock one of the mysteries.

Figure 4.102
Getting started with
Magic Carpet.

Figures 4.103 and 4.104 show typical scenes from Magic Carpet. The world is eerily lit, shrouded in a misty fog that prevents you from seeing everything at once. Adding to the fun is the fact that this is all about magic—some objects can't be seen until you are close enough to penetrate the invisibility spell that surrounds them. Figure 4.103 shows the opening scene. It shows an artificial rock formation, and all such rock arrangements indicate that manna may be found. Accumulating manna is the name of the game, in fact, so you'll want to keep your eye out for those rock formations! Figure 4.104 shows a Stonehenge-like formation, which contains not just manna but a few spells. When attacked, you cast appropriate spells to save your hide.

Figure 4.103
The opening view of
the Magic Carpet
world.

Figure 4.104
Locating manna is
as easy (and as
hard) as finding the
stone formations.

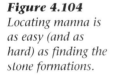

You'll also need to cast spells just to get things done. The citizens of this world need your help in bringing balance, and you can create a castle with a castle spell, as shown in Figure 4.105. Note the information bar at the top of the screen. At the left, it shows a small map of the world around your location. The various sections of the top bar contain useful information about the world and you. You can also look at a larger map, as shown in Figure 4.106. This view shows the map on the left, a small version of the current location at the upper right, and your current spells at the lower right.

Figure 4.105
A castle created with
a spell.

Figure 4.106
Finding your way
with the map.

Overall, Magic Carpet is more of a puzzle game than an action game, but it truly incorporates elements of both. The flying experience, for example, is fun and challenging, but you'll never crash and burn. My kids Justen and Chanel liked Magic Carpet a lot.

Under a Killing Moon

This is one of those games that breaks all the rules and defines a new way of playing games. Before Under a Killing Moon (UAKM), we had 3D games like DOOM that delivered smooth movement in a low-resolution, 3D environment, and we had 3D games like Myst that delivered static but splendidly detailed 3D images. UAKM delivers both high-resolution graphics and smooth movement in a 3D world.

However, UAKM is not very DOOM-like, nor is it quite like Myst. It is a detective story, and you must gather the traditional tools, evidence, weapons, and secrets from the universe of the game in order to reach the conclusion. Figure 4.107 shows the game interface. The upper left portion is where you see the 3D world of the game. Figure 4.107 shows the office of the detective, and you can move around freely using a mouse or joystick. Movement is smooth and fast, although you can change the size of the display area for a faster or slower computer.

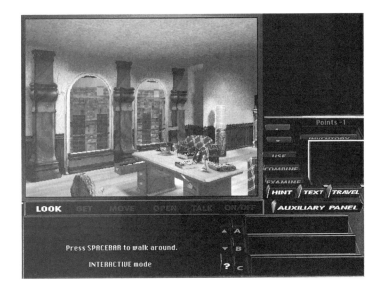

Figure 4.107
The game interface of Under a Killing Moon.

The row of words immediately below the display area defines what actions you can take. In the example, the only possible action is LOOK, but this changes depending on the significance of the object. You can GET objects, OPEN drawers (see Fig. 4.108), TALK with characters in the game, and turn things ON and OFF.

Figure 4.108
An open drawer; note the pen in it—it is an item the game requires you to locate and then GET.

This game is solid from a VR perspective—the images are very detailed, movement in the virtual environment is extremely smooth (although it varies with CPU speed, a 486/66 is more than adequate), and the sound effects are very detailed and helpful. Game play itself varies quite a bit. Movement in the environment is simple, but there are just too many repeating sound cues. I got awfully tired of hearing the same *spiel* every time I clicked on a desk drawer to open it or close it—there are six drawers, and listening to the narrator prattle on *12 times* was just too much.

That's probably the only real weakness in the game, however, and you can always turn off the sounds (but you won't want to; they are so good otherwise). The game incorporates live actors (see Fig. 4.109 for a view of our erstwhile detective[41]), mostly in long video clips that fill the gaps in the story line. For example, after you solve all the puzzles in the office and leave it for the outside world, you see a movie that fills in details of the story. The acting is hokey but fervent, and you'll probably be able to forgive the various name actors who are slumming in this game.

Figure 4.109
Under a Killing
Moon incorporates
live actors.

The game has an excellent interface, and that makes it a pleasure to play. Anything you need to do—put a stamp on a letter, write with a pen, check your inventory—is right at your fingertips. There is even a map for getting to the places you've visited before without having to go through a lot of rigid rigmarole (see Fig. 4.110). Overall, a fun game and an excellent use of 3D and VR technology.

---

[41]Most of the actors are name actors—Russel Means, Brian Keith, Margot Kidder—but the detective is none other than the producer of the game. An actor (any actor) would have been a better choice.

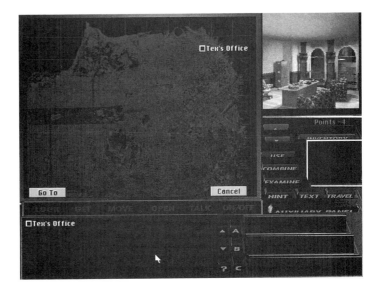

Figure 4.110
You can use the map to visit familiar places.

Gadget

Gadget is a bizarre but amusing game that is very, very hard to describe. It's a bit like Myst in that it has puzzles to solve, and a bit more like Myst in that it presents you with a sequence of finely rendered images as you move through the game. But I hesitate even to call it a game. Gadget is dark, mysterious, and more linearly arranged than Myst.

Figure 4.111 shows the opening locale for Gadget: room 306 in an unnamed hotel. A valet waits outside the door in case you try to leave the room before you've gathered everything from it that you will need (see Fig. 4.112). The valet is typical of the characters you'll meet in Gadget: stiff, formal, and very strange looking. Most of the characters do not speak to you verbally, but interact using text at the bottom of the screen. This is a bit retro, but the overall feel is so mysterious and magical that one is inclined to forgive such lapses of technique.

Figure 4.111
*The opening locale
in Gadget.*

Bring your room key to the reception desk, if you please

Figure 4.112
*A valet—typical of
the strange charac-
ters you'll meet in
Gadget.*

The renderings themselves are extremely detailed and well done. There are Quicktime video-animation sequences sprinkled here and there. Most are in black and white, either to preserve CPU capability or to deepen the mystery. Sometimes, it's hard to tell just what Gadget is up to—and, somehow, that just adds to the fun.

Gadget more or less guides you along the path you must take, dropping hints as you go. It is more like an interactive movie than a game. However, it predates the trend toward such movies, and is more creative than any other such product that I have seen. It's like an art movie, however, rather than a crowd pleaser: It will make you think, and it leaves many things unsaid.

To play along, you must talk to everyone you meet, even though some will only complain rather than offer useful information. It's hard to tell, though, what information is useful, what is accurate, what is nonsense, and what is meant as a form of poetry.

That is ultimately what makes Gadget charming: Just when you begin to be bored, and to think you know where the game/movie is going, the rug is pulled out from under your feet, and you have to regain your equilibrium.

The interface is nicely detailed, although all renderings use 256-color images (like Myst and many other products). Figure 4.113 shows a typical close-up with nice details.

Figure 4.113
A typical close-up image.

In the hotel room, you'll pick up your suitcase as you get ready to leave (see Fig. 4.114). However, the mystery begins on your way out, when you meet a small boy with a very similar suitcase (see Fig. 4.115). He pulls the old switcheroo on you, and you wind up with an almost empty suitcase which you must fill with secret devices in order to save humanity from a comet that is about to crash into the earth and destroy it. Figure 4.116 shows the items you'll be looking for.

Figure 4.114
Your suitcase.

Figure 4.115
The young,
mysterious boy.

Figure 4.116
The suitcase.

You'll meet that boy many times throughout the game/movie, and each time the mystery deepens. I won't spoil the fun by revealing any details, however.

Your mission really begins when you come down to the lobby of the hotel. A man in black gives you instructions (see Fig. 4.117). You set off for the train station (don't forget to drop your room key at the main desk, or you won't have a train ticket!), which, like most settings, is beautifully rendered (see Fig. 4.118).

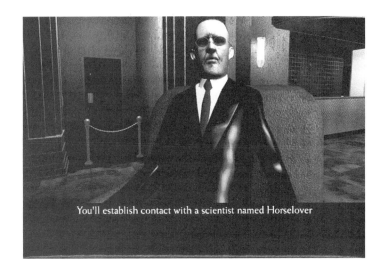

Figure 4.117
The mysterious man in black.

Figure 4.118
A rendering of the train station.

You'll spend a lot of time on the train exploring it and talking to the various folks who seem to inhabit it. Figure 4.119 shows a typical interior, and Figure 4.120 shows a typical passenger.

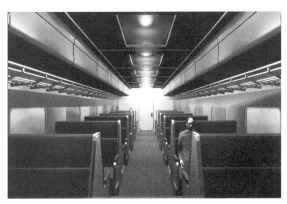

Figure 4.119
The interior of the train.

Figure 4.120
*One of the
mysterious train
passengers.*

That talk of a comet colliding with the Earth is just nonsense

Overall, I found myself glued to Gadget. I must admit that the technology used isn't of the highest order, but the story; the way it is told; and, most of all, the mystery make Gadget a wonderful way to while away an afternoon—or, better yet, a late evening. Gadget is like a D.W. Griffith movie: prescient, before its time. It's the first grand, artistic vision to find its way into the multimedia/VR mainstream, and deserves cult status.

Cyberwar

This is a very ambitious game that has great VR, but the game itself wasn't what I had hoped for. It is based loosely on the movie *Lawnmower Man*, with the main cybercharacter from the movie playing the role of Bad Guy in the game. However, most of the game actually consists of puzzles or tests of skill, and this just didn't fit in with the motif very well. Here we have this super-bad Cyberwar game package, and inside we have these rather tame puzzles.

We also had two specific kinds of trouble with the game. First, the printed documentation doesn't tell you how to exit the game. The key combination used to exit is odd enough that it surely should have been documented. We called tech support, and when they called back a day later, they told us how to exit: Press Ctrl-Esc. You have been warned.

The game graphics are very well done—the detail is as good as any game on the market. There is a great deal of 3D animation included on the four CD-ROMs that make up the game. You read that right: *four* CD-ROMs. The only other multi-CD game we encountered was Under a Killing Moon. Figure 4.121 shows another reference to the movie: an image of a face on the same "page" as the level-select controls. We thought this was a pretty cheap way to drag in the movie—it would have been much nicer to actually integrate the characters into game play!

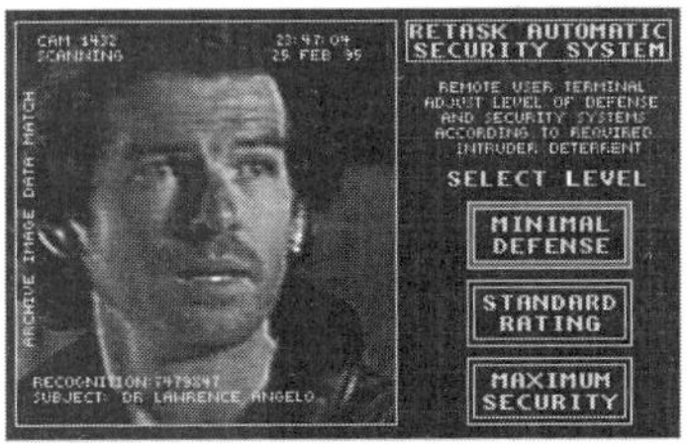

Figure 4.121
Selecting a level of play.

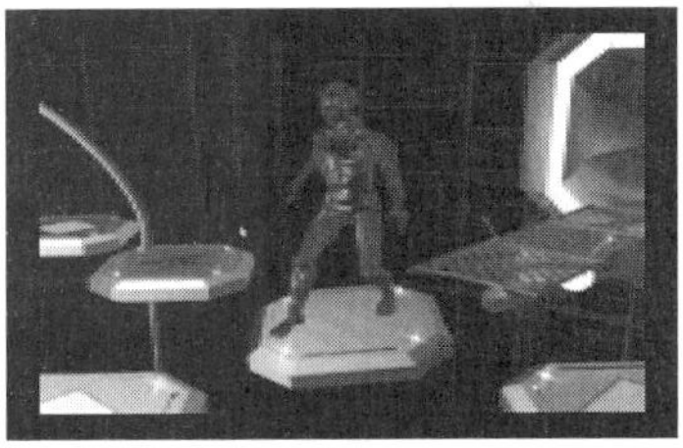

Figure 4.122
Attempting to solve a puzzle in the Reverse Engineering room.

The action shown in Figure 4.122 is typical of the tightly integrated animation sequences you'll find in the game. If VR and animation are your goals, the game will do well; if you actually want to play the game, that's a different story. It's OK, but it's not what the package promises.

Return to Zork

Return to Zork is a CD-ROM game that runs under DOS. There are two installation options. You can install a minimal set of files to your hard disk and run everything else from the CD, or you can install about 42M of files and Zork will run much faster. This speeds up performance, but not everyone has that kind of free disk space for a game. The installation program will automatically detect a Sound Blaster sound card and its current settings, although it can't auto-detect other digital audio sound cards. Have your sound card factory defaults handy, because you're going to need them during installation.

Some suggestions follow for optimizing performance of Return to Zork:

■ Set up your system to have as much free conventional RAM as possible. Return to Zork needs a lot of memory.

■ Use the XMS/EMS option. If you have XMS (expanded memory), set up as much free XMS memory as possible.

■ Often, SMARTDrive and other hard disk-caching software can increase performance.

- CD-ROM owners with lots of hard disk space should copy the project file to their hard disks.

- If you don't currently have a CD-ROM drive on your system and are thinking of purchasing one, you should get a double-speed drive capable of sustaining transfers of 300K/second. This will definitely improve performance of Zork and many other CD-ROM-based programs.

- Launching Return to Zork from Windows may diminish sound performance.

- Disk-compression software may be incompatible with Return to Zork's program and data compression, which could cause unreliable performance. Install Return to Zork on an uncompressed drive.

This game is extremely entertaining and playful. It offers high-quality graphics and animation that are different from Myst or Iron Helix. When you click on the screen, you invoke an animation that takes you to the next scene. It's similar to an interactive movie.

The accompanying manual is very well written and does a good job of describing how to play the game. It's a quick read, with only 28 pages. I prefer to play games using a mouse, and Zork does a good job of letting you use the mouse to your advantage. The cursors, which change depending on what you are doing, are big and easy to see and interpret. The game is easy to install and start playing. It has an intuitive interface that invites you to play.

The manual is supplemental rather than required reading. And if you get stuck and need a hint, call the Activision Hint Line at 900-680-HINT. Of course, you need to be 18 years or older or have your parents' permission to call. Calls are 95 cents per minute, and charges begin after the first 18 seconds.

The game begins with an entertaining sequence that combines video with an overlay of words. Anyone familiar with the original Zork game will enjoy the humorous references to the original game. No doubt about it, sound adds yet another dimension to the game, which increases the realism and draws you into a more immersive experience.

Figure 4.123
The opening video sequence for Return to Zork. Notice the words overlaid on the picture.

Figure 4.124
The Tele-Orb with the Wizard Trembyle, who provides colorful commentary throughout the game.

One of the most colorful characters you meet during the game is the Wizard Trembyle. He offers suggestions and warnings during the game.[42] Take note, because sometimes he warns you against areas that could contribute to your demise.

Figure 4.125
You can pick up and store items in your inventory during the game.

One of the nicer features of the game is that you can interact with the physical environment. If your cursor is over an item with which you can interact, you get action-interface options. You can put the item in your inventory, or combine items with other items in your inventory. Be creative! This combination of items offers the solution to many of the puzzles in the game.

Figure 4.125 shows the interface options for the rock. What is the normal reaction to an obnoxious vulture that keeps attacking you? Throw the rock at it, of course. This opens up other options, such as a closer examination of the vulture's roost. The possibilities are endless, which is what makes the game so fun.

If you click on the arrow to follow the path out of the Valley of the Vultures, you end up at the lighthouse. If you knock on the door, you get the keeper. This interaction with characters is unique to Return to Zork. The other CD-ROM games offer interaction with the environment but are devoid of any other human forms. Return to Zork is fun because it lets you visit with other life forms.

---

[42]It would be nice to be able to interrupt the video if you've seen it before or don't want to listen to all of it. I find it pretty frustrating to have to listen to the talking crystal ball repeat the same spiel over and over. I would like to be able to click while he's talking, interrupt the animation, and move on.

**Figures 4.126
and 4.127**
*The lighthouse and
its keeper.*

Figure 4.128
*Inside the light-
house, you can
explore up the stairs.*

Once inside, you have an opportunity to visit with the keeper or to travel up the stairs.
Navigation is indicated by a bright red arrow.

**Figures 4.129
and 4.130**
*You can interact
with most characters
in the game.*

You can have a conversation with the lighthouse keeper by selecting the Talk To icon from the Action Interface display. Once you select the Talk To icon and engage the keeper in conversation, you'll see a column of icons on the left side of the screen. If you click on these icons with the left mouse button, you can direct the tone of the conversation with your body language. What fun!

The map plots the path taken in your travels. Your current location is indicated by a blinking red dot. The map provides a useful overview for your explorations.

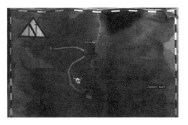

Figure 4.131
The map is one of the few permanent items in your inventory.

Figure 4.132
Some items located near the lighthouse.

If you get stumped and don't know how to proceed, take a closer look at some of the items in the surrounding area. The combination of some of these items often solves the puzzle of where to go next.

Figures 4.133 and 4.134
Traveling down the water with a brief stop in town.

I floated down the river and came to a cluster of small buildings. I knocked on each of the doors to gather any clues and pick up additional items for my inventory. But be sure to save frequently, in case you suddenly die.

You can access the Zork System menu by placing the cursor in the upper left corner of your screen at any point in the game. You'll know the cursor is in the right location when it changes to a Zork Disk icon. Then just click the left mouse button. Your options are to save, quit, load, restart; or change some of the effects like visual, music, sounds, or text. You also get the current game score.

Figure 4.135
This screen is accompanied by an evil laugh whenever you explore a dangerous area that proves to be lethal and leads to your early demise.

There are some areas you cannot explore with impunity. If you enter one of them, you die. If you saved your game, you can pick up where you left off.

So, as you can undoubtedly tell, I found Zork really amusing and restful. It was entertaining, and I enjoyed combining different inventory items. Sometimes the combination did nothing, and sometimes it provided an obvious solution to a puzzle.

The navigation isn't as direct as in DOOM, but I enjoyed the graphics and movie-like interaction with the game. And I especially enjoyed the characters I ran into. I would characterize this game as highly entertaining.

Quantum Gate

Quantum Gate is one of those games you'd like to like, but never do. The packaging is great, the concept is great, but the execution is, at best, average. The game just wasn't much fun to play.

The makers of this game could learn a lot from the folks who did Gadget. Quantum Gate is filled with every bit of technical wizardry available to the vendor, but it lacks a soul, a story that the technology can rally behind. The game uses live actors, but they seem lost in the interface, and the acting is, at best, stony and cold.

The look of the game, however, is spectacular. I suppose that if I limited myself to just the VR aspects of the game, I could be pleased. Figure 4.136 shows an example of the 3D graphics—they are outstanding, and operate in the manner of Myst or Gadget (that is, extremely high quality still images mixed with spots of video animation).

Figure 4.136
A scene from
Quantum Gate.

The integration of live actors is perhaps a bit too artsy. Figure 4.137 shows an example—one of the figures on the right is speaking, so the talking head is magnified at the left, and is a full video + audio clip. However, talking heads are boring, and nothing is done to spice it up—the actor hardly moves, and his words are not imbued with much meaning.

Figure 4.137
A live actor from
Quantum Gate.

Overall, I just couldn't get into the game. There is an action sequence portion of the game, but not a single machine we had on hand could cope with it—it appears to have trouble with various flavors of video cards. All in all, the 3D effects are great, but the game is flawed.

Megarace

Megarace, on the other hand, is a game that goes light on the technology (using basic, proven video/animation) and heavy on the cool stuff. This is a fun game in many respects. The fun starts with the announcer for the game—Lance Boil.[43] The character is played by a live actor, and it is an over-the-top performance not to be missed. Figure 4.138 shows Lance at his strutting best, introducing the show.

---

[43]One of many silly jokes in the game is the names.

Figure 4.138
Lance Boil,
announcer
extraordinary.

How many times have you started up a game, only to practically fall asleep as the story is explained to you? Most of the time, right? Megarace is the answer to a prayer. The intro is so good you'll want to sit through it twice before you even play the game, and you'll be tempted to play it every time you start up the game. It's funny, it's well-acted, and it's clever and witty, too. Just the tonic for a bad day at the office.

The game itself isn't bad, either. It's a race, all right, around a series of more and more challenging tracks. The cars are armed, naturally, so if someone gets in the way, you can always blow them away. If you are good, you can eliminate the competition by smashing into them and running them off the road—but don't crash too hard, or you'll lose big time.

The integration of VR is first rate, though rather low tech. As with the character of Lance Boil, the use of VR relies more on good concept than on high tech. Figure 4.139 shows an example of what I mean—the cityscape is vivid and gets its point across well. Figure 4.140 shows a frame from the opening animation. Yes, it's low resolution, but it's well done, with fine control of movement and camera angle. A lot of other games could learn something here: Pay attention to the details, and don't expect fancy technology to carry a game if the story isn't good in the first place.

Figure 4.139
A vivid, if low-res,
cityscape from
Megarace.

Figure 4.140
A frame from the
opening animation
of Megarace.

Iron Helix

Iron Helix is a CD-ROM game produced by Drew Pictures. It requires Windows to run and, like Myst, requires a 256-color palette. Like Myst, it is a compromise: You get point-and-click navigation and high-quality graphics.

Installation couldn't be simpler, and the program entertains you while you wait. A dinosaur named Timmy eats players who don't send in their registration cards—you'll see a hapless victim who didn't send in his card become Timmy's next meal.

The intent of the game's creators was simple: to keep game play as fast as possible while maintaining high-quality graphics.[44] The game makes good use of background music, which is suitably "spacey."

To play, you must send a probe aboard a heavily armed ship named the SS Jeremiah Obrian, and find the ship's cargo—an H-bomb that is armed and ready to be used. You are in the Science Ship Indiana, and your goal is to sabotage the deadly mission of the Obrian and avert a holocaust. To do this, you must board the renegade ship Obrian with your probe and gain security access to the rooms and computers. You must then search the ship for ways to prevent it from deploying its deadly weapon against a peaceful planet. But watch out! The ship has a robotic Defender that is heavily armed and capable of performing all ship functions. You must avoid the Defender and destroy it in order to win.

The interface through which the game is played is the Probe Control panel, which lets you direct the probe through the ship, plug the probe's arm into the Obrian's computer, and gather microsamples of organic life.

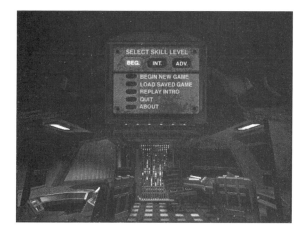

Figure 4.141
The opening sequence of the game begins with a video playing in the monitor at the top of the screen.

---

[44]The graphics were certainly creative and well done, but I found the dark corridors and rooms of the game rather plain and difficult to see. While highly detailed, they were singularly uninspiring.

Iron Helix takes advantage of a lot of animation and video sequences. The game begins with an introductory video that plays in the monitor at the top center of the screen.[45] When you click the mouse, the video stops and is replaced with a menu. You are given a chance to begin the game, save or load previous games, replay the introductory video, quit, or look at the About box. You can also select the skill level from this menu.

The game takes place through a control panel called the Probe Control Interface. The top left window of the control panel displays the areas of the ship through which you navigate. The window on the right displays messages about the ship or video displayed in the left window. For instance, if you come to a door (pictured in the top left window), the window at the top right displays a button that says Open Door. If you click the button to open the door and do not have clearance, you are informed that you do not have access.

The arrows at the bottom left of the panel are for navigation. You click on the arrows that are highlighted to go up, down, left, right, forward, or backward. The window at the bottom right displays maps of the ship. There are three map modes available.

Figures 4.142 through 4.144
The interface for Iron Helix is a control panel.

---

[45]I found this means of introducing you to the game's mission a refreshing break from having to read about it. Some games present background information in a manual or in a file on-screen. I enjoyed listening to a character lay out the story in a video. More and more games are moving to this method, and not a moment too soon.

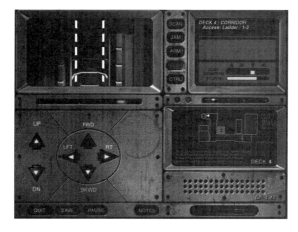

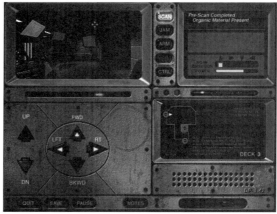

Iron Helix is a game of skill that requires you to spend some time reading the manual in order to play. The operations manual is 32 pages, and you would be well advised to look it over. The game offers a down-and-dirty quick start so you can begin playing Iron Helix immediately, but you probably won't get very far just poking around.[46] The Defender found me, and I died several times while I was just looking around.

System requirements follow:

- IBM 25MHz 80386 compatible or faster
- Microsoft Windows 3.1
- 4M RAM

---

[46]Iron Helix reminds me a lot of my introduction to science fiction. The first science fiction book I read was *Dune*, by Frank Herbert. Reading this book required that I frequently reference the glossary at the back. You can play Iron Helix by just poking around with the probe and trying doors, but it's a lot more fun if you get into the story and learn the nuances of the ship and its crew.

- Super VGA graphics (256 colors in 640X480 resolution or higher)
- Hard drive with 16M of free space
- CD-ROM drive (150 Kb/sec sustained transfer rate or better recommended)
- Double-speed CD-ROM recommended
- Sound Blaster or compatible

> If you don't have one or more of these required features, you will be unable to play Iron Helix.

King's Quest

I'm probably pushing the envelope a bit to include games at the low end of the VR spectrum, but if you subscribe to the trickle-down theory of VR, you'll understand what I'm up to. The King's Quest series of games had its start many years ago (many by computer-gaming standards, that is). The graphics were simple, but this was a game ahead of its time.

The interface has now evolved into the era of 3D. While the look is still cartoonish, the effect is artful and pleasing. Figure 4.145 shows the opening scene of the game—really just a painted background of a beach with an animated figure to move about on it.

Figure 4.145
The opening screen of King's Quest.

Figure 4.146 shows more of an effort at 3D—the inside of a store. Note that the speaker's face is blown up to give us more detail. It's an interesting, but not terribly effective, method of overcoming the inherent limitations of the game interface.

Figure 4.146
*A typical interactive
scene in King's
Quest.*

One of the basic problems any game designer has when incorporating 3D is to provide a good "look" at the low screen resolutions most games offer (a mere 320x200 in most cases). That's not many pixels to work with—try it some time. The cartoonish look avoids things like reflections and too much surface texture, but I still prefer the kind of details I found in Megarace, even if they are at low resolution. The game King's Quest is fun enough to play, but it doesn't make much use of 3D technology to get the job done.

Edutainment

Edutainment is one of those words that I wish we could do without. It's an odd duck, and sounds even odder than it looks. It describes software that is partly educational, and partly entertaining. As far as I'm concerned, if an educational CD isn't at least partly entertaining, there's no reason to spend money on it!

The titles in this section represent a wide variety of interests, topics, and styles. They range from a fanciful future technical manual (that is far more entertaining than the name suggests) to sports such as Golf.

Star Trek, The Next Generation

This is no game, but it has two very good things going for it: The content is extraordinary, and the technology is too. The content is styled after the computer displays of the Enterprise 1701 D, the ship used in the TV series. All the *Star Trek* backgrounds are used cleverly, and the voice of Majel Barrett (Gene Rodenberry's wife), the familiar voice of the on-board computer, is also the voice used throughout the technical manuals. Jonathan Frakes, who played Will Riker, narrates a tour of the starship that is thorough and fun—and that, like everything else, absolutely adheres to the high standards and detail of anything *Star Trek*.

Figure 4.147 shows a typical "page" in the technical manual. The use of the STNG computer display designs is evident, as is the amazing level of detail. There's no doubt about it—if you love and enjoy *Star Trek*, you'll love and enjoy this gem.

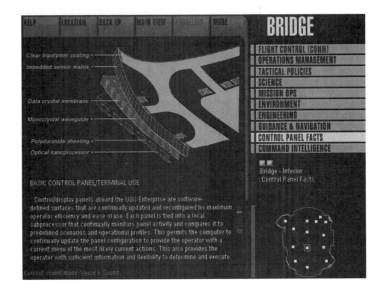

Figure 4.147
A page of the STNG technical manual.

The interface uses a variety of cursors to help you know where you are and what you can do. Figure 4.148 shows a portion of the Help page that explains the various cursors. You'll know when you can click on an object or scene for further detail, where the navigation hotspots are, how to move within a scene, etc. just by paying attention to the cursor. The Help system is excellent and makes full use of the STNG computer display interface.

Figure 4.148
A portion of the Help page showing the various cursors and navigation aids.

The scenes themselves are well done, and they utilize a dramatic new technology from Apple: QuickTime VR. This is a technique for taking 360-degree images of a scene, and then allowing you to navigate through the scene as though you were right inside it. Look at Figure 4.149, which shows a sequence of frames that illustrate how this works on the bridge of the Enterprise. However, these four frames don't really begin to give you an idea of how dramatic the sense of movement is. I would recommend you get this product just for the experience of working with QuickTime VR—it's that good.

Figure 4.149
A sequence of views showing movement in QuickTime VR.

The process of creating a QuickTime VR world involves stitching together a series of images that show the complete 360-degree view from one point in a space. Special software merges these images, and when viewed, the data is processed to remove any distortion introduced in the process—what you see looks as natural as if you were standing in the room, turning around to look. You control all motion, so that you look up, look down, turn left, and turn right. I have included the same sequence of images you see here in black and white in the color section of the book as well.

There are many excellent views of the Enterprise, inside and out, included in the technical manual. Figure 4.150 shows a view of the bridge area from outside the ship; note the level of detail, including details inside the ship. Figure 4.151 shows two views of Ten Forward—a long view of the bar, and a close-up of objects on the bar. Since the actual sets used for the TV show were used to create these images, the level of detail is almost always very high. In many cases, you can examine objects—even pick them up and turn them to see details. Figure 4.152 shows a view of the engine room. This, too, was photographed for the CD-ROM using the original sets.

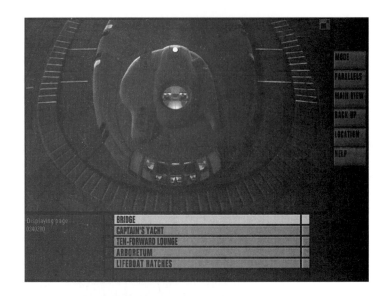

Figure 4.150
*A view of the bridge
from outside the
Enterprise.*

Figure 4.151
Ten Forward.

Figure 4.152
*A view of the engine
room.*

Golf 2.0

I'm sure that you are wondering if I have gone out of my mind: adding a golf game to
a book on virtual reality. But please don't throw out the book yet—I'm serious about
this.

Let me start by saying that I hate golf. No one can say that I have added this product out of some misguided love for the game of golf. No, sir! You would no sooner catch me out on the links than you would find me swimming the English Channel.

Even so, I was rather taken in by the Golf game from Microsoft. It's quite a nice application of virtual reality to a slice of everyday life.[47] Whatever one thinks of whacking a little bumpy white ball around the countryside, Microsoft has done a great job of adding VR to the concept. Figure 4.153 shows the program in action.

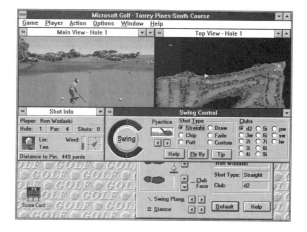

Figure 4.153
Microsoft Golf: VR where you least expect it.

The virtual stuff is on top, showing a scene of the golfer on a golf course at the top left, and an overview of the course at the upper right. If you like, you can fly above the entire course, one hole at a time, to get a look at what's there. The rest of the interface is just bells and whistles related to golf; if you like golf, I leave it to you, dear reader, to explore the details.

Links 386 CD

Yes, there is yet another virtual golf game out there. It's called Links 386, and it has everything for the golf enthusiast. There are more virtual golf courses than I could count, including such notables as Pebble Beach, Mauna Kea, Bighorn, Castle Pines, etc. Since I'm emphatically not a golf enthusiast, the course that appealed to me was the Devil's Island fantasy course. Figure 4.154 shows a sample course. As in Golf, you can fly above a hole or an entire course to see how it might play.

---

[47]Yes, that's a horrible pun. Just don't get teed off at me, OK? You'll see what I'm driving at momentarily.

Figure 4.154
Links 386 also provides virtual golf courses.

The game's interface is a lot like that used in Golf from Microsoft: You use the mouse to swing, and you have to work on your timing with either program, so there definitely is some skill involved in making good shots.

Setting Up Your Sound Card

All sound cards are not created equal. But all sound cards do have certain things in common. Most important, every sound card will require you to set it up before you can use it.[48] There are three steps involved in setting up your sound card:

1. Physical installation
2. Installation of utilities and drivers for DOS
3. Installation of utilities and drivers for Windows

    In many cases, steps 2 and 3 are combined. There is also often a fourth step:

4. Installation of games and other software that may come bundled with the sound card

Let's walk through the process of installing a typical sound card—the Sound Blaster

---

[48]Of course, if you bought your computer with the sound card already installed, you might find that the software and drivers for the sound card already function just fine. Congratulations if this is the case!

16. I chose this particular model because many readers will have exactly that card, and because it is fairly typical. If you have a different sound card, or a sound card from a different manufacturer, the exact details of your installation will be different. However, the basic ideas will be similar.

Physical Installation of a Sound Card

Adding a sound card to your computer is just like installing any other card. The process involves these basic steps:

1. Remove the cover from your computer.

2. Select an unused slot for the sound card. If the sound card will be connected to an internal CD-ROM drive, be sure to select the slot closest to the CD-ROM drive. Otherwise, the cables connecting the sound card and CD-ROM drive might interfere with other cards in your computer.

3. Remove the small cover for the slot with a Phillips screwdriver.

4. Check the documentation that comes with the sound card to see if you need to set anything on the card itself. There may be jumpers (see Fig. 4.155) or switches (see Fig. 4.156) to set.

Figure 4.155
Jumpers.

Figure 4.156
Switches.

5. Carefully insert the sound card into the chosen slot (see Fig. 4.157). Don't bend it, don't force it—gently but firmly seat the card into the slot. See Figure 4.158 for an example of how far into the slot the card should go. Replace the screw you removed in step 3 to hold the card in place.

Figure 4.157
A sound card positioned in its slot.

Figure 4.158
This is how far to insert the card.

6. Connect any cables that are required inside the computer. For example, you may need to connect your CD-ROM drive with a flat "ribbon" cable (see Fig. 4.159), and an audio cable may also be included if you bought a multimedia upgrade kit that included both a sound card and a CD-ROM drive (see Fig. 4.160).[49]

Figure 4.159
A ribbon cable carries data between a CD-ROM drive and your sound card (but not audio!).

---

[49]If you bought these two items separately, you may need to connect the CD-ROM drive's audio output to the sound card's input. Simply buy a 1/8-inch mini to 1/8-inch mini cable, and plug it into the CD-ROM drive's headphone output and the sound card's Line In input.

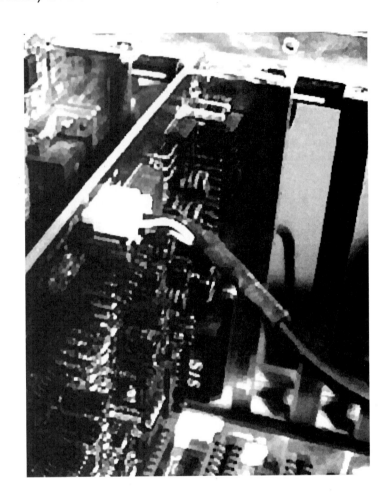

Figure 4.160
Many upgrade kits come with an internal audio cable for CD-quality sound.

7. Replace the cover on your computer.

Interrupts, I/O, and DMA

If it weren't for interrupts, memory I/O, and DMA channels, installing a sound card would be trivially easy. In many cases, you won't need to worry about it, but that's not why books get written! This section is here for those readers who can't use the default settings for their sound card.

First, let's define some terms:

> **Interrupt**—Many of the cards in your computer need to get the attention of the CPU from time to time. To get attention, the card sends an interrupt request[50] to the CPU. There are 16 interrupt lines, but a number of them are

---

[50]Hence the term IRQ: *interrupt request line.*

used for predefined purposes (such as printer and modem ports; see Table 4.2). Your sound card must use an interrupt that isn't already used by some other device in your computer.

I/O port or I/O address—A sound card needs a way for the PC to communicate with it. This is done through I/O ports. It must use a port that is not already being used by some other card. For example, if you have a network card, it may also use an I/O port, and must be at a different address to avoid conflict with the sound card.

Memory address—Many cards need a way to share data with the PC. This is typically done via a memory address. A card using this technique appears as memory to the PC. It must use a memory address that is not already being used by some other card. For example, if you have a network card, it may also use a block of memory, and must be at a different address to avoid conflict with another card that uses a memory address.

DMA channels—When a sound card plays sounds, it is moving very large amounts of data from memory to your sound card (via the I/O port). Most sound cards use Direct Memory Access (hence the acronym, DMA) channels to speed up the movement of this data.[51] DMA channels free the PC's CPU from work by automatically handling the movement of this data. There are only a handful of DMA channels and—as with interrupts, I/O address, and memory addresses—it is critical that only one card use any given channel.

Table 4.2. Interrupts and Their Uses.

Interrupt	Common Usage
0	Timer
1	Keyboard
2	Access to interrupts 9-15
3	COM 2 and COM 4 (if present)
4	COM 1 and COM 3
5	LPT2 (if present; can be shared with sound card)
6	Floppy disks
7	LPT1 (can be shared with sound card)
8	Real-time clock

continues

---

[51]Some high-end sound cards, such as the Turtle Beach cards, use alternative (and faster) methods for moving sound data around inside your computer.

Table 4.2. continued

Interrupt	Common Usage
9	Redirected IRQ 2
10	Not usually used by system; available for add-on cards
11	Not usually used by system; available for add-on cards
12	Not usually used by system; available for add-on cards
13	Math coprocessor
14	Hard disk
15	Not usually used by system; available for add-on cards

If your computer has only one COM port, that gives you an extra available interrupt. If you are not using a second printer port (LPT2), that also gives you an interrupt you can use. Some cards won't use interrupts higher than 8, and having an interrupt or two available in this low range can be important.

Not all cards can be set to any available interrupt. Often, the interrupt is selected by physically altering switches or jumpers on the card, and there may not be a jumper for certain interrupts. You might have to do some juggling to get interrupts for each card in your system.

CAUTION

Not every card in your computer uses interrupts; only some of them need an interrupt. For example, your video card probably does not use interrupts. On the other hand, some video cards come with a built-in mouse port—and the mouse port will need an interrupt. You will almost certainly have to check your computer's documentation carefully to determine which cards do and do not need interrupts.

In general, your sound card will almost certainly come with factory settings for interrupts, memory I/O, and DMA channels. You should first try these settings to see if they work—unless you already know that they won't.

Some sound cards will require you to use jumpers and/or switches. Some sound cards will allow you to use software to make these settings. And, naturally, some sound cards will use a combination of methods.

Installing DOS Drivers and Utilities

Let's step through the process of getting your newly installed sound card up and working. Merely putting the sound card into your computer isn't enough; the sound card requires some special software in order to function. This software is called a *driver*. That term may not mean much to you; it comes from the early days of computing. The key fact to know is that the driver is what allows programs to use the sound card to make sounds and music. The driver software sits between other software and the sound card.

One important job the driver does is to keep track of all that information about interrupts, memory I/O, and DMA channels. During installation, you will either tell the driver what settings you set (with jumpers and switches), or what settings should be set by the driver itself using software.[52] Let's see how the Sound Blaster 16 Setup program handles these tasks.

Before we start, note that the Sound Blaster 16 uses a combination of jumpers and software settings. The program that performs setup and configuration is SBCONFIG.EXE.

The first task is to set the address of the I/O port. Figure 4.161 shows the screen; note that there are four possible addresses that the Sound Blaster 16 can use—220 (default), 240, 260, and 280. You can also choose Auto Scan. Since the I/O address is set by software, Auto Scan will check your computer to see if any other card (such as a network card) is using any of these addresses for an I/O port, and then select an unused address for the sound card's port.

Figure 4.161
Selecting the I/O port address.

---

[52]There was a time when the only way to set the settings was to physically change a jumper or switch. More and more sound cards are moving over to using software programs to change settings. This is much, much more convenient—you don't have to pop open your computer and pull out the sound card every time you want to make a change. Of course, it is the higher priced sound cards that are using this technology first, so your budget may dictate some compromise.

The Setup software will choose whatever address you select to determine if it works properly (see Fig. 4.162). It will also test other settings, but those tests aren't shown here to conserve space.

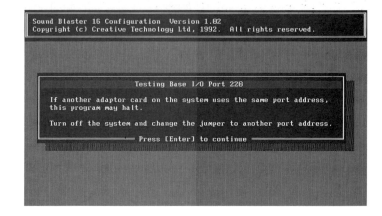

```
Sound Blaster 16 Configuration   Version 1.02
Copyright (c) Creative Technology Ltd, 1992.   All rights reserved.


                         Testing Base I/O Port 220

       If another adaptor card on the system uses the same port address,
       this program may halt.

       Turn off the system and change the jumper to another port address.
                        Press [Enter] to continue
```

Figure 4.162
Testing the I/O address.

If the address works properly, you will see a confirmation letting you know the port passes testing.

The address you just set was for the portion of the sound card that plays WAV files. Another part of the card is used for playing MIDI files, and it needs a port address as well. Figure 4.163 shows your choices; there are just two: 300 and 330. Both of these are *hexadecimal* addresses, by the way. That's a base-16 number system used by computers.[53] Note that the MIDI port is set using a jumper on the sound card; if the chosen port does not test OK, you'll need to pop the hood, pull the card, and change the jumper setting. Since you only have two choices, if there is a problem, you may need to change the other card, not the Sound Blaster.

The next step is to tell the configuration program which interrupt (also known as an IRQ) to use. The interrupt is set in software, so you can either accept the default or try various settings. There are four choices: 2, 5, 7, and 10 (see Fig. 4.164). Try to avoid using IRQ 2—it is used to access IRQs 9 through 15.

---

[53]When you and I count, we use the decimal number system—based on our 10 fingers. Computers operate using powers of two—2, 4, 8, 16, 32, 64, and so on. Thus, it makes sense for computers to count from 1 to 16. The numbers from 10 to 15 are represented by the letters A through F. To count from 1 to 10 in base 16: 1, 2, 3, 4, 5, 6, 7, 8, 9, A, B, C, D, E, F, 10. Many scientific calculators do conversions from decimal to hexadecimal and vice versa. Of course, you don't need to know any of this to choose a MIDI port; you just have to make sure that the MIDI port is one that nothing else in the computer is using.

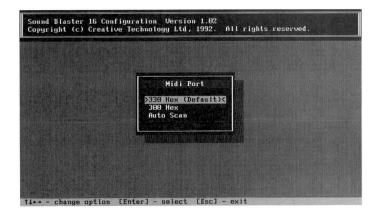

Figure 4.163
Setting the MIDI port address.

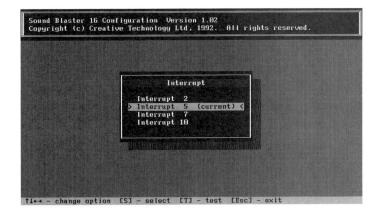

Figure 4.164
Selecting the interrupt for the sound card.

Interrupts 5 and 7 are normally used by printer ports (LPT2 and LPT1, respectively), but this is a case where the sound card and another device can share an interrupt setting.

You'll also need to set an 8-bit DMA channel for the sound card (see Fig. 4.165). There are just three choices: 0, 1, and 3. Few devices use DMA channels, so you are unlikely to run into a problem. It's usually safe to accept the default setting.

The Sound Blaster 16 is (as you might guess from the name!) a 16-bit sound card, and you will also be asked to select a DMA channel for 16-bit operation (see Fig. 4.166). The choices are 5, 6, 7, or none (that is, using only 8-bit DMA access). Again, accept the default. If there is some reason why your computer cannot use 16-bit DMA, the setting you select will fail during testing. This should not be a problem on new computers.

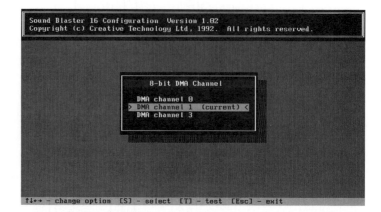

Figure 4.165
*Setting the DMA
channel.*

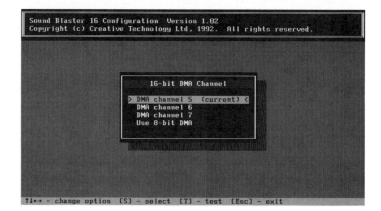

Figure 4.166
*Setting the 16-bit
DMA channel.*

When you have completed the configuration, the Setup program will modify your
AUTOEXEC.BAT and CONFIG.SYS files. This installs the DOS driver for the sound
card every time you reboot your computer.

Installing Windows Drivers and Utilities

You may or may not have to run a separate program to install Windows drivers for
your sound card. In the case of the Sound Blaster 16, the configuration program automatically modifies the Windows system files to install the sound card drivers. However, for some sound cards, there may be a separate step for Windows setup. Check
your documentation to see if this is necessary for your sound card.

In some rare cases, you may need to install the Windows drivers manually. You may
also have to install the driver manually if there is an update, or if your Windows setup
is incorrect.

Installing Additional Software

There are all kinds of extra software packages that sometimes are included with sound cards. If you purchased a multimedia upgrade kit, you may also have several software programs bundled with it—games, encyclopedias, clip art, music, and so on. In most cases, you will need to install each included package separately. Each package will have its own requirements and methods, and you'll need to check the documentation to determine how to perform the installations.

Often, bundles do not include the same documentation and packaging that is included with the full retail version of the product. For example, you may get a manual in a plain cover, or no manual at all. This can sometimes make it a bit of a challenge to get the software up and running, and you should be aware of this limitation when you go the bundle route.

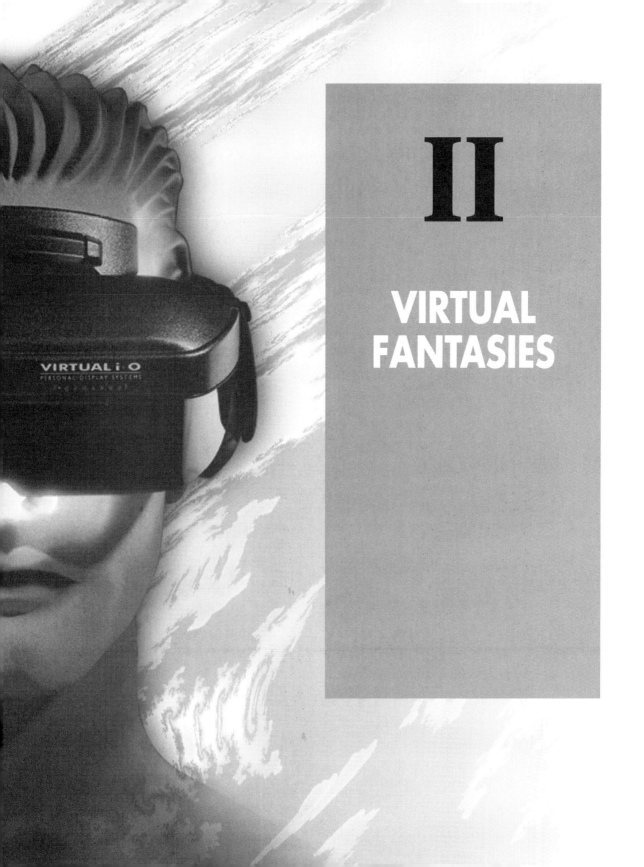

II

VIRTUAL FANTASIES

5

CREATING YOUR OWN REALITY

RECIPE

1 VR or 3D editing program
1 large serving imagination

Instructions: This chapter is about space—creating it, modifying it, moving around in it, and having a little fun with it. There will be practice in the art of creating a virtual universe by hand, as well as in the fine art of manipulating 3D models using the magic of inverse kinematics.

Don't Fence Me In

The whole idea behind creating your own reality is—*what*? What is the motivation? What makes it exciting and interesting and worth the time and effort to create your own alternative universe? After all, it's only virtual, right?

Let's face it—reality has its hang-ups. You can only go so far with reality. If you want to go to Paris, you have tickets, luggage, and the language to worry about. The whole idea of virtual reality is that there are no hang-ups, no fences, no limits beyond what's already in the software.

And as the hardware and software advance, those limits will always be farther out than they were yesterday.

Superscape: The Ultimate VR Tool?

If money were not an obstacle, this is the tool you would choose for making VR happen. I won't pull the wool over your eyes on this one. When it comes to VR, bigger and more expensive is definitely better.

When I wrote the first edition of this book, the whole point was to give you, the reader, a selection of inexpensive (mostly) tools that you could use on your own PC to work virtual miracles. This time around, a different point of view surfaced. What would it be like, I asked myself, to work with software that pushes the envelope of PC-based VR to the limit? In a word, it's cool.

For example, Figure 5.1 shows a simple Superscape world. It doesn't look all that impressive—no fancy structures, no dynamic motion. It contains a flashlight and a face. "Oh my," you are no doubt saying. "Mr. Author has flipped his lid—he thinks this is exciting." But there is something here that makes this little scene special. It shows exactly the kind of stuff you can do with Superscape that makes it powerful. With Superscape, you can truly mimic the real world, in many of the little ways that count.

What's so special about Figure 5.1? The flashlight is off. There are three buttons on the flashlight.[1] You can turn it on, off, or adjust the amount of illumination. Figure 5.2 shows the world with the flashlight turned on. This kind of detailed control is what makes Superscape such a great product. Even better, you could create a world with giant marching ants and a few miniature cars, and that giant face could look down on it all; the flashlight could be turned to illuminate any part of the scene, interactively. Superscape can handle the toughest task, and handle it well.[2]

Superscape will definitely spoil you. You will get used to the high resolution and the interactive power. You will get used to the tight integration of head-mounted devices and alternate input methods like the Spaceball.

At the same time, Superscape suffers from a mild case of what I call *Big Software-itis*. All Big Software has one thing in common: a small market. Software written for a small market has two key ingredients: lots of functionality oriented toward that specific market, and a weak user interface. Superscape suffers from this problem—but with a twist: If you've got the bucks for fancy input devices, you'll be fine. If you have to use the keyboard to move around in the virtual space, you will fry your brain before you will memorize all the cryptic methods you must use for moving around.

So the answer is obvious: If you have the money ($5,000 and more) for Superscape, you had better scrape up a few thousand more for a Spaceball 2003 or some other high-end input device. The combination is a killer—it's the only way to virtually fly. Add a good headset with motion tracking and hardware to generate dual stereo outputs for that headset, and you are in VR heaven.[3]

---

[1]You can just make them out if you look closely at the figure.

[2]At the same time, what makes VREAM such a good deal is the price—it's less than a tenth of what Superscape costs. However, you do get something for your money when you invest in Superscape. It's easier to use, operates at a higher resolution at design time, has a more complete programming language for animation, and has a faster, more efficient runtime. See Chapter 2, "Virtual Possibilities," for information about VREAM.

[3]Which raises an interesting point: Does a VR universe have a heaven and/or a hell? I guess it's up to the creator.

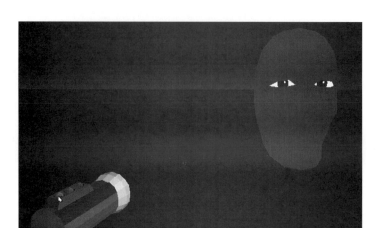

Figure 5.1
A Superscape virtual world with a face and a flashlight.

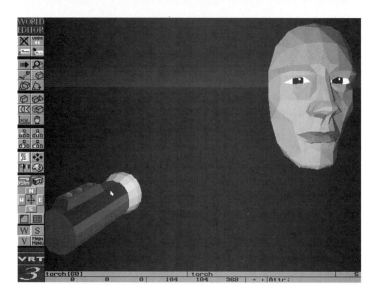

Figure 5.2
The flashlight has been turned on. Wow! Virtual reality lives.

Superscape has two key parts: an editing environment, where you can create, modify, and place objects in your universe; and a viewer, where you can interact with the universe. The editing environment consists of a Shape Editor and a World Editor, and the runtime module is called the Visualizer. Superscape also includes other tools—including a Layout Editor, Texture Editor, Sound Editor, and more. These additional tools aren't as cool as Superscape itself—but they are the ones you'll use anyway if you are using Superscape.

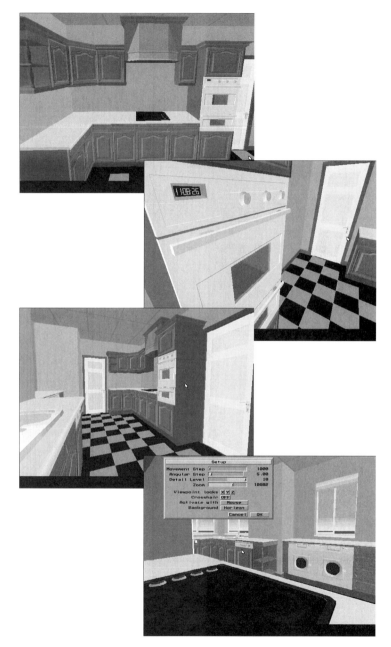

Figure 5.3
Four views of a kitchen created in Superscape. From top: A view of the stove top and range; a close look at the range and a door; looking down the length of the kitchen; a view from the stovetop, showing an interactive menu.[4]

---

[4]The Visualizer is realistic enough that when you pop up a menu, it's a bit jarring. That's how it should be!

Working in Superscape

Because Superscape supports a range of alternative input devices, we tested it using those devices we had on hand. By far, the niftiest is the Spaceball 2003 (see Fig. 5.4). With the Spaceball in one hand and a mouse in the other for selecting icons and menus, you can be extremely efficient navigating the complex tools that Superscape offers. It is significantly more cumbersome to use only the mouse and keyboard.

We also tried working in Superscape using an HMD (see Fig. 5.5). We found that the HMD was great in the Visualizer, but that it did not offer enough resolution for effective development in Superscape. This is unfortunate, because what the world really and truly needs is a good **and affordable** high-resolution 3D *development* environment. I have taken great pains to point out how challenging it can be to create 3D objects on a 2D screen. Yes, Superscape is powerful, but developing on a screen is tough. While a helmet may be too coarse, other solutions, like CrystalEyes LCD glasses, can give you what you need.

Figure 5.4
*The Spaceball 2003
from Spaceball
Technologies, Inc.*

If you will be using Superscape for development, I would urge you to look closely into the Spaceball for input. Superscape is hugely complex, and you can easily double your productivity by investing in the Spaceball.[5] We also tested the Logitech

---

[5]Donna found it somewhat harder to use than I did. The Spaceball is extremely sensitive, and it also helps if you have a natural ability with maps—you have to think in three dimensions of movement at all times. After several hours of use over several days, however, movement becomes almost second nature. It's very much worth sticking with the Spaceball—movement is very precise.

Cyberman (see Fig. 5.6), but that device didn't have the same tight control over position that the Spaceball does. At less than one-tenth the cost, of course, that's to be expected. The Cyberman is fun for games, but lacks the sensitivity and repeatability needed for serious VR development.

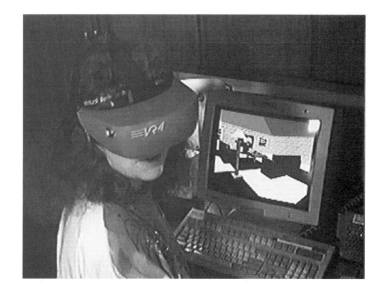

Figure 5.5
A head-mounted device in use by Donna Brown.

Figure 5.6
The Cyberman from Logitech.

Superscape World Editor

The main function of the World Editor is to construct a virtual world and the complex objects that furnish it. The building blocks of these objects are the shapes created in the Shape Editor. The World Editor lets you create, position, size, color, bend, rotate, and animate objects. When you finish constructing objects, you can use the Superscape Control Language (SCL) to give additional attributes to objects to control their movement, animation, lighting, distancing, interactivity, and intelligence.

The icon bar contains seven groups of icons arranged in two columns (see Fig. 5.8). They duplicate the functions used most often on the World Editor menus. You can either use the icon bar, or right-click to display the World Editor menu shown in Figure 5.7. You can access all features using the menus, while the icon bar only gives you access to the most-used features.[6]

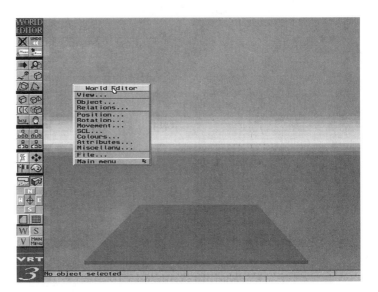

Figure 5.7
The Superscape World Editor.

General Object Features

Delete Object—Deletes the current object (and its children).

Rename Object—Renames a selected object.

Undo—The World Editor stores changes made when editing the world, which gives you the chance to undo those changes later in case of error.

---

[6]Just to be complete, there are also keyboard shortcuts for many features.

Virtual Reality Madness 1996!

Above: A scene from a Vistapro landscape animation.

Left: A fanciful VR landscape created in VisualPro and modified in Adobe Photoshop.

Below: A Vistapro landscape.

These pages contain graphics from vendors, screen captures, and output from various 3D and virtual reality software programs. They were assembled in Adobe Photoshop 3.0.

VR Madness

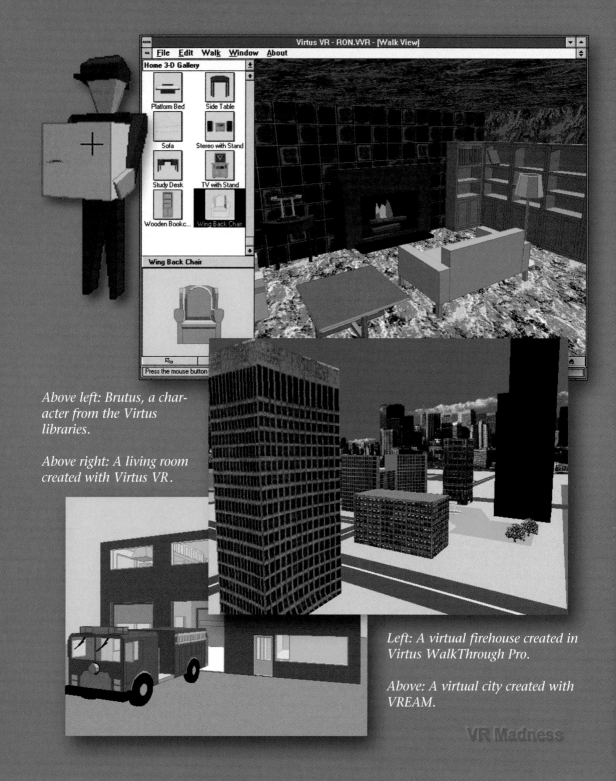

Above left: Brutus, a character from the Virtus libraries.

Above right: A living room created with Virtus VR.

Left: A virtual firehouse created in Virtus WalkThrough Pro.

Above: A virtual city created with VREAM.

VR Madness

Left: Multiple views of a virtual Chicago in VREAM's VRCreator.

Below: A virtual office created in 3D Studio.

Below left: A dizzying view of a virtual city created in 3D Studio.

VR Madness

Top left: Frame from a trueSpace animation.

Top right: A rendering created in Vistapro 4.0. Note reflections.

Above: trueSpace in action.

Left: The VR5 headset.

VR Madness

Right: A page from Star Trek, The Next Generation Technical Manual.

Below: The Fifth Dimension glove from General Reality.

WARP NACELLES

::Ship Exterior
:::Structural Features
:::Warp Field Nacelles
::::Warp Field Coils

MODE

PARALLELS

MAIN VIEW

BACK UP

LOCATION

HELP

WARP FIELD COILS

The energy field necessary to propel the USS Enterprise is created by
assisted by the specific configuration of the starship

POWER TRANSFER CONDUITS	
SUBSPACE FIELD GEOMETRY	
WARP FIELD COILS	

Below left: A frame from a fanciful animation created with 3D Choreographer.

Below: The hottest new game controller—the Spaceball Avenger.

VR Madness

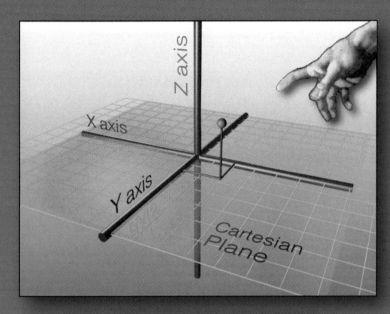

Left: The Cartesian coordinate system applied to three dimensions.

Lower left: The i-glasses! from Virtual I/O. No, they don't turn you orange, but they are the very best game headset under $1,000.

Lower right: Spreadsheets created in 3D Studio.

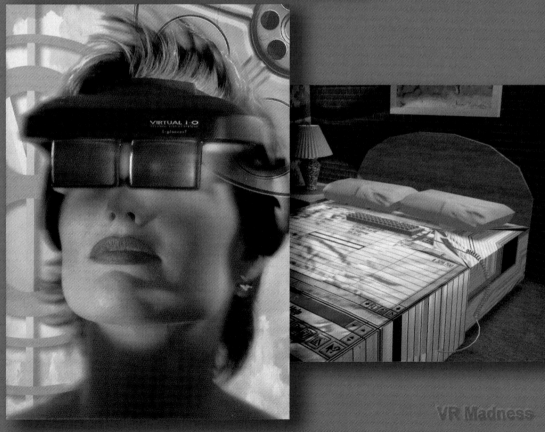

VR Madness

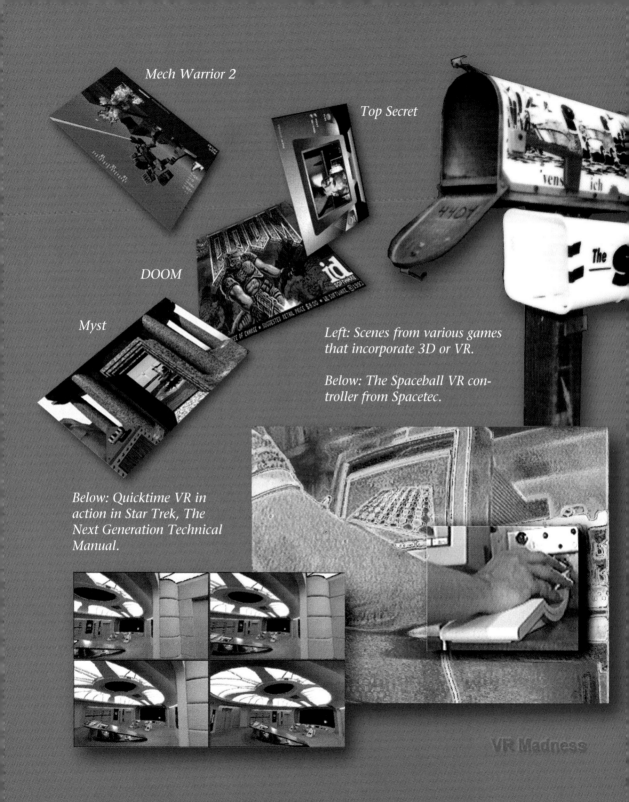

Mech Warrior 2

Top Secret

DOOM

Myst

Left: Scenes from various games that incorporate 3D or VR.

Below: The Spaceball VR controller from Spacetec.

Below: Quicktime VR in action in Star Trek, The Next Generation Technical Manual.

VR Madness

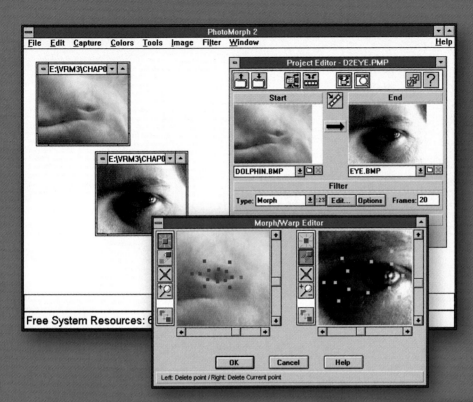

Above: A frame from the morph.

Left: Creating a morph in PhotoMorph 2.

Right: A wild depiction of 3D from the CrystalEyes folks.

Below: A space scene created in 3D Studio.

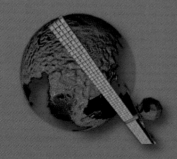

VR Madness

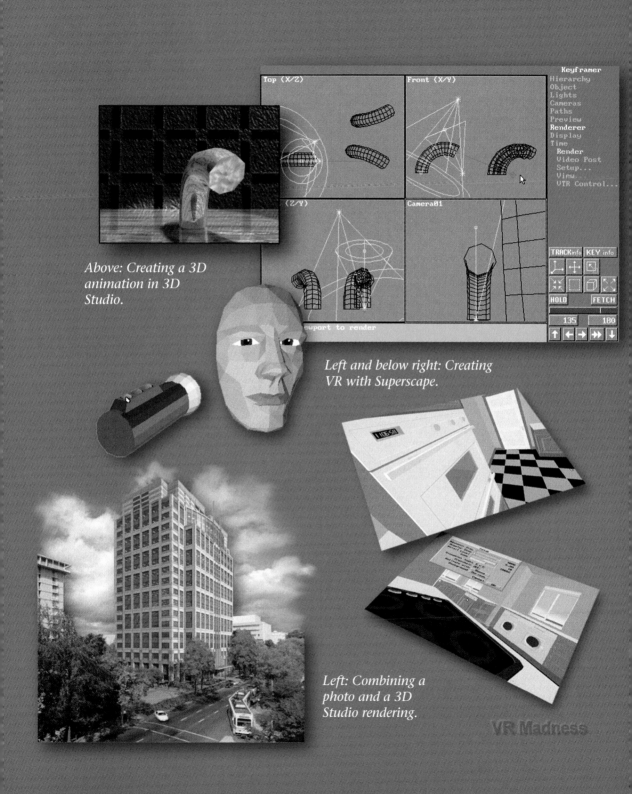

Above: Creating a 3D animation in 3D Studio.

Left and below right: Creating VR with Superscape.

Left: Combining a photo and a 3D Studio rendering.

VR Madness

Above: The VR4 headset in use with VREAM; screen enlarged at right.

Top left: Using the Mattel Power Glove with VREAM.

Top right: The Power Glove in use.

Left: The Logitech Cyberman.

VR Madness

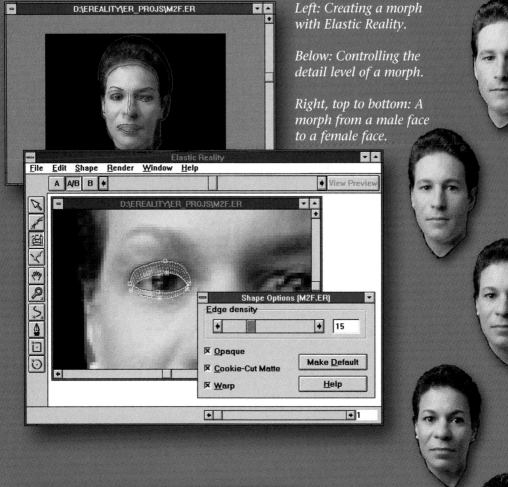

Left: Creating a morph with Elastic Reality.

Below: Controlling the detail level of a morph.

Right, top to bottom: A morph from a male face to a female face.

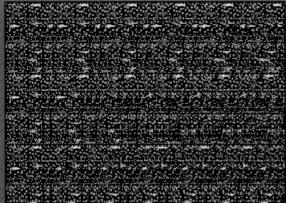

Left: A random stereogram created with Lifestyle Software Group's Stereograms software.

VR Madness

Left: Images of the eye, an example of an HTML web page.

Below: Chatting on the Internet in a 3D environment with WorldsChat.

Below left: Scenes from Cyberwar CD-ROM.

Left: Infrared LCD glasses from 3DTV.

Top right: Two examples of 3D screens for headsets in VREAM.

Middle: The VR4 headset.

Left top: A red/blue stereo image.

Left: Combined stereo pair showing right/left eye differences.

VR Madness

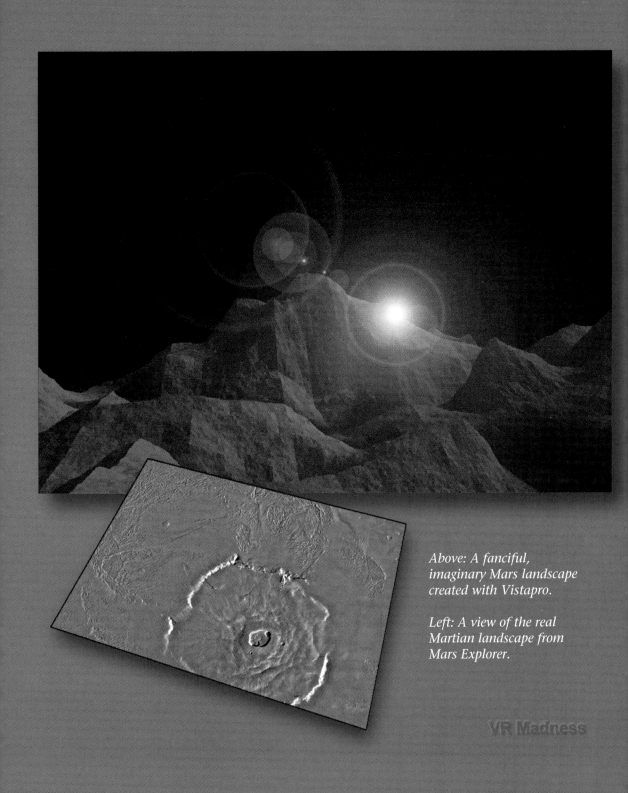

Above: A fanciful, imaginary Mars landscape created with Vistapro.

Left: A view of the real Martian landscape from Mars Explorer.

VR Madness

Left: A high-resolution rendering created in 3D Studio.

Right: A dinosaur animated with reverse kinematics in 3D Studio.

Below: Two models created with trueSpace.

VR Madness

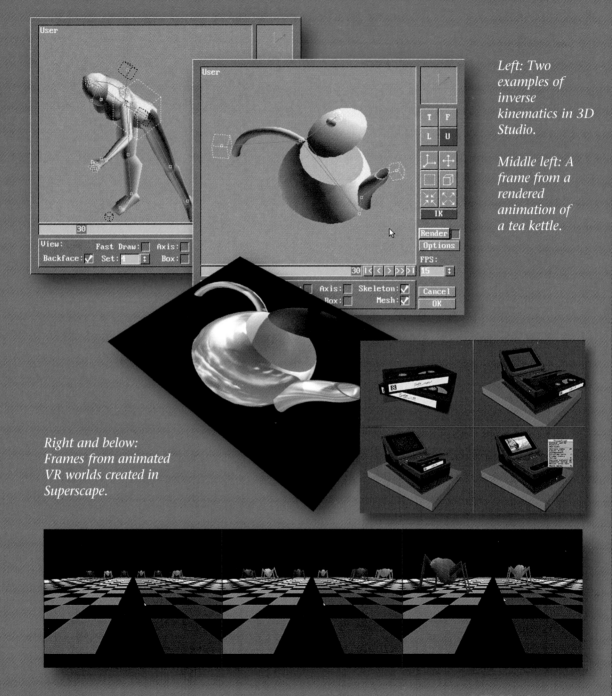

Left: Two examples of inverse kinematics in 3D Studio.

Middle left: A frame from a rendered animation of a tea kettle.

Right and below: Frames from animated VR worlds created in Superscape.

VR Madness

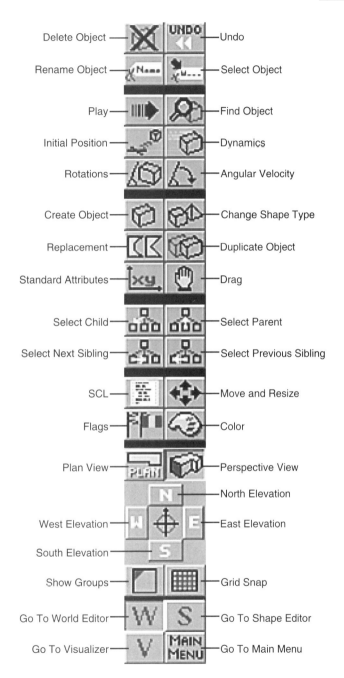

Figure 5.8
The Superscape World Editor icon bar.

Normally, the World Editor "remembers" several levels of Undo, although more simple functions may be undone than complex ones. By default, 100K of space is reserved for the Undo function. It is possible to change this value by editing the Preferences file, but the default should be enough for most purposes.

If there is not enough memory available to store all the changes being made, you are presented with an alert box warning that the operation cannot be undone. You can choose Cancel to stop the operation or Continue to continue the operation. If you choose to continue, this removes all information about previous Undo actions from the World Editor's memory.

Select Object—Lets you select an object by name from an object list. This is useful in large worlds where objects may be out of the viewing area.

Movement

Play—Switches activity on and off in the World Editor so that you can check the directional accuracy of motion attributes, and ensures that objects move and react the way you want. This icon also displays all the objects' motions and executes their SCL and animations, although at a slower speed than the Visualizer.

Initial Position—Sets the initial position of a moving object in the virtual world when the world is first loaded, or when the Reset (F12) key is pressed.

Rotations—Rotates an object according to its X, Y, or Z axis.

Find Object—Presents a list of objects from which you can select a specific object.

Dynamics—Lets you apply the following attributes to an object so that it reflects the dynamic features of the real world: gravity, fuel, climbing and falling, friction, restitution, driving velocity, externally modified velocities, maximum velocity, and whether the object can be "pushed."

Angular Velocity—Lets you add angular motion to an object using the angular-velocity attribute. This updates an object's rotation attribute, turning the object through a given amount every frame.

Creation and Position

Create Object—Creates a new object with the same dimensions (size) as the shape (the Superscape manual uses *shape* and *object* interchangeably) it is copied from. The new object can be moved anywhere in the world by using the standard attributes (which contain its position relative to its parent), by clicking the Place icon (which allows placement of the object using the mouse in elevation views), or by choosing Position from the World Editor menu.

Replacement—Creates a replacement object of the current object in the same position in the world as the original object. The duplicate object will have the same name as the original object, but with a unique numerical suffix, as is the case for normal duplicates. Any children of the original object are not duplicated. This feature is useful for replacing complex objects with progressively simpler replacements to improve processing speed.

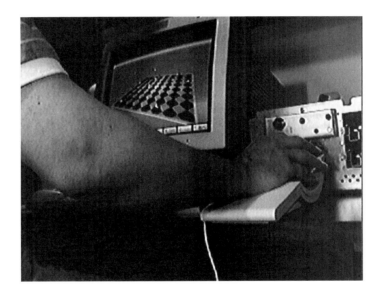

Figure 5.9
*A Superscape world
in the Visualizer.*

Standard Attributes—Each object has standard attributes, which are size, position, and shape type. These specify the minimum amount of information an object can have.

Change Shape Type—Changes a replacement object to use a simplified shape. As an object recedes into the distance, the eye cannot differentiate its separate facets, so it can be replaced by a simpler object that takes less time to process.

Duplicate Object—Duplicates the current object and gives it the current object's name followed by a "duplicate" number in brackets. The duplicate object has all the same attributes as the original object.

Drag—Drags a selected object to a new position. To drag several objects, click on the Drag icon, hold down the Shift key, and click on the required objects. Drag one object to the desired position, and the other objects will follow it.

Tree

The World Editor has facilities that let you step through the object tree structure. Moving up the tree selects the parent of an object; going down selects the first child of the object. Going right selects the next sibling of an object; going left selects the previous sibling of the object.

Select Child—Selects the first child of an object.

Select Next Sibling—Selects the next sibling of an object.

Select Parent—Selects the parent of an object.

Select Previous Sibling—Selects the previous sibling of an object.

Miscellaneous

SCL—Adds a Superscape Control Language (SCL) attribute to an object. SCL can perform some of the actions available through the World and Shape Editors, but offers a wider range of functions. These functions are in the main areas of position, angles and rotations, movement, animation, bending, visibility, color, lighting, and viewpoints. SCL can also be attached to objects to give them a high level of "intelligence" and the ability to react to external events.

Flags—Toggles an object's flag(s) on and off. Flags specify certain simple features of an object, and an object can have several different flags as part of the standard attribute. Some examples of flags are Moveable (makes object moveable), Replace (indicates object is a replacement), Enterable (allows moving objects to enter this object's bounding cube), and so on.

Move and Resize—Alters the position and size of objects in any view.

Color—Changes the color attributes of an object.

Object Viewing

Plan View—Looking down from above.

West Elevation—Looking from the left side.

South Elevation—Looking from the front.

Show Groups—Displays a visible group of objects.

Perspective View—Restores the object to its original orientation and position.

North Elevation—Looking from behind.

East Elevation—Looking from the right.

Grid Snap—Makes objects "snap" to a grid.

VRT Menu

Go to Visualizer—Goes to the Visualizer, which is used primarily as the "playback" software, to display and interact with virtual worlds created in the Shape and World Editors. The stand-alone Visualizer system has only input device configuration options.

Go To Shape Editor—Goes to the Shape Editor, which is used to create points in space and link them together to define two-dimensional faces or facets. These facets then are used to create three-dimensional shapes. After a shape is created, the Shape Editor lets you color it and add animation features.

Go to Main Menu—Displays the main menu.

The Superscape Shape Editor

The Shape Editor is for creating shapes, not objects. Objects are built from one or more shapes in the World Editor. Shapes are built in the Shape Editor.

The icon bar of the Shape Editor is similar to that of the World Editor, but it contains some variations, as shown in Figure 5.10.

Shape Management

Clear Shape—Removes the current shape from the current world.

Rename Shape—Gives the current shape a new name.

Go To Previous Shape—Displays the previous shape for this world. You can edit any of the shapes in the world at any time with the Shape Editor. In general, it's a good idea to store one shape before moving to the next.

Create Shape—Creates a bounding box within which you will create a shape. In other words, it adds a new shape to the world. It's up to you to define what that shape is by using points and facets.

Undo—Clears the most recent action. See "Superscape World Editor," earlier in this chapter, for additional details about Undo.

Select Shape—Selects the entire shape. After the shape is selected, you can perform point and facet operations on the entire shape.

Go To Next Shape—Displays the next shape for this world.

Store Shape—Saves recent changes to the shape. Many operations will lose changes if they are not stored, but Superscape is friendly about it—it always asks you if you want to store changes before moving on.

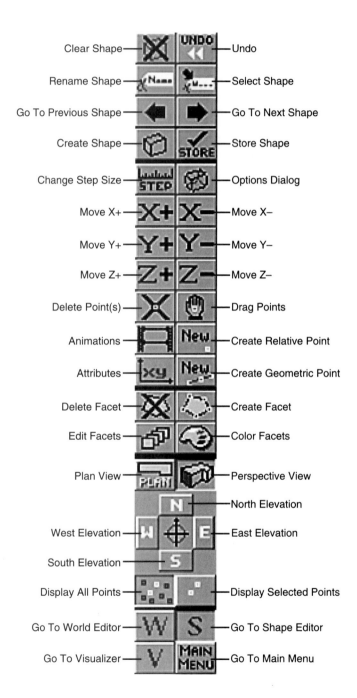

Figure 5.10
The Superscape
Shape Editor
icon bar.

Clear Shape — Undo
Rename Shape — Select Shape
Go To Previous Shape — Go To Next Shape
Create Shape — Store Shape
Change Step Size — Options Dialog
Move X+ — Move X−
Move Y+ — Move Y−
Move Z+ — Move Z−
Delete Point(s) — Drag Points
Animations — Create Relative Point
Attributes — Create Geometric Point
Delete Facet — Create Facet
Edit Facets — Color Facets
Plan View — Perspective View
North Elevation
West Elevation — East Elevation
South Elevation
Display All Points — Display Selected Points
Go To World Editor — Go To Shape Editor
Go To Visualizer — Go To Main Menu

Positioning

Change Step Size—The Plus/Minus buttons move the selected point(s) a distance equal to the current step size. By changing the step size, you can increase or decrease fine control over the position of points.

Move X+, Move Y+, Move Z+—These buttons are used for moving points in three dimensions—along the X, Y, and Z axes. There is one button for positive motion along each axis and another for negative motion. You also can move points by pressing the Alt key along with the arrow key(s). Also see the information for the Drag Points button.

Delete Point(s)—Deletes the currently selected point(s).

Animations—This is a very powerful tool. It enables you to create complex animations by moving the points of a shape to different positions at different points in time. Animation then must be activated in the World Editor. Animations can run by themselves, or they can be controlled during interaction with the virtual world in the Visualizer. Animations of complete objects occur in the World Editor; the Shape Editor only handles movement within the bounding box of the shape.

Options Dialog—Enables you to choose which display options are in effect for the current shape. For example, you can turn construction lines on or off, and you also can choose whether to display point numbers, face numbers, and so on.

Move X-, Move Y-, Move Z-—These buttons are used for moving points in three dimensions—along the X, Y, and Z axes. There is one button for positive motion along each axis and another for negative motion. You also can move points by pressing the Alt key along with the arrow key(s). Also see the information for the Drag Points button.

Drag Points—Enables you to move points by dragging them with the mouse.

Create Relative Point—Creates a point by specifying its position in X, Y, and Z coordinates.

Create Geometric Point—Creates a point between two relative points. Geometric points render faster than relative points.

Facets

Delete Facet—Deletes the selected facet(s). A *facet* is not exactly the same thing as a *face*. In Superscape, a *face* has two *facets*—one on each side of the face. You can set different properties and attributes for each facet. For example, a face can be transparent when viewed from one side, and colored when viewed from another.

Edit Facets—Enables you to change the properties of any facet.

Create Facet—Creates a facet from the currently selected points. In Superscape, you must be careful to select points in strict clockwise or counter-clockwise order. Otherwise, the facets will not fill the space correctly. The order in which you select the points determines which side of the face the created facet is on.

Color Facets—Applies a color from the current palette to a facet.

Object Viewing

Plan View—Looking down from above.

West Elevation—Looking from the left side.

South Elevation—Looking from the front.

Display All Points—Displays all points in the shape.

Perspective View—Restores the object to its original orientation and position.

North Elevation—Looking from behind.

East Elevation—Looking from the right.

Display Selected Points—Hides all points that are not currently selected. Points are selected by clicking on them; a second click deselects the point.

VRT Menu

Go To World Editor—Goes to the World Editor.

Go To Visualizer—Goes to the Visualizer.

Go To Main Menu—Displays the main menu.

The Superscape Visualizer

The Visualizer is the simplest part of Superscape—there is no icon bar, there are no tools. The Visualizer has just one job: to help you interact with the virtual environment.

As I mentioned previously, the Spaceball is by far the coolest way to move around. The intuitive capabilities of the Spaceball make it easy to move around, even in complex ways such as turning and rising simultaneously. This is a very satisfying way to interact with a virtual environment.

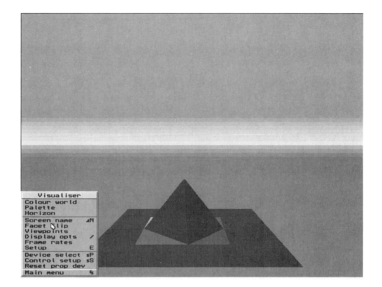

Figure 5.11
The Visualizer and its menu, showing a simple VR world.

However, you can also move around using the keyboard, and Superscape has a full complement of keyboard commands. You will sometimes want to use the keyboard commands, using them in tandem with either the mouse or a controller like the Spaceball. The following table shows the key commands for the Visualizer; additional commands are available in the various Editors.[7]

Key	*Command*
F1 to F10	Select viewpoints 1 through 10
F11	Revert to last viewpoint
F12	Reset World
Print Screen	Save screen to disk
Esc	Exit to main menu
1 to 0	Select viewpoints 11 through 20
=	Center cross hairs on and off
Backspace	Pause
E	Display setup dialog box
F	Move down
H	Move left
J	Move right
K	Move backward
L	Rotate down

continues

[7]When using an Editor, you will find that many commands can be carried out using either the keyboard or the mouse. Usually, you will find certain commands that are best with the keyboard, and others that are best with the mouse. Which is which depends on individual tastes.

Key	Command
M	Tilt right
N	Tilt left
O	Move down
P	Rotate up
Q	Rotate left
R	Move up
U	U-turn
W	Rotate right
,	Zoom out
.	Zoom in
/	Edit display options
Shift+P	Select devices
Ctrl+Esc	Exit
Alt+M	Display menu
Alt+S	Go To Shape Editor
Alt+W	Go To World Editor

On the numeric keypad:

0	Stop controlled object's movement
2	Decrease controlled object's forward velocity
3	Rotate controlled object up
4	Rotate controlled object left
6	Rotate controlled object right
7	Face forward
8	Increase controlled object's forward velocity
9	Rotate controlled object down
+	Increase controlled object's upward velocity
-	Decrease controlled object's upward velocity
Shift++	Increase resolution
Shift+-	Decrease resolution
Ctrl++	Increase texture resolution
Ctrl+-	Decrease texture resolution

One thing should be obvious immediately from this list of keystrokes: There is simply no logic, rhyme, or reason to it. You'll just have to use brute force memorization to keep track.[8] This list serves as a heads-up alert for anyone thinking about using Superscape: Expect to invest a good amount of time to learn it. You will recoup your investment—at the end of that time, expect to be able to create fantastic virtual worlds.

---

[8]Another example of Big Software syndrome: OK, here are the features; now you figure out how to use them.

How good is Superscape? Let's take a look at a few sample virtual worlds that were created with Superscape. Figure 5.12 shows the opening screen of Superscape VRT. It's pretty heady stuff, that hand reaching into the screen. Is it that good? It is—but only if you also have the hardware tools, the CrystalEyes goggles, and the Spaceball input device.

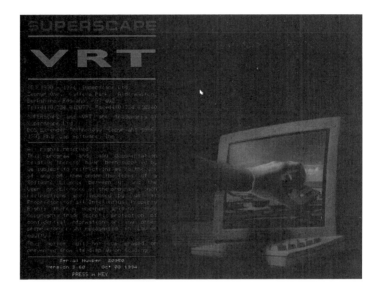

Figure 5.12
The Superscape VRT opening screen.

Figure 5.13 shows the main menu. The icons at the left give you access to the various Editors and files on disk, and the menu selections at the right do the same. If you want to use the Visualizer, click on the File menu selection, displaying the dialog box shown in Figure 5.14. You can load complete worlds (made up of multiple files), individual files, or backdrops; perform file maintenance; and so on.

Figure 5.13
The main menu.

Figure 5.14
File operations.

Each file has descriptive information stored with the file, which makes it easier to manage large projects. Figure 5.15 shows a sample dialog box displaying file information.

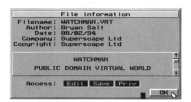

Figure 5.15
File information.

The Visualizer itself is designed to operate with a Super VGA screen that supports the VESA standard. The default setup is 640×480 and 256 colors. Figures 5.16 and 5.17 show two views of St. Paul's Cathedral in London, England. The model was built in the Superscape World Editor.

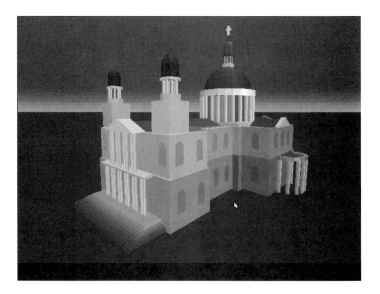

Figure 5.16
St. Paul's Cathedral,
in perspective view.

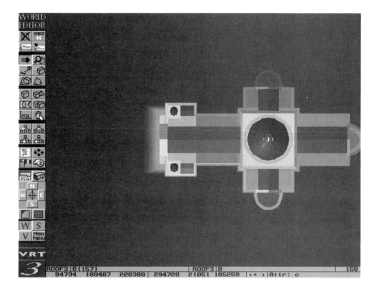

Figure 5.17
The cathedral in Plan view in the World Editor.

Figure 5.18 shows an accident simulation created in Superscape. In this model, two cars are animated, and clicking on various objects in the model causes other animations to run. Superscape is very flexible in this regard—you can animate objects, and you can also use sequential bitmaps for 2D animations on an object. You can even change textures on-the-fly.

Figure 5.18
A Superscape model with animation.

You can even create menu-driven applications using 3D virtual worlds and the Visualizer. Figure 5.19 shows a virtual world that has a computer monitor and a keyboard. The monitor displays a virtual world. To display other virtual worlds, you would click on the monitor. To go to a virtual world, you click on the keyboard. Figure 5.20 shows several frames from the virtual world shown on the monitor.

Figure 5.19
A virtual world that can act as a menu (see text).

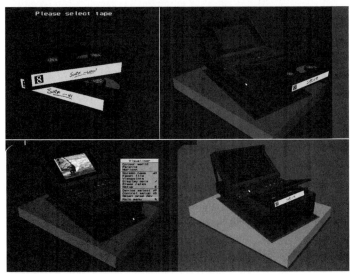

Figure 5.20
Frames from a virtual world accessed via a menu.

Clockwise from top left, the frames in Figure 5.20 show:

1. Two video tapes: one marked `Low Resolution`, one marked `High Resolution`.

2. Clicking on a tape animates it; it inserts itself into the player.

3. The player turns on, displaying the traditional blank video screen noise, as the tape continues to be inserted into the player.

4. The tape is playing, and the Visualizer menu (invoked by clicking the right mouse button) is displayed.

The model in question is very detailed. For example, after the tape is inserted, it spins into place, and then stops. Pressing the Play button causes the tape to play, and you can see the reels inside the tape cartridge spinning. There is an On/Off button, a Record button, and more—all of these active, and acting just like they do in the real world.

Remember my comment about animated giant ants? Look at Figure 5.21. It shows a Superscape model with exactly that. There are three frames shown (left to right). Note that the ants are fully animated. As soon as you enter the world, they march toward you.

Figure 5.21
Animated ants created and animated in Superscape.

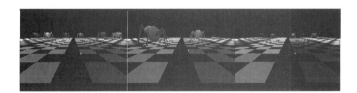

How about an office environment? Figure 5.22 shows a sample office world. Many of the objects in the scene (and more that aren't shown in the point of view shown in Figure 5.22) can be activated by clicking. The phone jumps off the hook, and doors (both the cabinets at the left and the door to the room) can be opened and closed by clicking and dragging with the mouse. A clock on the back wall keeps exact current time. The chair moves when you click it, and bounces off of walls and other objects appropriately. Objects in the drawers (which can be opened and closed) can be lifted and examined. If you click the pencil laying on the sheet of paper, the pencil jumps up and writes on the paper (see Fig. 5.23).[9] The light switch next to the door on the far wall is operational; it interactively brightens and dims the lights (see Fig. 5.24).

---

[9]The files PENCIL.AVI and PENCIL2.AVI show a rough approximation of the animation; you'll find them on the CD-ROM discs.

Figure 5.22
A virtual office.

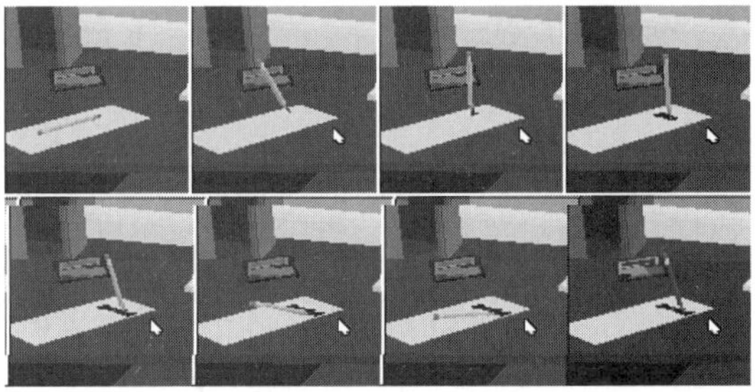

Figure 5.23
*An animated pencil
writes on a sheet of
paper.*

Figure 5.24
*You can even dim
the lights!*

That's a lot of cool functionality in one virtual world, but wait (as they say in those late-night TV commercials), there's more! Press the space bar, and a little box (the Movement Home box) appears at the mouse-cursor location (see Fig. 5.25). That little box tells you that the mouse can now be used for moving around, instead of just for pointing and clicking at objects. Figure 5.26 shows a detailed view of the little box. Figure 5.27 shows how to navigate—just move the mouse cursor out of the box, and the view shifts in that direction. To stop movement, move the cursor back inside that home box. Figure 5.28 shows a sequence of movements to the right.

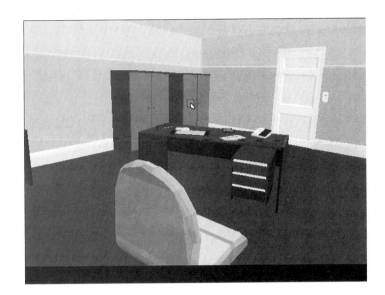

Figure 5.25
*Activating mouse-
movement control.*

Figure 5.26
*A close-up of
the Movement
Home box.*

Figure 5.27
*Initiating movement
to the right.*

Figure 5.28
*Moving with the
mouse.*

By now, you should be impressed with what you can do with Superscape—it's powerful and then some. Now let's take a reality check, and see what kind of effort it takes to create objects with Superscape VRT.

Working with Superscape VRT

Superscape comes with a bunch of manuals, and it looks pretty intimidating as you try to get started with it. I got a little worried when I first tried to use it—the interface looks quite different from other things I had tried to use.

That kind of a difference is often a warning sign, telling you that a product is funky. In this case, however, the differences were often improvements. You can't just sit down and immediately use Superscape, but as you learn how to work with it, it quickly begins to make sense. Even after my early fears, I give the interface a real A+ for workability.

However, that doesn't mean it's simple. The Superscape interface gets a good grade specifically because it makes a huge amount of power available to you. That means it's still going to take some time to get used to it.

The Superscape main menu is extremely non-intimidating,[10] as shown in Figure 5.29. It's really just a list of the major tools available to you. The three most important tools—the World Editor, the Shape Editor, and the Visualizer—are listed first, and then other tools are listed. We'll focus mainly on the Big Three in this tutorial.

Figure 5.29
*The Superscape
main menu.*

Creating a Shape

We'll begin with the Shape Editor. Before we create our first shape, let's look at some of the key features of the Shape Editor. When you first start it, you see a default shape: a cube (see Fig. 5.30). Because the facets of the cube are colored, and because the cube is the same size as its bounding box, it's not clear yet which is which. You'll see the difference when we create a shape later in this tutorial.

Accessing menus in the Shape Editor is easy—just click with the right mouse button to display the Shape Editor menu (see Fig. 5.31).

---

[10]Unless you look at how small it is, and remember that you just paid around $10,000 for this product! But have no fear—the main menu is just an entry point. There's enough functionality here to keep you busy for years.

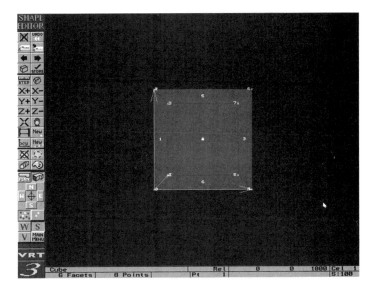

Figure 5.30
The default cube shape.

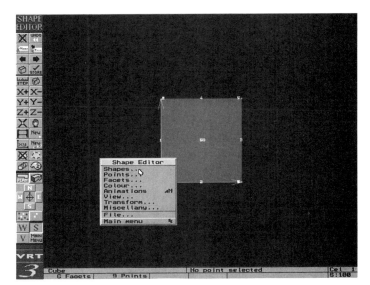

Figure 5.31
All menus are just a right-click away.

You can easily change your point of view by using the arrow keys. Figure 5.32 shows a view of our cube from slightly below and to the right.

You can also add a background[11] for the shape (see Fig. 5.33). The background will not appear when you place the shape into an object. It is used to guide your work. For example, you could load a digitized view of an object, and then create on top of that to get the most realistic results.

---

[11]Use the File menu option Load Backdrop after right-clicking.

You can also change the color of individual facets on the shape, as shown in Figure 5.34. Clicking on the icon that looks like a painter's palette displays the Color pick list shown in Figure 5.34. The color you pick will be applied to the currently selected facet(s).

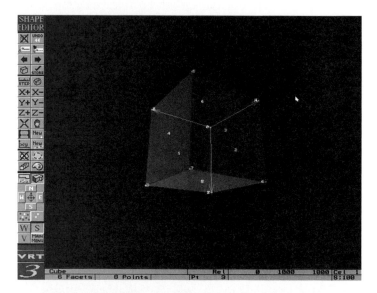

Figure 5.32
The point of view has been changed using the arrow keys.

Figure 5.33
You can use a background for tracing.

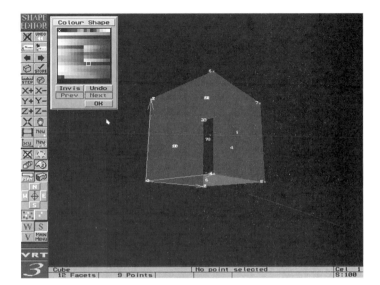

Figure 5.34
*Changing the color
of a facet.*

Enough theory! Let's get down and dirty, and create a shape of our own. Simply click
the Create Shape icon in the icon bar. You'll see the outline of a cube. This isn't a
cube like the last example—it's just the bounding box for our shape. To begin, click
the New Relative Point icon, which displays the dialog box shown in Figure 5.35.[12]
You are being asked to supply the X, Y, and Z coordinates for the new point. Look
ahead to Figure 5.36, and note that the origin of the coordinate system is at the lower,
front left of the bounding box. Creating a point at 250,250,250—as shown in Figure
5.35—creates a point relatively close to the origin because the bounding box is, by
default, 1,000×1,000×1,000.

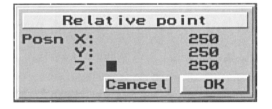

Figure 5.35
*Creating a
relative point.*

One point makes exactly nothing in 3D, so we'll need at least one more relative point
to make a line. By changing just one coordinate to 500, we get the results shown in
Figure 5.36.

---

[12]Relative points must be created first—geometric points can only be created when you have two
or more relative points to start from.

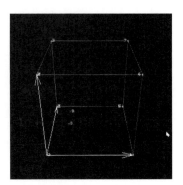

Figure 5.36
Two relative points
have been created.

Note that each of the points is marked by a small x and a number. By default, each point displays as an x, and every point has a unique number.[13] To select a point, click on it once, and the x changes to a tiny square. I have selected both points (numbers 8 and 9) in Figure 5.37.

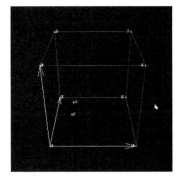

Figure 5.37
A selected point is
marked by a tiny
square instead
of an x.

With these two relative points selected, we can easily create a geometric point—just click on the New Geometric Point button. The new point, number 10, is created between the two relative points (see Fig. 5.38).

By adjusting the coordinates in the New Relative Point dialog box, you can easily create two more relative points at the corners of a square (see Fig. 5.39). The new points are numbered 11 and 12. In Figure 5.39, the mouse has been dragged around the two new relative points to select them. Once they are selected, you can create a geometric point between them: point number 13. I then continued to create two more geometric points on the other two sides of the square.[14]

---

[13]Facets also have numbers, and you can display them using the Options button in the icon bar.

[14]For perfectionists and detail freaks, that means I created point 14 between points 8 and 12, and point 15 between points 9 and 11.

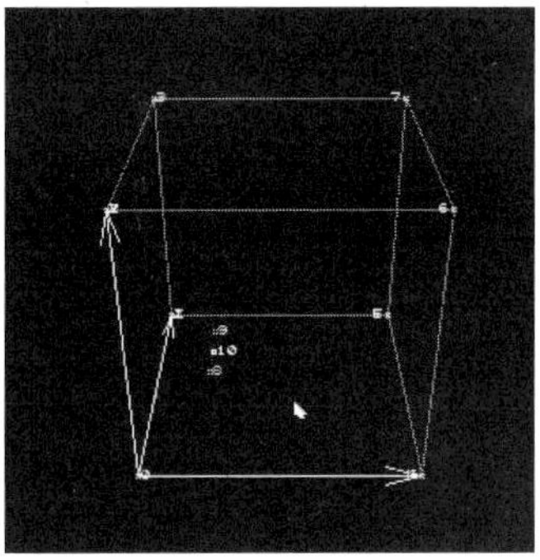

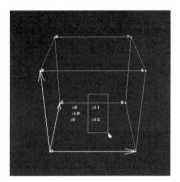

Figure 5.38
The new geometric point is midway between the two relative points used to create it.

Figure 5.39
Two additional points have been created.

Now we have a whole lot of points, and it's time to create some facets. This is also easy to do. Look ahead to Figure 5.40, which shows that we're going to create small triangular facets at the corners of the square. Clicking in counterclockwise order,[15] we click points 14, 8, and 9 to select them. Then click the Create Facet button to create the facet. That's all there is to it! Figure 5.40 shows three facets already created. Each facet, like each point, has a unique number.

All those numbers can get in the way of seeing your shape clearly, so you can turn them off. Select the Options button, and click the buttons for face numbering and point numbering to turn them off. The result is shown in Figure 5.41—the shape and the bounding box are now much less cluttered-looking.

---

[15]If you click in clockwise order, the facet will be created on the other side of the face, and you won't be able to see it unless you rotate the shape. Remember: All faces have two sides! To create a facet on the side facing you, click counterclockwise.

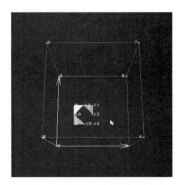

Figure 5.40
Three facets have been added to the shape.

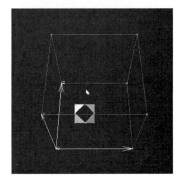

Figure 5.41
Point and facet numbering have been turned off.

We've done a lot so far, but our shape is not yet 3D—and that's what we're here for! It's easy to add points in the third dimension—just use the Z coordinate to create a new relative point above the existing points. You can use the X+, X-, Y+, Y-, Z+, and Z- buttons on the icon bar to position the new point exactly at the center of the existing shape (see Fig. 5.42).

By selecting the appropriate points (in counterclockwise order, of course), you can easily create new facets that connect the existing facets to the new point. Figure 5.43 shows the first such facet, while Figure 5.44 shows the object with all four new facets in place.

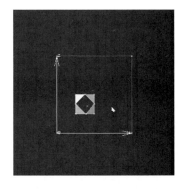

Figure 5.42
Creating a new point above the existing points.

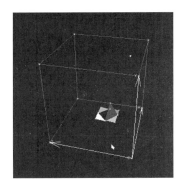

Figure 5.43
Adding a facet.

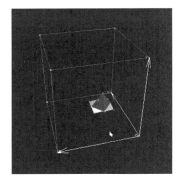

Figure 5.44
*All four new facets
are in place.*

We have one small remaining problem—the shape is much smaller than the bounding box that contains it. Ideally, the bounding box should be just big enough to contain the shape. This is easy to do—the Wrap Shape menu selection takes care of it in one step. The result is shown in Figure 5.45. The shape is really too small, however, and what we really want to do is to set its size. As shown in Figure 5.45, the Set Size button enables you to set the size of the object in each dimension.

Figure 5.45
*Wrapping the
bounding box to the
shape and setting a
new size.*

The result of resizing is shown in Figure 5.46. I changed each dimension by multiplying the previous length by 4, but you could also distort the shape by changing different dimensions by different multipliers.

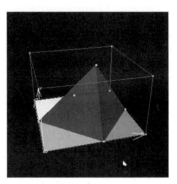

Figure 5.46
The shape has been
resized.

There are lots of other things you can do to a shape, but we'll explore just one more—animation. Shape animation is an extremely powerful tool, but it's super easy to use. You start by creating new frames using the Animation Controller (see Fig. 5.47). The Insert button will insert new cels[16] in the animation; 15 to 25 should be good for what I've got in mind.

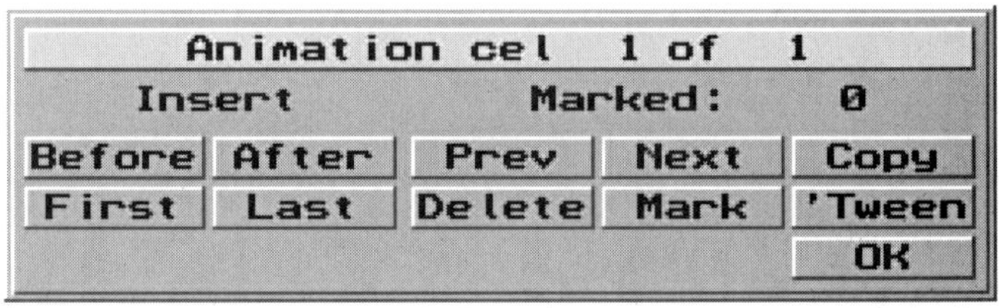

Figure 5.47
The Animation
Controller.

Animation consists of nothing more than moving around the points of the object. By default, all points are static; you must define which points are to become dynamic using the Points menu (see Fig. 5.48). To make a point dynamic, select the point and then click on Convert Stat-Dyn (static to dynamic).

With the Animation Controller active, you now go to the first cel (click the First button in the Controller) and move the dynamic points to their starting positions.[17] Now select all points that will move in the animation, and click the Mark button. This tells

---

[16]An animation cel is a single image. It is not the same as a frame, however; a frame can have several cels in it. Each cel is a single image of one or more objects. For example, if you have an animation of a bouncing ball and a waving stick, each frame could have one cel for the ball and another for the stick.

[17]If they are already where you want them, of course, you do nothing!

the Animation Controller which points are involved. Not all dynamic points will be involved in all animations—you can, after all, have several different animations for the same shape!

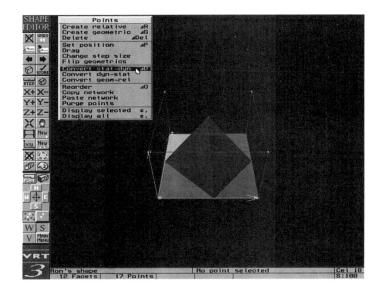

Figure 5.48
Defining dynamic points.

Now click the Last button in the Controller to move to the last cel. Move the dynamic points to their final location (see Fig. 5.49).

To create the intermediate cels, click the 'Tween button. This displays the various types of tweening, as shown in Figure 5.50.

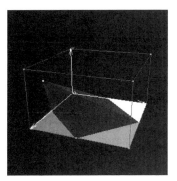

Figure 5.49
The end point of the animation.

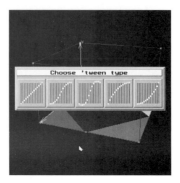

Figure 5.50
*Choosing the
'Tween type.*

There are five different kinds of 'tweening shown in Figure 5.50 (from left to right):

Linear—Points move at a constant speed and then stop.

Cosine—Points accelerate and decelerate at the start and finish of the animation.

Exaggerated—Points overshoot slightly at both ends.

Accelerate—Points accelerate and then stop.

Decelerate—Points decelerate to a stop.

These types of 'tweens allow you to create life-like motion for your animation. Figure 5.51 shows an intermediate cel in the animation. Figure 5.52 shows the animation in the World Editor.

The Shape in the World

You can move to the World Editor by clicking the W icon in the icon bar. The world will be pretty dull—no objects to speak of. The first order of business is to create an object based on our shape. It couldn't be easier: Click the Create Object button in the icon bar to display the dialog box shown in Figure 5.52. Then pick the shape of your choice, and click the OK button. As you can see at the right of Figure 5.52, you can preview each shape. This is convenient if you have a large library of shapes for your world.

The shape attaches itself to the cursor, and the view switches to the Plan view (see Fig. 5.53). Position the shape where you would like it to be, and click to place it.

To activate the animation, use the Movement submenu. You will create an animation (number 1; everything has a number in Superscape). You must then choose the Animation mode. The mode determines whether the animation runs at all, loops, operates interactively, and so on. You can also set the speed of the animation, starting and ending frames, and so on. As usual, Superscape offers complete control.

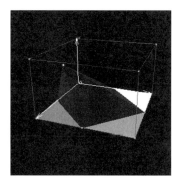

Figure 5.51
An intermediate point in the animation.

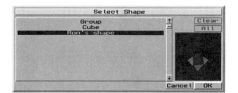

Figure 5.52
Selecting a shape in the World Editor.

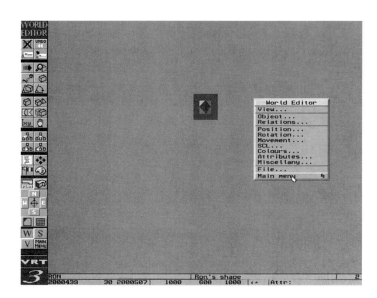

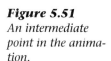

Figure 5.53
Placing a new object.

Virtual Is as Virtual Does

To interact with the simple world, go to the Visualizer by clicking the V icon. Figure 5.54 shows four views of the animation in progress in the Visualizer.

Figure 5.54
*Four views of the
animation.*

You can easily add textures to the object instead of the flat colors it has now. Access the Texture Editor from the main menu; you'll see something like Figure 5.55.

You can load a PCX file into the Texture Editor and build a library of textures. Figure 5.56 shows one of the texture files supplied with Superscape. There are only a few, so count on creating your own textures.

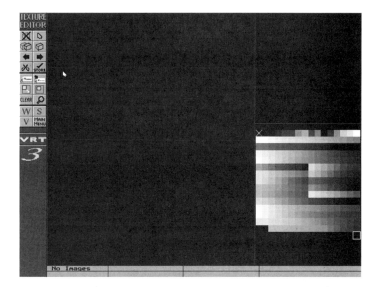

Figure 5.55
The Texture Editor.

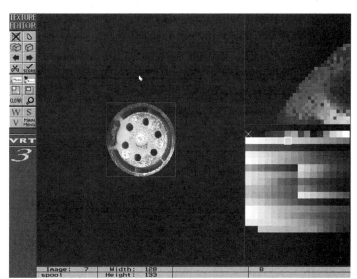

Figure 5.56
A texture from a Texture library.

A scanner is the ideal way to collect textures. Or, you can use PhotoCD discs and convert the PCD files to PCX using any competent image-editing software. I use Photoshop from Adobe, but Corel supplies a simple PhotoCD with its converted Corel Professional Photos on CD-ROM—and it works really well! Plus, you get a ton of useful images, and several of the CD-ROMs contain texture images.

Figure 5.57 shows the dialog box for applying a texture in the World Editor, and Figure 5.58 shows the result.

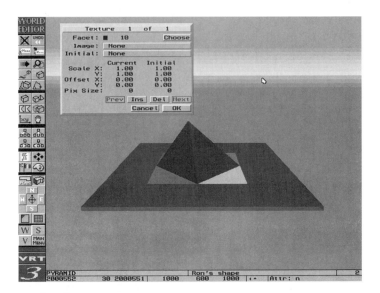

Figure 5.57
Setting a texture for a facet.

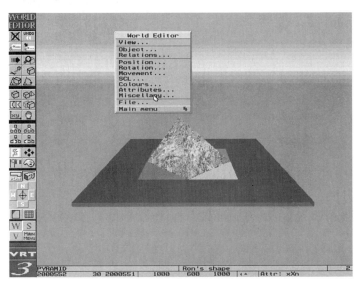

Figure 5.58
A texture has been applied to several facets.

All in all, Superscape was a pleasure to work with. It's awfully darn deep, however, so if you go this route, plan to take a few weeks to learn the ins and outs of the product. It's definitely a solid, professional effort. It's expensive, but if you need the best, this is it!

Give Me Some Space!

Virtual reality is very convenient. It doesn't have the same limitations as regular reality. Gravity, for example, is actually a serious bother when it comes to programming for VR. Friction is another real hassle. Sometimes, of course, these are highly desirable, and well worth the difficulties. If you are an industrial engineer designing parts for a new jet, things like friction and gravity are the point of the VR process—you want to learn about the performance of your designs in the real world by messing around with them in a virtual world. If the correspondence between real and virtual is not accurate, and that jet crashes...

For the rest of us, the stakes are so low as to be negligible. Fun is the order of the day. And when it comes to fun, things like gravity and friction can get in the way or be part of the game—rules become arbitrary. You can omit the rules, make up new rules, or give the rules a new twist. For example, if you would like to fly through the solar system, the distance between the planets in the real universe is inconveniently large. Things like the mass of propellant required to accelerate quickly, the effects of acceleration, and the speed of light all contribute to making a real-time simulation not much fun. But if we were to conveniently ignore such details, the solar system could be as accessible as an amusement park ride.[18]

On the other hand, there are times when you want something to look as natural as possible. When that's the case, you want tools that will give you the fine control you need.

---

[18]Time to discuss the moral side of virtual reality. I recently read an editorial regarding the existence of nature shows on television. Surely, the author suggested, if there were an unmitigated good on television, it would be nature shows. He then shot down that argument by pointing out that nature shows are actually quite artificial, and are giving people an incomplete—and often a staged—picture of reality. For example, nature shows are dramatic, while nature itself consists of vast stretches of very undramatic time punctuated by short, intense dramas. Only the latter are presented to the television viewer, and the result, the author suggested, is a twisted, inaccurate, and sometimes dangerous view of nature.

Can the same be said of virtual reality? Does the twisting and altering of the rules of the nature of reality carry some kind of price tag? I won't pretend to have an answer, and the whole issue is so uncertain that I almost don't have an opinion on the matter. If pressed, I would mention that overuse of carrots can lead to serious trouble, too. I can't buy the idea that adults are credulous enough to buy that nature shows represent reality. If we have become so civilized that we can be fooled extensively about the nature of reality itself, then, yes, we ought to back up a little and reconsider. Heck, a walk in the woods will disabuse just about anyone of false views of nature, and an occasional slip on a banana peel ought to be enough of a reminder of the effects of gravity for even the most jaded VR fanatic.

Lifelike 3D Animation

As I was considering which topics to include in this edition of *Virtual Reality Madness*, there was one item right at the top of my list: 3D animation. Strictly speaking, of course, this isn't virtual reality at all. But it's still an extremely important topic. Here's why:

■ With the hardware and software available today, high-resolution, real-time virtual reality is just way too expensive for ordinary computers.

■ Release 4 of 3D Studio puts big-time animation tools right on the desktop.

■ 3D animation of today is where the ideas for virtual reality of the future will be conceived, designed, and developed.

The road to virtual reality is a long one. Most of the key steps along the way will happen first in the relatively static world of 3D modeling and animation.

RECIPE

100 pounds 3D Studio, Release 4
1 tea kettle, dinosaur, or human figure
1 part inverse kinematics
1 T imagination

Instructions: This is a simply amazing meal—easy to prepare, but sure to be a hit with the most fastidious gourmet 3D enthusiast. With this recipe, you get all the power of a Hollywood animation studio for a tiny fraction of the price. Mix with inverse kinematics, apply liberal seasoning of imagination, and serve.

Until very recently, the cost of first-class 3D animation has been prohibitively high. How high? Anywhere from $100,000 to millions of dollars. At the high end are animations like those in *Jurassic Park* or the *Terminator* movies. At the "low" end are the animations in any number of commercials and movies. The bottom line is very simple: The more you spend, the more realistic and flexible the animations become.

This is changing fast. Although 3D Studio is expensive by normal software standards (it retails for $2,995), it's dirt cheap by 3D-animation standards. With each release, 3D Studio has moved closer and closer to the big guys. Release 3 added extremely natural lighting and rendering, and Release 4 adds powerful new tools for controlling animations without spending half your life on the details. Among these tools is one that stands out from all the rest: inverse kinematics. In this section, you'll build a simple model and animate it using inverse kinematics.

Inverse Kinematics

If ever there was a term less clear than *inverse kinematics* to the untutored observer, I have yet to see it. Let's break down these words to see what they mean.

Kinematics has as its root the Greek word for movement, *kinema*.[19] That's exactly what kinematics is all about. Until recently, getting 3D models to move naturally has been a very difficult task. For example, consider the human arm. In real life, an arm obeys a large number of physical rules. The wrist joint, for example, moves very differently than the elbow joint. To duplicate this motion, the animation artist had to be something of an expert in human movement, and then had to apply that knowledge to the animation using painstakingly careful adjustments to the model. For example, to lift an arm in a salute, the animator would first move the arm from the shoulder, and then carefully adjust the angle and rotation of the upper arm until it was correct. In the meantime, the lower arm, wrist, and all the finger joints simply came along for the ride.

Once the upper arm was correctly positioned, then the artist shifted attention to the lower arm and carefully positioned it. This all took time—and if the hand also had to be adjusted, every joint in the hand also had to be carefully placed. This took a long time, and the success was totally dependent on the skill of the operator to mimic human motion. When you consider that this process would need to be repeated hundreds of times just to create a very simple animation of the human figure, you see that it could take a long time to get the job done.

In the world of animation, time is money. The longer it takes to create an animation, the more it is going to cost. A tool that could dramatically cut the time to animate was desperately needed. That's why studios were willing to spend a small fortune (or even a large fortune!) on fancy animation software and powerful hardware to run it. Better to spend $100,000 on the software than several times that in development time.

The result is 3D Studio Release 4 and inverse kinematics. The key is that word *inverse*. In the example used here, the artist started with the upper arm, and then tediously

---

[19]This word is also the root for *cinema*—once known as moving pictures.

worked his way down to the fingers. With inverse kinematics, you start with a model. You define the range of motion for each joint: How far can it bend, how far can it rotate? And then comes the easy part: Move the finger, and the whole arm will follow. If you define the motion of each joint carefully, the animation itself is easy. All the hard work is done up front, one time, on the joints. To animate, you can quickly grab the end of the joint chain (a finger, a foot, the head, and so on), position it as desired, and everything will fall in line. The result is a much easier path to natural-looking 3D animation.

Figure 5.59 shows an example of inverse kinematics in 3D Studio. The black quadrant shows a female figure in a pose created simply by grabbing and moving the left hand, and then grabbing and moving the left foot. All other movement was automatic—a direct result of the rules set up for the joints.

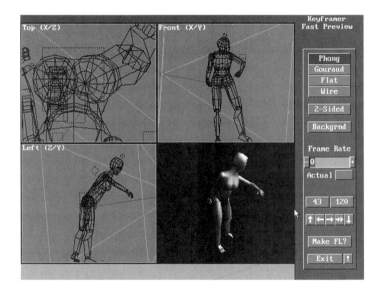

Figure 5.59
Inverse kinematics at work in 3D Studio.

Kinematics in a Teapot

Let's get down to virtual basics and look at how inverse kinematics work in a 3D Studio animation project. In this tutorial, you'll learn how to create a teapot, assign parameters to the joints interactively, and then animate the teapot using inverse kinematics.

The first step is to use the standard 3D Studio tools to create the various objects that make up the teapot. Figure 5.60 shows the basic features of the 3D Studio interface. There are four quadrants. Each quadrant can have a different view. Views include the traditional Top, Right, and Left, but you can also show the view from a camera or a light, or create custom User views. In Figure 5.60, we are about to create a sphere. The dialog box in the center is used to define how many segments the sphere will have. To create a smooth sphere, use more segments. In this example, the sphere will have 1,024 segments.[20] Note the menu at the right, which uses a hierarchy of nested menu choices. The available choices are always those at the bottom that are indented the farthest. At the bottom right, you see the various icons for generic actions such as zooming in and out, moving the viewpoint, changing orientation of the view, and so on. The current active choice is highlighted in yellow.

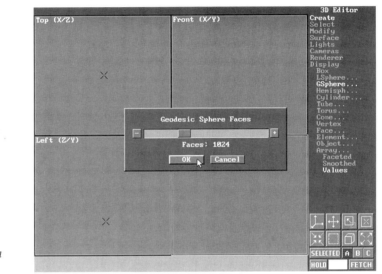

Figure 5.60
Beginning to create a sphere.

Let's move step by step through the process of creating a sphere. Most objects you can create with 3D Studio[21] use a similar process: Define some points, define some measurements, and—presto!—an object appears.

To create an object, start at the top menu and select Create. Then look at the indented menu selections and select GSphere. At the bottom level of the resulting hierarchy, select Smoothed.[22] Figure 5.61 shows the first step in the process: defining the center point of the sphere.

---

[20]There are two kinds of spheres you can create: GSphere and LSphere. The GSphere is simply a geodesic sphere, using triangular shapes to form an approximation of a perfect sphere. The LSphere uses shapes arranged more like lines of longitude and latitude on the earth.

[21]Boxes, toruses, hemispheres, tubes, cylinders, and so on.

[22]For objects with curves, you will want to pay attention to whether the object will be faceted or smoothed. Faceted objects will look like a diamond, while smoothed objects will have a smooth, curving surface when rendered. For this example, we want a smooth-faced teapot. Figure 5.61 shows the appropriate menu choice: Smoothed.

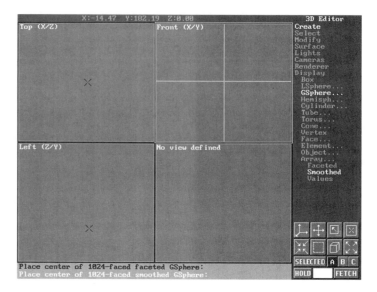

Figure 5.61
Smoothing the sphere.

To complete the definition of the sphere, you must click to set the radius, as shown in Figure 5.62.

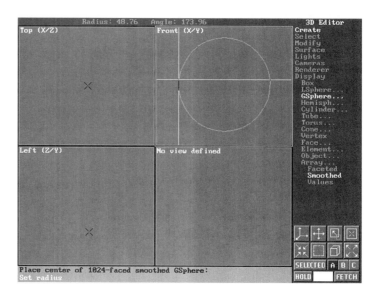

Figure 5.62
Setting the size of the sphere.

After you create an object, you must give it a name. In this case, the sphere[23] will eventually wind up as the base of the teapot, so I gave it the name *Kettle*. See Figure 5.63 for details on naming an object.[24]

---

[23]Actually, a portion of the sphere.

[24]If necessary, you can always change the name later in the File Attributes dialog box.

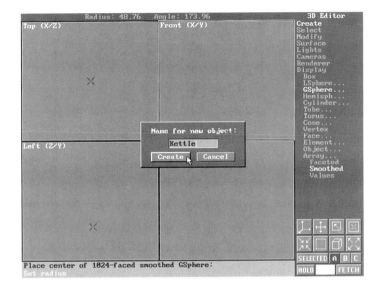

Figure 5.63
Naming an object.

After you enter the name, click the Create button. The object appears in Wireframe mode, as shown in Figure 5.64.

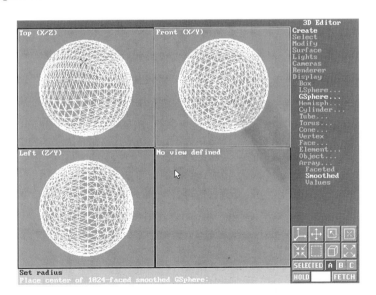

Figure 5.64
The newly created object.

A sphere, however, is not a kettle or a teapot. We need to modify the sphere to turn it into a teapot. In this example, you'll learn how to cut off the bottom half of the sphere to provide a flat bottom, and then cut a thin slice out of the remainder to create a lid. We'll use 3D Studio's Boolean[25] operations to make these changes.

To begin, we will create a box that holds the portion of the sphere we want to remove. Begin with the Create/Box menu selection (see Fig. 5.65). You are asked to mark the top left corner of the box.

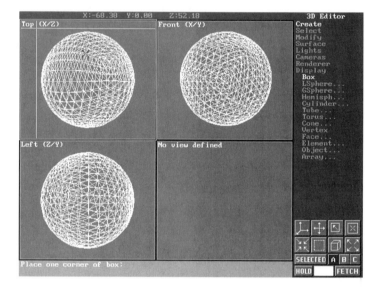

Figure 5.65
*Creating a box:
Planting the first
corner.*

Click to mark the first corner, and then move the mouse to the opposite corner and click again (see Fig. 5.66). Once you have marked the outline of the box (naturally, it should be slightly larger than the sphere!), you are asked to define the depth of the box. Figure 5.67 shows how to do this. Remember that the box's depth must extend from what will be the bottom of the kettle to below the sphere. The box won't be around long, so when you see the Name dialog box, give it the name *temp*.

If the box does not appear when you name it, it is located outside the current viewports. Click the Show All icon (identified in Fig. 5.67) to show all objects in the current viewport (see Fig. 5.68). The important point to note: Even though we carefully defined the depth of the box, we have not identified the position. The box will be created in the default position. We'll need to move it into the correct position. Note in

---

[25] I know: You are looking at this footnote because you expect me to provide the information and insights you need to understand why this is called a *Boolean operation*. Well, I can't do that easily, because, strictly speaking, this usage doesn't fit the dictionary definition of *Boolean*. The word itself, *Boolean*, is named after English mathematician George Boole, who became famous for his work in logic. To make an already too-long footnote only slightly longer, typical Boolean operations involve AND and OR statements. By definition, a Boolean operation must involve terms that can only have two states (usually TRUE or FALSE). By extension, this word is used to refer to anything that involves AND or OR statements.

Figure 5.68 that the Object/Move menu selection is active. Note also that the cursor has changed shape, showing the available directions of movement. The original cursor shape, shown enlarged in Figure 5.69, allows you to move in all directions. We only want to move the object upward, so press the Tab key until the cursor changes to the shape shown in Figure 5.70. This gives you tighter control over object movement.

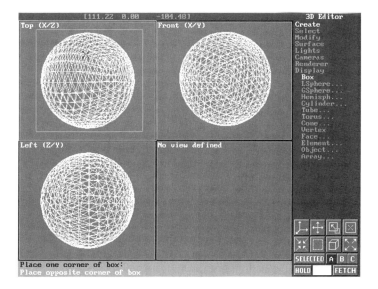

Figure 5.66
Marking the second corner.

Beginning of depth line

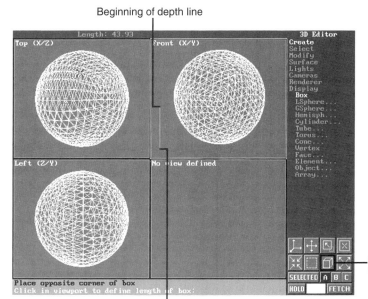

Figure 5.67
Defining the depth of the box.

Show All icon

End of depth line

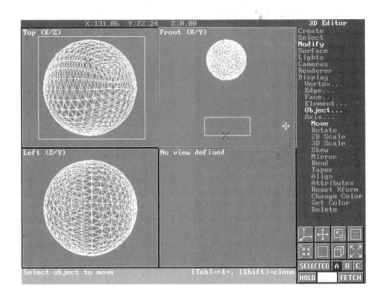

Figure 5.68
Moving the box.

Figure 5.69
The omnidirectional cursor.

Figure 5.70
The Up/Down cursor.

To move the object while the Object/Move menu is active, simply drag the mouse. You'll see a shadow object while you drag, as shown in Figure 5.71. Move the box until it is aligned as shown.

We now have the setup for our first Boolean operation. The box now marks the portion of the sphere that we want to cut. Use the mouse to select the Create/Object/ Boolean menu, as shown in Figure 5.72. The cursor changes to a small square box.

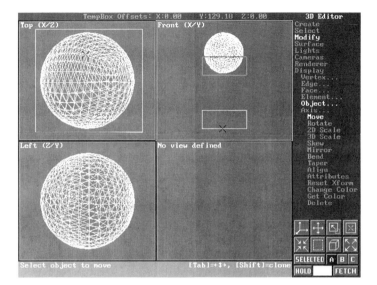

Figure 5.71
*Moving the box,
part 2.*

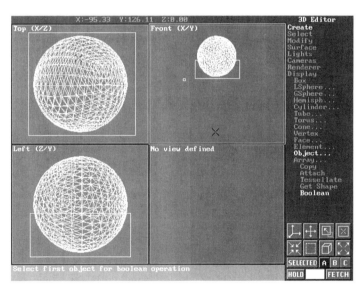

Figure 5.72
Boolean operations.

Click first on the sphere, and then on the box. The order is important! The first click defines the base object; the second click defines the object we plan to subtract. When you make the second click, the dialog box shown in Figure 5.73 appears. Make sure that Subtraction is highlighted in red, and then click the OK button.[26]

---
[26]If you want to play it safe, click the Hold button. This saves the current state of the model in a buffer. If something in the Boolean operation causes an error (Boolean operations are extremely complex, and they do sometimes go haywire), you can Fetch from the buffer and restore everything to the state it was in before the Boolean operation.

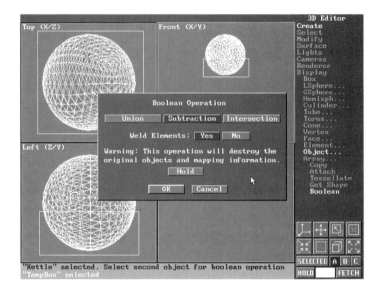

Figure 5.73
*The dialog box for
Boolean operations.*

The result of the Boolean operation is shown in Figure 5.74. It's still not a teapot, but we are well on our way!

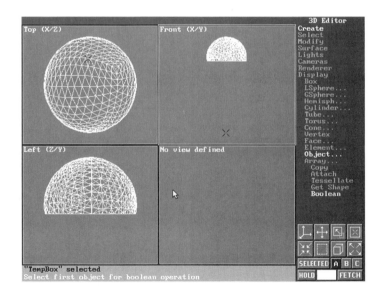

Figure 5.74
*Boolean subtraction:
The result.*

The next step is to separate the top of the slightly-more-than-half sphere and turn it into a lid for the teapot. We'll use a Boolean operation for this, too. Simply create a box like the last one, with one important difference: The depth of the box should be as small as possible. The resulting box should look like the one shown in Figure 5.75.

As before, if the box isn't located where you want it, use Object/Move to position it as shown in Figure 5.75.

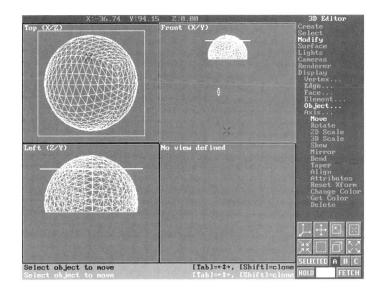

Figure 5.75
Creating another temporary box.

This very thin box marks the place where we will cut the leftover sphere into two parts. The process is the same as before: Create/Object/Boolean is the menu choice, and Subtraction is the process we use. Remember to click the leftover sphere first, and the box second. Figure 5.76 shows the result. I zoomed in on the Left view to show the cut. It is too thin to show up at normal magnification.

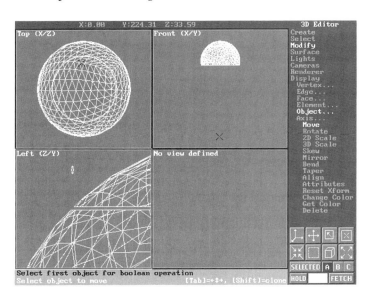

Figure 5.76
A cut made with a Boolean operation.

Even though we now have two pieces where we had one physical object, this is still one single object as far as 3D Studio is concerned. In this case, we don't want both to be the same object—we want them to move independently during the animation. To make the lid a separate object, click on the Create/Element/Detach menu selection, and then click on the lid. In 3D lingo, the lid is an *element*, not an *object*. To make it an object, we must detach it from its parent object (the kettle). After you click, you'll see the dialog box shown in Figure 5.77. Click on OK to detach. You won't see any difference in appearance, however.

Figure 5.77
Detaching an element.

To make it easier to work on these two different objects, move the lid upward. Use the Object/Move menu selection. To make it easier to move the lid back to its original position, press the Tab key until the cursor has the up/down shape shown earlier (see Fig. 5.70). The result of your move should look like Figure 5.78.

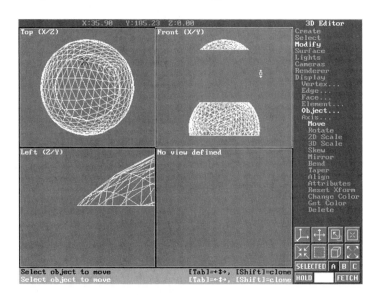

Figure 5.78
Moving the lid.

The lid needs a handle. Create a small GSphere with 144 faces and Smooth turned on; see Figure 5.79 for the size of the new sphere. Give it the name *Handle*. Then move the handle so that it touches the lid.

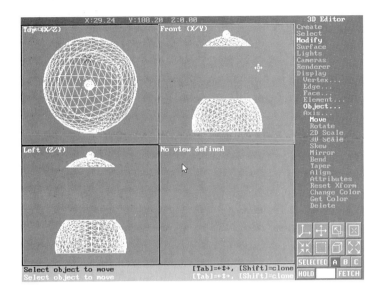

Figure 5.79
Adding a handle to the lid.

To attach the handle to the lid, use the menu selection Create/Object/Attach. Then click on the handle. The status line at the bottom says Select object to attach. The status line changes to Handle selected. Now select base object to attach it to. Click on the lid. The two objects are now one.[27] The combined object goes by the name of the base object: Lid. The result is shown in Figure 5.80.

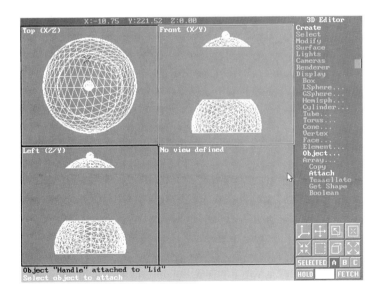

Figure 5.80
The new object: handle plus lid.

---

[27]Yes, you guessed it: They are now elements of a single object. To perform any operation on just one element, select Element rather than Object on the various menus.

This project is well on its way, but we still need a handle and a spout to really call it a teapot. Let's start with the spout. A real teapot has a curved spout, with a flare at the end. You'll learn several key 3D Studio features while we perform these operations.[28]

Let's create a tube to start the spout. Use the Create/Object/Tube menu selection, and then click the Values menu item to display the dialog box shown in Figure 5.81. *Sides* refers to the number of sides the tube will have when viewed from an end. *Segments* refers to the number of separate segments the tube will have when viewed from the side (top to bottom, as it were). Enter values for a 32-sided, 16-segment tube.[29]

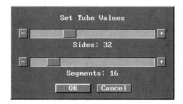

Figure 5.81
Setting values for a tube object.

To create a tube, you will define the inner radius, the outer radius, and the length of the tube. Figure 5.82 shows suitable inner and outer radii for the tube. The length should be about as long as the kettle itself is tall; Figure 5.83 shows one way to determine the length. Figure 5.84 shows the finished tube.[30] Give it the name *Spout*.

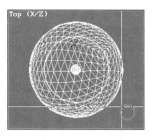

Figure 5.82
Creating the tube.

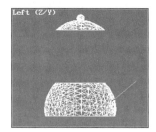

Figure 5.83
Defining the length of the tube.

---

[28]If you are getting impatient to get to the inverse kinematics, peek ahead!

[29]More sides will give you a smoother tube. More segments will give you a tube that can bend more smoothly.

[30]As before, if the tube gets created somewhere else, just move it into position. If you want to control where objects appear, use Modify/Axis/Place to set the default location.

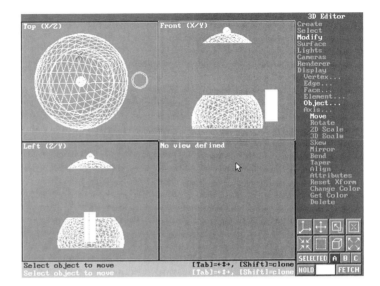

Figure 5.84
The finished tube.

Even when moved into position, the spout does us no good at all—it's pointing straight up, and we want it at an angle. We'll rotate the spout into position, and then bend and skew its shape until it looks more like a spout.

Before rotating, set a new pivot point, as shown in Figure 5.85, using the Modify/Axis/Place menu selection. The pivot point should be at the bottom left of the spout, nearest the pot. Simply click to place the pivot; a black x appears at the pivot point. Check all views to make sure that the pivot is actually at the edge of the tube! Normally, you must place the pivot in two separate views to position it correctly.

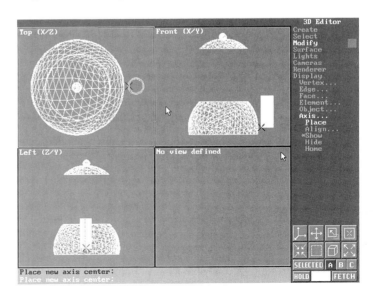

Figure 5.85
Moving the pivot point.

Now let's taper the spout, so that it is thinner at the top. Use the Modify/Object/Taper menu selection, and press the Tab key until the cursor has an arrow at the top (see Fig. 5.86). The taper should be about half the width of the tube, as shown in Figure 5.86.

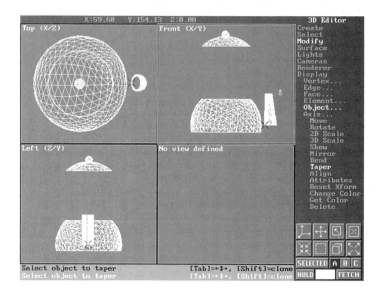

Figure 5.86
Tapering the tube.

Now use the Modify/Object/Rotate menu selection to rotate the spout into position. This is where the pivot point comes in handy—the spout rotates in position. If the pivot point were far away, an object might rotate clear out of view! Figure 5.87 shows rotation in action.

If your spout appears a little short at this point, you can use Modify/Object/2D scale to lengthen it. That's what happened to me! In Figure 5.88, the lengthened spout gets curved (by using the Modify/Object/Bend menu selection) to a more spout-like curve.

Figure 5.89 shows the result. This is good, but we can add a few additional details to the spout to make it look even more natural. We'll select some of the points[31] near the tip of the spout, and move them to add a reverse curve to the spout's tip. Use the menu selection Select/Vertex/Quad, and then click a series of points describing a fence around part of the tip, as shown in Figure 5.90.

---

[31]A point is called a *vertex* in 3D Studio lingo.

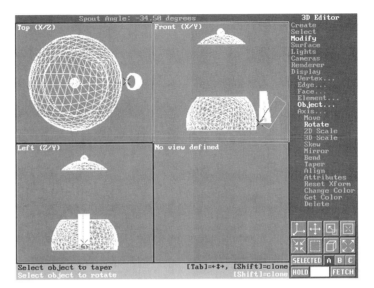

Figure 5.87
Rotating the spout into position.

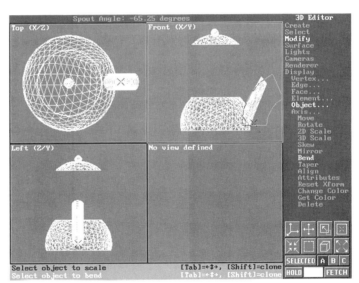

Figure 5.88
Bending the spout.

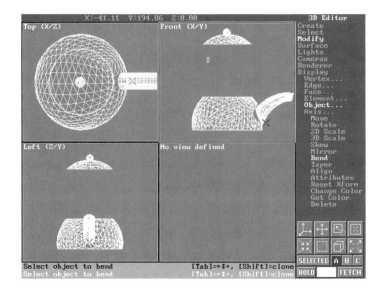

Figure 5.89
The spout with a curve.

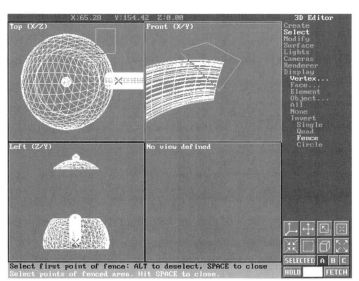

Figure 5.90
Selecting points.

The selected points will show up in red. To bend, use the Modify/Vertex/Bend menu selection, click the Selected button at the bottom right of the screen, and then press the Tab key until the cursor arrow points to the right. Then drag the cursor to bend, as shown in Figure 5.91. The point of this little diversion: To show that you can easily modify portions of an object or element by selecting just those points that you are interested in. This gives you tremendous power to modify the shape of objects. The result of the bend is shown in Figure 5.92.

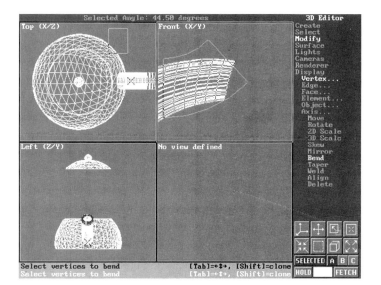

Figure 5.91
Bending the tip.

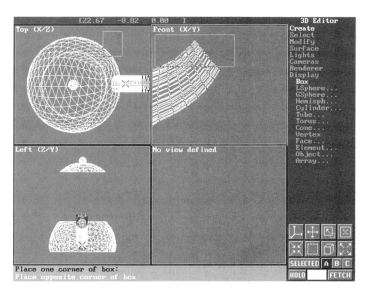

Figure 5.92
The bent tip.

To complete the tip, create a small box and use a Boolean operation to remove a small portion of the tip. The box is shown in Figure 5.93, and the result is shown in Figure 5.94.

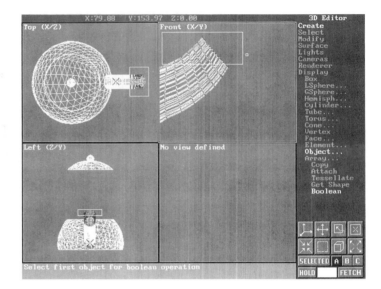

Figure 5.93
Creating the box for a Boolean operation.

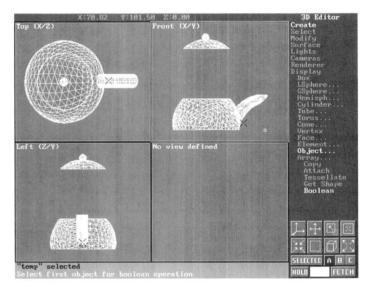

Figure 5.94
The tip of the spout after a Boolean subtraction.

The handle can be created from a torus.[32] Position the torus as you create it so that it winds up in the position shown in Figure 5.95.

---

[32]A *torus*, if you don't happen to know, is a doughnut shape.

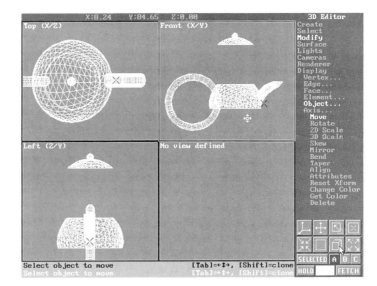

Figure 5.95
Creating and positioning a torus.

You can then create a series of boxes to remove portions of the torus, leaving a segment that makes a nice, modern-looking handle. See Figure 5.96 for the result.

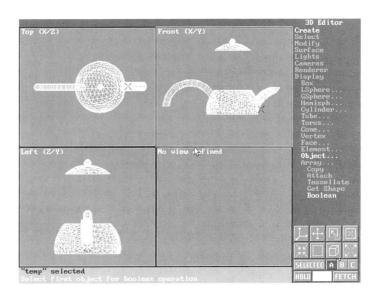

Figure 5.96
The handle from a torus.

Now we have all the objects for our teapot. To clean up, move the lid back down. The result is shown in Figure 5.97. Before you render the model, you'll need to choose materials for the objects in the model. I chose Black Matte for the lid, and Chrome Sky for the rest of the teapot. Use the menu selection Surface/Materials/Choose to pick a material, and Surface/Materials/Assign/Object to assign the material to an object. This completes the basic model. There's more work, however!

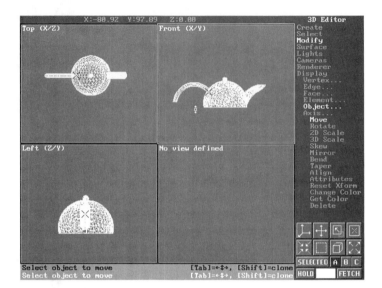

Figure 5.97
The completed teapot model.

Now, we'll add a camera and some lights to create a scene. Use the Cameras/Create menu selection, and click and drag in the Top viewport to create the camera and its target. The *target* is the place that the camera is aimed at. Figure 5.98 shows the process of creating a camera, while Figure 5.99 shows the result. To see what the camera sees, press Ctrl+V to display the dialog box shown in Figure 5.100. This dialog box enables you to change the view in the various viewports.

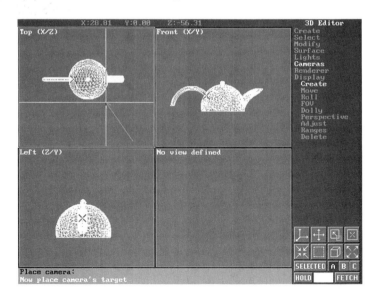

Figure 5.98
Creating a camera.

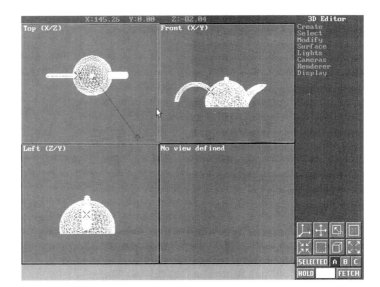

Figure 5.99
A camera in a viewport.

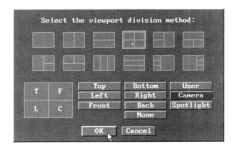

Figure 5.100
Changing the view in a viewport.

To change the view, click on the view type at the right of the dialog box, and then click in the viewport you want to change. In Figure 5.100, the Camera type is highlighted, and the bottom right viewport has been clicked to change it to a Camera view. Figure 5.101 shows the result. If the view in the Camera viewport isn't what you want, move the camera and/or its target until you see what you want.[33]

Let's take a look at the teapot. Click the Renderer/Render Viewport menu selection, and then click in the Camera viewport. This opens the Render Still Image dialog box shown in Figure 5.102. Accept the default settings, and click the Render button. Figure 5.103 shows a rendering of the object.

---

[33]Use the Cameras/Move menu selection to move the camera and/or target.

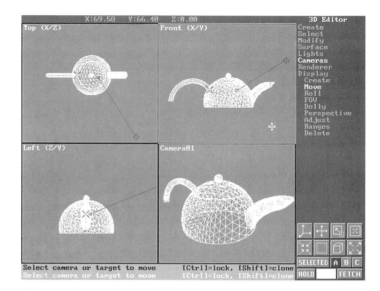

Figure 5.101
A camera viewport.

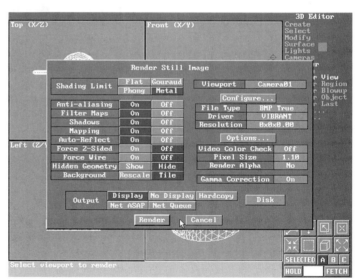

Figure 5.102
*The Render Still
Image dialog box.*

What happened to the lid? It's there, but you can't see it because we haven't added lights. The difference between the black lid and the background is too small to see, while the bright metal surface of the kettle shows up clearly. We'll add spotlights using the Lights/Spot/Create menu selection. Three lights provide good illumination: two in front of the teapot, and one above and behind to provide a highlight. You create a light the same way you create a camera: Click to position the light, and then drag and release to indicate the target. If the lights and targets don't show up where you want them (see Fig. 5.104), use Lights/Spot/Move to move both lights and targets. After you place a light, you'll see the dialog box shown in Figure 5.105; use the setting shown for each light. To adjust parameters after you create a light, use the menu selection Lights/Spot/Adjust.

Figure 5.103
The rendered teapot.

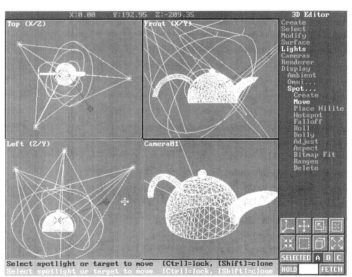

Figure 5.104
Adding three lights.

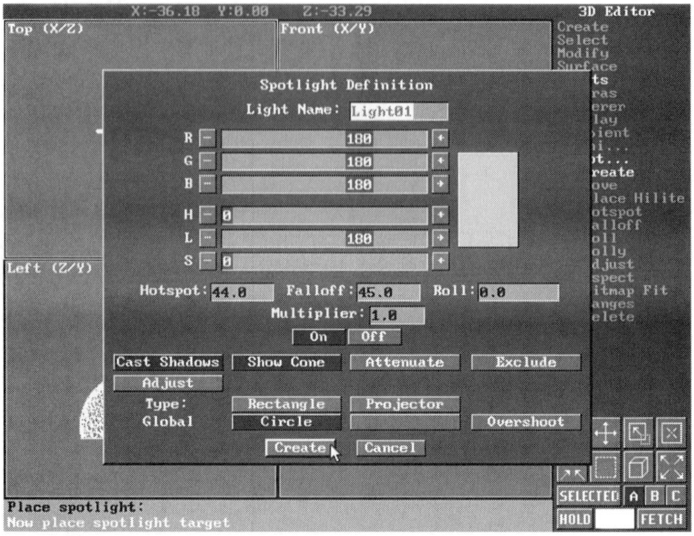

Figure 5.105
Adjusting parameters for a light.

After you add the lights, rendering gives a much better image, as shown in Figure 5.106. If you don't like the result you get in the rendering, you can adjust the direction, intensity, color, or other properties of the lights. You can also adjust the cone of light.[34] The outer band of the cone shows the outer limit of light (called the *falloff point*—that is, the point where the light falls off to zero), and the inner band shows the outer edge of the central hot spot. The cones are visible in Figure 5.104.

Figure 5.106
The teapot, properly lit.

---

[34]That's why Show Cone is highlighted in Figure 5.105.

Once you have the lights adjusted, however, these cones tend to get in the way. You can turn them off by using the Lights/Spot/Adjust menu selection—just click the Show Cone button if it is highlighted. This makes it much easier to view your scene, as shown in Figure 5.107. This will be especially important in the next phase. All our modeling work was done in the 3D Editor. Animation is next, and for that we'll use the Keyframer. Press the F4 key to enter the Keyframer. At first, it looks a lot like the 3D Editor (see Fig. 5.108). However, there are some very important differences. First, look at the bottom right—the new controls are for controlling animation playback. A careful look at the menu shows that it has changed, too. The Surface menu is gone, for example, and new menus like Hierarchy, Paths, and Time are available.

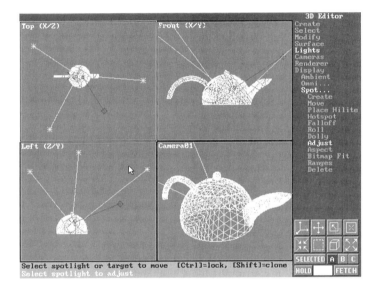

Figure 5.107
Removing light cones from the display.

Look more closely at Figure 5.108. There are small cubic objects with dashed lines located at various places. These are called *dummy objects*, and they can be created using the Hierarchy/Create Dummy menu selection. Dummy objects are invisible when you render, but they are very useful tools for the animator. You can link real objects and dummy objects. When you move the dummy object, the real object will follow.[35] Dummy objects can be moved and sized like real objects, but they have no surface materials or other visible properties.

In Figure 5.108, I created one dummy object for each moveable object in the teapot. One is located near the tip of the spout, another at the top of the lid, and one at the back of the handle. The dummy objects will be animated, and the real objects will follow along.

---

[35]You can also link lights and cameras to dummy objects, which is an excellent way to get a camera or light to follow a real object around a scene.

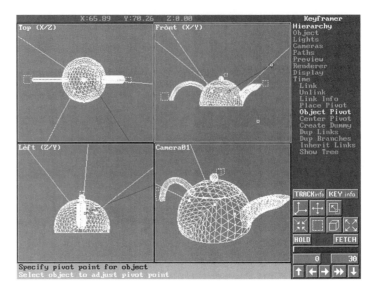

Figure 5.108
Working in the
Keyframer.

Before we can animate, however, we need to create *pivot points* for each of the objects. These are the points around which the object will rotate when it moves. The Hierarchy/Object Pivot menu selection allows you to place a pivot point for a single object. In Figure 5.109, I have placed the pivot point for the spout near the base, and central to the axis of the spout. Look for the dark X in the Top and Front views. Give the dummy object the name *SpoutX* to distinguish it from the real spout. The other two dummy objects will have the names *LidX* and *HandleX*.

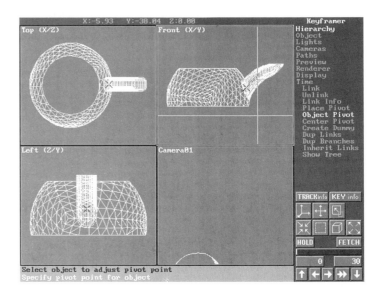

Figure 5.109
Placing object
pivots.

To use inverse kinematics on the model, we must also establish links between the various parts of the model. The kettle will serve as the main body, and the other parts are linked to that. The Hierarchy/Link menu selection does the job. When this menu item is first selected, the status line asks you to select a child object. Let's set up the linkage for the spout first. The child object is the dummy object at the tip of the spout. Click on the dummy object. The status line next asks you to click on the parent object; this is the spout. That's all you need to do to create a linkage between two objects. Repeat the process—this time, clicking on the spout as the child object and the kettle as the parent object. Now you have a linked chain of objects. To use inverse kinematics, you need at least three objects in a chain—a base (the kettle), something to move (the spout), and the end object (the dummy).

Next, create linked chains for the handle and the lid. In all cases, the kettle serves as the base, and a dummy object as the end object. When you are done, you have three linked chains:

Object	Chain 1	Chain 2	Chain 3
Base	Kettle	Kettle	Kettle
Moving	Spout	Lid	Handle
End	SpoutX	LidX	HandleX

This completes the ground work—now it's time for the fun of inverse kinematics. It takes a lot of effort to create a good model, but once you do, you then can have a lot of fun animating it. Press the F8 key to open the inverse kinematics dialog box. You'll see the screen shown in Figure 5.110. It's nothing impressive so far—this is just the door to the world of inverse kinematics. Click the button at the top left, Pick Objects.

This will pop you back to the Keyframer. Click on the kettle (the base object), and you will go back to the previous dialog box. Now, as shown in Figure 5.111, the various objects and their relationships are shown. Note that linked objects are shown indented. The farther the indent, the farther down the list the object resides. The dummy objects (SpoutX, LidX, and HandleX) are indented the most.

Two basic steps are involved in inverse kinematics. First, you'll define the various joints in the object and how they operate. Second, you'll actually animate the model. Let's start with the spout. At the bottom center of the dialog box, click the Start button (just above the Joint Precedence button), and then click on Kettle in the list. Now click the End button, and then click on SpoutX in the list. Kettle, Spout, and SpoutX should appear in white, as you see in Figure 5.111.

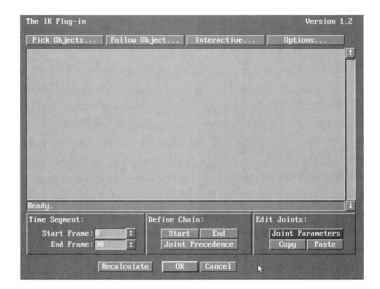

Figure 5.110
*Inverse kinematics,
at last!*

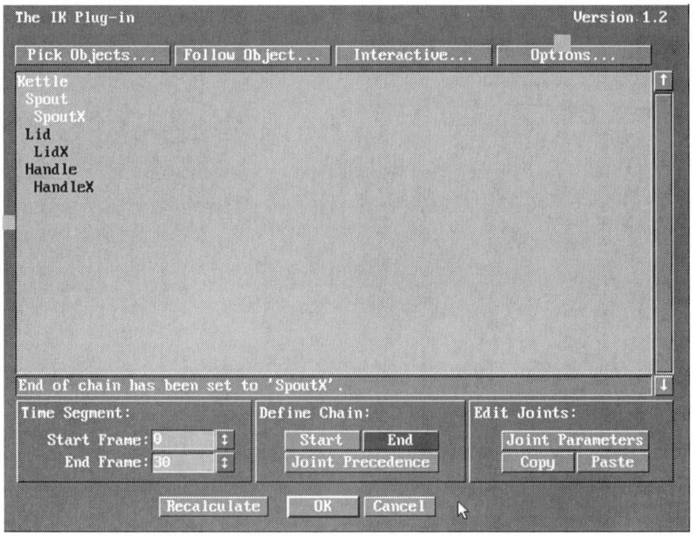

Figure 5.111
*Displaying the
relationships
between objects in
the hierarchy.*

Now click the Joint Parameters button at the lower right, and then click on Spout.
The dialog box shown in Figure 5.112 appears. Now we are getting somewhere! This
dialog box enables you to define the type and limits of joint movement interactively.

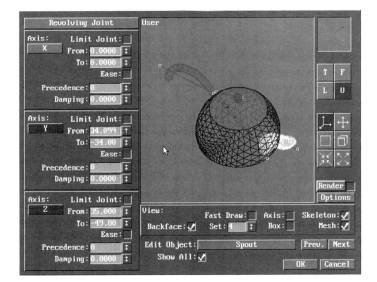

Figure 5.112
Setting joint parameters.

Note that the spout is shown in white, the kettle (base) appears in black, and other parts of the model are shown in gray. The tools at the right are similar to those in the 3D Editor, and are used to choose various views of the model, or to zoom in and out. This allows you to move the model to a view that makes it clear how the joints operate. The left of the dialog box has three areas—one for each axis of movement: X, Y, and Z. You can define a starting angle and an ending angle for each axis.

Let's start by turning off movement in the X axis for the spout. Just click the X button at the upper left. To adjust the From and To settings for the Y and Z axes, click on the small up/down arrows at the right of the numeric input for From and To. Figure 5.113 shows an adjustment of the To limit for the Y axis. Note that, in the figure, the spout has moved to a position corresponding to the displayed angle of movement. This allows you to see exactly how much a given joint angle will allow the object to move. You can set your own values or use those shown in Figure 5.113.

When you are working with complex models (our teapot is quite a simple one), it can be hard to visualize the model while looking at the wire mesh. The Render button, at the right of the dialog box, renders the model in a single color, as shown in Figure 5.114. This allows you to determine what's what when you make adjustments. Unfortunately, when you adjust settings, the model goes back to wire mesh.

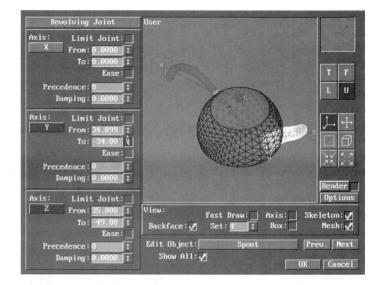

Figure 5.113
Adjusting limiting angles of movement.

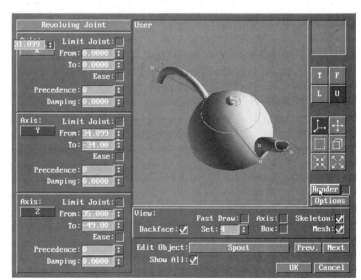

Figure 5.114
Rendering the 3D shape of the model.

After you set the various joint parameters, click the OK button to return to the list of objects.[36] Now set Kettle as the start object and LidX as the End object, and then click the Joint Parameters button. Click Lid to redisplay the Joint Parameters dialog box (see Fig. 5.115). You can set a range of motion in all three axes for the lid; Figure 5.115 shows my suggestions. Similarly, you can define joint parameters for the handle as well.

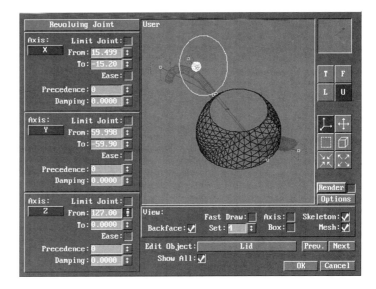

Figure 5.115
Adjusting movement of the lid.

After you create joint parameters for all three moveable objects (spout, lid, and handle), you must save them. Click the Options button to display the Options menu (see Fig. 5.116). Click the Save Joints button to save the parameters. This displays the dialog box shown in Figure 5.117, asking if you are sure. Click Yes.

Figure 5.116
Saving joints.

---

[36]We haven't covered the other joint parameters, and for a very good reason: They are quite complex. They are used to do such things as determine which axis of movement the joint prefers to move in, and which joints tend to move before other joints. These features can be used to generate more natural types of motion.

Figure 5.117
Verifying the save operation.

To animate the object, click the Interactive button near the top of the display. This opens the dialog box shown in Figure 5.118. I have clicked the Render button to show the model more clearly. Before beginning to animate, look at the slider control immediately below the image area. It should show the last frame of the animation, frame 30, as the current frame.[37]

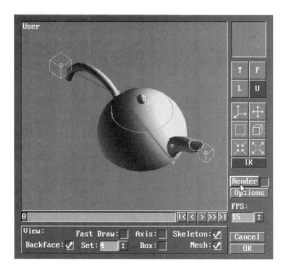

Figure 5.118
Ready to animate.

All the work we have done so far is now going to pay off big time. Animating the teapot is incredibly easy. All you have to do is drag the various dummy objects until the model is in the position you want it to be in. That's all there is to it—just click on a dummy object, drag, and then click to place it. Figure 5.119 shows a sample animation of the teapot. Figure 5.120 shows a rendered view of the same animation. Click OK to return to the List screen.

---

[37]By default, all animations begin with 30 frames. You can easily change this number in the Keyframer—just click on the number box at the bottom right, and type the new number of frames.

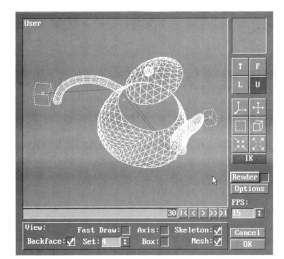

Figure 5.119
An animated teapot.

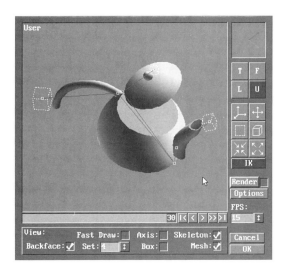

Figure 5.120
A rendered view of the teapot.

Click the Options button, and then click the Save Animation button to save the animation you have created. You can then click OK to return to the Keyframer. Figure 5.121 shows the result of your work—a very animated teapot in Wireframe view. You can preview the animation by pressing the F7 key to start the previewer (see Fig. 5.122). The buttons at the lower right enable you to play the animation in real time, with roughly rendered materials (note the bottom right viewport).

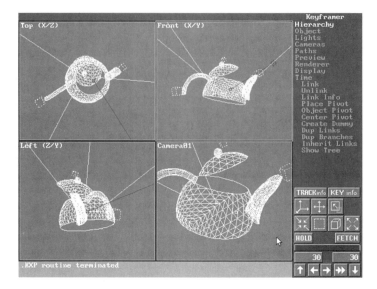

Figure 5.121
*Back in the
Keyframer again.*

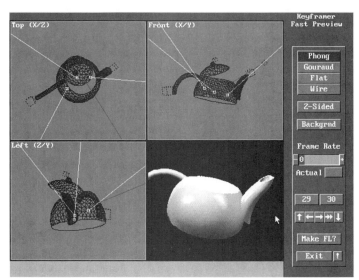

Figure 5.122
*Previewing the
animation.*

You can also render the animation in full, glorious color and detail by choosing the Renderer/Render View menu selection in the Keyframer. It is very similar to the same menu option in the 3D Editor. However, you can specify a range of frames for the rendering, and you can render to a FLC file (an animation file format) in addition to bitmap file formats. Figure 5.123 shows the Render Animation dialog box, and Figure 5.124 shows a frame from the completed animation.

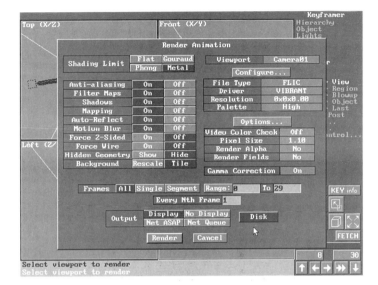

Figure 5.123
Rendering the
animation.

Figure 5.124
A frame from the
animation.

This little teapot is actually a very simple 3D model for animation. With some time and patience, you can build extremely complex models with 3D Studio. Are you a fan of *Jurassic Park*? Look at Figures 5.125, 5.126, and 5.127. They show a dinosaur model with separate objects for feet, lower legs, thighs, body, several tail parts, neck, and head. It would take a huge amount of time to animate such a complex model, but with inverse kinematics, all you need to do is move the paws, feet, and head to the appropriate position. Figure 5.128 shows a single frame from an animation of the dinosaur inside a cathedral.

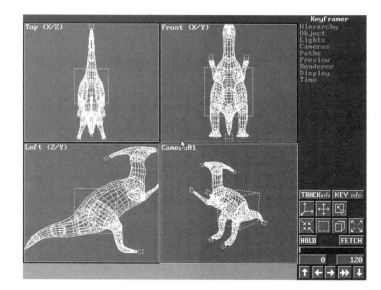

Figure 5.125
*A wireframe
dinosaur model.*

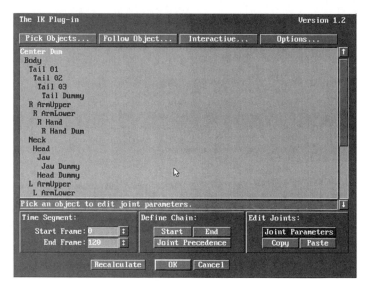

Figure 5.126
*A portion of the
joint list for the
dinosaur.*

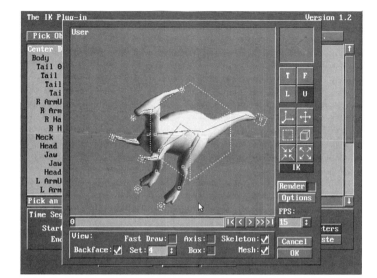

Figure 5.127
The dinosaur in the inverse kinematics Animation Editor.

Figure 5.128
A rendering of the dinosaur.

Even more complex models are possible; your imagination is the only limitation. How about a human model, for example, with dozens of separate parts, from finger joints to torso and head? Figure 5.129 shows a female model in a complex pose. The capability to quickly move the various limbs (always in a lifelike manner, thanks to carefully defined joint parameters), and to quickly render each attempt—these are tremendous advantages for a complex 3D animation. Figure 5.130 shows a close-up of Figure 5.129. Note that there are separate objects and joints for every digit of every finger in the hand. Each has been carefully defined for natural movement.[38]

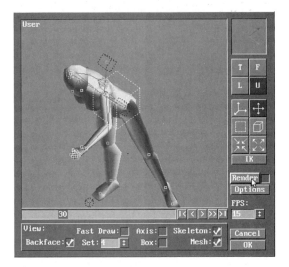

Figure 5.129
A human figure in a complex pose.

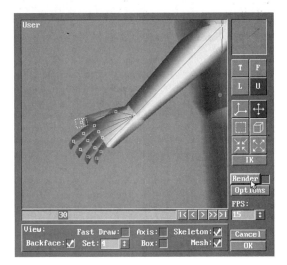

Figure 5.130
Detail of a human figure.

---

[38]This model is one example of several ready-to-go models that come with 3D Studio Release 4. See the Software Buyer's Guide on the CDs for information about third parties who offer a multitude of models, textures, and other goodies for use with 3D Studio.

The bottom line with 3D Studio is very simple to describe. Yes, it's expensive. But it also delivers the power, features, and tools that you need to develop top-notch 3D animations. It puts animation on the desktop at a reasonable price. Is 3D Studio for everyone? No. Is 3D Studio the right tool for a serious animator? Yes! 3D Studio gets my vote as one of the most powerful tools available today for 3D modeling and animation.

6

I CAN FLY!

Flights of Fancy

I love to fly.[1] And I know I'm not alone. So despite the fact that I've used up lots of superlatives describing various aspects of virtual reality, virtual flight is at the top of my list of Cool Stuff. As you learned in Chapter 1, it's not even hard to do. A fly-through is really an animation. This is not the same as an interactive virtual flight, where the visuals are recalculated for every frame. Because a fly-through is just an animation, it is relatively easy to play it back. You don't need hot hardware to play a fly-through, although a decent graphics subsystem doesn't hurt.

The holy grail of near-term virtual reality, however, is real-time, interactive movement—whether it be simulated flight, walking, driving, or whatever. On a personal computer—even one sporting a souped-up Pentium and all the hardware you can load into a single case—there just isn't enough horsepower to do all the processing that's required to move within a virtual space in real time and still handle such mundane tasks as updating the screen as fast as your eye *wants* it updated. Some systems come close, but the closer they come, the more they cost. Thus the value of the fly-through animation. If you insist on interactivity, you'll have to settle for lower quality graphics and/or lower frame rates. If you insist on high-quality graphics or high frame rates, you'll have to settle for an animated fly-through.[2]

On the other hand, these hot new Pentiums (90MHz is good, 120MHz and up is better) do deliver some excellent interactive fly-throughs. Your actual results will vary not just with the CPU, however, but with certain specific details of your graphics display subsystem. Most (and soon, all) interactive virtual reality software relies on something called the *VESA standard* when it comes to video display. In the bad old days, every video card required different drivers. This created sheer chaos, and the VESA standard was developed so that every video card could display graphics using a standard set of functions. With some video cards, you must load a VESA driver that translates these standard functions into a format that the video card can understand. With other video cards, VESA support is built right in. If virtual reality is your game (and it must be, if you have followed this far!), then a video card that handles VESA support on board is much better. Cards that use drivers require loading the driver

---

[1] And I'm not talking about airplanes! Maybe I should say, "I'd love to fly." But after spending so much time virtually flying, "I love to fly" is more accurate.

[2] You can simulate real-time interactivity using fly-through technology. Create an animation for every possible interactive choice, and then play the appropriate animation based on the interactive input. For example, if the user wants to enter a room, you would play an animation that moves through a door and forward into the room. If the user signals turn right, you play an animation of the viewpoint turning to the right. If the user signals turn left, you play that animation. I've included a sample of this kind of fly-through with the sample files for this chapter.

into the memory on your computer, and you really need as much memory as you can get these days—you don't want an extra driver taking up memory if it doesn't have to.

There is more to VESA than just the issue of a VESA driver. Yes, VESA is a standard. But that doesn't mean that every graphics card does equally well with it. Some cards will be slow—even ones that are otherwise very fast indeed. For example, the Matrox MGA Impression Plus, while absolutely lightning-like in Windows, is abysmally slow using the VESA standard. Software like VREAM and Superscape will absolutely crawl across your screen with such an adapter. The Jazz Jakarta, on the other hand, has built-in VESA, runs like greased lighting in both Windows and using the VESA standard, and is a much, much better choice.

In general, look for video cards that display very fast performance under DOS. Ignore Windows performance, except for programs like Virtus VR and Virtus WalkThrough Pro (since they run in Windows, of course). DOS performance will not guarantee fast VESA performance, but you are more likely to get it than with a card that is slow under DOS. With all the emphasis on speedy performance in Windows, many of these expensive, high-end video cards are actually quite slow in DOS, and that just won't do for VR. You have been warned!

Even if a fly-through isn't the Holy Grail of virtual reality, it is one of the most interesting and challenging aspects of virtual reality. It takes patience and a willingness to learn a huge number of details if you want to create a sophisticated fly-through, but you can also have fun with products like Vistapro. In this chapter, I'll show you how to fly with Virtus VR and 3D Studio. Then, for some really complicated excitement, you'll learn how to use Vistapro and 3D Studio together for some interesting effects. For other examples of fly-throughs, see Chapters 1 and 8.

Virtus VR Takes Off

Simply using Virtus VR, as you learned in Chapter 2, is like doing a fly-through. As a Windows product, Virtus VR is limited to the standard mouse for flying, but its clever interface makes flight simple, if not necessarily easy.[3]

Figure 6.1 shows the key to using Virtus VR: the instruction cube. It comes right in the Virtus VR package, is easy to assemble, and conveniently tells you all the important stuff about both world creation and flight.

---

[3]Virtus WalkThrough shares the same interface.

Each face of the cube gives you pertinent information about using Virtus VR. Well, almost every face is useful; the top face is little more than the product logo. The two most important faces are shown in Figure 6.1. They tell you how to use the mouse and the keyboard to fly through the universe.

Figure 6.1
The key to under-standing fly-throughs in Virtus VR is this little cardboard cube.

There are two mouse modes, and each mode gets one face of the cube. Mode 1 is the mouse alone. Mode 2 is the mouse and the keyboard used together. In both modes, you move by clicking with the mouse in the Walk window. Cross hairs mark the center of the window, as shown in Figure 6.2.[4] The following mode 1 mouse clicks are used to move in the environment:

Clicking above cross hairs   Moves forward

Clicking below cross hairs   Moves backward

Clicking right of cross hairs   Turns right

Clicking left of cross hairs   Turns left

You can move around quite a bit with just these clicks, but there are times when you want to move up or down, or tilt forward or backward, and so on. The Shift and Control keys come to your rescue. In mode 2, holding down one key or the other opens up

---

[4]It's been a while, but I wonder if you can place the scene shown in the figure. **Hint:** It's located in Waco, Texas. Another hint: That tank is about to roll through the walls. If the theme seems morbid, other famous (or should I say infamous) scenes are also included, such as Dealy Plaza in Dallas, Texas. VR and 3D technology are often used to reconstruct crime scenes for after-the-fact analysis.

new possibilities. For example, when you hold down the Shift key, the mouse clicks have different results:

Clicking above cross hairs	Looks up (pitch up)
Clicking below cross hairs	Looks down (pitch down)
Clicking right of cross hairs	Rolls right
Clicking left of cross hairs	Rolls left

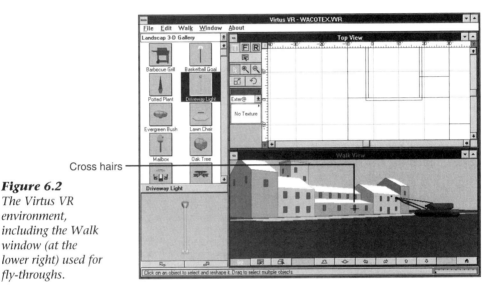

Cross hairs

Figure 6.2
The Virtus VR environment, including the Walk window (at the lower right) used for fly-throughs.

When you hold down the Control key, these movements become possible:

Clicking above cross hairs	Rises up
Clicking below cross hairs	Sinks down
Clicking right of cross hairs	Slides right
Clicking left of cross hairs	Slides left

Clicking in other areas of the Walk window yields a combination of moves. For example, clicking above and to the left results in a rotation to the left and a move forward. A very important fact: The farther away from the cross hairs you click, the larger the motion.

You can also click the small buttons at the bottom of the Walk window to move in basic ways. You can refer to the detailed information about Virtus VR and Virtus WalkThrough in Chapter 2 before continuing with the fly-through exercise if you haven't done so already.

Many of the scenes included as sample worlds with Virtus VR and Virtus WalkThrough contain prerecorded fly-throughs. You can play the prerecorded version, or you can create your own. Figure 6.3 shows the Walk menu, where the secret to fly-throughs is found: the Rewind, Play, and Record selections. It's not as fancy as a 3D VCR-style controller, but it gets the job done. You not only can use the mouse and the Shift and Control keys to move around, but you can record your movements for later playback. When you save a file, the recorded fly-through is saved with the file.

Figure 6.3
Control the Walk environment, including Play/ Record capabilities, by using the Walk menu.

Level Observer Ctrl+L
Wide Angle
√ Standard
Telephoto
√ Normal Speed
Fast
Faster
Fastest
Rewind
Play
Record
Sky Color...

To record a fly-through, you must click the Record button first. If you make a mistake, there is no way to edit the fly-through; you'll have to start over. To restart, just click the Walk/Stop menu option,[5] and then click Walk/Record again.

Let's take a look at what you can accomplish during a fly-through. Figure 6.4 shows the starting point of a short fly-through I created.

To begin the fly-through, I clicked several times in the area above the cross hairs, and slightly to the right. This moved me closer to the tank, as shown in Figure 6.5.

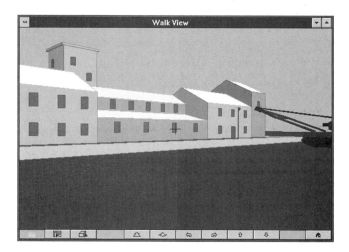

Figure 6.4
The beginning of a fly-through.

---

[5]The Rewind menu option changes to Stop when you are recording.

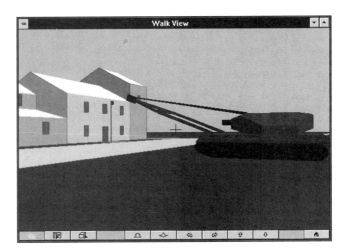

Figure 6.5
Moving forward into the scene.

If you continue to move forward, you can get as close to objects as you want. Unless the object has texture, however, you won't get any additional details (see Fig. 6.6).

You can also use the Shift and Control keys to move to true flight positions, as shown in Figure 6.7. You can move to almost any position; the virtual universe is a big place inside Virtus VR. You only need the patience to keep clicking the mouse to move as far as you want. The models can be quite complex, as you can see by looking at Figure 6.8.

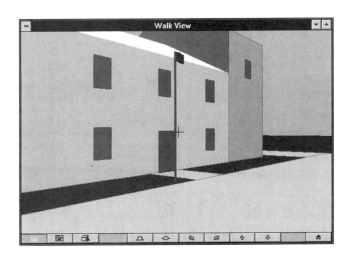

Figure 6.6
Object detail does not increase beyond a certain level, no matter how close you get.

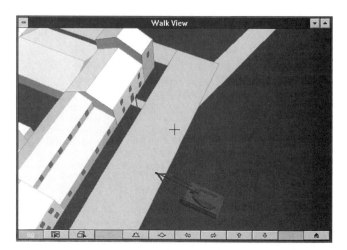

Figure 6.7
*Looking at the scene
from above.*

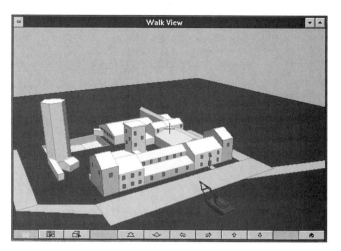

Figure 6.8
*Virtus VR models
can be complex.*

You can also explore interior spaces. The Waco, Texas model doesn't contain any interior objects (see Fig. 6.9).

You can, of course, use the libraries to add objects or people to interior spaces. Figure 6.10 shows a conference table added to the room shown in Figure 6.9.

When you have completed the fly-through, you can save it to disk with the rest of the file, or you can record it as a FLC file.[6] Look for the Snapshot option on the File menu (see Fig. 6.11). This allows you to save the current Walk view as a bitmap file, or the current recorded fly-through as a FLC file (see Fig. 6.12).

---

[6]That's Autodesk's animation file format.

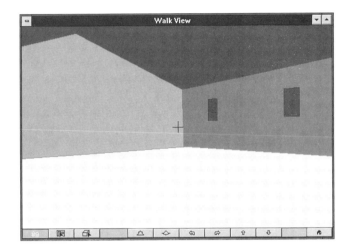

Figure 6.9
The beginning of a fly-through.

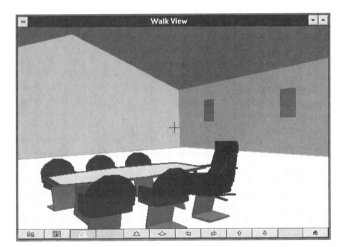

Figure 6.10
Adding a conference table gives the room some scale.

Figure 6.11
The Snapshot menu option.

<u>N</u>ew	Ctrl+N
<u>O</u>pen...	Ctrl+O
<u>C</u>lose	Ctrl+W
<u>S</u>ave	Ctrl+S
Save <u>A</u>s...	
Re<u>v</u>ert to Saved	
<u>P</u>rint...	Ctrl+P
Print Set<u>u</u>p...	
Snapsho<u>t</u>	▶
E<u>x</u>it	Alt+F4

Figure 6.12
You can save bitmaps or animations.

<u>B</u>MP...
<u>A</u>nimator Pro...

If there is not a recorded fly-through, the Animator Pro menu option is grayed out.

If you choose to save the animation, the dialog box shown in Figure 6.13 appears. You can set the size of the animation to any of the preset options, or you can use a custom size. Remember that larger animations require faster computers to play back smoothly. The animation can be in color or grayscale, and you have the option of specifying which portion of the animation to save to disk.

If you click the Smooth Path option, the program adds frames to make the animation smoother.

If desired, you can import the FLC file into a Video for Windows-compatible Editor, add sound to the animation, and save it as an AVI clip.

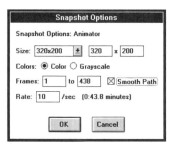

Figure 6.13
*Options for saving
an animation to
disk.*

Setting Up a 3D Studio Fly-Through

You can create a complete virtual space in 3D Studio,[7] but there are easier ways of going about the process. You can import DXF files[8] created with other software, such as AutoCAD, and many other engineering and architectural programs. Many low-end programs also export 3D images in DXF format, such as 3D Concepts and Generic CADD. For this example, I chose the 3D image file from Chapter 3—the house and yard. This image has quite a genealogy. It started as a floor plan in the Home Design series from Autodesk and was turned into a 3D file (with a 3DD extension) in 3D Plan. It then was loaded into 3D Concepts and saved as a DXF file. Now it can be loaded into 3D Studio.

---

[7]**Note:** This fly-through was created with Release 2 of 3D Studio. However, this does not affect the situation at all. Most of what you need to pull off a good fly-through isn't built into 3D Studio— whether you use Release 2, 3, or 4, most of what you need to do involves concepts, not version-specific tools.

[8]DXF files are the standard of the 3D universe. They are most commonly used by AutoCAD but are now supported by a wide variety of software packages. Like most file format standards, DXF owes its standardization to nothing more than the success of the program.

3D Studio can load DXF files directly, using the File/Load menu option (see Fig. 6.14). If you accept the default values, the file will be loaded with many of the image characteristics intact. For example, objects will still be objects—the refrigerator will not decompose into its separate parts.

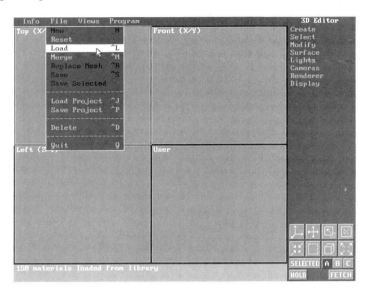

Figure 6.14
Loading a DXF file into 3D Studio.

Figure 6.15 shows the house file loaded into 3D Studio. All the pieces are there, although not always in ways that you might expect. The walls, for example, are constructed of many, many tiles. Unfortunately, this creates a lot of visual clutter, as you can see in Figure 6.15. You can get some relief from this by setting Display/Geometry to hide *backfaces* (faces on the hidden side of objects). 3D Studio also allows you to set individual objects for box display. The object is displayed as, yes, a box, which is very fast, but there are no details. If you aren't working on a particular object, this is a convenience.

Although the file is largely intact,[9] one key element of virtual reality is missing at this point. There are no surface colors or textures on any of the objects. 3D Studio allows you to associate specific materials with objects. In fact, it has a Material Editor you can use to specify the characteristics of a wide variety of materials. The Material Editor is sophisticated, and only the basic features are discussed in this chapter. See Chapter 8 for more information on materials engineering in a virtual space.

---

[9]There were a few bugs in the loaded image. For example, several faces on the bathtub object were missing and had to be corrected by hand. In other cases, the face normal of an object was set incorrectly. The *face normal* is the direction in which a face faces. If it faces away from the camera, then you won't see anything there unless the material you chose for that face or object is two-sided. If you ever see missing objects, or missing parts of objects, it's a safe bet that some face normals are facing the wrong way. You can easily set all of an object's faces to normal by using the Unify Normals command.

3D Studio comes with a large number of ready-to-use materials, and for the most part you can use them for this example. Specifying existing materials is easy. Choose Surface/Material/Choose to select a material, and then use Surface/Material/Assign/Object to apply it to an object.[10]

3D Studio supports *extended objects*. That is, you can group objects together. 3D Studio calls the component objects *elements*. In the file used for this example, objects with similar characteristics are grouped together.[11] Grouped objects don't have to be "physically" together—they can be anywhere in the virtual space.

Figure 6.16 shows that doors, door frames, and window frames are actually one object. The floor plan in the Top view shows this clearly, even including the bifold doors in the bedroom at the lower right. You can assign the material Teak to all of these at one time by using the menu choice Surface/Material/Assign/Object, or you can assign specific materials to any one element using Surface/Material/Assign/Element.[12]

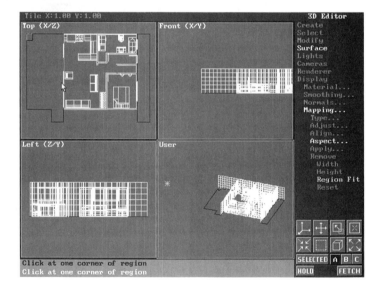

Figure 6.15
The DXF file has been loaded into 3D Studio.

---

[10]You can apply materials to portions of an object as well. 3D Studio is extremely flexible about such things once you learn the ins and outs of the menus.

[11]This was done in the original floor plan software when groups of objects were given similar physical characteristics, such as color.

[12]This is typical of the depth (and complexity) of 3D Studio. The menu structure is not something you can learn in a day or a week; knowledge of the pathways and byways comes with experience over several months.

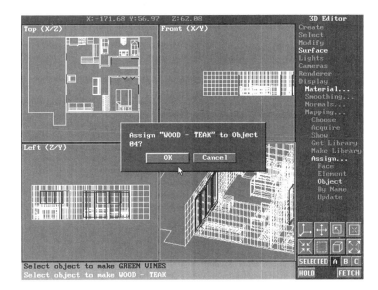

Figure 6.16
Assigning the material Wood - Teak to a 3D Studio object.

You must repeat this process for every group of objects in the virtual space.[13] You can draw on the extensive library of materials included with 3D Studio, or you can make up your own.

After you add materials, the next task is to create lighting. 3D Studio offers a range of lighting options, but the most interesting is Spotlights, since it casts shadows. You can place spotlights in the same locations that you would find them in many homes—near the ceiling or in the center of a room. Figure 6.17 shows the dialog box for setting the attributes of a typical spotlight.

The *hotspot* refers to the portion of the light cone that is the brightest, while *falloff* refers to the zone where the light fades from bright to dark. To simulate a typical room light, the values for both should be large—large enough to brighten just about the entire room the light is in. Figure 6.18 shows the lights in place. Each light is connected to a target that determines the direction in which the light shines. For this example, the target is the floor directly underneath the light. The Top view at the upper left shows the lights in Plan view, while the User view at the bottom right shows the lights (and their targets) in 3D perspective view.

---

[13]Perhaps you could try some Blue Marble for the bathroom fixtures, or a nice Almond for the appliances in the kitchen. If you don't find the color, texture, or material you want, you can probably create it using the various tools in the Material Editor.

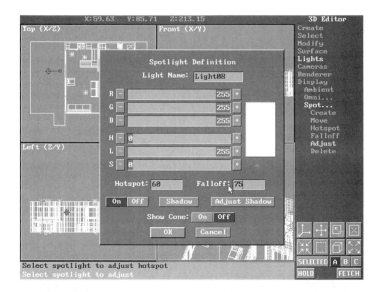

Figure 6.17
Setting the attributes
for a spotlight.

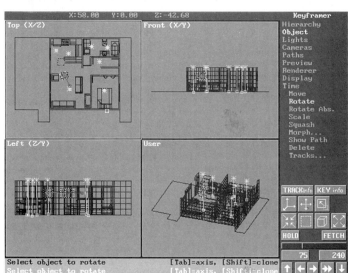

Figure 6.18
Adding lights to a
virtual space.

We have the set, we have the lights—the next step is a camera.

Flying the Camera

Before you can fly the camera, you need to create one with the Camera/Create menu choice. As with lights, you place both the camera and the target at which it is aimed.[14] Figure 6.19 shows a camera and a target. I set the camera for the beginning of the fly-through, on the patio outside the doors. It is at approximately eye height. The target is only a short distance away. This was a deliberate choice—it wouldn't work very well to have the target very far away, since the camera will be moving about in a relatively cramped space. You can, however, set the target arbitrarily far from the camera. For example, you could move the camera a large distance away and use a zoom-lens setting to bring the subject closer in the Camera view.

Once the camera has been created, you have all the ingredients needed for the fly-through. Move now to the Keyframer by pressing the F4 key. In the Keyframer, you can create animation frames for the fly-through.

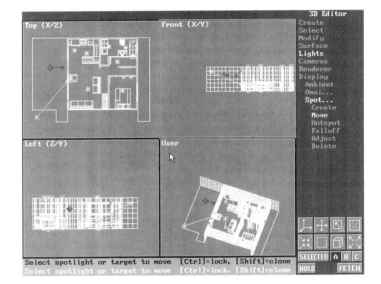

Figure 6.19
Adding a camera and target to the virtual space.

---

[14]3D Studio has some interesting support for camera features. One of my favorite features is the capability to set the focal length of the lens, using the same values you would use for a standard 35mm lens. For example, for interior shooting, you would typically use a wide-angle lens. For this example, I used a 28mm lens. A wider lens would show more of the room, but it also would add distortion—just like a real lens.

Strictly speaking, 3D Studio does not allow you to fly cameras as part of an animation. Nor can you move or fly a camera target. The trick is to create a dummy object using the Hierarchy menu. A *dummy object* has many of the characteristics of a real object—you can move it, scale it, rotate it, and so on—but it is invisible when the scene or animation is rendered. Figure 6.20 shows the Keyframer screen, and a dummy object has been created. It is marked by a dotted outline to make it stand out from normal objects.[15]

Once you have created the dummy object, link the camera and the target to it using the Hierarchy/Link menu option. Do this once for the camera and once for the target. After you create the links, be careful to move only the dummy object—not the camera or target individually.

It is very easy to create the path the camera will follow for the fly-through. There are at least two useful ways to do it, and I will explain both of them. The first method involves setting specific camera positions at regular frame intervals. In this example, I set a new camera position every 15 frames. The second method involves setting the initial camera position in frame 1 and the final camera position in the last frame, and then creating camera positions along the default path and moving them into position. The second technique requires a deeper knowledge of how 3D Studio works, but it can be very useful as a first draft for a path.

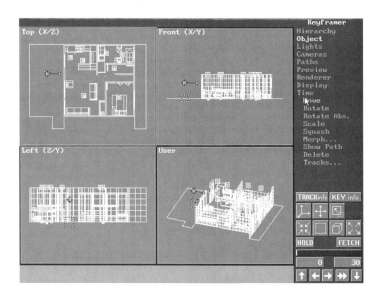

Figure 6.20
Adding a dummy object to the scene.

---

[15]It is obvious that the dummy object was created in the Top view. That is the only view where the dummy object and the camera line up. This is a hazard of using a 2D interface to create 3D objects: you can only work in one plane at a time. If you look at the Front or Left view, you can see that the dummy object was created at the default zero level in the 3D space. It's a simple matter to move the object in, say, the Front view to put it in the same position as the camera. In fact, since it is invisible, you can put it right over the camera with no ill effects.

You can use the Time menu or the buttons at the bottom right of the Keyframer screen to move to specific frame numbers. You can also set the total number of frames to be used for the animation. A typical animation uses 15 frames per second. To make the fly-through move at a natural speed, you need to calculate the distance of the total flight and decide how long it should take. In this example, it should take about eight seconds to move from the patio to the bathroom, which will require 240 frames. The final version of this fly-through, which you can find on the CD-ROMs, is somewhat longer and uses 360 frames.

At each camera position (every 15 frames, in this example), there are two camera settings to adjust: position and rotation. For example, after the camera "walks" in through the patio door, it must turn left. If you do not rotate the camera to follow the change in direction, it will give the appearance of facing sideways. Sometimes this will be the effect you want, but it is often awkward for the viewer.

To change the camera position, use the Object/Move menu option. Then click on the dummy object and move it to the new location. Fifteen frames is just one second, so you shouldn't move it too far. In fact, sometimes you may want to leave the position of the dummy object unchanged and simply change the rotation. This mimics a person turning in place. As a general rule, if you move fast, don't use rotation. If you use a fast rotation, don't use much other movement.

To change the camera rotation, use the Object/Rotate menu option. You then can click on the dummy object to rotate it. There are three axes of rotation available; press the Tab key to change from one to the next. Use the Top view for best results and control. Most rotation will be from side to side, either to match changes in the camera path, or to look at interesting objects in the virtual space. You can simulate looking up and down by applying rotations in the Left or Front view, depending on which direction the camera is facing at the time.

Figure 6.21 shows a set of views in the Keyframer that have been set up for working with a camera path. The view at the upper left shows the patio, and the camera is inside the dummy object at the upper left. The Front view shows the entire home, with the camera located just to the left of the house. The lower left view is a Plan view that shows the entire camera path,[16] starting at the top left center of the view and moving toward the bottom of the view. The view at the bottom right is a view through the camera lens from the current camera position on the patio.[17]

---

[16]To see the camera path, you must use the Paths or Camera menu and click on Show Path. Normally, an object's path is hidden.

[17]This view is of frame 4, so the camera hasn't really begun to move yet. It is still very close to its starting position.

You can use the Paths/Move Key menu option to adjust the camera position at key frames. 3D Studio will automatically alter the intervening points between the key frames.[18] To see a very rough approximation of your animation, make the Camera view the active view by clicking in it, and then click on the double-arrow icon at the bottom right to play the animation. For a complex scene, playback may be delayed in order to draw all the objects in the scene. If this is the case, playback speed may vary, depending on how many objects are in the scene at any given frame.

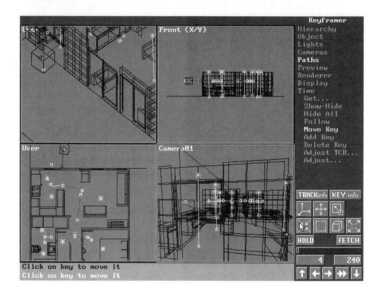

Figure 6.21
The Keyframer set up for working with a camera path. Note the existence of a path in the lower left view, marked User.

To see a rough but real-time preview, click the Preview/Make menu option. This will take some time to create, but not nearly as long as it takes to render the scene.

You also can have a little fun with a fly-through. Before you render the animation, find places in the scene where you can personalize the virtual space. For example, you might want to hang a painting or display a vase full of flowers. Adding details to just a few objects can transform a dull, dreary scene into one that is interesting.

For example, I couldn't resist adding a painting to this particular fly-through. Despite the presence of furniture and appliances, the walls were inescapably bare. Figure 6.22 shows how it is done.

The view at the bottom right shows the painting selected; these are the darkest lines in the viewport. The object that will be the painting itself is the only object selected, but there is also a frame around it. You can see one corner of the frame in the Top

---

[18]A *key frame* is any frame in which you have established a position for the object. In this example, that would be 15, 30, 45, and so on.

viewport. Note that the painting is recessed inside the frame to help yield a 3D appearance. In addition to this painting, I added a wall mirror to the bathroom.

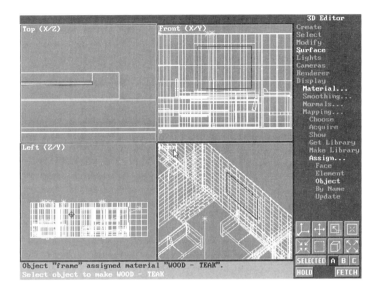

Figure 6.22
Adding a painting to a scene.

But these are just objects, created in the 3D Editor and modified slightly until they are just the right size.[19] The Material Editor is where the magic takes place. Figure 6.23 shows a Material Editor screen.[20] The currently selected material is called "Painting of Me." This is the material that gets applied to the thin rectangle inside the frame (see Fig. 6.22). It has the following characteristics:

- The shininess factor is set to 82 out of 100. This ensures that the painting will reflect the scene around it, just as you would expect of a real painting behind glass. You also could create a glass object, but this is easier.

- For safety's sake, I made this a two-sided material. That means that no matter which way the face normals point, you will see the painting. This is a cheap but common trick.

- Two of the four buttons at the bottom of the image are highlighted: Texture Map and Reflection Map. The Texture Map is set to a file, RON.TGA, which is an image of me taken from a video file that accompanied an earlier book. The Texture Map slider is set to 100, which means that only the image file will be

---

[19]All these added objects started out with the Create/Box command. I did a little nipping and tucking with the Create/Object/Boolean command to make everything fit properly.

[20]Please excuse the appearance of the scroll bars near the center of the image, and of the samples at the top of the image. They don't actually look like that. In order to capture the screen, I had to use a 16-color VGA graphics mode. Normally, you would use the Material Editor in a 256-color mode.

used to cover the surface of the object. If the slider were set to a lower number, the colors set above for Ambient, Diffuse, and Specular would show through to some degree.

■ The Reflection Map is set to Automatic. This tells 3D Studio to handle reflections of the surrounding space automatically. The Reflection Map slider is set to 25, which means that only a partial reflection will occur—this is intended to imitate the behavior of real glass, which only reflects a similar small percentage of the light that strikes it.

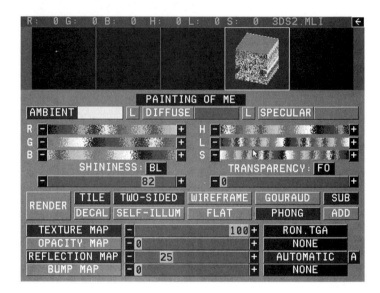

Figure 6.23
Creating a material with texture and reflection maps.

To save this material in the Material library, use the Materials menu at the top of the screen. Choose Put Material from the drop-down menu. You must re-put a material if you change it in any way after creating it.

If you create a reflection map for a flat object, there are special rules to follow when you assign the material to an object. The most important rule is to make sure that you attach the material with a reflection map only to the actual faces that will do the reflecting. If you apply it to the whole object, 3D Studio will decide which face to apply reflections to, and it may not be the one you want!

Figure 6.24 shows the dialog box that appears if you click the Automatic button. For most reflection maps, you can use an Anti-Aliasing setting of Low—objects in a reflection map are usually small, and don't require much anti-aliasing. However, for objects that are flat, you must click Yes for Flat Mirror, or you will not get acceptable results. 3D Studio uses a different reflection algorithm for flat objects.

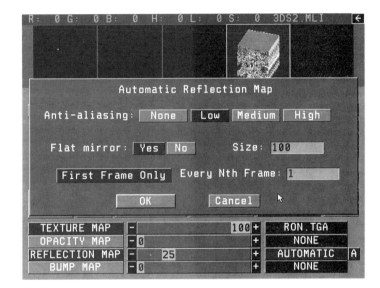

Figure 6.24
*Automatic Reflec-
tion Map settings for
a material used with
flat objects.*

If the object with the reflection map will be stationary, then click the First Frame Only button to activate it. This instructs 3D Studio to create the maps used for reflections only once, which avoids a lot of unnecessary rendering time.

For the mirror in the bathroom, I modified an existing 3D Studio material called Chrome Sky. The settings are similar to that for the painting, but there is no texture map, and the reflection map is set to 100 percent. This material is also two-sided,[21] and the settings for Automatic Reflection Map are the same as shown in Figure 6.24.

The fly-through animation file is on the CD-ROMs with the files for this chapter. Figures 6.25 through 6.28 show various scenes from the animation.

---

[21]More out of laziness than necessity.

Figure 6.25
Frame 5 from the
360-frame anima-
tion of the house fly-
through.

Figure 6.26
Frame 83 from the
360-frame anima-
tion of the house fly-
through.

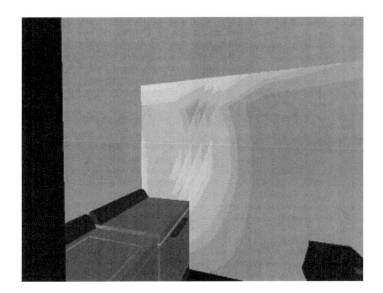

Figure 6.27
Frame 283 from the
360-frame anima-
tion of the house fly-
through.

Figure 6.28
Frame 360 from the
360-frame anima-
tion of the house fly-
through

Fly-Through via Helicopter

The last section was more of a walk-through than a fly-through, but this section will
more than make up for that with an exciting helicopter fly-through of Crater Lake,
Oregon. It will take the combined resources of both Vistapro and 3D Studio, but it's
worth it.

RECIPE

1 copy Vistapro 3.0
1 fly-through animation
1 copy 3D Studio
1 or more objects to animate
1 large dose patience[22]

Instructions: This is a complex, gourmet-level recipe, and all the instructions won't fit here on the card. See the accompanying text for details of preparation. This recipe is a real crowd pleaser, and is excellent for large parties such as demonstrations and presentations.

Chapter 1 covered the details of creating an animation with Vistapro, and you'll build on that in this section. The basic steps in the complete process follow:

- Create the fly-through animation using Vistapro and Flight Director.
- Analyze the data in Flight Director to determine the lighting angles on the helicopter at various points in the animation.
- Record the relative positions of the sun and the helicopter in a table for reference in 3D Studio.
- Create a helicopter as an object in 3D Studio, as well as a screen and a camera. Position the helicopter between the camera and the box.
- Create a material that uses the fly-through animation as a texture map.[23]
- Apply the material to a box the same relative size as the animation (320×240 and 320×200 are the two most common sizes).
- Create a light and position it according to the table you created from studying Flight Director for frame 1.
- Animate the helicopter to create realistic lighting and motion.
- Render!

---

[22]This is a frequently needed ingredient in VR recipes—keep plenty on hand in the cupboard.

[23]Yes, you can use an animation as a texture map. You can save the animation as a FLC file, or you can use a series of bitmaps by providing a list of the bitmaps in a text file.

Admittedly, this is a long list of tasks, but the results are well worth it. The entire process isn't as tedious as it sounds; some of these steps are easy. Others, of course, will tax your patience heavily.

Analyze the Data

Figure 6.29 shows the map portion of the Flight Director screen after the path has already been created. Since the goal is to track the relationship between the helicopter and the sun, I have taken the liberty of putting icons into the map image to indicate their relative positions at the start of the animation. The sun is located to the east (north is at the top of the map), and stays there throughout the animation.

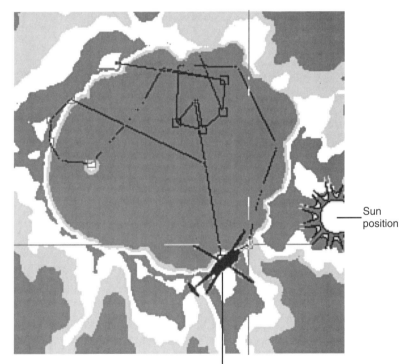

Sun
position

Helicopter at frame 0

Figure 6.29
A path in Flight Director.

The helicopter, however, twists and turns as it follows its path. If you don't add a light that moves, the helicopter won't look very realistic. The lighting on the scene will be coming from one direction, and the lighting on the helicopter will be coming from a different direction. This is subtle, but it is an important consideration if realism is your goal.

It would be more precise to consider the sun angle for each and every frame, but that's not realistic—there are 615 frames in the animation! Instead, you only need to identify key points along the path where the sun angle on the helicopter changes. Figure 6.30 shows the key points along the path, with the frame numbers for those points.[24]

There's a second level of analysis that you may also want to perform: banking. The Flight Director will bank the virtual aircraft during turns. This causes an apparent tilt of the landscape. If you want the last touch of realism, you can record the bank angles for various frames and then use that list to adjust the bank angle of the helicopter in 3D Studio.

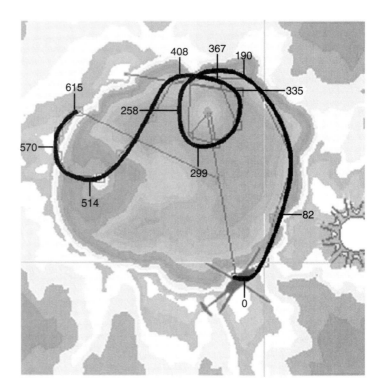

Figure 6.30
Key frames along the path of the helicopter flight.

Record Relative Positions

The easiest way to record the sun angle is to create a chart. Figure 6.31 shows the kind of chart I use, although when I do it at my desk, the pretty helicopter and sun pictures are replaced with an arrow and a small circle, drawn by hand. In Figure 6.32,

---

[24]Finding the frame numbers is easy. As you move along the path in Flight Director, it displays the frame number on the screen.

the far left column is a frame number. In the middle column, the sun is held constant on the east side of the box, and the position of the helicopter at each frame changes.[25] These positions are easy to determine—the process doesn't require much thinking. With so many variables to keep track of, a minimum of thinking is a good thing.

The next step is to normalize[26] for the helicopter; the reason for this will be evident in a moment. To normalize, use your imagination to rotate the helicopter and the sun together until the helicopter is facing straight up. This keeps the angle between the helicopter and the sun constant, resulting in a nice, neat, normalized column of figures (the right column).

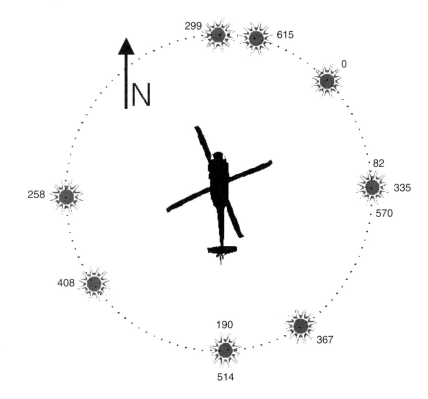

Figure 6.31
Determining and normalizing the angle between the sun and the helicopter.

You're almost done now. The final step is to combine all the images from the right column into a single image, as shown in Figure 6.32. I added the frame numbers to the diagram to make it easier to work with the illustration in 3D Studio. If you want

---

[25]The position of the helicopter is assumed to be tangent to the direction of motion for this example. If you set targets for nodes, this will change the situation. The direction the helicopter is facing, toward the target, is used as the position instead of the tangent.

[26]*Normalizing* is a common mathematical operation. Normally, it means keeping one variable constant and adjusting all the other variables appropriately.

to look ahead, Figure 6.36 shows how this drawing corresponds to the location of the light in various frames.

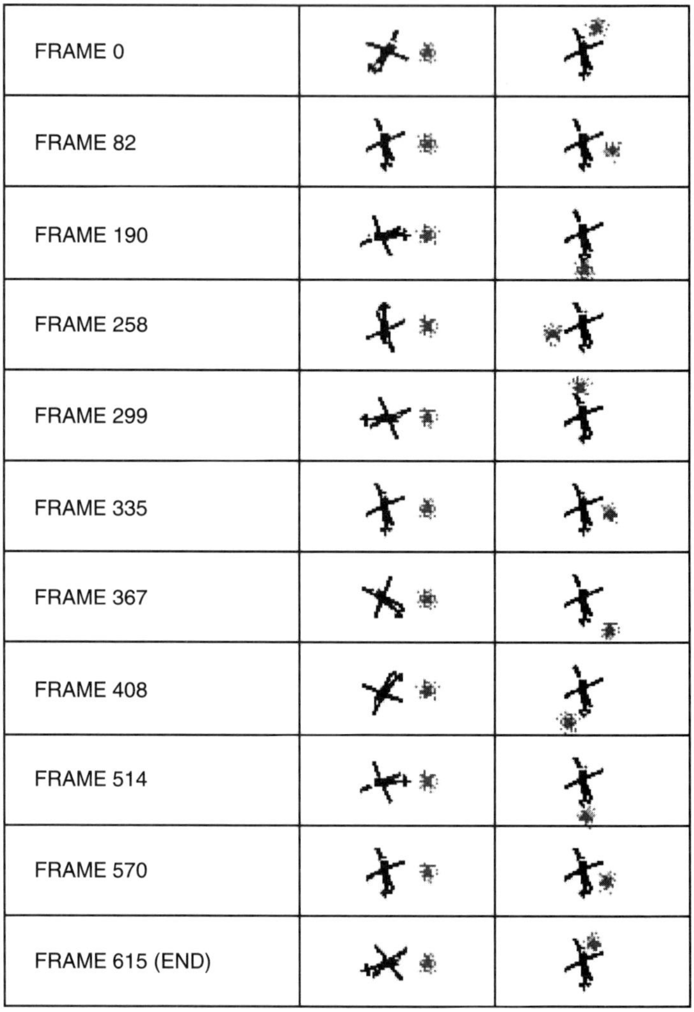

FRAME 0		
FRAME 82		
FRAME 190		
FRAME 258		
FRAME 299		
FRAME 335		
FRAME 367		
FRAME 408		
FRAME 514		
FRAME 570		
FRAME 615 (END)		

Figure 6.32
An illustration to keep at hand while working in 3D Studio.

If you want to also add bank angles for that extra touch of realism, you'll need to step through the frames in Flight Director and record the frames in which the bank angle changes. Table 6.1 shows the variation of the bank angle for the first 100 frames of the animation.

Table 6.1. Bank-Angle Changes in an Animation.

Frame	Bank Angle
0	–8
2	–7
4	–6
7	–5
12	–4
14	–3
16	–2
19	–1
21	0
28	1
31	2
48	1
53	0
62	–1
65	–2
70	–3
72	–4
92	–3
96	–2

Use the slider at the bottom right of the Flight Director screen to step through the frames and examine the bank angle. The bank angle is displayed at the right center of the screen.

Create a Helicopter and Other Objects

There are two ways to create a helicopter in 3D Studio: from scratch, or out of the box. Fortunately, 3D Studio includes a sample file with a helicopter already in it, which you can use for this demonstration. Figure 6.33 shows the helicopter loaded into the 3D Editor. The "screen" that will be used for the animation also is evident, particularly in the Top and Left views—it's right there in front of the helicopter. It's a simple box, but a very thin one. The animation image size is 320×200, so you should use the same proportion for the screen. Create it in the Front viewport to make life easy.

The helicopter is made of three separate objects:[27] the main rotor, the tail rotor, and the helicopter body. There are two levels of animation involved. The rotors, naturally, must rotate in relation to the body. The body then must move up and down, and bank left and right to make realistic movements as determined by the analysis of the animation path.

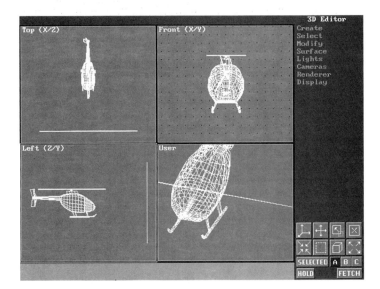

Figure 6.33
A helicopter and a screen in 3D Studio's 3D Editor.

The rotor animation should be considered part of the process of creating the helicopter. That way, it will be there when you need it. To create the rotor animations, determine the number of frames to use for one revolution; I used a setting of 30 frames, but you might prefer a faster or slower rotor. I chose 30 frames because that seemed to provide a sense of rotor motion. After moving to frame 30, I rotated each of the rotors through 360 degrees. That would only result in one rotation. To create a repeating rotation, click the Key Info button at the bottom right of the screen and then on the rotor. This displays the Key Info dialog box (see Fig. 6.34).

Click the Repeat button to make this a repeating animation. That's all there is to it. Do the same for the rear rotor. Then use the Hierarchy/Link menu option to link each of the rotors to the helicopter body. Now you have a helicopter, complete with rotors that rotate without any further fuss.

---

[27]Each of the objects has some individual elements, but they can be ignored for the purposes of this description. For example, the main rotor and the rotor shaft were created as separate objects, but they are joined together during all phases of the animation and thus can be considered as one object.

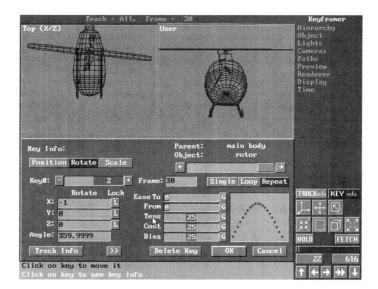

Figure 6.34
The Key Info
dialog box.

There are two more objects to create: a camera and a spotlight.[28] The camera requires only a little care to set up:

- Create the camera with the Camera/Create menu option. Place the camera directly behind the helicopter body. A longer lens setting works best; try something in the range of 85mm to 135mm. Adjust the camera position with the Dolly command until the right and left edges of the screen are just outside the Camera viewport.[29] Ignore the extra space at the top and bottom—the screen is matched to the image size, and if you also set 320×200 as the output size, the extra space will not appear in the rendered frame even though you can see it in the viewport. See Figure 6.35 to see what the Camera viewport should look like at frame zero.

- Figure 6.35 also shows the correct position of the spotlight for the beginning of the animation. In the Top view, it is located at the right of the helicopter and slightly forward. In the Front view, you can see that the light is also located slightly above the helicopter. This angle, too, is derived from the sun position in the original file.

Just for fun, I have tilted the helicopter aggressively forward. This is not necessary, but it gives the opening frame a sense of action and urgency. As a final touch, also link the spotlight target to the helicopter body. This will ensure that the helicopter is always illuminated.

---

[28]It doesn't have to be a spotlight, but a spotlight creates shadows that add interest to the scene.
[29]You did remember to press Ctrl+V to bring up the Viewport dialog box and make one of the views a Camera view, right?

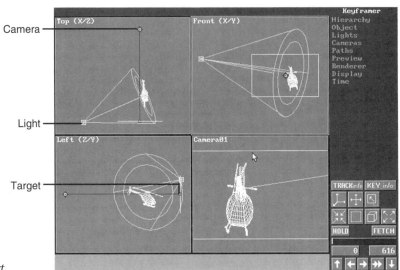

Camera

Light

Target

Figure 6.35
Setting up the
Camera viewport.

Animation as a Texture Map

You can use an animation as a texture map using the same procedures as described earlier for bitmaps. Use the Material Editor to create a new material, and select the FLC file created with the PCX2FLC utility (it comes with Vistapro) as the texture map. Set the Texture Map slider to 100 percent. During rendering, each frame of the animation will use the corresponding frame from the fly-through animation in the FLC file. It's all automatic.

All you need to do is use the Material/Object/Assign menu option to apply the material to the screen. If you want to avoid checking face normals, make the material two-sided.

Lighting

The light is the key to a realistic final result. With all of the analysis already performed, it's easy to animate the light correctly. With a worksheet similar to Figure 6.32 at hand, you can easily animate the light correctly. Look at Figure 6.36—it shows the desired result. If you look closely, you'll see that the key points along the light's path correspond to the points in Figure 6.32. To arrive at this happy conclusion, move to each frame listed in Figure 6.32 and move the light to a point corresponding to the orientation shown in the right column of Figure 6.32. When this is complete, display the path for the light. It should look like Figure 6.36. You may need to add key points, or move a few around, to get the best results.

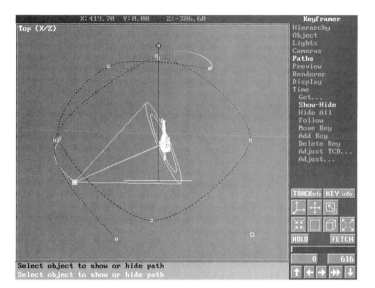

Figure 6.36
The fully animated spotlight.

Animate Helicopter

There are two kinds of movement that you can apply to the helicopter. One is simple bobs and weaves based on the animation. The other is bank adjustments to adjust for turns. If you plan to add the bank adjustments, you should make them first. These are simple adjustments—move to the frames where the bank angle changes, and adjust the bank angle one degree plus or minus as needed. Once this is done, you can add all the bobs and weaves you want.

To change the bank angle, work in the Front viewport. Use the Rotate command to make the changes; press Tab to change the axis of rotation to the correct one. For bobbing and weaving, you can tilt forward and backward, or move the helicopter around. Figure 6.37 shows the path for the helicopter. The path doesn't show the numerous rotational changes—only the bobbing and weaving.

If you only make position changes in the Front view, you will keep the helicopter in the correct relationship to the screen—no closer, and no farther.

NOTE

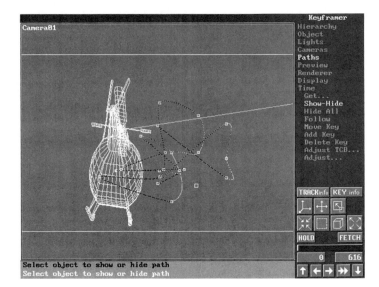

Figure 6.37
The path for the helicopter body.

Render

Figure 6.38 shows four views of the helicopter at frame 503, near the end of the animation. Figure 6.39 shows a rendering (at 640×480, instead of the smaller 320×200 used for the animation) of the image for this frame. You also can render the animation at 160×100 if you want to have a much shorter rendering time and can settle for a lower resolution.

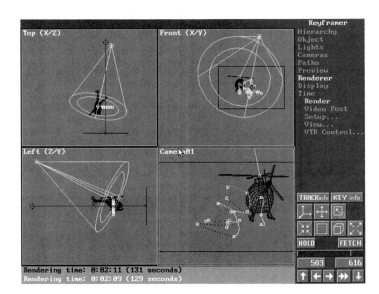

Figure 6.38
Frame 503 in the Keyframer.

Figure 6.39
A rendering of frame 503.

Gallery

Figures 6.40 through 6.50 show the key frames identified for the lighting changes. Even if you don't play the animation from the CDs, you can see from these figures how the lighting angle, banking angle, and position changes are used to provide a realistic-looking helicopter addition to the fly-through.

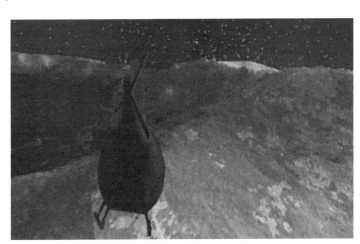

Figure 6.40
Frame 0 of the animation. The light is coming from forward and to the right of the helicopter.

Figure 6.41
Frame 82 of the
animation. This
figure shows a bank
of −4 degrees.

Figure 6.42
Frame 190 of the
animation. This
figure shows a bank
of −5 degrees, and
the helicopter has
been moved to a low
position in the
frame. The lighting
is now coming from
behind the camera.

Figure 6.43
Frame 258 of the
animation. The light
is now on the
opposite side of the
helicopter from
where it started.

Figure 6.44
Frame 299 of the animation. In this frame, the light is directly ahead of and slightly above the helicopter.

Figure 6.45
Frame 335 of the animation. The helicopter has come full circle: 360 degrees. The lighting is now back at the right side of the helicopter. The bank angle is zero.

Figure 6.46
Frame 367 of the animation. The light is nearly behind the camera again.

Figure 6.47
Frame 408 of the animation. A minor shift from the previous figure: the light is now behind and to the left. The bank angle is −6. This frame is a good example of how a correct bank angle adds to the realism of animation.

Figure 6.48
Frame 514 of the animation. I added some spice at this point in the animation—the camera has begun to zoom in on the helicopter. The light is nearly exactly behind the camera.

Figure 6.49
Frame 570 of the animation. The zoom is complete. I moved the helicopter to the lower right corner of the frame more to keep it out of the way during the zoom than for any other reason.

Figure 6.50
Frame 615 of the
animation. To
conclude the
animation, the
helicopter jumps
quickly to the center
top of the frame,
and looks over the
entire lake after
coming over the crest
of the ridge. This
was an attempt to
add a touch of
breathlessness to the
animation—a
feeling of swooping
into the overview.

7

HARDWARE FOR VIRTUAL WORLDS

The Hardware Universe

Playing with virtual reality on your computer falls into two very distinct categories: Doing it with special VR hardware and doing it without. When it comes to VR hardware, there's some very good news: the times are changing. The advance guard of cool hardware is here at last. Just a year ago, this wasn't true—we were still waiting for the goodies. Here's what I said a year ago about the state of the field in VR hardware:[1]

> *Most VR hardware is expensive, and if I weren't writing this book, there's absolutely no way we would have been able to afford many of the devices you are going to read about in this chapter. So far, the main explanation we have offered for the current state of VR has been that CPU power hasn't caught up to the requirements of serious VR. In this chapter, we encounter another big reason: the cost of hardware for serious VR.*

Both of these reasons no longer apply. CPU power has advanced dramatically with the Pentium chip, and the P6 moves us a quantum leap forward in 1996. Costs for headsets in particular are coming down—not as fast as the cost of the CPUs, but the downward trend is unmistakable. You now can buy good VR hardware for the cost of a basic stereo system. You can buy *really* good VR hardware for less than $2,000.

There are also many alternatives from many different companies. Most of those companies are new, and are banking on success in the consumer marketplace. However, there are companies that have been around for years, such as 3DTV. This one company is doing (and has done) more to put affordable VR hardware and software in the hands of consumers than any other I have encountered. They are pioneers in the field of "garage virtual reality" and are worth a close look before you make any buying decisions.[2] Many (but not all) of 3DTV's products are low cost. They are often cleverly designed, work well, and usually avoid any frills or fancy packaging.

You can find detailed information about 3DTV products in Chapter 12, "The Virtual Workshop," where you can find out what is possible with affordable (mostly) VR hardware. There are, as you would expect, some compromises that you must make in the name of affordability. In this chapter, we'll be looking at a wide range of VR hardware products, from consumer level to the kind you might think twice about before

---

[1]That was in the second edition of the book. When I wrote the first edition, affordable, consumer VR hardware was as rare as jabberwocks and bandersnoots.

[2]The name alone (3DTV) should clue you in to the fact that they are pioneers. Back when this company got started, TV (video) was really the only way to do 3D, and VR was still a dream for the future. You'll still find TV-oriented products in their catalog, including 3D videos, adapters to use LCD glasses with your TV and VCR, and cameras for recording 3D video.

buying just for fun. The focus here is on what's hot and new. For additional information on most of these products, including prices and how to contact the manufacturer, see the VR Hardware Buyer's Guide on the CD-ROMs that come with this book.

Hardware for VR

Before we get to the details, let's look at an overview of the types of hardware that are available in various price ranges. Here's how things shake out in the VR universe; these are prices for hardware only:

When You Spend $100, You Get

An inexpensive pair of LCD glasses (see Fig. 7.1). This gives you basic 3D, but probably with significant flickering. Images will likely be low-resolution and are available only on a computer screen.

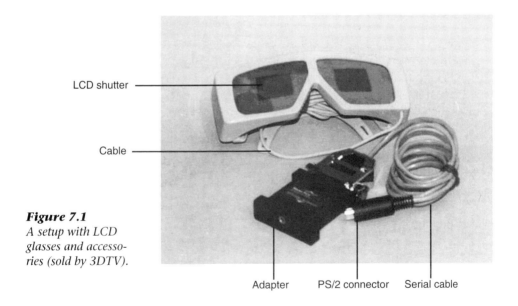

Figure 7.1
A setup with LCD glasses and accessories (sold by 3DTV).

When You Spend $500, You Get

The same setup as for $100, but with a little black box to double the refresh rate and greatly reduce flickering. Images are still low-resolution and appear only on your computer screen.

When You Spend $1,000, You Get

Better quality LCD glasses, such as CrystalEyes (see Fig. 7.2). Images are medium resolution, and flicker is greatly minimized. You'll also need a monitor that can handle 120Hz vertical refresh, such as a Nanao F550i.

or

Low-resolution, game-oriented HMD, with or without motion tracking. Examples include the CyberMaxx from VictorMaxx and the VFX1 from Forte.

Figure 7.2
No, CrystalEyes won't make VR look quite this good.

When You Spend $2,000, You Get

A real head-mounted device (CyberEye, from General Reality; see Fig. 7.3), also called an HMD. The 3D image will appear to float in the air around you, with medium resolution. Head tracking will be present, but at low resolution.

Figure 7.3
The General Reality CyberEye headset.

When You Spend $5,000, You Get

Essentially the same thing you get for $2,000. That's what is so nice about the HMD from General Reality: it performs like much more expensive HMDs. One thing you can add at this price point: a sturdier HMD, able to take more abuse, and perhaps with more adjustments to fine-tune fit and visuals. You also might be able to get a slightly wider field of view. Head tracking will almost certainly be present, but resolution and response might not be as rapid as you would like.

When You Spend $10,000, You Get

Same HMD, but with a slightly higher resolution. Also, now the system can keep track of your head position at high resolution and with quick response, altering the point of view to correspond to your movement.

When You Spend $50,000, You Get

True high-resolution HMDs live in this territory, with wraparound viewing instead of just a narrow band right in front of you. Head tracking is very sophisticated.

When You Spend $100,000, You Get

At this price, you get it all—HMD, head tracking, and perhaps even a data glove and some pneumatic legs to make your artificial world jump and twirl.

or

An arcade game with full-body motion detection and sophisticated graphics (see Fig. 7.4).

Figure 7.4
*A full-blown arcade
VR system.*

There are even less expensive ways of getting to more or less real 3D. Some games, for example, use red/blue glasses to create a 3D effect (see Fig. 7.5[3]). The image you view

---

[3]This is black and white; you'll have to use your imagination!

has two superimposed images—one in red and one in blue. The colored lenses make sure the correct image goes to the correct eye. It works, but everything is purple; Figure 7.6. is my black-and-white attempt to show you how awful it looks. A non-stereo image is shown in Figure 7.7 for your reference. Affordable, yes, but of limited use—for reasons that should be obvious! Nonetheless, for games, such simple technology does have a place.

Figure 7.5
Red/blue glasses for crude 3D viewing.

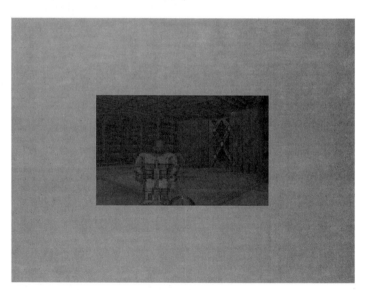

Figure 7.6
A red/blue stereo image.

Figure 7.7
A non-stereo image similar to Figure 7.6.

The Party Line

I have a bone to pick with traditional VR, and this is the perfect place to discuss the issues. The traditional definition of virtual reality goes something like this:

> **Virtual Reality provides an interactive environment that simulates a real environment.**

However, this little definition usually carries a lot of baggage with it that isn't spelled out. If you and I were to walk down the hallowed halls of just about any institution doing VR research, we'd find the following assumptions tagging along in any discussion of VR:

- Helmet devices are required for VR
- Body suits are desirable for VR
- Head tracking is required for VR
- Alternate input devices should be as natural as possible

I hate to spoil the party, but this is a pile of virtual hogwash. Such narrow definitions of VR might work in the narrow hallways of research, but out here in the real world where you and I want to use VR and VR-related stuff in meaningful ways, different rules and assumptions have to apply. This is never more true than when it comes to hardware. Here's Ron's Rule about VR hardware:

Ron's Rule: If it costs too much, it's irrelevant (for now).

In other words, go ahead—spend your big bucks on military and research VR hardware. But don't make me wait until that $100,000 headset comes down to $199 to have some fun! I want something now.

What Really Matters

What really matters is what you and I can do. Pure VR makes no more sense than pure multimedia or a pure sports car. There will always be purists, of course, and may they always have the money they need for the pursuit of purity. I'm talking here about the rest of us. What matters is being able to use this stuff, either for fun or in meaningful but affordable ways.

I know I've just made a few enemies but, darn it, VR isn't just some high and mighty technology. Pure VR is just a small part of the entire technology related to VR, and the ways that you and I will use VR probably won't be foreseen by the purists. We will be striking out in new directions, finding new uses, and integrating the technology into our lives. So we're the ones who should have the control, right?

Now that we have that little business squared away, let's consider the possibilities.

Where Is the Hardware Going?

At the high end, the hardware is going where the money is pointing, as is the case with all "high technology." If the military has the money to pay for fancy head-mounted systems, then the hardware is going toward goals that the military sets. However you might feel about the military and its goals, what this means for VR in general is that there is a force driving the leading edge of development ahead. Medicine is another driving force behind VR. It's a lot safer for a surgeon to learn to use a virtual scalpel first! Any given technology might have just one or two examples in development, with a price tag in the millions, maybe even the mega millions.

The direction of high-end hardware is not always evident; military implies security and secrecy. However, much of the research is being done at colleges and universities, and enough is out in the open to suggest some amazing possibilities. There is research into the use of low-power lasers to "write" a VR environment right onto your eyes from a small, lightweight face unit, for example. Currently, researchers would be happy to get a monochrome heads-up display working, but the possibilities are striking for VR.

At the middle level, VR (much of it fairly traditional) is feeding off the needs of industry. There are chemists using headsets to visualize molecular structure, for example. There's also an entertainment angle—headsets and VR arcades for trade shows, for example. While the high end might see just a handful of prototypes, the middle level is about numbers—hundreds or thousands of units make for a successful technology at the middle level. To buy your VR toys, you need relatively serious money—from $5,000 to $100,000.

The middle level is where you will find primitive body suits, data gloves, stereo HMDs, and all the other stuff that was fantasy just a few years ago.

At the lower level—mostly under $1,000, to be considered affordable—there are actually only a few VR devices that will make you say, "Wow!" Most of the affordable technology is still making very serious compromises.[4] Of course, most of this stuff didn't even exist at these prices last year, so we are making progress. But you shouldn't expect a really fantastic VR experience with affordable hardware. Interesting, yes; stimulating, yes; but true VR, no.

What you *will* find in the affordable range are VR alternatives to the mouse; basic head tracking; and simple 3D, head-mounted hardware (headsets and HMDs).

---

[4]Translation: If you find a headset under $1,000, you won't find yourself using it for anything but game playing.

How Much Does Hardware Matter?

I'm of two opinions on this. On the one hand, as part of writing this book, I've had the chance to play with some of the high-end hardware. On the other hand, there's a lot you can do without any special hardware at all.

I wasn't able to review every piece of VR hardware out there. My rules for hardware were simple: We had to try it out on our own PCs if we were going to recommend it to you. Special-purpose VR hardware is great for its intended audience, but we wanted to stick to stuff that you or I could connect to a PC and use.

If you are on a budget and want to play with VR, there are some very good software-only products that will give you both enjoyment and a learning experience. Such products won't meet the purists' definition of VR: immersion in an environment plus interactivity. But, if you are like me, you will be fascinated by what you find and by what you can do.

If you have the money to explore hardware, there are some good options. VR hardware is quite sophisticated and, for most of us, that means that building your own is out of the question. You need to know a fair amount about computers and electronics to pull off creating your own VR hardware—it's not for the average garage mechanic. What this means is that if you just want toys, you can get them relatively cheaply—certainly for less than $1,000 and occasionally for less than $100. If you want stuff that works well, you will occasionally find it for less than $1,000, but usually between $1,000 and $2,000, with some stuff running up to $5,000 and more *each*. That's serious money for any hobby, so anyone without a business purpose for VR is hereby forewarned: It's going to cost you.

A good example is alternative input technology. A Logitech Cyberman, which costs less than $100, is fun but hardly something to build entire virtual worlds with. A Spaceball 2003, on the other hand,[5] costs about $2,000 and is something you can really use and control during development.[6]

Where you fit into the hardware universe will be a combination of desire and funds—there's no way around that until two things happen:

■ The market for VR hardware gets bigger, bringing economies that follow from increased production.

---

[5]Quite literally on the other hand, actually. Normal use is to put a mouse in your right hand and a Spaceball in your left. The mouse controls the cursor, and the Spaceball controls the (virtual) world.

[6]Speaking of development, good hardware just about demands good software, such as Superscape. Let's see: $2,000 for the input device, another $5,000 or so for the software, and perhaps $2,000 for a headset—that's $9,000 and we haven't even bought the computer yet!

■ The technology advances to the point where cheaper components can be used.

Until then, I can only tell you that there is some seriously fun hardware out there, but some of it will cost you serious money. Only you can decide if the thrill is worth the cost. In a few cases, you'll be delighted to know that there are a few relatively inexpensive products that will make you happy.

Winner!

Throughout this chapter, where I have found a technology that really does the job well, I've identified it with this icon.

This icon identifies hardware that, whatever its cost, does the job so well that I'd buy it for my own use. That's a pretty strict criterion; I don't spend money for stuff unless it's awfully darn good.

Input Devices

The line between input and output devices isn't always clear, because a good VR system has to handle both seamlessly, and input and output are often tied together in feedback loops. So I will sometimes draw arbitrary lines between the two, just for the sake of keeping things neatly disorganized.

One only has to look at the wide variety of alternate mouse devices to understand that no one input device will work for everyone. In the not-too-distant future, when VR input is as common as mouse input, we'll no doubt see a bewildering array of interesting input devices. Until then, there are a few basic designs from which to choose.

Freedom and 3D

The job of a VR input device is to enable you to work fluidly in three dimensions. There are many different tasks that an input device is called on to perform, such as

■ Changing the point of view

■ Selecting or picking up objects

■ Moving objects

■ Rotating objects

■ Digitizing real-world objects

■ "Throwing" and dropping objects

■ Interacting with menus, toolbars, icons, buttons, and so on

You are probably used to thinking and talking in terms of 3D by now. The three dimensions usually are described as coordinates in space, with the axes called X, Y, and Z. X and Y are typically considered to be the two dimensions of a flat plane, while Z represents up and down movement. However, this is arbitrary—the letters can and do refer to different directions in different software packages. Figures 7.8, 7.9, and 7.10 show these three dimensions in a fanciful way.

Figure 7.8
The X dimension.

Figure 7.9
The Y dimension.

Figure 7.10
The Z dimension.

However, there are actually *six* things to consider, and they are called the *six degrees of freedom*. The first three are the familiar directions of 3D space—X, Y, and Z:

> **X**—Left/right
>
> **Y**—Forward/backward
>
> **Z**—Up/down

The second three will be familiar to anyone who has played with a flight simulator or flown a plane:

> **Roll**—Rotation about an axis along the length of the "airplane."
>
> **Pitch**—Raising or lowering the nose of the airplane.
>
> **Yaw**—Rotating about an axis that goes vertically through the airplane.

Figures 7.11, 7.12, and 7.13 show these three movements graphically.

Figure 7.11
Rolling.

Figure 7.12
Pitching.

Figure 7.13
Yawing.

An input device must do all six jobs well, and there are very few that pull it off.

Mouse and Keyboard: Dead?

One can only hope that these two instruments of VR torture will be dead soon, but they are still alive and well. From a designer's point of view, the mouse and keyboard have their place—the input requirements during the design phase are complex. At runtime, however, these arcane input devices have no place. Stumbling through 3D space with 2D input devices is a situation whose days are numbered.

However, as you learn in this chapter, that number is still pretty big—it still costs a few thousand dollars to get first-class VR-level input. There are some good toys, like the Logitech Cyberman, to see us through.

Cyberman: Budget Input

The Cyberman is one of those quiet little surprises known only to folks who have been around VR for a while—there is just about zero effort to market the Cyberman to the mainstream computer/multimedia community. Although the Cyberman supports all six degrees of freedom, it is most often used with games. It lacks the fine degree of control required for serious VR, but for games like DOOM, it can be a lot of fun.

Figure 7.14 shows the Cyberman out on our back porch—not, I assure you, where we use it. Its real home is next to the kids' computer, where it gets used occasionally for DOOM and other games. Because the Cyberman doesn't make for a very good mouse, it only gets used in those situations where it's the best choice.

Figure 7.14
*The Logitech
Cyberman.*

The primary limitation of the Cyberman is that it's hard to control. Figure 7.15 shows how you hold the Cyberman while using it. Although the wrist is supported on the base, the weight of your hand can't really rest on the Cyberman's control handle. If you do put the weight of your hand down, that's the same as moving down—and you can't control your position or direction if you do that. This means that there is always some tension in your hand.

A second problem is the looseness of the control handle. It offers little or no resistance, so it's hard to judge how far you are moving it.

These problems, however, are not fatal flaws—they just relegate the Cyberman to the toy category. But toys are fun, and the Cyberman is fun. When matched with the right software, in fact, it's a blast. Having one control for every direction of motion is a great convenience.

Figure 7.15
*The Cyberman
in use.*

The Logitech 3D Mouse

Although the Cyberman is budget technology in every sense of the word, another product from Logitech deserves a close look: the 3D mouse. This unit, shown in Figure 7.16, shows the unit itself (at the bottom right) and the sensors that detect its movement in 3D space.

Figure 7.16
*The Logitech 3D
mouse.*

The 3D mouse is simplicity itself. You move the unit in 3D space, and the sensor detects the position of the mouse and relays position data to the software.

Winner! ## Spaceball 2003

Simply put, the Spaceball 2003 is the input device of choice for VR development. You can spend more, you can spend less, but everyone who has tried it agrees that it's hard to beat the smooth, intuitive performance of the Spaceball.

The Spaceball is very futuristic-looking, as you can see in Figure 7.17. The ball itself doesn't actually move; it responds to the pressure of your fingertips in the six degrees of freedom described earlier in this chapter.

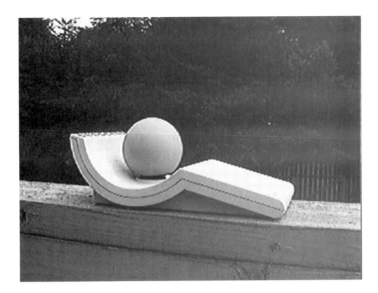

Figure 7.17
The Spaceball 2003.

Figure 7.18 shows the Spaceball sitting at our test computer; that's it at the right side of the monitor. The scene on the monitor is from the runtime of Superscape. It's a platform with bumper cars, into which falls a soccer ball that the cars then bop around.

Figure 7.18
The Spaceball ready to use.

Figures 7.19 and 7.20 show the Spaceball in use. The sloped platform provides great support for your hand and wrist, so the Spaceball is much more stable to use than the Cyberman. You do not hold the Spaceball like a joystick; light finger pressure is all that is required for input. This makes it very easy to control movement in all six directions.

The row of buttons, shown most clearly in Figure 7.20, allows applications that support the Spaceball to provide easy access to key features.

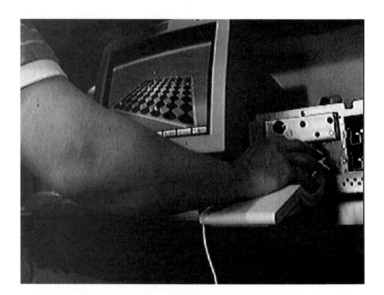

Figure 7.19
The Spaceball provides full support for your hand.

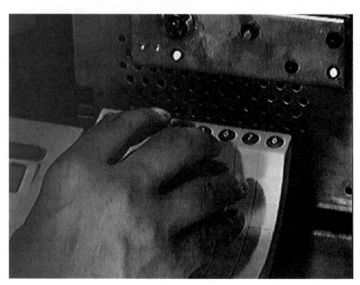

Figure 7.20
This close-up shows the function buttons on the Spaceball.

The normal way to use the Spaceball is to have both it and the mouse connected to your computer, with the keyboard between them. The manual suggests that you use your customary hand for the mouse, and the other hand for the Spaceball. However, I did just the opposite and liked it.

Using the Spaceball is a lot like being able to reach into the screen and move the objects there directly, but that's not an exact analogy. As I became more familiar with using the ball, I had a sense of having a vehicle within the virtual space that I could control somewhat like you probably control a helicopter. Since you can use the Spaceball to move simultaneously in several different directions—rotation and tilt while dropping and moving forward—it's really just not like anything else you've ever tried on a computer.

To start with, however, you might want to stick to one degree of freedom at a time. Multi-degree movement is a lot easier after you develop an intuitive sense of the ball. Once you do, however, movement is as smooth as you have ever experienced. Now for the bad news: the Spaceball 2003 is expensive—$1,995 worth of expensive. If games are more your style, however, there's also some good news: the Spaceball Avenger.

Spaceball Avenger

If the cost of the Spaceball concerns you, boy have I got some good news. For less than a tenth of the cost, you can purchase a game controller that uses the same basic technology as the Spaceball. It's called the Spaceball Avenger, and it's shown in Figure 7.21.

Figure 7.21
The Spaceball Avenger game controller.

There are three key things you should know about the Avenger:

- It uses a serial port instead of a game card. This is necessary to support the high data rate of the unit. The up side: smooth movement in every direction (X, Y, Z, yaw, pitch, roll), and multi-axes movement without pausing. That means you can roll left, pitch forward, and move ahead all at one time—even while firing away at the enemy in a game like Descent.

- The Spaceball unit itself, at the upper left in Figure 7.21, works exactly like that on the Spaceball 2003. However, the construction isn't as solid. It isn't flimsy, either, so this isn't a problem in normal use. The Spaceball 2003 is simply a very high-quality product by comparison. We had no trouble with the low-cost Spaceball Avenger at all during our testing. Because the Spaceball doesn't actually move (you just kind of press it in the direction you want to go), it's not subject to much stress.[7]

- The unit comes with a whole bunch of buttons for controlling games. They are called *rapid action buttons* (RABs). There are seven buttons. Since the Avenger uses the serial port, the unit is capable of using all these buttons to control many aspects of a game right from the hand unit. For many games that otherwise require heavy keyboard input (like Descent, for example), the Avenger comes as a very pleasant surprise. The RABs are preconfigured for each game, but you can change the configuration if you get a better idea. In our tests, the buttons were used very effectively—someone really took the time to figure out the best way to use these buttons for each game. Overall performance is simply outstanding.

The technical support staff at Spacetec IMC were very helpful to folks who had to make the call. Most problems were setup problems that were easily resolved.

One key point about the Avenger: If you do get one, remember that it's for use with games that support it. Newer games are not a problem, but some of your older games might not run with it. Our Avenger came with complete support for the following games:[8]

Game	*Button*	*Movements*
DOOM	Btn A: Turbo fire	Forward and back
	Btn B: Fire	Spin in place
	Btn C: Open (doors, etc.)	Left/right slide

---

[7]We didn't do any destructive testing (that is, see what happens when you really torque it) because we wanted to continue playing games.

[8]Support for additional games is planned, and Spacetec is working with various game vendors to add support.

Game	Button	Movements
	Btn D: Forward thrust	
	Btn E: Weapon up	
	Btn F: Pause activity	
DOOM II	Btn A: Turbo fire	Forward and back
	Btn B: Fire	Spin in place
	Btn C: Open (doors, etc.)	Left/right slide
	Btn D: Forward thrust	
	Btn E: Weapon up	
	Btn F: Pause activity	
Heretic	Btn A: Turbo fire	Forward and back
	Btn B: Fire	Spin in place
	Btn C: Open (doors, etc.)	Left/right slide
	Btn D: Forward thrust	
	Btn E: Head lock	
	Btn F: Pause activity	
Wolfenstein 3D	Btn A: Turbo fire	Forward and back
	Btn B: Fire	Spin in place
	Btn C: Open (doors, etc.)	Left/right slide
	Btn D: Undefined	
	Btn E: Single axis	
	Btn F: Pause activity	
Blake Stone	Btn A: Turbo fire	Forward and back
	Btn B: Fire	Spin in place
	Btn C: Open (doors, etc.)	Left/right slide
	Btn D: Weapon up	
	Btn E: Single axis	
	Btn F: Pause activity	
Corridor 7	Btn A: Turbo fire	Forward and back
	Btn B: Fire	Spin in place
	Btn C: Open (doors, etc.)	
	Btn D: Undefined	
	Btn E: Single axis	
	Btn F: Pause activity	

Game	Button	Movements
X-Wing	Btn A: Track	Forward and back
	Btn B: Fire	Turn left/right
	Btn C: Mouse control	Pitch up/down
	Btn D: Weapon switch	Roll left/right
	Btn E: Change fire mode	
	Btn F: Pause activity	
Spear of Destiny	Btn A: Turbo fire	Forward and back
	Btn B: Fire	Spin in place
	Btn C: Open (doors, etc.)	Left/right slide
	Btn D: Undefined	
	Btn E: Single axis	
	Btn F: Pause activity	
Descent	Btn A: Flares	Forward and back
	Btn B: Primary weapon	Spin in place
	Btn C: Secondary weapon	Left/right slide
	Btn D: Forward thrust	Move up/down
	Btn E: Map	Look up/down
	Btn F: Pause activity	Cartwheel (roll 360)
Dark Forces	Btn A: Secondary weapon	Forward and back
	Btn B: Fire	Spin in place
	Btn C: Open (doors, etc.)	Left/right slide
	Btn D: Weapon up	Jump up/crouch down
	Btn E: Forward thrust	Look up/down
	Btn F: Auto leveling	
Rise of the Triad	Btn A: Map	Forward and back
	Btn B: Fire	Spin in place
	Btn C: Open (doors, etc.)	Left/right slide
	Btn D: Swap weapon	Jump up/crouch down
	Btn E: Aim head lock	Look up/down
	Btn F: Pause activity	

Game	Button	Movements
System Shock	Btn A: Left mouse	Forward and back
	Btn B: Right mouse	Spin in place
	Btn C: Grab/open + dbl clk	Left/right slide
	Btn D: Cursor control down	Go up/down ladders
	Btn E: Re-center cursor	Look up/down
	Btn F: Throw grenade	Lean left/right

Overall, of all the game controllers we tried (and oh, how we tried them!), the Avenger was the only one to really get us excited. We played with joysticks, some of them costing more than $100, and none of them were nearly as much fun as the Avenger.

CyberStick

Speaking of joysticks, one that we tried but weren't all that hot on is the CyberStick. This is a joystick without a base (see Fig. 7.22). It has the traditional wire, and the wire attaches to your game card, but you hold the CyberStick in the air. Instead of being tied to a joystick base, you are free to move around while you use the CyberStick.

Figure 7.22
The CyberStick.

It sounded like a wonderful idea. The unit is very light, and it's very easy to hold in the hand. Being able to move around with the unit was particularly nice when we played a game with the headsets. It's tough being tied down with a joystick when you are wearing a headset. You get the feeling of being immersed in the game when you use a headset, and it's nice to be able to move around.

However, we found that the CyberStick wasn't easy to use. The motion that results from tilting and turning the Stick wasn't even or as predictable as we felt it needed to be. In our opinion, the unit needs better quality components. Too much effort was made to keep the price low, and the unit only really works if it moves at least as smoothly and effectively as a good joystick.

However, keep your eye on this product. It's from General Reality, which has otherwise done a great job with high-quality VR products. Look for improvements during 1996, and don't count this unit out yet. For now, however, if you want a go-anywhere cyber controller for games, the Spaceball Avenger is the clear winner.

Glove Input

We use our hands for lots of things, from driving to writing and typing. It would seem only natural to use them for virtual reality using gloves with built-in sensors. It's a great idea, of course, but it has turned out to be very costly to implement. As a result, there are only a few glove-based input devices. And all but one are very expensive.

The low end of glove technology is very low priced: the Mattel Power Glove. This former toy has developed a second life as a VR input device. The Power Glove isn't high tech, of course, but it is an interesting and fun input device. It allows crude interaction with a VR environment. A number of devices and software products that support the Power Glove are offered by the 3DTV company, and you can find information in Chapter 12 on how these items work together. A number of mainstream VR products, such as VREAM, also support the Power Glove. Used Power Gloves are available at prices of $30 and up, depending on their condition.

Until this year, there wasn't much of a middle level for glove input. Unlike the Power Glove, which has a few simple sensors that detect when you bend your fingers, real glove technology requires dozens of accurate, miniature sensors. The human hand is a marvelously complex instrument, and merely keeping track of all the things it does requires a very high degree of technical sophistication.

The CyberGlove from Virtual Technologies, for example, contains up to 22 sensors. There are three flex sensors and one finger-angle sensor for each finger, plus sensors for thumb crossover, palm arch, wrist flex, and wrist angle. All of this has to be packaged into a lightweight glove that still allows you to use your hand.

The Fifth Dimension Glove

A South African Company, Fifth Dimension, has finally introduced a mid-priced glove alternative. Figure 7.23 shows the glove (known as the 5th Glove) in a rather picturesque setting. The glove senses how much each finger bends and sends the data to a computer interface card you install inside your computer. So far, there isn't much software that supports the glove, but the American distributor of the glove, General Reality (makers of a truly fine HMD, the CyberEye, also shown in Fig. 7.23[9]), has sent copies to all the major software vendors. Look for applications to begin supporting this and other mid-priced gloves by the end of 1995.

Figure 7.23
The 5th Glove in use with the arcade-hardened version of the CyberEye HMD.

The 5th Glove comes in one size, and uses hook-and-loop fasteners to allow adjustment for different sizes of hands. It comes with two extra flex sensors, which you can attach as needed for additional input, where supported by software—elbow, knee, etc. Up to four gloves and 16 flex strips can be attached to the single interface card. There is a small unit at your wrist that is light in weight (see Fig. 7.24). The standard glove is for the right hand, but you can special order left-hand gloves.

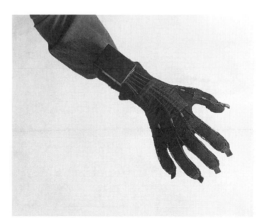

Figure 7.24
A detailed view of the 5th Glove.

---

[9]The unit shown in the figure is *arcade-hardened*. It costs more than the base unit, but it is made with stronger materials than the standard unit so that it will stand up under heavy use with an arcade game.

The performance of the glove lies somewhere between the low end of the Power Glove and the high end. Accuracy is good, but not perfect. Results will vary from one hand to the next. For now, it's really the only alternative, and if you have a project that will really benefit from the glove and are willing to write your own software for it, it can be a good choice. However, until more software supports it (and you can simply ask the vendor whose software you own, or plan to buy, if they support it), this glove, like the expensive ones, will be used primarily in niche markets.

The glove package sent to me by General Reality included a right-hand glove, an interface card for my PC, a connecting cable (lightweight, much like a typical phone cord), a single floppy disk with software, and three pages of instructions. The instructions were complete as far as installation and setup; I had the card and glove working within five minutes of opening the box. The interface card needs a small block of upper memory, and the configuration software gives you more than 100 choices for the address. You do need to set a DIP switch if the default memory block at the address range E000-E03F isn't available. Utility software is included with the glove that makes finding an available address range easy, so don't sweat it if you aren't intimately familiar with such things.

The installation routine adds a program group to Program Manager (see Fig. 7.25). There are two Help files that document the SDK included on the floppy disk. These are functions that a programmer can use to interface with the glove. There is one SDK for the glove data, and another for gesture recognition.

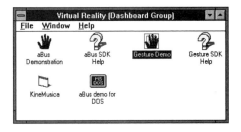

Figure 7.25
The suite of Windows programs that comes with the 5th Glove.

I tested the various programs that come with the glove, and I learned a lot about the capabilities of the glove by doing so. However, at the time I am writing this, there was no major software package to test the glove with (as noted earlier).

> **Demo Program**—The aBus Demonstration program displays a simple window, as shown in Figure 7.26. A graphic of a hand responds to the movements of your hand in the glove. Figure 7.27 shows several hand positions.

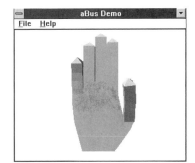

Figure 7.26
The aBus Demonstration program.

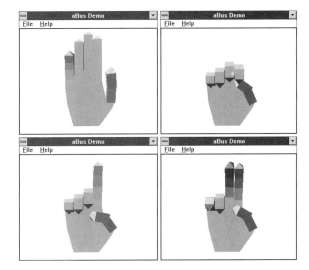

Figure 7.27
Various hand positions as reported by the glove.

Gesture Recognition—The 5th Glove comes with a library of functions that enable it to recognize a gesture. You can train the glove to recognize gestures. Figure 7.28 shows the sample gesture program (written in Visual Basic). I have created and trained the glove for four different gestures, as shown in the list at the left in the figure. You can use the Insert button to add a new gesture, as shown in Figure 7.29. To add the gesture, you name the gesture, move your hand into position, and then click the Sample button.[10] The software then recognizes the gesture. Figure 7.30 shows gesture recognition in process. Recognition was reasonably reliable.

---

[10]If you are using a glove for the right hand, of course, you'll need to use your left hand to move the mouse and click. This is awkward, but not all that difficult.

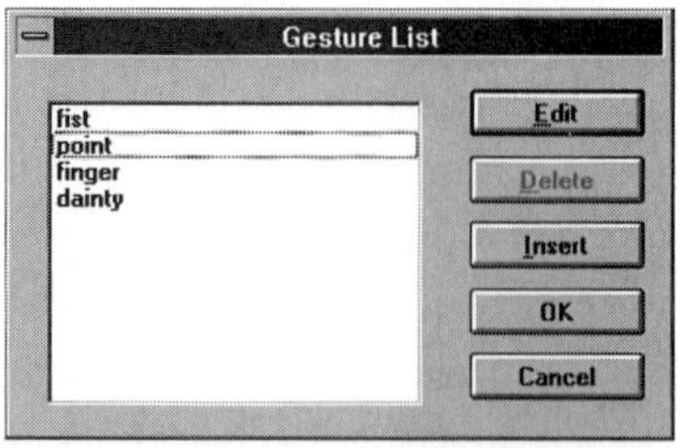

Figure 7.28
The sample gesture program included with the 5th Glove.

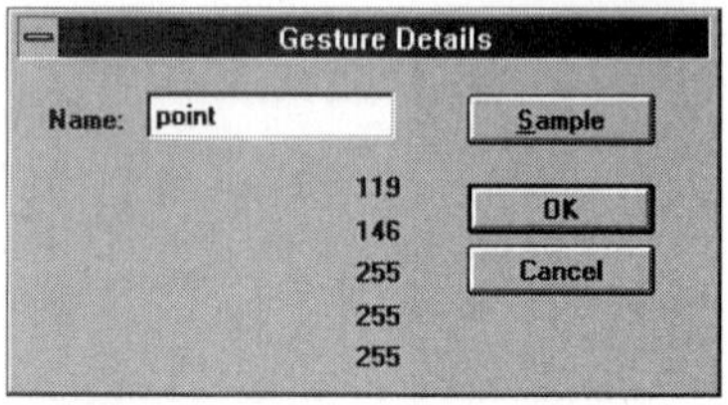

Figure 7.29
Adding a new gesture.

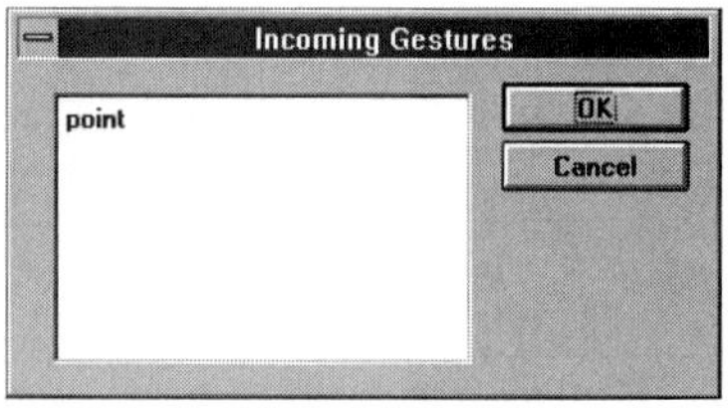

Figure 7.30
A gesture being recognized.

Finger Music—The KineMusica demo is a series of Visual Basic programs that use glove input to activate various musical games. Figure 7.31 shows the different games available, such as Binary Ballet and Dancing Drums. Figure 7.32 shows a typical game (Dancing Drums) in progress. I have assigned a different General MIDI drum sound to each finger, and whenever the value for a finger bend reaches the right bar, the sound is heard. Figure 7.33 shows a scene from Binary Ballet, where movement of the first through third fingers is used to animate the valves of a virtual French horn.

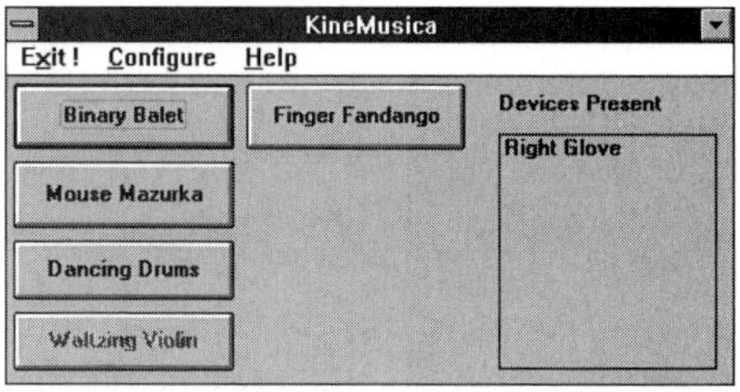

Figure 7.31
KineMusica.

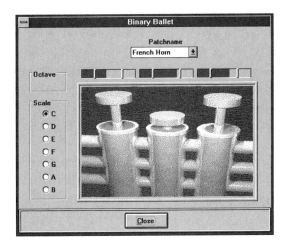

Figure 7.32
Dancing Drums.

Figure 7.33
Binary Ballet.

Overall, the 5th Glove is a very useful product in search of software support. With other gloves coming into the market during 1996, only time will tell which will survive. If you want to do your own glove programming, the 5th Glove and its SDK are a relatively easy way to get into the game. The SDK is reasonably well thought out and accessible. See Tables 7.1 and 7.2 for a list of some key functions and other features of the SDK.

Table 7.1. 5th Glove SDK Basic Functions.

Function	Description
CalibrateDeviceBent	Sets calibration limit for bent hand.
CalibrateDeviceStraight	Sets calibration limit for open hand.
CardPresent	Determines whether interface card is present.

continues

Table 7.1. continued

Function	Description
GetDevice	Returns the bus address of a device, and loads calibration values for the device. Used prior to a ReadDevice call.
GetDeviceCount	Returns the total number of devices present.
GetDeviceList	Returns a list containing addresses the type codes for all devices on the bus.
GetDeviceName	Returns the name of a device.
ReadDevice	Returns a scaled reading from a device on the bus. Use GetDevice to get a device address before using this.
ReadDeviceIIR	Returns a filtered and scaled reading. Takes longer than a ReadDevice call, but is more reliable.
ReadRawDevice	Returns the actual 12-bit data value from a device.

Table 7.2. 5th Glove SDK Gesture Functions.

Function	Description
SetGestureTable	Sets a pointer to the gesture lookup table. The table is maintained by the calling program and is a list of finger positions that define the gestures.
SetHandID	Sets the ID of the device to use for gesture recognition.
SetHitLevel	Determines when the hand is considered to be still (gestures are only reported when the hand is still, and this allows you to set a time limit).
SetNotifyWindow	Sets the handle of the window that will receive messages regarding gestures.
SetSampleDelay	Sets the sampling delay in milliseconds.
SetStillnessCount	Sets the number of consecutive samples during which the hand must be still before the gesture is interpreted.
SetStillnessLevel	Another function for setting stillness level.

There are also a few simple structures defined: one group for the finger positions of the glove, and one group for the various gestures that have been defined:[11]

```
typedef int DIGITS[5];
typedef struct tagGESTURES {
    WORD NumEntries;
    DIGITS Gesture[1];
} GESTURES, FAR* LPGESTURES;
```

Anyone with intermediate experience with programming in C could handle programming for the 5th Glove. Any Visual Basic programmer who has worked with the Windows API (especially if you've accessed structures) could handle the programming as well. In fact, Visual Basic seems like an ideal environment for working with the 5th Glove.

I did notice a few idiosyncrasies while using the glove. My hands are fairly large, and this caused a slight misalignment between the base of my fingers and the strain sensors used to determine how much the fingers bend. The result was that sometimes the values reported for a finger position were influenced by the bending of a nearby finger. This wasn't a fatal problem, but I did have to learn to make minor adjustments. As a general rule, you will be most successful when you bend the finger from the tip, not from the base.

Glove Data

All that a glove really does is track the relative movement of the parts of your hand. Gloves like the 5th Glove simply track the amount of finger-bend movement; it cannot detect the angle between fingers—that's for more sophisticated hardware. This means that you can easily use a pointing gesture, but you can't get the glove to make a peace or victory sign (first two fingers in a V shape).

The movement of the hand in space is another issue entirely. To pick up an object in a virtual world, for example, you can't just close your hand; you have to position your hand next to the object. That involves keeping track of the hand's position in space. That requires more sensors.[12] Given that individual

---

[11]These definitions are in C, but the SDK also comes with OBJ files you can use with just about any language if you supply your own definitions.

[12]VR is a sensor-intensive process. The whole issue of sensing position, velocity, and other variables is a big part of the research going on at the cutting edge of VR. The weight, resistance, cost, bulkiness, and electrical requirements of sensors will become a more and more important part of making VR a success.

sensors can cost as much as $2,000, it's going to be a while before we see the complete package. The industrious sort of person, of course, can buy the sensors and add them to the glove. That's more like garage virtual reality, and outside the scope of this book.[13]

MicroScribe

There's more than one way to create realistic 3D computer models. You can build them from scratch in a 3D modeling program, or you can use a 3D digitizer to generate digital data from a real-world model. Figure 7.34 shows the MicroScribe-3D from Immersion Corporation. It is a mechanical arm that senses and reports movement in three dimensions. With appropriate software running on your computer, you simply trace out the shape of a 3D object, and the software generates a 3D model from the data points. It's a bit like making a tracing of a drawing, but you do it in three dimensions.

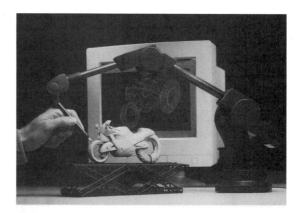

Figure 7.34
Digitizing a 3D physical model with the MicroScribe.

You can construct models using points, lines, polygons, or splines. The software for the unit can export the data in standard 3D file formats such as DXF, OBJ, and TXT. Drivers are available for AutoCAD and 3D Studio. Resolution is 0.005 inch, and the unit can work in a 50-inch sphere. Sampling rate is 1,000 samples per second. MicroScribe-3D uses a serial interface for connecting to your computer.[14]

---

[13]But, at the very least, you know it can be done if you get the itch.

[14]Since the average computer only has two usable serial ports, you can only have two serial devices attached. This is a bit inconvenient, because you sometimes want more than two cool VR devices attached at the same time.

In addition to using the MicroScribe as a digitizer, you can use it to move around in 3D space in products like Superscape. You can use it to grab objects, control views, control light sources, and define animation trajectories. In other words, it also makes a useful 3D mouse.

Input and Motion Sensing

One of the least known, but in some ways most spectacular, uses for input is motion-sensing technology. You see this technology much more often than you might realize. It was even used in the O.J. Simpson trial. The company that prepared VR animations of the scene of this and many other crimes used actors. The actors moved on a special stage, while connected to special devices. Their movements were recorded and used to animate models in a VR world.

The products from Adaptive Optics are premiere examples of this kind of technology. There are two principal kinds of animation in use: body movement and facial expression.

Body Movement

Recording of body movement is usually done in a special environment where there are no distractions for the input equipment. The equipment itself is quite expensive—a prefabricated setup with all the bells and whistles typically costs more than $100,000. That's one of the reasons we don't see more of this kind of technology in use: It simply costs a lot of money for the hardware and software you need for this technology.

The process starts with the hardware. Figure 7.35 shows a typical imaging unit; two units are required to track accurately in 3D space.

Figure 7.35
An Adaptive Optics imaging unit.

The imaging units are set up so that they view the actor from different angles. They are video units, and the recorded images are fed into a computer for analysis. The computer takes the input, processes it, and determines the 3D coordinates of the actor's joints. These coordinates, over time, describe the motion of the actor. The motion is then fed into an animation program, and used to animate a model. Figure 7.36 shows an actor at work. Figure 7.37 shows the equipment setup required for the recording. Note that a large space is required, and that the background must be free of any major clutter.

Note that, in both figures, large white dots have been placed at the actor's joints. These dots are tracked by the software visually, and are used to generate the motion data.

Figure 7.36
An actor creating an
animation.

Figure 7.37
The setup required
for an animation.

Facial Expression

Tracking of facial expressions is very similar to body-motion tracking. Instead of applying white dots to body joints, dots are attached to key areas of the face, as shown in Figure 7.38. Note that the expression of the actor is duplicated on the computer monitor behind him.

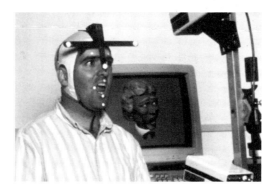

Figure 7.38
Tracking facial expressions.

Figure 7.39 shows a slightly different approach to expression tracking. It shows a head-mounted camera that can be fine-tuned to track facial expression accurately. It follows the actor's head movements naturally, and allows greater precision.

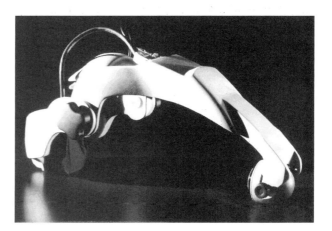

Figure 7.39
FaceTrax—a real-time, non-contact, facial expression capture system from Adaptive Optics.

Performance Animation

As with body tracking, you have probably seen animations created with facial-expression tracking without ever realizing it. Taken together, these and other motion-capture systems are called *performance animation*, referring to the actor or performer at the heart of the process.

Another company that offers performance animation hardware is Polhemus. Its system is called UltraTrak, and it uses completely different technology for motion capture. Instead of video cameras, it uses a central transmitter that emits a magnetic field. The performer's movements are measured by sensors attached to the body, and connected to a motion capture server—a 486 computer with four to eight motion-capture boards, each of which can support up to two receivers.

The transmitter is mounted in the middle of the performance area. It can be mounted overhead, on a pedestal/tripod, or on a table. The Polhemus systems run about $25,000 for a system with 10 receivers.

The results of using performance animation technology are outstanding. If ever the cost of this technology comes down, you can bet your bottom dollar that you'll find me playing with it. I'm as fascinated as the next person by dancing cereal boxes and talking cars, and this is just the technology to accomplish it!

The Rest of the Story

Creative solutions for VR development and exploration are underway, and some of the devices that have been developed for input are quite interesting.

For example, consider the Immersion Probe. It's part pen, part robot, and completely off-beat. We did not have one available for testing, but it is an interesting alternative for anyone working in a CAD environment.

The key to proper use of the Immersion Probe: the tip. Rotation, position, and tilt—all of this movement information is relative to the tip of the unit. It's like having a cursor in 3D space.

But there are plenty of other alternative input devices out there; the Immersion Probe is just one clever idea, and time alone will tell us which ideas are the best.

Winner!   ## For the Birds?

With a name like Flock of Birds, you might expect something fanciful or magical, but this product is simply a high-quality sensor—or, more precisely, multiple sensors. That multiplicity is the key ingredient in Flock of Birds—getting a bunch of sensors to work together is quite a challenge.

Flock of Birds is position-sensing technology. That means that there are two pieces involved: a transmitter and a receiver. The transmitter goes on the object to be tracked, and the receiver keeps track of it. Transmitters and receivers are shown in Figure 7.40.

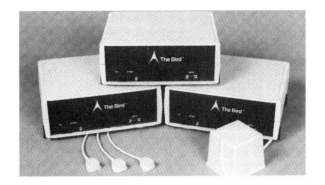

Figure 7.40
*Transmitters (front)
and receivers for
Flock of Birds
position trackers.*

There are many issues involved in sensor tracking, and just about all of them conspire to make the job hard and complicated. Consider the following facts:

■ Each sensor must transmit in such a way that it can be identified reliably. It wouldn't do if the receiver(s) became confused about which sensor is which.

■ Sensor sample rate is critical to success. However, the more sensors you have, the harder it is to check in with each one of them. If you sample 100 times per second for one sensor, for example, you can only sample each of two sensors 50 times per second. Every new sensor adds to the overhead.

■ The environment can interfere with sensor accuracy. Metals and magnetized materials can throw sensors out of whack, for example.

■ The range at which sensors can be tracked accurately can be surprisingly small. Until recently, distances of more than two to three feet were about the maximum extent for safe tracking.

The bottom line: Keeping track of sensors is a big job, and that's what accounts for the high cost. Flock of Birds is one of the more successful technologies. The product employs DC, not AC fields, so it is less sensitive to metals and magnetized materials. Flock of Birds also handles sample rates in a unique way to ensure that sampling rates are not decreased as new sensors are added—thus, the name *Flock of Birds*. The accuracy range is also quite large—up to eight feet.

Besides its uses in VR, Flock of Birds is often used for character animation. You simply attach a bunch of sensors to a person at key points, and then use the output as input to an animation program. If you want to animate a 3D model of a person to make it dance, for example, simply attach sensors to an accomplished dancer, record the movements, and then input them to your animation program.[15]

---

[15]We aren't talking about just any animation program here. You'll need special-purpose software, such as Alias Power Animator (416-362-9181) or Kinemation from Wavefront (805-962-8117).

But Flock of Birds isn't the only sensor game in town. Polhemus offers 3Space Insidetrack, which is billed as a "PC insertable tracking system." It uses a board inside your computer, an external receiver, and multiple tracking devices. Figure 7.41 shows the various components that make up the system.

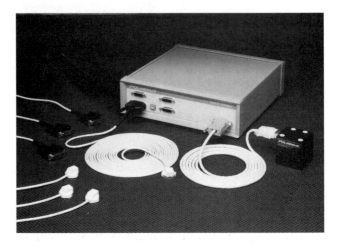

Figure 7.41
Polhemus' 3Space Insidetrack—3D tracking hardware for the PC.

You can also use sensor products with software such as VREAM, Sense8, 3D Studio, Superscape, and many special-purpose packages. Contact the manufacturer of a given software package to determine whether it supports Flock of Birds or Polhemus 3Space Insidetrack.

Computing for the Handicapped

One area in which virtual reality research shows some great promise is in alternative computing tools for the handicapped. For example, head-tracking, an important capability for high-end VR, has useful applications for handicapped computer users. Origin Instruments, for example, offers the HeadMouse—a Microsoft mouse-compatible box that allows you to use your head movements to control the mouse cursor (see Fig. 7.42).[16]

---

[16] The HeadMouse is also compatible with the Apple Macintosh mouse and the IBM OS/2 mouse.

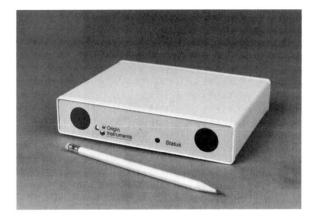

Figure 7.42
*The HeadMouse—a
head-controlled
pointing device.*

The HeadMouse is a wireless optical sensor that tracks a tiny, disposable target that is placed on the user's head or glasses. The unit can be combined with an on-screen keyboard to allow input without any use of the hands. As with most systems for the severely handicapped, a mouse click is achieved by lingering in one position for a set period of time or by using an external switch. A wireless transmitter is available for such a switch.

Origin Instruments also sells the Dynasight sensor, which measures the 3D position of a target. In most cases, the sensor is used to track head movement and is coupled to interactive stereo displays. This offers simple but effective head tracking for applications that support response to head movement.

GAMS Unique 3D Input

GAMS stands for *gesture and media system*, and it's the magic wand of VR interactivity. A system of ultrasonic speakers is arranged around a room-sized space, and the operator is free to move around in the space with one or more wands. GAMS tracks the movement of the wand, and the wireless receiver can respond to clicks on the wand.

GAMS has a wide variety of potential uses, from performance artists controlling MIDI devices by moving a wand in 3D space to immersive data visualization. Speaking of visualization, the best way to understand GAMS is to see it in use. I've included an AVI file on the CD-ROMs that shows GAMS in action as part of an alternative musical experience.[17]

---

[17]Yes, it's as strange as it sounds. Check it out.

Figure 7.43
*The GAMS unit
in use.*

Output Devices

If input is the overlooked part of the VR hardware story, then output is the exact opposite. Output is where most of the world's attention is focused. The reason: The glamour and allure of expensive headsets and 3D environments.

But let's face it—there's something to be said for glamour and allure. After all, that's what puts the coolness in cool, right? The more flash and pizzazz we get out of these PCs of ours, the better. As virtual reality moves forward, it does so with thrill after thrill, not unlike a carnival ride. There's plenty of time to settle in and get serious when VR becomes a mature technology. For now, there are four key areas to focus on when it comes to output devices:

- Graphics resolution
- Field of view
- Stereo imaging
- Head tracking

Graphics Resolution

A standard VGA screen is 640 pixels wide and 480 pixels high. If you use Windows, you know that this is a confining space—it's hard to run multiple programs. Even worse, a standard VGA screen supports only 16 different colors. You can't create a very realistic virtual world in 16 colors. Figure 7.44 shows a virtual world in 16 colors. It's harsh, and bitmaps lack detail.

Figure 7.44
A low-resolution view in Virtus VR.

There's another side to the VGA story, however—a video mode that is 320 pixels wide by 200 pixels high, with 256 colors. Figure 7.45 shows a virtual world using 256 colors, and it's obvious how much clearer the various objects are. In particular, shading is much more effective. Look at the photorealistic image on the back wall to see the clearest difference. The 256-color version is much better.

Figure 7.45
A high-resolution view in Virtus VR.

This video mode, called MCGA, is simply a trade-off—give up some pixels, gain some colors. Giving up pixels, of course, means giving up resolution. Many early virtual reality products supported this low-resolution mode because any PC with a VGA card supports it. Many virtual reality products still do, and for an equally good reason:

> The more pixels there are to push around, the more computing horsepower you need to push 'em.

In order to achieve high-resolution graphics, hardware and software has to break through several boundaries:

- The hardware must have the power to display large numbers of pixels quickly.
- Both hardware and software must support 256 (or more) colors.

If you are using your computer screen for VR display, the key component is your video card. The faster it operates, the smoother your VR environments will respond. Most of today's video cards come packed with power to spare. If you don't have a video card of recent vintage, you can upgrade at a cost of $150 to $500. Diamond, VideoLogic, ATI, and many other companies offer a lot of power for a small investment, while companies like Matrox offer video cards with built-in 3D capabilities. Look particularly for video cards that support Intel's standards for 3D graphics.

Head-mounted units face a different set of requirements. An HMD usually has two small screens in it—one for each eye. The small space and lightweight requirements of an HMD limit the size of these screens. This, in turn, limits the number of pixels the screens can have. Until the density of pixels on the small, relatively inexpensive color LCD screens used in HMDs improves, there is a very definite limit to what you can achieve with an HMD.

Many 3D systems use special glasses and your computer display. For such systems, resolution is limited by your video card and monitor—not by the glasses.

Field of View

Field of view refers not to how many pixels are used, but to how wide the display appears to your eyes.[18] A computer monitor has a very narrow field of view—it sits right

---

[18]Yup, that means that the situation is loaded. You can get a wide field of view with a few very fat pixels (and a coarse, low-resolution image), or with a lot of skinny pixels (and a high-resolution image).

in front of you, and it occupies only a small portion of your field of vision. Thus, while it is certainly convenient to use the computer monitor you already have for virtual displays, it isn't very lifelike at all.

To get a wider field of view, you can start with a larger monitor. The average computer has a monitor that measures 14 or 15 inches diagonally. You could upgrade to a 17-inch monitor, or even something like a 21-inch monitor. Even if you do, you won't increase your field of view substantially, and you'll spend a lot more for the larger monitor.

Not that I'm arguing against large computer monitors—I use a 21-inch monitor myself, and the large screen area is a major improvement. I wouldn't give it up for anything! But, from a VR standpoint, the improvement doesn't make a fundamental difference—the screen still occupies only a fraction of your field of view.

To get a wider field of view, you need to build a huge monitor (something wall-sized and negatively curved would do nicely), use a projection system (onto something wall-sized and curved), or use a head-mounted device.

Huge monitors are simply too costly to be practical. A monitor with a 30-inch diagonal measurement would set you back about $5,000 to $10,000—not exactly affordable.

Projection systems are more practical but still fairly costly. You could route the output of your VR computer to a projection TV, but you'd be sacrificing a lot of detail. A television has much less resolution than a standard VGA screen. Standard projection systems don't fit the needs of VR. State-of-the-art VR projection systems are often found in commercial and military aircraft training simulators.

Which brings us to HMDs, the only under-$5,000 devices supporting a wide field of view. The lack of support for high-resolution in such "affordable" HMDs takes some of the pleasure out of the wide field of view. However, you can use an HMD to explore a virtual environment and have lots of fun doing it. But there's sometimes not enough detail visible to develop a virtual world—you can't read menu text with many HMDs!

Bottom Line: One of the hardest things to create in a virtual world is a wide field of view for the user. We take the width of our visual field for granted, but it will be a while before affordable VR gives us something to fill in our peripheral vision. Wide fields of view remain a costly option for most uses.

Stereo Imaging

If there is one thing about VR that gives me a real kick, it's good 3D images in stereo. Whether you do it with glasses and your computer monitor, a hood on the monitor, or an expensive HMD, there is nothing quite like seeing a virtual world in 3D.

Going to true stereo, such as with a head-mounted device, automatically doubles the load on your computer. Instead of one output for both eyes, you need two outputs: one for each eye. A standard computer is completely unprepared to generate stereo visual output for an HMD. Affordable stereo comes in the form of special glasses.

Your VR software must be set up to create output for the glasses. This consists of displaying two images simultaneously—one for each eye. In some cases, one image is over the other; in other situations, the images are beside each other. Glasses, headsets, and hoods use electronics, mirrors, or other techniques to make sure that the correct image gets to the correct eye.

There are now many different devices using various formats, at many different price points. In some cases, you can use a high-end output format (such as the CrystalEyes over-under format) with less costly equipment. Check the documentation of any hardware and software product for supported formats *before* you buy it!

Not all VR software supports the various kinds of glasses that are available. Different kinds of 3D glasses are covered in various sections of this chapter, and additional information can be found in Chapter 12.

Head Tracking

You normally interact with your computer by using a mouse. The computer doesn't care where the mouse is—all motion is relative. You can move the mouse around on the floor, on a book, on the desk, and so on. The cursor simply moves when the mouse moves.

If you are in a virtual world, however, it is highly desirable to let the computer know where you are looking. If you look up, the computer should detect that movement, and display what you would see looking up in the virtual world. If you turn your head to the right, the computer should be able to keep track of that, and switch your viewpoint in the virtual world at the same time.

Head tracking can be accomplished in a variety of ways, but most of the good ones aren't cheap. The keys to good head tracking are to allow the user complete freedom of movement, and to update the virtual display in real time. This, however, takes some serious hardware and some very serious computing power. Most affordable head-tracking units have a very noticeable lag time. That means that when you turn your head, it takes a distressing few seconds for the computer to make the virtual world catch up. Some users of such systems report vertigo from the lack of synchronization.

Figure 7.46
Imagine the vertigo you would feel experiencing this scene in a virtual world!

Headsets, Head-Mounted Devices (HMDs), and Goggles

These three terms often mean the same thing. There used to be significant differences, but as new (and lower cost) units come into production, the various kinds of devices borrow features from each other.

The term *headset* traditionally was all inclusive. However, as more types of units come out, there is sometimes a need to be more specific. In this book, when I use the term *headset*, I'm referring to just about anything you can stick on your head.

The term *head-mounted device*, usually shortened to *HMD*, also is fairly generic, but it normally refers to the more bulky units that more or less completely cover your head. It means different things to different folks, mostly because at this stage of the VR game everyone throws terminology around without really thinking about how the terms have been used over the years.

Goggles usually look something like glasses, are light in weight, and don't normally cover the head—just the top portion of the face at the most. Goggles are a possible alternative to HMDs. The most common kind of goggles use LCD in the eyepieces. A cable is attached, which causes the LCD for each eyepiece to go black alternately. If the image source—a TV or your computer monitor—is synchronized to the goggles, separate images for each eye can be obtained. This allows you to see a useful but sometimes flickery form of 3D.[19] However, some headsets use HMD technology but put it

---

[19]A new product from 3DTV, the StereoSpace, deals with this problem by doubling the refresh rate. See the VR Hardware Buyer's Guide on the CDs that come with this book.

in a goggle-sized package, such as the i-glasses!, covered later in this chapter. Are these goggles, or are they HMDs? Shakespeare said it best when he said that "A rose by any other name would smell as sweet." A headset by any other name will still deliver images to your eyes. The real question is how good those images are.

But as HMDs start to look more like goggles, and as goggles add features and start to look more like HMDs, it is sometimes hard to know what categories to use to refer to the various kinds of hardware out there. So hard, in fact, that I am loathe to even try to sort it all out. I'm going to use a much simpler criterion: I'm looking for stuff that works. I'm interested in things like comfort, width of field, and image resolution—in other words, package these features any way you like, but how do they *work?* Call it whatever you will, just deliver the features that I need.

As far as prices are concerned, if there was a headset out there for $100, everyone would be doing VR. Unfortunately, the arrival of low-cost goggles and HMDs is somewhere off in the indefinite future. At the top end, the military can spend $80,000 and more for HMDs that include full head-tracking, stereo inputs, and crystal-clear resolution. It's just not realistic to expect the same features in a consumer headset.

VR4

Head tracking is actually an input issue. The computer must receive data from sensors on the HMD[20] that provide precise information about head angle, distance, rotation, and so on. With individual sensors running as high as several thousands of dollars, you might not expect to find this feature in consumer technology. For example, I tested the VR4 HMD, from Virtual Research Systems (408-748-8712), for one week. At more than $6,000 per unit—and that's without head tracking—the VR4 isn't exactly consumer-level equipment. Figure 7.47 shows the VR4 in use by my wife Donna while she is working with VREAM. The unit includes stereo headphones, and the large cable at the back of Donna's head is the connection at the base unit. The base has two audio and two video inputs, but of course, you need a source to provide true 3D input.[21]

Figure 7.48 shows the headset from the front. It looks big, and you might be wondering how comfortable is it to wear and use. That cable at the back acts as a counterweight to the front of the unit. It isn't exactly lightweight, but the careful balancing of the unit makes it reasonably comfortable. As long as you keep the cable behind you, the unit balances very comfortably. If you start to move around, the long cable can occasionally get in your way. However, it's long enough and stiff enough that it tends not to interfere.

---

[20]Or headset, or goggles, or whatever we are calling them this week.

[21]For units like the VR4, that means a stereo video output card in your computer; conventional VGA card output will not work for stereo input to the VR4.

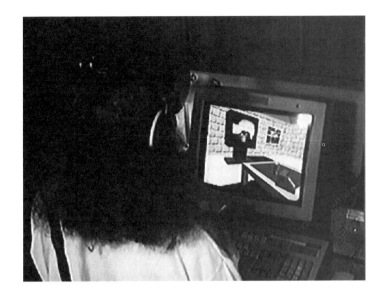

Figure 7.47
*The VR4 headset
in use.*

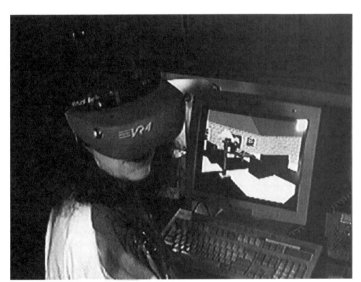

Figure 7.48
*The VR4 headset
from the front.*

To understand how the VR4 functions, it helps to know what's inside. Figure 7.51 shows the unit upside down, and you can see the two video units nestled inside the front of the unit. There are small controls at the sides of the unit that allow you to adjust the distance between the two videos. You can also slide the front back and forth to adjust for comfort.

Figure 7.49
The VR4 and the Spaceball 2003 being used to control vrTrader, a virtual reality stock trading program from Avatar.

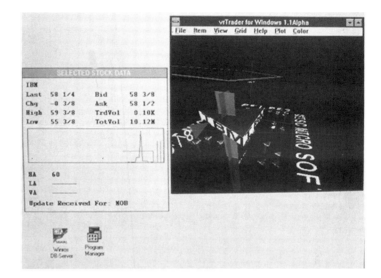

Figure 7.50
*A screen view of
vrTrader.*

Figure 7.51
*A look at the inside
of the VR4.*

Figure 7.52 shows an even closer look at the two video units. There is a thick lens on each to allow you to see the video image clearly at close range.

At a price of $6,000, the VR4 is fairly expensive. It is designed for heavy use, and much of the cost has gone into using rugged components. The unit is lightweight and sturdy when compared to much of the competition. It's still too much for household use in terms of cost, weight, resolution, and just about any other key parameter.

What the world really needs is obvious: that $100 headset. But we have a way to go yet before we have the HMD equivalent of the Sony Walkman.[22] While it would be great to have something like the VR4 around (we really miss it now that it is gone), as a practical matter, that's too much technology for home use.

Figure 7.52
A close look at the video units inside the VR4.

Figure 7.53
Another HMD model from Virtual Research.

---

[22]Unless you are willing to count the Virtual Vision Sport (see Fig. 7.54), which gives you a set of goggles that provides TV reception for one eye, and is coupled to a belt pack, which is the tuner.

Figure 7.54
The Virtual Vision Sport, featuring a TV view for one eye.

CyberEye

There are less expensive units than the VR4. One of the most important is the CyberEye from General Reality.[23] The CyberEye sacrifices wide-angle view for higher resolution in a smaller area and costs around $2,000. Figure 7.55 shows one potential use for the CyberEye, or a product like it, sometime in the future. Yes, that's a pretty fanciful anticipation of the future—who wants to stumble along wearing a headset and typing? What's *really* exciting about the CyberEye is that it delivers the same mid-level resolution and clear, crisp images that the VR4 does. The unit is lighter in weight and meant specifically for personal use. It's not as rugged as the VR4, but it doesn't need to be as rugged if it's not used in an arcade or other public situation.

---

[23]Don't you just love the names that VR companies come up with? I suppose this is a pun on General Electric.

Figure 7.55
A fanciful use for
the CyberEye
headset.

I really and truly enjoyed using the CyberEye. In some ways, I liked it better than the VR4. It's much lighter in weight, for example, and is not at all a burden to wear. While it does have a cable, the cable is much, much lighter than the one used with the VR4 and is very easy to keep out of the way. The cable was a bit on the short side, however. The CyberEye is fine when you are using it sitting down or standing in one location. You won't be able to walk around with it unless you clip the small base unit to your belt.

What impressed me the most about the CyberEye were the crystal-clear images. As we move down the cost ladder to the true consumer units (those under $1,000), you won't hear me saying things like that. If you have the money and want a really and truly good game-playing headset, you simply can't beat the CyberEye. Of all the units we tested, it actually delivers the goods. For example, while using the unit to watch television, images are clear and pleasant to view. I can't say that any of the consumer units matched it, either for TV or computer-game viewing. Better yet, the CyberEye is excellent for use with products like VREAM or Superscape. And it goes both ways— you can use it with a mono VGA card (you'll need an NTSC converter for some models), or you can install a special stereo-output card in your computer for true high-quality 3D and VR. At double to triple the cost of the consumer units, the CyberEye delivers enough value to be well worth your consideration if you have the budget for it. It's far enough ahead of the consumer units to be in a class by itself.

The ads from General Reality boast that the CyberEye delivers the crisp images and performance of units in the $5,000 to $10,000 range. Having tried exactly those kinds of units, I can verify their ad claims: the CyberEye definitely delivers the goods. If I had $5,000 to spend on a headset, I'd spend $2,000 on the CyberEye and the rest on other goodies. There is no question that the CyberEye is the unit of choice. It's the top of the consumer end and fills the mid-level niche at the high end. It is probably the best value in headsets today. There are other units (for example, see the VIM Personal Viewer from Kaiser in the VR Hardware Buyer's Guide on the CDs with this book), but none of them beat the price and performance of the CyberEye.

Headsets for Games

The preceding headsets have one thing in common: They aren't willing to sacrifice performance for a lower price. Now we move into a different category of headset. The four headsets listed in this section (i-glasses!, VFX1, CyberMaxx, and Virtual Boy) are all intended not so much for general VR as for use with games.

The first thing you'll notice about these headsets is the great variety in design; no two are alike. The i-glasses! are like a pair of glasses on steroids. The VFX1 is about as futuristic-looking as any headset on the market. The CyberMaxx has the look and feel of the traditional headset. The Virtual Boy is a cross between a headset and old-time aviator goggles.

But they, too, have something in common: They all draw the line at games.[24] You won't be tempted to try using these devices to operate your computer. As a class, they all have lower resolution images. Most of them rate as true VR headsets, however, because they include motion tracking as well as 3D viewing. If your VR interests run to games, or if you are willing to settle for games, then you can have some fun with these units. However, you do get what you pay for, so don't expect to experience the thrills of a high-end headset/HMD. The real question is how these headsets perform in the arena they were designed for: games. That's where I'll focus my attention. If you want a true VR experience, you'll need to jump up to something like the CyberEye (see the preceding section) at double, or even triple, the price.

i-glasses!

Beyond the cute name, the i-glasses! from Virtual I/O offer a good-looking package of features and performance. As you can see from Figure 7.56, the unit is light and compact, and can easily be used by someone who wears eye glasses.[25] Of all the game-oriented units I tested, the i-glasses! were at the top of the heap in almost every category. The image is bright and crisp, although not as good as what the CyberEye from General Reality offers. Construction of the unit is very good, and the packaging

---

[24]Not totally, exactly true. You can also use most of these units to watch television, but some of them are marginal for this use. It takes quite a bit of resolution to handle a television image—and television has much less resolution than even a simple VGA screen! I'll believe that these units can handle a computer when I *first* see them handle something as simple as TV.

[25]This isn't the most dramatic of the images sent to us by the manufacturer; for a more dramatic take on the i-glasses!, look in the color section of the book.

and documentation are first rate and complete. The good images are a real plus, but the best part of the i-glasses! is the quality of the motion tracking. It is extremely smooth and accurate, and is slanted toward game-like performance. For instance, when you look left in Descent, you don't just see the image drift left; you get a bounce and feel that are just what you'd expect from your floating spaceship. The motion tracking of this unit is nothing short of phenomenal, and it makes the headset a pure joy to use with games. The result is that the i-glasses! are the only game-oriented headset to merit a Winner designation.

Figure 7.56
The i-glasses! in use.

The theory is that the two eyepieces present you with a video image. If you use the unit for TV viewing, you'll see the same image in each eye. If you use the unit with a 3D game, each eye gets one half of a stereo pair of images. The unit also has stereo sound built in. The video image appears to float in front of you, more or less like a large-screen TV hanging in mid-air. As shown in Figure 7.56, the unit is somewhat transparent, and you can see through the image to the real world. For VR applications, however, you will want to clip on what Virtual I/O calls a *blast shield*. It's nothing more than a plastic shade that blocks out the exterior world, and allows you to immerse yourself in the VR world. Figure 7.57 shows the shield in place.

Figure 7.57
The i-glasses! with
the shield in place
for VR viewing.

The key advantages of the i-glasses! are its light weight and the price/performance ratio. You wouldn't expect to see the same clarity as you would get with a full VR headset such as the CyberEye, but you do get the best images in this class of headset. Head-tracking quality is superb.

Here are some key specs on the i-glasses!:

- Field of view for each eye is 30 degrees.

- Fixed focus at apparent distance of 11 feet.

- No IPD (interpupilary distance) adjustment, and Virtual I/O claims none is needed. I tried the unit and found it workable, but I would have preferred having this adjustment available.

- 100 percent stereo overlap of right and left eye images.

- Can be worn with eyeglasses.

- Computer connection passes through to your monitor so you can view both simultaneously.

For additional technical specs, see the VR Hardware Buyer's Guide on the CDs.

VFX1

The VFX1 headset from Forte Technologies features an innovative design, as you can see from Figure 7.58. The front portion flips up away from your eyes if you need to check in with the real world (see Fig. 7.59), and the headphones look more like high-end, stand-alone headphones than the little ones commonly found attached to headsets.

The VFX1 costs a bit more than other game-oriented headsets, but it also tends to feature better construction details. The LCDs are twin 789×230-pixel units.[26] The apparent field of view is 35 degrees vertical and 53 degrees horizontal.

The over-the-head design helps to distribute the weight of the headset evenly. This headset includes head tracking for games, and a two-axis *CyberPuck* that is used in place of a joystick or mouse for navigation (see Fig. 7.59).

One unique feature of the VFX1 is that it uses an interface card installed in your computer, rather than connecting to the VGA output or an NTSC[27] video output (see Fig. 7.59). The interface card uses the VGA feature connector, so you must have a VGA card that has such a feature connector. Most do, but a few do not.[28] The headset

---

[26]These are standard 0.7-inch LCD panels found in most game-level headsets.

[27]Some headsets require NTSC output, which is the kind you get from the typical VCR and some televisions. This is often referred to as *composite output*. Very few computer video cards output this kind of signal; the Jazz Jakarta is one that does, and it is also one that I recommend highly. Other choices for creating an NTSC signal are external boxes that convert VGA output to NTSC, or a card that sits alongside your regular video card.

[28]A word of caution about the feature connector! Not all feature connectors are created equal. You should contact the dealer or Forte to see whether the video card you use mates properly with the VFX1's interface card.

itself attaches to the interface card using a 26-pin D connector. You can connect your sound card's output to the input of the interface card to get sound to the headphones.

The VFX1 also includes a built-in microphone. It is designed for player-to-player communication, but I fail to see the need for it in most situations.

For additional technical specs, see the VR Hardware Buyer's Guide on the CDs.

Figure 7.58
The VFX1 headset.

Figure 7.59
The underside of the VFX1 headset's eyepieces, the CyberPuck, and the interface card.

CyberMaxx

The CyberMaxx headset was one of the first game-oriented models to hit the streets. The first version was admittedly on the weak side, with relatively low-resolution LCD screens. The current model offers the standard medium-resolution LCD screens featured on the other game headsets.

Unfortunately, resolution isn't everything, and the visual quality of the CyberMaxx images lags behind the category leader, the Virtual I/O i-glasses!. Like the other game headsets, the CyberMaxx features built-in head tracking, and it works with all the popular games. Its strongest point is that it has been around for a while; if a game supports any headset at all, it's going to support the CyberMaxx.

The CyberMaxx also has a few other features that the i-glasses! lack. For example, you can adjust the interpupilary distance (fancy lingo for *distance between the screens to match the distance between your eyes*). I couldn't quite get the i-glasses! to sit perfectly, but I could get both screens on the CyberMaxx aligned perfectly.[29]

The headset itself has both vertical and headband adjustments, making it possible to align everything (headphones, screens, motion tracking) easily. Total weight is 14 ounces—not heavy, not light.

The CyberMaxx uses the now-standard 0.7-inch LCD screens, with 180,000 pixels per screen. Tracking ranges up and down 90 degrees (45 degrees in each direction) and 360 degrees horizontally. Resolution is to 0.1 degrees theoretically, but in practice it's a bit rougher than that.

For additional technical specs, see the VR Hardware Buyer's Guide on the CDs.

Virtual Boy

Yes, you read that title correctly: Virtual Boy. The folks who brought us the Game Boy (Nintendo) now bring us the lowest-cost VR product out there. Already available in Japan, the U.S. introduction of these units was too late for us to test one,[30] but from the description, you get (exactly) what you pay for. Figure 7.60 shows the Virtual Boy setup, including the goggles and the base unit.

---

[29]Not without a little difficulty, however. It's nice to have the interpupilary distance adjustment, but if you go too far, it can get off the track and it takes some clever hand work to get it back on. **Hint:** If you get the screens too far apart, gently push one of the screens with your finger, then twist the adjustment, and it should catch.

[30]The unit was scheduled to ship in August 1995, so they should be out by the time you are reading this.

Figure 7.60
The Nintendo
Virtual Boy.

Retailing for $179, Virtual Boy would not be expected to deliver the same images and performance as the other HMDs and goggles we've been talking about so far. And it does not. It uses a completely different technology.

The hardware behind the goggles is a RISC-based, 32-bit system. It uses two mirror-scanning LEDs[31] to create a 3D image pair. The LEDs are red, so the image you see is a red image. That's the first trade-off for the low price: you don't get a color image.[32] Figure 7.61 shows the view into the goggles, and you can see the red light of the LEDs (but not an image). In use, you'll see a red, 3D image against a dark black background.

Figure 7.61
Looking into the
Nintendo Virtual
Boy's goggles.

---

[31]*Light emitting diodes.*

[32]Unless you are picky and point out that the monochrome image is red, not white.

The game-playing experience includes stereo sound as well. The controller (shown in Fig. 7.60) uses both hands. Movement within a game depends on the game itself, and the system uses only games specifically designed for it.

The technology used for the 3D monochrome display was created by Reflection Technology, Inc., and is licensed exclusively by Nintendo for the video game market. The Virtual Boy is a complete stand-alone unit; it does not attach to a TV set. It is powered by six AA batteries. Accessories include an AC adapter and a rechargeable battery adapter, sold separately.

Cyberscope

On the other hand, there is an affordable way to get stereo VR. It's called the Cyberscope, and it's a clever and functional solution to the problem of inexpensive stereo. Figure 7.62 shows the Cyberscope in use on a 17-inch monitor.[33]

Figure 7.62
The Cyberscope attached to a monitor.

Unlike goggles and HMDs, the Cyberscope is stationary. You attach it to your monitor, and you must look through the eyepieces for a 3D effect. Before you start thinking that this is just plain weird, I have to tell you the most important part: It works, and it works well. And at about $150, you can't beat the price for flicker-free VR/3D.

---

[33]You may also have noted that the top is not on our computer, to the right of the monitor. We have to install so many different pieces of hardware that we gave up keeping the lid on ages ago.

Figure 7.63 shows the inside of the unit. There is a light baffle running down the center (its purpose will be clear in a moment), and a series of mirrors at the back near the eyepieces.

Figure 7.64 shows the screen without the Cyberscope attached. The view shows a VREAM runtime session, and the screen is divided into left and right halves. The image of each half is rotated 90 degrees. The light baffle keeps the two images from interfering with each other, and the mirrors rotate the view back to horizontal and present the correct image to each eye. *Voilà*—instant 3D. Not all VR software supports the Cyberscope, but for software that does, such as VREAM, 3D is quite easy to achieve.

Figure 7.63
The interior of the Cyberscope.

Figure 7.64
A view of a VREAM screen set up for the Cyberscope.

You look into the eyepieces of the Cyberscope from above. In Figure 7.65, you can see the light from the screen, but the camera has the screen out of focus. I have included a video clip on the CD-ROMs that shows this entire sequence, and it makes the process very clear.

Figure 7.65
The Cyberscope
from above.

The Cyberscope, in our opinion, provides the best 3D value for the money.

Feedback

99.99999 percent of computer output goes to the eyes, but that does leave approximately .00001 percent for other senses, such as touch. TiNi Alloy offers *tactors*—small fingertip devices that provide tactile feedback. Figure 7.66 shows a single tactor and control unit.

The tactor strip can be attached to a mouse button, a key on the keyboard, or any physical device. The feedback consists of a kind of "buzz" provided by small actuators in the tactor. You cannot feel actual objects; you just get your fingertip stimulated when the software triggers the tactor.

We did not find any software that supports the tactor directly, so it is of interest primarily to researchers and hobbyists who want to experiment with tactile feedback. The physical interface is simple—just plug the control unit into a serial port. As a programmer, all you need to be able to do to activate the tactor is to send any kind of data through the serial port. Programs such as Visual Basic make this very easy to do.

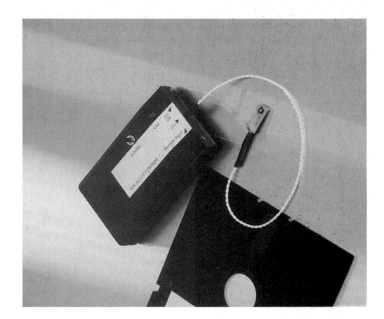

Figure 7.66
A tactile feedback
device from TiNi
Alloy and distrib-
uted by Mondo-
tronics.

Summary

We had a lot of fun with almost every aspect of VR, but it was very clear that the hardware toys were the most fun. Whether it was me, Donna, or the kids, there was a heightened sense of excitement every time we tested a new piece of hardware. The helmet was clearly the Big News, but it wasn't much of a surprise. Probably the biggest surprise was how much we liked the innovative Cyberscope; we kind of expected it to be funky, not functional, but it was very useful and easy to set up and use.

But there was also a note of caution behind the excitement. As exciting as 3D is initially, it fades to normal pretty quickly. I would like to see 3D visual technology overtake what we have now the same way that stereo-sound technology wiped out mono. The cost of stereo versus mono sound, however, wasn't large. The current cost of 3D visuals—at least the really fancy stuff—is so large that one must wonder if it will ever arrive in the consumer marketplace.

There are now several products on the edge of consumer acceptance. The Cyberscope is probably a little too awkward for popular use, however, and LCD glasses must overcome the flicker problem if they are going to make it. But both these technologies are very affordable, and it only takes a small amount of enthusiasm to overcome the minor problems and awkwardness, and have some fun.

On the other hand, if you can get your hands on an HMD, go for it!

8

SEEING IS BELIEVING

The human visual system is mostly an electrochemical/mechanical device.[1] We seldom think of it that way, of course; we just know that we can see, and we take that pretty much for granted. Each aspect of our visual system has some interesting flaws and loopholes. The eye itself, being mostly mechanical, has the most weaknesses. These can be exploited to fool the eye into thinking that what it sees is real when it is not. This means that a visual virtual reality need not be perfect to be perceived as real, which makes the job easier.[2]

There are numerous examples of optical illusions; Figure 8.1 shows an example. The two horizontal lines don't look like they are straight and parallel, but they are. If you doubt it, just lay a ruler against the lines to verify it.

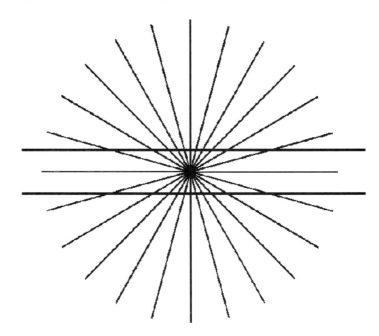

Figure 8.1
An example of an optical illusion. The lines are parallel but don't appear to be so.

There is actually a wide variety of ways in which the eye can be fooled. By taking advantage of these flaws, the eye can be made to see color where there is none,[3] to

---

[1] I know; you think I should say "biological" in there somewhere. Strictly speaking, perhaps I should. However, biology is just a short way of saying "an amazingly tiny, sophisticated, and self-repairing electromechanical device," right?

[2] Perhaps someday we'll even bypass the eye entirely—see William Gibson's book, *Virtual Light*, for speculation along that front.

[3] The most common example involves spinning disks with concentric semicircles on them. The disk is white, and the circles are black.

not see objects that are really there,[4] or to see the same object in completely differ-ent ways. For example, Figure 8.2 shows a drawing of a cube. Depending on how your eyes perceive the cube, you can see it from either the bottom or the top.[5]

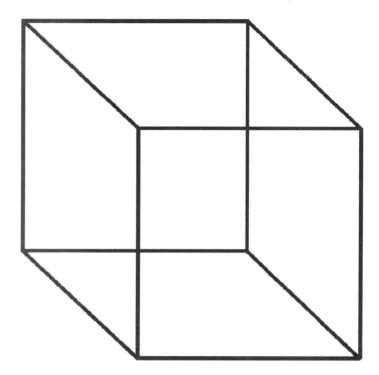

Figure 8.2
Another example of an optical illusion. The cube will sometimes appear to have its top toward you, and sometimes its bottom.

Figure 8.3 shows one of the most famous optical illusions, and one that is purely psychological in origin. What do you see when you look at Figure 8.3: the pedestal of a table (white) or two faces (black)?

In this chapter, you'll learn how the eye can be fooled into thinking things are real, and you'll also learn about *morphing*, the art and science of making it appear as though one object is being turned into another.

---

[4]The most common reason to not see things that are there is the development of an afterimage. Try staring at a tile floor sometime—the lines between the tiles will come and go, as the afterimage tends to cancel them out. This works best when the tiles and the lines between them are of contrasting colors or values.

[5]If you don't see both forms, just stare at the image for a while—the image will usually flip by itself without you having to do anything.

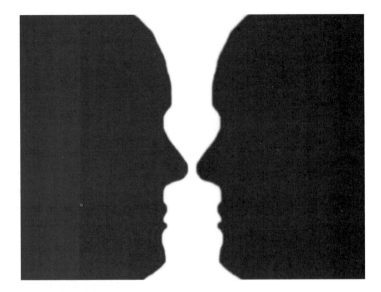

Figure 8.3
*What do you see? A
table pedestal or
faces?*

Seeing Is Not Believing

There are two elements of perception involved in seeing an object in a virtual reality. The first element, the physical and electrical systems, has been analyzed by various branches of science so that it is reasonably well understood. The second element, our attitudes (the willingness to believe), is perhaps an even more important consideration.

The folks who analyze literature for a living use the term *suspension of disbelief* to describe the process of becoming involved in a story. When you open a book, sit in a movie theater, or observe a play, you know for a fact that what you are observing does not reflect reality.[6] The book is just words on a page; the movie is just flickering light on a screen, and the actors are not who they seem to be. When you sit down at your computer to create or interact with a virtual space, you must likewise willingly suspend your disbelief. You must allow yourself to be deceived.[7]

It is impossible to quantify such things. The mechanics of seeing—which are better understood than attitudes—suffer from no such limitation.

---

[6]On the other hand, actors who play roles on television shows are forever receiving mail from fans who clearly don't understand that the character they see on television does not exist.

[7]I like the phrase "allow yourself to be deceived" better than "suspension of disbelief" for several reasons. One: It is more accurate. Two: It avoids indirection. (That's an indirect way of saying, "it is direct." Get the point?) Three: I like going against the grain.

Motion

The first trick that is used to fool the eye is *sequential imaging*. You know the technique by the more common names in use: *animation*, *movies*, and *video*. All these media use the same basic method to convince your eye that motion is occurring—putting a series of images in front of your eyes so fast that your eyes are fooled. The rate at which the images are presented is critical to the process. Movies and animation normally use a rate of 24 images per second, whereas video uses 30 frames per second.[8]

Digital video—video that has been converted to digital form and stored on a CD-ROM or a hard disk—is an emerging technology that has an increasing role in virtual reality. Digital video, however, must move from its current limitations—15 frames per second—in order to play a larger role.[9] The wide acceptance of digital video (thanks in large part to Video for Windows technology) is leading to rapid advances.

The frame rate is critical to the success of sequential imaging. However, not all parts of the eye respond to the trick equally well—and this has some important ramifications for virtual reality technology. To simulate reality more effectively, a VR display system should wrap around the user's head. This adds peripheral vision to the simulation. But peripheral vision uses a different part of your eye, and that part doesn't work like the part that you use to see directly in front of you.

The eye has two kinds of light receptors: rods and cones. *Cones* are located mostly in the center of your eye, and they are very good at distinguishing colors. *Rods* are located mostly around the edges of the eye, and they are very good at distinguishing differences in brightness. Therein lies the problem. The most noticeable defect when using frames to simulate motion is the change in brightness that occurs when you change from one frame to the next. The sequence goes like this:

- Frame 1 is displayed.
- Nothing is displayed.
- Frame 2 is displayed.

---

[8]Strictly speaking, this is not exact. Video is an *interlaced technology*. This means that half the image is put onto the screen first—every other horizontal line of pixels. This is called a *scan*, and the horizontal lines are called *scan lines*. In the second scan, the rest of the image is put onto the screen. These two scans constitute a single frame; each of the scans is commonly referred to as a *field*. Thus, each frame has two fields. The process is called *interlacing*, and if you have ever tried to work with a 1,024×768 video card using an interlaced signal, you know that the result of interlacing is flickering.

Thus, while video technology is the easiest to extend into virtual reality, it brings with it some potential flickering problems. Recent advances in television technology, such as HDTV, look more like the displays normally used on computers, which do not use interlacing and are thus much more stable.

[9]And that is happening now, as technology such as MPEG hardware—like the Jazz Jakarta or Sigma Designs' Real Magic video cards—deliver a full 30 frames per second.

The problem is that nothing is in the middle. Depending on the medium, it will be more or less obvious. A movie uses a shutter to block the light while the frame is advanced, whereas video intermixes the frames somewhat. In either case, the rods at the outer part of the eye are particularly susceptible to the change in brightness that is associated with frame changes. This means that your peripheral vision is most likely to be affected by a visual system with excess flicker. It also means that a wraparound display must be better at flicker reduction than the typical computer monitor.

Flicker can be annoying. The key to getting rid of it is to increase the frame rate. Since most headsets rely on video technology, which uses a frame rate of 30 frames per second,[10] new standards will have to be developed to smooth out the flicker. Computer monitors started out around 60 cycles per second (Hz), but the current standard is 72 or more. At 72 Hz, a monitor appears fairly steady, even to the rods in your retina. However, some monitors use frequencies of up to 90 Hz for rock-steady displays.

If a monitor is using a refresh rate of 90 cycles per second (Hz), then it must repaint every pixel 90 times each second. For a large monitor, that's a lot of pixels. For a headset that uses a wraparound display, that's also a lot of pixels. The more pixels, the more it is going to cost to keep the flicker at a low level.

The Third Dimension

Once the object and the virtual world are in motion, the next consideration is to convince the eye that the world exists in three dimensions. This is easier said than done. The history of motion 3D can be summed up in a few lines:

- Red/blue glasses
- Polarized glasses
- Shutter glasses
- Stereo headsets (HMDs)

Before we look more closely at these technologies, we need to answer a question: How do red/blue glasses, LCD glasses, and head-mounted devices manage to create a 3D effect on your flat computer screen? In real life, each eye sees a slightly different view of an object. Your brain merges these two views into a 3D view of the world. The trick with all kinds of glasses and HMDs is to make sure that each eye sees a different view of an object—then your brain will do what it usually does, and construct a 3D view of the virtual world.

---

[10]With two fields per frame because of interlacing, that's actually a "flicker rate" of 60 per second.

This whole 3D trick is based on a physical principle called *parallax*. Let's take a look at how this works; you can follow along at home. Get yourself a standard finger, pencil, or pen. Hold it in front of your nose (see Fig. 8.4). Close or cover your right eye, and note what you see. Figure 8.5 shows a view through a video camera that corresponds to what I see in my office through my left eye. Now close or cover your left eye. Figure 8.6 shows what I see in my office through my right eye.

Figure 8.4
Learning about parallax.

Figure 8.5
The view through the left eye.

Figure 8.6
The view through the right eye.

These two images, by the way, constitute a *stereo pair*. This is a pair of images which, if we can somehow project each image to the correct eye, will appear to be a realistic 3D image. All you need to make a stereo pair of images is two cameras—one for each eye position. In a virtual world, the cameras are virtual cameras—not real ones—but the principle is the same. By carefully setting the point of view for a pair of cameras in a virtual world, a very realistic 3D effect results.

You can create all kinds of 3D images with stereo pairs. The purplish blob in Figure 8.7 (OK, so it's in black and white here) shows a superimposed stereo pair you can view with red/blue glasses. It shows Mount St. Helens, and was created using a software product called Vistapro (see Chapter 1, "Virtual Reality Has Arrived"). To view the image, you must be wearing glasses that cover your left eye with a red lens and your right eye with a blue lens. The colored filters make sure that each eye sees only the view that is appropriate for it.

Another example illustrates a different kind of stereo pair. The images in Figures 8.8 and 8.9 show detail from a pair of stereo images created in a high-end 3D software product, 3D Studio. You might not be able to see much difference between the two images, but if they are properly presented to the correct eyes, your brain will still manage to see them correctly as 3D (see Fig. 8.10).

Figure 8.10 shows Figures 8.8 and 8.9 overlapped to show that they are, in fact, different.

Figure 8.7
A red/blue pair.

Figure 8.8
The view through the left eye.

Figure 8.9
The view through the right eye.

Figure 8.10
The two images
combined into one
to show differences.

Combined-Image 3D

We've established the basic mechanism for stereo (3D) vision: Your brain combines any two images it receives in separate eyes and creates the 3D effect right there in your head. This means that if we can

■ Capture two sets of images, one for each eye, and each from a different viewpoint, and

■ Find a way to present the separate images to the correct eyes

we can engage the brain to create a 3D image. Most 3D systems that use this method actually combine the two images into one image, and then use special glasses to send only the correct half of each image to the correct eye. The three kinds of glasses listed earlier use different techniques to achieve this result. The mechanism used to create images for each kind of glasses also differs.

Red/Blue Glasses

This is the easiest form of 3D technology, but it is also the least effective. To view the 3D image, you must wear glasses that use a blue film in one eye and a red film in the other. The source image contains overlapping blue and red versions of the scene. Figure 8.7 shows such an image in black and white, but you can make out the two images.

To create the image, all that is needed is something called a *stereo pair*. This is just a fancy term for two images that represent what your own eyes would see if they had been there instead of the camera that took the pictures.[11] One image is encoded using blue colors only, and the other image is encoded using only red colors. When

---

[11]This is not always exactly true. To enhance the 3D effect, you can increase the distance between the two cameras. Instead of using a few inches between the cameras to mimic the distance between our eyes, you can move the cameras several feet—or even more—apart. If the cameras are moved too far apart, this can destroy the 3D effect, however.

you view the image, the red image goes to one eye, and the blue image goes to the other eye—thanks to the colored filters in the glasses. The result is a so-so 3D image.

Polarized Glasses

Polarized glasses also put both images into a single image, but instead of using color, this technique relies on the capability to polarize light.[12] It is most commonly used with movie projection. When the image for one eye is projected onto the screen, light polarized at a specific angle is used. The corresponding lens on the glasses has a filter on it that will only allow light polarized at that angle to enter. The image for the other eye uses a polarization angle that is different by 90 degrees. The corresponding lens on the glasses also has a matching polarizing angle. The result is that each eye sees only the image intended for it.

A significant advantage of the polarized technique is that you can use real colors in each image, so the resulting 3D view is much better than with red/blue glasses. The disadvantage, of course, is the need for equipment to polarize the light.

Shutter Glasses

Shutter glasses take a kind of brute-force approach to the problem. Each lens contains a shutter that simply blocks the view of the eye on that side when the shutter is closed. This method works well with video sources—if you recall, a video frame is actually made up of two fields. If we put the image for one eye in one field, and for the other eye in the other field, the shutter can be used to block the "wrong" field for each eye. The result is that each eye sees only the information that is intended for it.

The downside to shutter glasses is that they effectively cut the vertical resolution in half. This method also requires heavier, more complicated, and costlier glasses than either of the other methods. This disadvantage is offset by the fact that little or no special equipment is needed to encode the images.

The glasses themselves aren't like regular glasses—they aren't made of just glass. They are made from the same material used in LCD computer screens, watches, etc. When an electrical current is applied, the lens can be made transparent or opaque. By applying current to one or the other lens, the computer can control which lens is open quite precisely. There are special crystals inside the lenses that twist when an electric

---

[12]If you are not familiar with the polarization of light, here is a simple explanation. Light behaves like a wave. Normally, light waves vibrate every which way. A polarizer restricts the vibrations to one direction—for example, up and down. A beam thus polarized can be used for one image, and one polarized to a side-to-side vibration can be used for the other image. Each side of the glasses has a set of ultra-tiny, parallel slits that only allow light matching the polarization to enter the slits.

current is applied. Twisted one way, they let light through. Twisted another way, they block the light.

You might not be aware of it, but your computer monitor gets a new image 56, 60, 72, or more times each second. Let's slow down the process and see what happens when you use LCD glasses to display a stereo pair.

In the first 60th of a second, the left image of the stereo pair is displayed on your computer screen (see Fig. 8.11). At the same time, a signal is sent to the LCD glasses. This causes the left lens to go clear, and the right image to go dark. As a result, only your left eye sees the image (see Fig. 8.12).

Figure 8.11
The left image of a stereo pair.

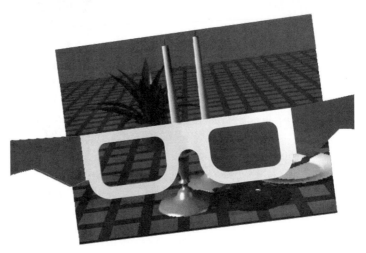

Figure 8.12
The left eye is clear, the right is closed.

In the second 60th of a second, the right image of the stereo pair appears on the computer screen (see Fig. 8.13). A signal goes to the LCD glasses, telling them to switch— the left lens goes dark, the right lens goes clear. Now the right eye sees the image intended for it (see Fig. 8.14).

Figure 8.13
The right image of a stereo pair.

Figure 8.14
The right eye is clear, the left is closed.

This switching continues at the rate of 60 times per second. Without glasses, you would see both images at one time (see Fig. 8.15). The LCD glasses are connected to your computer by a wire, and that wire is used to send the electric signals that alternate dark and clear in both lenses. Each eye sees the correct image about 30 times a second. A normal video display uses at least 60 images per second, and even that may cause a little flicker—72 times per second is about right for smooth display. At 30 times per second, LCD glasses flicker noticeably, but the 3D effect is quite clear.

Figure 8.15
Both images
combined into one.

You can purchase a frequency doubler from 3DTV (the Stereospace), which works with some software products to output images at 120 times per second, so each eye sees a reasonably steady 60 images per second. However, only very high-quality monitors will support 120 Hz refresh rates.

Headsets (HMDs)

Headsets offer a much more effective way of presenting 3D information to the eye. Instead of putting both images on a single screen, a headset usually has a separate screen for each eye built into the headset. A separate image is built for each eye, and then sent to the appropriate tiny screen inside the headset. Lenses allow you to see the image clearly, even though the tiny screen is no more than an inch or two in front of your eye.

The positive side of this equation is that flicker is easier to tackle. Instead of having one large screen that must be kept flicker free, even while displaying images at double speed, each eye has its own miniature TV screen. This cuts the flicker problem in half.

The negative side of headsets, at least so far, is the size and weight involved. Some of the lightest headsets are also the least powerful—they manage to stay small by using extra tiny (and very low resolution) screens. This cuts the weight—and the price—but it doesn't deliver much "reality."

Options

As a general rule, there are two points in the 3D process where costs and technology get in the way: creating the image and decoding the image. The best balance of quality, cost, and convenience is probably shutter glasses. Red/blue glasses are easy to use, but image quality is inferior. Polarizing is effective but requires a projection system. Shutter glasses cost more than other kinds of 3D glasses, but they provide the capability to create images at a minimal cost.

Multiple Images

The ideal VR system would put a separate image in front of each eye. Wraparound, head-mounted displays will make this possible. Currently, this technology is going through a process that laptop LCD screens went through several years ago. The manufacturing capacity of the industry is waiting for demand, and demand is waiting for the manufacturing capacity to increase and bring down prices.

Until there is an advance that will move this stalemate off dead center, the cost of even modest-quality, head-mounted displays will be high—more than $1,000. There are some HMDs at lower prices, but they are basically just televisions that hang in front of your eyes.

Bending Reality to Fit

Let's back away from 3D a bit to look at a fascinating technology that has only recently moved from the realm of the super computer to the desktop: morphing. *Morphing* is the art of appearing to transform one object or picture into another. You'll learn about two products in this chapter: Elastic Reality—quite possibly the coolest piece of desktop software anywhere—and PhotoMorph.

RECIPE

1 copy Elastic Reality
1 starting image or video clip
1 ending image or video clip
A dash of flash and panache
1 Media Player, VidEdit, or Adobe Premiere

Instructions: This is gourmet cooking at its best—easy to whip up, but your guests will inevitably be stunned by the subtle flavors of this dish. Served in all the best video studios and a Hollywood favorite for years, this scrumptious product is now available for home use.

There are a number of commercial and shareware morphing products on the market. My favorite, hands down, is Elastic Reality. In the first edition of this book, the Best in Class was another excellent product: PhotoMorph. This is still a wonderful product—see the next section of this chapter for the details—and version 2.0 of PhotoMorph is included on the CD-ROMs. Elastic Reality marks an important watershed in desktop morphing. Formerly available only for the SGI (Silicon Graphics) platform, Elastic Reality has been used for many of the special effects you see on TV and at the movies. Whether Elastic Reality is busy morphing Dracula into a bat in an Energizer Bunny commercial or creating the amazing morphs in the movie *Wolf*, it is one powerful piece of professional software.

This presented a problem while I was testing the software and writing about it. There are levels of cool when it comes to software. Some software is mildly cool and quite enjoyable. Other software is very cool and hard to put down—Vistapro is a good example. Rarely, a product comes along that I can only call mega cool—so hot, so exciting, that you simply cannot put it away. To shut it down becomes an offense against one's inner child. One can only be dragged kicking and screaming from such fun. I'm a bit jaded—after all, I have access to just about everything in VR—but I still fell head over heels in love with Elastic Reality. There was no way I wanted to stop playing with it and start writing about it. There was always one more special effect to try, one more feature to explore. Therefore, be warned: This is addictive stuff. If you bought the first edition of this book and became hooked on Vistapro, that was nothing. Elastic Reality bends and twists reality so cleanly that you'll find yourself always wanting just one more morph.

If you somehow manage to satisfy your cravings for the ultimate morph, you are still not home free. Elastic Reality does much more than mere morphs. It is a real studio in a box; you can create mattes or traveling mattes, create composites, do A/B rolls, and incorporate backgrounds. This is a powerful, flexible, and versatile package.

Figure 8.16 shows two images taken from a professionally done morph created with Elastic Reality.

As clean and impressive as the morphs you create with Elastic Reality are, they are not that hard to do. Follow along as I show you how it's done.

Elastic Reality runs under Windows. If you are familiar with typical Windows programs, it will be easy to use Elastic Reality. Figure 8.17 shows the opening window for the program.

Figure 8.16
Even Ulysses S. Grant can be made to smile with Elastic Reality.

All the tools above and to the left of the main window are gray—you can't use the tools until you load one or more images. If you load one image, you can use Elastic Reality to warp the image—enlarge eyes, puff out cheeks, or otherwise animate a still image. If you load two images, you can morph from one image to the other, as the following example shows.

Figure 8.18 shows a completed project loaded into Elastic Reality. Note that you can see both images at the same time, as well as the control lines that define the level of detail in the morph. Look in the color section of this book to see how the program uses color to distinguish the morphing lines for each image. In black and white, you can't tell which of the lines over the faces belongs to which image.

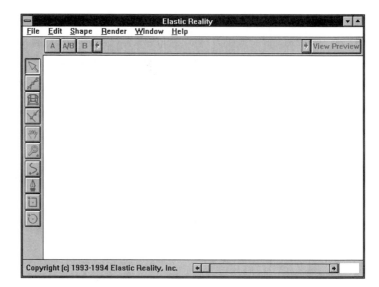

Figure 8.17
*The opening window
of Elastic Reality.*

I have created control lines for each image. Figure 8.19 shows the starting image of a man, including the control lines. Figure 8.20 shows the image without the control lines.

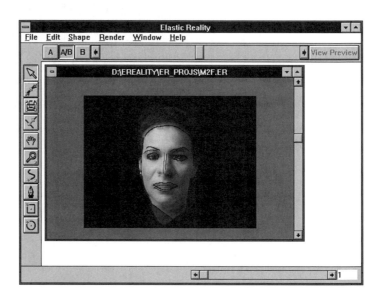

Figure 8.18
*A completed Elastic
Reality project,
showing both
images at the same
time.*

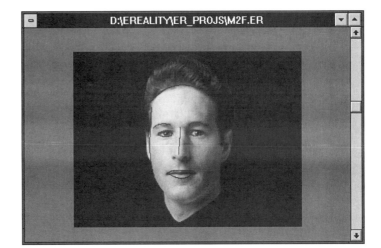

Figure 8.19
*The starting image
for the morph, with
control lines.*

Figure 8.20
*The starting image
for the morph.*

There are probably an infinite number of ways you can arrange control lines for any given morph. Learning what kinds of lines to use and where to put them gives you a great deal of power and control. In Figure 8.21, I have added control lines for all the major features and outlines involved:

- A line down the middle of the nose
- A line outlining the top of the head
- A line outlining the hairline
- A line outlining the lips
- A line outlining each ear

- A line down the middle of each eyebrow
- A line around each eye

For every control line in the starting image, you'll need a corresponding line in the ending image. Figure 8.21 shows the ending image with control lines, and Figure 8.22 shows just the image. Note how the lines in Figure 8.21 are on or near the same physical features used in Figure 8.19.

Figure 8.21
The ending image for the morph, including control points.

Figure 8.22
The ending image for the morph.

Let's look at how a single pair of control lines was created for this morph. Figure 8.23 shows a close-up of the man's eye. I used the Freehand tool to roughly outline the eye. I then used the Reshape tool to carefully align the control line with the outline of the eye. A control line is made up of segments, with control points where the segments join. You can use the same techniques to adjust and reshape a control line that you would use on a Bézier curve in a typical desktop publishing illustration package like Corel or Illustrator.

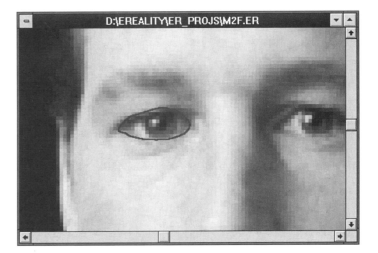

Figure 8.23
Using the Freehand and Reshape tools to add a control line.

This control line defines the starting image of the eye. It will control the position and size of the eye during the morph. If the morph occurs over 30 frames, the eye will move 1/30th of the distance toward its final position in the final image for each frame.

Starting and ending control lines must have the same number of segments. The easiest way to make sure that this is so is to use the Clipboard. Click the control line to select it, and then copy it to the Clipboard (choose the Edit/Copy menu selection). Click the B button at the top left to see the ending image, and then choose Edit/Paste to insert a copy of the control line. You can then use the Reshape tool to change the size and shape of the control line to match the eye in the ending image. Figure 8.24 shows the result.

By pressing the A/B button, you can view both images at the same time (see Fig. 8.25). You can see both images overlapped, as well as both of the control lines. When the images are overlapped, the differences between the two control lines are easy to see. One is lower than the other, and one is taller than the other.

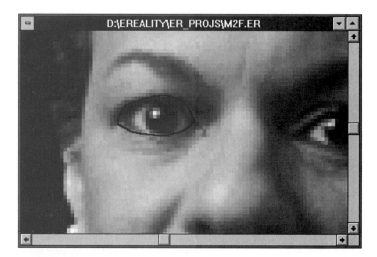

Figure 8.24
The control line has been copied to the ending image and reshaped to fit.

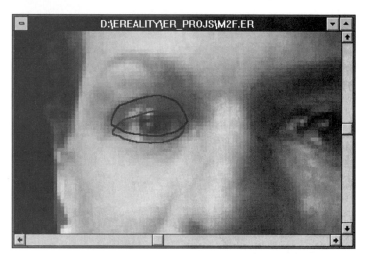

Figure 8.25
Viewing both images with the A/B button pressed.

We have now created the starting and ending control lines for the morph, but there is more to do. Click on the smaller of the two control lines (the one from the starting male image) to select it. This displays a bounding box around the control line (see Fig. 8.26).

While holding down the Shift key, click on the second (ending) control line. Now both control lines display their bounding boxes (see Fig. 8.27).

Now comes the magic part—while both control lines are selected, press the J key (for Join). This tells Elastic Reality to join the two control lines for morphing purposes. The line you select first is always the starting control line, and the line you click second is always the ending line.

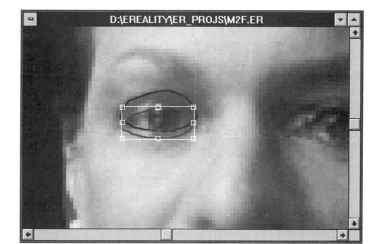

Figure 8.26
Selecting a control line displays its bounding box.

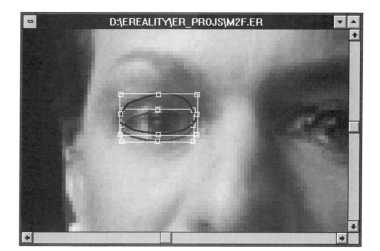

Figure 8.27
Both control lines are selected.

Figure 8.28 shows the result. The bounding boxes are now made up of dashed lines. The starting box has long dashed lines, and the ending box has shorter dashed lines. This allows you to keep track of which is which.

You can control the level of fine detail during the morph by setting the edge density. Click on the Correspondence tool to display the current edge density (see Fig. 8.29). This shows up as yellow dashed lines between the two control lines. To change the edge density, click the Window/Shape Options menu selection. This displays the dialog box shown in Figure 8.30. Use the slider bar at the top to increase or decrease edge density. Increasing edge density will improve the way that Elastic Reality controls the morph from one frame to the next.

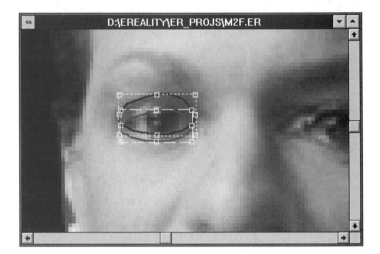

Figure 8.28
*The control lines are
now part of a
morph.*

Earlier, I mentioned the Reshape tool. Let's look at how you can use this tool to easily change the shape of a control line.[13] Figure 8.31 shows a close-up of the control line for the woman's lips. Note that the control line is defined by a series of points shown as small white squares.

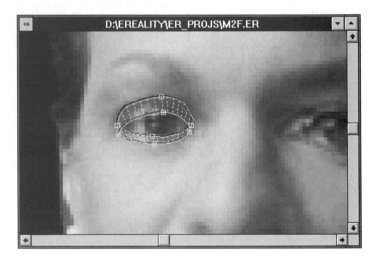

Figure 8.29
*Displaying edge
density.*

---

[13]Control lines aren't the only way you can control morphing. You can also use the Ellipse and Rectangle tools to add closed control shapes. Control lines can be open, as for the nose; or closed, as for the eyes. Ellipses and rectangles are always closed.

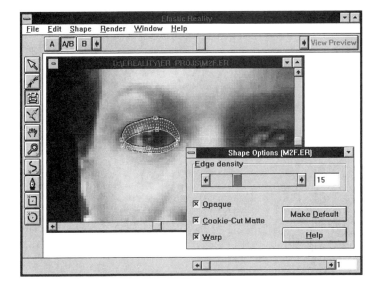

Figure 8.30
Changing edge density.

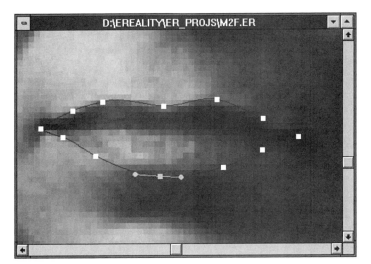

Figure 8.31
A close-up view of another control line.

In Figure 8.31, one of the points has two small circles next to it, connected by lines (look at the bottom of the lower lip). You can change the shape of a control line in two ways. You can move the points themselves, or you can use those two little circles to change the way that the shape curves. These curves are called Bézier curves.[14] Figure 8.32 shows the result of dragging out the little circles (called *handles*).

---

[14]Named after a Frenchman; approximate pronunciation is *Bezz-ee-ay* curves.

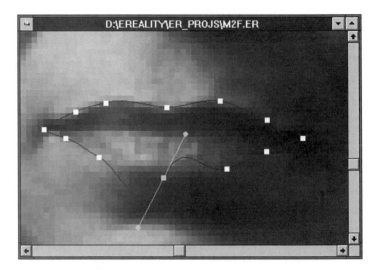

Figure 8.32
Changing the shape of a control line using handles on a point.

When you have created control lines for all the main features in your images, you are ready to create your morph. Figure 8.33 shows a close-up view of the two images and the control points using the A/B button. I created morphing pairs using the J key for each corresponding pair of control lines.

Figure 8.33
A close-up view of the control lines for both images.

Note that in Figure 8.33 there is a slider control at the bottom right. The slider is all the way to the left, indicating frame 1 of the morph. To see a wireframe preview of the morph, drag the slider slowly from left to right.[15]

To create a single-frame preview, position the slider in the middle of the control at frame 15 (by default, a morph consists of 30 frames, but it's easy to change this number using the Window/Output Options dialog box). Press Ctrl+P (or use the Render/ Render Preview menu selection) to activate preview mode, and wait a few seconds for the preview to complete. Figure 8.34 shows what frame 15 looks like. To create the final morph, use the Window/Output options to set the type of output you want— bitmaps, AVI files, and many popular (and many obscure!) other file formats. Use the Render/Render Final menu selection to output to disk. Look in the color section to see a series of frames from the morph.

Figure 8.34
The middle frame of the morph.

As pleasing as these results are, this is just a small part of what you can accomplish with Elastic Reality. You can also create many different kinds of special effects. Let's look at just one quick example.

Figure 8.35 shows the Sequence Editor. This is used to load multiple images. The top line is for the A image or sequence, the second for the B image or sequence, the third

---

[15]You can also play the wireframe animation automatically. Use the Window/Wireframe Controller menu selection to display the Wireframe Controller dialog box.

for a matte, and the fourth for the background. You can have one or more lines with an image or sequence, depending on the effect you want to create.[16]

In Figure 8.35, an A image and a background image have been added using the Insert menu selection on the menu bar. The A image will appear over the background image of a lightning flash.

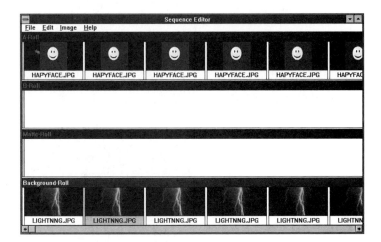

Figure 8.35
Using the Sequence Editor.

Figure 8.36 shows the A image in the Elastic Reality window. I have added a circle around the smiley face, and there is a second circle partially visible at the upper left. These are a morphing pair; note the dashed lines that make up their bounding boxes. By setting the background as a cookie-cutter matte, only the portion of the A image within the starting bounding box will appear over the background. I also used the Window/Render Options dialog box to change the relationship of the two control lines—the ending control line at the upper left will control the position of the starting image rather than provide a morph. I created a simple 30-frame animation of the ending circle; Figure 8.37 shows an intermediate frame of the animation with the ending circle just below and to the left of the starting circle.

---

[16]For the previous example, in which we morphed a man's face into a woman's, the man's face was loaded into the A Roll sequence, and the woman's face was loaded into the B Roll sequence. Now you know why we pressed the A, A/B, and B buttons to view the images!

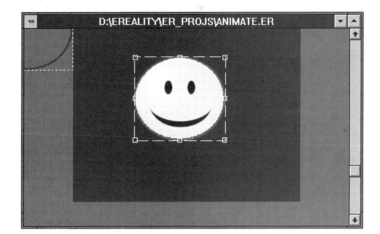

Figure 8.36
Starting and ending control shapes are in place.

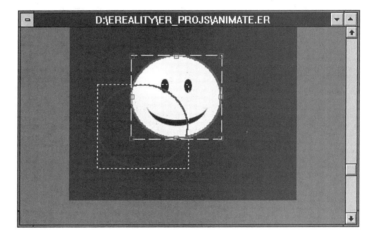

Figure 8.37
The ending control shape has been moved in frame 13.

Pressing Ctrl+P to render frame 13 results in the image shown in Figure 8.38. This image retains the control shapes for your reference. Figure 8.39 shows the actual image with the control shapes removed.

Figure 8.38
*A preview of frame
13 of the animation.*

Figure 8.39
*A rendering of
frame 13.*

Using this technique, you can easily overlay objects from one image, animation, or video clip onto another image, animation, or video clip.

If you really want to explore Elastic Reality—and there is plenty to explore that I don't have room to even touch on here—there is only one way to do it: cold, hard cash. But if there was ever one program that you might want to buy instead of lunch, this is it.

The Morph the Merrier

Good morphing software must not only follow the basic rules for morphing but must be sensitive to various nuances of the morphing process. PhotoMorph does an excellent job of balancing all these requirements, and the newest edition adds a host of extra features that create some exciting possibilities. You'll find a complete copy of PhotoMorph 2.0 on the CD-ROMs.

RECIPE

1 copy PhotoMorph 2.0
1 starting image
1 final image
10-100 little square dots
1 Media Player or VidEdit

Instructions: This is a real taste treat. However, the recipe calls for a light touch—sort of like working up a soufflé or a puff pastry. Take two images, roughly similar in outline if possible, then dot lightly with square-dot sprinkles. Careful positioning is a must! Serve the AVI output in Windows, or slice into BMPs or DIBs for animation software.

I have included a number of PhotoMorph examples on the CD-ROMs. One of the neatest features of PhotoMorph is that it outputs AVI files. You can view these easily by using the Windows Media Player. Along with Vistapro, PhotoMorph is very high on my personal must-have software list. Look for a new version of PhotoMorph to appear on the market soon, which fully supports Windows 95 and adds a number of new, exciting features.

Figure 8.40 shows the basic PhotoMorph program windows. The main window has a separate window in it called the Project Editor. Most of your work takes place in the Project Editor. As you open image files to use in the Project Editor, they appear in the main window behind the Editor.

PhotoMorph is a bit like two programs in one. You can load bitmaps into the main window, where you can perform various operations on them as needed. You can add borders, change the contrast of an image, convert file types, and so on. You will probably still use your favorite photo-paint software for major image manipulation, but you can always perform simple adjustments at the last minute in PhotoMorph.[17]

---

[17]One nice feature of PhotoMorph is that you can use 32-bit image files. Such files contain their own masking channel, which means that PhotoMorph will automatically work only on the part of the image within the mask.

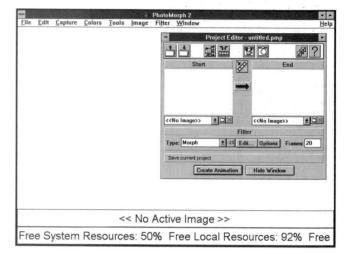

Figure 8.40
The basic
PhotoMorph
windows.

Morphing is simple, and morphing is complex. The simple side involves the method used for morphing. You simply place a point on an image and then tell the morph program where that point should wind up in the final image. After entering a series of points, you let the software perform the morph. The complex side involves the art of placing those points where they will do the most good.

Let's look at an example. There are two files on the CD-ROMs that you can use for this example. They are DOLPHIN.BMP and EYE.BMP. To load these images into the Project Editor, click on the small folder icons to the right of the file names. Load DOLPHIN.BMP into the left frame, marked **Start**. Load EYE.BMP into the right frame, marked **End**. This loads the two image files into the main window and into the Project Editor (see Fig. 8.41).

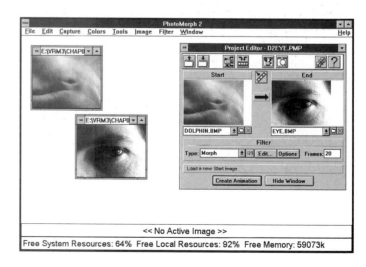

Figure 8.41
Two images loaded
into the Project
Editor.

There are many controls in the Project Editor, and you'll learn about those in the next section. For now, simply click the Edit button at the right of the Filter type Morph. This displays the editing window (see Fig. 8.42).

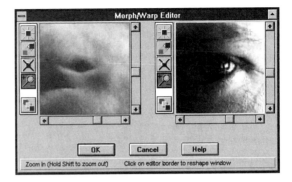

Figure 8.42
The editing window.

When you enter the Morph Editor, there are five buttons at the left of each of the images. From top to bottom, these buttons are

■ Create a New Dot

■ Move a Dot

■ Delete a Dot

■ Enlarge/Reduce Image

■ Go To Next Image

Clicking a button changes the operating mode of the window. For example, when you click the top button (Create a New Dot), any time you click in that image, a new dot will be created.[18] If you click the Enlarge/Reduce button, the cursor changes to a magnifying glass and will alter the scale of that image until you click a new icon. The editing window is resizeable, but you must use the Enlarge/Reduce icon to change the scale of an image.

I used the Magnification icon to enlarge the eye portions of both images—this is where most of the morphing takes place. Note that there are square dots in both images.

I carefully adjusted the position of each key dot in both images. If a dot was at the corner of the eye in the dolphin image, I made sure that the corresponding key dot in the other image was also exactly at the corner of the eye. Because the sizes of the eyes are different in the two images, this involved a lot of moving around of the dots.

---

[18]As a general rule, you should create one dot at a time. Adjust that dot's position in both images before you create another dot. If you create too many dots at once, you will lose track of which dot is which.

When I had the dots where I wanted them,[19] I saved the changes by clicking the OK button and returned to the Project Editor. I clicked the Create Animation button, and it took a few seconds for the AVI file to be generated.[20] This file (D2EYE.AVI) is on the CD-ROMs. Figure 8.43 shows a sequence of frames from the morph. As you can see, the images blend smoothly.[21]

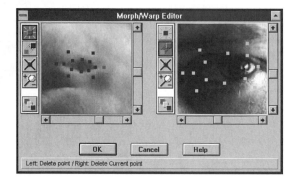

Figure 8.43
A frame from the morph animation.

More Than Morphing

Before we move on, let's take a moment to list and describe the basic features and controls you'll find in PhotoMorph. Most of the morphing work is done in the Project Editor, which is shown in Figure 8.44. There is a row of buttons across the top of the window, and two image windows marked Start and End. The currently open images are listed under both of these windows for easy access. The little folder icons next to the file names enable you to easily add more image files to the list.

 Load Project—Loads a project file from disk.

 Save Project—Saves the current project to disk.

 Animation Controls—Displays additional controls related to AVI file creation, such as compression method. This is a toggle control (see Fig. 8.45).

---

[19] Where to put the dots is the subject of much of this chapter—don't expect to just lay down a few dots and get a world-class morph right away. By the end of this chapter, you will learn enough skills to give you a good idea of where to put those dots for your own morph. However, you will probably find that there is a certain irreducible amount of trial and error in the morphing process.

[20] One of the nice features of PhotoMorph is the speed with which it creates the morph output.

[21] This is much clearer if you play the AVI file itself. Still, black-and-white images cannot convey the subtlety of the morph.

Figure 8.44
The PhotoMorph Project Editor.

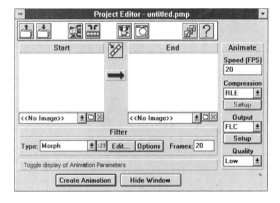

Figure 8.45
Animation file creation controls (at the right).

 Storyboard Controls—Toggles display of controls related to storyboarding (see Fig. 8.46).

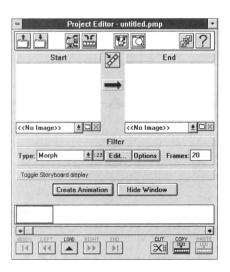

Figure 8.46
Storyboard controls (at the bottom).

AVI Player—Displays the AVI player (see Fig. 8.47). This is a toggle control.

Figure 8.47
AVI Player.

 Preview Window—Displays the Preview window (see Fig. 8.48).

Figure 8.48
The Preview display.

 Preferences—Opens the Preferences dialog box (see Fig. 8.49).

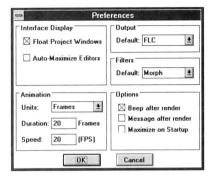

Figure 8.49
Setting preferences.

 Help—Accesses Help files.

Below the images is the Filter section (refer to Fig. 8.44). There are several controls here: the type of the filter (Warp, Morph, Distort, and others), a 123 button, an Edit button, an Options button, and a Frames control.

The filter type dictates what you see after you click the Edit button. Each filter has its own settings. In the previous example, we did a morph. Later in this section, you'll see how the other filters work. The 123 button steps you through the various phases of a project—you can use more than one filter by using the Storyboard option. For example, you could warp a starting image, and then use the warped image to morph into yet another image.

The Edit button takes you to the editing screen where you place and move those little square dots for a morph or warp, or change filter settings for the other filters.

The Option button allows you to change the options for a given filter.

The Frames control tells PhotoMorph how many frames to create in the AVI file. More frames means a smoother morph.

At the bottom of the window are two buttons: Create Animation and Hide Window. The former creates the output file, and the latter hides the project window.[22]

There is also a button between the Start and End windows. This button adds a new set of key frames to the storyboard (see Fig. 8.50).

---

[22]You can redisplay it from the menus.

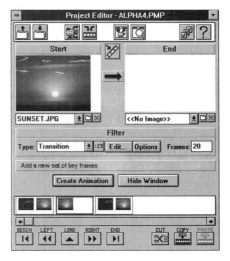

Figure 8.50
Adding new key frames to the storyboard.

Let's take a look at some of the different kinds of filters included with PhotoMorph. In Figure 8.51, I have loaded an image of an elk into the Start window.[23] I have used the Filter drop-down box to change the filter type to Distort. Figure 8.52 shows what you will see when you click the Edit button if the filter type is Distort.

Figure 8.51
An image loaded in the Start window.

[23]You might have noticed that the background behind the elk is dark. This is not an accident; it's on purpose. PhotoMorph supports 32-bit images. The background has been masked in an image-editing program that also supports 32-bit imaging. This means that, when PhotoMorph uses this image, filters will apply only to the unmasked area. Figure 8.50 showed this; go back and take a look. I have also included a color version of this figure in the color section of the book, where the masking effect is easier to see.

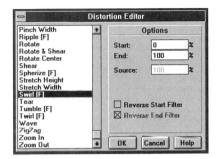

Figure 8.52
Choosing the type of distortion.

You can choose any distortion type you want. For this example, I chose Swirl. Figure 8.52 shows the settings for this type of distortion. If you choose other kinds of distortions, you may see different values at the right side of the dialog box. Figure 8.53 shows what you see when you click the Options button. You can change the effect of the distortion (or any other filter) by using the Options button. In this example, the rate of apparent movement has been altered to slow it down at the beginning of the swirl.

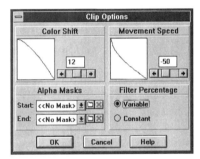

Figure 8.53
Setting filter options.

Once you have the setting you want for Edit and Options, it's a simple matter to create the output file. Simply click the Create Animation button at the bottom of the Project Editor. You'll see a dialog box asking you for the file name (see Fig. 8.54), and while the file is being created, you'll see a progress dialog box (see Fig. 8.55). Figure 8.56 shows a single frame from the animation.

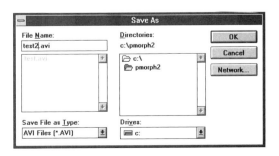

Figure 8.54
Entering a file name.

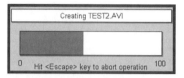

Figure 8.55
Progress meter.

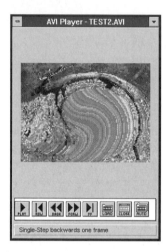

Figure 8.56
*A frame from the
Swirl effect.*

Let's try another filter: Warp. Use the drop-down box for Filter Type to change to warping (see Fig. 8.57). Click the Edit button to edit the warp. You'll see the same editor you encountered earlier when we did a morph (see Fig. 8.58). A warp is a lot like a morph, but it uses the same image for start and end. You enter the control dots just like you did for a morph, but instead of morphing from one image to another, you simply bend or warp the start image.

Figure 8.57
*Editing a Warp
filter.*

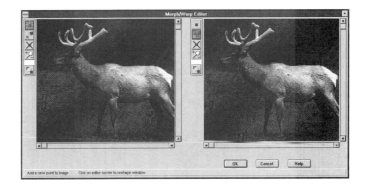

Figure 8.58
*Setting Warp as the
filter type.*

Figure 8.59 shows the starting points for a warp. I have added control points along the elk's back. Figure 8.60 shows ending points that will make the elk's back much higher, like the hump of a camel.

Figure 8.59
*Starting points for
the warp.*

Figure 8.60
*Ending points for
the warp.*

Figure 8.61 shows a frame from the midpoint of the warp, and Figure 8.62 shows the final result. Figure 8.63 shows a different warp, which uses a different set of control points arranged in a straight line above the back. Warps offer a limitless set of possibilities for modifying illustrations.

Figure 8.61
The midpoint of the warp.

Figure 8.62
The endpoint of the warp.

Figure 8.64 shows yet another kind of filter: Colorize. This allows you to choose from the wide variety of color operations shown at the left of the dialog box. The right side of the dialog box shows a preview of the effect. You can use the slider under the preview to see any frame of the animation.

Figure 8.63
A different warp, for comparison.

Figure 8.64
Using a Colorize filter.

You can also overlay one image over another, as shown in Figure 8.65. An image of an apple has been loaded into the Start window, and the Elk image is loaded into the End window. Figure 8.65 shows the editing window for an overlay, where I have chosen the Luminance type of overlay (the black around the apple will disappear, showing the underlying elk image, as shown in Fig. 8.66).

Figure 8.65
The Overlay filter.

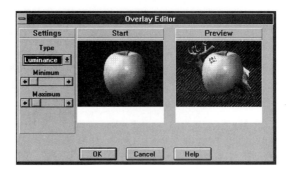

Figure 8.66
The result of the overlay.

Figure 8.67 shows the Transition Editor, yet another kind of filter. This example shows the Explode filter. The apple image will explode, revealing the car image beneath it. For fun, I applied a melt subfilter to the apple, and a random noise filter to the car. Figures 8.68 through 8.71 show frames from the resulting animation.

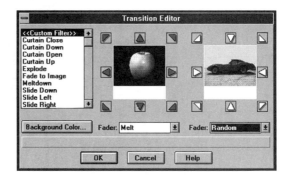

Figure 8.67
An Explode transition.

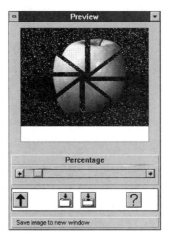

Figure 8.68
The start of the explosion.

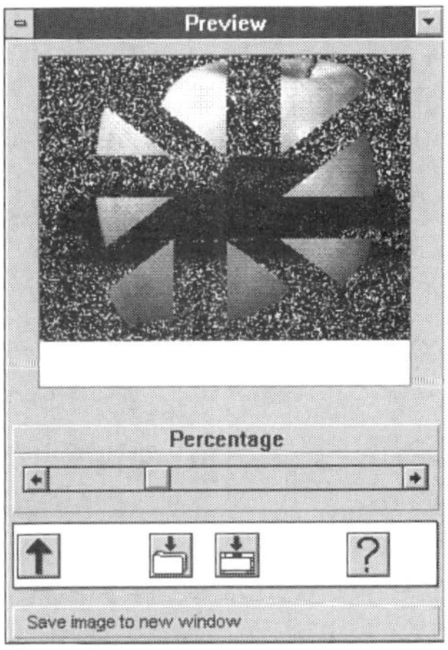

Figure 8.69
The apple continues to explode, and the car is just visible now.

Figure 8.70
The explosion is nearly done, and the car is clearly visible.

Figure 8.71
The final frame of the animation.

As you work with PhotoMorph, it keeps all the current files for the project available in the workspace, as shown in Figure 8.72. If you need to lighten an image, change contrast, or perform other basic operations, you can simply click on the image to bring up a floating menu.

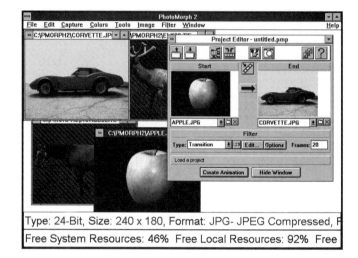

Figure 8.72
The PhotoMorph
workspace in action.

Video + Video = Video

Morphing still images, while fun and exciting, is just one step along the way to getting the most out of morphing. The really cool morphs—the ones you see at the movies and on TV—involve motion. If we are going to use morphing to create alternate reality, motion is required. The impact is much more dramatic than it is for still images.

PhotoMorph allows you to use two AVI video clips for input, and will produce a morph AVI as output. To pull this off, you are going to have to follow the same rules (and tedious procedures) that the Big Guys in Hollywood have to follow:

Rule #1—All motion must be planned for and controlled.

Rule #2—Careful attention to detail is the only way to ensure a smooth morph.

Rule #3—If at first you don't succeed, modify, modify, and then modify again.

Let's look at a motion morph. The following example is taken from the sample images that come with PhotoMorph 2.0 on the CDs, so you can follow along at home. To begin, of course, you must have installed the software from the CDs to your hard disk.

Run PhotoMorph by double-clicking. In the Project Editor, load two AVI clips: one into the Start image and one into the End image. Figure 8.73 shows the file CHRIS26.AVI as the starting image and EDIE26.AVI as the ending image. You load video clips in the same way that you load a single image. The direct approach is simplest: click on the small folder icon just below the right bottom corner of the image window. This displays a File Open dialog box, and you can select any valid AVI file.

Figure 8.73
Loading AVI files for morphing is as easy as loading single image files.

In this example, both video clips contain extremely similar motion and framing. In both cases, the person's head rotates slowly, and each is a head-and-shoulders shot. This is in keeping with Rules #1 and #2—control and detail are what make a morph successful. Even so, there are some problems evident in the beginning frame match-up. The man has long hair, but it's arranged in a ponytail, while the woman's hair is fuller and has nothing to tie it down. In addition, the man's ear is exposed, while the woman's is not. These are issues that must be dealt with during the morph, plus any additional issues that appear in later frames.

When you have loaded both images, the process of adding morph points can begin. When you perform a morph on a pair of images, you create only one set of control points. You might imagine that you'll need a separate set of control points for each matching pair of frames in the video clips. Fortunately, PhotoMorph uses Smart Points to make the job simpler. *Smart Points*, used only in video morphs, repeat automatically from frame to frame. You still have to drag them around, of course, but you don't have to remember how many points you put in frame 1 when you go to edit frame 2.

You can also perform a "morph" without setting any control points at all. However, that's nothing more than a fade from one image to another; it's not really a morph at all. Almost any video editor will do that much for you. As you'll see shortly, morphing can be much more effective than a simple fade.

When you click on the Edit button to enter control points, the Morph/Warp Editor window looks very familiar (see Fig. 8.74). There's one important difference, however: the scroll bar below the images. The scroll bar is used to move from frame to frame in both video clips.

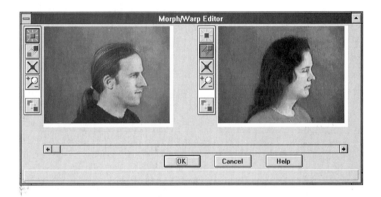

Figure 8.74
*Editing a video clip
morph.*

As you can see in Figure 8.74, the scroll bar starts out at the far left, which means you begin with frame 1 of each video clip—a very good place to start. Your job is to place control points as you would for any morph, paying special attention to boundaries and features. Figure 8.75 shows the first point: right on the nose. However, because a motion morph only keeps each frame on-screen for a fraction of a second, you do not need to control the points, or place as many points, as you might for a simple morph. Figure 8.76 shows a good starting set of points. [24]

There are a few things worth noting about the placement of the control points. First, there are two points used to define the man's ear. Normally, I would probably use at least six, because quite a bit of movement would occur during the morph between

---

[24]It might even be too many, but I'm conservative.

the ears in both images. However, as the head turns, the ear will disappear, so I only have to control it for a limited number of frames.[25] There are two corresponding points defining the woman's ear (or as much of it as is visible through her hair). They are much closer together. That means that, during the morph frames where ears are visible, there will be a size change based on the location of the control points in both images.

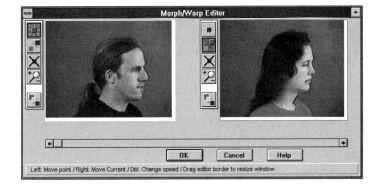

Figure 8.75
Placing the first control point.

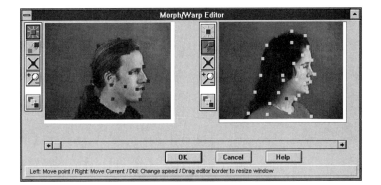

Figure 8.76
A starting set of control points.

The next step is to move forward through the video clips as far as you can without losing track of what the points are for. Figure 8.77 shows frame 4 of both clips. The heads have started to turn, so the control points no longer line up with the features in the images. The next task, therefore, is to move the control points so they match up with the proper features and boundaries in the images.

---

[25]You can delete control points later in the morph if they are no longer needed. The points will still remain in the earlier frames.

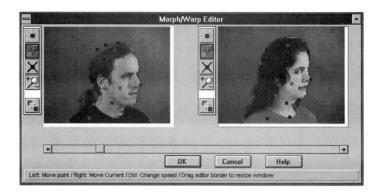

Figure 8.77
Moving to a new set of frames in the clips causes misalignment of the control points.

Figure 8.78 shows the control points adjusted for frame 4. There are still two points for the ears, and I have realigned all points to correspond to relevant features. A second eye has begun to reveal itself in both images, so I have shifted one of the control points to take over the job of tracking that eye. The important thing is that the control points for any frame correspond to similar features in both images.

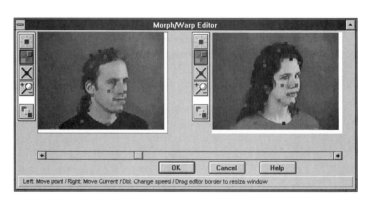

Figure 8.78
The control points have been adjusted for the new position of features in both images.

If you now look at frames 2 and 3, you see that the control points for these frames are in positions between those of frames 1 and 4. The control points in frames 1 and 4 act as keys, and PhotoMorph calculates intermediate control points for frames that you do not edit manually. In fact, if you only move some points on a given frame, only those points you actually change or create will be key points. PhotoMorph will add Smart Points on all frames between key points.

This process continues until you reach the end of the video clip. The number of key points you will have to create or adjust depends completely on the nature of the morph. For example, if there is little change in position or rotation, you may set key points every 15 frames, every 5 frames, or some other number. You'll have to determine the best interval yourself—Rule #3 in action.

Figures 8.79 through 8.82 show the rest of the key points I set for this example.

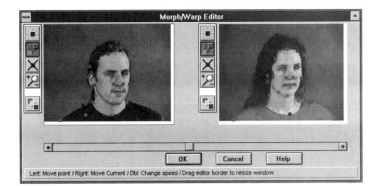

Figure 8.79
Control points for frame 7.

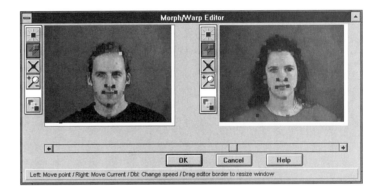

Figure 8.80
Control points for frame 10.

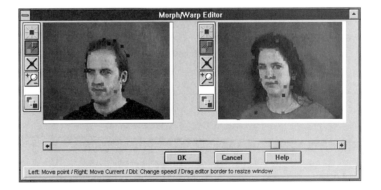

Figure 8.81
Control points for frame 13.

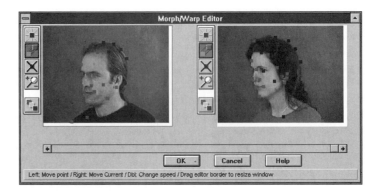

Figure 8.82
*Control points for
frame 16.*

After you set control points at all the key frames you need, click the OK button in the
Morph/Warp Editor. This returns you to the Project Editor, where you can click the
Create Animation button. You can view the completed animation using either Me-
dia Player or PhotoMorph's built-in viewer.

To see the advantages of a morph over a simple fade, let's look at some sample frames
from both kinds of transitions. Figure 8.83 shows two frames. The image on the left
is taken from a simple motion fade. Note that there is a distinct shadow of the woman's
hair at the left of the neck and to the right of the face (not the woman's left/right;
your left/right). The image on the right is taken from a morph. Note that the hairline
has been adjusted outward from the face—a proper morph between the two different
hairlines. There is still some ghosting, and that can be solved by adding a few additional control points.[26]

Figure 8.83
*Left: Simple fade.
Right: Morph using
control points. Note
that morph controls
change more tightly.*

---

[26]Rule #3 in action again.

Similar advantages of the morph over the fade are clear in Figure 8.84. The hair is again more clearly defined and less ghostly. More important, the face outline is much clearer, and more truly intermediate between the two faces.

Figure 8.84
Left: Simple fade.
Right: Morph using
control points. Note
that the hair is
much better defined
using a morph, and
that the face outline
is clearer.

Figure 8.85 shows an even clearer example of why a morph does a better job. The crispness of the morph image compared to the fade makes the best case yet for taking the time to create control points.

Figure 8.85
Left: Simple fade.
Right: Morph using
control points. Note
that details are
much clearer in the
morph.

This is just one small example of what you can accomplish with the advanced features of PhotoMorph 2. Here's just a sample of the features in PhotoMorph 2:

- Change image bit depths
- Change image file formats
- Flip, mirror, invert, crop, scale, and rotate images
- Apply filters to images, such as sharpen, blur, despeckle, emboss, median, trace edges, noise, maximum, minimum, and (my favorite!) Old Movie

- Have up to three filters/morphs/warps/transitions going on at one time
- Create a sequence of morphs in one animation
- Preview the morph without having to create the entire file
- Motion warping
- Colorizing
- Distortions, such as ripple and wave
- Create overlay using alpha channel or chroma/luma keys
- Create transitions such as fade, melt, and random

I'm excited about PhotoMorph, as you can probably tell. The program's design, engineering, and features are all excellent, and it's even easy to use. It's high on my list of recommended software.

Summary

In this chapter, you learned about how the eye can be deceived into believing that images are more or less real. However, tricks and techniques are only part of the story—the eye's owner must be willing to be deceived. As demonstrated by morphing, the extra time it takes to smooth out the unreality of artifice can be well worth your while.

9

THE MODEL
IS THE
THING

Today's virtual reality hardware and software are models of reality. This takes us back to Chapter 2, where the subject was *artificial reality* versus *virtual reality*. In many ways, the phrase *artificial reality* is much more appropriate for the technology available today. The original idea of virtual reality was of an electronic (or otherwise) simulation that was, at its best, indistinguishable from everyday reality.

The reality of virtual reality is quite different. The reality involves the kinds of computers we use today, the limitations of hardware and software, and the sheer quantity of information that our brains process routinely—as fast as computers are, they can't duplicate what our brains can do. Speed is great, but when it comes to simulating reality, it's all about bandwidth and detail.

Nonetheless, there are some wonderful products out there in Virtualville. One of the most important is VREAM. We looked at VREAM in Chapter 2, but we are going to take a much more in-depth look in this chapter. After a few introductory comments, we'll get down to brass tacks and tackle some serious virtual construction.

Granularity

Weather forecasters use models to simulate the earth's weather systems. These models are extremely complex, and they consist of software running on some of the fastest and largest computers in use today. Such weather software models reality, but we all know how accurate such computers are! Who hasn't had a foot of partly cloudy to shovel off the front sidewalk, or been caught in a downpour of partly sunny? The truth is, often enough, these expensive, complex models aren't even close to reality.

Weather is complex, chaotic, and, in truth, pretty much unpredictable beyond a brief period into the future. A model necessarily leaves out many of the details. One term used to describe the accuracy of a model's predictions is *granularity*. This term comes from the concept of graininess. For example, photographs use grains of silver compounds to create an image. Some grains are dark and others are light. The smaller the grains are, the more closely the image will resemble the original. Figure 9.1 shows an image constructed of very large grains, and Figure 9.2 shows an image constructed of very small grains.[1]

Granularity is easy to spot in a picture, but it is not always so easy to see in a model of something. Back to the weather simulation: granularity here involves, among other things, the distance between the sensors used to record weather information. If the

---

[1]So, OK, these are not grains in a photographic film. But you get the point, right?

sensors are 100 miles apart, that means aspects of weather smaller than 100 miles or so will not be part of the model—a grain is 100 miles in size. In addition, weather is chaotic—a very small change in one location can lead to (unpredictable!) large changes elsewhere.

Figure 9.1
*An image con-
structed of large
grains.*

Figure 9.2
*An image con-
structed of small
grains.*

The granularity of time is also a consideration when you create a model. If those weather stations sample the weather once a day, the model will have large time grains. If the weather stations sample the weather every hour, that's a much higher granularity and a much more accurate model.

Both kinds of granularity are crucial factors when modeling any aspect of reality—not just the weather. Reducing the size of the grains in a model costs money, however. There is a general rule at work here: More grains means more CPU power, more bits of data, more time, and more money.[2]

A 486/66- or Pentium-driven computer, even with a cutting-edge video display and the fastest hard disk available, isn't going to be able to create a simulation of reality that will fool anyone. The emphasis is on *virtual* and *artificial*, not on *reality*. Even if you spend $100,000 or more, the hardware can only do so much.[3] This chapter,[4] therefore, will be about what you and I can do on a reasonably fast computer, on our own, and not about what you could do "if only."

You may have noticed that this chapter is a long one. That's because the VREAM tutorial is long and detailed. If, at any time during the tutorial, you start to think to yourself, "Wow, this sure is long and detailed," think again, in terms of granularity. VREAM simulates a lot of the things you know from everyday reality, like gravity. The price you pay for this detailed granularity is the time it takes to "engineer" all the virtual details. Don't blame VREAM if it seems complex. Put the blame where it really belongs: on real life.

What If...

What if virtual reality were actually so close to everyday reality that you couldn't easily tell the difference? What would it mean? I've been wondering that for years—and there are a lot of science fiction writers and futurists who have been wondering, too. Even screenwriters and the folks who create commercials have been speculating. Thanks to TV, there's a tremendous amount of VR in our lives, although some of it is pure hogwash.

---

[2] It doesn't always cost more money, however. Today's computers are a hundred or more times faster than the original IBM PC, but they cost about the same. It has always cost about $2,500 for a decent computer—we just keep getting better computers at that same price.

[3] Of course, if you've got a few million to spare and a lot of time on your hands, you might do a pretty good job.

[4] And, in many ways, most of this book, too!

There are, for example, the beer ads that feature futuristic environments in which sports contests are held. There are all those headsets to be seen in all those ads—unconstrained by the realities of weight and bandwidth, among other things. There are television shows like *VR5*, where a totally spectacular VR world manages to wend its way across a dial-up phone line and an acoustic coupler modem! The reality that's virtual here has nothing to do with headsets and data gloves.

It is fun to conceive of the future before it arrives. Unfortunately, the future has a funny way of ending up quite unlike what anyone expected. Just look back at the concept of "future" that was current in the '50s and '60s (let's not forget *The Jetsons!*), and you'll see what I mean. All the advances in all the sciences haven't changed the fundamental unpredictability of the future.

Even so, what would it be like to have VR—really good VR? In some ways, we already know. You might not realize it, but you have been exposed to some cutting-edge VR already—in your neighborhood movie theater. Not every time you go, mind you, but sometimes, yes, it's virtually real in that dark room full of flickering lights and magic.

It's the magic, you see, that makes the difference between virtual reality and artificial reality. Having HMDs, data gloves, 3D stereo, head tracking—that's all just the mechanics of VR, and constitutes mere artificial reality. It's like a plastic apple—it's interesting until you pick it up and try to bite into it.

Without the magic—what the literature instructor in college calls a *willing suspension of disbelief*—VR is all mechanics and no soul. True, good mechanics make it easier, just as *Star Wars'* special effects made that movie so much more fun. But without the spookiness of Darth Vader, the boyish charm of Luke, and the mystery of Obi Wan, it would have been just another pile of nuts and bolts.

The purpose of art—and VR is no less an art than any other—is to stir the imagination, and the model is just one piece of the puzzle. Keep that in mind throughout this chapter as we look at the model and how it is created.

VREAM Scream

Let's get down to those (virtual) brass tacks right now. The time has come to walk you through a VREAM tutorial. To show you how the real VR stuff gets done. Here's a word of warning to the wise: It's a jungle out there. Like any jungle, it's full of both adventure and wild animals.

The adventure is easy to spot—you'll be able to create fully interactive virtual worlds with VREAM. The power you need is there.

The wild animals are fun to look at, but they can be dangerous if you don't know how to act with them. And what are these wild animals? They are the very powerful tools you'll be using in VREAM. If you aren't careful, they'll snap out and bite you. I'll point out the wild animals during the tutorial. Once you learn how to feed and care for them, they'll be your pets and you'll really start to have some fun!

VREAM Facts

If you haven't already read through the initial VREAM tutorial in Chapter 2, I strongly suggest that you look at it now. It covers all of the VREAM tools, and provides many useful insights into how you can use them. This tutorial builds on the concepts and ideas presented in the earlier tutorial.[5]

There are some new concepts, however, that come into play, and those are covered here. The first is one of those wild animals I warned you about earlier: the VREAMScript language. When you create a model in the VREAM World Editor, it gets saved to disk as a text file full of VREAMScript commands. For example, here's a command that describes a cube named RemoteCtl:[6]

```
Cube,S,
  1.300000,-3.900000,0.850000,
  0.400000,-3.900000,0.850000,
  0.400000,-2.700000,0.850000,
  1.300000,-2.700000,0.850000,
  1.300000,-3.900000,1.300000,
  0.400000,-3.900000,1.300000,
  0.400000,-2.700000,1.300000,
  1.300000,-2.700000,1.300000,
  0.000000,0.000000,0.000000,
  4,4,4,4,4,9;
  ACTIVATE_SOLID,S,1;
  ACTIVATE_WIREFRAME,S,1;
  NAME,S,RemoteCtl;
  VISIBILITY_VALUE,S,1;
  WIREFRAME_COLOR,S,8;
```

You can also use the VREAMScript language to create interactive commands. The following command causes one object to move (Frankie the robot) when a different object (RemoteCtl) is the target of a hand push:

```
Link,S,RemoteCtl,Frankie,0,0,20;
  HAND_PUSH,C,1;
  AUTO_TRANSLATE,R,0.000000,0.000000,0.000000,
    1,0.000000,0.000000,0.000000;
```

---

[5] I will, of course, repeat all the Really Important Stuff that might have gotten fuzzy since you read Chapter 2.

[6] In fact, this cube is one from the robot that you'll learn how to build in this very tutorial.

These VREAMScript commands look arcane and obscure. Fortunately, the VREAM World Editor offers easier methods for dealing with VREAMScript, and you'll learn several of those in the tutorial. However, there will be times when the easiest way to make a change is to edit an existing VREAMScript command. As you become more skilled with VREAM, the time will come when you want to do that. All VREAMScript commands are documented in great detail, but it does take a lot of time to become familiar with such a large body of commands—especially when they are so complex.

That's what makes the VREAMScript language a wild animal. As you start to learn VREAM, you will sometimes run into what appears to be a limitation of the program. That's the bite on the hand. In most cases, once you learn the full power of the VREAMScript language, you'll discover that there is a way to accomplish your goal. That's taming the wild animal.

Don't expect to learn everything there is to know about VREAM in this tutorial. Do expect to get a clear idea of the kinds of things you can do with VREAM. This tutorial is a launching point for your own investigation and exploration.

Virtual Refreshments

Refreshment doesn't refer to beverages, but to refreshing your memory about how to move around in a 3D space. More than most 3D software, VREAM requires you to think in three dimensions at all times. The orientation of the three dimensions are

> **X**—Left to right
>
> **Y**—Front to back
>
> **Z**—Top to bottom

VREAM doesn't use real-world measuring systems—everything is measured in VREAM units. You can translate a VREAM unit into any real-world system you want: feet, meters, miles, light years, or whatever, but you'll have to do it in your imagination. VREAM doesn't care.

You'll also often need to move and rotate objects, and you'll use yaw, pitch, and roll to do that. Think of an imaginary airplane when you think of yaw, pitch, and roll:

> **Yaw**—Turns left or right
>
> **Pitch**—Dips nose down, pulls nose up
>
> **Roll**—Left wing goes down, right wing goes up

In more technical terms, each of these motions is a rotation about a particular axis. For the sake of completeness, and for those who like to think about such things, consider the following:

Yaw—Rotates about Z axis

Pitch—Rotates about X axis

Roll—Rotates about Y axis

VREAM 3D World Editor Tools

One of the major components of the World Editor are the tools in the toolbar. They enable you to create and edit objects in your virtual world.

The toolbar contains two kinds of tools: Drawing/Creating tools and Editing tools. To select a tool, just use your basic button-pushing skills: Position the cursor over the button and click with the left mouse button. You will then have to watch the bottom of the screen for instructions specific to each tool. For example, when you create a cube, you'll be asked for the width, depth, and height in sequence. You provide these measurements, of course, by clicking and dragging in the 3D space. For some VREAM tools, you'll use the prompt line to enter information. Chapter 2 provided a basic overview of the VREAM tools. In this chapter, we're going to look at the gory details. You will probably notice that some of the tools are covered more than once. There is a simple reason for this: Some of the tools can do more than one thing. Later, as you work through the tutorial, you may want to refer back to these detailed tool descriptions for additional information.

Drawing/Creating Tools

The left side of the toolbar is composed of Object Draw tools that are used to create object primitives, groups, and rooms.[7]

 ## Point Tool

The Point tool creates a single-point object or multiple-point objects by defining each point individually. Each point is defined by a single point in space, and is displayed on the screen as a single pixel. This tool is intended to be used as a reference object in the Environment Editor rather than as a finished object in worlds. For example, points

---

[7] I like this idea of creating an entire room. VREAM was the first product I encountered that had such a logical feature. The implementation is a bit weird if you like things like windows and doors, but it works great.

can be placed throughout the environment, and then locked onto with the Point-Tracker feature when drawing other object primitives. Think of the points as a sketch that you can erase when you complete the final drawing.

 ### Line Tool

The Line tool lets you create a single-line object or multiple-line objects by defining the two endpoints for each line. You can draw a series of line endpoints by using the second endpoint for the current line as the first endpoint for the next line.

 ### Polyline Tool

The Polyline tool lets you create a single polyline object that contains multiple line segments by defining the endpoints for each line segment in the polyline. The Polyline tool is similar to the Line tool in that you use the second endpoint for the current line segment as the first endpoint for the next line segment. The main difference between the Polyline tool and the Line tool is that the Line tool enables you to create multiple single-line objects, whereas the Polyline tool enables you to create a single polyline object consisting of multiple line segments.

 ### Surface Tool (Three-Sided Surface)

The Three-Sided Surface tool lets you create a single surface (polygon) object that contains exactly three sides, by defining the three points that define the surface. The VREAM Environment Editor also contains a Four-Sided and an N-Sided Surface tool, but the Three-Sided Surface tool is more efficient for defining three-sided objects.

Each individual surface object must be a *convex surface*—that is, a surface that contains interior angles at each of its vertices that are less than 180 degrees. In order to create a *concave surface* (one containing an interior angle greater than 180 degrees), you can group together two or more convex surfaces.

 ### Surface Tool (Four-Sided Surface)

The Four-Sided Surface tool lets you create a single surface (polygon) object that contains exactly four sides by defining the four points that define the surface.

Like the Three-Sided Surface tool, each individual surface object must be a *convex surface* (a surface that contains interior angles at each of its vertices that are less than 180 degrees). In order to create a concave surface, you can group together two or more convex surfaces.

 ### Surface Tool (N-Sided Surface)

The N-Sided Surface tool lets you create a single surface (polygon) object that contains from 3 to 256 sides. The number of sides of the polygon, along with the positions of the N points in space that comprise the polygon, are defined by you. If you exit from the N-Sided Surface tool before setting at least three points, no surface object will be created.

Arc Tool

The Arc tool lets you create an arc object based on the definition of a center point for the arc, the radius arc, the start and stop angles for the arc, and the number of segments along the circumference of the arc. The arc objects will have varying resolutions based on the number of segments used along the circumference of the arc. A high-resolution arc containing many sides along its circumference will appear more rounded, but will also require more processing.

Circle Tool

The Circle tool lets you create a circle object by defining the center point of the circle, the radius circle, and the number of segments along the circumference of the circle. By letting you define the number of segments along the circumference, this tool gives you the option of creating circle objects of varying resolutions. For example, a high-resolution circle (one containing many sides along its circumference) will appear more rounded, but will also require more processing.

One of the features of the Circle tool is that you can draw perfect polygons containing a number of sides equal to the number of segments specified for the circle. Suppose that you enter a value of 16 or more for the number of segments; you will create a rounded polygon approaching a circle. However, if you enter a smaller value for the number of segments, the Circle tool can be used to create perfect polygon surfaces of varying sides. For example, a perfect pentagon will be generated if you create a five-sided circle, and a perfect hexagon will be generated if you create a six-sided circle.

Tetrahedron Tool

The Tetrahedron tool lets you create a tetrahedron object based on the definition of a base point for the tetrahedron, along with the height, width, and depth of the tetrahedron. You are prompted to set each of these values.

Pyramid Tool

The Pyramid tool lets you create a pyramid object based on the definition of a base point for the pyramid, along with the height, width, and depth of the pyramid. You are prompted to set each of these values.

Wedge Tool

The Wedge tool lets you create a wedge object based on the definition of a base point for the wedge, along with the height, width, and depth of the wedge. You are prompted to set each of these values.

Cube Tool

The Cube tool lets you create a cube object based on the definition of a base point for the cube, along with the height, width, and depth of the cube. You are prompted to set each of these values.

Cone Tool

The Cone tool lets you create a cone object based on the definition of a center point for the base of the cone, the radius of the base of the cone, the height of the cone, and the number of sides along the circumference of the cone. You can select a number from 3 to 256 for the number of sides of the cone; the default value is 16. You are prompted to set each of these values.

You can define the number of sides along the circumference of the cone, which lets you create cone objects of varying resolutions. A high-resolution cone (one containing many sides along its circumference) will appear more rounded, but will also require more processing.

Cylinder Tool

The Cylinder tool lets you create a cylinder object based on the definition of a center point for the base of the cylinder, the radius of the base of the cylinder, the height of the cylinder, and the number of sides along the circumference of the cylinder (an integer value from 3 to 256; the default is 16). You are prompted to set each of these values.

You can define the number of sides on the circumference of the cylinder to create cylinder objects of varying resolutions. A high-resolution cylinder (one containing many sides along its circumference) will appear more rounded, but will require more processing.

Sphere Tool

The Sphere tool lets you create a sphere object based on the definition of the center of the sphere, the radius of the sphere, and the number of longitudinal and latitudinal segments of the sphere. You are prompted to set each of these values.

You can create sphere objects of varying resolutions by defining the number of longitudinal and latitudinal segments of the sphere. A high-resolution sphere (one containing many longitudinal and latitudinal segments) will appear more rounded, but will also require more processing.

Torus Tool

The Torus tool lets you create a torus object based on the definition of the center of the torus, the radius of the torus, the radius of the tube comprising the torus, the number of tube segments, and the number of torus segments. You are prompted to set each of these values.

You can create torus objects of varying resolutions by defining the number of torus and tube segments. A high-resolution torus (one containing many sides and tube segments) will appear more rounded, but will also require more processing.

 ### Revolution Tool

The Revolution tool lets you create a surface-of-revolution object based on the definition of a polyline object (to serve as the object to be revolved), the center of the surface of revolution (around which the polyline will be revolved), the angles through which the revolution will take place, and the number of sides that will comprise the circumference of the surface revolution. You are prompted to set these values.

In order to use this tool, you must have already created a single polyline object using the Polyline tool. You can create partially revolved objects by specifying start and stop angles that cover less than a 360-degree rotational area.

You can create revolution objects of varying resolutions by defining the number of revolution sides. A high-resolution revolution (one containing many sides along its circumference) appears more rounded, but also requires more processing.

 ### Extrusion Tool

The Extrusion tool lets you create a surface-of-extrusion object based on the definition of a polyline object (to serve as the object to be extruded), the direction and magnitude of the extrusion, and the number of levels that will comprise the surface of the extrusion. You are prompted to set each of these values.

In order to use this tool, a single polyline object must have been previously created using the Polyline tool. The Extrusion tool will extrude the selected polyline into 3D space based on a direction and magnitude defined by you.

You can create extrusion objects of varying resolutions by defining the number of extrusion levels. A high-resolution extrusion (one containing many levels) will contain more component polygon surfaces along its extruded length, but will also require more processing.

 ### Mesh Tool

The Mesh tool lets you create a general polygon mesh object that is bounded on four sides by straight lines. The mesh object consists of multiple four-sided polygons that are interconnected to form a meshed surface. You are prompted to define the mesh by entering the four bounding corners of the mesh, along with the number of rows and columns of lines that will be used to comprise the polygons of the mesh.

The mesh object primarily consists of rows and columns of lines in 3D space joined together to form a surface of multiple, four-sided polygons. If, for example, a mesh object is created having 5 rows and 4 columns, then a mesh is created having 20 vertex points (5×4=20) bounding 12 internal polygons. Each of the 20 points within the mesh can be individually manipulated. This lets you form a flat mesh surface into a bumpy terrain by individually changing the position of the vertex points along the mesh surface. Additionally, the individual polygons within the mesh object can be set to different colors using the Surface Color option from within the Attribute menu.

You can create mesh objects of varying resolutions by defining the number of rows and columns within the mesh. A high-resolution mesh (containing many rows and columns) will contain more component polygon surfaces, but will also require more processing.

 ## Solid Cut Tool

The Solid Cut tool lets you cut a hole in a currently existing surface object. The Solid Cut tool is capable of cutting a four-sided rectangular hole in a four-sided surface object primitive. You will be prompted to set the four solid cut points.

You can use the Solid Cut tool to create multiple types of effects when building virtual worlds with the VREAM system. It is especially useful for cutting holes for windows and doors out of surfaces that are used to build room objects. This lets the viewer easily see inside a room from the outside, or view the area outside a room from the inside.

 ## Texture Tool

The Texture tool lets you create a single texture object that is bounded by exactly four sides, by defining the four points that define the texture and by selecting the PCX image file that will be displayed as the texture. You are prompted to set the four texture points.

You can use the Texture tool to incorporate photorealistic textures into virtual reality worlds. *Textures* are digitized representations of real-life images such as a picture of a person or the wooden grain of a table. Texture information usually represents two-dimensional (flat) data, but within the VREAM system, two-dimensional texture information can be applied to a polygonal surface residing in three-dimensional space.

You can create a texture object by defining a four-sided polygon in space and by selecting a PCX bitmap image file to be applied to the surface area comprising the four-sided polygon. A PCX bitmap file must be created that contains the desired image to be displayed as the texture. The PCX file format is a standard graphics file format supported by a wide variety of graphics paint programs. The PCX file can be created in many ways: by scanning a picture using a digital scanner, by drawing an image from scratch using a paint program, or by converting an image from another file format into a PCX file using a graphics-conversion program.

Text Tool

The Text tool lets you create a text object by defining the characters to be contained in the text object, the position of the text in space, the font style to be used in creating the text, and the font size to be used in the text. You can set the font style and font size prior to selecting the Text Tool button. Do this by selecting the Font Style and Font Size options from the Editor menu. You will be prompted to define the actual characters to be displayed in the text object and the position of the text object. Use the keyboard to enter the text characters and the 3D cursor to define the position of the text.

The text object can contain any text passage you want, up to 80 characters (including spaces). VREAM uses a set of standard-stroked[8] font files to provide the information required to generate text characters in different font formats. The Text tool internally constructs the specified text passage using standard lines to create the words in 3D space. Even though the text object is actually a two-dimensional (flat) object, it can be used as detail lettering on all types of objects such as signs, billboards, books, and so on. And because the text object is an actual object primitive within VREAM, it can be given attributes like all other objects. This means that a text object can be given motion so that it rotates and moves, its size and color can be altered, it can be picked up and moved around with the 3D Hand, and it can be used as the condition or response object of a dynamic link. Additionally, certain font styles can be extruded into 3D space to easily create three-dimensional text. This can be done with the Extrusion tool.

Group Tool

The Group tool lets you create a group object consisting of one or more previously created objects. To use the Group tool, select one or more objects that were previously created within the active environment. Define a group object by clicking the Group Tool button after the desired objects have been selected, and then enter a name for the group object in response to Group tool prompts.

The Grouping feature lets you combine multiple objects (3D primitives, groups, and rooms) and create a group of object primitives that can be treated by the system as a

---

[8]A *standard-stroked font* is one that has no crossing lines or other elements that would prevent it from being projected into the third dimension cleanly.

single object. For example, four elongated cube objects can be grouped with one flat-tened cube object to create a table with four legs. This single group object can be assigned attributes, resized, moved, and used to serve as the condition or response object for a dynamic link, just like any other standard object.

 ## Ungroup Tool

The Ungroup tool lets you break a group object down into its component objects. To use the Ungroup tool, one or more group objects must have been previously created and selected within the active environment. To ungroup a group object, select the desired group object(s) and click the Ungroup Tool button.

The Ungrouping feature lets you break down group objects into their next level of hierarchical object components. For example, a group named MAINGROUP may be comprised of a cube object primitive and a group object named SUBGROUP. When the group MAINGROUP is ungrouped, it will be broken down into the cube object primitive and the group SUBGROUP. Note that the group SUBGROUP will not be broken down, because it is one hierarchical level removed from the affected group. Select the group SUBGROUP to break it down into its component parts.

 ## Room Tool (Custom Room)

The Custom Room tool lets you create a room object consisting of one or more pre-viously created 2D surface object primitives. The 2D surface object primitives that can be used to create a custom room using the Custom Room tool are the three-sided surface, four-sided surface, N-sided surface, arc, and circle. One or more 2D surface objects must have been created and selected within the active environment in order to use the Custom Room tool.

The Room feature combines multiple 2D surface objects, thereby creating a room of 2D surface object primitives that can be treated by the system as a single object. For example, six four-sided surfaces can be roomed together to form an enclosed rectan-gular room. This single room object can be assigned attributes, resized, moved, and used to serve as the condition or response object for a dynamic link, just like any other standard object.

Room objects are special objects within the VREAM system. They are created as a single entity (constructed from surface objects), but they can hold other objects inside them that can be independently manipulated. Rooms can be constructed with doors and windows, which allows the viewer to see inside the room from the outside, or to look outside the room from the inside.

You create room objects by combining 2D surface objects (as the walls of the room) so they collectively enclose a common space that is defined as the inside of the room.

These 2D surface objects that comprise the walls of the room can be combined in a variety of ways to create a room. Rooms can be created in the shape of rectangular boxes, pyramids, cylinders, spheres, and many other shapes.

Room Tool (Room from Object Primitive)

The Room from Object Primitive tool lets you create a room object from a previously created 3D object primitive. The room object will be formed in the exact shape of the 3D object primitive. The 3D object primitives that can be used to create a room with this tool are the tetrahedron, pyramid, wedge, cube, cone, cylinder, and sphere. To use this tool, exactly one 3D object primitive must have been selected within the active environment. Define the room object by clicking the Room Tool button after you have selected the desired object, and then enter a name for the room object when prompted by the Room tool.

The Room from Object Primitive feature lets you automatically convert a single 3D object primitive into a single room object containing multiple 2D surface objects that serve as walls for the room. For example, a single cube object can be converted to a room object that contains six four-sided surface objects defining the walls of the enclosed, rectangular room. This single room object can be assigned attributes, resized, moved, and used to serve as the condition or response object for a dynamic link, just like any other standard object.

Room objects are special objects within the VREAM system. They are created as a single entity (constructed from surface objects serving as walls of the room), but can hold other objects inside them that can be independently manipulated. Rooms can be constructed with doors and windows, which lets the viewer see inside the room from the outside or view outside the room from the inside.

There are generally two ways of creating room objects with the VREAM system: using the Custom Room tool, which requires that the surfaces that define each wall be individually created and formed into the shape of an enclosed room; or using the Room from Object Primitive tool, which allows you to easily create room objects from a single 3D object primitive. This is possible because the VREAM system internally breaks the selected 3D object primitive down into its component surfaces and then reconstructs those surfaces in the form of a room object.

Unroom Tool

The Unroom tool lets you break a room object down into its component surface object primitives. To use the Unroom tool, select one or more room objects that were previously created and are within the active environment. To unroom a room object, select the desired room object(s) and click the Unroom Tool button.

The Unroom feature breaks down room objects into their next level of hierarchical object components. In the case of a room object, this next level of components will always consist of surface object primitives (three-sided surfaces, four-sided surfaces, N-sided surfaces, arcs, and circles). So, when a room is unroomed, the resultant objects in the environment will always be surface object primitives. However, unlike a group object that can contain other groups, a room is limited in the kinds of objects it can contain. For example, a room cannot contain another room or a group, but a room can be contained by a group. This lets you break down a group into one or more rooms, but does not let you break down a room into one or more groups.

Editing Tools

The right side of the toolbar consists of the Object Edit tools that are used to edit existing objects and to change the current viewer's position in space.

Move Tool

The Move tool lets you move objects from one position in space to another within the same environment. You must have created and selected one or more objects within the active environment in order to use the Move tool. You define the distance and direction in which the object(s) are to be moved by drawing a vector in 3D space. The direction and magnitude from the beginning point of the vector to the ending point of the vector will define the change in distance and direction for the object(s). You are prompted to set each of these values.

Rotate Tool

The Rotate tool lets you rotate objects from one orientation in space to another. In order to use the Rotate tool, you must have created and selected one or more objects within the active environment. You define the desired rotation for selected objects by entering values into a dialog box defining the yaw, pitch, and roll of the object(s). You are prompted to set each of these values.

The values used to define yaw, pitch, and roll offsets of the selected object(s) are indicated in degrees. These values represent the amount that the objects are to be rotated (around their natural centers) in each of the respective directions. Note that the values entered in the Rotate dialog box define relative offset values for the yaw, pitch, and roll of the selected object(s), based on its current orientation in space. So, if you enter a yaw value of 10 degrees, the current orientation of the selected object will be updated by 10 degrees in the yaw direction. If you again enter a yaw value of 10 degrees for the same object, it will be rotated another 10 degrees in the yaw direction, making the total offset from the original orientation 20 degrees.

Copy Tool

The Copy tool lets you copy objects within the active environment and define the precise location in space of the newly copied objects. The Copy tool performs a function similar to the Move tool, except that the Copy tool generates an exact duplicate of a selected object in addition to moving it in the specified direction and distance.

To use the Copy tool, you must have previously created and selected one or more objects within the active environment. You then select the objects to be copied and define the distance and direction in which the object(s) is to be moved by drawing a vector in 3D space. The difference in direction and magnitude from the beginning point of the vector to the ending point of the vector will define the change in distance and direction for the object(s). You are prompted to set each of these values.

Note that when an object is copied, most of its attributes are copied along with it. However, certain attributes, such as the name of the object, must be updated so that links and other references that affect the initial object will not be confused by the existence of the copy.

 Rectangular Array Tool

The Rectangular Array tool lets you create multiple copies of objects within the active environment. These copies are arranged in a uniform pattern of rows and columns called a *rectangular array*. You define the number of copies to be made by entering the number of rows and columns of objects to be created. The Rectangular Array performs a function similar to the Copy tool, except that Rectangular Array generates multiple copies of a selected object with one operation, evenly spacing the resultant objects to your specifications.

To use the Rectangular Array tool, you must have previously created and selected one or more objects within the active environment. You first select the objects to be copied, and then are prompted to specify the number of object copies to be created and their locations. You will also be prompted to enter the number of rows of objects to be created, the number of columns of objects to be created, the distance between objects within each row, and the distance between objects within each column.

Note than when an object is copied (using either the Rectangular Array tool or the Copy tool), most of its attributes are copied along with it. However, certain attributes must be updated, such as the name of the object, so that links and other references that affect the initial object will not be confused by the existence of the copy.

 Change Tool (Single Point)

The Single Point Change tool lets you change the position of a single point within the environment. This single point can be contained by one or more than one object. You can alter the shapes of objects in the environment by changing the position of the points that comprise them. To use the Single Point Change tool, you must have previously created and selected one or more objects within the active environment. After you select the Single Point Change tool, you select the object point to be changed (from one of the selected objects) by selecting it with the 3D cursor in Point-Tracker mode. You then define the distance and direction in which the point is to be moved by drawing a vector in 3D space. The difference in direction and magnitude from the beginning point of the vector to the ending point of the vector will define the distance and direction of the change for the object point. You are prompted to set each of these values.

There are two Change functions available from within the VREAM World Editor Change tool. The Single Point Change tool (which we are currently discussing) lets you change the position of a single point in the environment, whether it belongs to one or multiple objects. The Surface Point Change tool lets you change the positions of multiple points in the environment by selecting one or more object surfaces that contain the desired points. Both Change Tool functions are useful when building VREAM worlds.

Change Tool (Surface Points)

The Change Surface Points tool lets you change the positions of multiple points within the environment by selecting the surfaces that contain the desired points, and then by defining a vector to describe the position change. You are prompted to set each of these values.

Resize Tool

The Resize tool lets you change the size of one or more objects within the active environment. The Resize tool will expand or contract a selected object from the natural center of the object outward. Thus, the center of the object will remain in the same position in space, but the position of the points surrounding the center of the object will be updated.

Delete Tool

The Delete tool lets you delete one or more objects from the active environment. It provides a mechanism for verification and confirmation of the selected objects prior to deleting them. You will be prompted to verify the Delete operation, at which time you may choose to continue or to cancel the deletion. If the deletion is performed, a confirmation prompt is displayed showing the number of objects that were successfully deleted.

Viewer Distance Tool

The Viewer Distance tool lets you move immediately to a specified distance from the current location while maintaining the same orientation in space. This may have the effect of moving the viewer forward or backward, left or right, or up or down within the scene, providing a new view of the current environment.

 ### Viewer Position Tool (Predefined Position)

The Predefined Viewer Position tool lets you move immediately to a new, predefined position and orientation in space, so that you can view the current scene from a new perspective. When you select the Viewer Position Tool button from the toolbar, VREAM displays a dialog box containing 16 viewer-position options. Fifteen of the options allow the viewer to jump immediately to a new, predefined position and orientation in space. One of the options lets you define a new, unique viewer position and orientation in space.

The Viewer Position tool complements the Viewer Walk tool, which lets you walk through the environment in real time using a variety of interface devices such as a joystick or keyboard. The Viewer Position tool lets you immediately jump to an exact location in space, and is useful in obtaining a new perspective of a scene without taking the time to walk to that new position.

The Viewer Position tool can also be used with the Viewer Distance tool to quickly gain new perspectives of the environment from varying distances. The Viewer Position tool lets you position and orient the viewer in space; the Viewer Distance tool lets you move the viewer into or out of the scene while maintaining the same orientation in space.

 ### Viewer Position Tool (Unique Position)

The Unique Viewer Position tool lets you move immediately to a new unique position and orientation in space, viewing the current scene from a new perspective. After selecting the Viewer Position Tool button, you are prompted to select one of 16 viewer-position options from the dialog box. Fifteen of the options let you jump immediately to a new, predefined position and orientation in space, and one of the options lets you define a new, unique viewer position and orientation in space.

 ### Viewer Walk (or Viewpoint) Tool

The Viewer Walk tool lets you walk through the current active environment. This feature gives you virtual reality capabilities within the VREAM 3D World Editor, and lets you walk through environments as they are being built.

The VREAM 3D World Editor lets you operate within two modes: Edit mode and Walk mode. Edit mode is used to perform editing functions, such as drawing objects, assigning attributes, or assigning links. While in Edit mode, you remain primarily stationary in space. You have the capability to jump to a new location in space using the Viewer Position and Viewer Distance tools, but you cannot walk through the environment in real time.

When you select the Viewer Walk button, you activate Walk mode in the VREAM 3D World Editor. The viewer lets you walk through the environment using any active interface devices that have been enabled to control the viewer, such as a joystick or the keyboard. While in Walk mode, any active interface device used to control the viewer will let you control all three degrees of translational and rotational freedom of the viewer, which lets you move or rotate in any direction in space. However, you do not have access to the World Editing functions while in Walk mode. To continue editing the current environment, you must exit Walk mode and return to Edit mode.

Note that in order to use interface devices in Walk mode, you must have previously defined and enabled them using the World menu.

At a minimum, you will need a keyboard (for viewer control) and a mouse (for cursor control) while building worlds within the 3D World Editor. The keyboard provides access to the complete range of viewer movement and rotation functions, and the mouse handles the VREAM Hand (you can find more information about the Hand later in this chapter).

Alternate Output Devices

One of the areas in which VREAM really shines is in the use of alternate output devices, including CrystalEyes, the Cyberscope, and HMDs. As with input devices, you must use the World menu to set a specific output device for your world. Figure 9.3 shows the output VREAM uses for a Cyberscope, while Figure 9.4 shows the output for CrystalEyes. As you can see, VREAM creates two images—one for each eye. In each case, the device takes care of making sure that only one image goes to each eye.

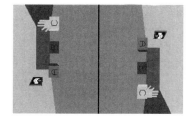

Figure 9.3
VREAM output for a
Cyberscope.

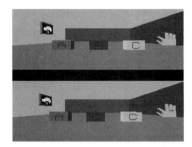

Figure 9.4
VREAM output for a
CrystalEyes headset.

See Chapter 12 for a low-cost method of using the CrystalEyes output with LCD shutter glasses, courtesy of 3DTV Corporation. See Chapter 7 for information about many different kinds of input and output hardware.

VREAM Startup

You'll need to be in DOS to run VREAM.[9] Type the following at the DOS prompt:

VREAM

Then press Enter.

In a moment or two, you'll see the VREAM GAGOS,[10] as shown in Figure 9.5. This screen-filling image has just three active buttons on it. The first button takes you to the VREAM World Editor, the second button takes you to the VREAM runtime, and the third button takes you back to DOS. Click the top button to enter the World Editor (see Fig. 9.6).

The World Editor consists of the following:

Title bar—Shows the name of the program.

Menu bar—Provides access to the various menu selections. If you are used to Windows-style menus, get ready for some surprises. For example, once you click on a menu selection, you can't click on a different one—you must go all the way back out of the menu, and then start again.

Status bars—Tell you what's happening. The first line shows, from left to right, the current environment number, how far the cursor can move (span), cursor lock status, selection mode (2D/3D), sorting mode (object or surface), and colors. The second line shows position data. There are three modes:

---

[9]Don't try to run VREAM in a Windows DOS box with versions of Windows prior to Windows 95.
[10]That's short for *Grand and Glorious Opening Screen*. Yes, my tongue is firmly in my cheek.

Viewer (position of your point of view), Cursor (position of the 3D cursor), and Track (cursor position is always one of the existing points). In Viewer mode, the six numbers show X, Y, Z, Yaw, Pitch, and Roll. In Cursor mode, the six numbers show X/Y/Z relative to viewer, and X/Y/Z of the cursor. In Track mode, the six numbers show the same values as for Cursor mode.

Compass—Shows the current direction of the view.

Work area—This is where you create and edit.

3D cursor—Looks as shown when it's in front of an object. Changes to a cross when it's behind a surface or object to aid you in 3D navigation.

Reference grid—Not an actual object. It's just there to help you keep oriented.

Toolbar—These are the VREAM tools. See Chapter 2 and the section "VREAM 3D World Editor Tools," earlier in this chapter, for detailed information about using these tools.

Prompt line—VREAM prompts you for actions here. Keep an eye out; VREAM often wants you to click the left mouse button when you least expect it.

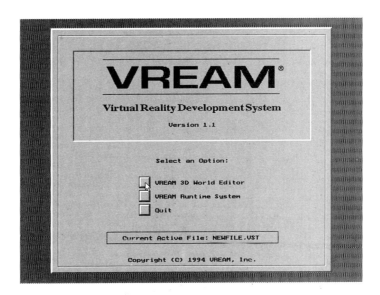

Figure 9.5
The VREAM
opening screen.

Oh—if you get into trouble and want to back out, don't try the Esc key. Instead, click both mouse buttons simultaneously.[11]

---

[11]Well, not exactly simultaneously. Since the left mouse button is often used to confirm an action, you want to develop the habit of clicking the right button just a hair sooner than the left. Otherwise, you'll wind up accidentally continuing instead of aborting.

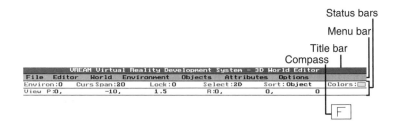

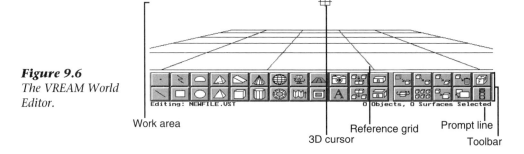

Figure 9.6
The VREAM World Editor.

There are a few other things you need to keep in mind as you work with VREAM:

Selecting—To select an object, click on it. To deselect (*clear*, in VREAM lingo) it, click on it again. You can also use the Objects menu to choose Select All or Clear All.

Controlled move—To move the selected object(s) freely, hold down the Alt key and drag the mouse.

Vectors—VREAM uses the concept of vectors over and over. You'll learn more about this during the tutorial. If you aren't familiar with vectors, don't worry: You'll learn. If you *are* familiar with them, rejoice: You'll get to use them a lot.

VREAM World Building

Let's get one thing straight before we start messing around with VREAM: This is going to take a while. VREAM is complicated. It can do an amazing number of things. So be patient. Take this tutorial step by step until you get a feel for what VREAM is doing. VREAM is magical but, like any magic, there's a lot of science and knowledge behind the scenes. This tutorial will focus on teaching you the behind-the-scenes stuff. It will focus on making you a well-rounded VREAMster. I'm not going to rush through it, so relax and enjoy the ride. We'll get there eventually.

What, pray tell, shall we build? If you've been reading the footnotes or peeking ahead, you already know: a robot. We'll build the robot, arm by arm, leg by leg. We'll make it walk. We'll make it turn around. We'll make it respond to a remote control. Then we'll sit back, take a deep breath, and reflect on just what this means for you and your VR future.

VREAM dialog boxes aren't quite like Windows dialog boxes. From the VREAM World Editor, click on the File menu, and then on the Open menu selection (see Fig. 9.7). This opens the dialog box shown in Figure 9.8. To enter a file name at the top, you'll need to click the mouse in that space, then type the file name, and then press Enter to finish editing. After you press Enter, the dialog box won't go away as you might expect. However, you will get the cursor back! It was gone while you were typing the name. Remember: This is DOS, not Windows, so you'll have to learn how things work as you go along. The VST extension is standard for VREAM worlds. Click the Open button when you have the correct file name entered.

You can also simply double-click on the file name in the scrolling list at the center of the dialog box. I just wanted to point out that VREAM takes input different from the way Windows dialog boxes take input. You'll use this input technique over and over as you work with VREAM.

Figure 9.7
Using the VREAM menus.

Figure 9.9 shows what the robot will look like when you are done. Yes, we're going to build every piece you see there, and then carefully link them together so that the robot appears to walk.[12]

---

[12]I say "appears to walk" because that's closer to the truth. The robot won't know anything about gravity and motion in general, or walking in particular. It'll be up to us to manipulate it so cleverly that it appears to walk.

Figure 9.8
Selecting a file to open.

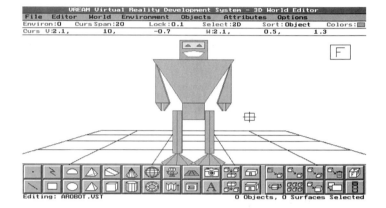

Figure 9.9
The robot.

Here's a quick summary of what we'll do in this tutorial:

Step 1: Build each of the component parts needed for the robot. This will include a head, two eyes, a background for the eyes, a mouth, a torso, a pelvis, two arms, two grasping appendages (hands) for each arm (four in total), two legs, and two feet.

Step 2: Mark various surfaces on the various parts so that VREAM can tell how to paint them properly on your screen. This helps VREAM understand what goes in front of what. As you'll see in the tutorial, VREAM is pretty clumsy when it comes to determining what object is in front of another. So we're going to give it some hints to help out.

Step 3: Group the various parts logically. We'll link the feet to the legs, and the legs to the pelvis. We'll link all the head stuff together. We'll link the grabbers to the arms, and the arms to the torso. Then we'll group the groups into one big happy robot.

Step 4: Create automatic motions that move the robot's legs in a walking motion.

Step 5: Create links so that the robot changes direction, instead of walking off the screen, never to be found again.

Step 6: Create a remote control that allows us to start and stop the robot's motion.

Enough talk—let's get started! Use the File/New menu selection to start a blank file. You'll see a dialog box similar to the one used for opening a file (see Fig. 9.10). Click in the space at the top, type the file name **MYROBOT.VST**, press Enter, and then click the Create button. You'll wind up in the World Editor with a blank world. The file name MYROBOT.VST will show up in the lower left corner.

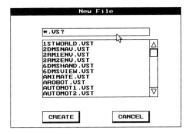

Figure 9.10
Selecting a file to open.

Before we start drawing, let's set things up properly. Use the Editor/Status Bar/Status Bar Mode menu selection to display the dialog box shown in Figure 9.11.[13] Make sure that the Display Cursor Position option is checked, and then click the Set button. This allows you to use the right side of the bottom status line to see exactly where the cursor is located. You'll see an example of this shortly.

The next step is to set up a cursor lock. Many software products call this a *grid*. A grid defines points that the cursor "locks" to; other software calls this a snap or snap-to feature. For this tutorial, we'll use a grid of .1 VREAM units. The Editor/Cursor/Cursor Lock menu selection causes the prompt line to make the following request:

`Cursor Lock: Current Value=0.000000, enter new value(0).`

Type a value of **.1**, and then press Enter. Look at the bottom status line. Cursor positions are now indicated with only one digit to the right of the decimal point. Previously, you could have moved the cursor anywhere—to a 3D point such as –5.23847, 4.298374, or 0.13847. Now you are limited to points like –5.2, 4.3, and 0.1.

---

[13]You can also press the F3 key to toggle the status lines. It will change from Viewer mode to Cursor mode to Tracker mode and then back to Viewer mode. You'll need to wiggle the mouse to move the cursor to complete the change into a new mode.

Figure 9.11
*Setting the status
bar mode.*

Now we are ready to start. Since this is probably your first time working with VREAM, we'll go through the first few steps in the process detail by detail, so that you get a comfortable feel for the VREAM interface. Once we've established the ground rules, I'll move ahead faster.

Building the Robot: The Head

Let's start with the robot's head, and work our way down. Click the Cube icon in the toolbar (see Fig. 9.12). Note that the prompt line says

Cube tool

`CUBE: Enter base point.`

> This is how you create objects in VREAM: Click the icon, and then follow the prompts. Pay close attention to that prompt line. Sometimes it will ask you to do things you might not have anticipated.

We don't want to enter just any point; we want to enter a very specific starting (base) point. Verify that the status bar is in Cursor mode—look for cur at the left of the bottom status line. Now look at the right side of the bottom status line as you move the cursor. It shows the position of the cursor in 3D space.

Look closely at the bottom status line in Figure 9.12. There are three numbers on the right-hand side after the letter W. The first number is the X coordinate, the second number is the Z coordinate, and the third number is the Y coordinate.[14] Keep that order in mind: XZY. Repeat it often. XZY. XZY. XZY. Get used to it, because we'll be referring to this part of the status bar over and over and over again.

---

[14]Yes, it would have been nice if the VREAM folks would have put these in X, Y, Z order. Why didn't they? That is one of the great mysteries of software development.

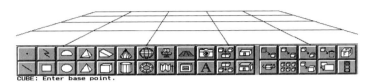

Figure 9.12
Entering a base point for a cube.

A careful analysis of Figure 9.12 reveals the following values:

X—0.5

Z—0

Y—4

Move the cursor carefully until you match these values. You may have to experiment a bit to get a feeling for which mouse movement changes which value. This will probably seem awkward for a while, but by the time we finish building the robot, you'll be an expert at moving in three dimensions.

To move the mouse in and out of the work area, press and hold the right mouse button. Watch the status line to see the coordinate of the Z dimension change. You'll also see the cursor get smaller as it moves away, and larger as it moves toward you. These are very useful visual cues, but it's the status bar values that count.

When you have the correct coordinates in the status bar, carefully click the left mouse button[15] to set the base point. The prompt now changes to

CUBE: Enter Width.

---

[15]I say *carefully* because, if you aren't careful, the coordinates will change and you probably won't even notice! If this does happen, remember that you can click both mouse buttons simultaneously to abort any procedure.

Figure 9.13 shows how to indicate width. The correct coordinates for the cursor are

X—0.5

Z—0

Y—4

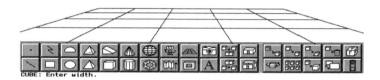

Figure 9.13
Entering the width.

When you have these exact values in the right side of the bottom status line, carefully click the left mouse button.

The prompt changes again, to

CUBE: Enter Depth.

Figure 9.14 shows how to enter the depth. Remember to press and hold the right mouse button to move the cursor forward into the work area. The values for depth are

X—0.5

Z—1

Y—4

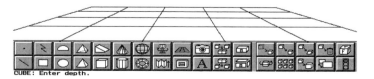

Figure 9.14
Entering the depth.

If you are doing the math in your head, you know that we are building a cube that will be one VREAM unit on a side. When you have the exact values in 3D space, click the left button.

The prompt changes again, to

`CUBE: Enter Height.`

Drag the mouse upward (see Fig. 9.15) until the values in the status line are

> **X**—0.5
>
> **Z**—1
>
> **Y**—5

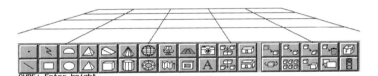

Figure 9.15
Entering the height.

Click to enter the height. That's it—we've followed the prompts, and now we get our reward (see Fig. 9.16).

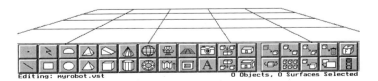

Figure 9.16
The cube appears.

Now select the cube by clicking it. Figure 9.17 shows what a VREAM object looks like when it is selected: The corners get little black boxes. Use the Attribute/General/Name menu selection; you will see a prompt that says

```
OBJECT NAME: Current value is '', enter new value.
```

Figure 9.17
Selecting an object.

Enter the name **Head**, and then press Enter. Note that, after you press Enter, the prompt line says

```
OBJECT NAME: 'Head' entered, click Left to continue.
```

VREAM does this a lot. It is asking you to click the left mouse button. You'll see this kind of prompt often, and I won't mention it again. When it happens, just click to continue.

This is a good time to save your work; use the File/Save menu selection.

Building the Robot: The Torso

When I look back at what we've covered so far, just to add a cube for the robot's head, I think that you, dear reader, might be worrying about how complicated this procedure has become. Part of this is due to the fact that I have explained the construction of that little cube in great detail. There are so many choices, so many tools, so many options, that I thought it best to go into even excruciating detail so as not to get lost along the way. From now on, when we encounter something we've done before, I'll be much briefer.

The torso of the robot will also be made out of a cube. Later, when we have added more parts, we will go back and reshape the torso. The torso cube is built just like the head cube, but with different coordinates at each step. Here are the coordinates for the various points you must click:[16]

Point	Coordinates	Comments
Base	–1.4, –0.3, 4	Wider and in front of head
Width	1.4, –0.3, 4	2.8 units wide
Depth	1.4, 1.3, 4	.3 units deeper than head, total 1.6
Height	1.4, 1.3, 2	2 units high

---

[16]Refer back to the head instructions if you are unsure about any of the details.

Figure 9.18 shows what the torso should look like. It's a very good idea to name objects as you create them. Use the Attributes/General/Name menu selection to enter the name **Torso** for this object.

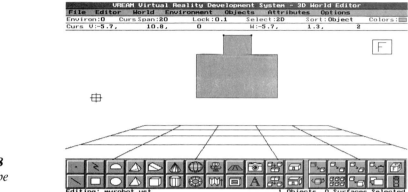

Figure 9.18
The torso cube added.

Building the Robot: The Pelvis

The pelvis is also made out of a cube. Here are the coordinates for the various points you must click:

Point	Coordinates	Comments
Base	–0.5, 0, 2	Matches head in depth
Width	0.5, 0, 2	1 unit wide
Depth	0.5, 1, 2	Same as head
Height	0.5, 1, 1	1 unit high

Figure 9.19 shows what the torso should look like. Use the Attributes/General/Name menu selection to enter the name **Pelvis** for this object.

I have deliberately made the pelvis larger than it needs to be so that we can experiment with the Resize tool. To resize the pelvis, click on it to select it.[17] VREAM tools almost always operate on the currently selected object(s). If you click a tool when no object is selected, VREAM displays a dialog box telling you of your mistake.

---

[17]You should see those little black boxes at the vertices (points) of the cube when it is selected. If you select the wrong object, just click on it again to deselect it.

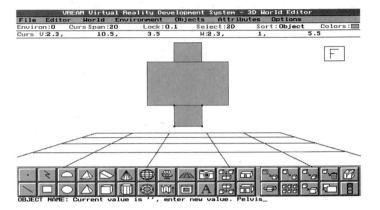

Figure 9.19
The pelvis cube added.

Resize tool

If you selected the pelvis and clicked the Resize tool, you'll see the dialog box shown in Figure 9.20. VREAM doesn't allow you to resize by dragging. You resize an object one dimension at a time, or in all dimensions simultaneously. In this case, we are going to shrink the pelvis on two dimensions. For the first resize operation, click on the X check box.[18]

Figure 9.20
The Resize dialog box.

The dialog box disappears, and the prompt line reads

RESIZE: 1 Objects selected. Enter magnification value.

Enter the value **.8** and press Enter. The pelvis shrinks slightly in width. To shrink the height of the pelvis by the same amount, click the Resize tool again, and click the Z check box. The dialog box disappears, and the prompt line says

RESIZE: 1 Objects selected. Enter magnification value.

Enter the value **.8** and press Enter. The pelvis shrinks slightly in height. Look at Figure 9.21 to see the result of shrinking two of the three dimensions.[19]

---

[18]If you recall correctly, you remember that the X axis runs from left to right. This operation will resize the width of the object.

[19]Right—the depth of the cube remains the same.

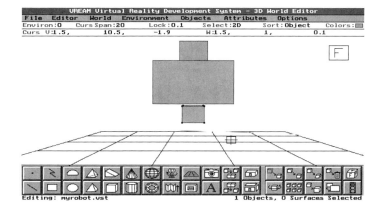

Figure 9.21
The pelvis is resized.

Shrinking the height of the pelvis, however, has created a minor problem. The pelvis is now floating below the torso. Our task is to move the pelvis upward exactly .1 VREAM unit.[20] We'll use the Move tool to accomplish the task. Click the Move tool on the toolbar. The prompt line reads

Move tool

MOVE: 1 Objects selected. Enter reference point.

VREAM is asking you to click on a reference point. For a move, the reference point can be anywhere, so click with the 3D cursor visible anywhere in the work area. I clicked at the point 1.4, 1, 1, and the prompt changed to

MOVE: 1.400000,1.00000,1.00000 selected, enter move point.

The trick here is to watch the right side of the bottom status line very closely. Move the 3D cursor just .1 unit upward, making sure that you do not move it sideways, to the coordinates 1.4, 1, 1.1 and click. This locks in the move, as shown in Figure 9.22.

Building the Robot: Modifying the Torso

A while back, I promised that we would make the torso into a more interesting shape. Now is that time. To do this, you'll need to move into Tracking mode. You can do this with the menu,[21] or simply use F3 to toggle among the three modes.[22]

---

[20]Why one tenth of a unit? It started out as 1 unit high. We shrank it to 80 percent of that value, or .8 units high. It shrank uniformly, which means the top is .1 unit lower, and the bottom is .1 unit higher.

[21]Editor/Status Bar/Status Bar Mode.

[22]Remember that you must move the mouse at least a little bit to move into the next mode. If you have trouble going from Tracker mode to Cursor mode, move the cursor to the status lines, press F3, and then move the mouse. Sometimes, VREAM appears to stubbornly skip past Cursor mode when you start in Track mode and use the F3 key.

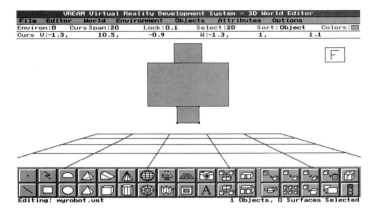

Figure 9.22
The pelvis back in position.

Figure 9.23 shows Tracker mode in operation. This mode can seem confusing at first, but it's very powerful and well worth some practice to get the hang of it. You can move the cursor all over the place in Tracker mode, but you are limited to locations where points already exist. The coordinates that show up in the status line (bottom line, right-hand side, as always) are always the coordinates of the point nearest to the 3D cursor in 3D space. For example, look closely at the torso in Figure 9.23. The torso itself is selected, as indicated by the small black squares at the corners. However, inside the torso, near the upper right corner, is a larger black square. This square corresponds to an upper corner on the back side of the torso. In other words, I was able to use the Tracker mode to select a point that I can't even see in this view! This is extremely convenient when you want to line things up.

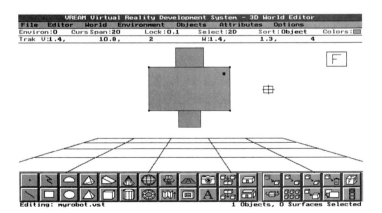

Figure 9.23
Using Tracker mode.

If I wanted to use Tracker mode to select the front corner of the torso, I would simply hold down the right mouse key and drag the mouse until the large black square jumped from the back corner to the front corner.

Let's use the Change tool to move some of the points on the torso. Click the Change tool to display the dialog box shown in Figure 9.24. Click on the Single Point check box to set the type of change. We are going to change one point at a time. The other selection allows you to move all points on a surface at one time.

Change tool

Figure 9.24
Setting the change type.

The prompt line changes to

`CHANGE SINGLE POINT: 1 Objects Selected. Select point to change.`

This is where Tracker mode becomes very handy. Move the 3D cursor in 3D space until you are able to select the front lower left point on the torso, as shown in Figure 9.25. You'll know you have selected the correct point when the status line coordinate is –1.4, –0.3, 2.

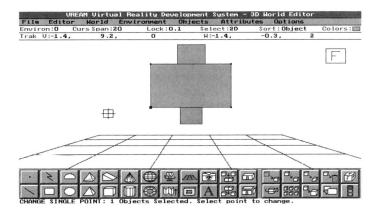

Figure 9.25
Selecting a point in Tracker mode.

The prompt line changes to

CHANGE SINGLE POINT: Enter reference point for move.

VREAM is asking you to enter a starting point for the move. In most cases, including this one, click again on the same point: –1.4, –0.3, 2. The prompt changes to

CHANGE SINGLE POINT: Enter target point for move.

You now want to select the front top-left corner of the pelvis as the target. Its coordinates are –0.4, 0, 2. Watch the status line to make sure that you have selected the correct point; you don't want to select the back corner! Figure 9.26 shows the proper point selected. Click to complete the operation. VREAM moves just this one point, as shown in Figure 9.27.

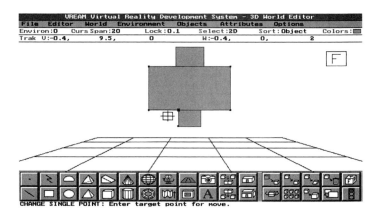

Figure 9.26
Selecting a target point.

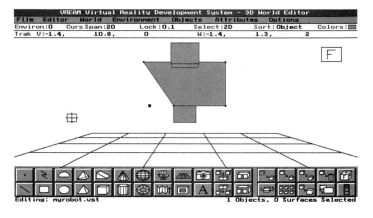

Figure 9.27
The point has moved.

The torso looks odd, doesn't it? That's because we've created such an odd shape that VREAM is confused. The back of the torso seems to have disappeared—even though we can see the back lower corner selected as a black square! Don't worry about it—VREAM does get confused about how to display complex objects. There are menu choices that allow you to help VREAM understand which surfaces are in front of other surfaces, but we don't need to do that here—we won't be leaving the torso in this condition.

We are going to move the other three bottom points of the torso to the corresponding points on the pelvis. The point at the bottom right gets moved exactly like the one we just moved. The coordinates, however, are for a different point on the pelvis: 0.4, 0, 2. Figure 9.28 shows the result.

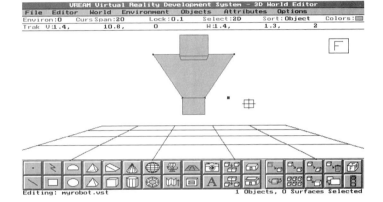

Figure 9.28
The revised front of the torso.

It will be much easier to change the points on the back of the torso if we change our viewpoint so that we are looking at the back of the robot. This is easy to do. Click the Position icon on the toolbar. This opens the dialog box shown in Figure 9.29. Simply click on the check box for Back view, and then click the Set button at the lower left. Figure 9.30 shows what you will see if you do this correctly. Note that the Compass, at the top right, shows Ba, indicating that you are in the Back view.

Position tool

Once you are at the Back view, it's easy as pie to move the two lower points on the torso to match the two corresponding points on the pelvis. The key things to watch for: Make sure that you are in Tracker mode, and make sure that you select points on the back of the pelvis to move to! The lower left point on the torso gets moved to the top left back point on the pelvis: 0.4, 1, 2. The lower right point on the torso gets moved to the top right back point on the pelvis: –0.4, 1, 2. Note that, in both cases, these are similar to the coordinates we used in the Front view. The only difference is the depth coordinate (Z), which is 1 instead of 0. Figure 9.31 shows the end result.

Figure 9.29
Changing the viewer position.

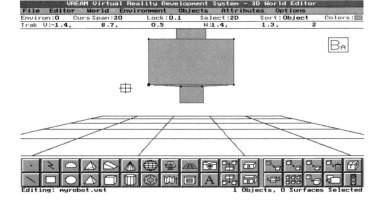

Figure 9.30
Viewing from the back.

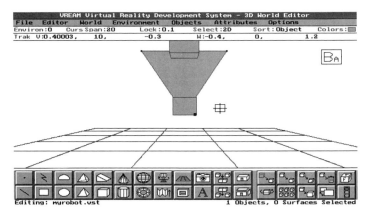

Figure 9.31
Torso tapering completed.

Viewpoint tool

Before we continue, let's switch back to Front view. Click the Viewpoint tool but, this time, click the Front check box and then click the Set button to make the change.

Building the Robot: Arms and "Hands"

Our model has a slight resemblance to a robot at this point. It's time to add some details: arms and "hands." We won't use real hands with four fingers and a thumb, however. We'll add grabbers instead.

Let's add some variety, and use the Wedge tool to create an arm. The method is similar to creating a cube, but the final result is a wedge, with its base at the start of the depth line and its tip at the end of that line. Here's the drill for creating the wedge:

Wedge tool

Click the Wedge tool. The prompt line changes to

`WEDGE: Enter base point.`

Move to –1.4, 0.3, 2 and click to establish the base of the arm. The prompt changes to

`WEDGE: Enter width.`

Move to –0.9, 0.3, 2 and click to establish the width of the base of the arm. The prompt changes to

`WEDGE: Enter depth.`

Move to –0.9, 0.7, 2 and click to establish the depth. The prompt changes to

`WEDGE: Enter height.`

Move to –0.9, 0.7, 4 and click to establish the height of the arm. Figure 9.32 shows the result. As with all objects, be sure to give it a unique name so that you can refer to it later. I recommend the name RightArm. Don't use spaces or punctuation in object names. You can use the Objects/View Object Hierarchy menu selection to display all current objects and the relationships between them.[23] Figure 9.33 shows the dialog box that displays the object hierarchy. Note that you can select or deselect (clear) objects in this dialog box.

The easiest way to create the other arm is to copy the one we already made. Click on the arm to select it, and then click the Copy tool. The prompt changes to

Copy tool

`COPY: 1 Objects Selected. Enter reference point.`

---

[23]So far, we haven't created any relationships between objects, hierarchical or otherwise. We'll do that later when we group objects.

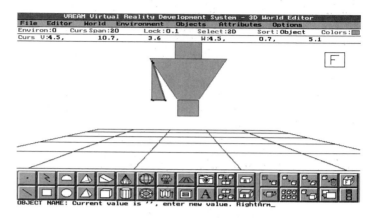

Figure 9.32
An arm is added.

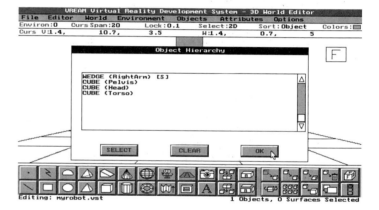

Figure 9.33
The Object Hierarchy dialog box.

Copying is like moving: You can use any two points to mark the position of the copy with respect to the original. However, it's much easier to use real points. Move the cursor to –1.4, 0.3, 4 (the top of the existing arm) and click to set the start point. The prompt changes to

```
COPY: -1.400000,0.300000,4.000000 selected, enter copy point.
```

Move the 3D cursor to the point 1.4, 0.3, 4 and click. A copy of the arm appears, as shown in Figure 9.34. Give it the name LeftArm.

*Rotate
tool*

The left arm must be rotated to be a mirror image of the right arm. If the arm isn't already selected, click on it to select it. Then click the Rotate tool on the toolbar.

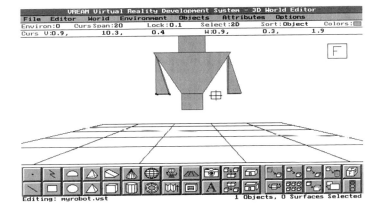

Figure 9.34
A copy of the arm.

This displays the dialog box shown in Figure 9.35. There are two choices: Set Unique Midpoint and Use Natural Midpoint(s). For this rotation, we can go ahead and use the natural midpoint of the wedge. Later, we'll be setting unique midpoints to gain control over the rotation. Click the Set button. This displays the dialog box shown in Figure 9.36.

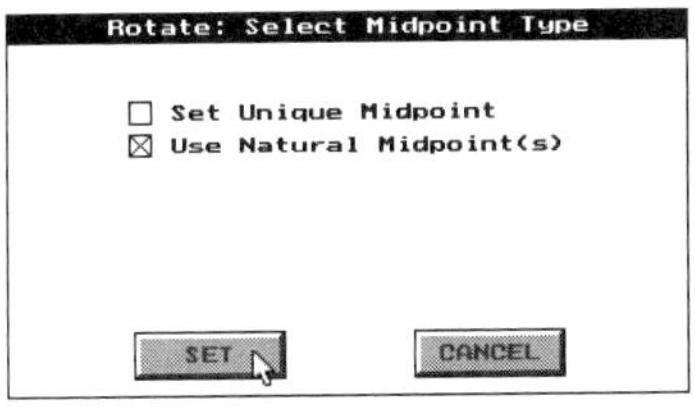

Figure 9.35
Selecting the type of midpoint.

Figure 9.36
Setting the rotation amount.

You can rotate the object in one, two, or three dimensions at one time. In this case, we want to yaw the arm 180 degrees, so click in the Yaw box, enter the number **180**, and then press Enter. Click the Set button to carry out the rotation. Figure 9.37 shows the result.

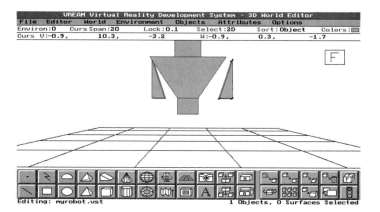

Figure 9.37
The rotated arm.

Now we need to move the arm next to the torso's shoulder. Click the Move icon, and then use Tracker mode to set the reference point for the move at the top front of the arm wedge and click.[24] Switch to Cursor mode (press the F3 key), and then move the 3D Cursor to 1.4, 0.3, 4 to set the target point and click. The arm moves to the correct location, as shown in Figure 9.38. This is a good point to save your work again, using the File/Save menu selection.

Wedge tool

The grabbers (hands) will be made up of a pair of small wedge shapes. We'll start by creating a wedge .2 units wide, .4 units deep, and .4 units high. Here are the coordinates for the wedge; just follow the prompts in the prompt line:

Base point—-1.4, 0.3, 1.5

Width point—-1.2, 0.3, 1.5

Depth point—-1.2, 0.7, 1.5

Height point—-1.2, 0.7, 1.9

Rotate tool

Figure 9.39 shows the result. Use the Attributes/General/Name menu selection to give the new object the name Rhand01. The wedge needs to be rotated into position using the Rotate tool. Click the Rotate tool, and then click the Set button in the dialog box to use the natural midpoint. In the Rotation dialog box, click in the Pitch box, type the value **180**, and then click the Set button. This rotates the grabber, as shown in Figure 9.40.

---

[24]This move would be very difficult without Tracker mode, because the X coordinate of the arm is at 1.733334.

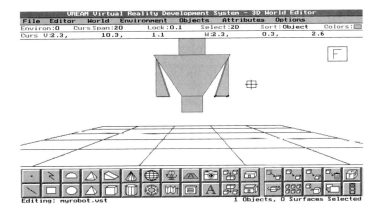

Figure 9.38
The completed left arm.

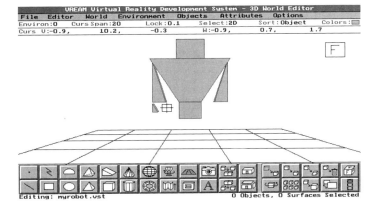

Figure 9.39
Adding a wedge for a grabber.

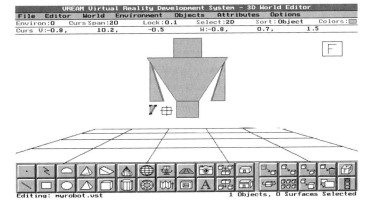

Figure 9.40
Rotating the grabber.

Copy tool

This still isn't quite where we want the grabber, but if we make a copy now, we can save a few moves later. Click the Copy tool. Then, using the rightmost point as a reference point, make the target point .4 or .5 units to the right. This creates a copy of the grabber, as shown in Figure 9.41. Give the new object the name RHand02.

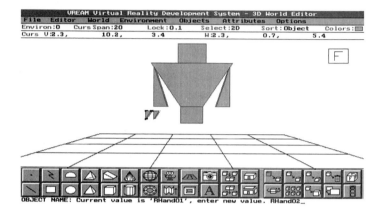

Figure 9.41
The second half of the grabber.

Rotate tool

All that remains is to rotate one of the grabbers so that it faces the other, and then move them into position.[25] Rotate the left grabber 180 degrees in Yaw, using the natural midpoint. Figure 9.42 shows the result. The two wedges are now properly oriented for the grabber.

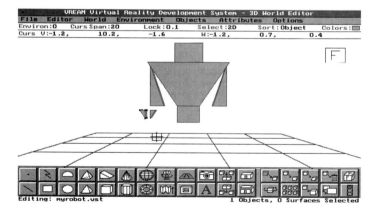

Figure 9.42
Rotating the grabber.

---

[25]Yes, I know, this is all terribly detailed. If you are following along, however, I'm sure you appreciate the details!

Now use Tracker mode to move each half of the grabber up to the arm. Align the two grabbers, as shown in Figure 9.43, using the Move tool.

Move tool

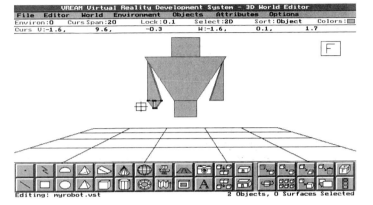

Figure 9.43
The correct orientation for the grabber parts.

We can copy both grabber parts at the same time to the other arm. Click to select each half of the grabber, and make sure that nothing else is selected.[26] Then use the Copy tool to make the copy. Figure 9.44 shows where to set the reference and target points for the move. Note that the target is at the extreme left of the grabber, and that the target is at the extreme left of the other arm. Figure 9.45 shows the result.

Copy tool

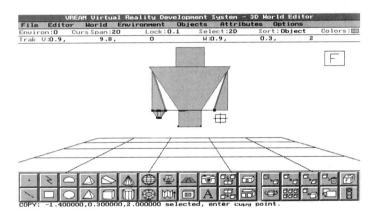

Figure 9.44
Copying the grabber.

Don't forget to give names to the grabbers on the robot's left-hand side: LHand01 and LHand02 will do fine. It doesn't matter which one gets which name—only that each one has a unique name.

---

[26]The menu selection Objects/Clear All will clear all selections.

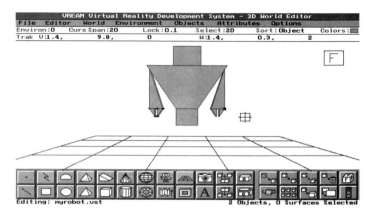

Figure 9.45
Both grabbers are
complete.

Building the Robot: Legs and Feet

Cylinder
tool

We're going to use yet another object type to build the legs for the robot: cylinders. They are created like any other object: by specifying the limits of the space they will occupy. There are some variations, however. For example, instead of the width, we'll specify a radius for the cylinder. To create the cylinder, click the Cylinder tool and use the following responses for each prompt (use the 3D cursor to move to the indicated points in 3D space[27]):

Center of base—–0.6, 0.5, –0.5

Radius of base—–0.4, 0.5, –0.5

Height point—–0.4, 0.5, 1.6

Number of sides—6

Figure 9.46 shows the result. Use the menu selection Attributes/General/Name to give the leg the name RightLeg.[28]

Cone
tool

The foot will be made from a cone. Click the Cone tool, and use these responses (use the 3D cursor to move to the indicated points):

Center of base—–0.6, 0.5, –1

Radius of base—0, 0.5, –1

Height point—0, 0.5, –0.5

Number of sides—8

---

[27]And watch that status bar to tell where you are!

[28]Yes, the leg is on the left, but, from the robot's point of view, it's his right leg. OK?

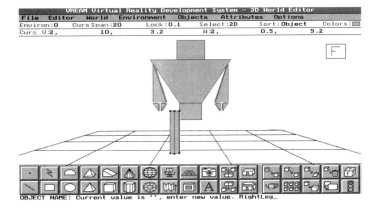

Figure 9.46
The leg added.

Figure 9.47 shows the right leg and foot added. Don't forget to give the right foot the name (sorry to be so original here) RightFoot.

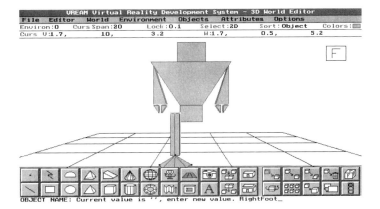

Figure 9.47
The foot added.

To make the other leg and foot, we'll copy the ones we just created. Select both the leg and the foot, and then click the Copy tool. The prompt changes to

Copy tool

COPY: 2 Objects Selected. Enter reference point.

VREAM is asking you to enter the start point for the copy. Since we want to make the new copy at a distance exactly equal to the distance from the left side of the leg (from our point of view, not the robot's!) to the right side of the pelvis, the reference point can be anywhere on the outside of the leg (see Fig. 9.48). Click on the point –0.8, 0.5, 1.6. The prompt changes to

COPY: -0.800000,0.500000,1.600000 selected, enter copy point.

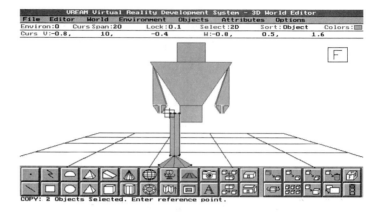

Figure 9.48
Setting a reference point.

The copy point is at the edge of the pelvis, as shown in Figure 9.49. Move the 3D cursor to 0.4, 0.5, 1.6 and click. Figure 9.50 shows the result: another leg and foot. Give them names: LeftLeg and LeftFoot.

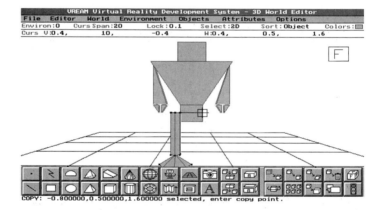

Figure 9.49
Setting a target point.

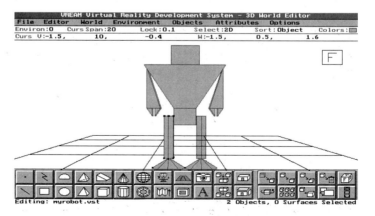

Figure 9.50
The second leg and foot added.

We are almost done with the physical construction of the robot. All we need now is a face to give it some personality.

Building the Robot: The Face

It will be easier to work on the face if we move in closer to it. The secret: that little traffic light icon at the bottom right of the toolbar. Clicking the Viewpoint icon changes it from a red light (at the left in Fig. 9.51) to a green light (at the right).

View-point tool

Figure 9.51
Using the Walk icon.

When the Viewpoint icon is active (that is, a green light), you can use keystrokes to move around in 3D space.[29] When you are done, either click both mouse buttons simultaneously or press F9 to return to normal (non-walk) mode. Table 9.1 shows the most commonly used keystrokes. For this example, press the X key 5 to 6 times to move up, and press the S key 5 to 6 times to move forward. Figure 9.52 shows the result. Don't worry if you don't see exactly this view on your monitor—if you are close to the face, you are fine. Note also that your view may not show the torso and head in the exact same relationship—VREAM may render either the torso or the head on top of each other.[30]

Figure 9.52
Moving closer to the face.

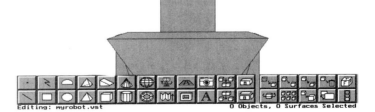

---

[29]Meanwhile, the toolbar itself and the menus become inactive.

[30]Later in this tutorial, you'll learn how to gain more control over this aspect of VREAM.

Table 9.1. VREAM Keys for Movement/Rotation.

Key	Movement/Rotation
Q	Slide left
A	Move back
Z	Move down
W	Slide right
S	Move forward
X	Move up
E	Rotate left
D	Nose down
C	Tilt left
R	Rotate right
F	Nose up
V	Tilt right

Surface tool

Click the Surface tool to display the dialog box shown in Figure 9.53. There are three kinds of surfaces you can create: three-sided, four-sided, and N-sided (where N can be any number). The first part of the face will be a rectangular background for the eyes, so click the 4 Sided Surface check box, and then click the Set button. The prompt changes to

```
4 SIDED SURFACE: Enter point #1.
```

Figure 9.53
Choosing the type of surface tool.

The rectangular surface must be located on the front surface of the head, so the first point should be at 0.4, 0, 4.9. We will create this surface object by placing points in a counterclockwise direction. Why? The front surface of an object faces you *only* if you create it in a counterclockwise direction—that's why. Figure 9.54 shows the location of this point. Move the 3D cursor to the point, and click to set it.

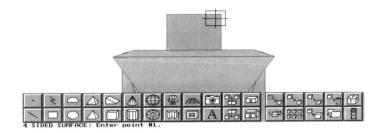

Figure 9.54

Setting the base point for a surface object.

Get into the habit of creating all objects, holes, surfaces, and so on in a counter-clockwise direction. This ensures that you won't run into display problems later. Creating in a counterclockwise direction means that the front of the object will be facing you. In the case of openings, it means that VREAM won't choke on the result!

The prompt line will now ask you to enter points 2, 3, and 4. These four points define the rectangle. Yours should look like the one shown in Figure 9.55. Like all other objects, give it a name: EyeBlock.

The EyeBlock isn't very visible—it's the same gray as the robot's head.[31] To make it stand out, let's give it a white background. Make sure that nothing else is selected, and then click on the eye background to select it. Then use the Attributes/Display/Solid Color menu selection to display the dialog box shown in Figure 9.56.

The current color of the EyeBlock (gray in the middle) has a darker box around it, and is also shown at the top of the dialog box. Let's be boring—click on the white box at the right of the dialog box to change the solid color to white.[32] Figure 9.57 shows the result.

---

[31]Of course, this whole section is in black and white, so it could have been any color, right? Well, it really *is* gray.

[32]Hey, if you want to be daring, go ahead—pick a color.

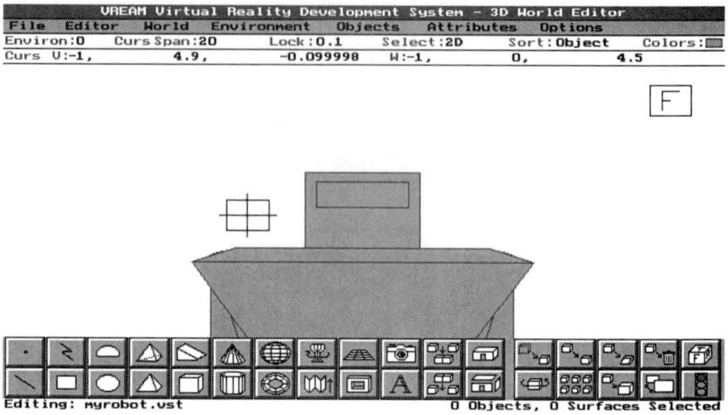

Figure 9.55
*The completed
surface object.*

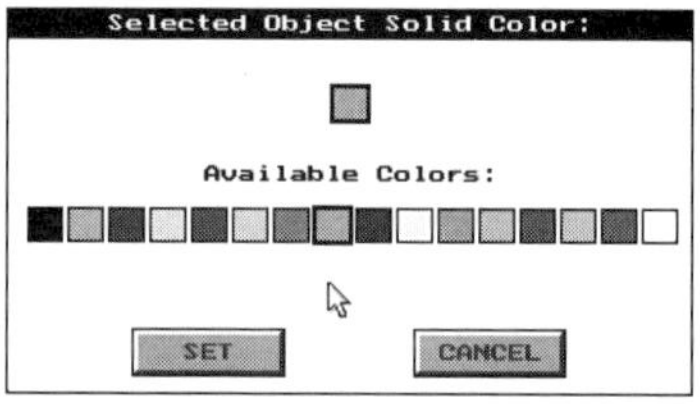

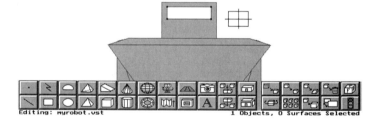

Figure 9.56
*Setting the solid
color of an object.*

Figure 9.57
*Changing the solid
color.*

*Surface
tool*

Next come the eyes. We'll create triangles (*three-sided surface objects,* in VREAM lingo)
for the eyes. Click the Surface tool, but this time click the 3 Sided Surface check box.
(Refer to Fig. 9.53 to see the dialog box.) Create a triangular eye, as shown in Figure
9.58, by clicking the three points of the triangle. Give it the name RightEye. As with
the EyeBlock, make sure that the coordinates are on the front of the head. This puts
the eyes in the same plane as the EyeBlock. You may have to move the EyeBlock out
of the way to see the eye; Figure 9.59 shows this situation.

If you have trouble selecting an object, use the Object/View Object Hierarchy menu selection to show objects by name. Click on the desired object's name, and then click the Select button to select it. Click OK when you are done selecting.

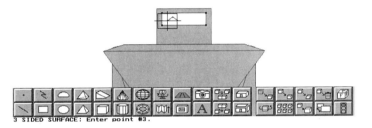

Figure 9.58
Using a triangle for an eye.

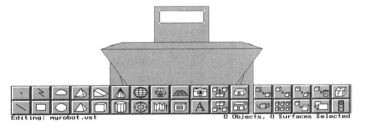

Figure 9.59
The EyeBlock hides the eye.

Use the Copy tool to make a copy of the eye; give it the name LeftEye. Figure 9.60 shows the result.

Copy tool

Now let's create a mouth. You might be tempted to create a smile (I was), but there's an important VREAM concept that gets in the way of this apparently simple task: All objects and surfaces must have positive curvature. This means that you can create a shape like the one shown in Figure 9.61, but you cannot create a shape like the one in Figure 9.62. Figure 9.63 shows what happens when you create a shape with negative curvature: VREAM gets confused. It's not designed to handle such shapes.[33]

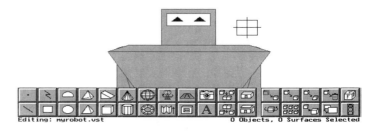

Figure 9.60
Two eyes on the EyeBlock.

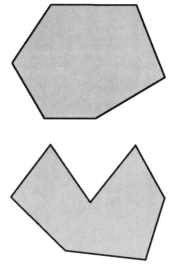

Figure 9.61
A shape with correct (positive or convex) curvature.

Figure 9.62
A shape with incorrect (negative or concave) curvature.

---

[33]This is common among VR modeling packages; don't blame VREAM!

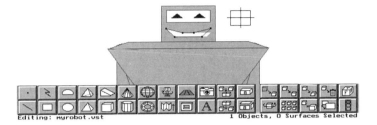

Figure 9.63
The result of using negative curvature.

To create shapes that appear to have negative curvature, you must combine two or more shapes which, taken together, give you the shape you want. Then you can use grouping (discussed shortly) to combine the separate objects. To create the mouth, click the Surface tool and select N Sided Surface (see Fig. 9.64).[34]

Surface tool

You can be as creative as you want with the shape of the mouth—just keep the curvature positive. Figure 9.65 shows my artistic effort. As with all the face features, make sure that the 3D cursor is at the same plane as the front surface of the head.[35] Give the mouth the name (drum roll, please) Mouth. If you want, make the mouth white with a red outline. To change the outline color, use the Attributes/Display/Wireframe color menu selection. This completes the face. As a matter of fact, this completes the first phase of our work: We have built all the parts for the robot. Save your work. It's time to start looking at how to group the parts together into a coherent whole.

Figure 9.64
Select N Sided Surface.

---

[34]The N means that you can create a surface with any number of sides. It comes from mathematics.

[35]If you did not know the coordinates of the front surface of the head, you could find them by using Point-Tracker mode, couldn't you?

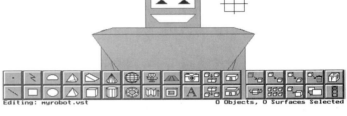

Figure 9.65
The mouth has been added.

Building the Robot: Grouping

Let's take a break from building the robot and discuss how (and why) one groups objects within VREAM. There are two key reasons for grouping:

- To link related objects. For example, we can group the leg and the foot so that when the leg moves, the foot will follow it.

- To enable objects that touch each other to display properly. Throughout this tutorial, you have probably noticed that VREAM often gets confused about which object is in front of which other objects. Grouping can fix this problem. It's not easy, mind you, but it can be done. This process is called *sorting*, and it's critical to get it right.

Linking Related Objects

Group tool

Grouping related objects is the easier of these two tasks. The example I used earlier, grouping the leg and the foot, is a simple example. But even grouping large numbers of objects is easy. You simply select the objects you want to group, and then group them. To group, click the Group tool.

Ungroup tool

If you need to ungroup, you can use the Ungroup tool. For example, if you have grouped objects, but then need to change one object in the group, you need to ungroup, make the change, and then group again. Any properties you assigned to the group, however, will be undone when you ungroup, and must be reapplied.

In many cases, however, you will find that you need to make special arrangements before grouping. This has to do with object and surface sorting, the topic of the following section.

Grouping to Control Sorting

You've seen plenty of evidence proving that, without some kind of help from you, VREAM will have a tough time displaying objects properly. For example, the head and the torso share a common surface. VREAM isn't clever enough to figure out which object is in front of the other—that would slow VREAM down quite a bit. The result is that you need to give VREAM hints about how to accomplish proper display. The key is sorting. By telling VREAM which surface on an object sorts ahead of other surfaces on that or other objects, you can control this properly.

The key to this technique is identifying a surface on one object to serve as a reference. These are called *group surface joints*, and they come in three flavors:

Relative surface joint—The surface of *one object* in a group is identified and marked so that the object sorts correctly *relative* to one other object in the group.

Absolute surface joint—The surface of *one object in a group* is identified and marked so that the object sorts correctly for *all other* objects in the group.

Group relative surface joint—The surface of *one object in a group* is identified and marked so that the group sorts correctly *relative* to other objects *or groups*.

Yes, these are terribly technical definitions, and I will do my best to clarify them for you. Note carefully the words in italics; they'll help you tell the difference between these different kinds of joints. Let's look at some examples that show how these various kinds of joints are used. Then we'll apply them to the tutorial.

You may have noticed that we've been giving every object a name. This is especially critical when it comes to surface joints. VREAM will choke and die if you try to create joints for objects that do not have names. Always name your objects! You can use the Object/View Object Hierarchy menu selection to verify that all objects have names.

Relative Surface Joint

The relative surface joint is one of the most commonly used joints. However, it should never be used if you can use the absolute surface joint (next section).

VREAM renders different kinds of joints at different speeds. The absolute surface joints render the fastest, and if you can use an absolute joint, you should. Use a relative joint only if an absolute joint won't work for you. Group relative joints render slowest of all, but they are sometimes necessary.

The purpose of the relative joint is to force one object in a group to display (sort) itself properly in relation to another object. Consider the case of a simple chair, which has a back, a seat, and four legs. Your job is to tell VREAM which surface on the LEG faces the SEAT. This surface defines a plane that will completely separate the two objects. Obviously, this would be the top surface of the leg. To set the joint, you would

- Select the LEG.
- Select the top surface of the LEG by holding down the Alt key, and then clicking on the top surface.[36]
- Select the SEAT.
- Use the Attributes/Group/Group Surface Joint menu selection to display a dialog box in which you choose Relative Surface Joint.

We'll perform this operation later (sort of[37]), when we group the arms and the torso. In general, to create a relative surface joint, you must select

- An object
- A surface on the object that defines a plane completely separating two objects
- A second object

Absolute Surface Joint

Absolute surface joints are the preferred method of joining objects. They are also much easier to create than other kinds of surface joints. Whenever possible, use an absolute joint.

How can you tell whether you can use an absolute surface joint? The main requirement is that you are able to define a single surface that faces all the other objects in a group. In the case of a chair, the SEAT faces all four LEGs. You could select the bottom surface of the SEAT as an absolute surface joint. You would then group the SEAT

---

[36]If necessary, you would use the Viewpoint icon or the Compass to change the viewpoint so that you can see that top surface.

[37]No pun intended, I assure you.

and the LEGs, and then group that group and the BACK into a group.[38] That makes the SEAT/LEGs group a subgroup.

To actually create the absolute surface joint, you would do the following:

- Select the SEAT.
- Select the bottom surface of the SEAT by holding down the Alt key, and then clicking on the bottom surface.
- Use the Attributes/Group/Group Surface Joint menu selection to display a dialog box in which you choose Absolute Surface Joint.

We'll perform this operation later, when we group the legs and the feet. In general, to create an absolute surface joint, you must select

- An object.
- A surface on the object that defines a plane completely separating the object from all other objects in a group.

Group Relative Surface Joint

A group relative surface joint is a lot like a relative surface joint. However, instead of sorting a single object relative to a selected surface, the entire group is sorted.

The purpose of the group relative joint is to force one group of objects to display (sort) itself properly in relation to another object or group. In the case of the chair, you could group the legs and the seat, and then define the top of the SEAT as the group relative joint with respect to the BACK. To set the joint, you would

- Select the SEAT/LEGs group.
- Select the top surface of the SEAT by holding down the Alt key, and then clicking on the top surface.[39]
- Select the BACK.
- Use the Attributes/Group/Group Surface Joint menu selection to display a dialog box in which you choose Group Relative Surface Joint.

We'll perform this operation later, when we group the head and the torso. In general, to create a group relative surface joint, you must select

- A group.

---

[38] I know, too many groups, but how else would you say it?

[39] If necessary, you would use the Viewpoint icon or the Compass to change the viewpoint so you can see that top surface.

- A surface on the group that defines a plane completely separating two objects or groups.
- A second object or group.

Grouping the Robot

When you are grouping a complex object, the best strategy is to start at the extremities and work your way toward the center. This makes it easier to tell what kinds of groups to create, and will generally result in better sorting and proper display of objects. In the case of the robot, we'll start with the legs and arms, and move toward the torso/pelvis.

> Surface joints won't show up in the display until we actually group objects with the Group tool. Until then, any display problems you have noticed will continue to occur. Another way to put that: If you are having problems getting objects to display properly relative to each other, you should create a surface joint between them, and then group them.

Grouping the Head

Before we proceed, let's create a simple group first: the head and face. The face objects are all surface objects. By default, they are double-sided, and are likely to show up on both sides of the head. We need to change their visibility value so that they only show on the front of the head. Select the face objects (two eyes, the EyeBlock, and the mouth), and then use the Attributes/Display/Visibility Value menu selection to display the dialog box shown in Figure 9.66. Check the Front check box, and then click the Set button. You won't see any immediate difference, but when we've grouped the face objects and the head, the face will now only show on the front of the head.

Next, let's change the group level of the face objects. This will ensure that the correct surface objects are visible above other surface objects. Click to select the mouth, or use the Object/View Object Hierarchy menu selection to select it by name. Then click on the Attributes/Group/Group Level menu selection, which changes the prompt to read

```
OBJECT LEVEL: Current value is '0', enter new value.
```

VREAM Virtual Reality Development System - 3D World Editor
File Editor World Environment Objects Attributes Options
Environ:0   Curs Span:20   Lock:0.05   Select:2D   Sort:Object   Colors:▨
Curs V:1.25,   4.8,   1.5   W:1.25,   -0.1,   6.1

F

Object Visibility Value

☒ Front
☐ Back
☐ Both

SET   CANCEL

Editing: myrobot.vst   4 Objects, 0 Surfaces Selected

Figure 9.66
Setting an object's
visibility.

The new value for the mouth is 1. Repeat this for EyeBlock, setting its object level to 1. Then select each of the eyes, and set their object level to 2. The higher object level will make sure that the eyes display above the EyeBlock, avoiding problems such as that shown in Figure 9.67. Now we can create the group. Select both eyes, the EyeBlock, the mouth, and the head (see Fig. 9.68). Click the Group icon; and the prompt changes to

Group
tool

GROUP: 5 Objects Selected. Enter name of group object.

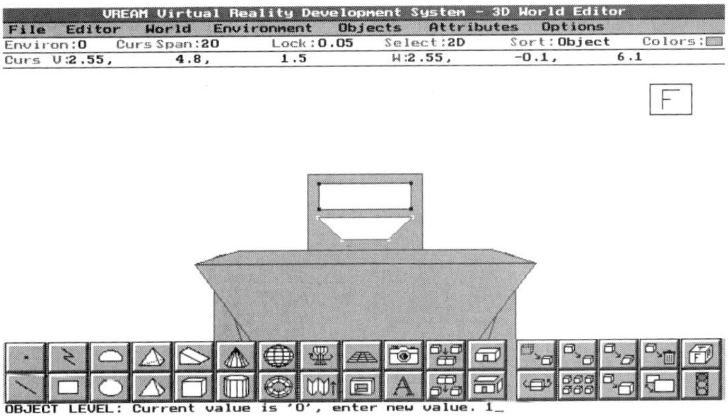

VREAM Virtual Reality Development System - 3D World Editor
File Editor World Environment Objects Attributes Options
Environ:0   Curs Span:20   Lock:0.05   Select:2D   Sort:Object   Colors:▨
Curs V:2.55,   4.8,   1.5   W:2.55,   -0.1,   6.1

F

Figure 9.67
The EyeBlock hides
the eyes.

OBJECT LEVEL: Current value is '0', enter new value. 1_

Type the name **GHead** and press Enter. The five objects now behave like one—if you click anywhere on the head or on any of the face surface objects, the entire collection is selected. That's the nature of a group. The individual objects lose their separate identities, and the entire collection acts like a single object for selection purposes.[40] This is a good time to save your work to your hard disk.

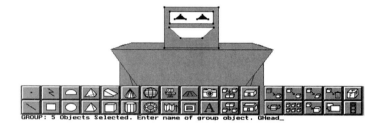

Figure 9.68
Selecting objects for a group and naming the group.

Grouping the Legs

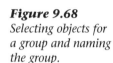

Position tool

Viewpoint tool

The first joint to create is one between a leg and a foot. Right now, all we can see is the head and shoulders. Click the Position tool, click on Front, and then click the Set button to change back to standard Front view. Then click the Viewpoint tool to activate Walk mode. Press the Z key until your point of view is below the robot, as shown in Figure 9.69. The important point is that we must be able to see the bottom surface of the leg in order to select it.

Figure 9.69
Changing the viewpoint.

---

[40]Many operations, however, will not operate on a group. In such cases, you'll need to Ungroup, operate on each object individually, and then Group.

This will be an absolute surface joint. Start by clicking on the left leg (that's the robot's left), as shown in Figure 9.70. Then press and hold the Alt key, and click on the bottom surface of that leg. Figure 9.71 shows the result. Note that when you select a single surface, that surface is outlined with larger black boxes, and the color of the surface changes. The surface we have selected is small and these changes aren't easy to see but, in later examples, you'll see it more clearly.

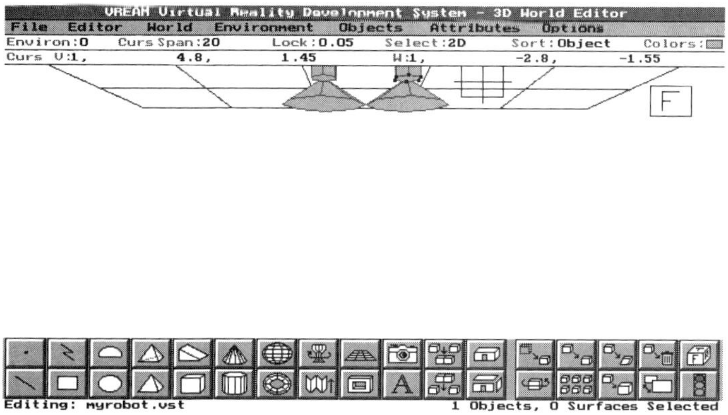

Figure 9.70
Selecting the robot's left leg.

Figure 9.71
Selecting a single surface.

We now have the requirements for an absolute surface joint: a selected object and a selected surface on that object. Use the Attributes/Group/Group Surface Joint menu selection to display the dialog box shown in Figure 9.72. It shows the three types of surface joints. Click on Absolute, and then click on Set. VREAM asks for confirmation, as shown in Figure 9.73.

Figure 9.72
Making a joint
absolute.

Figure 9.73
Confirmation of
joint type.

Group
tool

Deselect all objects[41] and then select the robot's left leg and left foot. Click the Group tool, and the prompt changes to

GROUP: 2 Objects Selected. Enter name of group object.

Enter a name of **GLeftLeg**. The G stands for *group*. If you peek at the Objects/View Object Hierarchy menu selection's dialog box, you'll see that groups have names, too. Now repeat this entire sequence for the right leg and right foot, and give the group the name GRightLeg.

Grouping the Arms

Position
tool

Use the Position tool to change back to Front view. Click the Position tool again, and this time click on Unique (see Fig. 9.74). This allows you to set a new viewpoint by clicking in the 3D space. The prompt line will ask you for a starting point; use 0, –5, –1.5. For a target point, use a point that is up and closer to the robot, such as 0, –2, 0. The view changes to that shown in Figure 9.75. Your view may differ a bit, depending on the exact coordinates you chose.

This allows us to see the bottom surface of the arms. These are the surfaces we'll use to properly group the arms and the grabbers. Click on the robot's right arm (that's the left side from your point of view), and then hold down the Alt key and click on the bottom surface of the arm wedge (see Fig. 9.76).

---

[41]**Hint:** Use the Objects/Clear All menu selection.

Figure 9.74
Setting a unique viewpoint.

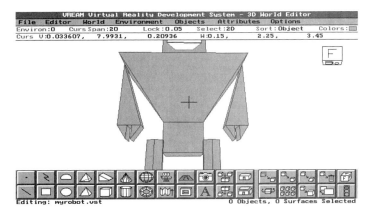

Figure 9.75
The new viewpoint.

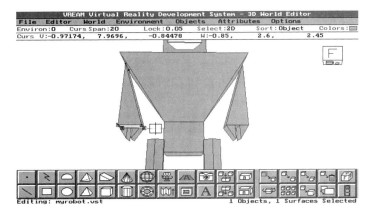

Figure 9.76
Selecting a single surface.

As we did with the leg, this will be an absolute surface joint, so there is nothing more to select. Use the Attributes/Group/Group Surface Joint menu selection to display the Select Joint Type dialog box (see Fig. 9.77). Click on Absolute, and then click the Set button.

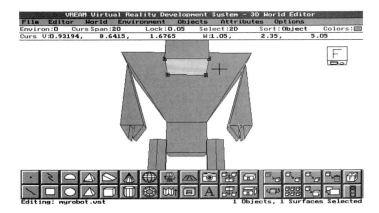

Figure 9.77
Setting the joint type.

Group tool

Now let's group the arm and the grabbers. Clear all selections, and then select the arm wedge and the two grabber wedges. Click the Group tool. When the prompt asks for a name for the group, type **GRightArm** and press Enter. Repeat this process for the robot's left arm, and give it the name GLeftArm.

Grouping the Head and Face Objects

The head group is next. Make sure that nothing is selected, click anywhere on the head group to select it, and then hold down the Alt key and click on the bottom of the head to select that surface (see Fig. 9.78). Then click on the torso to select it. Use the Attributes/Group/Group Surface Joint selection to display the Select Joint Type dialog box. Because the head is a group, click on Group Relative as the joint type, and then click the Set button.

Figure 9.78
Selecting the bottom surface of the head group.

Grouping the Groups

Now let's add an absolute surface joint to the pelvis. Note how we are working toward the center with these various joints. Figure 9.79 shows the drill: Select the pelvis, and then hold down the Alt key and click on the top surface.[42] Use the Attributes/Group/Group Surface Joint menu selection to display the Select Joint Type dialog box, click on Absolute, and then click the Set button.

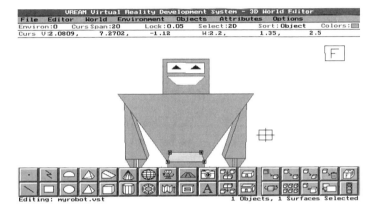

Figure 9.79
Selecting the top of
the pelvis.

We have grouped the parts for each of the legs and arms. Now let's group the parts for the body: the head group, the torso, and the pelvis. Clear all selections, and then select the head group, the torso, and the pelvis. Click the Group tool, and give the body the name GBody.[43]

*Group
tool*

This would be a good time to make an editorial comment. We've done a lot of stuff so far, and we're not done yet. We built the model. Now this stuff with joints is taking forever. Are you getting frustrated? These steps might seem tedious right now, but as you work with VREAM over time, you'll realize that there is a lot of power in all these joints. It's well worth the time to make them.

So let's make more of them! The arms are next. Clear all selections, and then click on the robot's right arm to select it. Hold down the Alt key and carefully click on the inside surface of the arm wedge (see Fig. 9.80). Click on GBody to select it. Because the arm is a group, you'll need to make the joint type Group Relative.[44]

---

[42]One nice thing about the "problems" that VREAM has with displaying objects before you add surface joints: It makes it easy to pop an object to the front and select surfaces.

[43]Note that all group objects have names that start with G. This isn't required, but it will make it easier to tell which objects are groups, and which are not.

[44]Use the Attributes/Group/Group Surface Joint menu selection, and click on Group Relative.

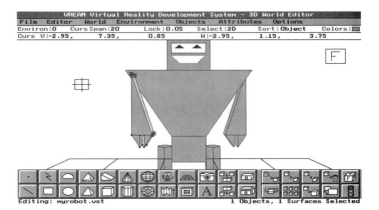

Figure 9.80
Selecting the inside arm surface.

Repeat for the robot's left arm, and remember to also select the GBody before you set the joint type. If you forget, VREAM will give you an error message telling you that you didn't select the GBody.

The legs are next. Use the Viewpoint icon to go into Walk mode, and then use the Z key to move downward until you are looking at the legs. Use the S key to move forward until you can clearly see the inside surface of both legs (see Fig. 9.81).

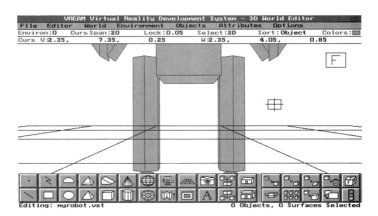

Figure 9.81
Zooming in on the legs.

Select the robot's right leg, and then carefully select the inside surface (see Fig. 9.82). Since the leg is a group (leg plus foot), this is another group relative joint. Click on the GBody to select it, too, and then use the Attributes/Group/Group Surface Joint menu selection to make it a group relative joint. Repeat for the other leg.

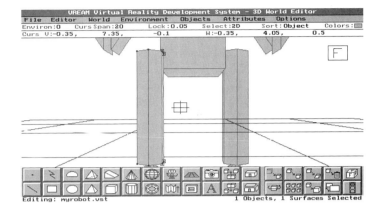

Figure 9.82
Selecting the inside surface.

That last joint was, in fact, the last joint. It's time to group everything we've got into the robot. Use the Object/Select All menu selection to select all objects. Then click on the Group tool, and give the whole shootin' match the name Frankie.[45] This is a good time to save your work.[46] Figure 9.83 shows our work so far. Note that, with the grouping, all the various parts of the robot now display correctly.

Group tool

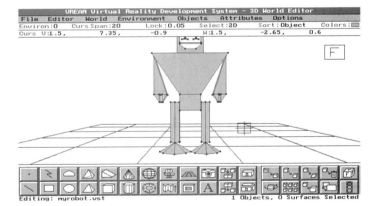

Figure 9.83
The completed robot model.

However, we're not done yet. We have a robot, and we have defined all its joints, but we haven't made it do anything. The next section is where the real fun starts. All so far is but prelude; the best is yet to come.

---

[45] Hey, if you have a better name, use it!

[46] If you feel industrious, you can construct a room for Frankie to move around in. You can apply textures, add objects, or do whatever else you want. However, we won't be exploring those options in this tutorial.

The Robot in Motion

Ungroup tool

Believe it or not, the first thing we have to do next is to *ungroup* the robot! In order to operate on the various objects and subgroups, we must be able to select them individually. Click the Ungroup tool, and the prompt changes to

`UNGROUP: 1 Groups Selected, click left to ungroup, right+left to quit.`

Click to proceed. Use the Object/Clear All menu selection to clear all selections.

Rotation

Click on the robot's left leg to select it, as shown in Figure 9.84.

To add motion to objects, you'll be using the Attributes/Motion submenu. Figure 9.85 shows this menu in action. The first job is to click on Object Axis.[47] This displays the dialog box show in Figure 9.86. Click OK to continue. All this does is set the group's axis at the default location.[48]

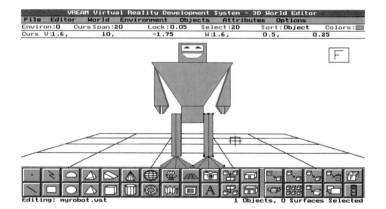

Figure 9.84
Selecting the left leg.

We are going to rotate the leg. Click on the Attributes/Motion/Auto Rotate menu selection to display yet another submenu (see Fig. 9.87). This menu allows you to set *values* for auto-rotation (how many degrees per frame), to set *limits* for auto-rotation (start and stop angles), and to select *true rotation* (rotation stays the same even if the

---

[47]Later, you are going to repeat this process for the other leg. This is where you start from: setting the object axis of the leg.

[48]If you wanted it at a different orientation, you would rotate the object to that orientation, and then click this menu choice.

object moves). The first thing we'll do is click on Maintain True Rotation. In the dialog box that pops up, there are two choices: to maintain, or to not maintain, true rotation. Click on Maintain True Rotation, and then click on Set to complete the choice.

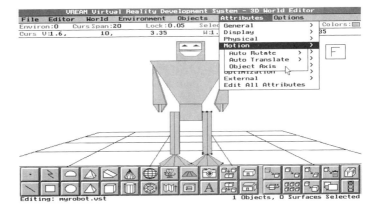

Figure 9.85
The Motion submenu.

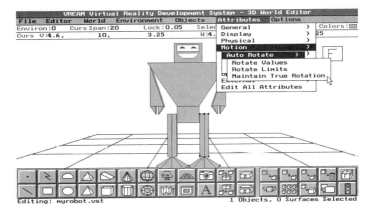

Figure 9.86
Setting the object axis.

Figure 9.87
The Auto Rotate submenu.

Now click on the Attributes/Motion/Auto Rotate/Rotate Values menu selection; the dialog box shown in Figure 9.88 appears. Every rotation must have a point around which it rotates. You can choose between using a natural midpoint or setting a unique midpoint. We want the leg to rotate from the top, so we need to select Set Unique Midpoint. Click Set to continue. The prompt line reads

`AUTO ROTATE: Center at 0,000,0,000,0.000. Enter a new one.`

Figure 9.88
Setting the type of midpoint.

You are asked to set a point for the center of rotation. Go into Tracker mode and select the top left point on the leg shown in Fig. 9.89. Click to continue; the dialog box shown in Figure 9.90 appears. Click on Pitch, and enter a value of **10**. This is the number of degrees the object will rotate for each frame of the animation at runtime.[49]

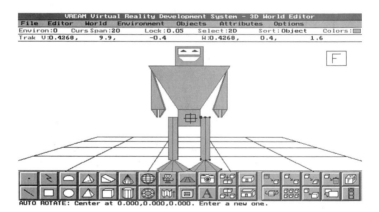

Figure 9.89
Setting the center of rotation.

Figure 9.90
Setting the amount of rotation.

---

[49]If you have a very fast computer, such as a Pentium, you might want to try a lower value—otherwise, the robot may move too fast to appear natural.

At this point, the leg will rotate through a full 360 degrees of pitch change—around and around. We need to set limits so that the motion is more natural. Now click on the Attributes/Motion/Auto Rotate/Rotate Limits menu selection. The dialog box shown in Figure 9.91 appears. Click next to the word Pitch to turn on the Pitch limits. Enter a value of **–30** as Limit 1 and **30** as Limit 2.[50] Repeat all of this to set the object axis for the other leg, with one difference: Set the rotation for pitch per frame to –10 instead of 10, so that the legs will move alternately, imitating a walking motion (one forward, one backward). **Important:** Save your work, because you'll be needing it in a moment.

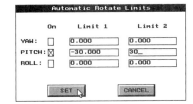

Figure 9.91
Setting rotate limits.

To view the walking motion, click the Viewpoint tool, and watch the robot's legs. Figure 9.92 shows the legs in action. When you are done, use File/Revert to go back to the point where the robot's legs are straight.[51]

Viewpoint tool

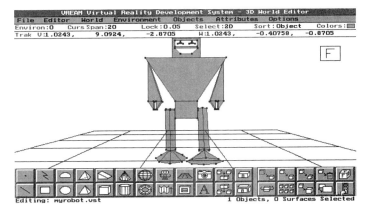

Figure 9.92
The legs in motion.

---

[50]Always put the lower limit in Limit 1.

[51]That's all the rotational motion we're going to add as part of the tutorial. If you are interested in some extra credit, you can do the same thing for the arms. However, swap the 10 and –10 values for the arms, so that they rotate alternately to the leg on the same side as each arm. That is, if the left leg has a value of –10 for pitch, give the left arm a value of +10.

Translation

Rotate tool

Our next move is to rotate the robot so that we can walk it from side to side using Auto Translation.[52] Select the robot, and then click the Rotate tool. In the dialog box that appears, set a Yaw value of 90 degrees. The robot will now face to the right (see Fig. 9.93).[53] Click to select the entire robot.

Click on the Attributes/Motion/Auto Translate/Translate Values menu selection to display the Midpoint Type dialog box. Select Use Natural Midpoint. The dialog box shown in Figure 9.94 appears. We're going to move the robot along the X axis, so enter a value of **1**.[54]

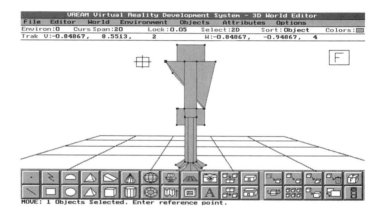

Figure 9.93
Turning the robot.

Figure 9.94
Turning Auto Translate on.

If we did nothing else, the robot would start moving and never stop. We need to set translation limits. Click on the Attributes/Motion/Auto Translate/Translate Limits menu selection to display the dialog box shown in Figure 9.95. Click to turn on the X axis, and then enter values of **–9** for Limit 1 and **9** for Limit 2.[55] This means that,

---

[52]*Translation* is just fancy VREAM lingo for *move*.

[53]Your robot isn't going to look like mine—I opted for the slim look.

[54]1 means On and 0 means Off.

[55]Limits are relative to the position of the robot at the time you set the limits.

when the robot gets to either limit, it will stop and reverse direction. Save your work, especially if you plan to view the robot's motion, because you'll need to use File/ Revert to get back to the base position of the robot. Note that, as the robot moves back and forth, it always faces the same way. It is walking backward in one direction, forward in the other.

Figure 9.95
Setting translation limits.

Links

It's nice to have an animated robot at your disposal. Now, we'll use links to make the motion better, and to give the user interactive control over the robot. Figure 9.96 shows the Links submenu. Our first job: to turn links on. Click on the Links On/Off selection. Click on Runtime Links On to turn links on, and then click Set.

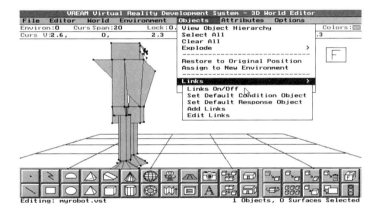

Figure 9.96
The Links submenu.

The first link will make the robot turn around when it reaches the end of its walk. To properly control this rotation, start by clicking to select the entire robot. Then click on the Attributes/Motion/Object Motion menu selection, and click the Set button to set the axis at the current orientation. Next, use the Attributes/Motion/Auto Translate/Maintain True Translation menu selection to turn True Translation on. Next, go through the steps for setting translation limits, and set them to zero on the X axis. We're going to control the limits using links instead.

Now click on the Objects/Links/Add Links menu selection. The dialog box shown in Figure 9.97 appears. Click in the Select New Cond./Resp. Objects check box. This tells VREAM that we intend to click to select the objects for the condition and the response. The *condition object* determines when the link takes effect, and the *response object* is affected by the link.

Figure 9.97
Choosing the link-selection method.

The prompt line changes to

LINKS: Select the condition object.

Click on the robot. The prompt line changes to

LINKS: Frankie chosen, select the response object.

Click on the robot. It will serve as both the condition and response object. The prompt says

LINKS: Frankie is condition, Frankie is response, click L to continue.

Click the left mouse button to continue. The dialog box shown in Figure 9.98 appears. It lists the various conditions that are available. Scroll to Object Position, click to select it, and click the Set button.

Figure 9.98
Selecting the condition.

Enter the following values into the dialog box that appears asking you for the position coordinates (see Fig. 9.99):

X Low—–9

Y Low—–11

Z Low—0

X High—9

Y High—6

Z High—7

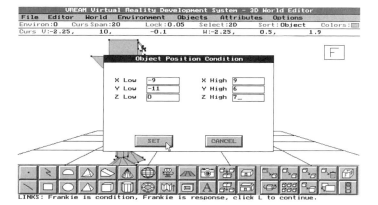

Figure 9.99
Entering position values.

These coordinates define a three-dimensional box. The next dialog box asks whether you want the condition to be triggered when the robot goes inside the area defined, or outside the area defined. Click on Outside Area. Another dialog box appears, as shown in Figure 9.100.

Figure 9.100
Selecting the response.

This dialog box asks you for the response action. Scroll to and select Object Rotate. When the condition is met (that is, when Frankie moves out of the 3D box), we're going to rotate Frankie so that he faces the opposite direction. Click Set to continue.

The dialog box shown in Figure 9.101 appears; enter a value of **180** for Yaw. Yet another dialog box appears, asking for the midpoint type. Click on Use Natural Midpoint, and then click Set.

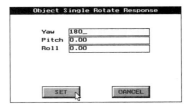

Figure 9.101
Setting response value.

Yes, another dialog box appears, as shown in Figure 9.102. Click in the Activate On Change check box, and then click Set.

Figure 9.102
The Select Link Activation dialog box.

Yes, another dialog box appears, as shown in Figure 9.103. Click in the Direct Link check box, and then click Set. Finally, when a dialog box asks for the link number, enter a value of **10**.[56]

Figure 9.103
Setting link type.

Viewpoint tool

If you should need to use the Viewpoint tool to move around, you may want the robot to sit still. Use the World/Auto Motion On/Off menu selection to toggle automatic motions. Save your work! To have fun, go to the runtime system. Choose File/End, and then click on Runtime.[57]

---

[56]Every link has its own number; links are evaluated in numerical order. High-priority links should have lower numbers.

[57]Links are only active in the runtime system.

Adding a Remote Control

Let's have some fun with the robot, its motion, and its links. Start by creating a cube object, as shown in Figure 9.104, and give it the name RemoteCtl. If you want, give it some snazzy colors.[58] The remote control will do just that: control the robot remotely. We'll set things up so that pushing the remote with the hand will stop the robot, and grabbing the remote with the hand will start it moving again.

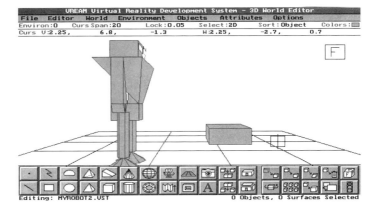

Figure 9.104
Creating a remote control.

It's time for the Links submenu again (see Fig. 9.105). Click on Add Links, and choose Select New in the dialog box that appears.

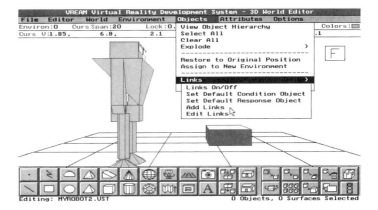

Figure 9.105
Adding a link to the remote control.

---

[58]I used blue for the box and yellow for the top surface.

Click RemoteCtl to select it as the condition object, and then click on the robot to make it the response object. When asked to select a condition for RemoteCtl, choose Hand Push (see Fig. 9.106). This displays the Choose Object Pushed Condition dialog box, which offers two choices: Not Pushed and Pushed. Since we want the robot to respond when we push, click Pushed and then click Set.

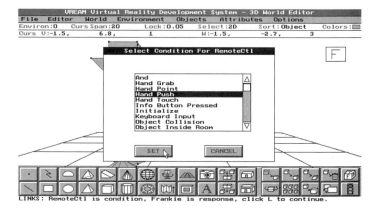

Figure 9.106
Selecting Hand Push.

Next, VREAM asks you to select the response. Click on Auto Translate (see Fig. 9.107). To finish up, enter **0** (zero) in the Translate box, click Set, click Set again (use Natural Midpoint), click Set again (Activate on Change), click Set again (Direct Link), enter a link number of **20**, press Enter, and click Set one last time. A hand push in the runtime will now stop the robot.[59] However, we need a way to get it started again. Time for one last link!

Figure 9.107
Selecting the response.

---

[59]To do a hand push, click both mouse buttons simultaneously.

Here's the drill for adding the last link: Start with the menu selection Objects/Links/Add Links. Click Set (New Cond/Resp), select RemoteCtl as the condition, and select Frankie the robot as the response. Select Hand Grab as the condition (see Fig. 9.108), Set, Set, select Auto Translate as the response, Set, select the X box, type **1**, and press Enter. Set, select Keep Current Midpoint, Set, Set (Activate on Change), Set (Direct Link), and enter **30** into the Link Number box, press Enter, and click on Set.

Figure 9.108
Selecting Hand Grab as the condition.

Go to the runtime system and give it a try. Click and hold the left button on the remote to carry it around with you as you move; this is a *hand grab*. To stop the robot, let go of the remote and push both mouse buttons simultaneously to point the hand's finger. This is a *hand push*. When you want the robot to start again, grab the remote. You might need to move forward and backward until you are the right distance from the remote to push it or grab it. See Table 9.1, which shows the movement keys. Table 9.2 shows the methods for controlling the hand.

Table 9.2. Controlling Hand Movement.

Mouse	Movement
Mouse left	Hand left
Mouse right	Hand right
Mouse down	Hand down
Mouse Up	Hand up
Mouse down+right button	Hand back
Mouse up+right button	Hand forward
Mouse left+right button	Hand roll left

continues

Table 9.2. continued

Mouse	Movement
Mouse right+right button	Hand roll right
Mouse right+middle button	Hand yaw left
Mouse left+middle button	Hand yaw right
Mouse down+middle button	Hand pitch left
Mouse up+middle button	Hand pitch right
Mouse left button	Hand grab (all fingers close)
Mouse right+left buttons	Hand push (index finger bends)
Mouse right+middle buttons	Hand point (thumb in)

Perhaps obviously, the movements involving a middle button are only available with mice that have three buttons.

This concludes the tutorial for VREAM. I hope that you have enjoyed it—it certainly was a lot of work to get it done! You have learned two very important things about VREAM: it is very powerful, and capable of full interactive VR. It is also very complex, and takes time to learn to use well.

III

VIRTUAL REALITIES

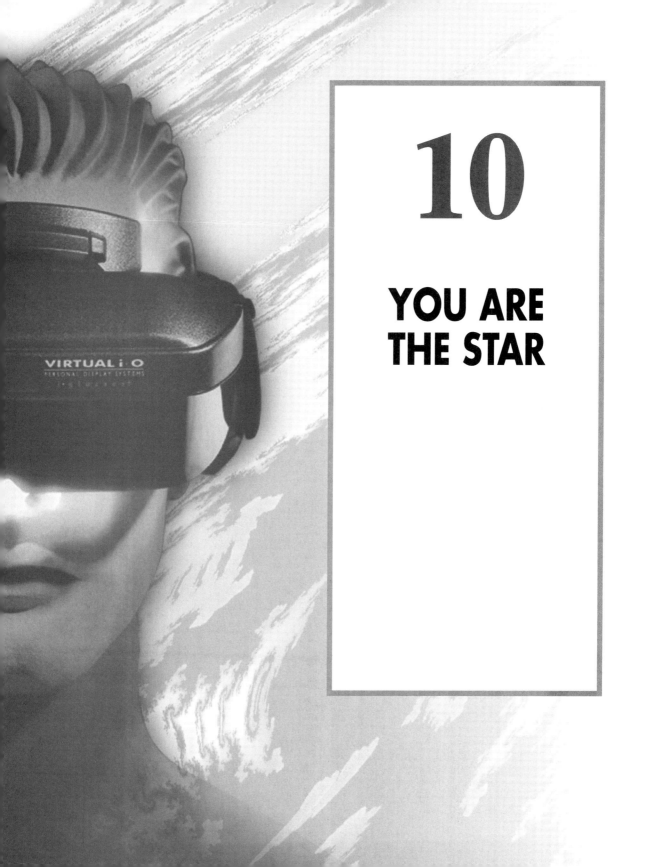

10

YOU ARE
THE STAR

One of the key skills you'll need in the new world of virtual reality is the ability to work with video. Today's technology allows you to combine not just one video image with another, but animation as well. This means that you can create an animation in a product such as 3D Studio or trueSpace, and then add video to it.

For example, you might create a virtual world in 3D Studio, and then add an image of yourself to the animation—truly making yourself the star of your virtual world. You can also do the reverse: create a video clip, and then add one or more virtual objects or creatures. Both approaches use the same basic technique: overlay. Either the video or the animation serves as the background, and the other image is overlaid on top of it. This can be done easily using video-editing software such as Adobe Premiere or ATI's Media Merge.

In other words, this chapter is about combining video with virtual reality.[1] This involves putting real objects into a virtual space.[2] For example, using these techniques, you can put a video of yourself into a landscape of Crater Lake, Oregon (created with Vistapro), or next to a 3D Studio animation of a dinosaur. Although I won't go so far as to say that it's trivially easy to accomplish these feats, I can show you what it takes to get into this part of the virtual reality universe. You will learn how to set up a simple video studio,[3] and see an example of an overlay that combines a virtual spaceship and a video.[4]

Video Basics

Everyone agrees about one thing when it comes to using video on a computer:

Video allows you to show what you mean, instead of just describing it.

---

[1]Which raises a question: What does one call such a hybrid? *Virtual video* springs to mind but isn't terribly accurate. I lean toward *VVR—video virtual reality*. Let's face it: Just about everything else has a three-letter acronym.

[2]"Objection, your honor! Video objects are not real objects," the defense attorney says, jumping from his seat. "Overruled," the judge says, adding, "Everyone knows that video is real. Don't you watch reality TV?"

[3]That's an interesting concept: Setting up your own video studio. Be honest now: Did you ever think you would be reading a book, thinking to yourself, "Hmmm...should I set up a video studio this weekend?" The fact that one can now rationally consider such possibilities points out how far we've already come toward virtual reality.

[4]As the popularity of video increases, more and more software supports video in one format or another. For additional ideas on what you can do with VR and video, consider such products as Elastic Reality and Autodesk's Animation Studio. Both will support video clips and 3D animations as well as bitmaps.

If you have a new product, you can show your customers how it works and how it will benefit them. If you supply technical equipment, now you can show your users how to perform maintenance. In both cases, using video to get your message across is smart, because it's almost impossible to describe something that the reader hasn't seen before. In the case of virtual reality, the virtual spaces you create may never have been seen by anyone before.

These advantages of video led to Stage One of video on a PC: the video clip. A *video clip* is a self-contained bit of video that shows one thing and one thing only. This is good, but it's not enough.

Products like Adobe Premiere and ATI's Media Merge take us to Stage Two: the video production. With video-editing software, you can now show not only what you mean, but you also can tell a story—and you have the tools to tell it very well.

For example, some folks have complained that the size of a PC video window is small— usually somewhere between 160X120 and 320X240. At most, this covers one quarter of a standard VGA screen. If what you have in mind is watching the latest Indiana Jones movie, this argument has some merit. But the video window normally shares the screen with such things as interactive menus and buttons, text blocks, and bitmaps. That makes a video in a window even better than full-screen video. For example, you could create a virtual space, add video elements to it, and then place it within the context of a text story line; or combine it with still images, add music or narration, and so on.

Learning to work with video is like any other skill: A little time and repetition will go a long way toward making you good at it. The first time you work with video and/or animation, you'll want to select a project that you can finish. To begin, you'll need a video capture card, such as the Intel Smart Video Recorder Pro, which allows you to digitize video from a camcorder or VCR. You capture short clips, which you then assemble into a video production. Your animated background is treated just like any other video clip.

Video Concepts

In one sense, all of us are video experts. Think about how much television you've seen over the years: every commercial, every sitcom, every movie you have ever seen has been part of your education for working with video on a computer. Like most of us, the only thing lacking is a framework of knowledge that will help you decide what video techniques to use in your own productions. That will come with time, of course, but this section will give you a jump start.

There are five key areas that you should think about before you begin to produce video:

Moving Images—Video shows movement. Use that movement to your advantage. Don't rely on static, boring subjects in your video clips—when was the last time you saw a commercial that didn't jump and dance and dazzle you? With Media Merge, you can mix and match static and dynamic content.

Transitions—A video production is made up of several video clips. How you make the transition from one clip to the next is important.

Content—Video moves and is therefore interesting in its own right. Don't use that as an excuse to use boring material. Seek out subjects that are interesting—that will double the impact of your final production.

Timing—Unlike a book or a document, a video production rolls along in real time. Timing of various events—music, narration, dramatic moments, and so on—is critical.

Pace—Finding the right pace for your video is important. Short clips that whiz by will confuse viewers and long, similar clips risk boredom.

Each of these topics is described in detail in this section.[5]

Moving Images

Video is movement. Unlike static images, video allows you to show life in action. To create videos with impact, you'll want to put as much action in your videos as possible.[6] The key to using movement is simple: Tell your story with actions, not words, whenever possible.

For example, there will be times when you simply must use a video clip of a *talking head*. That's any video that simply shows someone talking. Instead of sitting that person behind a desk, why not have him look up as he starts speaking, or perhaps he could be walking or pointing at the subject he is talking about. Even adding an interesting background—a seacoast, a factory floor, a busy workplace—adds visual interest.

Another important aspect of movement involves movement within the frame from one scene to the next. One scene can contain a subject at the upper left; the next can use a subject at the lower right. Use such motion to add interest—but be careful not

---

[5]My earlier book, *PC Video Madness*, includes an extended treatment of a variety of video issues, including how to use a camera, how to light a scene, and other topics.

[6]That is not strictly true, although if you will only be doing television commercials, you can assume that it is always true. Action is a good thing; too much action is usually confusing. In general, it is easier to err on the side of too little action.

to overdo it with stuff coming from all directions. For example, you could have a series of three subjects move into the frame from the left, and then have one subject come in from the right to offer a summary.

Finally, movement is not the ultimate answer for every video clip. You may want to emphasize something by allowing it to be perfectly still during a clip.

Transitions

The best videos are made up of a number of video clips. Normally, you won't just chop from one video clip to the next; you'll add transitions between clips. Transitions include such effects as wipes and fades,[7] and video-editing software makes it very easy to add transitions to your video productions.

There are three major types of transitions:

- Same-subject transitions
- New-subject transitions
- Breaking transitions

You should use different kinds of wipes and fades for each type of transition.

A same-subject transition occurs when you have two clips that are very closely related. For example, the first clip might show a complete picture of a product, while the next clip shows a close-up of a particular part of the product. Generally, you should use soft, unassuming effects for same-subject transitions. A dissolve is a good technique to use in these situations.

A new-subject transition occurs when you have two clips that do not relate closely but have some relationship to each other. For example, the first clip might show how to load paper into a new printer, while the second clip might show how to attach a fax device to the printer. Both clips are about the printer, but they are also about different topics. This is a more abrupt change, and you can signal the abruptness of the change by using an appropriate transitional effect. In this example, a wipe would be a good choice.

A breaking transition occurs when two clips are about very different subjects. For example, if you have a series of six clips that show different aspects of a printer, and then you have five clips that show different aspects of a copier, you should use a transitional effect to make it clear that a major break is occurring. You may also want to add a title sequence to alert the viewer to what is going on. In this example, the Media

---

[7]*Wipes* and *fades* are transition effects used between scenes in video production. You see them all the time on your TV, especially during commercials. Most video-editing software offers a huge variety of transition effects.

Merge Boxes effect (the new video clip fades in using small, random boxes) would work well—especially if you use color between the videos. You could easily put title text on a solid color.

Content

There is sometimes a temptation to rely on the movement in a video image to keep the viewer's interest. It's true that video alone is interesting simply because it moves. But if you want your productions to stand out, keep a sharp eye out for interesting content as well.

People make particularly interesting video subjects, but not if they are nervous about the experience. Help the subject of the video relax by minimizing the impact of the videotaping process—don't constantly start and stop recording. Set everything up in advance, and let your subject act naturally.

For inanimate objects, get as close as you can to the object. Fill the frame! PC video sizes are small, and you don't want to lose detail if you can avoid it. If the subject is large, keep the background simple so the outline of the subject is clear.

Take some close-up shots of various details. You can use some of them later during production to emphasize these details.

Timing

As you work with video, you will automatically develop a sense of timing. It is one of the most important assets you can have for creating video productions that are strong and effective. Knowing when to end a video clip and start the next one is something of an art. However, there are a few basic rules that will get you started:

- A good starting point usually involves action. You don't need a lot of tape prior to the beginning of the action. In fact, the only reason to use any slack time at the beginning or end of a clip is to use it as part of a transition, such as a fade from black.

- Every clip has a start and an end; you just have to find out where they are. Don't settle for just any ending point. Here's a trick: Count the action beats in a clip. A *beat* is anything that happens—he picks up a pen, he touches his hat, he pauses for effect, he points at the audience. Everything that happens is a beat. End a clip on a strong beat.[8]

■ Good things come in threes. A three-beat clip is often perfect. Or try two clips to set up the idea, and then hit hard with a third clip. Use same-subject transitions between the three clips and follow the third clip with a new-subject transition.

Pace

It's very important to find the right pace for each video production you create. I am speaking here of the overall video, not individual clips. If the video moves too slowly—if the story is being told too slowly—your viewers will lose interest. If the video is too fast, your viewers will miss important information.

Keeping a video at a useful pace can be difficult if you don't have experience with video production. Fortunately, there's a simple cure. Find someone you trust to view your material and give you feedback about the pacing. Here are some questions you can ask yourself to get started:

■ Does each video clip move the story along?

■ Is each video clip part of the same story?

■ Is there any part of a clip that seems to be just hanging out, serving no useful purpose?

■ Is each video clip long enough to make a clear point? Is it short enough to hold interest?

The Viewer Over Your Shoulder

With experience, you will learn to be your own best viewer. Until then, sit down to look at your video in progress with an imaginary viewer looking over your shoulder at your work. Ask yourself whether the video you are creating will be interesting and useful to that viewer.

Your Own Video Studio

If you already own a video camera of any description, you now have half of what you need to put yourself in a virtual space. The other (and less costly) half is a card for

---

[8]Sometimes, the clip must serve other masters. For example, a clip may have a natural ending, but the script requires that you hold that subject for more time. Perhaps the narration is complex at that point, and the clip has to last at least long enough to explain the subject. If the clip is truly boring, you might be able to use one of those detail shots I mentioned earlier. While you are in the field videotaping, it's always a good idea to collect more shots than you think you'll need.

your computer that will capture video. Setting up the physical studio is the easiest part of all.

Video Camera

I have yet to meet a video camera (camcorder) that isn't up to the task. Whether you have a large, VHS camera or one of those miniature 8mm or VHS-C cameras, there are only two output signals that you will encounter in North America: Composite and S-Video.[9] Most video capture cards will handle either, and all of them will handle a Composite signal. There's no need to understand the technical nature of these signals.[10] All you need to know is that S-Video uses a higher resolution than Composite, and that either one is fine for video capture, because at 160X120 or 320X240, you're hardly pushing the capabilities of either kind of signal.

Video Capture Card

Of all the video capture cards on the market, there is one card that I use and like: the Intel Smart Video Recorder Pro.

Simply put, the Smart Video Recorder Pro is the best of its class. It is one of a few cards that capture and compress in one step. The ISVR Pro (as it is affectionately known) is easy to install and use,[11] and it has excellent image quality. It is also very reliable and comes with the Indeo codec[12]—an excellent choice for compression.

I tend to favor the ISVR Pro for much of my own work, because the real-time compression from the on-board, clock-doubled i750r chip saves a lot of time. For example, compressing with the Cinepak codec after capture can add 30 to 60 minutes of compression time for each minute of video. Cinepak is a great codec, however, with excellent playback quality, and there are times when the wait is well worth your while.

The Studio

Once you have a video camera and a video capture card, it's time to set up your studio. I set up mine in my garage, but you can use any space that has at least one blank

---

[9]Neither of these has anything to do with RF signals. Radio Frequency signals are used for broadcast television. Newer televisions have the usual RF input as well as Composite and, sometimes, S-Video inputs.

[10]For example, I don't.

[11]The bane of video capture cards is that they must use things like IRQs and memory addresses. Unfortunately, it is up to you to find unused IRQs and memory addresses. You may have to check your installed hardware to determine what IRQs and memory addresses are available.

[12]*Codec* stands for either *encode/decode* or *compress/decompress*—it depends on who you ask.

wall. One advantage of the garage is that I can often just open the garage door to get plenty of natural light. Figure 10.1 shows my basic setup.

The only critical piece is that square thing in the middle of the picture. It's a piece of bright blue fabric used for Chroma key. With the solid color in the background, it's easy to use video-editing software to blend in any object I can videotape. I added weights to the bottom of the cloth to keep it from fluttering (especially when the garage door is open!), and you might also want to add a long, thin strip of wood to the bottom edge. This adds weight and helps keep the cloth from showing fold marks.

Figure 10.1
A simple video studio setup in a garage.

I added a few other bits and pieces to complete my simple studio. I invested in a simple color monitor (a Panasonic 1379 is a good and inexpensive choice) that I use to preview the video image, a microphone, and a video tripod.[13] The tripod is a critical piece of equipment. Without it, camera jitters can ruin your video footage and make it useless.

This setup is easy to use. Place the object—yourself, for example—in front of the blue screen, and turn on the camera. That's all there is to it. If you want to have the object appear to move within the virtual landscape, you can move the camera instead of the object. For example, if you want the object to start out at the lower left of the video frame, and then move to the upper left, tilt the camera instead of moving the object. This gives you very tight control over the location within the video frame.

---

[13]Don't settle for just any old tripod. A video tripod uses a fluid head that makes for smooth panning and tilting. Regular tripods don't have this feature.

Going Virtual with Media Merge

You now have everything you need to go virtual: the software, the hardware, and a studio to create the video. It's time to do some serious virtual video. There are four steps involved:

- Create the virtual space.
- Make the videotape.
- Capture the video.
- Merge it!

Create the Virtual Space

There are a variety of ways to create a virtual space, but not all of them will work with the methods described in this chapter. File formats are the backbone of the process of combining video and virtual reality.

The captured digital video file doesn't present any problems. It can be loaded directly into any video-editing software. The problems, if any, crop up when you try to use the animation output from the software you use to create the virtual space. If the animation isn't in the same format as the video (the AVI file format), the animation must be converted to an AVI file. That's not a problem if the software can output using the FLI or FLC file formats. For example, Vistapro outputs single frames as PCX files, but it comes with a utility program that will convert the PCX files into a FLC file. If you don't already know what file formats your software supports, check the documentation.

It's easy to use Media Merge's Scene Editor or Premiere's Project Window to combine the video file with the animation file, but it's not so easy to make the blend look realistic. For example, as you learned in Chapter 6, the lighting in the virtual space must be matched when you videotape the real object that you plan to include. If you don't do that, the difference in lighting angles can be jarring to the viewer. If the lighting angles are too complex, you can minimize the effect by using an overhead light in both the virtual space and for the videotaping. Such lighting casts minimal shadows, and movement of objects causes only minor changes to shadows.

If the animation of the virtual space uses a camera and you change the camera angle, you'll need to duplicate the camera angle when you videotape.

All of this may sound like a lot of bother, but it's really just basic bookkeeping. A little time taken to jot down frame numbers and camera or light angles, for example, can add a real sense of reality to your creation. The techniques you use can be based on the examples in Chapter 6.

Make the Videotape

There are several levels of camera technique that you can use when you are photographing a real object that will be added to a virtual space. These range from the simple to the complex:

- Stationary camera, stationary target
- Stationary camera, moving target
- Moving camera, stationary target
- Moving camera, moving target

Each of these has different uses and applications, and a different level of difficulty.

Stationary Camera, Stationary Target

This is the easiest way to get started. Because neither the camera nor the target is moving, the logistics are very simple: Position the object/target, aim the camera, and make the tape. If you need to move the lighting during filming, that adds a bit of complexity, but once you start the camera, you've got two hands free.

Stationary Camera, Moving Target

There are different ways of moving an object, and each of them creates different challenges. If the object is moving in the same place—that is, it does not change its distance from the camera—the only question is the mechanism for moving the object. You do not want any of the support system showing up in the video. If you must have a visible support, make sure that the support is covered with the same color and kind of fabric you used for the background. You can, for example, make a glove for your hand, drape cloth across your arm or shoulder, and move the object the old-fashioned way: by hand.

If the distance between the camera and object changes, the issues become more complex. The biggest priority is to keep the object in focus. If your camera has auto focus, that will keep the object in focus in most situations. However, there are several special situations where auto focus may not be adequate. For example, some auto-focus systems use the center of the frame for focusing. If the object is at the edge of the frame, the camera may try to focus on the background cloth—a hopeless task, since the cloth is uniform in color and lighting.

Moving an object away from the camera also presents special problems. The farther away you are from the object, the bigger the background must be. This can create a practical limit to how large an object you can videotape. For example, putting all of your body into the frame requires a very large background—most likely from floor to ceiling. If possible, use a continuous strip of background material and curve it to cover part of the floor and ceiling—this will avoid any creases that may be difficult to remove in your video-editing software. Most fabric is only 60 inches wide, and this can cause problems, too.

If you are serious about using large objects, you have two choices: build a larger studio, or remove the background in each frame using a program like Photoshop.

Moving Camera, Stationary Target

Instead of moving the object, you can move the camera so that it looks like the object is moving. This is the technique that was used to animate the various star fighters in the movie *Star Wars*. The movie studios rely on computers and motorized camera transports to work their magic. If you try this technique, you will have to think through the necessary camera motions very carefully, and you will probably need to move the camera by hand. This can be very unsteady, and you would need to create tracks to even out the camera movement. Some motions can be done using a tripod, but they aren't the useful ones. Panning and tilting will seldom give you the effect you want.

There is another type of moving-camera shot, however, that is easy to take. This involves just the opposite of what I have been describing so far. Instead of adding video to a virtual space, you can add virtual objects to a video. In this case, you are free to do whatever you want to do with the camera. When you have the tape you want, you can add the virtual object. For example, if you create a bizarre space alien in Imagine, and then animate it in the foreground,[14] you can use Media Merge to put the alien into any video. Or, you might hold the camera while walking along a path, and then add a floating spacecraft or a pair of robot arms to the foreground. Let your imagination run wild.

Moving Camera, Moving Target

There should seldom, if ever, be a need for this combination. Almost any movement can be accomplished using either a moving camera or a moving target.

Capture the Video

Once you have your videotape, the next step is to capture the video sequence to your hard disk. You'll need a pretty fast computer to handle video capture. I recommend at least a 486/33, although the Intel Smart Video Recorder may work satisfactorily with slower hardware because it offloads some of the work to its on-board, video-

---

[14]With an appropriate single-color background, of course.

compression chip. A fast hard drive is critical. I use a disk with an average seek time of 10ms.[15] Any disk with a seek time of less than 15ms is acceptable, but 12ms or less is better. A fast video display card is very desirable for playback, but it won't have much impact on capture.

Here are some hints on video capture from my book *PC Video Madness*:

■ Test the capabilities of your system before you try to capture for any real projects. Start easy—try to capture at 160X120 using 256 colors and 15 frames per second as a beginning. If that works, try 24 and then 30 frames per second. Verify that you are getting reliable performance. Then you can try such things as 24-bit color codecs like Indeo and Cinepak. You won't get the benefits of 24-bit color, of course, unless you have a video display adapter that can handle it.

■ If you use the Intel Smart Video Recorder, set the following options in VidCap for capture: Indeo codec, highest quality setting, and key frames set to 1. This almost always gives you the best results. The key frame setting is critical for the Indeo codec version 2.12 to correct a potential problem with ghosting when the frame contents change dramatically from one frame to the next. After capture, use VidEdit to save the file using No Change as a compression option and using the data rate of your choice.

■ Use a permanent capture file. To create a permanent file, start by defragmenting your hard disk with a utility like Speed Disk from The Norton Utilities.[16] Then run VidCap, and from the File menu choose Set Capture File. The dialog box allows you to set the size of the capture file. Allow from 10 to 25 megabytes per minute of capture, depending on such things as image size, frame rate, and bit depth. If you will be using the Intel Smart Video Recorder or another board that compresses in real time, you'll need less space—usually at least one-third less than for uncompressed (also called *raw*) capture. After you capture a video sequence to the permanent capture file (which will now always stay defragmented until you erase it), use Save As in VidEdit to save the file with an appropriate name after you have made any necessary changes. This preserves the capture file for future use.

■ Unless you need to play the video files from a CD-ROM, don't use the Pad for

---

[15]The *ms* stands for *milliseconds* and refers to average seek time. I use a Micropolis 2112A, with a 1.05-gigabyte IDE drive. The SCSI version, the 2112, is also a good choice.

[16]Having a fragmented hard disk slows down access times because files wind up being in several pieces. In the case of a large video file—say 50 megabytes or so—a fragmented hard drive can mean that the file is cut into hundreds of pieces.

CD-ROM feature in the Compression options. However, the 150K data rate is a good target if you want the file to be playable on a variety of machines. Any file with a data rate of more than 300K per second may not play well on the majority of machines—such high data rates demand the fastest computers, hard disks, and video systems. In general, don't compress until you create the final video—use uncompressed files throughout development to preserve image quality.

Merge It!

Once you have the two files, you can merge them with your video-editing software. The process is extremely straightforward, but it will vary from product to product. I have included an example created with ATI's Media Merge to show the basic steps common to most video editors:

1. Load the file with the virtual space animation in one time line. For this example, it is a Vistapro landscape animation.

2. Load the file with the video object in a second time line. For this example, it is a video of myself.

3. Load any additional video objects into the appropriate additional time lines. In this case, I wanted a dashboard effect; I used a bitmap between the video of me and the landscape animation. With most video editors, you can think of this process as stacking layers of video/animation.

4. Set the overlay properties for each video object. Select the background color of the video as the Chroma key color.[17] You will usually have to adjust the falloff (the range of similar colors used for the Chroma key) until the background disappears completely. If a feathering option is available, you may want to experiment with it to see if it improves the appearance of the overlay.

5. Check the appearance of the results before you save the results to disk. In Media Merge, look in the Composite time line at the top of the window. Figure 10.2 shows the kind of results you can expect. The composite only uses 8-bit color, so don't be alarmed if the images there don't look as detailed as you were expecting. If what you see is what you want, use the appropriate menu selections in your video editor (File/Produce menu selection in Media

---

[17]A *Chroma key* is a color that will allow underlying video/animation clips to show through. For example, I used a blue fabric background behind me when I shot the video of myself. I clicked in Media Merge to select this background color as the Chroma key color.

Merge) to create the final product. In Figure 10.2, the video in track 1 is already a composite video: I added a still image of a cockpit as an overlay using a Chroma key. I then loaded the resulting video in for a second overlay. I could have overlaid all three videos in one step, of course. In this case, I wanted to do several versions using the same cockpit. The dashboard bitmap is shown in Figure 10.3.

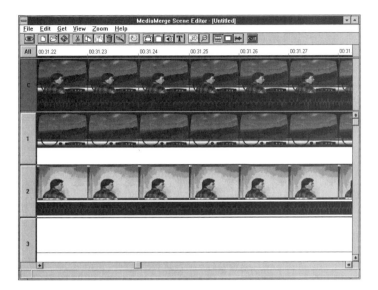

Figure 10.2
Several video files loaded into the Scene Editor.

Figure 10.3
A bitmap used to create a dashboard for the composite video.

Figures 10.4 and 10.5 show single frames from the video produced using the files loaded into the Media Merge Scene Editor for Figure 10.3. These images have been compressed, so the detail is not as crisp as in the original. Note that all three elements of the composite are integrated into the images: the Vistapro landscape, the dashboard, and the video of me, Mr. Author (or, in this case, tour guide—play the file MEETME.AVI on the CD-ROMs in the VRMAD directory).

Figure 10.4
A single frame from the produced video.

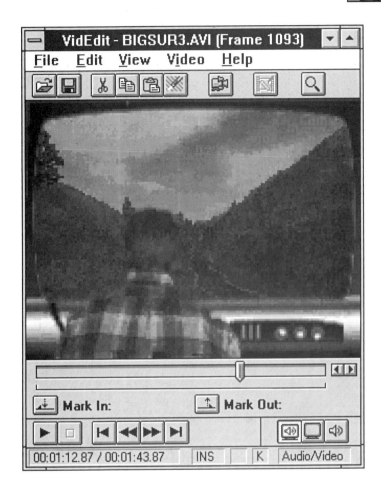

Figure 10.5
Another single frame from the produced video.

Figure 10.6 shows a frame from the original video I made in my garage studio. The surface behind me is the blue cloth I used as a backdrop. It is not quite exactly uniform in color, but most video editors allow you to make adjustments for this (use the Falloff slider in Media Merge).

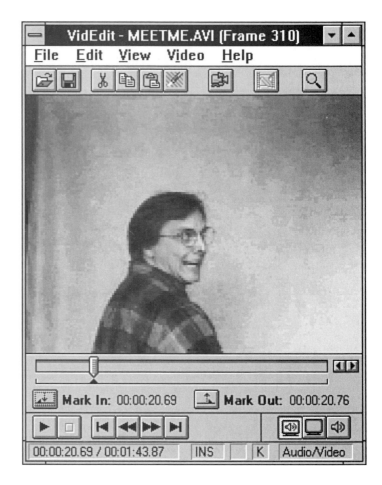

Figure 10.6
A frame from the
original video,
before making the
composite.

Summary

The list of possibilities for working with a combination of virtual-space animation and video files is endless. The capability to layer multiple images with video-editing software gives you a powerful tool for creating never-before-seen images. Whether you add video to a virtual space or enhance a video by adding virtual objects, you will likely find yourself on the cutting edge of computer technology for quite some time.

11

VIRTUAL VIRTUOSITY

From total immersion to 3D morphing, from flights of fancy to detailed pseudo-realities, virtual reality is as much an art as a science. Life on the cutting edge has always been that way. There are never any prefabricated solutions out on the cutting edge. Virtual reality is as different from humdrum, everyday programs like spreadsheets and word processors as heaven is different from earth.

Once upon a time, of course, spreadsheets and word processors were new, fun, and exciting. But the various programs from the various vendors look more and more alike with each new version. Virtual reality, on the other hand, is a mere babe in the woods.[1] Like multimedia a couple of years ago, virtual reality still has room for the home-grown product, for the enthusiast to go places no one has ever gone before.

Today's VR tools, as limited and experimental—and sometimes costly—as they are, still offer enormous possibilities to anyone who is willing to put in the time and effort to stretch the limits. Out there, in the trenches, the Cezannes, Van Goghs, and Picassos of virtual reality are sweating out the details in front of their computers, trying to find a sense of style, a way of doing things that breaks completely new ground.

These are the virtual virtuosos. These are the people who aren't willing to wait until someone else gives them the tools to build new worlds—they'll build them now, either by finding new ways to use the tools available or by creating their own tools out of their impatience.

In this chapter, you learn about stretching and bending tools to get what you want, when you want it. This chapter features 3D-modeling software: 3D Studio from Autodesk and trueSpace from Caligari. Both products have been covered elsewhere, but in this chapter I've applied a sense of fun to the use of the software. Ever been threatened by a column of glass? Ever wanted a tour of your own solar system? This is your chapter: a morph here, a reflection there, and pretty soon you can have your own virtual fantasy.

More specifically, you'll build a cylinder in a sparklingly technological-looking environment and then make it come to life. It will bend down toward you and then shake its "head" threateningly at you. After the example, I'll show you some possibilities for adding even more pizzazz to the animation.

The results will be first class, because 3D Studio is used by many professionals to create the artificial realities you see on television, in commercials, and in movies.

Then we'll go into orbit with trueSpace, where you'll learn about things like hierarchical animation.

---

[1] And not just any woods, of course. These are the forests of fantasy, the wispy dreams of mankind are fuel for the campfires, and we're all savages thinking that anything is possible.

The Column That Ate the Animator

RECIPE

1 copy 3D Studio Release 2 or later[2]
1 highly developed sense of imagination
1 conception of a virtual space and its inhabitants

Instructions: The recipe can only suggest where to go with this gourmet item. Begin by visualizing a scene that has some impact—something that hits you in the gut. For example, pretend that you have been hired to create a scene in a movie where an inanimate object comes to life. What would it look like? How would it move? Then work at it and work at it until it appears to come to life in an animation. Serve only when really, really ready.

You will create just a handful of objects in this scene, but the results will make it look like it took forever to do. Begin by setting the values for a cylinder using the Create/Cylinder/Values menu selection, as shown in Figure 11.1.

To create the cylinder itself, use the Create/Cylinder/Smoothed menu selection. When asked, use the name Cyl01. Make the cylinder tall and thin, as shown in Figure 11.2. Apply the material Blue Glass[3] to the object.

Let's cover a little background information before proceeding. To animate the column, you're going to use a little trick. You will actually use a morph[4] to transform the column into various versions of itself. Instead of animating a single column, you will create different versions of the column and then morph from one to the next.

---

[2]This recipe was cooked up with 3D Studio Release 2, but the morphing features are still an outstanding tool for anyone working in 3D. In the current version, Release 4, you also have the option of using inverse kinematics (see Chapter 5 for details).

[3]These are just suggestions; feel free to adjust the mapping and materials to suit your own concept of a column that will come to life. By the way, you need not specify the same material for the object copies—morphing has no effect on the surface characteristics of an object.

[4]See Chapter 8 for more information about morphing.

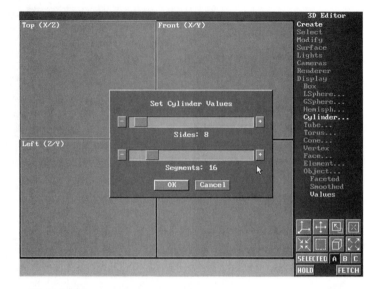

Figure 11.1
Setting values for a new cylinder.

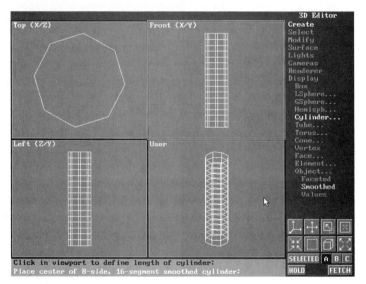

Figure 11.2
Creating a tall, thin cylinder.

Create four copies of the column. The easiest way to do this is by cloning. Use the Modify/Object/Move menu selection, but hold down the Shift key when you select the column for moving. This creates an exact copy of the column, including the surface material. Name each of the cylinders appropriately, such as Cyl02, Cyl03, and so on. You can use any of the viewports for the moving and cloning operations, as shown in Figure 11.3.

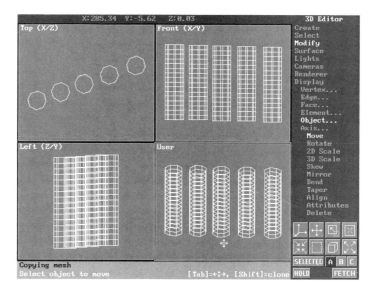

Figure 11.3
Five identical cylinders.

Now use the Modify/Object/Bend menu selection to bend cylinder #2 30 degrees. Make sure that the cursor that appears has a little arrow pointing up. If the arrow points in a different direction, press the Tab key until it points up. Figure 11.4 shows the cylinder as it looks during the bend operation. A shadow cylinder shows the degree of bending. Check for the exact degree of bending in the status line at the top of the screen.

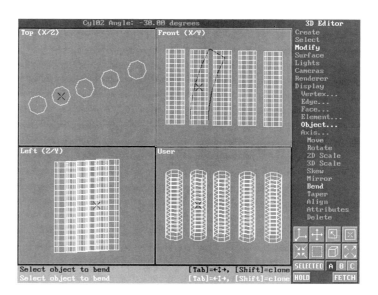

Figure 11.4
Bending a cylinder.

Now move to cylinder #3, and bend it to 60 degrees. Bend cylinder #4 to 90 degrees and cylinder #5 to 120 degrees. After you have bent all the cylinders, the screen should look something like Figure 11.5.

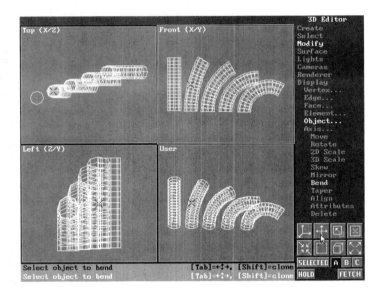

Figure 11.5
Different degrees of bending on the cylinders.

Press the F5 key to go to the Keyframer, 3D Studio's animation tool. Use the Display/Hide/Object menu selection to hide each of the bent cylinders.[5] The only remaining object is the original cylinder, as shown in Figure 11.6.

This is the point where you apply the morphing. Move to frame 30, and then go to the Object/Morph/Assign menu selection. Click on Cyl01, which will display the dialog box shown in Figure 11.7. This is a list of the objects in the scene that are valid morph objects for Cyl01.

Click on Cyl02 and then click OK. The cylinder now appears bent, as shown in Figure 11.8.

Move to frames 60, 60, and 120, and morph the cylinder to cylinders 3, 4, and 5. In frame 120, the cylinder appears nearly bent over (see Fig. 11.9).

---

[5]Simply click on each cylinder to hide it.

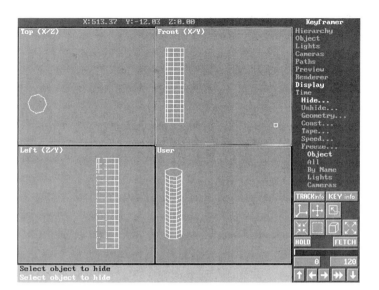

Figure 11.6
The bent cylinders have been hidden.

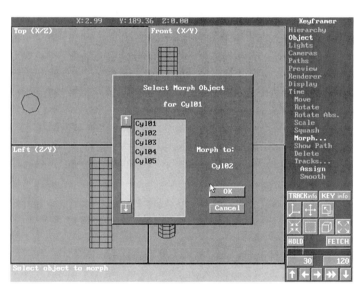

Figure 11.7
Selecting an object to morph to.

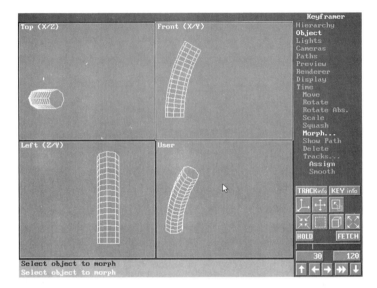

Figure 11.8
*The cylinder appears
bent in frame 30.*

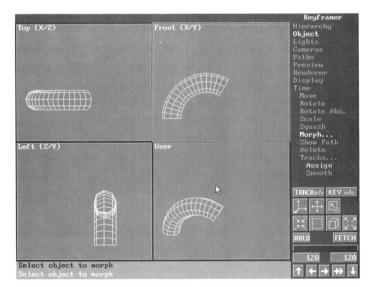

Figure 11.9
*The completed
morph.*

Throughout the morph, the cylinder did not move. It did not, for example, move to the location of cylinder #2 when morphed to that cylinder. Morphing is actually a limited action. It does not affect the surface properties of an object, nor does it affect position. In fact, morphing does only one thing. A morph merely moves the vertices of one object to the (relative) positions of the vertices in the second object. In other words, all that a morph does is change the shape of an object to match the shape of a second object.

One side effect is that you can only morph objects that have the same number of vertices. When you click on an object to morph it, you are presented with a list of the objects in the scene that have the same number of vertices. If you want to morph, say, a sphere into a cube, you will first have to add vertices to the cube—lots of them, as a matter of fact, because the typical sphere may have hundreds, while a stock cube has only eight.

One of the best ways to create objects with the same number of vertices is to copy them, as we have done here, and then make changes to the copy. Another method is to use the 3D Lofter (another 3D Studio tool) to create the two shapes, and then loft them into 3D objects. This offers more flexibility but can take much more time.

Now you can set about getting the most out of the morph. Return to the 3D Editor by pressing the F3 key. Use the Cameras/Create menu selection to open the dialog box shown in Figure 11.10.

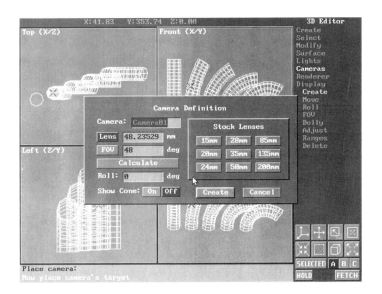

Figure 11.10
Adding a camera to the scene.

There are a number of lenses to choose from, and the lens you select will affect the appearance of the bending column. A wide-angle lens[6] will make the column look far away—it won't show the effect to its best advantage. A telephoto lens[7] will show the column close up, but if we get too close, the morphing will not be seen in its entirety. In this case, the so-called normal lens is best—50mm. Select this lens by clicking on it.

---

[6]The lens focal lengths from 15mm to 35mm are considered wide angle.
[7]The lens focal lengths from 85mm to 200m are considered telephoto.

To make one of the viewports show what the camera sees, press Ctrl+V to display the dialog box shown in Figure 11.11. Click the Camera button, and then click in one of the viewports at the lower left of the dialog box. The viewport marked with a U would be a good choice, because the User point of view isn't needed when you have a Camera viewport.

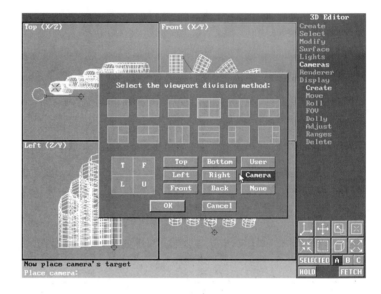

Figure 11.11
Changing the contents of a viewport.

Place the camera at a low level, looking up at the column. You should also add a light to the scene. A spotlight would be nice because it casts shadows, which adds depth to the scene. Figure 11.12 shows the light and the camera in position in the 3D Editor.[8]

The light from above, however, may not be enough. This leaves the underside of the column in shadow as it bends. Because the camera sees mostly the underside of the column, it would be a very boring animation—not at all appropriate for a movie scene. You can add a second spotlight below the bending column, as shown in Figure 11.13. Note that this illuminates the area right in front of the camera at the end of the sequence.

The animation as it now stands is OK, but it lacks punch. A bending column, after all, doesn't have much personality. If we want this column to really look like it is coming alive (and we'll have to if we ever want to see our payment from the movie's producer), we'll have to add more motion. Time to head back to the 3D Editor.

---

[8]You may need to change the position of both objects, depending on exactly where and how the column moves during the morph.

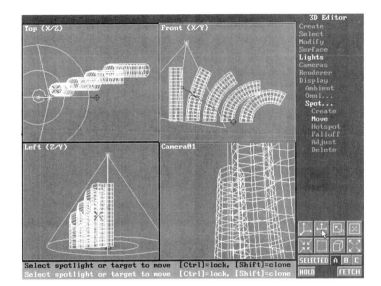

Figure 11.12
The scene with a light and camera added.

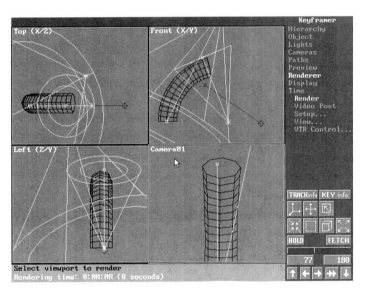

Figure 11.13
Adding a second spotlight under the column.

Create two copies of cylinder #5—the one that is bent farthest. Figure 11.14 shows the two additional objects (best seen in the Top viewport) after they have been bent a second time—this time, sideways.

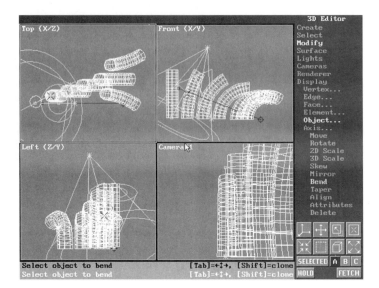

Figure 11.14
Adding two more bent cylinders.

These two new cylinders can be used to add some rather interesting morphs. Return to the Keyframer and add 60 additional frames (for a total of 180). Move to frame 135 (see Fig. 11.15) and add a morph to one of the new objects.

Move to frame 165 and add a morph to the other object, and then move to frame 180 and morph to cylinder #5. Now hide the two new objects using the Display/Hide/Object menu selection. Figure 11.16 shows how the cylinder looks in Wireframe view in frame 165.

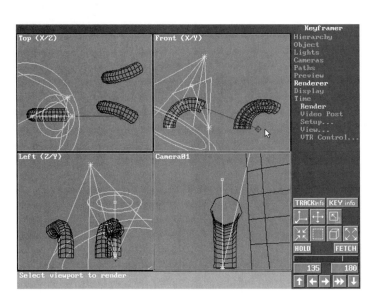

Figure 11.15
The view in the Keyframer before hiding the new objects.

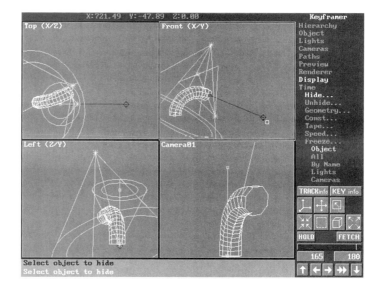

Figure 11.16
A view of the cylinder bending both down and to the side.

If there is anything about the animation that you are not satisfied with, the easiest way to make adjustments is with the Track Editor. To use the Track Editor, click the Track Info button at the lower right, and then click on the cylinder. This displays the Track Info dialog box (see Fig. 11.17).

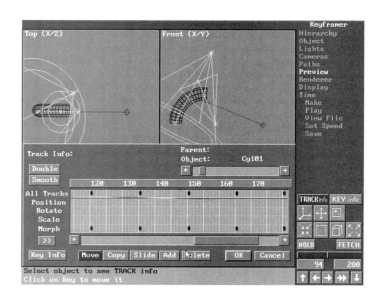

Figure 11.17
The track info for the cylinder.

Note that there is a dot at each frame where you created a morph. To edit a morph, simply click the Key Info button at the lower left of the dialog box, which displays the Key Info dialog box (see Fig. 11.18).

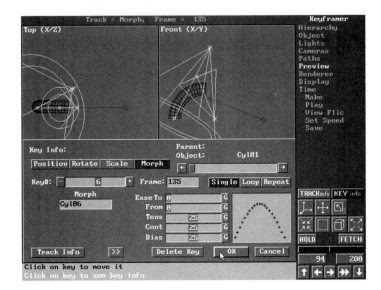

Figure 11.18
The Key Info
dialog box.

Using the Key Info dialog box, you can change the object you are morphing to, and you can also change the Ease To settings. This can give you a high degree of control over the pace of motion during the morph. The Ease To value affects the velocity with which an object (or, in this case, a morph) approaches a key frame. If the value is 0, there is no change in velocity. If the value is 50 (the maximum), the change in velocity will be as high as possible.

The Ease From setting also affects velocity. A high setting (50 is also the maximum here) increases velocity leaving the key frame.

In other words, if you increase the Ease To setting, the pace of the morph speeds up as it reaches the key frame. If you increase the Ease From setting, the pace of the morph is fast as it leaves the key frame and then slows down. You can use these controls to change a boring, same-speed morph into a dynamic, unpredictable virtuoso performance.

There are three other settings in the same area of the Key Info box that can be useful:

    Tension—This control determines how abruptly a transition occurs. A setting of 50 means the transition is very abrupt; 25 is average; and 0 means that motion will even go in reverse, if necessary, to make the transition as smooth as possible.

Continuity—This control determines how smooth the changes will be at the key frame. A setting of 0 means the change will be abrupt—all in one frame. A setting of 25 means the change will be smooth, and a setting of 50 forces an overshoot prior to and after the key frame.

Bias—This control determines whether the settings that apply to a given key frame will apply equally to entry and exit, or favor one or the other. A value of 50 emphasizes entry, a setting of 25 is neutral, and a setting of 0 favors exit.

These settings, which were designed primarily to control motion, can have either interesting or ruinous effects on a morph—experimentation is the only useful guide.

As interesting as we have managed to make the morph so far—a snake-like column wobbling dangerously from side to side—we are not done. We can add substantial mood to the morph by creating a suitable background. If you recall, the specifications called for a "sparklingly technological-looking environment." The first order of business is to create the background object. I opted for a simple background, consisting of a floor and one wall (see Fig. 11.19).

The objects are simply boxes created in the 3D Editor using the Create/Box menu selection. I adjusted the size and position of the boxes to make sure that they filled the Camera view. I then assigned suitable materials to each of them—Blue Marble to the floor, and a material I created for the wall using pattern #150 as a texture map. Figure 11.20 shows a rendering of the scene.

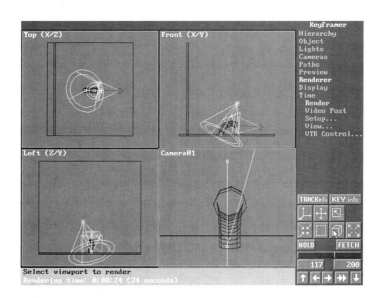

Figure 11.19
Adding objects for a background.

Figure 11.20
A rendering of the first frame in the morph.

All three objects can be seen in this rendering. The blue glass is nearly transparent, however, and may not be an ideal choice. We'll return to this subject in a moment. For now, see Figure 11.21, frame 107 of the animation. The cylinder is bent at a little bit more than 90 degrees.

In Figure 11.22, the cylinder is bent completely to one side.

Figure 11.21
Frame 107 of the morph.

Figure 11.22
Frame 134 of the morph.

There are some things you can do to improve the appearance of the animation. I made the following changes, and then rendered the image in Figure 11.23:

- Added an automatic reflection map to the blue glass material and increased its shininess.
- Added a bump map to the blue marble to create some highlights and shadows in the surface and added automatic-reflection mapping.
- Added shininess to the pattern of the wall and added a bump map.

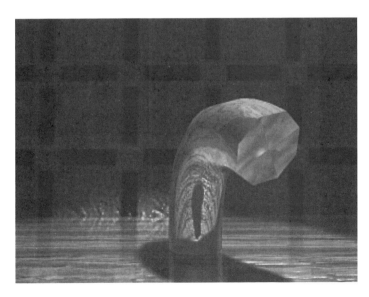

Figure 11.23
Frame 135 with changes to the characteristics of the materials.

As you can see, this adds quite a bit of atmosphere to the scene. We are almost there, but not quite. For a final touch, add a spotlight that illuminates the wall in the background. Place the light so that it is above and nearly in the same plane as the wall—this causes harsh shadows that emphasize the texture of the wall. The final result is shown in Figure 11.24 and can be found on the CD-ROMs as BEND.AVI.

What's Next?

This scene is really just a basic morph in 3D Studio. I have added a few extra touches to give the animation more impact. But there are more things that you could do. For example, you could join a face to the top of the cylinder using the Create/Object/Boolean menu selection. 3D Studio comes with a large number of sample files, several of which contain heads or faces that would be useful in this situation, or you could create your own from scratch.

You could also add other objects to the scene and have the cylinder interact with them. For example, a ball could roll in from the side and then get eaten by the cylinder when it bends down.

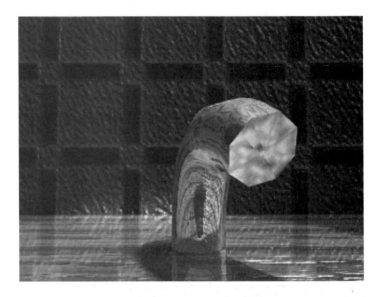

Figure 11.24
A light has been added to emphasize the texture of the background wall.

You can also replace the simple pattern of the back wall with a rock wall that looks like a dungeon, or a sparkling, futuristic metallic look. You can add objects—lights, paintings, decorations, and architectural details—to the back wall or the floor.

For some real fun, you could create hands, arms, and a futuristic or fantastic head for the bare tube and use inverse kinematics to make it look truly threatening (see Chapter 5 for the full scoop on inverse kinematics).

The bottom line is this: The more you put into a scene, the more you are going to get out of it. Of course, knowing when you are done—when adding even one more detail would be too much—is just as important!

trueSpace Virtuosity: Virtual Planets

When we speak of virtual worlds, we often get stuck in things that look a lot like everyday life—corridors and offices, streets and roads. This is fine, but there aren't any predefined limits to what a virtual world can be. Let's take a different approach to the problem and use trueSpace to create an alternate solar system just for us.[9]

Before we start, however, a few words about the differences in the two products are in order. 3D Studio packs a tremendous amount of power under the hood. That means that it has layer upon layer of features—which translate into layer upon layer of menus. trueSpace is less ambitious, so it has less to navigate through. Caligari, the maker of trueSpace, has taken full advantage of this. It has made the interface simpler, and that means it's easier to maneuver around and get things done. I've used 3D Studio for years, and I still run into areas of the program that I missed before. I usually have to pull out the documentation to figure out how to use new features. With trueSpace's unique interface, most tools can be figured out on-the-fly. This means you can have fun with trueSpace even if you don't know what you are doing. It can be great fun to just poke around with the tools, uncovering new and exciting toys as you go.

In this exercise, we'll create a bunch of planets, give at least one planet some moons, and put them all into orbit around a sun. Along the way, you'll learn more about creating surfaces in trueSpace.

Figure 11.25 shows the starting point: an empty virtual universe in trueSpace. I have taken the liberty of creating a new Perspective window using the Window tools at the bottom right. If you haven't already been through the trueSpace tutorial in Chapter 3, you might want to use it to get familiar with the basics. There is a demo version of trueSpace on the CDs with this book, which you can use to follow along with the tutorial.

The first step is to use the Primitives panel (see Fig. 11.26) to add a sphere roughly at the center of the small Perspective window (see Fig. 11.27). To add the sphere, simply click on the Sphere tool in the Primitives panel; you'll get a sphere of default size and orientation.

---

[9]This tutorial was created with version 1.0 of trueSpace, but the animation and hierarchy features used in the tutorial are essentially the same in version 2.0, a demo of which is included on the CD-ROMs.

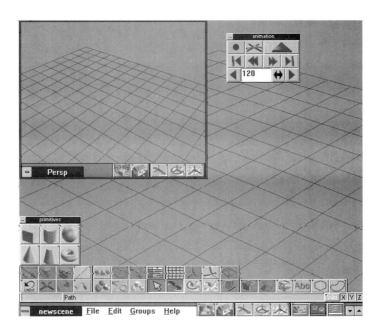

Figure 11.25
*trueSpace's main
window and
toolbars.*

Figure 11.26
*The Primitives
panel, used for
creating simple 3D
objects.*

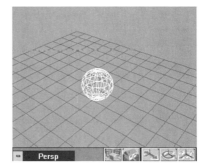

Figure 11.27
*A single sphere has
been added.*

If the sphere isn't in the location you want, you can use the tools shown in Figure
11.28 to (from left to right) select it, move it, rotate it, or scale it.[10]

---

[10]The last tool is for navigating hierarchies; remember it for later.

Figure 11.28
Tools for manipulat-
ing objects.

A single sphere doesn't make for much of a universe. The next step is to add a smat-
tering of planetary objects—spheres of different sizes. To change the size uniformly,
hold down both left and right mouse buttons while you drag to resize. Figure 11.29
shows the central "sun" sphere and two smaller "planetary" spheres.

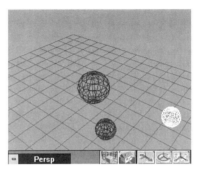

Figure 11.29
Three spheres added
to the universe.

If you make a mistake, there are two easy ways to back out. You can use the Undo
selection on the Edit menu (see Fig. 11.30), or you can click the Undo button (see Fig.
11.31).

Figure 11.30
The Edit menu.

Figure 11.31
The Undo button,
left, is a quick way
to back out of a
mistake.

Continue adding spheres, moving farther out from the "sun" as you go. You may want
to adjust the sizes of the spheres, as I have done in Figure 11.32. In Figure 11.32, there
is a central sun, two small inner planets, and several larger planets. The last planet
out (lower right) has two small moons. Remember that you are seeing in 3D; the nearer
objects appear larger than they really are.

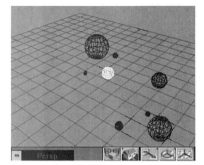

Figure 11.32
*All the objects are
present for the solar
system.*

Figure 11.33 shows the system from above, and you can see the relative sizes and positions of the objects more clearly. To change to this view, you can either create a new Top view window, or change the view temporarily using the second button from the left in the Perspective window.

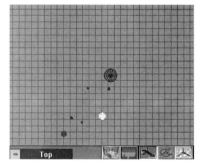

Figure 11.33
*The view from
above.*

Our little solar system is static so far—there is no movement, no animation. Clicking on the Path tool[11] opens the small dialog box shown in Figure 11.34. From left to right, the three buttons at the top are

- Move points
- Create points
- Remove selected point(s)

The number next to the word *Segments* refers to the number of frames that will be created between the path points you create. This means you don't have to click for every frame and every point; you can let trueSpace handle the intervening points and frames.

---

[11]See Chapter 3 if you are unsure about which tools are which.

To create a path for the selected object (the object in white is the selected object), simply select the object, click the Path tool, and then click on the middle top button. Now, every time you click in the workspace, trueSpace creates a new Path point, plus 10 intervening frames. Figure 11.35 shows a partially drawn path for one of the planets. Since these are orbits, they will be circular or elliptical.[12]

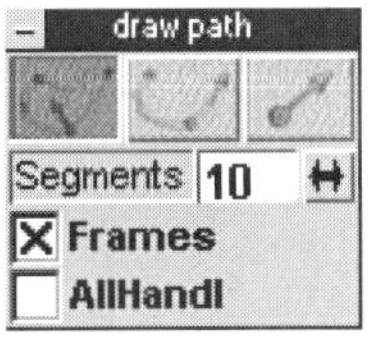

Figure 11.34
The dialog box for creating and editing paths.

Figure 11.35
A partially drawn path.

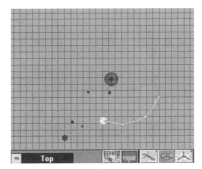

Figure 11.36 shows the completed path, and Figure 11.37 shows the path for one of the inner planets. As you can see in Figure 11.38, the path can be anything you want it to be, including the highly elliptical orbit shown.

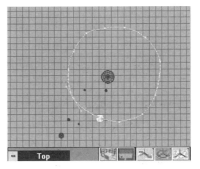

Figure 11.36
A completed path.

[12]You can also create paths of certain basic shapes, such as a circle.

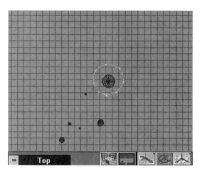

Figure 11.37
A path for an inner planet.

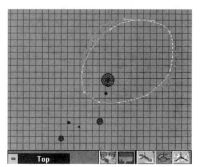

Figure 11.38
A highly elliptical path.

Figure 11.39 shows a path in the Perspective window. Because the view is 3D, you are seeing the path in perspective. In general, I prefer to modify a path in a "regular," non-perspective view, such as Top or Front.

Figure 11.40 shows a rendering of the scene. The 3D nature of the objects is much clearer in a rendering. The materials that are used for the object surfaces and the background color are default values; we'll be changing them to get a more realistic[13] appearance.

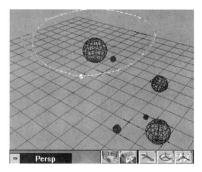

Figure 11.39
A path in the Perspective window.

---

[13]Or at least more interesting!

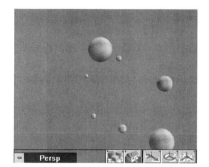

Figure 11.40
A rendering of the scene so far.

To see the animation in action as a wireframe model, click the Animation tool. This displays the Animation Controller (see Fig. 11.41). You can also right-click on the same tool to display the Animation Parameters dialog box (see Fig. 11.42).

Figure 11.41
Use the Animation Controller to control playback and position.

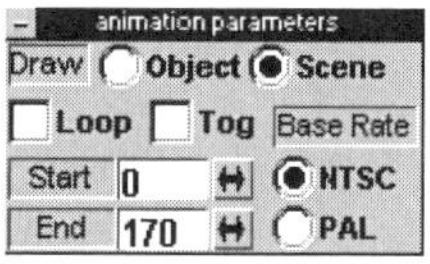

Figure 11.42
The Animation Parameters dialog box controls many aspects of animation.

By default, the animation is set to animate only the currently selected object. To animate all objects that have a path, click on Scene instead of Object in the Animation Parameters dialog box. Another item to note: The default endpoint of the animation will be the number of frames in the animation of the currently selected object. If the total animation has more frames, you can enter the number by hand.

To play the animation, click on the large, upward-pointing arrowhead at the top right of the Animation Controller.

Right now, the animation is incomplete—some of the objects do not have paths. The outermost planet with the two moons is the culprit, and there's a reason. We want the two moons to orbit the planet while the planet orbits the sun. This involves hierarchical relationships.[14]

---

[14]Big words, but less intimidating than you might think. Like any hierarchy, there's one entity in charge, and one or more levels of responsibility lower down. A monarchy is a hierarchy taken to extremes, but it's a good model for most animation work: there's one central object in any hierarchy, and as many levels as it takes to get down to the peasants who do all the real work.

It's easy to create a hierarchy in trueSpace. Begin with the Big Cheese, the Parent, the King: the object that is at the top of the hierarchy. In this case, that's the outermost planet.[15]

Look closely at Figure 11.43. A lot has happened to the animation, but it might not be immediately evident. First, notice that the outer planet has a path; that's no big deal—we've done this before. No, the really big news is that the outer planet and the two little moons are all in white. White means selected. How did this happen?

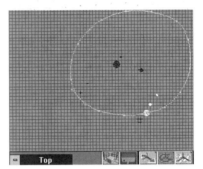

Figure 11.43
Creating a hierarchi-cal animation.

The process is trivially easy. First, select the outermost planet by clicking on it. Now click the Glue Child button (see Chapter 3 for a complete map to trueSpace buttons). Now click on the inner moon. Presto—you've just created a hierarchy; congratulations. Wasn't that easy? It was so easy and so much fun, let's add another level to the hierarchy. If you haven't done any random clicking, the Glue Child button is still down. Now click on the second little moon. Wow—now we have a two-level hierarchy.

Now add the path, and the whole hierarchy will follow the path. That's what actually is going on in Figure 11.43—those aren't the starting positions for any of the planets you can see. But the little moons need orbital paths of their very own. Again, it's easy. We just have to navigate up and down the hierarchy until we have selected only the member we want. Again, this is easy—just use the arrow keys. The left- and right-arrow keys move sideways in the hierarchy, and the up- and down-arrow keys move up and down. If the planet and its two little moons are all white (selected, in other words), press the down arrow. You will move down a level, and just the two little moons will be white; the planet will be beige. White means selected; beige means part of the current hierarchy, but not selected. In Figure 11.44, only the inner little moon is selected. The process of moving around in the hierarchy couldn't be much easier. To select just the outer little moon, press the down arrow again.

---

[15]Strictly speaking, if we planned to move the sun around, it would be the Top Enchilada, so that the planets would follow it around like little Taquitos.

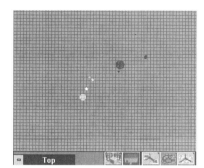

Figure 11.44
Selecting just one member of a hierarchy.

Figure 11.45 shows a nice elliptical path for the outer moon. Add a path for the inner moon and, presto, a moving hierarchy.

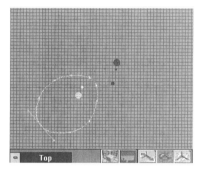

Figure 11.45
Adding a path for one of the little moons of the outermost planet.

All the animations we have been creating have different numbers of frames. The complete animation is as long as the longest individual animation. However, the object with the shortest animation will simply stop moving after one execution. The Animation panel comes to the rescue (see Fig. 11.46). Each object (or hierarchy, such as our NoName hierarchy in Fig. 11.46) has its own horizontal band in the panel. To create a repeating animation, just click the far right button on the bottom of the Animation panel, and then click on the horizontal bar corresponding to the animation. We want everything to repeat, so repeat the process for all animations.

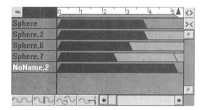

Figure 11.46
The Animation panel.

We now have the basics of what we want: an animated solar system of our own design. Figures 11.47 and 11.48 show two frames from a wireframe animation. However, let's face it—it's a boring little solar system, full of pink planets and a pink sun,[16] with a dull gray background. All of our animation work deserves a much spicier color scheme. To do this, we must create materials or select from existing materials in the library.

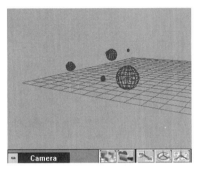

Figure 11.47
A frame from the animation, in Wireframe mode.

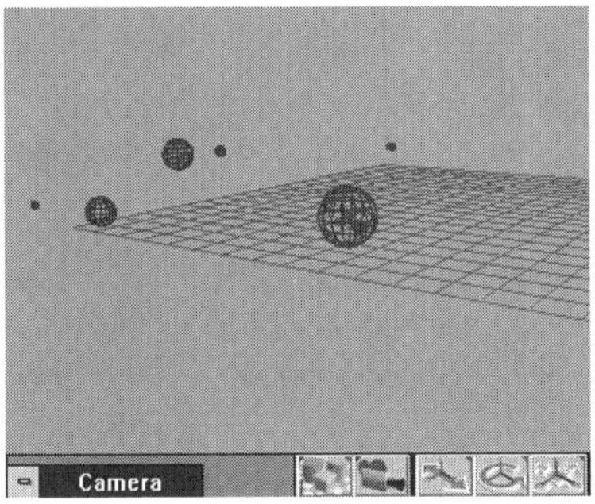

Figure 11.48
A frame from a different part of the animation.

To access the material controls, right-click the Paint tool. This displays several dialog boxes, shown in Figures 11.49 through 11.52. This may look intimidating, but the dialog boxes work together in a simple way. When in doubt, pass the mouse cursor over a button or dialog box, and watch the status bar for helpful information. There are just too many buttons to remember here and in trueSpace overall. This little trick makes it much easier to learn how to use trueSpace.

The color picker is just like any other color picker. First, pick a color from the large hexagon. Then lighten or darken it by clicking in the vertical bar. This becomes the primary color for the material. If you change the color (or any other material parameter), you will see an immediate update in the Material dialog box.

---

[16]Refer back to the earlier rendering, which, while in black and white, is pretty darn boring.

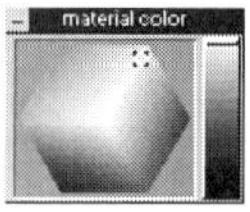

Figure 11.49
The color picker.

Figure 11.50
The current material.

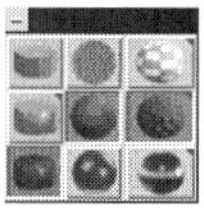

Figure 11.51
Setting material characteristics.

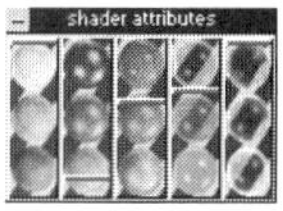

Figure 11.52
Adjusting the shader attributes.

The dialog box in Figure 11.51 is unnamed, and perhaps that's wise, because it contains quite a variety of buttons and controls. They are arranged in three columns. The far-left column controls faceting. From top to bottom, you'll get facets, auto-smoothing, and all smooth surfaces.[17] The second column controls shading from simple to fancy metallic, and the third column controls surface texture/bumpiness.

The Shader Attributes dialog box provides visual cues for adjusting a variety of material properties. There are five columns, with a slider in each column. To vary a property, move the slider up or down as needed. The five properties are

> Self-illumination
>
> Shininess
>
> Roughness
>
> Transparency
>
> Refraction

For the sun, we can take advantage of self-illumination—set it all the way to the top. You'll find that maximum self-illumination tends to override other settings, so you may not need to change anything else except color—yellow for my sun, and the color you want for yours. Figure 11.53 shows a rendering for the scene, with the sun glowing away nicely. But the background is still gray, and the planets are still smooth and, well, pink. However, they are nicely lit by the sun!

---

[17]*Smooth* means you won't see the edges between facets.

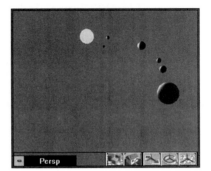

Figure 11.53
*A rendering showing
the sun as a self-
illuminating object.*

What we need now are some nice planetary textures and colors for the planets. You can, if you want, dig out planetary maps for your own solar system, but this is strictly a do-it-yourself solar system, so we'll have to improvise. Figure 11.54 shows a material that uses a bumpy texture. It has a nice planetary look, and I tuned it a bit by using the Shader Attributes dialog box. Figure 11.55 shows the dialog box that allows you to select various surface textures; I chose orange because it was the most planetary-looking.

Figure 11.54
*A material with a
planet-like texture.*

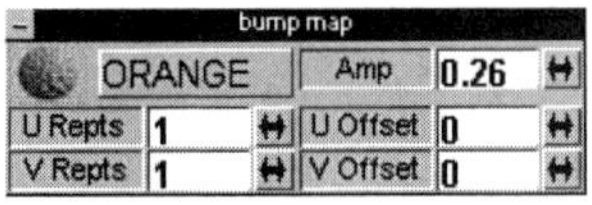

Figure 11.55
*Selecting a surface
texture for a
material.*

I used this texture, with some variations, for all the planets but the outermost one. I kind of liked the weird texture shown in Figure 11.56, which I dug out of the sample textures supplied with trueSpace.

Figure 11.56
*A nice, exotic,
planetary texture.*

Figure 11.57 shows a rendering of the scene with the planets and the sun all having textures. Nice, but, wow—that gray background has got to go!

Figure 11.57
All the objects now have a material texture.

It's easy to do; just right-click the Render button in the Perspective window to display a few global settings (see Fig. 11.58), one of which is the background. I created the background shown in Figure 11.59 using an Image Editor—just some random white, blue, and red dots for stars, and then an airbrush to create a nebula or two. Instant space background.

Figure 11.58
Adjusting the background.

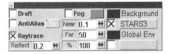

Figure 11.59
A background that looks nice and spacey.

To save the animation as an AVI file, I simply clicked the Render to File button (a variant of the Render tool). Figure 11.60 shows the dialog box that allows you to set parameters for the AVI file. Make sure that you click on All Frames in the Animation section of the dialog box, and enter a valid AVI file name. You'll also need to set a size for the animation (I used 320×240 because it's a standard size for video clips), as well as a frame rate (15 or 30), and verify that the Pixel Aspect Ratio is 1.0. Click the Render button when all is ready.

Figure 11.60
Setting values saving the animation to a file.

This will display YADB (Yet Another Dialog Box),[18] shown in Figure 11.61. You can accept the default, no compression, but you wind up with a huge file that no one can play. Compression makes it possible to hit frame rates of 30 per second with an animation that uses a steady background (that's this one). I have chosen Cinepak in the example, but any compression codec you favor will do (such as Indeo or MS Video 1). Set a quality level (the higher the number, the better the image, but the greater the demands it will put on your system during playback). Click OK when you have it all decided.

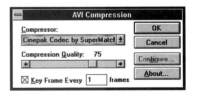

Figure 11.61
Setting the compression method.

Now, all you have to do is sit back and wait—compression may take anywhere from a few seconds to a minute per frame, depending on a variety of factors. But the end result is a lot of fun, as you can see from the sample rendered frame in Figure 11.62. A full-size rendering is shown in Figure 11.63.

This is just the beginning of what you can do with trueSpace. The combination of a reasonably complete set of tools, a clever and easy-to-learn interface, and first-rate rendering make trueSpace an excellent startup tool for anyone interested in 3D animation, rendering, or artificial reality.

---

[18]Of course, trueSpace can't hold a candle to VREAM when it comes to dialog boxes, now can it?

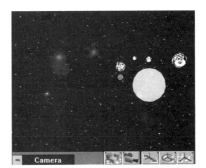

Figure 11.62
*A sample frame
from the animation.*

Figure 11.63
*A larger rendering of
a single frame,
uncompressed for
best image quality.*

12

THE VIRTUAL WORKSHOP

Two of the most exciting areas of the virtual workshop are the Internet and World Wide Web (WWW). As faster modems and faster point-to-point connections become standard, it's now possible to move large amounts of data across the net without totally slowing down the on-line process. This means that 3D worlds, virtual worlds, and multimedia content are becoming regular features of the net.

If you are not already on the Internet, we've provided some ideas farther on in this chapter, in the section "You Are Not Alone." You'll learn a few Internet basics, and how to get yourself onto the Internet. However, you will probably want to pick up a reference on the Internet for complete information; the net itself is just too large for me to give it adequate coverage in just one section of one chapter.[1]

The emerging standard in the world of 3D on the net is called VRML. *VRML* stands for *Virtual Reality Markup Language*. It plays the same role on the net that HTML plays, but with a VR twist. HTML is used to create pages on the World Wide Web. Figure 12.1 shows a typical web page created with HTML.[2] VRML is used to create pages, home or otherwise, that allow you to explore interactively in 3D. Figure 12.2 shows an example of a VRML page. The most obvious fact: It's all graphics, and no text. For this reason, folks often mix VRML and HTML files.

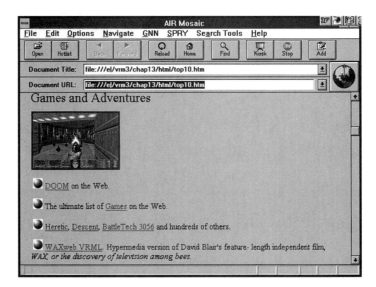

Figure 12.1
An example of an HTML page in use.

---

[1] I took the easy way onto the net myself (I guess I have to confess that I'm lazy!). I just bought Internet in a Box, installed it, and used the default Internet provider. You can't beat the speed of it all; within minutes, I was up and on the net.

[2] As a matter of fact, it's an early version of the home page we are creating for this book. You can find it at http://www.mcp.com/sams/vrmadness. Any web browser, such as Internet in a Box's AIR Mosaic, will get you there.

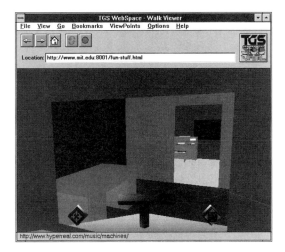

Figure 12.2
*An example of a
VRML page in use.*

One of the first tools for browsing VRML files is called WebSpace, and it is a featured product in this chapter. It's available online from either of the following World Wide Web sites:

- `http://www.sgi.com/Products/WebFORCE/WebSpace/`
- `http://www.cts.com/~template/WebSpace/`

You'll also find several VRML browsers on the included CD-ROMs. If you are not already on the Internet, you can explore using the files on the CD-ROMs. If you are on the Internet, you can explore a multitude of 3D and virtual worlds on the net. We have supplied Internet connection software and a World Wide Web browser on the CD-ROMs if you would like to get yourself connected. Check the CDs for details.

WebSpace

WebSpace is a VRML browser that has been available on the SGI (Silicon Graphics) platform for some time, and there has been a steady growth in the number of VRML worlds available for browsing. However, the company TGS is now shipping PC-compatible versions of WebSpace. I will warn you, however, that browsing in 3D is a CPU-intensive activity, and any computer less than a Pentium is going to be very slow at browsing. We tested the software on a 486/66, and it took several seconds to make a movement—not ideal at all! You can have some fun with the software on a 486, but you will have to be very patient.

In this section, you'll learn what VRML is, and how to use WebSpace to cruise through 3D worlds.

RECIPE

1 Pentium-based PC running Windows
1 copy WebSpace
1 Internet connection

Instructions: Fire up your PC at top speed, then gently add WebSpace browser to your regular Mosaic browser. Allow entire mixture to flow out of the bowl and into the net, where you will find delicious pastries, rich gourmet offerings, and some lighter refreshment. Don't leave it on the burner too long, however, as your on-line costs might soar!

WebSpace Overview

WebSpace is just one of many of the VRML browsers we will see over the next few years, but it has one key advantage: It's here now. A *browser*, for anyone who is not already familiar with Internet lingo, is simply a program that allows you to view or interact with an Internet file. You can have image browsers, HTML browsers (files of the type *.HTM), and, of course, VRML browsers (files of the type *.WRL).

That means that the only real job that WebSpace or any other VRML browser has is to display the graphic image that the VRML file describes, and then allow you to move around in the virtual space inhabited by the object. The interface itself is utter simplicity. There are just three controls at the bottom of the WebSpace window. Figure 12.3 shows a typical WebSpace session. You are looking at a house with a few trees in front of it. The foreground objects aren't VRML objects at all—they are the WebSpace controls. Let's take a close look at these controls.

The following list shows the WebSpace controls isolated from the background. There are three of them, as shown in figure 12.3. From left to right, they are

Jump control

Move control

Slide control

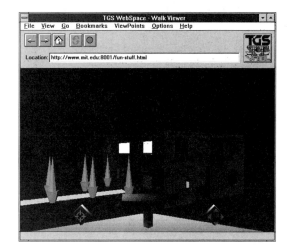

Figure 12.3
A VRML world in
WebSpace.

Jump Control

This control allows you to move immediately to any object you can see in your current view. To use it, just click on the control to activate it, and then click on the object you want to jump to. If you change your mind, click on the Jump control again to deactivate it.

Move Control

The Move control allows you to move forward and backward, to rotate your point of view, or to do both at the same time. It works like a virtual joystick. Click on the Move control and drag upward to move forward; drag downward to move backward. To rotate left, click on the control and drag left. To rotate right—but by now you've got the idea. If you want to rotate without moving forward or backward, be sure to drag in a horizontal line from the Move control. If you want to rotate left and move forward, drag up and to the left. This sounds more complicated than it actually is—in actual use, it's as easy as pie.[3]

Slide Control

The Slide control can move you up or down, left or right, but without rotation or forward/backward movement. It is especially handy for up and down movements, so that you can look into containers, rise above the crowd, etc. To use it, click and drag in the direction you want to slide. You can move the mouse exactly horizontally or vertically, or you can move at an angle.

---

[3]On the other hand, whoever was it that started this business of "easy as pie?" I tried making a pie, and I didn't think it was easy. Maybe they meant "as easy to eat as pie." I'll buy that.

WebSpace in Action

Let's take a tour of the VRML file supplied with WebSpace. Begin by running
WEBSPACE.EXE, the VRML browser from TGS. This is a shareware version; if you want
to register it to receive support or updates, you'll need to contact TGS. That's easy to do
if you are on the Internet—just go to their home page (http://www.cts.com/~template/),
shown in Figure 12.4.

Figure 12.4
*A VRML world in
WebSpace.*

When you visit TGS on the web, you can read more about WebSpace, learn about
new VRML pages you can visit, register your version of WebSpace, and many more
things. TGS' home page also provides links to a wide variety of VR-related Internet sites.

Before we dive into WebSpace, I'd like to take a moment for a reality check. WebSpace
comes in many versions, including Windows, Windows 95, and Windows NT. It
started out, however, on a very high-end platform: SGI (Silicon Graphics). Even a fast
486 is really no match for this kind of software, at least in the early versions of
WebSpace; this may improve over time. In our experience, you'll need at least a
Pentium computer to actually enjoy what WebSpace has to offer. We experienced
delays of 5 to 45 seconds on a 486/66 running Windows NT, depending on the complexity of the virtual world/object.[4]

---

[4]At the time I wrote this chapter, WebSpace was still in beta, so there is some chance the version you
get will be more responsive. This also means that the version you get might not have exactly the
same look or features as what you see here; be prepared to make minor adjustments as we go along. I
also had to work with the Windows NT version, as the Windows 3.*x* and Windows 95 versions were
not even in beta release at the time I wrote this chapter.

When you first run WebSpace, you'll see a lot of black and little else (see Fig. 12.5). To learn about WebSpace, load the sample file included with it: URLHOUSE.WRL. Use the File/Open menu selection to open this file. WebSpace will churn the disk for a bit while it loads the file, and then you'll have a delay while it constructs the 3D space in the window.[5] Then you'll see a 3D model in the WebSpace window, as shown in Figure 12.6.[6]

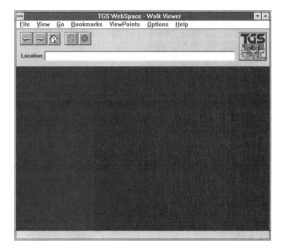

Figure 12.5
The WebSpace
opening screen.

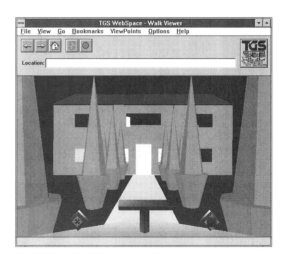

Figure 12.6
Loading a 3D world
into WebSpace.

---

[5]The length of the delay will depend on your computer's speed. On a 486/66, expect a long delay—perhaps 10 to 30 seconds. Faster computers will use less time to load.

[6]The exact orientation of the house in the viewer may differ for you.

Now all you have to do is learn to move around in the 3D world, using the three controls described earlier. For example, if you want to move closer to the house, simply click on the Move control, and then drag upward. Drag a little to move slowly; drag a lot to move quickly. If you have a slower computer,[7] be careful—you can wind up moving a long way while you wait for WebSpace to display the new position. Start with small moves, and see how it goes.

You can also use the Jump tool to move. For example, click the Jump tool, and then click in the window at the lower left of the house (refer to Fig. 12.6). You'll move to approximately the point shown in Figure 12.7. If you look closely through the window, you can see a portion of a piano; click again on the Jump tool, and then on the piano. You'll move to a position similar to the one shown in Figure 12.8.

Figure 12.7
Jumping to the window.

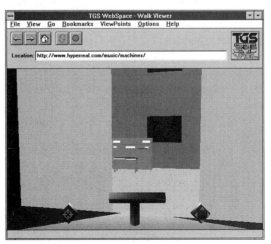

Figure 12.8
Jumping to the piano.

---

[7]Defined for this piece of software as anything less than a Pentium 90.

This is fun, but you might be wondering: What's the point? What can I do? The answer is that you can do plenty. Just as text or an image can be a "hot link" in an HTML file, so can objects in a VRML file. For example, clicking on that piano would take you to a web site having to do with music—specifically:

`http://www.hyperreal.com/music/machines/`

To get the benefits of hot links, you'll need the registered version of WebSpace. You can register most easily by visiting the TGS home page and looking for the registration instructions. You'll need a Web browser to get there, but you need a browser to jump the hot links, too!

Objects that have web links change color when you pass the mouse cursor over them. Figure 12.9 shows what happens to the piano when the mouse is on it. Notice that, even in black and white, the piano is obviously lighter in color. Just what color an object changes to varies from one VRML file to another.

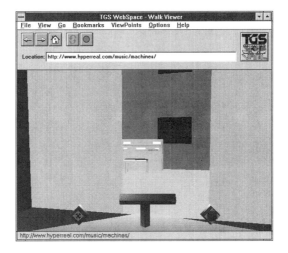

Figure 12.9
The piano is a hot link—the color changes when the mouse is on it.

In addition to all the moves you've learned so far, you can also look up and down without changing your position. There is a tiny red bar on the right side of the Move control. Click it and drag up to look up, and drag down to look down. Figure 12.10 shows what happens when you look up from the position shown in Figure 12.9.

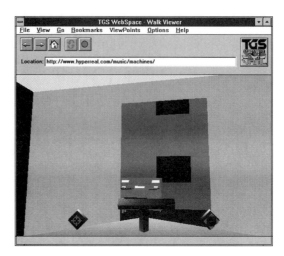

Figure 12.10
You can look up by
dragging the control
at the right side of
the Move control.

There are many places in the house that you can visit; Figures 12.11 and 12.12 show two of them. You might want to explore moving around the house (as well as outside it) until you feel comfortable navigating with WebSpace.

Figure 12.11
Looking down from
a balcony in the
virtual house.

WebSpace is slow, but it opens up a whole new range of possibilities for the Internet. In the next section, you'll learn about a simple but effective method for not only connecting to a VR experience on the Internet, but also for talking to other folks in that virtual environment.

We'll also be seeing more VRML browsers in late 1995 and in 1996; you can visit our home page to learn more about them.[8]

---

[8]Again, the number to call is: http://www.mcp.com/sams/vrmadness

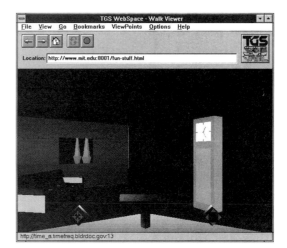

Figure 12.12
*A room in the
virtual house.*

WorldsChat

RECIPE

1 copy WorldsChat
1 Internet connection
8M RAM (16M is advised)
16-bit sound card (optional)
An urge to chat in 3D

Instructions: Choose a digital alter image to represent you in cyberspace, teleport to the WorldsChat space station, and make new friends from around the world. Makes a great mixer.

There is a mad rush to put virtual reality on the Internet, and Worlds Inc. is one of the first.[9] They have created an amazing and thoroughly addictive interactive program: WorldsChat.

---

[9]Thanks to Tim McNitt for a major contribution to this section.

WorldsChat is virtual social gathering.[10] You navigate through a 3D environment and chat with avatars[11] representing people from around the world. It's a reasonably realistic social experience, right down to the often superficial party atmosphere and chitchat. It is possible to meet interesting people and engage in thoughtful conversation, but it takes time and effort. Just imagine being thrust into a room with people from around the world whom you've never met. It takes a while to get past the "where are you from and how old are you" introductory chat. Fortunately, if the conversation gets boring, you can zoom around the space station or look out the windows at the stars and planet.

The WorldsChat Window and Controls

Figure 12.13 shows the WorldsChat application. It's fairly simple to use; descriptions of the main controls and tools follow.

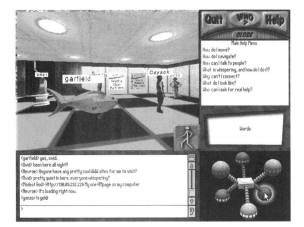

Figure 12.13
The WorldsChat window and controls.

Main View screen—This is your view of the world as seen through the eyes of your avatar. Clicking the mouse once suspends mouse navigation and brings up a Walk icon in the lower right of the Main View screen. Clicking on the Walk icon resumes mouse navigation.

Text box—The lower part of the text box displays outgoing messages as you type. The ear-shaped icon to the right is used to send *whispers* (explained later). The larger area above this icon displays the most recent incoming messages and any outgoing messages you have already sent. To view more of the earlier messages, use the scroll bar or the up/down arrows to the right of the text box, or click on the Earlier Messages icon above the up arrow.

---

[10]Drinks and hors d'oeuvres not included.

[11]*Avatars* are 3D images/objects that stand in for the various folks you can chat with.

Help box—To end your visit to WorldsChat and close the application, click Quit. Who? lists the people in your immediate vicinity with whom you can chat. Help brings up a menu of brief Help topics. Close (below Who?) closes the text in the Help box (it does not close WorldsChat).

Map—This displays a diagram of the space station. Passing the mouse cursor over a section highlights it and displays its name in the box above the map. Clicking on a section of the station teleports you to that section.

Entering the World

When you open WorldsChat, you begin in the Avatar Gallery (see Fig. 12.14). Instead of selecting an avatar right away, you might want to take the opportunity to learn how to move around.[12] You can move using either the mouse or the arrow keys on your keyboard. You can use the up- and down-arrow keys or the mouse to move you forward and backward. Use the left- and right-arrow keys or the mouse to rotate your avatar. To move sideways, hold down the Shift key, and then move the mouse left or right.

Figure 12.14
The WorldsChat opening screen—the Avatar Gallery.

After you are comfortable moving around, it is time to choose an avatar to represent you in cyberspace (see Fig. 12.15). To select an avatar, click the left mouse button once to get a cursor, and then click on the portrait of the avatar you want to view. You will then see a rotating 3D model of the avatar. If you want to choose this avatar, click on the Embody Me[13] button. Otherwise, you can click on Keep Looking.

---

[12]It's often easy to spot the newbies in WorldsChat, as their avatars stumble around bumping into walls or other avatars.

[13]Now there's a button name we never expected to see.

Figure 12.15
Viewing an avatar.

After you select an avatar, the next step is to choose a username[14] by which others in WorldsChat will know you. A username must be more than two characters, but less than 12. If the username you choose is already in use by someone else in WorldsChat, you will be asked to select another name.

Choosing an Avatar and Username: Social Psychology on the Internet

Internet etiquette is a subtle and ever-changing skill. In cyberspace, just as in the real world, first impressions are often determined by appearance and name. How others respond to you initially may depend on the avatar and username you select. It can be an interesting study in human psychology, but be careful! If you select an avatar of the opposite sex, for example, and are found out, be prepared for a possibly hostile reaction from the other users.

If you select a username that is crude, you might find it hard to get into a conversation. It is difficult enough to get to know people in an Internet chat group without imposing additional barriers. Likewise, people who engage in obnoxious or rude behavior quickly find themselves being ignored.

On the same screen where you type your username (see Fig. 12.16), you also have the options of turning off the sound and music. After you make your selections and enter a username, click on Enter WorldsChat, and the program will attempt to connect you to the Worlds server. If the connection is not made, you will then have the option of continuing in single-user mode.[15] If you are connected to the server, you will soon find yourself in the main meeting room (the hub center), or on one of the six platforms out under the stars.

---

[14]Pronounced *USE-er-name*.

[15]Useful for learning your way around the station, but it gets pretty lonely.

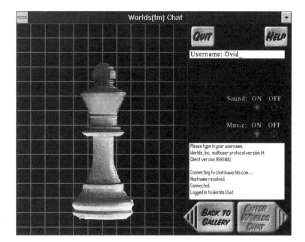

Figure 12.16
Choosing a username and selecting sound and music.

Cyberspace Communication

The avatars are visible in the large portion of the WorldsChat window. You communicate with them by using the text box at the lower left of the window. At present, the program supports text only.[16] Type a message, and it is displayed on the screens of the other users you are chatting with. Worlds Inc. is promising to upgrade to a voice interface in the near future.[17] You can see and communicate with the six avatars closest to you.[18] Just type your message and press Enter to send it to the group.

After you are connected to WorldsChat, you can enter into a conversation by typing **Hi, everyone**. If you move next to an avatar, say hello, and get no response, don't be dismayed. They might already be having a conversation with someone else, and might not want to be disturbed.[19]

Keeping track of who is talking to whom is an art. Following conversations in a chat group takes some getting used to. Several distinct conversations may be going on at the same time, and all appear on your screen together. It's up to you to sort out which comments belong to which conversation. You'll know you are getting good at it when you find yourself actively involved in several conversations at one time. Keeping up with multiple conversations requires concentration and fast typing. If the room you are in is crowded, you might not get all of a particular conversation. In that case, you might want to move to one of the small meeting rooms.

---

[16]Won't it be fun when you can record a comment in a WAV file and send that? Cool!

[17]Trying to keep up with a conversation when you are a slow typist is frustrating. Also, in a text conversation, you can never quite be sure that the avatar named Sue with whom you are chatting is really a female. This can lead to some very peculiar interchanges.

[18]If you want to know which users are in your group, you can view their names by clicking on the Who? button at the top right of the window.

[19]See the next section, "Whispering."

Whispering

You can send a private message to a single individual by whispering. To whisper, type the username of the person you want to whisper to exactly as it appears above that person's avatar. Whispers are case sensitive, so it is important to use upper- and lowercase letters just as they are shown above the avatar. After the username, type a colon, followed by the message. For example, a whisper intended for username Alice might look like the following:

```
Alice: Have you seen the Mad Hatter today?
```

To send the whisper, press the Tab key or click on the ear-shaped icon to the right of the message box.[20]

There are a few shortcut functions for whispers. After you send a whisper to an avatar, you don't have to type the username again to send the same avatar another whisper. Just type the message and press Tab or click on the ear icon. WorldsChat remembers who you last sent a whisper to. Another fast way to send a whisper is to click on the name above an avatar. That name shows up in the message box, followed by a colon.

Whispers can be sent to anyone anywhere on the space station. If you are in Geometry, and Alice is in Words, you can send her a whisper and she will receive it. This is a great way to find someone if you don't know what room they are in.

Exploring the World

The WorldsChat space station is a cool place to explore. The view through your avatar's eyes is the same as it would be if you were inside the station. If you want to see what your avatar looks like, you can click on the Help button at the upper right of your screen, and then select What Do I Look Like? An image of your avatar then is displayed in the Help window (see Fig. 12.17).

To move around the station, use the mouse or the arrow keys to go through doorways and up or down the escalators[21] to other platforms or to the hub. The fastest way to move to another section is to click the left mouse button to get a cursor, and then click on a section of the map at the lower right of your screen. Your avatar will instantly be teleported to the new section. When you have a mouse cursor available, mouse navigation is suspended. To resume mouse-navigation mode, click on the Walk icon at the lower right of the View screen.

---

[20]If you press Enter, the whisper will be sent as a regular message, and anyone in your nearby group can read it. It can be pretty embarrassing if you intend to send a whisper and instead the message gets broadcast to everyone.

[21]Be sure to check out the escalators. After you "step" onto one of them, you can relax and let it carry your avatar to the new level. It's a small thing, but little touches like this are what make WorldsChat fun to explore.

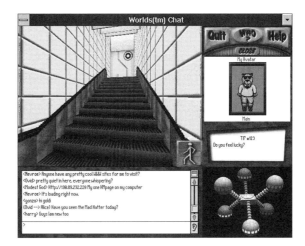

Figure 12.17
Viewing your avatar.

In Hub Center, there are two billboard panels at opposite corners of the room. Clicking on a billboard brings up a text window[22] or a detailed Help screen. At either end of the room are doorways leading to a corridor that completely encircles the hub. Doorways lead off the corridor to each of the six platforms (see Fig. 12.18).

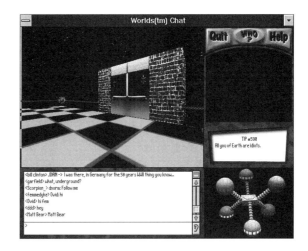

Figure 12.18
A doorway to smaller meeting rooms.

---

[22]A likely place for paid advertising to show up someday. Don't complain too much, though—the program is free.

Each platform has five doorways leading to small meeting rooms. These rooms are great for semi-private meetings for a small group. In Geology, the doorway leads to a large open space under the stars instead of a meeting room.

The designers of WorldsChat included a few surprises in the program—some intentional, some not. I'm not going to give away any secrets, however—you are on your own. Enjoy!

VR on the Internet

In addition to virtual worlds that you can explore using WebSpace, there is a ton of information about virtual reality topics on the Internet and the WWW. These range from university sites where research into VR is ongoing, to home pages for companies with VR products, to fanciful and exploratory pages that set new standards for virtual reality.

I have included a file on the CD-ROMs that represents the home page for this book, but it's mainly intended for folks who don't have an Internet connection—it's a sample of what you would be able to do if you had the connection. If you do have an Internet connection, you ought to visit our home page, where you'll find the latest and greatest stuff we've been able to find. Here's a short list of the kinds of links you will find on our home page:[23]

Games and Adventures

- DOOM custom levels and information.
- The ultimate list of games on the Web.
- Heretic, Descent, BattleTech 3056, and hundreds of other games.
- WAXweb VRML. WAXweb is the hypermedia version of David Blair's feature-length independent film, *WAX, or the discovery of television among bees*.

Internet VR Viewers (VRML)

- One of the hottest viewers for VRML is WebSpace from Silicon Graphics and Template Graphics Software.

---

[23]Not all of these links may be on our home page at the time you connect with it—the web is notoriously fluid, and some of the sites may go away, or other, even better, ones may appear. We'll always have the latest, greatest, and best links we can find on our home page.

- Another VRML viewer is Worldview from Intervista. Many tools for building virtual worlds with VRML are in production. One of the first on the market was Home Space Builder from Paragraph International.

- VREAM, Inc. has created WIRL (Web Interactive Reality Layer), a VR web viewer for browsing worlds created with its product, VRCreator. VREAM's products go a step beyond many of the other browsers, providing a more interactive environment.

- Avril is another VR browser (as well as a world builder); it is from Lepton International.

Miscellaneous VR Stuff

- WorldsChat from Worlds Inc. Pick your avatar and enter a 3D world where you can communicate with other computer users around the world.

- Usenet groups on VR include sci.virtual-worlds, sci.virtual-worlds.apps, alt.3d, alt.cyberspace, alt.cyberpunk, and comp.graphics.

Other VR Listings

- **VR Resources:** Charles R. Durham has put together the most comprehensive listing of VR resources available on the Internet.

- **EERIE:** VR List School of Engineering and Research in Computer Science and Electronics, Parc Scientifique Georges Besse, France.

- **Atlantis:** Another VR Web supersite.

- Lara Ashmore's **VR page**.

- Jon Neill's **Virtual WWW list**.

- Sandy Ressler's **Hot Virtual Reality Sites**.

- **Yahoo Entertainment:** Virtual Reality.

- The **NASA Virtual Reality** page.

Publications

- On-line magazine: *VR World*.

- *NewType Gaming Magazine*.

- Eric Scroger's *Virtual Reality 3D* rendered comics.

You Are Not Alone

These are exciting times for both virtual reality and the Internet.[24] Two of the hottest areas of computing are undergoing a merger. Virtual reality is the result of the evolution of the user interface from command line (DOS) to 2D graphical (Windows) to 3D and VR. Combine this with the Internet and you have 3D virtual worlds where you can interact with other people from around the world.

Imagine logging onto a home page, and instead of a screen full of text and graphics, you find yourself in a 3D rendering of an arboretum. To interact in the arboretum, you upload a 3D model (usually called an *avatar*[25]) of yourself. You wander around the arboretum, enjoying the scenery, listening to the birds. Along the way, you meet other people,[26] shake virtual hands, and chat a bit about the weather. Perhaps the two of you go on to talk about recent research into black holes, or explore the possibilities of cybersex. Whatever your choice, it's as private as you want it to be.

This isn't just fanciful thinking—the technology exists for most of what I've described, and it is available at a reasonable cost. In fact, much of the software is available as shareware or freeware, downloadable over the net. At the time of this writing, many software developers are tripping over one another to be the first to get their products out. A few products are in beta testing, some are in alpha, and many others are just promises of things to come. Things are happening fast, and they are happening on the net.

What Is the Internet?

The Internet is made up of millions of computers all over the world, linked together in various ways. The nerve centers of the net are the large file servers at universities, large corporations, and government agencies. There are also thousands of smaller computers at libraries, small businesses, and owned by individuals, that are part of the net. Collectively, these servers store unimaginable amounts of data. The beauty of it is that these servers are all wired together, so that information can be rapidly[27] sent from one to another.

---

[24]Thanks to Tim McNitt for a major contribution to this section.

[25]In Hindu mythology, an avatar is an earthly manifestation of a deity. The term over-reaches just a bit, if you ask me. But then, you didn't ask, did you?

[26]Actually, their avatars.

[27]Well, as rapidly as a modem can move it.

So what kind of data is stored on these servers? You name it! Whole libraries are available. You can search these libraries using various powerful tools designed for the Internet. Freeware, shareware, and demo versions of software can be accessed and downloaded. You can browse huge repositories of images, sounds, and even movie clips.

Of course, it isn't the machines and data that make the Internet so cool, it's the many people who spend countless hours creating the content and the connections. The Internet has a wonderful tradition of sharing. Most of what you will find there was created by people who received little or no compensation for their work—just the satisfaction that comes from connecting with others.

How Do I Connect?

There are many ways to get connected. Each has its advantages and disadvantages. Probably the ideal is to be a student at a university, or an employee at one of the companies that house one of the large file servers. Being affiliated with an institution, you can probably get free access to a computer and log onto the net from there. Besides being free, another major advantage of connecting in this way is speed. The larger servers are linked together with incredibly fast connections. The disadvantage of connecting in this way is that you might have limited access. Some institutions put restrictions on when you can log on the net, or on what kinds of activities you can engage in once there. Many universities have a no-games policy for students.

The next best thing to free access at work or at school is to find free dial-up access though a local library or school. Again, there might be restrictions on usage, and finding this kind of access isn't easy.

Most of us have to settle for paying for our Internet access through a commercial Internet provider. Many such services have sprung up around the country in the last few years, providing full Internet access for a monthly or hourly fee. Aside from the fact that you have to pay for it, the other major disadvantage here is the lack of speed, since you will be working though a modem. Even at 28,800 baud, a 4M file takes a *llllooooonnnngggg* time to download. Large software files, images, and even video files are common on the net, but until we all have T-1 lines[28] into our homes, we will just have to put up with the wait.

---

[28]That's phone company lingo for "a really, *really* fast connection."

Fortunately, the commercial on-line services such as CompuServe, America Online, and Prodigy have seen the light[29] and are beginning to open up their services to the wider world. So it pays to shop around to find the best deals on the services you want.

Internet Services

Electronic mail (e-mail) is the most basic Internet service. E-mail allows you to send and receive messages with anyone else connected to the net—anywhere in the world. If you have compatible software, you can also send and receive data files as messages.

In addition to sending and receiving single messages, you can also subscribe to mailing lists. They are an offshoot of e-mail, and they allow you to receive all the messages on a particular topic sent by a group of people. The normal way to subscribe to a mailing list is to send mail containing certain required text. What text? Well, you usually have to know someone on the mailing list to find that out![30]

Usenet newsgroups are the next level in the Internet hierarchy. Think of Usenet as public e-mail. Basically, you send messages to the newsgroup, and anyone who drops by can read them. Usenet and mailing lists are used for discussions and are the best way of keeping up to date on a particular topic.

Several tools, such as Internet Relay Chat (IRC) allow you to hold real-time keyboard conversations on-line. You can even talk to others on the net with products like Internet Phone.

Want to log onto a remote computer and run a program on that computer? That's what Telnet does. You can dial up and search a database, play a game, etc.

There are several methods for searching for and retrieving information on the net. File Transfer Protocol (FTP) is used for establishing connections between machines when you want to transfer files. You log onto the remote machine as a user, browse through the file archives until you find the file you want, and then download it. You can search the universe of FTP files with a tool called Archie. Another useful tool is Gopher, an information search-and-retrieval system that presents information like the table of contents of a book.

At the high end of the net, you'll find the web—that's where you'll find interactive multimedia, on-line video (why, there are even sites with live video cameras whose output you can view on-line. Whew!), and other goodies. Mosaic is the tool of choice for the web. I use AIR Mosaic, which comes with Internet in a Box.

I could go on, but by now I hope you have a general idea of what the Internet is and how you can use it. If you want more, products like Internet in a Box are easy ways to get up on the net fast.

---

[29]Not to mention the potential for profits.

[30]Isn't the Internet fun?

The Virtual Future

The virtual future holds a lot of promise, but there's no telling how much of the promise will actually come true. You can, however, get a real taste of that future today. You can even do it without spending a lot of money. Consider the recipe that follows. The ingredients are inexpensive. You might not get quite the razzle and dazzle you get from one of the game headsets, but you won't be limited to playing games, either. There's lot to be said in favor of the new game headsets (for one things, they transform the very nature of computer games), but there's also a lot to be said for tinkering around and coming up with something that is all your own. That's what the virtual workshop is all about. Chapter 7 covered the goodies you'll find in the virtual playground—ready-made headsets, expensive position-tracking devices, and other ready-to-wear VR hardware. But these have little place in the VR workshop, where assembling your own outfit is all the rage.

RECIPE

1 PCVR parallel port interface
1 pair LCD 3D goggles
1 Mattel Power Glove
1 3D software package

Instructions: This recipe looks much more intimidating than it really is. Over the last year, the ingredients have become much more economical. With only a little fine-tuning, you can attach a few cables and be virtual, interactive, and 3D all in one shot. Add software and simmer for hours of enjoyment.

You might think it would cost a lot of money to acquire that list of ingredients, but that's not the case. For example, consider the costs of a basic 3D system from a company called 3DTV:

LCD[31] goggles	$100 to $150
3D software	Free or $$$[32]
Goggle interface	Included

You can augment this basic setup with:

Mattel Power Glove[33]	$30 to $100

That means your total initial investment in VR hardware can be from $100 to $250. At the time the first edition of this book was written (early 1993), the same equipment would have cost you about $500.

In the rest of this chapter, we'll be looking at a lot of products from a variety of companies. There are more and more companies offering the kind of hardware you want in a virtual workshop. There was a time, just a couple of years ago, when 3DTV was the only standard in the garage VR universe. Times have changed. 3DTV's long-standing support for 3D and VR technology continues to make it a relatively safe bet in this emerging market. 3DTV has made a serious effort to provide low-cost 3D and VR products, and I've been happy with the products they have offered. Some of them are downright fun, and I've always gotten the most bang for the buck out of its products. We'll take some time to look at the key products from 3DTV, and then look at a few other items that are guaranteed to catch your eye.

Keep in mind that an emphasis on low cost means you won't be getting polished, full-color documentation with some products; keep your thinking cap on! If your idea of a good deal is to trade away the spit and polish and get low prices and a photocopied manual, 3DTV is the place to shop for VR. Besides, the president (Michael Starks) is nuts about 3D and VR, and his enthusiasm comes across in the usefulness and design of his company's products.

---

[31]*LCD* stands for *liquid crystal display*. This is the same technology that is used in watches, laptop computer screens, and hand-held calculators. The idea is simple: When an electrical current is applied to and then removed from the liquid crystal, it toggles between transparent and opaque. In typical applications, the crystals are shaped into letters and numbers. Electrical currents are turned on and off to make portions of the LCD panel opaque, thus making readable text or numbers. Also, note that this price is a special one for readers of this book; standard prices are higher.

[32]That $$$ can be as much as you care to spend, or you can download shareware programs such as Rend386 from the CompuServe forum CYBERFORUM. For complete information about Rend386, look for the book *Virtual Reality Creations* from the Waite Group Press. It is written by one of the authors of Rend386, David Stampe. You can create stereo images with Vistapro as well.

[33]This item is no longer manufactured, but it remains in heavy circulation among VR enthusiasts. You can find them locally by watching the classified section of your newspaper, or you can buy them on the very active VR market. Several companies are stocking large quantities of used Power Gloves. I ordered one, and when it arrived, it still had all the original equipment and manuals.

Really Virtual

Of course, you don't have to stick with the basics. The next step up in LCD goggles is high refresh rates. Until about a year ago, you had to spend several thousand dollars to get that—only the fancy LCD glasses, such as the CrystalEyes line, supported high refresh rates (and therefore minimal flicker). A new product from 3DTV, the Stereospace Model 1, makes high refresh much more affordable. The unit and a pair of higher quality LCD glasses will run you about $400 to $450. The Stereospace is a little black box that allows you to use inexpensive LCD glasses with all kinds of powerful VR and 3D software from VREAM to Superscape. They use the same kind of input as the CrystalEyes hardware, but work with conventional LCD glasses (although you can gain a better image by going to mid-level LCD glasses, I had no trouble using an off-the-shelf pair of LCD goggles). CrystalEyes has released several low-cost versions of their product, so you now have a choice. See the details of products from both manufacturers in the VR Buyer's Guides on the CD-ROMs.

Why am I a fan of the Stereospace? The biggest problem with LCD goggles in the past has been flicker. The Stereospace allows the goggles to operate at twice the frequency of conventional units. The higher the frequency, the less flicker, and the more effective the 3D effect. Let's look at the nature of LCD goggles, and then return to the Stereospace.

LCD Goggles

LCD goggles work on a very simple principle. They are a pair of glasses with LCD panels in place of lenses. As explained in Chapter 8, "Seeing Is Believing," most 3D systems must find a way to present different images to each eye. By switching electrical current to alternate LCD panels, the computer can control which eye sees the computer screen. Here's what's happening:

- The computer displays an image for the left eye on the monitor. At the same time, it sends a timing signal to the interface that controls the glasses, usually through the parallel port.
- When the glasses receive the timing signal, they open one LCD panel and close the other.[34]
- The computer displays the image for the right eye on the monitor and sends another timing signal.
- The glasses switch panels—the one that was open is now closed, and the one that was closed is now open.

---

[34]This system does not guarantee that the correct panel will be open. Most such systems have a simple way for you to reverse the currently open panel—often nothing fancier than a simple toggle switch.

This process continues at a very high speed. If you were to view the monitor without the glasses, you would see both images at once—sort of like double vision. You need the glasses to make sure that each eye only sees what it is meant to see. Figure 12.19 shows an example of how this process works; see also the discussion in Chapter 8 on LCD glasses.

Figure 12.19
LCD glasses work by showing images to alternate eyes.

The glasses are often referred to by VR enthusiasts as *Sega goggles*, because Sega was one of the first companies to come out with such a product. However, this is not an accurate name at all, because most such goggles are now used on computers, not game machines.

Figure 12.20[35] shows a pair of LCD goggles that I received from the 3DTV Corporation.

I found it very easy to set up and use the glasses. In fact, it took just a few minutes to get up and running with the glasses. The glasses can be interfaced to your computer using any one of several different black boxes. I tested several, including the PCVR interface from 3DTV. It consists of a switch box[36] (see Fig. 12.21) and cables. The PCVR is ideal if you will be using the Power Glove, because you can connect both the glasses and the Power Glove to the PCVR. If you will not be using the Power Glove and just want 3D, you can try one of the less expensive products listed in one of the "Alternative" sections later in this chapter.[37]

---

[35]Many of the figures in this chapter were created using PC Video Capture technology. For those who are interested, the videos were recorded on Hi8 tape with a Canon A1 camcorder, and then captured with a Video Spigot card from Creative Labs. The images were captured at 640×480 as single frames and saved as 24-bit bitmaps.

[36]It is a conventional printer/modem switch box modified with additional components.

[37]For the latest product info, contact 3DTV; their address and phone number are in the VR Buyer's Guide on the CD-ROMs.

Figure 12.20
*3D LCD glasses
from 3DTV
Corporation.*

Figure 12.21
*The PCVR interface
unit for 3D glasses
and Power Glove.*

The front panel of the PCVR looks a bit intimidating, but most of what you see never needs any attention. To use the PCVR, you must make the following connections:

- ■ Connect the PCVR to the parallel port of your computer, using the cable supplied.
- ■ Connect the 3D goggles to the front of the PCVR (cable supplied).
- ■ Connect the Power Glove cable (supplied) to the back of the PCVR.
- ■ Connect the power cord (supplied) to the back of the PCVR, and plug it in.

- ■ (Optional) Connect your printer cable to the PCVR.
- ■ (Optional) Add a cable between your video display card and your normal video cable, and connect one end to the PCVR for better frame synchronization.

Figure 12.22 shows the rear panel of the PCVR, with the various connection ports just described.

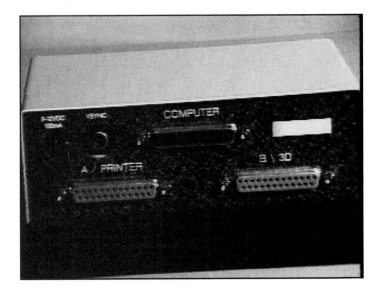

Figure 12.22
The rear panel of the PCVR.

The front panel of the PCVR has a large rotating switch. This works just like the rotating switch on a printer switch box—to use your parallel printer, rotate the switch to the Printer setting. To use the Power Glove, rotate the switch to the B 3D setting.

There are also two indicator lights. A red light indicates that the power is on, and a yellow light tells you when the proper synchronization signal is present for the glasses.[38] Just in case the timing signal is off, there's a switch you can use to make sure that the right and left eyes get into proper synchronization.

The whole process is much simpler to do than it is to describe. Once you connect the cables, you should be up and running. One place where you can run into trouble is with a nonstandard port address for your parallel port, but that's easy to fix. If you connect everything correctly, and don't get a yellow light, check the "3D Software" section later in this chapter.

---

[38]The yellow light also lights up when data is being sent to your printer—just thought you should know.

Figure 12.23 shows the goggles in use.[39] I expected the cable to get in the way, but it is light, thin, and very flexible, and wasn't much of a problem. However, a cable is a cable, and it is at best a minor annoyance.

Figure 12.23
The 3D LCD goggles in use. Note the connecting cable dangling from the left side of the goggles. This is the cable that connects to the PCVR.

There is a noticeable flicker when you use the goggles. This is not unexpected, considering that the goggles are basically flickering on and off to do their job. To reduce flicker, keep room lights low, and don't crank up the brightness setting on your monitor. Generally, I found that the 3D effect was quite good.[40]

Stereospace Model 1

But if you really want to get the most out of a $150 pair of goggles, the Stereospace and some serious VR software is really the way to go. I tested the Stereospace with standard LCD goggles and two software packages: VREAM and Superscape.

You can use the Stereospace with any software that supports the under-over method of 3D. As shown in Figure 12.24, this technique outputs two completely separate images from your video card, with a black bar separating the two images. The top image is for the left eye, and the bottom image is for the right eye. The viewing hardware must pull apart the single video image and route the correct portion of the overall output to each eye. Most such hardware senses the black bar between the two images

---

[39]That's Ron's wife, Donna Brown, under those goggles.

[40]If you want better image quality and minimal flicker, you'll need to spend more for either the Stereospace from 3DTV, or one of the CrystalEyes units.

to tell when to switch from one eye to the other. In other words, the hardware reads each horizontal scan line in the video signal. If the scan line contains data, it continues sending lines to the current eye. When it encounters the black lines at the middle of the image, it stops sending to the current eye and gets ready to send to the other eye. When it encounters the first scan line of the second half of the image, it begins sending to the new eye.

Figure 12.24
An over-under split-screen 3D image.

There is an important advantage to using this technique, and it has to do with refresh rates. The average computer video card is outputting data at about 60Hz to 72Hz (cycles per second). If you were to take a complete image and route it to one eye, and then take another complete image and route it to the other eye, you cut that refresh rate in half. For example, if your computer outputs 60 screens per second (60Hz vertical refresh), that means your eyes get a new image every 1/60th of a second. If you alternately route images to each eye, each eye sees a new image every 1/30th of a second—half as often. In short: flicker city.

The over-under 3D format allows each eye to see a new image every 1/60th of a second. The obvious disadvantage: The resolution is cut in half.

Until recently, all LCD glasses have used the alternate technique; over-under was just for the Big Guys. The Stereospace changes that. It takes as input the standard over-under video format. It then doubles the video rate to 120Hz, and then converts to alternate format. This means that each eye sees images updated at a full 60Hz—if you have a good multisync monitor that can handle the 120Hz refresh. I use a 17-inch Nanao F550i, and it works fine at this rate. The Stereospace has a readout on the front panel that tells you what refresh rate it is working at.

If your monitor won't handle the full 120Hz, you can cut back your video card's output to a lower refresh rate (56Hz, 53Hz). However, you probably will need a recent monitor to make use of the Stereospace. There are exceptions, but you shouldn't count on it.

The front panel of the Stereospace contains controls that allow you to tune the effect. You can adjust the vertical alignment of the two images, and you can easily toggle back and forth between standard mode (for viewing non-3D screens) and 3D mode.

Overall, I was extremely impressed with the results I got from using the combination of true VR software, LCD goggles, and the Stereospace. At $400 for readers of this book (goggles plus Stereospace plus a few free, if simple, goodies), this is an excellent way to enjoy true 3D with your virtual reality software.[41]

Of course, you'll need to use software that supports the over-under format. To check if your software supports it, look for support for the CrystalEyes HMD. That's one of the most common hardware units supporting the over-under format. If your software supports CrystalEyes, it will support the Stereospace. Then check the manual that comes with your monitor; if it supports 90Hz or better, there's a very good chance it will support the Stereospace.[42] You'll also get better results using a recent vintage of video card; most high-quality video cards support a wide range of refresh rates.

The Mattel Power Glove

3D is fun, but getting right into the action is better. Using the Power Glove, you can interact with your computer in completely new ways.

However, before I get you all excited about the possibilities, a few words of caution are in order. The Power Glove, after all, started out as a toy. Real computer gloves use sophisticated tracking methods to allow fairly precise interpretation of your hand movements. For example, one model of a professional glove uses fiber-optic cables strung along your fingers. The surface of the cables is etched to allow a slight loss of light. The more the cable is bent by your finger, the greater the loss of light. Separate cables are used for each knuckle and joint on your hand. The result is a precision tool, and the cost is many thousands of dollars.

The Power Glove, on the other hand,[43] uses cruder techniques for detecting finger movements. The Power Glove offers much lower precision in tracking finger movement—it can detect when your fingers are straight and when they are bent, and that's about it. Instead of fiber optics, it uses resistive, coated mylar—as your finger bends, the resistance of the coating changes. This is simply not as effective as fiber optics. But the price is much better: about $30 to $50 for a typical used Power Glove. (They

---

[41]I spoke personally with the president of 3DTV and have arranged for readers of this book to receive two key discounts. First, if all you want is LCD goggles, you can get goggles, a PC interface (serial or parallel port), and some basic free software (what you get is up to 3DTV) for $150. Second, if you want to work with VR products, you can get goggles, Stereospace Model 1, and basic free software for $400. Both these prices represent significant discounts (about 40 percent at the time of this writing). You must mention this book to qualify for the discount; call 415-479-3516 to place orders or get more information.

[42]In most cases, you'll be able to achieve a better refresh rate than the rated maximum for your monitor. However, don't push your monitor too far past its rated capacity; such activity is seldom covered in your warranty!

[43]Pun, as usual, intended.

are no longer manufactured.) If you buy reconditioned Power Gloves from a reseller, you may pay as much as $100 to $125, but you are guaranteed to get results. Power Gloves you purchase at garage sales will be as is—let the buyer beware. Try before you buy, or you could get a very fancy unmatched glove that won't even keep your fingers very warm in the winter.

Figure 12.25 shows the Mattel Power Glove. The unit consists of a glove for the hand, a sending unit attached to the back of the hand, and a data-entry section over the wrist. It is connected to the computer by a cable at the base of the wrist section. You will need to build your own interface or purchase a commercial interface such as PCVR in order to use the glove with your PC or Mac.

The underside of the glove is shown in Figure 12.26, attached to a hand. The straps are easy to attach using the hook and eye (more commonly, but incorrectly, known by the trademarked term *Velcro*) straps.

Figure 12.25
The Mattel Power
Glove.

I have very long fingers, but I had no trouble using the glove—as you can see, the finger tips are open, allowing long fingers to simply stick out. This was not uncomfortable.

In normal use, you must do two things before using the glove with your software: flex and center. *Flexing*—making a fist a few times, as shown in Figure 12.27—allows the glove to adjust to the size of your hand.

Figure 12.26
The underside of the Power Glove.

Figure 12.27
Flexing the glove to adjust to the size of your hand.

Centering is done by relaxing your hand and leveling it with the fingers spread in a relaxed manner (see Fig. 12.28). When the glove is comfortable and level, press the Center button on the control panel of the glove with your other hand. A beep will confirm that you are centered.

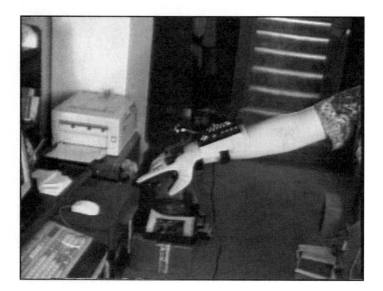

Figure 12.28
*Centering the glove
should be done with
a relaxed hand.*

Proper centering requires that you point the glove at the middle of the stationary receivers. The little black box attached at the back of the hand generates ultrasonic signals that the stationary receivers translate into positional information. Figure 12.29 shows the stationary receivers. There are three of them, and they must be oriented as shown. Normally, you drape them over your monitor. Because the average computer monitor is smaller than the average TV, you may need to add a book or something similar to balance the receiver properly on your monitor. Later illustrations show the use of a large dictionary for exactly this purpose.

To center properly, make sure that the glove points at the middle of a rectangle defined by the three black boxes of the receiver.[44]

To verify that the glove is working properly, either plug it into a Nintendo Entertainment System (for which it was originally designed) or check to see that the LEDs[45] at the upper right of the receivers follow the movement of the glove.

You can also test the glove visually if your software displays the current position and gesture of the glove on-screen. Pointing is a good test (see Fig. 12.30). This is a gesture that is very useful in most VR products, and is one of the few gestures that read very clearly with the Power Glove.

---

[44]Yes, you only need three points to define a rectangle.

[45]*LED* stands for *light-emitting diodes*, and are not to be confused with LCDs, which emit no light of their own.

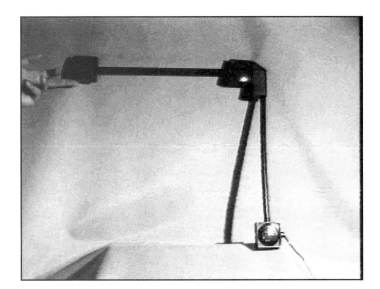

Figure 12.29
The stationary receivers used with the Power Glove.

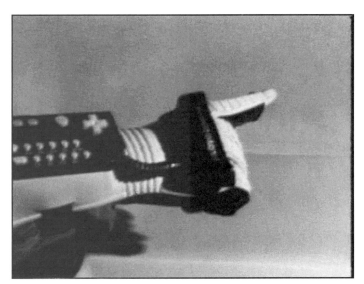

Figure 12.30
The pointing gesture.

Using the Power Glove

Once you have the Power Glove centered, you can begin using it with your software. Different software uses different glove gestures to manipulate objects. Figure 12.31 shows the glove in use.

In general, we found that the glove was easiest to use standing up. This makes typing awkward, and you can't type very well with the hand wearing the glove. This is part of the price you pay for using the glove.

Figure 12.32 shows the glove in use with the Rend386 program. The glove is in the centering position. If you look carefully, you can see that the glove on the screen matches the position and orientation of the real glove.

Figure 12.31
*Using the Power
Glove.*

Figure 12.32
*Using the Power
Glove with software.*

Figure 12.33 shows the glove made into a fist and the corresponding fist of the glove in the software.

If you move to the left of the screen (see Fig. 12.34), the on-screen glove follows. If you make a pointing gesture (see Fig. 12.35), the on-screen glove points, too.

Figure 12.33
The physical glove and the on-screen glove match gestures.

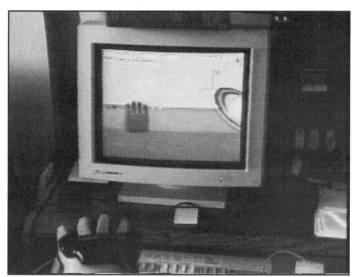

Figure 12.34
Moving the glove side to side.

Figure 12.35
*Making a pointing
gesture.*

Moving the glove toward and away from the screen moves it into and out of the scene.

Connecting for 3D

The PCVR is just one way to connect your 3D goggles to your computer. The folks at 3DTV[46] make several other devices that work just as well—and if you won't be using a Power Glove, these are quite economical. In fact, they make a whole bunch of useful and interesting 3D/VR products; see the VR Buyer's Guides on the CD-ROMs for more information.

Alternative #1: The PC3D

The goggles kit that comes with the PC3D is normally $250, a full $100 less than the PCVR kit. As a reader of this book, you qualify for a purchase price of $150, but you must mention this book to get the deal.

The PC3D is a serial interface for the goggles and is extremely compact (see Fig. 12.36). It is extremely easy to use. It takes its power from the serial port, so all you need to do to use it is to connect it to your serial port and plug in the 3D glasses. As with the PCVR, if your computer doesn't use standard port addresses, or if you aren't using COM1 as your serial connection, you may have to edit a few lines in the configuration file of the software.

---

[46]You may be wondering why I keep mentioning 3DTV—am I ignoring other companies? It's because this is an infant industry, and 3DTV is by far the most prominent supplier of inexpensive VR technology. If it weren't for 3DTV, VR would not be as accessible as it is.

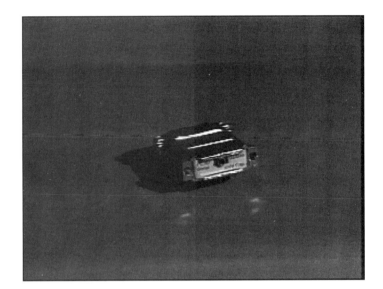

Figure 12.36
The PC3D serial interface for 3D goggles.

Alternative #2: The Model 3000

The Model 3000 is an interesting device. The unit I tested was a prototype (see Fig. 12.37). This unit costs $175 (in addition to the cost of goggles).

The Model 3000 is an interesting hybrid. It interfaces your goggles with the video port only—there is no parallel port connection involved. It senses the sync signal by tapping into the video cable using an adapter supplied with the unit. It also comes with a power unit for its AC connection.

The Model 3000 also supports viewing of 3D video from your VCR. To use it in this manner, you need only run a cable from the video out of your VCR to the Model 3000. You can then plug the 3D goggles into the Model 3000. 3DTV markets a number of 3D videotapes, which are listed in the VR Hardware Buyer's Guide on the CD-ROMs.[47]

How does 3D video look? When the source material is recorded using a 3D video camera, the effect is the best I have ever seen. Converting 3D movies to videotape is not as effective.

---

[47]The quality of the tapes is mixed, and the content is idiosyncratic. However, when the content and quality of the material is just right, the effects are some of the best 3D I have ever seen.

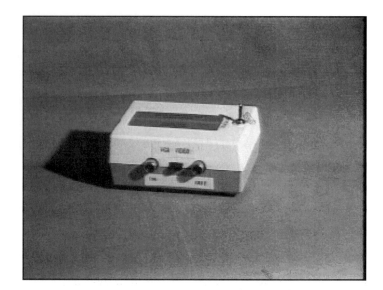

Figure 12.37
The Model 3000 3D goggle interface.

3D Software

The world of 3D software is in its infancy. It wasn't until 1993 that inexpensive hardware became commonly available and, as in the past, software is busy trying to catch up to what the hardware can do.

Keep in mind that there is simply no way to provide adequate illustrations for 3D in the book. I have included some sample 3D software on the CDs, but if you don't have at least LCD glasses and an interface, you won't be able to do much of anything with it.

Software Options

OK, so you spring for a set of LCD glasses and some kind of interface. What can you do with them? Software options are currently limited, but the range of products has increased significantly since the first edition of this book. Of course, if you had a lot to spend, the range was always better, but the list of products in the key under-$500 range has expanded enormously. Two of the more interesting ones are Vistapro, whose virtual reality aspects were covered in Chapter 1, and Rend386 (shareware). Each program takes advantage of 3D goggles in a completely different way.

If you are willing to invest in a Stereospace Model 1, your horizons open up. Many VR development and runtime tools support the over-under video format. I tested the Stereospace with VREAM and Superscape, but many other VR products also support the format.

Stereo Pro

Stereo Pro is a simple product that does a simple job, but does it really well. Stereo Pro works with LCD glasses to display 3D still images.

A 3D still image is actually made up of two images, called a *stereo pair*. One image is for the left eye, and one image is for the right eye. The trick, as with all 3D products, is to make sure that each eye sees the image intended for it. Stereo Pro handles the process of alternating the presentation of the images and coordinates timing of the LCD glasses.

Figure 12.38 shows an image for the left eye, and Figure 12.39 shows an image for the right eye. Figure 12.40 shows the two images superimposed; this is how they look on the computer monitor if you are not wearing the LCD glasses. If you are wearing the LCD glasses, of course, you see a single 3D image.[48]

Figure 12.38
The left-eye image.

---

[48]There is some slight ghosting of the image for the other eye, since LCD glasses are not perfectly opaque when the shutter is closed.

Figure 12.39
The right-eye image.

Figure 12.40
The combined images.

The Stereo Pro software ships with several 3D images, but to get good use out of this product, you will want to create your own 3D images. Vistapro, covered elsewhere in this chapter, is one of many different products you can use to create stereo pairs. Most 3D modeling and rendering software will create stereo pairs. For example, here is a stereo pair I created in 3D Studio (see Figs. 12.41 and 12.42). Figure 12.43 shows the overlapped version. trueSpace is also a good product for creating 3D stereo pairs.

Figure 12.41
Left-eye image.

Figure 12.42
Right-eye image.

The trick for stereo pairs is to set up two cameras that simulate the human eye. To get useful images, you can't simply position two cameras a few inches apart; the actual distance varies. In general, I find that an angle of about 2 to 5 degrees between the cameras is good; the focal points of the cameras should meet at about the middle of the depth of the field. Figure 12.44 shows a 3D Studio session with two cameras; this is the model that was used to create Figures 12.41 and 12.42.

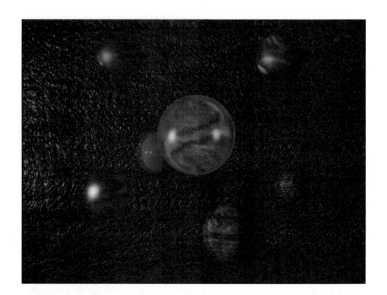

Figure 12.43
Overlapped images.

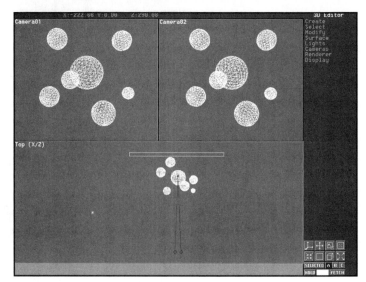

Figure 12.44
Setting up for a 3D stereo pair in 3D Studio; note the camera angle at the upper left.

3D Flic Player

Here's my basic position on 3D software: 3D is cool, but moving 3D is even cooler. The 3D Flic player is a perfect case in point. As much fun as stereo pair images are, creating an animation is a lot more fun for me.

If it's hard to convey the quality of a 3D still image in a book, it's even harder to do so with an animation. I created an animation in 3D Studio of the comet Shoemaker-Levy 9 crashing into Jupiter. To make it a 3D animation, I added a second camera as I would for a still stereo pair, and then rendered the animation a second time.

That gave me two complete FLC files with perfect stereo alignment, but I needed a way to play them back. Good old 3DTV came to my rescue with a product called 3D Flic. This program will play back a right/left stereo pair of FLC files for viewing with LCD goggles.

Figure 12.45 shows a left frame from the animation, and Figure 12.46 shows a right frame. The complete animation is provided on the CDs, as is the 3D Flic player. If you can create your own 3D FLC files (using Vistapro, trueSpace, 3D Studio, or any other software capable of creating camera positions), you can view them with 3D Flic.[49]

Figure 12.45
Left-eye frame from a 3D animation.

---

[49]3DTV normally charges for 3D Flic, but they agreed to put a free copy on the CDs for two reasons: one, so you can play with it; two, so you'll go out and buy LCD glasses from them. This is capitalism at its best, eh?

Figure 12.46
*Right-eye frame
from a 3D anima-
tion.*

Games

There are now many 3D and VR games available, but only a subset of those games allows you to play in *true* 3D, using LCD goggles or an HMD. This is changing rapidly with the introduction of HMDs like the i-glasses!, however. Look for a flood of new games in 1996 and beyond.

The unfortunate side of this is that few of the games support an output format suitable for good old inexpensive LCD goggles. They appear to expect all of us to fork over the big bucks for the fancy headsets, even though the goggles can provide many of the same benefits with less glitz and less cash.

There is a simple solution to this problem. If you own LCD goggles, call up the game manufacturers (or send e-mail, or snail mail, or whatever!) and tell them that you want 3D games. Unless they know the market exists, they won't create for it.

Until then, you'll have to settle for things like 3D versions of the breakout game. One exception: 3DTV's 3D Go game (see Fig. 12.47).

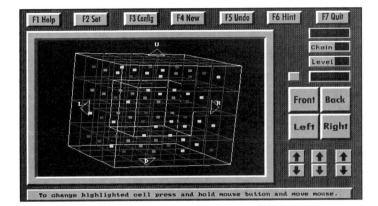

Figure 12.47
*3DTV's 3D Go
game.*

Vistapro

To use Vistapro with 3D glasses, you can create stereo pairs in the normal manner (see Chapter 1 for the gory details). However, instead of combining the pair into a single red/blue color image, you would convert each of the PCX files to the GIF format and then combine them using the PCGV program supplied by 3DTV for viewing with 3D goggles.

You can also generate a pair of FLC files (animations) in Vistapro, one for each eye, and view that using 3DTV's 3DFLIC software. This is extremely effective, but it does take time to create the two separate animations.[50]

VREAM

It's unbelievably easy to create 3D stereo with VREAM, since VREAM supports many different kinds of 3D hardware. If you have the Stereospace, you can set the method of stereo reproduction as CrystalEyes (the over/under method). The Stereospace will automatically convert that into high-refresh-rate 3D output for your LCD glasses. VREAM also supports the Simsalabim Cyberscope, a hood that provides excellent low-cost 3D viewing.

---

[50]The longest I ever created was a 1,000+ frame animation that took over a full day for each animation on a 486/66 computer.

Summary

In this chapter, you learned about technology that is at the cutting edge of affordable VR hardware and software. Throughout this book, I have tried to present tools that are within the reach of the average computer user. The barriers—cost and complexity—that kept VR tools out of the mainstream of computing are falling all around us. You have the opportunity, right now, to get involved in the development and use of virtual worlds.

Whatever the implications of adding virtual reality capabilities to personal computers may turn out to be, you are in a position to start finding out today. A whole new world of support for VR on the Internet is opening up, and it offers a wonderful ground-floor opportunity for anyone involved with virtual reality.

A

THE *VIRTUAL REALITY MADNESS 1996 CD-ROMS*

The three CD-ROMs that accompany this book contain a wealth of VR-related software, including complete award-winning programs such as

- Virtus WalkThrough Stereo
- Superscape Visualizer
- The Journeyman Project Turbo
- PhotoMorph 2
- Virtek 3-D Ware Personal Edition
- Vistapro 1
- Distant Suns 1
- Total Internet Access Kit, including Netscape Navigator

For more information on installing and using these products, see the section "The *Guide to the CD-ROM* Programs," later in this appendix. This section also contains information about the electronic manual for each product.

These programs are included on the CD-ROM through special arrangements with these companies:

Virtus Corporation
118 MacKeanan Drive, Suite 250
Cary, NC 27511
(800) VIRTUS1

Virtual Reality Laboratories, Inc.
2341 Ganador Court
San Luis Obispo, CA 93401
(805) 545-8515

Superscape International
2483 E. Bayshore Road, Suite 103
Palo Alto, CA 94303
(415) 812-9380

North Coast Software
PO Box 459
Barrington, NH 03825
(603) 664-6000

Sanctuary Woods Multimedia Corp.
1875 S. Grant St., #260
San Mateo, CA 94402

Virtek International Corporation
Barclay House
35 Whitworth Street West
Manchester, England M1 5NG
+44-161-237-9929
Internet: sales@virtek.com

EarthLink Network, Inc.
3171 Los Feliz Blvd., Suite 203
Los Angeles, CA 90039
(213) 644-9500

In addition to these amazing programs, these three discs contain:

■ VR Hardware and Software Buyer's Guides

■ Test-drive versions of VR games

■ Virtual worlds to explore

■ Working demos of commercial programs

■ Video clips and images of cutting-edge VR applications

■ Pictures and video clips seen in the book

The menu programs on the discs allow you to easily navigate through the included software—you can run or install programs, explore worlds, play animations and videos, and view pictures.

The *Guide to the CD-ROM* Programs

Disc 1 and Disc 2 contain easy-to-use *Guide to the CD-ROM* menu programs. Disc 3 contains only the game *The Journeyman Project Turbo*. Before you can run the menu for one of the first two CD-ROMs, you must run the setup program on that disc.

The setup program will create a Program Manager group with icons for running the software. It will also copy software drivers to your hard drive that allow you to view animations.

Windows 95 Users: When you insert Disc 1 or Disc 2 into your CD-ROM drive, an introductory screen appears that gives you the choice of running the setup program or the CD-ROM menu.

1. Start Windows, if you haven't already done so, and follow these steps:

2. Insert Disc 1 into your CD-ROM drive.

3. Switch to Program Manager or File Manager. Select **F**ile from the menu, and then select **R**un. Windows 95 users should click on the Start button, and then click on **R**un.

4. In the Run dialog box, type `D:\VRSETUP.EXE` in the box and click on OK. If your CD-ROM drive is not drive D, then substitute the correct letter. For example, if your CD-ROM drive is G, type `G:\VRSETUP.EXE`.

5. The opening screen of the setup program appears. Click on the Continue button.

6. The program installs animation drivers to your hard drive and creates a Program Manager group named *VR Madness 1996*.

> **Windows 3.1x:** When the setup for Disc 1 is complete, you'll need to install Microsoft's Video for Windows playback drivers. Double-click on the *Install Video for Windows* icon in the *VR Madness 1996* group and follow the prompts within this program. When the Video for Windows setup is complete, it restarts Windows to allow the new drivers to load.

If the first setup has completed successfully, you're ready to explore the first CD-ROM! Double-click on the *CD-ROM Menu Disc 1* icon to explore Disc 1.

To set up and explore Disc 2, insert it into your CD-ROM drive, follow the preceding steps, and additional icons for this disc will be created in the *VR Madness 1996* group.

See the section "Running Disc 3" for instructions on setting up *The Journeyman Project Turbo*, which is on Disc 3.

Running the *Guide to the CD-ROM*

When you start the Windows menu program, you'll see an opening screen—click anywhere on the screen to begin exploring the disc. Each screen of the menu program is referred to as a *page*. Just think of the program as being like a multimedia book. You can jump directly to sections that interest you, or you can move through the program one page at a time.

Your Windows video setup must be capable of displaying at least 256 colors, or the menu program and animation clips will not display properly. Graphics with lots of colors look pretty ugly on a 16-color display; if you can only display 16 colors, consult your system's manual for information on how to switch to a different video driver with more colors. If you can switch to a driver that displays 16-bit or 24-bit color, graphics and animations will look like they were intended to look.

You can navigate through the disc in several different ways. In the bottom right area of each page, you'll find yellow navigation buttons. To move to the next or preceding page, click on one of the left- or right-arrow buttons. You also can use the left-arrow and right-arrow keys for the same functions.

If you click on the question mark symbol in the lower right area, a series of Help screens appears. Pressing the F1 key also displays this Help screen.

On some pages, you won't see the arrows that let you move to the next or preceding page; you'll see an upward-pointing arrow instead. Each upward-pointing arrow moves back to the main menu page.

To exit from the menu, click on the word EXIT at the bottom of the screen. You also can press the Alt+F4 keys to exit the program.

Installing and Running Programs

The menu programs allow you to easily install all of the software on Discs 1 or 2—even the DOS software. Follow the instructions in the menu program to run a program after installing it—some of the DOS programs may require that you exit Windows first.

Some programs require a large amount of memory to run properly—if you are running the Guide menu and you can't run another program properly, exit the menu program and then try to run the other program.

Each of the complete VR products mentioned at the beginning of this appendix have an electronic manual included on the disc. You can read or print this manual from within the CD-ROM menu, or you can double-click the manual's icon in the *VR Madness 1996* group.

Running Disc 3

The Journeyman Project Turbo is the only product on Disc 3. Follow these steps to install and set up the software:

1. Start Windows, if you haven't already done so.

2. If you're not running Windows in 256 colors, you need to change the screen driver in Windows Setup. If you're unsure of how to do this, refer to your Windows manual or the manual that came with your video card. Restart Windows after making this change.

3. Insert Disc 3 into your CD-ROM drive.

4. From Program Manager, choose **F**ile and then **R**un from the menu.

5. Type `D:\JMSETUP.EXE` and press Enter. If your CD-ROM drive is not drive D, then substitute the correct letter. If your CD-ROM drive is G, for example, type `G:\JMSETUP.EXE`.

After the setup program has completed, double-click the *Journeyman* icon in the *Journeyman Project* Program Manager group. For optimal performance, it's advisable to quit any other applications that you have open before running *The Journeyman Project Turbo*.

If your system has a high-resolution video card, you may get an error message on your monitor.

■ Check that you are using a 640×480 Windows video driver capable of displaying 256 colors, and that the driver is compatible with your video card.

■ Check that you are running the latest version of your video card's driver. If not, or if you are unsure, contact the video card manufacturer.

If you experience audio problems, make sure that your sound card is installed properly for Windows 3.1 or higher. Also, make sure that the sound card and CD-ROM driver are Multimedia PC compatible. If sound problems persist, check the following:

■ Ensure that your external speakers or headphones are connected to the output jack of your sound card.

■ Ensure that your sound card has the proper sound driver software assigned to it in Windows (refer to the documentation that came with the sound card).

Troubleshooting and Support

If you experience any problems with running the menu program, double-click on the Troubleshooting icon in the *VR Madness 1996* group. This opens a file with hints and tips for solving your Windows problems.

If you have problems with Virtus VR Stereo, Superscape Visualizer, The Journeyman Project Turbo, PhotoMorph 2, Virtek 3-D Ware Personal Edition, Vistapro 1, Distant Suns 1, or the Total Internet Access Kit, contact the vendor of that particular software product. Double-click on the *Product Support* icon in the *VR Madness 1996* group to see contact information for these vendors.

If you have problems with the discs themselves, the *Guide to the CD-ROM* menu, or the book, you can contact our support department. Please be prepared to give information on your computer system and a detailed account of the problem you're experiencing.

Internet Email:

support@mcp.com

CompuServe

GO SAMS to visit the Macmillan Computer Publishing forum and leave a message in the *Multimedia/VR* message area (Section 13).

Mail:

Macmillan Computer Publishing Support
201 West 103rd Street
Indianapolis, IN 46290

Telephone:

(317) 581-3833

Fax:

(317) 581-4773

I

INDEX

PLUG YOURSELF INTO...

THE MACMILLAN INFORMATION SUPERLIBRARY™

Free information and vast computer resources from the world's leading computer book publisher—online!

FIND THE BOOKS THAT ARE RIGHT FOR YOU!

A complete online catalog, plus sample chapters and tables of contents give you an in-depth look at *all* of our books, including hard-to-find titles. It's the best way to find the books you need!

- ● **STAY INFORMED** with the latest computer industry news through our online newsletter, press releases, and customized Information SuperLibrary Reports.

- ● **GET FAST ANSWERS** to your questions about MCP books and software.

- ● **VISIT** our online bookstore for the latest information and editions!

- ● **COMMUNICATE** with our expert authors through e-mail and conferences.

- ● **DOWNLOAD SOFTWARE** from the immense MCP library:
    - Source code and files from MCP books
    - The best shareware, freeware, and demos

- ● **DISCOVER HOT SPOTS** on other parts of the Internet.

- ● **WIN BOOKS** in ongoing contests and giveaways!

TO PLUG INTO MCP: →

GOPHER: gopher.mcp.com

FTP: ftp.mcp.com

WORLD WIDE WEB: http://www.mcp.com

Finally.
A Powerful, Easy
3-D World Builder.

Der Rosenkavalier opera set by Darwin Reid Payne.

VIRTUS
WALKTHROUGH PRO
PROFESSIONAL 3-D VISUALIZATION

Virtus Corporation has led the industry in practical applications of virtual environment creation software since 1990. We build worlds fast—on machines that people can afford.

Explore the form and function of 3-D space adding surface textures, controlling lighting and roaming anywhere in your new worlds.

Advanced product features include:

- **VRML Export Support**
  Take advantage of this exciting new file format to publish your worlds on the Internet.

Take advantage of this exclusive offer for only

$249.00
SRP $495

Call 1-800-847-8871 to order.

- **Stereo Support**
  New feature enables you to use commercially-available headmount displays and other hardware.

- **Realistic Texture Mapping**
  Quickly add realism to your model by applying BMP textures to the surfaces. Use our textures or create your own.

- **Smooth Shaded Polygons**
  Gauraud shading adds realism to curved objects. Apply this rendering to single objects in a model or apply it to an entire scene.

- **3-D Surface Selection**
  Select surfaces for editing in the 3-D Walk View to change their color or textures — fast.

- **Import/Export Features**
  Import–BMP, TIFF and 2-D DXF as trace layers
  Export–BMP, Illustrator 1.1, TIFF, 3-D DXF, 2-D DXF, VRML and Virtus Player.

Call us today to order!
1-800-847-8871

Virtus Awards

Questions?
Virtus Corporation
118 MacKenan Drive, Ste 400
Cary, NC 27511
Tel: 919/467-9700
Fax: 919/460-4530
http://www.virtus.com

VIRTUS

Add to Your Sams Library Today with the Best Books for Programming, Operating Systems, and New Technologies

The easiest way to order is to pick up the phone and call
1-800-428-5331
between 9:00 a.m. and 5:00 p.m. EST.
For faster service please have your credit card available.

ISBN	Quantity	Description of Item	Unit Cost	Total Cost
0-672-30737-5		World Wide Web Unleashed, 2nd Edition	$39.99	
0-672-30570-4		PC Graphics Unleashed (Book/CD-ROM)	$49.99	
0-672-30413-9		Multimedia Madness!, Deluxe Edition (Book/2 CD-ROMs)	$55.00	
0-672-30638-7		CD-ROM Madness (Book/CD-ROM)	$39.99	
0-672-30590-9		The Magic of Interactive Entertainment, 2nd Edition (Book/CD-ROM)	$44.95	
0-672-30516-X		Corel Photo-Paint 5 Unleashed (Book/CD-ROM)	$45.00	
0-672-30612-3		The Magic of Computers (Book/CD-ROM)	$45.00	
0-672-30717-0		Tricks of the DOOM Programming Gurus (Book/CD-ROM)	$39.99	
0-672-30707-3		Fractal Design Painter 3.1 Unleashed (Book/CD-ROM)	$49.99	
0-672-30697-2		More Tricks of the Game Programming Gurus (Book/CD-ROM)	$49.99	
0-672-30322-1		PC Video Madness! (Book/CD-ROM)	$39.95	
❏ 3 ½" Disk		Shipping and Handling: See information below.		
❏ 5 ¼" Disk		TOTAL		

Shipping and Handling: $4.00 for the first book, and $1.75 for each additional book. Floppy disk: add $1.75 for shipping and handling. If you need to have it NOW, we can ship product to you in 24 hours for an additional charge of approximately $18.00, and you will receive your item overnight or in two days. Overseas shipping and handling adds $2.00 per book and $8.00 for up to three disks. Prices subject to change. Call for availability and pricing information on latest editions.

201 W. 103rd Street, Indianapolis, Indiana 46290

1-800-428-5331 — Orders   1-800-835-3202 — FAX   1-800-858-7674 — Customer Service

Book ISBN 0-672-30865-7